Adobe®
Creative Suite 4
Design Premium
Digital
Classroom

Aquent Creative Team

WILEY

Wiley Publishing, Inc.

A Q U E N T

Adobe® Creative Suite 4 Digital Classroom

Published by
Wiley Publishing, Inc.
10475 Crosspoint Boulevard
Indianapolis, IN 46256

For general information on our other products and services or to obtain technical support, please contact our Customer Care Department within the U.S. at (800) 762-2974, outside the U.S. at (317) 572-3993 or fax (317) 572-4002.

Please report any errors by sending a message to errata@aquent.com

About the Authors

The Aquent Creative Team is comprised of Adobe Certified Experts and Adobe Certified Instructors from Aquent Graphics Institute (AGI). The Aquent Creative Team has authored many of Adobe's official training guides, and works with many of the world's most prominent companies helping them to use creative software to communicate more effectively and creatively. They work with marketing, creative and communications teams around the world, and teach regularly scheduled classes at AGI's locations, and are available for private and customized training seminars and speaking engagements. More information at agitraining.com

Credits

Writing
Jeff Asura, Chad Chelius, Fred Gerantabee,
Greg Heald, Jeremy Osborn, Christopher Smith,
Jennifer Smith, Jerron Smith, Robert Underwood

Series Editor
Christopher Smith

Senior Acquisitions Editor
Jody Lefevere

Technical Editors
Cathy Auclair, Larry Happy, Sean McKnight,
Haziel Olivera, Eric Rowse, Caitlin Smith

Editor
Marylouise Wiack

Editorial Director
Robyn Siesky

Business Manager
Amy Knies

Senior Marketing Manager
Sandy Smith

**Vice President and Executive Group
Publisher**
Richard Swadley

Vice President and Executive Publisher
Barry Pruett

Project Coordinator
Lynsey Stanford

Graphics and Production Specialist
Lauren Mickol

Media Development Project Supervisors
Christopher Leavey, Jeremy Osborn

Proofreading
Jay Donahue

Indexing
Broccoli Information Management

Stock Photography
iStockPhoto.com

Acknowledgments

Thanks to our many friends at Adobe Systems, Inc. who made this book possible and assisted with questions and feedback during the writing process. To the many clients of Aquent Graphics Institute who have helped us better understand how they use Adobe's creative software and provided us with many of the tips and suggestions found in this book. A special thanks to the instructional team at AGI for their input and assistance in the review process and for making this book such a team effort.

Contents

Photoshop Lesson 1: Exploring Photoshop

Photoshop Lesson 2: Getting to Know the Workspace

Photoshop Lesson 3: The Basics of Working with Photoshop

Photoshop Lesson 4: Making the Best Selections

Photoshop Lesson 5: Painting and Retouching

Photoshop Lesson 6: Creating a Good Image

Dreamweaver Lesson 1: Dreamweaver CS4 Jumpstart

Dreamweaver Lesson 2: Setting Up a New Site

Dreamweaver Lesson 3: Adding Text and Images

Dreamweaver Lesson 4: Styling Your Pages with CSS

Dreamweaver Lesson 5: Managing Your Web Site:
Reports, Optimization, and Maintenance

Flash Lesson 1: Flash CS4 Jumpstart

Flash Lesson 2: Getting Started with the Drawing Tools

Flash Lesson 3: Creating Basic Animation

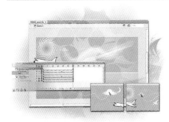

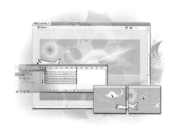

Flash Lesson 4: Delivering Your Final Movie

Fireworks Lesson 1: Adobe Fireworks Jumpstart

Contents

Illustrator Lesson1: Illustrator CS4 Essentials

Illustrator Lesson 2: Adding Color

Illustrator Lesson 3: Working with the Drawing Tools

InDesign Lesson 1: InDesign CS4 Essential Skills

InDesign Lesson 2: Building Documents with Master Pages

InDesign Lesson 3: Working with Text and Type

InDesign Lesson 4: Working with Styles

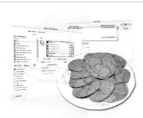

InDesign Lesson 5: Working with Graphics

InDesign Lesson 6: Document Delivery: Printing, PDFs, and XHTML

Starting up

About Adobe Creative Suite 4 Design Premium Digital Classroom

Adobe Creative Suite 4 (CS4) Design Premium is the leading software package for creating print, Web, and interactive content. It includes the perfect creative tools for designing and manipulating images, creating print layouts, building and maintaining Web sites, and creating interactive and animated content. CS4 Design Premium includes the tools you need to express your creative ideas.

The *Adobe Creative Suite 4 Design Premium Digital Classroom* helps you to understand the capabilities of these software tools so you can get the most out of your software and get up-and-running right away. You can work through all the lessons in this book, or complete only specific lessons that you need right now. Each lesson includes detailed, step-by-step instructions, along with lesson files, useful background information, and video tutorials.

Adobe Creative Suite 4 Design Premium Digital Classroom is like having your own expert instructor guiding you through each lesson while you work at your own pace. This book includes 26 self-paced lessons that let you discover essential skills, explore new features, and understand capabilities that save you time. You'll be productive right away with real-world exercises and simple explanations. Each lesson includes step-by-step instructions, lesson files, and video tutorials, all of which are available on the included DVD. The *Adobe Creative Suite 4 Design Premium Digital Classroom* lessons are developed by the same team of Adobe Certified Instructors and experts that have created many of the official training titles for Adobe Systems.

The lessons in this book cover the essential skills for using the software programs that are part of the Adobe Creative Suite 4 (CS4) Design Premium. To gain a more in-depth understanding of any of these software packages, turn to these Digital Classroom titles:

- Dreamweaver CS4 Digital Classroom
- Flash CS4 Digital Classroom
- Photoshop CS4 Digital Classroom
- InDesign CS4 Digital Classroom
- Illustrator CS4 Digital Classroom

Prerequisites

Before you start the *Adobe Creative Suite 4 Design Premium Digital Classroom* lessons, you should have a working knowledge of your computer and its operating system. You should know how to use the directory system of your computer so that you can navigate through folders. You also need to understand how to locate, save, and open files, and you should also know how to use your mouse to access menus and commands.

Before starting the lessons files in the *Adobe Creative Suite 4 Design Premium Digital Classroom*, make sure that you have installed About Creative Suite 4 Design Premium. The software is sold separately, and not included with this book. You may use the free 30-day trial version of the Adobe Creative Suite 4 Design Premium Digital Classroom applications available at the *Adobe.com* web site, subject to the terms of its license agreement.

Adobe Photoshop CS4 versions

Photoshop CS4 comes in two versions: Adobe Photoshop CS4 and Adobe Photoshop CS4 Extended. The Extended version offers everything you find in Photoshop CS4, along with additional tools for editing video, motion-graphics, 3-D content, and performing image analysis. This section of this book that covers Photoshop CS4 addresses both versions of the software. Where appropriate, we have noted any features that are available only in the Extended version. Adobe Photoshop CS4 is used to refer to both versions of the software throughout the book.

System requirements

Before starting the lessons in the *Adobe Creative Suite 4 Design Premium*, make sure that your computer is equipped for running Adobe Creative Suite 4 Design Premium, which you must purchase separately. These are the minimum system requirements for using the Adobe Creative Suite 4 Design Premium applications:

Windows OS

- 2GHz or faster processor
- Microsoft® Windows® XP with Service Pack 2 (Service Pack 3 recommended) or Windows Vista® Home Premium, Business, Ultimate, or Enterprise with Service Pack 1 (certified for 32-bit Windows XP and Windows Vista)
- 1GB of RAM or more recommended
- 9.3GB of available hard-disk space for installation; additional free space required during installation (cannot install on flash-based storage devices)
- 1,024x768 display (1,280x800 recommended) with 16-bit video card
- DVD-ROM drive
- QuickTime 7.4.5 software required for multimedia features
- Broadband Internet connection required for online services

Macintosh OS

- PowerPC® G5 or multicore Intel® processor
- Mac OS X v10.4.11–10.5.4
- 1GB of RAM or more recommended
- 10.3GB of available hard-disk space for installation; additional hard-disk space required during installation (cannot install on a volume that uses a case-sensitive file system or on flash-based storage devices)
- 1,024x768 display (1,280x800 recommended) with 16-bit video card
- DVD-ROM drive
- QuickTime 7.4.5 software required for multimedia features
- Broadband Internet connection required for online services

Starting the Adobe Creative Suite 4 Design Premium applications

As with most software, Adobe Creative Suite 4 Design Premium is launched by locating the application in your Programs folder (Windows) or Applications folder (Mac OS). If you are not familiar with starting the program, follow these steps to start the desired Adobe Creative Suite 4 Design Premium application:

Windows

1   Choose Start > All Programs > Adobe Photoshop, Dreamweaver, InDesign, Flash, Fireworks, or Illustrator CS4. If you have a Creative Suite installed, you will navigate to that folder to locate the Photoshop, Dreamweaver, InDesign, Flash, Fireworks, or Illustrator CS4 folder.

2   Close the Welcome Screen when it appears.

Mac OS

1   Open the Applications folder, and then open the Adobe Photoshop, Dreamweaver, InDesign, Flash, Fireworks, or Illustrator CS4 folder. If you have a Creative Suite installed, you will open that folder to locate the Photoshop, Dreamweaver, InDesign, Flash, Fireworks, or Illustrator CS4 folder.

2   Double-click on the Adobe Photoshop, Dreamweaver, InDesign, Flash, Fireworks, or Illustrator CS4 application icon.

3   Close the Welcome Screen when it appears.

Menus and commands are identified throughout the book by using the greater-than symbol (>). For example, the command to print a document is identified as File > Print.

Resetting Adobe Photoshop CS4 preferences

When you start the Adobe Photoshop section of this book, note that Photoshop remembers certain settings along with the configuration of the workspace from the last time you used the application. It is important that you start each Photoshop lesson using the default settings so that you do not see unexpected results when working with the lessons in this book.

As you reset your preferences to the default settings, you may wish to keep your color settings. This is important if you have created specific color settings, or work in a color calibrated environment. If you do not work in a color calibrated environment or have not set up specific (custom) color settings, you can jump ahead to the section "A note about color warnings."

Use the following steps to reset your Adobe Photoshop CS4 preferences and save your color settings. If you are confident that you do not need to save your color settings, you can skip to the section, "A note about color warnings."

Saving Adobe Photoshop CS4 color settings

1   Launch Adobe Photoshop.

2   Choose Edit > Color Settings, and then press the Save button. The Save dialog box opens. Enter an appropriate name for your color settings, such as the date. Leave the destination and format unchanged, then press the Save button. The Color Settings Comment dialog box opens.

3   In the Color Settings Comment dialog box, enter a description for the color settings you are saving, then press OK. Press OK again in the Color Settings dialog box to close it. You have saved your color settings so they can be accessed again in the future.

4   Choose File > Quit, to exit Adobe Photoshop CS4.

Steps to reset Adobe Photoshop CS4 preferences

Press and hold the Ctrl+Alt+Shift keys (Windows) or Command+Option+Shift keys (Mac OS) simultaneously before launching Adobe Photoshop CS4. A dialog box appears verifying that you want to delete the Adobe Photoshop settings file. Release the keys, then press OK.

Restoring previous Adobe Photoshop CS4 color settings

1   Start Adobe Photoshop CS4. Choose Edit > Color Settings. The Color Settings dialog box appears.

2   From the Settings drop-down menu, choose your saved color settings file. Press OK. Your color settings are restored.

A note about color warnings

Depending upon how your Color Settings are configured, there may be times when you will receive a Missing Profile or Embedded Profile Mismatch warning when working in the Photoshop section of this book. Understand that if you reset your preferences before each lesson (without restoring your color settings) you should not see these color warnings. This is because the default color setting of North America General Purpose 2 has all warning check boxes unchecked.

If you do receive Missing Profile and Embedded Profile Mismatch warnings when working in the Photoshop section of this book, choose the Assign working option, or Convert document's colors to the working space. What is determined to be your working space is what you have assigned in the Color Settings dialog box.

Resetting the Dreamweaver workspace

When you get to the Dreamweaver section of this book you can make certain that your panels and working environment are consistent. Do this by resetting your workspace at the start of each Dreamweaver lesson. To reset the Dreamweaver workspace, choose Window > Workspace Layout > Designer.

Resetting the Flash workspace

When you get to the Flash section of this book you can make certain that your panels and working environment are consistent. Do this by resetting your workspace at the start of each Flash lesson. To reset the Flash workspace, choose Window > Workspace > Essentials.

Resetting Adobe Illustrator CS4 preferences

When you start Adobe Illustrator, it remembers certain settings along with the configuration of the workspace from the last time you used the application. It is useful for you to start each of the Adobe Illustrator lessons in this book using the default settings so that you do not see unexpected results. You can use the following steps to reset the Adobe Illustrator CS4 preferences.

Steps to reset Adobe Illustrator CS4 preferences

1   Quit Illustrator.
2   Locate and rename the AIPrefs (Windows) or Adobe Illustrator Preferences (Mac OS), as follows.

- In Windows: Rename the AIPrefs file (for example, to AIPrefs.old) in the Documents and Settings/*(user)*/Application Data/Adobe/Adobe Illustrator CS4 Settings folder.

- In Windows Vista: Rename the AIPrefs file (for example, to AIPrefs.old) in the Users/ *(user)*/AppData/Roaming/Adobe/Adobe Illustrator CS4 Settings/*(language_location)* folder.

- In Mac OS: Rename the Adobe Illustrator Preferences file in the Users/*(user)*/Library/ Preferences/Adobe Illustrator CS4 Settings folder.

3   Start Illustrator. Illustrator creates a new preferences file.

To restore custom settings, delete the new AIPrefs file and restore the original name of the previous AIPrefs file.

Resetting the InDesign workspace and preferences

To make certain that your panels and working environment are consistent when working in the InDesign section of this book, you should reset your workspace at the start of each InDesign lesson. To reset your workspace, choose Window > Workspace > Typography. The selected workspace determines which menu items display, which panels display, and which options display within the panels. If menu items that are identified in the book are not displaying, choose Show All Menu Items from the menu in which you are working to locate them, or choose Window > Workspace > Advanced to show all panel options.

You can reset the settings for InDesign at the start of each lesson to make certain you match the instructions used in this book. To reset the InDesign preferences, start Adobe InDesign, and immediately press Shift+Alt+Ctrl (Windows) or Shift+Option+Command+Control (Mac OS). In the dialog box that appears, press OK to reset the preferences.

Fonts used in this book

Adobe Creative Suite CS4 Digital Classroom includes lessons that refer to fonts that were installed with your copy of Adobe InDesign CS4. If you did not install the fonts, or have removed them from your computer, you may substitute different fonts for the exercises or re-install the software to access the fonts.

If you receive a Missing Font warning, replace the font with one available on your computer and proceed with the lesson.

Loading lesson files

The *Adobe Creative Suite 4 Design Premium* DVD includes files that accompany the exercises for each of the lessons. You may copy the entire lessons folder from the supplied DVD to your hard drive, or copy only the lesson folders for the individual lessons you wish to complete.

For each lesson in the book, the files are referenced by the file name of each file. The exact location of each file on your computer is not used, as you may have placed the files in a unique location on your hard drive. We suggest placing the lesson files in the My Documents folder or the Desktop (Windows) or at the top level of your hard drive or on the Desktop (Mac OS).

Copying the lesson files to your hard drive:

1   Insert the *Adobe Creative Suite 4 Design Premium* DVD supplied with this book.

2   On your computer, navigate to the DVD and locate the folder named CS4lessons.

3   You can install all of the files, or just specific lesson files. Do one of the following:

   • Install all lesson files by dragging the CS4lessons folder to your hard drive.

   • Install only some of the files by creating a new folder on your hard drive named CS4lessons. Open the CS4lessons folder on the supplied DVD, select the lesson you wish to complete, and drag the folder(s) to the CS4lessons folder you created on your hard drive.

Macintosh users may need to unlock the files if they are copied from the accompanying disc. This only applies to Mac OS computers running older versions of Mac OSX operating system. If you receive warnings that the files are locked after copying them to your computer, select the CS4lessons folder, then choose File > Get Info. In the CS4lessons info window, click the You can drop-down menu labeled Read Only, which is located in the Ownership & Permissions section of this window. From the You can drop-down menu, choose Read & Write. Click the arrow to the left of Details, then click the Apply to enclosed items... button at the bottom of the window. You may need to click the padlock icon to change these permissions. After making these changes, close the window. This is only necessary if working on a Macintosh computer and if you receive a warning about the file(s) being locked after copying them to your hard drive.

Working with the video tutorials

Your *Adobe Creative Suite 4 Design Premium* DVD comes with video tutorials developed by the authors to help you understand the concepts explored in each lesson. Each tutorial is approximately five minutes long and demonstrates and explains the concepts and features covered in the lesson.

The videos are designed to supplement your understanding of the material in the chapter. We have selected exercises and examples that we feel will be most useful to you. You may want to view the entire video for each lesson before you begin that lesson.

Setting up for viewing the video tutorials

The DVD included with this book includes video tutorials for each lesson. Although you can view the lessons on your computer directly from the DVD, you can also copy the folder labeled *Videos* from the *Adobe Creative Suite 4 Design Premium* DVD to your hard drive.

Copying the video tutorials to your hard drive:

1   Insert the *Adobe Creative Suite 4 Design Premium* DVD supplied with this book.

2   On your computer desktop, navigate to the DVD and locate the folder named Videos.

3   Drag the Videos folder to a location onto your hard drive.

Viewing the video tutorials with the Adobe Flash Player

The videos on the *Adobe Creative Suite 4 Design Premium* DVD are saved in the Flash projector format. A Flash projector file wraps the Digital Classroom video player and the Adobe Flash Player in an executable file (.exe for Windows or .app for Mac OS). The file extension may not be visible depending upon the preferences for your operating system. Projector files allow the Flash content to be deployed on your system without the need for a browser and without the need to install any other software.

Playing the video tutorials:

1   On your computer, navigate to the Videos folder you copied to your hard drive from the DVD or to the folder on the DVD.

2   Open the Videos folder and double-click the Digital_Classroom_CS4.exe (Windows) or Digital_Classroom_CS4.app (Mac OS) to view the video tutorial.

3   Press the Play button to view the videos.

The player has a simple user interface that allows you to control the viewing experience, including stopping, pausing, playing, and restarting the video. You can also rewind or fast-forward, and adjust the playback volume.

A. Go to beginning. *B*. Play/Pause. *C*. Fast-forward/rewind. *D*. Stop. *E*. Volume Off/On. *F*. Volume control.

Playback volume is also affected by the settings in your operating system. Be certain to adjust the sound volume for your computer, in addition to the sound controls in the Player window. If you have difficulty viewing the videos directly from the DVD, try copying them to your hard drive. If you have a slower hard drive, try viewing the files directly from the DVD. The best viewing option varies depending upon your computer configuration.

Additional resources

The Digital Classroom series goes beyond the training books. You can continue your learning online, with training videos, at seminars and conferences, and in-person training events.

DigitalClassroomBooks.com

You can contact the authors, discover any errors, omissions, or clarifications, and read excerpts from the other Adobe Creative Suite 4 books in the Digital Classroom series at *digitalclassroombooks.com*.

Seminars, conferences, and training

The authors of the Digital Classroom seminar series frequently conduct in-person seminars and speak at conferences, including the annual CRE8 Conference. Learn more about their upcoming speaking engagements and training classes at *agitraining.com*.

Resources for educators

If you are an educator, contact your Wiley education representative to access resources for this book designed just for you including instructors' guides for incorporating Digital Classroom books into your curriculum.

What you'll learn in this lesson:

- Navigating Adobe Bridge
- Using folders in Bridge
- Making a Favorite
- Creating metadata
- Using automated tools

Using Adobe Bridge

Adobe Bridge is the command center of the Creative Suite. In Adobe Bridge, you can manage and organize your files, utilize and modify XMP metadata for faster searches, and quickly preview files before opening them.

Starting up

Before starting, make sure that your tools and panels are consistent by resetting your preferences. See "Resetting preferences" on pages XXV–XXVI.

You will work with several files from the br01lessons folder in this lesson. Make sure that you have loaded the CS4essons folder onto your hard drive from the supplied DVD. See "Loading lesson files" on page XXIX.

See Lesson 1 in action!

Use the accompanying video to gain a better understanding of how to use some of the features shown in this lesson. The video tutorial for this lesson can be found on the included DVD.

What is Adobe Bridge?

Adobe Bridge is an application included with Adobe Photoshop and the other Adobe Creative Suite 4 components. Adobe Bridge helps you locate, organize, and browse the documents you need to create print, web, video, and audio content. If you have Photoshop or any one of the Creative Suite applications, you can start Adobe Bridge using the File menu, or you can select the Launch Bridge button ().

You can use Bridge to access documents such as images, text files, and even non-Adobe documents, such as Microsoft Word or Excel files. Using Adobe Bridge, you can also organize and manage images, videos, and audio files, as well as preview, search, and sort your files without opening them in their native applications.

Once you discover the capabilities of Adobe Bridge, you'll want to make it the control center for your Photoshop projects. With Bridge, you can easily locate files using the Filters panel and import images from your digital camera right into a viewing area that allows you to quickly rename and preview your files. This is why the recommended workflow throughout this book includes opening and saving files in Adobe Bridge. Reading through this lesson will help you to feel more comfortable with Adobe Bridge, and will also make you aware of some of the more advanced features that are available to you for your own projects.

Adobe Bridge contains more features when installed as part of one of the Creative Suites. The tools and features demonstrated in this lesson are available in both the single product install and the Suite install, unless otherwise noted.

Navigating through Bridge

In order to utilize Adobe Bridge effectively, you'll want to know the available tools and how to access them. Let's start navigating!

1   Even though Adobe Bridge is accessible directly from the File menu in the Creative Suite applications, you'll launch it separately for this part of the lesson. To launch Adobe Bridge in Windows, go to the Start button, choose All Programs, and select Adobe Bridge CS4. On the Mac OS, navigate to the Applications folder, open the Adobe Bridge CS4 folder, and double-click on Adobe Bridge CS4 to launch the application.

If you have a CS4 Suite installed, you will have to open the Adobe Suite folder in order to locate the Adobe Bridge application.

2   Click on the Folders panel to make sure it is forward. Click on Desktop (listed in the Folders panel). You see the br01lessons folder that you downloaded to your hard drive. Double-click on the br01lessons folder and notice that the contents of that folder are displayed in the Content panel, in the center of the Adobe Bridge window. You can also navigate by clicking on folders listed in the Path bar that is located in the upper-left corner of the content window.

You can view folder contents by double-clicking on a folder, or by selecting the folder in the Path bar.

You can navigate through your navigation history by clicking on the Go back and Go forward arrows in the upper-left corner of the window. Use the handy Reveal recent file or go to Recent folder drop-down menu (🕑) to find folders and files that you recently opened.

3   Click on the Go back arrow to return to the desktop view.

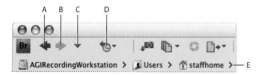

A. Go back. B. Go forward. C. Go to parent or Favorites.
D. Reveal recent file or go to recent folder. E. Path bar.

4   Click on the Go forward arrow to return to the last view, which is the br01lessons folder.

Using folders in Adobe Bridge

Adobe Bridge is used for more than just navigating your file system. Bridge is also used to manage and organize folders and files.

1   Click on the tab of the Folders panel in the upper-left corner of the Bridge window to make sure it is still forward. Then click on the arrow to the left of Desktop so that it turns downward and reveals its contents.

2   Double-click on My Computer (Windows) or Computer (Mac OS) to reveal its contents in the center pane of the Bridge window. Continue to double-click on items, or click on the arrows to the left of the folder names in the Folder panel, to reveal their contents.

You can use Adobe Bridge to navigate your entire system, much like you would by using your computer's directory system.

Managing folders

Adobe Bridge is a great tool for organizing folders and files. It is a simple matter of dragging and dropping to reorder items on your computer. You can create folders, move folders, move files from one folder to another, and copy files and folders to other locations; any organizing task that can be performed on the computer can also be performed in Adobe Bridge. This is a great way to help keep volumes of images organized for easy accessibility, as well as easy searching. The advantage of using Adobe Bridge for these tasks is that you have bigger and better previews of images, PDF files, and movies, with much more information about those files at your fingertips.

3 Click on Desktop in the Folder panel to reveal its contents again.

4 Click on br01lessons to view its contents. You'll now add a new folder into that lessons folder.

5 Click on the Create a new folder icon (📁) in the upper-right corner of the Bridge window to create a new untitled folder inside the br01lessons folder. Type the name **Music Extras**.

Creating a new folder in Bridge.

You can use Adobe Bridge to organize images. Because you can see a preview of each file, you can more easily rename them, as well as relocate them to more appropriate locations in your directory system. In the next step, you will move files from one folder to the new Music Extras folder you have just created.

6 Click once on the image named IMG_1381.JPG, then hold down the Ctrl (Windows) or Command (Mac OS) key and select image IMG_1426.JPG. By holding down the Ctrl/Command key, you can select non-consecutive items in Adobe Bridge. The two images appear simultaneously in the Preview panel, located in the upper-right corner of the Bridge window.

You can easily reduce and enlarge the size of your thumbnails by pressing Ctrl+plus sign or Ctrl+minus sign in Windows or Command+plus sign or Command+minus sign in Mac OS.

7 Click and drag the selected images to the Music Extras folder. When the folder becomes highlighted, release the mouse. The files have now been moved into that folder.

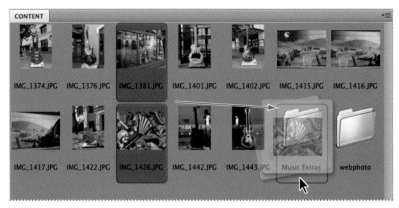

You can select multiple images and organize folders directly in Adobe Bridge.

8 Double-click on the Music Extras folder to view its contents. You see the two images that you moved.

9 Click on br01lessons in the Path bar to return to the br01lessons folder content.

Making a Favorite

As you work in Photoshop, you will find that you frequently access the same folders. One of the many great features in Bridge is that you can designate a frequently used folder as a Favorite, allowing you to quickly and easily access it from the Favorites panel. This is extremely helpful, especially if the folders that you are frequently accessing are stored deep in your file hierarchy.

1 Select the Favorites panel in the upper-left corner of the Bridge window to bring it to the front. In the list of Favorites, click on Desktop. Because the br01lessons folder is going to be frequently accessed in this lesson, you'll make it a Favorite.

2 Place your cursor over the br01lessons folder in the center pane (Content), and click and drag the br01lessons folder until you see a horizontal line appear in the Favorites panel. When a cursor with a plus sign (**♦**) appears, release the mouse. The folder is now listed as a Favorite.

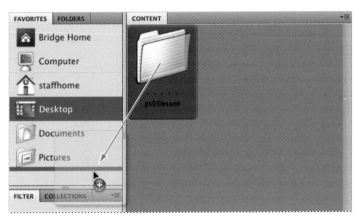

Drag a folder to the bottom of the Favorites panel to make it easier to locate.

3 Click on the br01lessons folder shown in the Favorites panel to view its contents. Note that creating a Favorite simply creates a shortcut for quick access to a folder; it does not copy the folder and its contents.

If your Favorite is created from a folder on an external hard drive or server, you will need to have the hard drive or server mounted in order to access it.

Creating and locating metadata

Metadata is information that can be stored with images. This information travels with the file, and makes it easy to search for and identify the file. In this section, you are going to find out how to locate and create metadata.

1 Make sure that you are viewing the contents of the br01lessons folder in the center pane of Adobe Bridge. If not, navigate to that folder now, or click on the br01lessons folder in the Favorites panel.

2   Choose Window > Workspace >Reset Standard Workspaces. This ensures that you are in the Essentials view and that all the default panels for Adobe Bridge are visible. Alternatively, you can click and hold on the Workspace drop-down menu, in the Application bar at the top of the Bridge workspace. You may need to maximize your Bridge window after you reset the workspace.

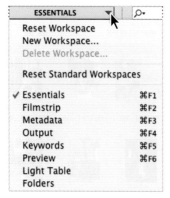

Resetting the workspace using the Workspace drop-down menu.

3   Click once on IMG_1374.JPG, and look for the Metadata and Keywords panels in the lower-right area of the Adobe Bridge workspace.

4   If Metadata is not in front, click on the Metadata panel now. In this panel, you see the image data that is stored with the file. Take a few moments to scroll through the data and view the information that was imported from the digital camera that was used to take the photo.

Click and drag the bar to the left of the Metadata panel farther to the left if you need to open up the window.

5   Select the arrow to the left of IPTC Core to reveal its contents. IPTC Core is the schema for XMP that provides a smooth and explicit transfer of metadata.

6   Here you see a series of pencils. The pencils indicate that you can enter information in these fields.

If you are not able to edit or add metadata information to a file, it may be locked. Right-click on the file and choose Reveal in Explorer (Windows) or Reveal in Finder (Mac OS). In Windows, right-click on the file, choose Properties, and uncheck Read-only; in Mac OS, right-click on the file, choose Get Info, then change the Ownership and Permissions to Read and Write.

7 Scroll down until you can see Description Writer, and click on the pencil next to it. All editable fields are highlighted, and a cursor appears in the Description Writer field.

8 Type your name, or type **student**.

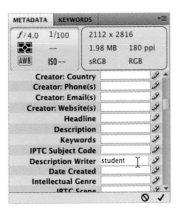

Reveal the IPTC contents and enter metadata information.

9 Scroll up to locate Creator: City. Click on the pencil icon to the right of the Creator City text box, type the name of your city, and then press the Tab key. The cursor is now in the State text field. Enter your state information.

10 Check the Apply checkbox (✔), located in the bottom-right corner of the Metadata panel, to apply your changes. You have now edited metadata that is attached to the image, information that will appear whenever someone opens your image in Bridge or views the image information in Adobe Photoshop, using File > File Info.

Using keywords

Keywords can reduce the amount of time it takes to find an image on a computer, by using logical words to help users locate images more quickly.

1 Click on the Keywords tab, which appears behind the Metadata panel. A list of commonly used keywords appears.

2 Click on the New Keyword button (⊕) at the bottom of the Keywords panel. Type **guitar** into the active text box, and then press Enter (Windows) or Return (Mac OS).

3 Check the empty checkbox to the left of the guitar keyword. This adds the guitar keyword to the selected image.

4   With the guitar keyword still selected, click on the New Sub Keyword button (👋). Type **Gibson** into the active text box, then press Enter (Windows) or Return (Mac OS).

5   Check the empty checkbox to the left of the Gibson keyword. You have now assigned a keyword and a subkeyword to the IMG_1374.JPG image.

Notice that the keywords you added appear at the top, under Assigned Keywords.

6   Click on the New Keyword button (🔁) at the bottom of the Keywords panel; a blank text field appears. Type **Austin** and press Enter (Windows) or Return (Mac OS). Then check the checkbox next to Austin to assign the keyword to this image.

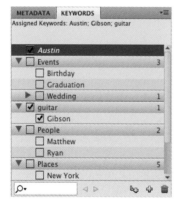

Add keywords to the keyword list, and then apply them to selected images.

You can add as many keywords as you like to an image, and you can keep them organized by adding sets. To add new sets, click on the folder icon at the bottom of the Keywords panel; this helps you organize keyword categories.

7   Right-click (Windows) or Ctrl+click (Mac OS) on the Wedding keyword, and choose the option Rename. When the text field becomes highlighted, type **Conference**, press Enter (Windows) or Return (Mac OS).

You can also enter information directly into the image by opening the image in Adobe Photoshop, and then choosing File > File Info. The categories that appear on the left include Description, Camera Data, IPTC Contact, and IPTC Content, among others. Once it is entered in the File Info dialog box, the information is visible in Adobe Bridge.

Opening a file from Adobe Bridge

Opening files from Adobe Bridge is a great way to begin the work process in Adobe Photoshop. Not only is it very visual, but important data stored with the files also makes it easier to locate the correct file.

1   Make sure you are viewing the contents of the br01lessons folder, and then double-click on image IMG_1402.JPG to open the file in Adobe Photoshop.

Sometimes you will find that double-clicking on a file opens it in a different application than expected. This can happen if you are working in generic file formats such as JPEG and GIF. To avoid this problem, you can right-click (Windows) or Ctrl+click (Mac OS) on the image, and choose Open With to select the appropriate application.

2   Choose File > Close to close the file in Photoshop and return to Adobe Bridge.

3   You can also click once to select an image and then choose File > Open, or use the keyboard shortcut Ctrl+O (Windows) or Command+O (Mac OS).

Searching for Files Using Adobe Bridge

Find the files that you want quickly and easily by using the Search tools built directly into Adobe Bridge, and taking advantage of the Filter panel.

In this example, you have a limited number of files to search within, but you will have the opportunity to see how helpful these search features can be.

Searching by name or keyword

Note that in the Default view of Adobe Bridge, you have a Search text box ready and waiting to use. To search for a file by keyword, simply type the name **criteria** into the text box and press Enter (Windows) or Return (Mac OS).

1   Type **guitar** into the Search text box and press Enter (Windows) or Return (Mac OS). Because you are looking within the active folder only, you should get a result immediately. The image file, IMG_1374.JPG, to which you added the guitar keyword, appears.

The remaining steps show you how to broaden your search.

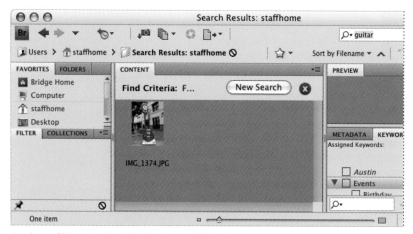

Search your folders using the tools built right into Adobe Bridge.

2   Click on the Folders tab to make sure that this panel is forward, and then click on your computer name. On the Windows platform, this might be called your C: Drive; in Mac OS, it might be called Macintosh HD.

3   Make sure the guitar text is still in the Search text box and press Enter (Windows) or Return (Mac OS) again. Now the entire hard drive is searched. In your case, maybe you are a musician, and you may find more guitar-related files. But in this example, the same image file is found.

4   Press the X to the right of the New Search button in the Content pane to cancel the search.

Using the Filter panel

If you have ever been in the position where you knew you put a file into a folder, but just can't seem to find it, you will love the Filter panel.

Using the Filter panel, you can look at attributes such as file type, keywords, and date created or modified, in order to narrow down the files that appear in the content window of Adobe Bridge.

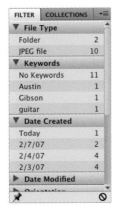

Find files quickly by selecting different criteria in the Filters panel.

Automation tools in Adobe Bridge

Adobe Bridge provides many tools to help you automate tasks. In this section, you will learn how to access and take advantage of some of these features.

Automated tools for Photoshop: Web Photo Gallery

If you want to share images online, you can use the Web Photo Gallery, which creates a web site that features a home page with thumbnail images and gallery pages with full-size images. You select the images you want to include in the site and Adobe Bridge does the rest, from automatically creating navigation images, like arrows, links, and buttons, to creating Flash files. This is a fun feature that you can take advantage of quickly, even if you have no coding experience. If you have coding experience, or if you want to edit the pages further, you can open the pages in Adobe Dreamweaver or any other HTML editor to customize them.

1   Make sure that you are viewing the contents of the br01lessons folder. If you do not see the contents of the br01lessons folder in the content window in Bridge, choose the Favorites panel and click on Desktop. Click on the br01lessons folder. If you stored the lesson files elsewhere, use the navigation tools in Bridge to locate your lesson files.

2 In the Content window, click once on image IMG_1374.JPG, and then use the scroll bar to locate the image named IMG_1443.JPG. Hold down the Shift key and click on the last image; this selects both images and all the images in between.

3 Click and hold down on the Output drop-down menu in the Application bar, and choose Output to Web or PDF; the workspace changes to reveal an Output panel on the right.

Select multiple images and then select the Output
drop-down menu.

If you cannot see all the options in the Output panel, click and drag the vertical bar to the left of the panel to increase its size.

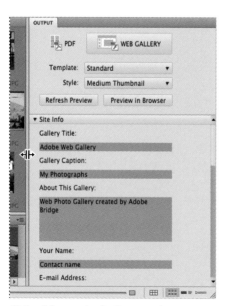

Click and drag to resize the Output panel.

4 Press the Web Gallery button at the top of the Output panel.

5   Click and hold on the Templates drop-down menu, and choose HTML Gallery. As you can see, there are a lot of options to choose from, including Lightroom Flash Galleries. In this example, you will keep it simple.

6   From the Styles drop-down menu, choose Lightroom.

7   In the Site Info section of the Output panel, type a title in the Gallery Title text box; for this example, you can type **My First Web Gallery**.

8   You can also add photograph captions if you like, as well as text in the About This Gallery text box, to include more information. In this example, those are left at their defaults.

9   Using the scroll bar to the right of the Style Info section, click and drag to scroll down through the rest of the options. Note that you can add additional contact information, and define colors that you want to use for different objects on the page, including text.

10   Press the Browser Preview button that is located in the upper half of the Output panel; your web site is automatically created.

The completed web site, using Web Gallery.

Saving or uploading your Web Gallery

So now you have an incredible Web Gallery, but what do you do with it? The Web Photo Gallery feature creates an index page, individual gallery pages, and images, and so you need someplace to put them. You have a couple options available if you click the scroll bar to the right of Style information and drag down until you see the options for Gallery Name. Note that you can choose to save your Gallery to a location on your hard drive, or input the FTP login information directly in Adobe Bridge to upload your file directly to a server. In this example, you will save the Web Gallery to the folder named webphoto in your br01lessons folder.

1 Scroll down to the bottom of the Output panel, where you see two options for output: Save to Disk, and Upload.

2 Click the radio button for *Save to Disk*, and then press the Browse button and navigate to the br01lessons folder. Select the already-created folder named webphoto, and press Choose; then press the Save button.

A dialog box appears, indicating that you have successfully created a Web Gallery; press OK.

You have successfully saved your Web Gallery. Use Adobe Bridge to navigate and open the contents of this folder to see that a folder named My First Web Gallery is inside your webphoto folder. Open the contents to see that your components are neatly organized so that you can open them in your web editor and customize them, or send them to your web site administrator for uploading.

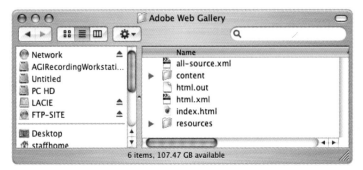

The completed web site, when saved to the hard drive.

Automated tools for Photoshop: PDF contact sheet

By creating a PDF contact sheet, you can assemble a series of images into one file for such purposes as client approval and summaries of folders.

1   Make sure that you are viewing the contents of the br01lessons folder. If you do not see the contents of the br01lessons folder in the content window in Bridge, choose the Favorites panel and click on Desktop. Click on the br01lessons folder. If you stored the lesson files elsewhere, use the navigation tools in Bridge to locate your lesson files.

2   In the Content window, at the bottom of the workspace, click once on image IMG_1374.JPG then use the scroll bar to locate the image named IMG_1443.JPG. Hold down the Shift key and click on the last image; this selects both images and all the images in between.

3   If your Output panel is no longer visible, click on the Output button and choose Output to Web or PDF. In the Output panel, click on the PDF button.

4   From the Template drop-down menu, choose 5 x 8 Contact Sheet.

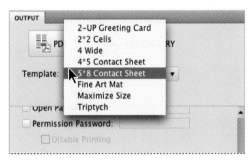

Choose to create a PDF contact sheet from the Template drop-down menu.

5   In the Document section of the Output panel, choose U.S. Paper from the Page Preset drop-down menu.

Scroll down and notice that you have options for final size, document quality, and even security in the Output panel. You will leave these items at the default and scroll down to the Playback Options section of this panel.

6   Because this PDF is to be used as a contact sheet, and not a PDF slide show, uncheck the three options that relate to a PDF presentation: *Open in Full Screen Mode*, *Advance Every 5 Seconds*, and *Loop After Last Page*.

7   Scroll down to the bottom of the Output panel and check the checkbox to *View PDF After Save*; then press the Save button. The Save As dialog box appears.

8   In the Save As dialog box, type **contact** and browse to save the file in your br01lessons folder; press Save.

A dialog box appears, indicating that you have successfully created a PDF contact sheet; press OK. The contact.pdf file is saved in your br01lessons folder and your contact sheet is launched in Adobe Acrobat for you to view.

9   After examining your contact sheet in Adobe Acrobat, choose File > Close to close the contact.pdf file.

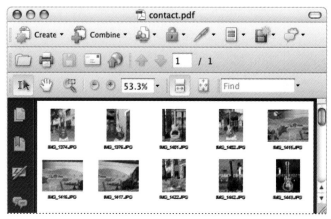

The completed PDF contact sheet.

Changing the view

You can work the way you like by adjusting the look and feel of Adobe Bridge. Changing the view can help you focus on what is important to see in the content section of the Bridge workspace. Whether you need to focus on content or thumbnails, there is a view that can help you.

1   Before experimenting with the views, make sure that you are in the default workspace by selecting Window > Workspace > Reset Standard Workspaces.

2   Click on the Click to Lock to Thumbnail Grid button (⊞) in the lower-right corner of the Bridge workspace. The images are organized into a grid.

3 Now click on the View Content as Details button (▬≡) to see a thumbnail and details about creation date, last modified date, and file size.

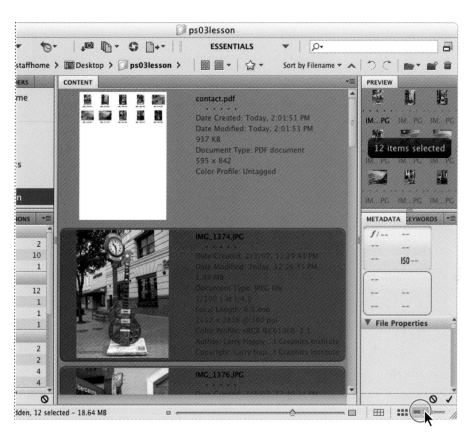

Changing the view of Adobe Bridge.

4 Choose the View as List button (≡) to see the contents consolidated into a neat list, which you can easily scroll through.

5 Click on the View Content as Thumbnails button (⠿) to return to the default thumbnail view.

6 Experiment with changing the size of the thumbnails in the Content panel by using the slider to the left of the preview buttons. Don't forget, you can also change the thumbnail size by pressing Ctrl+plus sign or Ctrl+minus sign (Windows) or Command+plus sign or Command+minus sign (Mac OS).

Adobe Bridge Home

Adobe Bridge Home delivers up-to-date learning resources for all your Adobe Creative Suite 4 components in one convenient location. Watch in-depth video tutorials, listen to podcasts by leading designers, learn about training events, and more.

1   Access Bridge Home by selecting the Favorites panel to bring it forward.

2   Select Bridge Home from the Favorites panel. If you are connected to the Internet, a helpful page appears in the Content panel that allows you to find cool tips and tricks on your favorite Adobe products, as well as giving you access to tutorials and online forums. You are never without help if you use Adobe Bridge Home.

Self study

As you work with Bridge, create some new Favorites of folders that you frequently use. You might also want to practice removing Favorites: highlight the Favorite and choose File > Remove from Favorites. Also, explore creating a PDF slide show when in the Adobe Media Gallery workspace. By turning on the Playback options in the Output panel, you can create a full-screen presentation of the images in the Content panel of Adobe Bridge.

Review

Questions

1   How do you access Photoshop automation features from within Adobe Bridge?

2   Where do you find the metadata for an image, and how do you know if the metadata is editable?

3   Which panel in Adobe Bridge enables you to organize your files on your computer?

4   Which panel allows you to create Web Galleries, PDF presentations, and contact sheets?

Answers

1   You can access automated tools for Adobe Photoshop by choosing Tools > Photoshop.

2   You find metadata information in the Metadata and Keywords panels in the lower-right corner of the Bridge workspace. Metadata is editable if it has the pencil icon next to it.

3   You can use the Folders panel to organize your files.

4   You must be in the Output panel to create Web Galleries, PDF presentations, and contact sheets.

What you'll learn in this lesson:

- How to work with multiple documents
- Creating a simple composition
- New masking features
- Introduction to 3D feature

Exploring Photoshop

In this lesson, you are offered the opportunity to dive right into Adobe Photoshop CS4 and put together an exciting composition. This lesson was created to help current users (or fast learners) quickly discover some of the hottest new features in Photoshop CS4.

Starting up

Before starting, make sure that your tools and panels are consistent by resetting your preferences. See "Resetting Adobe Photoshop CS4 preferences" on pages XXV-XXVI.

Note that users of all levels can follow this step-by-step exercise, but if you are a new user, it is recommended that you start with Photoshop Lesson 2, "Getting to Know the Workspace," and return to this lesson when you have completed the remaining lessons.

You will work with several files from the ps01lessons folder in this lesson. Make sure that you have loaded the CS4lessons folder onto your hard drive from the supplied DVD. See "Loading lesson files" on page XXIX. Now, let's take a look at what's new in Photoshop CS4.

See Lesson 1 in action!

Use the accompanying video to gain a better understanding of how to use some of the features shown in this lesson. The video tutorial for this lesson can be found on the included DVD.

Taking a look at the final project

In this lesson, you'll create a 3D postcard. The composition for the postcard will come from several different sources, allowing you to use some of the new cloning tools, mask features, and adjustments in Adobe Photoshop CS4.

1 Choose File > Browse in Bridge, or click on the Launch Bridge button (Br) in the Application bar. You will be using Adobe Bridge to locate your images for this lesson, but it can also help you to search, organize, and manage your documents. Refer to Lesson 3, "Using Adobe Bridge," to find out more about Adobe Bridge.

2. In Bridge choose Window > Workspace > Essentials to see the entire workspace.

If you are unfamiliar with Adobe Bridge, simply click on the Folders tab in the upper-left corner of the workspace to navigate from one folder to another. If you saved your lesson files on the desktop, use the slider and click on Desktop; all the folders on your desktop appear in the Content panel.

3 Navigate to the ps01lessons folder and double-click to open the file named ps0101_done.psd. A 3D image of a postcard appears. If you receive a warning dialog box about your video card, click OK.

The completed 3D postcard.

It may not look 3D, but this image can be rotated, repositioned, and even have its light source edited.

4 Click on the 3D Rotate tool (🔄) and click and drag to reposition the artwork. You will find out more about the new and improved 3D features in Photoshop in Lesson 13, "Introducing 3D."

5   Now that you have seen the final image that you will create, choose File > Close. When the Warning dialog box appears, click No, you do not want to save the file.

Starting the composition

The finished postcard composition was created from three different source images. In this part of the lesson, you will start to pull those images together.

1   Choose File > Browse in Bridge, or click on the Launch Bridge button () in the Application bar.

2   Navigate to the ps01lessons folder and click once on the file named ps0101.psd; then Ctrl+click (Windows) or Command+click (Mac OS) on the file named ps0102.psd. Both thumbnails are selected in Bridge.

3   Choose File > Open to open both the images at once in Photoshop CS4. If your preferences were not reset you might receive a Color Profile warning dialog box. Press OK.

If files do not open in Photoshop CS4, choose File > Open With, and then select Adobe Photoshop CS4.

In order to see both images at once, you will use the new Arrange Documents button (▦) in the Application bar in Photoshop.

The Application bar runs across the top of your Photoshop work area, and is discussed in more detail in Lesson 2, "Getting to Know the Workspace."

4   Click and hold on the Arrange Documents button in the Application bar and select 2 Up from the drop-down menu; both images appear side-by-side.

View both images by using the Arrange Documents button.

If you used previous versions of Photoshop, you might find the new system of docking image windows different than what you are used to. If you would rather have your image windows "float" as in previous versions, choose Float All in Windows from the Arrange Documents drop-down menu.

5 Select the Move tool (⬩+) and then click on the ps0102.psd image. Click and drag the ps0102.psd image on top of the ps0101.psd image window. Release the mouse when the cursor changes to a plus sign (+), or when you see a grey outline of the ps0102.psd image on top of the ps0101.psd image. If you receive a message that the layer is locked, try again, as you did not drag the file over far enough.

Click and drag the ps0102.psd image on top of the ps0101.psd image.

6 Choose Window > Layers to see that the ps0101.psd image now has two layers.

7 Double-click on the text Layer 1 in the Layers panel to the right of the layer thumbnail and type **boy** to give the new layer an appropriate name.

8 Click once on the ps0102.psd image to make it the active window, and then choose File > Close to close the file. If you are asked to save changes, click No.

9 If you can not see the entire window press Ctrl+0 (zero) or Command+0 (zero) to fit the window into the screen.

10 With the Move tool still selected, click on the newly placed ps0102 layer and drag, repositioning the child's head to be closer to the lower-left corner. If his hand on the right is not visible, click and drag the image up slightly, as shown in the figure.

Reposition the new layer so that the child's head is in the lower-left corner of the image.

You will now take a moment to save this as a work file.

11 Choose File > Save As, to open the Save As dialog box. Using the Save In drop-down menu, navigate to the ps01lessons folder. Type **ps0101_work** in the File Name text box and choose Photoshop (PSD, PDD) from the Format drop-down menu. Then click Save. Leave the file open for the next part of this lesson. If the Photoshop Format Options dialog box appears, press OK.

Using the new Mask panel

Adding masks in Photoshop has been an available feature since the use of channels in the very first version of Photoshop. Over time, both the creation and editing of masks have been improved to make these features more accessible and easier to use, as is apparent with the addition of the Masks panel in Photoshop CS4.

1 Select the Lasso tool (☌) from the Tools panel, and click and drag a rough selection around the boy's head and visible body. The selection does not have to be perfect, as you will refine the edge in the next part of this lesson.

Because you want to select the image to the bottom edge of the window, you should drag outside of the image area.

2   Choose Window > Masks, if the Masks panel is not visible. With the selection still active, click on the Add a Pixel Mask button (⟳) in the upper-right corner of the Masks panel.

A very rough mask is created, eliminating the area outside of your selection; you will now refine that selection.

With an active selection, click on the   *The selection is converted into a mask.*
Add a Pixel Mask button.

In the Masks panel, you can choose to set the Density (opaqueness of the mask) or the Feather (softness of the edge), using the sliders. To achieve even more control, you can select the Mask Edge button. In this lesson, you are briefly introduced to the Refine Edge dialog box; you can find more details about selections in Lesson 5, "Making the Best Selections."

3   Click once on the Mask Edge button to open the Refine Edge dialog box. The selection appears with a white background, to help you see your selection. Now use the sliders, or enter values in the appropriate text box, to make the following adjustments.

- Change the Radius to 5. The Radius determines how much of an area will be affected by the adjustments you are making.

- Make sure the Contrast is set to 0 (zero).

- Set Smooth to 3.

- Change Feather to 10. This softens the hard edge.

- Use the Contract/Expand slider to adjust your selection so that it is as close to the edge of the boy as possible. Make this a visual change based upon your selection. In this example, the selection had to be contracted to −25 pixels to bring it closer to the boy.

4 Press OK to close the Refine Mask dialog box.

You have added a layer mask that can be disabled or edited at any time.

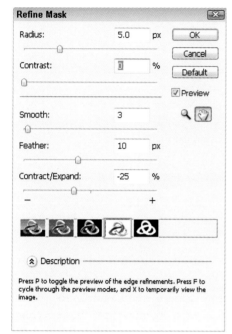

Refine the selection (mask).

The selection edge is softened with feathering.

Disable and re-enable a layer mask by Shift+clicking on the mask thumbnail in the Layer's panel.

5 Using the Move tool (✛), click and drag the boy layer down slightly so as not to see the feathered edge along the bottom.

You can find out in Lesson 9, "Taking Layers to the Max," how you can paint on a layer mask to fine-tune selections.

6 Choose File > Save to save this file. Keep it open for the next part of this lesson.

Adding a graphic image with the Clone tool

In this next part of the lesson, you will add a graphic element as a new layer and change the blending mode. This will add a subtle texture to the image.

1   When a new layer is added, it appears by default on top of the active layer. Because this graphic is going to be positioned between the Background layer and the boy layer, you should select the Background layer. Do this by clicking on Background in the Layers panel.

2   Hold down the Alt (Windows) or Option (Mac OS) key and press the Create a New Layer button in the Layers panel. By holding down the Alt/Option key, you are offered the opportunity to name a layer before it is created. In the New Layer dialog box, type **graphic** in the Name text box, then press OK.

3   Choose File > Browse in Bridge or click on the Launch Bridge button (Br) in the Application bar.

4   If you are not already in the ps01lessons folder, navigate to it now. Then double-click to open the file named ps0103.psd. An image of a circular graphic appears.

5   Click and hold on the Arrange Documents button (▦) in the Application bar and select 2 Up from the drop-down menu; both images appear side-by-side.

6   Click on the tab (at the top of the image window) for the ps0103.psd image, and then select the Clone Stamp tool (♨) from the Tools panel. Alt+click (Windows) or Option+click (Mac OS) on the center of the circle graphic ps0103.psd. This sets the source for the Clone tool.

7   Now click on the tab for the ps0101_work.psd image to make it the active image, and position the cursor just above the boy's head. Note that in CS4 you see a pixel preview of the clone source before you start painting. You can make adjustments to the preview using the Clone Source panel, available under the Window menu item. In this lesson, you will keep the preview at its default. You can find out more about the Clone Source panel in Lesson 6, "Painting and Retouching." Before you start cloning, you will change the blending mode. The blending mode affects how the underlying image interacts with the cloned pixels that you will be creating.

8 With the Clone Stamp tool selected, choose Overlay from the Mode drop-down menu in the Application bar. Then type **20** in the Opacity text box. The cloning that you do will now be overlaid on top of the Background layer at a light opacity.

In order to get a nice, painterly feel to the text that you apply, you will make your brush a little softer.

9 With the Clone tool selected, click on the Brush Preset arrow. It is to the right of the Brush preview in the Application bar. Then double-click on the Soft Round 200 pixel brush.

By double-clicking on a brush, you select it and simultaneously close the Brush panel.

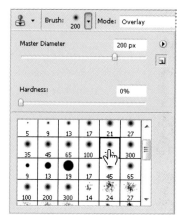

Select the Soft Round 200 pixel brush.

10 Using the Clone Stamp tool, lightly start brushing above the boy's head.

Because of the pixel preview (on the cursor), it may appear that you are painting on top of the boy's head, but the pixels are actually being painted on the graphic layer, which is under the layer with the image of the boy.

You see a light copy of the graphic appearing. The benefit of using a light opacity is that you can brush (by clicking, dragging, and releasing the mouse) lightly in some areas, or repeatedly in other areas to increase the opacity of the cloned pixels. Using the Clone Stamp tool, paint the outside edges of the graphics lightly, but paint repeatedly over the center part of the image to make those clone pixels more opaque.

Paint repeatedly in the center area, above the boy's head, to build up the opacity.

11 When you have cloned the graphic to your satisfaction, click on the image tab for ps0103.psd to activate that window, and then choose File > Close. If you are prompted to save changes, choose No.

12 Choose File > Save. Keep the file open for the next part of this lesson.

Don't like what you created with the Clone Stamp tool and want to try it again? The benefit of working on a new blank layer is that you can choose Select > All and then press the Delete key to delete the cloned pixels, and start cloning again.

Adding an adjustment layer to the composition

Adjustment layers are not new to Photoshop. They have been used for several versions as a method for making non-destructive editing changes to layers. In this lesson you find out how to create an adjustment layer using the new Adjustments panel. For more details about adjustment layers, read Lesson 9, "Taking Layers to the Max."

1 If the Layers panel is not visible, choose Window > Layers.

2 Click on the layer named boy. The default is for an adjustment layer to appear on top of the active layer.

3 Click on the Create New Fill or Adjustment Layer button (●) at the bottom of the Layers panel and select Black & White. An adjustment layer is applied, on top of the boy layer, and the image changes to look as though it is a grayscale image.

The Adjustments panel is now be visible. New in Photoshop CS4, you make revisions to the active adjustment layer using this panel. If you do not see the Adjustments panel, choose Window > Adjustments.

Creating a new adjustment layer.   *All layers beneath are affected.*

In the Adjustments panel, you can change the options that are available for the Black & White adjustment. For this part of the lesson, you will just use the Click and Drag adjustment feature.

4 Select the Click and Drag in Image button (☝). Then position the cursor over the boy's shirt in the image.

5 Click and drag to the right to see that you are visually adjusting the color interpretation of his red shirt to make it a lighter gray. Photoshop is interpreting and adjusting the tonality in the whole image based on where the you click.

6 Click and drag to the left to create a darker gray. No specific settings are required for this part of the lesson. Experiment by clicking and dragging on various parts of the boy image to change the lights and darks in the grayscale image.

In order to apply the grayscale to only the layer immediately beneath, you can *clip* the adjustment.

7   Click on the This Adjustment Affects All Layers Below button (●) at the bottom of the Adjustments panel. The only layer being affected by the Black & White adjustment layer is the boy layer.

Click on the This Adjustment Affects   *The grayscale applies only to the layer directly underneath it.*
All Layers Below button.

8   Choose File > Save to save this file, and keep it open for the next part of this lesson.

Adding a text layer

Adding text is the final step before converting this image into a 3D object. In this part of the lesson, you will create text that will be positioned off to the right of the postcard. For this lesson you will simply set the text as instructed, but if you want to discover more possibilities with text, read Lesson 4, "The Basics of Working in Photoshop."

1   Make sure that the topmost (Black & White) layer is selected; then select the Type tool (T) and click off to the right of the boy in the image area. The cursor appears.

2   Type **Bike**, and then press the Enter (Windows) or Return (Mac OS) key and type **On!**

3   Press Ctrl+A (Windows) or Command+A (Mac OS) or choose Select > Select All to activate both words. You will now take advantage of some keyboard shortcuts to help speed up the font size and typeface selection.

4 Hold down Ctrl+Shift (Windows) or Command+Shift (Mac OS) and then repeatedly press the > (Greater Than) key to make the text incrementally larger. Continue pressing the > key until your text is approximately 36 points. If you are not in favor of using keyboard shortcuts, you may simply type **36** into the Font size text box in the Application bar.

To make text incrementally smaller, you use the < (Less Than) key instead of the > key.

5 Change the leading, or space between the lines of text, by pressing Alt+up arrow (Windows) or Option+up arrow (Mac OS). If you decrease the space too much, you can press Alt+down arrow (Windows) or Option+down arrow (Mac OS) to increase the leading, the vertical space between the lines of type. You do not need any specific settings for this step; simply set the leading to the amount you feel works well.

6 Click and drag to highlight the font name in the Application bar at the top of the image area, and then press the up or down arrow key to change your font selection to the font that is on the list before or after the current font selection. This is an easy visual method to use when selecting a font. No specific font is required; in the example, the Poor Richard font is selected.

7 To change the color of the text to white, click once on the Set the Text Color box in the Application bar. When the Color Picker appears, click on a white (or light) color in the upper-left corner of the color pane. Press OK. The text is now white.

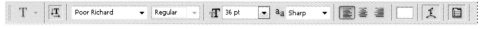

Change the text to 36 points, and then select the font and text color.

8 If necessary, switch to the Move tool (⊹) and reposition the text to be centered in the sky area off to the right in the image.

9 Press Ctrl+S (Windows) or Command+S (Mac OS) to save this file. Keep it open for the next part of this lesson.

Making a 3D postcard

You will now convert your flat image into a 3D postcard. You will do this by using the new 3D features and tools that have been added to Photoshop CS4. You will experiment more with the new and improved 3D features in Lesson 13, "Introducing 3D."

Converting multiple layers into one smart object layer

Because the 3D features work with an individual layer, you will first convert the multiple layers in this image into one smart object layer. A smart object layer can embed multiple layers into one layer. You can re-open the separate layers by double-clicking on the smart object layer in the Layers panel. Find out more about smart objects in Lesson 10, "Getting Smart in Photoshop."

1   Click once on the bottom (Background) layer, and then hold down the Shift key and click on the topmost layer (Bike On!). All layers are now selected.

2   Click and hold on the panel menu (arrow in the upper-right corner of the Layers panel) and select Convert to Smart Object from the panel drop-down menu. The layers are consolidated into one layer. As a default, the smart object layer takes on the name of the topmost layer.

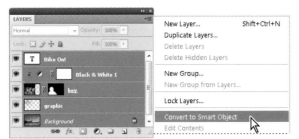

Select all layers.   *Convert them to one smart object layer.*

Turning your image into a 3D texture

You will now take the smart object layer that you have created and apply it as a texture to a 3D object. In this example you will create a simple 3D postcard.

To avoid clipping off some of the layer, you will expand the canvas. This makes your work area a little larger, and creates some needed space for 3D rotation.

1   Choose Image > Canvas Size; the Canvas Size dialog box appears.

2   Type **125** in the Width text box and then choose percent from the measurement units drop-down menu. Then type **125** in the Height text box, and press OK. An additional 25 percent of transparency appears around the image.

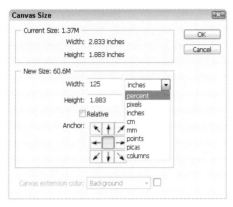

Increase the canvas size.   *The result.*

3   With the smart object Bike On! still selected, choose 3D > New 3D Postcard from Layer. You may not see any change occur at this time.

4   Choose the 3D Rotate tool ( ) from the Tools panel, and then click and drag the image. The image rotates in space, much like an actual postcard might. Experiment with the rotation until you find a satisfactory position; no specific coordinates are required for this.

The completed file.

Congratulations! You have completed the tour of Adobe Photoshop CS4. Read to discover more details about the features you were introduced to in this lesson.

What you'll learn in this lesson:

- Opening a file using Adobe Bridge
- Using Photoshop tools
- Navigating in your image area
- Using panels

Getting to Know the Workspace

In this lesson, you'll learn how to best use the Adobe Photoshop CS4 work area. You will also discover how to open a document using Adobe Bridge, how to use the Tools panel, and how to easily navigate images.

Starting up

Adobe Photoshop is an image-editing program that can open an image captured by a scanner or digital camera, or downloaded from the web. It can also open captured video images and vector illustrations. In addition, you can create new documents in Photoshop, including vector graphics, which are scalable image files (for example, the images can be enlarged or reduced in size with no loss of clarity).

Before starting, make sure that your tools and panels are consistent by resetting your preferences. See "Resetting Adobe Photoshop CS4 preferences" on pages XXV-XXVI.

You will work with several files from the ps02lessons folder in this lesson. Make sure that you have loaded the CS4lessons folder onto your hard drive from the supplied DVD. See "Loading lesson files" on page XXIX.

See Lesson 2 in action!

Use the accompanying video to gain a better understanding of how to use some of the features shown in this lesson. The video tutorial for this lesson can be found on the included DVD.

Opening an existing document in Adobe Bridge

As mentioned previously, Adobe Bridge is a standalone application that can be accessed using the File menu in any of the Creative Suite 4 applications, or by using the Launch Bridge button (Br) that is found on the Application bar or control panels of most of the Creative Suite 4 applications.

1 Launch Adobe Photoshop CS4. If the Welcome menu appears, choose Close.

2 Choose File > Browse in Bridge. If the Folders panel is not in the foreground, click on it now to bring it forward, then click on Desktop, the first list item in the Folders panel.

3 Open the CS4lessons folder that you have already copied onto your desktop, and then open the ps02lessons folder.

4 Locate and then double-click on the image named ps0201.psd to open it in Photoshop. An image of a girl with a dandelion appears.

As you practice with the files throughout this book, you will find that you are instructed to save a work file immediately after opening the original file.

5   Choose File > Save As to save a copy of this document to your ps02lessons folder.

6   Navigate to the ps02lessons folder. In the File name text field, type **ps0201_work**, and choose Photoshop from the Format drop-down menu. Click Save.

Discovering the Tools panel

When you start Photoshop, the Tools panel appears docked on the left side of the screen—it is not a floating Tools panel, as it was in earlier versions of Photoshop. There are four main groups of tools, separated by functionality on the Tools panel: selection, cropping, and measuring; retouching and painting; drawing and type; and 3D and navigation.

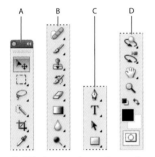

A. Selection, cropping, and measuring tools.
B. Retouching and painting tools.
C. Drawing and type tools.
D. 3D and navigation tools.

Selection, Cropping, and Measuring Tools

ICON	TOOL NAME	USE	WHERE IT'S COVERED
	Move (V)	Moves selections or layers.	Lesson 4
	Marquee (M)	Makes rectangular, elliptical, single row, and single column selections.	Lesson 4
	Lasso (L)	Makes freehand, polygonal (straight-edged), and magnetic selections.	Lesson 4
	Quick Selection (W)	Paints selections.	Lesson 4
	Crop (C)	Crops an image.	Lesson 6
	Eyedropper (I)	Samples pixels.	Lesson 5

Retouching and Painting Tools

ICON	TOOL NAME	USE	WHERE IT'S COVERED
	Spot Healing (J)	Removes imperfections.	Lesson 5
	Brush (B)	Paints the foreground color.	Lesson 5
	Clone Stamp (S)	Paints with a sample of the image.	Lesson 5
	History Brush (Y)	Paints a duplicate of the selected state or snapshot.	Lesson 5
	Eraser (E)	Erases pixels—or reverts to a saved history state.	Lesson 5
	Gradient (G)	Creates a gradient.	Lesson 5
	Blur (R)	Blurs pixels.	Not referenced in this book
	Dodge (O)	Lightens pixels in an image.	Lesson 4

Drawing and Type Tools

ICON	TOOL NAME	USE	WHERE IT'S COVERED
	Pen (P)	Draws a vector path.	Lesson 4
T	Horizontal Type (T)	Creates a type layer.	Lesson 3
	Path Selection (A)	Allows you to manipulate a path.	Lesson 6
	Rectangle (U)	Draws vector shapes.	Lesson 2

3D and Navigation Tools

ICON	TOOL NAME	USE	WHERE IT'S COVERED
	3D Rotate (K)	Rotates 3D objects.	Not referenced in this book
	3D Orbit (N)	Changes the view of 3D objects.	Not referenced in this book
	Hand (H)	Navigates the page.	Lesson 2
	Zoom (Z)	Increases and decreases the relative size of the view.	Lesson 2

Can't tell the tools apart? You can view tooltips that reveal a tool's name and keyboard shortcut by positioning your cursor over the tool.

The Tools panel is in a space-saving, one-column format. Click on the gray title bar area above the Tools panel to bring the Tools panel into the two-column view. Click on the title bar again to bring the Tools panel back to the default, single-column view. Keep the Tools panel set to whichever format works best for you

Hidden tools

Some of the tools in the Tools panel display a small triangle at the bottom-right corner; this means that there are additional tools hidden under the tool.

1   Click and hold the Blur tool to see the hidden Sharpen and Smudge tools.

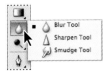

Selecting a hidden tool.

2   Drag to the Smudge tool (👆) and release. The Smudge tool is now the visible tool.

Most tools have options that you can adjust, using the Options bar that runs across the top of your document window. In this case, you will change an option for the Smudge tool before using it on your image.

3   Click on the arrow to the right of Brush in the Options bar to open up the Brush Preset picker. Using the Master Diameter slider, slide to the right until you reach approximately the 100 mark, or type **100** into the Master Diameter text field.

Now you can try painting with the tool you just customized.

4 Click and drag over the seeds flying away in the image. Use freeform brush strokes, as you want the smudging to look like part of the image is being stirred up by the wind. Have fun with this part of the lesson and smudge any part of the image you like. Don't worry; your next step is to revert the file back to its last saved version.

Smudging the seeds.

5 Choose File > Revert. The image is returned to its last saved version.

Navigating the image area

To work most efficiently in Photoshop, you'll want to know how to zoom (magnify) in and out of your image. Changing the zoom level allows you to select and paint accurately and helps you see details that you might otherwise have overlooked. The zoom function has a range from a single pixel up to a 3200 percent enlargement, which gives you a lot of flexibility in terms of viewing your images.

You'll start by using the View menu to reduce and enlarge the document view, and end by fitting the entire document on your screen.

1 Choose View > Zoom In to enlarge the display of ps0201_work.psd.

2 Press Ctrl+plus sign (Windows) or Command+plus sign (Mac OS) to zoom in again. This is the keyboard shortcut for the Zoom In command that you accessed previously from the View menu.

3 Press Ctrl+minus sign (Windows) or Command+minus sign (Mac OS) to zoom out. This is the keyboard shortcut for View > Zoom Out.

Now you will fit the entire image on the screen.

4 Choose View > Fit on Screen, or use the keyboard shortcut Ctrl+0 (zero) (Windows) or Command+0 (zero) (Mac OS), to fit the document to the screen.

5 You can also display artwork at the size it will print by choosing View > Print Size.

Using the Zoom tool

When you use the Zoom tool (🔍), each click increases the view size to the next preset percentage, and centers the display of the image around the location in the image that you clicked on. By holding the Alt (Windows) or Option (Mac OS) key down (with the Zoom tool selected), you can zoom out of an image, decreasing the percentage and making the image view smaller. The magnifying glass cursor is empty when the image has reached either its maximum magnification level of 3200 percent or the minimum size of one pixel.

1 Choose View > Fit on Screen.

Fitting the image on the screen.

2 Select the Zoom tool, and click four times on the dandelion to zoom in. You can also use key modifiers to change the behavior of the Zoom tool.

3 Press Alt (Windows) or Option (Mac OS) while clicking with the Zoom tool to zoom out. You can accurately zoom into the exact region of an image by clicking and dragging a marquee around that area in your image.

4 With the Zoom tool still selected, hold down the mouse and click and drag from the top left of the dandelion to the bottom right of the dandelion. You are creating a rectangular marquee selection over the dandelion. Once you release the mouse, the area that was included in the marquee is now enlarged to fill the document window.

Dragging a marquee over the dandelion.

5 Double-click the Zoom tool in the Tools panel to return to a 100 percent view.

Because the Zoom tool is used so often, it would be tiresome to continually have to change from the Zoom tool back to the tool you were using. Read on to see how you can activate the Zoom tool at any time without deselecting your current tool.

6 Select the Move tool (⊕) at the very top of the Tools panel.

7 Hold down Ctrl+spacebar (Windows) or Command+spacebar (Mac OS) Note that on the Mac OS you must hold down spacebar before the Command key, otherwise you trigger Spotlight; the Move tool is temporarily converted into the Zoom In tool. While still holding down Ctrl/Command+spacebar, click and drag over the dandelion again, then release. Note that although you have changed the zoom level, the Move tool is still active.

You can zoom out by holding down Alt+spacebar (Windows) or Option+spacebar (Mac OS).

8 Choose View > Fit on Screen.

Using the Hand tool

The Hand tool allows you to move or pan the document. It is a lot like pushing a piece of paper around on your desk.

1 Select the Zoom tool (⌕), and click and drag on an area surrounding the dandelion.

2 Select the Hand tool (✋), then click and drag to the right to push the picture to the right. Notice that when the Hand tool is active, four view buttons appear in the Options bar (at the top of the work area) that allow you to change your current view to Actual Pixels, Fit Screen, Fill Screen, and Print Size. You can also select the Hand tool from the Application bar. Mac Users must choose Window > Application Bar to see the Application bar.

View options are available in the Options panel.

3 Select the Zoom tool and hold the spacebar. Notice that the cursor turns into the Hand tool. Click and drag left to view the dandelion again. By holding down the spacebar, you can access the Hand tool without deselecting the current tool.

4 Double-click the Hand tool in the Tools panel to fit the entire image on your screen. This is the same as using Ctrl+0 (zero) (Windows) or Command+0 (zero) (Mac OS).

Using the Rotate View tool

The Rotate View tool allows you to rotate the image view of a document to match the way you would typically draw or paint on paper or canvas. This does not change the orientation of a document, only the view. Note that this feature only works with OpenGL enabled document windows (see note on page 34.)

1 Click and hold on the Hand tool to display the hidden Rotate View tool.

2 Drag to the Rotate View tool and release. The Rotate View tool is now the active tool.

3 Click on the gray area just outside the boundary of the open image and drag to the left. As you are dragging, you see an image of a compass displayed in the center of the image, indicating the orientation of the image. The image is now rotated in a counter-clockwise direction.

4 Click and drag again, but this time hold down the Shift key while dragging. The image is now rotated in 15-degree increments, giving you precise control of the image rotation The image view can also be adjusted in the Options bar by typing in a numeric value or by dragging the line in the Rotation icon.

5   Double-click on the Rotate View tool or click the Reset View button in the Options bar
to return the view to normal.

Dragging to rotate the view of the image.

The ability to use the Rotate View tool is dependent upon the capabilities of your computer. The Rotate View tool relies on technology called OpenGL, which is used in high-performance graphics cards. When you install Photoshop, it looks to see if your computer's graphics card supports OpenGL and turns on the preference in Photoshop that enables OpenGL performance. If your computer's graphics card doesn't support OpenGL, then you will not be able to use the Rotation tool. In addition, you must be running Windows Vista or Mac OS X 10.4.11 or later to use the OpenGL features.

NAVIGATION SHORTCUTS	WINDOWS	MAC OS
Zoom In	Ctrl+plus sign Ctrl+spacebar	Command+plus sign Command+spacebar
Zoom Out	Ctrl+minus sign Alt+spacebar	Command+minus sign Option+spacebar
Turn Zoom tool into Zoom Out tool	Alt	Option
Fit on Screen	Ctrl+0 (zero) or double-click the Hand tool	Command+0 (zero) or double-click the Hand tool
Hand tool (except when Type tool is selected)	Press spacebar	Press spacebar

Tabbed windows

In Photoshop CS4 you now have control over how your windows appear in the workspace. You can work with floating image windows, or choose to tab your windows across the top of the workspace. If you are working on the Windows OS tabbed windows are the default. In this section you find out how to use the new tabbed workspace.

1. If you are a Macintosh user and want to experiment with tabbed windows choose Window > Application Frame.

2 Click the Launch Bridge button (Br) to switch to Adobe Bridge.

3 Double-click the ps0202.psd file to open the image in Photoshop. The image is displayed as a separate tab within Photoshop, allowing you to click on the tab to switch between active images.

Multiple open images appear as tabs at the top of the screen.

4 Click on the ps0202.psd tab to make it active; then click and drag the tab away from its tabbed position and release the mouse button. The image window is now floating.

5 Click the title bar of the floating window and drag upwards until your cursor is next to the tab of the other image. When you see a blue bar appear, release the mouse button. The image is now back to a tabbed window. Keep in mind that you can stop a window from tabbing accidently by holding down the Ctrl (Windows) or Command (Mac OS) key while dragging the floating window.

If you are a Windows user would prefer not to take advantage of the tabbed window feature, you can choose Edit > Preferences > Interface. In the Panels & Documents section uncheck Open Documents as Tabs and press OK.

To quickly move all floating windows back to tabbed windows, choose Window > Arrange > Consolidate All to Tabs.

Maximizing productivity with screen modes

Now that you can zoom in and out of your document, as well as reposition it in your image window, it's time to learn how to take advantage of screen modes. You have a choice of three screen modes in which to work. Most users start and stay in the default—standard screen mode—until they accidentally end up in another. Screen modes control how much space your current image occupies on your screen, and whether you can see other Photoshop documents as well. The Standard Screen mode is the default screen mode when you open Photoshop for the first time. It displays an image on a neutral gray background for easy and accurate viewing of color without distractions, and also provides a flexible work area for dealing with panels.

1 Click on the tab of the ps0201_work.psd image to make that image active.

2 Position your cursor on the vertical line that runs down the left side of the panel docking area. Click on the line and drag to the left. Notice that this not only expands the panel docking area, but it also dynamically changes the image window when you release the mouse. The document window is resized when dock widths change.

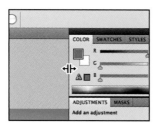

The image area dynamically changes as the panel docking area is resized.

3 Press the Tab key; the Tools panel and other panels disappear, creating much more workspace. Press the Tab key again to bring the Tools panel and other panels back.

4 Press Shift+Tab to hide the panel docking area while keeping the rest of the panels visible. Press Shift+Tab to bring the hidden panels back. Both the Tools panel and the panel docking area should now be visible.

As you position your cursor over various tools, you see a letter to the right of the tool name in the tooltip. This letter is the keyboard shortcut that you can use to access that tool. You could, in fact, work with the Tools panel closed and still have access to all the tools.

You will hide the panels once more so that you can take advantage of a hidden feature in Photoshop CS4.

Press the Tab key to hide the panels. Then position your cursor over the thin gray strip where the Tools panel had been, and pause. The Tools panel reappears. Note that the Tools panel appears only while your cursor is in the Tools panel area, and it disappears if you move your cursor out of that area. Try this with the panel docking area to the right of the screen, and watch as that also appears and disappears as your cursor moves over it.

By changing the screen modes, you can locate over-extended anchor points and select more accurately up to the edge of your image. Changing modes can also help you to present your image to clients in a clean workspace.

5 Press the Tab key again to display all the panels.

6 Press **F** to cycle to the next screen mode, which is Full Screen Mode With Menu Bar. This view surrounds the image out to the edge of the work area with a neutral gray (even behind the docking area) and displays only one image at a time, without tabs and centered within the work area. You can access additional open images by choosing the image name from the bottom of the Window menu.

You can also change your screen mode by clicking and holding on the Change Screen Mode button in the Application bar and selecting Full Screen Mode With Menu Bar.

The Change Screen Mode button accessed in the Application bar.

7   Notice that the gray background area (pasteboard) now extends to fill your entire screen, and your image is centered within that area. One of the benefits of working in this mode is that it provides more area when working on images.

The Full Screen mode with Menu bar.

8   Press **F** on the keyboard again to see the last screen mode, Full Screen Mode. You may receive a warning dialog box in this screen mode, indicating that you can exit the screen mode by pressing the F or Esc key because all the interface elements are hidden.

Full Screen mode.

This is Full Screen mode. A favorite with multimedia folks, it allows you to show others your document full-screen with no distracting screen elements. All menus and panels are hidden automatically in this mode; however, they are still accessible by hovering the cursor over the area where the panels normally reside. The panels temporarily reappear for easy access. If you'd like to see the panels while in this mode, simply press the Tab key to display and hide them.

9   Press the **F** key once to cycle back into Standard Screen mode, or click and hold on the Screen Mode button in the Application bar at the top of your screen and select Standard Screen Mode. Stay in this mode throughout this lesson.

Using panels

Much of the functionality in Photoshop resides in the panels, so you will want to know how to navigate them and find the ones you need quickly and easily. In Photoshop CS4, the panel docking area has become streamlined with added functionality. In this lesson, you will learn how to resize, expand, and convert panels to icons and then back to panels again. You will then find out how to save your favorite workspaces so that you don't have to set them up every time you work on a new project.

The default panel locations.

Putting the new panel system to use

To maximize your workspace, convert your panels to icons. You can get an idea of what the complete icon view for panels looks like by switching to the Basic workspace.

1　Click and hold down on the Workspace button on the right side of the Application bar and select Basic. A warning message appears, verifying that you want to change your menu and keyboard shortcut sets. Select Yes. Notice that all the panels are now converted to small icons. Move your cursor over the icons to see tooltips indicating the names of the panels associated with each icon.

Select the Basic workspace.

2　Click on the Navigator panel icon (✳); the Navigator panel opens.

The Navigator panel shows the entire image. A red box (called the proxy view) in the image area of the Navigator panel identifies the area currently being viewed in the active window. You can change the proxy view by clicking and dragging the red box to other locations in the Navigator panel. The view percentage—how much of the whole image you're currently able to see—is shown in the lower-left corner of the Navigator panel. To zoom in or out, you can either type in a new percentage or use the slider at the bottom of the panel.

Move the proxy view (red box) to navigate your image.

3   In the Navigator panel, drag the bottom slider to the right to approximately 200 percent to zoom into the image. The image on-screen updates once you release the mouse.

Use the slider to adjust the zoom level.

The box to the left of the slider automatically updates the percentage of zoom.

4   Move your cursor over the image in the Navigator panel. The cursor becomes a pointer (✋). Click anywhere over the preview image in the Navigator panel to move the area that is being previewed.

5   Now, move the cursor over the proxy view (red rectangle). Your pointer turns into the Hand tool (✋). Drag the proxy view to the top left. This allows you to quickly scroll to that part of the image. Next, you will control your zoom with a key modifier.

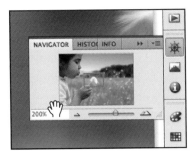

Reposition the proxy view.

6   Hold Ctrl (Windows) or Command (Mac OS) while hovering with your cursor over the Navigator panel; your cursor becomes the Zoom tool (🔍). Click and drag over the part of the image that contains the dandelion. When you release, the exact location of the region you created is enlarged to the maximum level.

Use Ctrl/Command to zoom.

7   Press Ctrl+0 (Windows) or Command+0 (Mac OS) to fit the image to the screen.

Choosing other panels

Now you will focus on a different panel, the Actions panel. To move from the Navigator panel to the Actions panel, select the Actions panel icon (▣). The Navigator panel changes back to an icon as the Actions panel appears. Actions are very useful tools; Photoshop comes with many predefined actions installed that can help you perform common tasks. You can use these actions as is, customize them to meet your needs, or create new actions. Actions are stored in sets to help you stay organized.

1   Select the arrow to the left of Default Actions to expand the folder, then use the scroll bar to locate the action named Sepia Toning (layer).

2   Select the Sepia Toning (layer) action by clicking on it, and then press the Play Selection button (▶) at the bottom of the Actions panel. The image is immediately converted to a sepia-toned image.

3   Now, select the History panel icon (▤). The Actions panel disappears and the History panel appears. Select the first state in the History panel that has the filename to its right; this is the state of the image when it was initially opened. The image file is reverted back to the original image data. You can read more about the History panel in Photoshop Lesson 5, "Painting and Retouching."

Expanding your panels

If you do not like deciphering what the panel icons represent, you can expand your panels. You can do this automatically with a preconfigured workspace, or you can choose to expand only the panels you want to see.

1   Click and hold on the Workspace button on the Application bar and select Essentials. The Essentials workspace is the default workspace in Photoshop and provides a workspace with all the panels expanded.

2   Collapse panels to button view by clicking on the dark gray bar (title bar) at the top of the panel docking area. Click on the dark gray bar again to expand them.

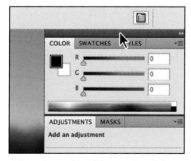

Collapse the panel by clicking on the title bar.

In addition, you can collapse specific panel groups by clicking on the gray bar above each panel group to collapse and expand them.

Customizing your panels

A panel group is made up of two or more panels that are stacked on top of each other. To view the other panels in a group, select the name on the tab of the panel. You will now learn how to organize your panels the way that you want.

1   Select the tab that reads Swatches; the Swatches tab is brought forward.

2   Now, select the Color tab to return the Color panel to the front of the panel group.

3   Click on the tab of the Color panel, and drag it away from the panel group and into the image area. The panel looks slightly transparent as you drag it away from the group. Release it—you have just removed a panel from a panel group and the docking area. Rearranging panels can help you keep frequently used panels together in one area.

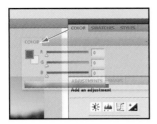

The Color panel as it is dragged away from a panel group.

4   Click the title bar area at the top of the Swatches panel and drag it over the Color panel. It appears slightly transparent as you drag. As soon as you see an outline around the Color panel, release the mouse. You have now made a panel group.

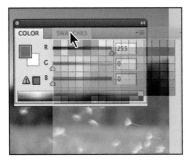

The Actions panel dragged over the History panel.

You'll now save a custom workspace. Saving a workspace is a good idea if you have production processes that often use the same panels. Saving workspaces is also helpful if you are in a situation where multiple users are sharing Photoshop on one computer.

5   Click on the workspace button at the far-right side of the Application bar and choose Save Workspace.

6 In the Save Workspace dialog box, type **1st Workspace**, and make sure that Panel Locations is checked. Press Save.

7 Whenever you want to reload a workspace, whether it's one that you created or one that comes standard with Photoshop, simply click the Workspace button in the Application bar and select the desired workspace from the list.

8 You have completed the "Getting to Know the Workspace" lesson. You can choose File > Save and then File > Close to close this file, or keep it open while you continue through the Self study and Review sections.

Self study

Choose File > Browse to access a practice file in your ps02lessons folder. You can double-click on ps0202.psd to explore workspaces further.

1 The Application bar contains several buttons that provide quick access to commonly used features inside Photoshop. One of those buttons, called Arrange Documents, allows you to arrange several open document windows in different ways. Explore the different views that Photoshop provides by choosing various icons found under the Arrange Documents button.

2 Using the Navigator panel, zoom into the image. Try holding down the Ctrl or Command key for the Zoom tool shortcut, available in the Navigator panel. Once you are zoomed in, navigate to different parts of the image using the proxy view (red box).

3 Click on the tabs of various panels and practice clicking and dragging panels from one group to another. You can put your panels back in order when you are finished experimenting by clicking on the Workspace button in the Application bar and choosing Essentials.

4 Use the Window menu to open the Info, Navigator, Histogram, and Layers panels, and then save a new workspace called color correction.

5 Take a look at some of the pre-built workspaces Photoshop has already made for you. They will change the panel locations, and some will highlight things in the menu that are relevant to each workspace. For instance, try selecting What's New in CS4 to see all the new features become highlighted in the menus.

Review

Questions

1 What is the Full Screen mode?

2 Name two ways to fit your image to the screen.

3 What happens in the default workspace when you exit one panel and select another?

4 How do you save a workspace?

5 Can you delete a workspace?

Answers

1 The Full Screen mode displays a document window on a black background and hides all interface elements from view.

2 You can fit your image to the screen by using the View menu, or by double-clicking the Hand tool (✋), right-clicking while you have the Zoom (🔍) or Hand tool selected, or by pressing Ctrl+0 (zero) (Windows) or Command+0 (zero) (Mac OS).

3 When you leave one panel to select another, the initial panel returns to its original location in the docking area.

4 You can save your own workspace by clicking on the Workspace button in the Application bar and choosing Save Workspace.

5 Yes, you can delete a workspace by clicking on the Workspace button in the Application bar and choosing Delete Workspace. Note that you cannot delete any of the default workspaces.

Lesson 3

What you'll learn in this lesson:

- Combining images
- Understanding document settings
- Removing backgrounds
- Saving files

The Basics of Working with Photoshop

In this lesson, you'll learn how to combine images while gaining an understanding of image resolution and file size. You'll also learn about file formats and options for saving your files for use on the web or in print.

Starting up

Before starting, make sure that your tools and panels are consistent by resetting your preferences. See "Resetting Adobe Photoshop CS4 preferences" on pages XXV-XXVI.

You will work with several files from the ps03lessons folder in this lesson. Make sure that you have loaded the CS4lessons folder onto your hard drive from the supplied DVD. See "Loading lesson files" on page XXIX.

In this lesson, you'll use multiple images to create a composite image that you will then save for both print and online use.

See Lesson 4 in action!

Use the accompanying video to gain a better understanding of how to use some of the features shown in this lesson. The video tutorial for this lesson can be found on the included DVD.

A look at the finished project

In this lesson, you will develop a composite using several images, while addressing issues such as resolution, resizing, and choosing the right file format.

To see the finished document:

1 Choose File > Browse in Bridge to open Adobe Bridge, or click the Launch Bridge button (Br) in the Application bar. Using Adobe Bridge, navigate to the CS4lessons folder on your hard drive and open the ps03lessons folder.

2 Double-click on the ps04_done.psd file, and the completed image is displayed in Photoshop.

The completed lesson file.

3 Make sure that the Layers panel is active by choosing Window > Layers.

4 Click on the visibility icon (👁) to the left of the cow layer to hide the layer. Click the box where the visibility icon used to be to make the layer visible again.

Layers allow you to combine different elements into a single file while retaining the ability to move and modify each layer independently of the others. In this chapter, you'll be creating multiple layers in Photoshop just like the ones in this finished file.

5 You can keep this file open for reference, or choose File > Close to close the file.

Opening an existing document

Now you will assemble all the images that are part of the final combined image.

1   Return to Adobe Bridge by choosing File > Browse in Bridge or selecting the Launch Bridge button in the options bar.

2   Navigate to the CS4lessons folder you copied onto your system, and open the ps03lessons folder.

3   From the ps03lessons folder, select the file named ps0401.psd. Hold down the Ctrl key (Windows) or Command key (Mac OS), and also select the ps0402.psd and ps0403.psd files. Choose File > Open or double-click any one of the selected files. All the selected images open in Adobe Photoshop.

If you receive an Embedded Profile Mismatch warning when opening the images, you may have forgotten to reset your preferences using the instructions on page 3. If you receive the warning, choose the Use Embedded Profile option, and then click OK.

Understanding document settings

In this section, you will move images from one file to another to create your mock-up. Before you combine the images, you need to be familiar with each document's unique attributes, such as size, resolution, and color mode. Moving layers between documents that have different resolutions may create unexpected results, such as causing the images to appear out of proportion.

Viewing an image's size and resolution

1   Click on the tab of the image of the barn, ps0401.psd, to make it active. Press Alt (Windows) or Option (Mac OS) and click the file information area in the status bar, located in the lower-left corner of the document window. The resolution of the barn image is displayed as 885 pixels wide by 542 pixels tall.

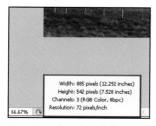

Width: 885 pixels (12.292 inches)
Height: 542 pixels (7.528 inches)
Channels: 3 (RGB Color, 8bpc)
Resolution: 72 pixels/inch

Image size and resolution information.

2   If the picture of the rooster, ps0402.psd, is not visible, choose Window > ps0402.psd or click on the tab for that image at the top of the screen to make it the active window. After confirming that this is the active document, select Image > Image Size to open the Image Size dialog box.

The Image Size dialog box appears.

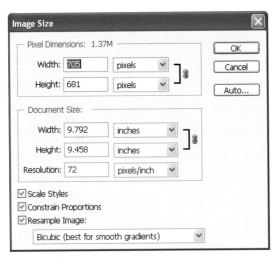

Image size plays an important role when combining images.

The Image Size dialog box is divided into two main areas: Pixel Dimensions and Document Size. Pixel Dimensions shows the number of pixels that make up the image. For web graphics, the pixel dimensions are more relevant than the document's actual printing size. Document Size shows the resolution information, as well as the actual physical size of the image.

The most important factors for size and resolution of web images are the pixel dimensions and the pixels per inch (ppi). If you are designing content for the web, you should reference the top (Pixel Dimensions) section of the Image Size dialog box. As a print designer, you should reference the bottom (Document Size) section of the Image Size dialog box.

3   The image size of the rooster is 705 pixels by 681 pixels. At this size, the rooster is taller than the barn, which would be apparent when you combine the two files. While this might work for an Attack of the Roosters horror movie, you're interested in making the rooster smaller.

4   Make sure that the *Resample Image* and *Constrain Proportions* checkboxes are both selected. In the Image Size dialog box, type **200** pixels for height in the Pixel Dimensions portion at the top half of the dialog box. Press OK to apply the transformation and close the Image Size dialog box.

5   The rooster is now an appropriate size to combine with the barn image.

Combining the images

For this project, you'll use several methods to combine the images.

Using Copy and Paste

1 If necessary, click the tab of the rooster image, ps0402.psd, to make it active.

You can have many documents open at once in Photoshop, but only one of them is active at any given time.

2 Choose Select > All to select the entire image. This creates a selection marquee around the outside edge of the image. You can learn more about selections in Photoshop Lesson 4, "Making the Best Selections."

3 Choose Edit > Copy to copy the selected image area. The image is now in your computer's clipboard, ready to be pasted into another document.

4 Select the tab of the barn picture, ps0401.psd, to make it the active document. Choose Edit > Paste to place the image of the rooster into the picture of the barn.

The rooster appears on top of the barn, and the background surrounding the rooster blocks part of the image. Both these items will be addressed in future steps in this lesson.

The image of the rooster is now in the middle of the barn.

5 Select the tab of the rooster image, ps0402.psd, and choose File > Close to close the file. Do not save any changes.

Dragging and dropping to copy an image

In this section, you'll drag and drop one image into another.

1 Click on the Arrange Documents button (▦), in the Application bar, and choose 2 Up from the drop-down menu to view both the cow (ps0403.psd) and the barn (ps0401.psd) pictures at the same time. The Arrange commands allow you to determine how windows are displayed on your monitor; the Tile command allows you to see all the open images.

2 Select the Move tool (⊹), and then select the picture of the cow, which is the ps0403. psd image. Click and drag the cow image over to the barn image. When your cursor is positioned over the picture of the barn, release your mouse. The cow picture is placed into the barn picture on a new layer.

Like using the Copy and Paste command, you can use the Move tool to copy images from one document to another.

Click and drag the cow image into the picture of the barn.

3 Select the tab of ps0403.psd and choose File > Close to close the file containing the picture of the cow. Do not save any changes to the file.

4 With the composite image of the barn, rooster, and cow active, choose View > Fit on Screen, or use the keyboard shortcut Ctrl+0 (zero) (Windows) or Command+0 (zero) (Mac OS). This fits the entire image into your document window.

The barn picture combined with the other images.

5 Choose File > Save As to save this file. When the Save As dialog box appears, navigate to the ps03lessons folder and type **farm_done** in the Name text field. Choose Photoshop from the format drop-down menu and press Save. If the Photoshop format options dialog box appears, press OK.

Transforming and editing combined images

Although you have combined three images together, they still require some work. The background remains in the two imported images, and the picture of the cow is out of proportion when compared with the barn.

In order to use the transform options, the affected area must reside on a layer. Layers act as clear overlays on your image and can be used in many ways.

In this section, you will do the following:

• View the stacking order of the layers that were automatically created when you combined the images;

• Remove the background from the copied images;

• Refine the edges of the combined images;

• Name the layers to organize them.

Changing the size of a placed image

While you could have adjusted the image size prior to dragging and dropping it into the barn picture, you can also make adjustments to layers and the objects that reside on the layers. Here you will adjust the size and position of the placed images.

1 Make sure the Layers panel is visible. If you do not see the Layers panel, choose Window > Layers.

The Layers panel, with the layers that are part of the combined file.

2 Double-click on the words Layer 1, to the right of the image thumbnail of the rooster in the Layers panel. When the text field becomes highlighted, type **rooster**, and then press Enter (Windows) or Return (Mac OS) to accept the change. Repeat this process to rename Layer 2, typing the name **cow**.

The layers renamed.

3 With the cow layer selected in the Layers panel, choose Edit > Free Transform, or use the keyboard shortcut Ctrl+T (Windows) or Command+T (Mac OS). Handles appear around the edges of the cow. Keep the cow selected. If you do not see handles press Ctrl+0 (Winodws) or Command+0 (Mac OS) to fit the image into the window.

4 Press and hold Alt+Shift (Windows) or Option+Shift (Mac OS), and then click and drag any one of the handles on the outside corner edges of the cow toward the center. The image size is reduced.

Notice that the scale percentages in the Options bar change as you scale the image. Reduce the size of the cow image to approximately 50 percent of its original size. Holding the Shift key maintains the proportions as you scale, while the Alt or Option key scales the image toward its center.

5 In the Options bar, click the Commit Transform button (✔), or press Enter (Windows) or Return (Mac OS), to accept the changes.

6 If you do not see the Rooster image, use the Move tool to reposition it. In the Layers panel, click to activate the rooster layer, and then choose Edit > Free Transform.

7 Press and hold Alt+Shift (Windows) or Option+Shift (Mac OS) and reduce the size of the rooster to approximately 60 percent, using the Options bar as a guide to the scaling you are performing. Click the Commit Transform button, or press Enter (Windows) or Return (Mac OS), to accept the changes.

The cow layer being reduced in size, using the Free Transform command.

Removing a background

Photoshop CS4 makes it easy to remove the background of an image. Here you'll use a method that works well with solid backgrounds, such as the white behind the cow and rooster.

1 If necessary, click in the Layers panel to select the cow layer.

2 In the Tools panel, click to select the Magic Eraser tool (🖎). You may need to click and hold on the Eraser tool to access the Magic Eraser tool.

3 Position the Magic Eraser tool over the white area behind the cow, and click once to remove the white background.

Use the Magic Eraser tool to remove the background behind the cow.

4 In the Layers panel, click to activate the rooster layer.

5 Position the cursor over the white area adjacent to the rooster, and click once to remove the white background.

Understanding the stacking order of layers

Layers are much like pieces of clear film that you could place on a table. The layers themselves are clear, but anything placed on one of the layers will be positioned on top of the layers that are located beneath it.

1   Confirm that the rooster layer remains selected. Click to select the Move tool (⊕) from the Tools panel.

2   Position the Move tool over the rooster image in the document window, and drag the rooster so your cursor is positioned over the head of the cow. Notice that the rooster image is positioned under the cow. This is because the cow layer is on top of the rooster layer in the Layers panel.

3   In the Layers panel, click and hold the rooster layer. Drag the layer up so it is positioned on top of the cow layer. Notice in the document window how the stacking order of the layers affects the stacking order of the objects in the image.

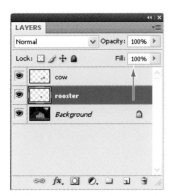

Click and drag the rooster layer up to place it on top of the cow layer.

4   Using the Move tool, click and drag the rooster to position it in the lower-left corner of the image, in front of the fence and along the side of the barn. If your image seems to *jump* when you are trying to position the image, choose View > Snap to prevent the edge of the image from snapping to the edge of the document.

5   Click to activate the cow layer, and then, continuing to use the Move tool, click and drag the cow to position it in the lower-right corner of the image. Position the cow so it appears to be grazing on the grass without hanging outside the image area.

6   Choose File > Save. Keep the file open for the next part of this lesson.

Refining the edges of copied images

When the images were copied, they maintained very hard edges, making it very clear where the picture of the cow or rooster stops and the original image starts. This hard edge makes the images look contrived. You will blend the images so they look more natural together.

1   Click to select the cow layer in the Layers panel. Choose the Zoom tool (🔍) from the Tools panel, then click and drag to create a zoom area around the entire cow. The cow is magnified to fill the entire display area.

2   Choose Layer > Matting > Defringe. The Defringe dialog box opens.

3   In the Defringe dialog box, maintain the default setting of 1 pixel, then click OK. The Defringe command blends the edges of the layer into the background, making it appear more natural.

The cow before it is defringed.   *The cow after it is defringed.*

4   Press **H** on the keyboard to choose the Hand tool (✋). Using the Hand tool, click and drag the window to the right to reveal the content positioned on the left side of the image. Stop dragging when the rooster is visible.

5   In the Layers panel, click to activate the rooster layer, then choose Layer > Matting > Defringe. The Defringe dialog box opens.

6   In the Defringe dialog box, once again maintain the default setting of 1 pixel, and then click OK. The Defringe command affects only the selected layer.

Notice that both the rooster and the cow now look more naturally blended into the background.

7   Press Ctrl+Z (Windows) or Command+Z (Mac OS) to undo the application of the
     Defringe command. Notice the hard edge around the perimeter of the rooster. Press
     Ctrl+Z or Command+Z again to re-apply the Defringe command.

8   Double-click the Hand tool in the Tools panel to fit the entire image in the document
     window. This can be easier than choosing View > Fit on Screen, yet it achieves the
     same result.

9   Choose File > Save As. In the Name text field, type **ps0401_work**, keep the format as
     Photoshop (PSD), then click Save. If the Photoshop Format Options dialog box appears,
     click OK without changing any settings.

Adding text

You will now add text to the image.

1   With the farm_done file still open, click to select the cow layer in the Layers panel.

2   In the Tools panel, click to select the Type tool (T) and click in the upper-left corner of
     the image, just above the roof of the barn. Notice that a layer appears on top of the cow
     layer in the Layers panel.

3   In the Options bar, select the following:

     • From the font family drop-down menu, choose Myriad Pro. If you do not have this font,
       you can choose another.

     • From the font style drop-down menu, choose Bold Italic.

     • From the font size drop-down menu, choose 72.

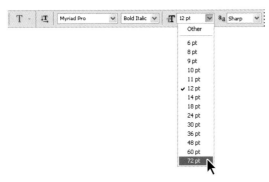

Choose font attributes in the Options bar.

4   Click once on the Set Text Color box (■) in the Options bar. The text Color Picker
     appears. Click on white or any light color that appears in the upper-left corner of the
     color pane, then press OK to close the Color Picker window.

5   Type **Big Red Barn**; the text appears above the roof of the barn. When you are finished
     typing, click on the Commit checkbox (✓) in the Options bar to confirm the text.

6 With the text layer still active, click the Add a Layer Style button (*fx*) at the bottom of the Layers panel, and choose Stroke. The Layer Style dialog box opens, with the Stroke options visible; click on the color box and choose a red color. Press OK to accept the color, and then click OK again to apply the stroke. A stroke is added to the border of the text.

7 Choose File > Save. Keep the file open for the next part of this lesson.

Saving files

Adobe Photoshop allows you to save your files in a variety of file formats, which makes it possible to use your images in many different ways. You can save images to allow for additional editing of things such as layers and effects you have applied in Photoshop, or save images for sharing with users who need only the finished file for use on the web or for printing. In all, Photoshop allows you to save your file in more than a dozen unique file formats.

As you work on images, it is best to save them using the default Photoshop format, which uses the .PSD extension at the end of the filename. This is the native Photoshop file format, and retains the most usable data without a loss in image quality. Because the Photoshop format is developed by Adobe, many non-Adobe software applications do not recognize the PSD format.

Additionally, the PSD format may contain more information than you need, and may be a larger file size than is appropriate for sharing through e-mail or posting on a web site. While you may create copies of images for sharing, it is a good idea to keep an original version in the PSD format as a master file that you can access if necessary. This is especially important because some file formats are considered to be *lossy* formats, which means that they remove image data in order to reduce the size of the file.

Understanding file formats

While Photoshop can be used to create files for all sorts of media, the three most common uses for image files are print, the web, and video production. Following is a list of the most common formats and how they are used.

PRINT PRODUCTION FORMATS	
PSD (Photoshop document)	The Photoshop format (PSD) is the default file format and the only format, besides the Large Document Format (PSB), that supports most Photoshop features. Files saved as PSD can be used in other Adobe applications, such as Adobe Illustrator, Adobe InDesign, Adobe Premiere, and others. The programs can directly import PSD files and access many Photoshop features, such as layers.
TIFF or TIF (Tagged Image File Format)	TIFF is a common bitmap image format. Most image-editing software and page-layout applications support TIFF images up to 2GB in file size. TIFF supports most color modes and can save images with alpha channels. While Photoshop can also include layers in a TIFF file, most other applications cannot use these extended features and see only the combined (flattened) image.

PRINT PRODUCTION FORMATS

EPS (Encapsulated PostScript)	EPS files may contain both vector and bitmap data. Because it is a common file format used in print production, most graphics software programs support the EPS format for importing or placing images. EPS is a subset of the PostScript format. Some software applications cannot preview the high-resolution information contained within an EPS file, so Photoshop allows you to save a special preview file for use with these programs, using either the EPS TIFF or EPS PICT option. EPS supports most color modes, as well as clipping paths, which are commonly used to silhouette images and remove backgrounds.
Photoshop PDF	Photoshop PDF files are extremely versatile, as they may contain bitmap and vector data. Images saved in the Photoshop PDF format can maintain the editing capabilities of most Photoshop features, such as vector objects, text, and layers, and most color spaces are supported. Photoshop PDF files can also be shared with other graphics applications, as most of the current versions of graphics software are able to import or manipulate PDF files. Photoshop PDF files can even be opened by users with the free Adobe Reader software.

WEB PRODUCTION FORMATS

JPEG (Joint Photographic Experts Group)	This is a common format for digital camera photographs and the primary format for full-color images shared on the web. JPEG images use lossy compression, which degrades the quality of images and discards color and pixel data. Once the image data is lost, it cannot be recovered.
GIF (Graphic Interchange Format)	GIF files are used to display limited (indexed) color graphics on the web. It is a compressed format that reduces the file size of images, but it only supports a limited number of colors and is thus more appropriate for logos and artwork than photographs. GIF files support transparency.
PNG (Portable Network Graphics)	PNG was developed as an alternative to GIF for displaying images on the web. It uses lossless compression and supports transparency. Some web browsers do not support PNG images, which has limited its widespread use.

VIDEO PRODUCTION FORMATS

TIFF or TIF	*See Print Production Formats, above.*
TARGA (Truevision Advanced Raster Graphics Adapter)	This legacy file format is used for video production. The TARGA format supports millions of colors, along with alpha channels.

Choosing a file format

In this section, you will save your file to share online and for printing. You will use two common formats, JPEG and Photoshop PDF.

Saving a JPEG file

To save a copy of your image for sharing online, whether on a web site or to send through e-mail, you will save it using the JPEG file format.

1   Choose File > Save As.

2   In the Save As dialog box, type **farm** in the File name text field. From the Format drop-down menu, choose JPEG. If necessary, navigate to the ps03lessons folder so the file is saved in this location, then press the Save button. The JPEG Options dialog box appears.

3   In the JPEG Options dialog box, confirm the quality is set to maximum, and leave the format options set to their defaults. Press OK. This completes the Save process for your file.

4   Choose File > Close to close the file.

Because JPEG is supported by web browsers, you can check your file by opening it using any web browser, such as Firefox, Internet Explorer, or Safari. Open the browser and choose File > Open, which may appear as Open File or Open Location, depending upon the application. Navigate to the ps03lessons folder and double-click to open the file you saved.

Saving for print

In this part of the lesson, you will change the color settings to choose a color profile more suitable for print to help you preview and prepare your file for printing. You will change the resolution of the image before saving it.

Changing the color settings

You will now change the color settings to get a more accurate view of how the file will print.

1   Choose File > Open Recent > farm_done.psd. You can use the Open Recent command to easily locate the most recently opened files. The file opens.

2   Choose Edit > Color Settings. The Color Settings dialog box appears.

3   From the Settings drop-down menu, choose North America Prepress 2. This provides you with a color profile based upon typical printing environments in North America. Press OK to close the Color Settings dialog box.

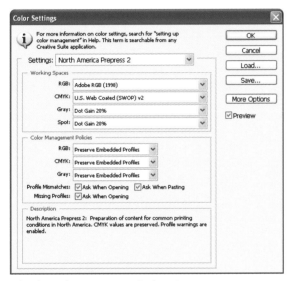

Select the North America Prepress 2 color setting.

4   Choose the Zoom tool (🔍) from the Tools panel, and then click and drag to create a zoom area around the text at the top of the image. The text is magnified to fill the entire display area.

5   Choose View > Proof Colors. Notice a slight change in the color of the red stroke around the text, as the colors appear more subdued. The Proof Colors command allows you to work in the RGB format while approximating how your image will look when converted to CMYK, the color space used for printing. While you will work on images in the RGB mode, they generally must be converted to CMYK before they are printed.

The title bar reflects that you are previewing the image in CMYK.

Adjusting image size

Next you will adjust the image size for printing. When printing an image, you generally want a resolution of at least 150 pixels per inch. For higher-quality images, you will want a resolution of at least 300 pixels per inch. While this image was saved at 72 pixels per inch, it is larger than you need. By reducing the physical dimensions of the image, the resolution (number of pixels per inch) can be increased.

1 Choose Image > Image Size; the Image Size dialog box appears. The image currently has a resolution of 72 pixels per inch.

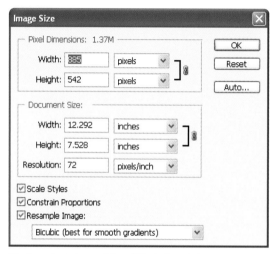

The image is at a low resolution of 72 pixels per inch.

This low resolution affects the image quality, and should be increased to print the best image possible. For this to occur, the dimensions of the image will need to be reduced so the image will be of a higher resolution, but will be smaller in size.

Resampling *changes* the amount of image data. When you resample up, you increase the number of pixels. New pixels are added, based upon the interpolation method you select. While resampling adds pixels, it can reduce image quality if it is not used carefully.

2 In the Image Size dialog box, uncheck *Resample Image*. By unchecking the *Resample Image* checkbox, you can increase the resolution without decreasing image quality.

You can use this method when resizing large image files, like those from digital cameras that tend to have large dimensions but low resolution.

3   Type **300** in the Resolution field. The size is reduced in the Width and Height text boxes to accommodate the new increased resolution but the Pixel Dimensions remain the same. For quality printing at the highest resolution, this image should be printed no larger than approximately 2.9 inches by 1.8 inches. Press OK.

In this image, you are not adding pixels, you are simply reducing the dimensions of the image to create a higher resolution.

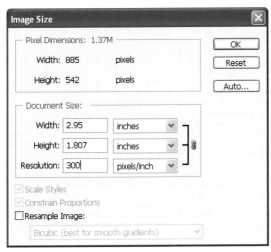

Increase resolution without decreasing quality.

4   Choose File > Save. Keep this file open for the next part of this lesson.

Saving a Photoshop PDF file

Images containing text or vector shapes may appear fine in low resolution when viewed on a computer display, even if the vector information is rasterized. When the same images are used for print projects, they should retain the resolution-independent vector elements. This keeps the text and other vector graphics looking sharp, so you do not need to worry about the jagged edges that occur when text and shapes are rasterized. To keep the vector information, you need to save the file using a format that retains both vector and bitmap data.

1   With the farm_done.psd image still open, choose File > Save As. The Save As dialog box appears.

2   In the Save In menu, navigate to the ps03lessons folder. In the Name text field, type **farm print version**. From the Format drop-down menu, choose Photoshop PDF, then press Save. Click OK to close any warning dialog box that may appear. The Save Adobe PDF dialog box appears.

3   In the Save Adobe PDF dialog box, choose Press Quality from the Adobe PDF Preset drop-down menu, then click Save PDF. If a warning appears indicating that older versions of Photoshop may not be able to edit the PDF file, click Yes to continue.

4   Your file has been saved in the Adobe PDF format, ready to be used in other applications such as Adobe InDesign, or shared for proofing with a reviewer who may have Adobe Acrobat or Adobe Reader.

5   Congratulations! You have finished the lesson.

Self study

1   Using the farm image try adjusting the stacking order of the layers in the composite image.

2   Scale and move the layers to place the cow and rooster in different positions.

3   Add your own images to the composition, adjusting their position and scaling.

4   Save the images as PDF and JPEG files using the different compression options and presets to determine the impact these have on quality and file size.

Review

Questions

1   Describe two ways to combine one image with another.

2   What is created in the destination image when you cut and paste or drag and drop another image file into it?

3   What are the best formats (for print) in which to save a file that contains text or other vector objects?

Answers

1   **Copy and Paste:** Select the content from your source document and choose Edit > Copy. Then select your destination document and choose Edit > Paste to paste the artwork into it.

    Drag and Drop: Make sure both your source and destination documents are visible. With the Move tool selected, click and drag the image from the source file to the destination file.

2   When you cut and paste, or drag and drop, one image into another, a new layer containing the image data is created in the destination file.

3   If your file contains text or vector objects, it is best to save the file in one of these three formats: Photoshop (PSD), Photoshop (EPS), or Photoshop (PDF).

What you'll learn in this lesson:

- Using the selection tools
- Refining your selections
- Transforming selections
- Using the Pen tool
- Saving selections

Making the Best Selections

Creating a good selection in Photoshop is a critical skill. Selections allow you to isolate areas in an image for retouching, painting, copying, or pasting. If done correctly, selections are inconspicuous to the viewer; if not, images can look contrived, or over-manipulated. In this lesson, you will discover the fundamentals of making good selections.

Starting up

Before starting, make sure that your tools and panels are consistent by resetting your preferences. See "Resetting Adobe Photoshop CS4 preferences" on pages XXV-XXVI.

You will work with several files from the ps04lessons folder in this lesson. Make sure that you have loaded the CS4lessons folder onto your hard drive from the supplied DVD. See "Loading lesson files" on page XXIX.

See Lesson 4 in action!

Use the accompanying video to gain a better understanding of how to use some of the features shown in this lesson. The video tutorial for this lesson can be found on the included DVD.

The importance of a good selection

You have to select it to affect it is an old saying in the image-editing industry. To make changes to specific regions in your images, you must activate only those areas. To do this, you can use selection tools such as the Marquee, Lasso, and Quick Selection tools, or you can create a selection by painting a mask. For precise selections, you can use the Pen tool. In this lesson, you'll learn how to select pixels in an image with both pixel and pen (vector) selection techniques.

You'll start with some simple selection methods and then progress into more difficult selection techniques. Note that even if you are an experienced Photoshop user, you will want to follow the entire lesson; there are tips and tricks included that will help all levels of users achieve the best selections possible.

Using the Marquee tools

The first selection tools you'll use are the Marquee tools, which include Rectangular, Elliptical, Single Row, and Single Column tools. Some of the many uses for the Rectangular and Elliptical Marquee tools are to isolate an area for cropping, to create a border around an image, or simply to use that area in the image for corrective or creative image adjustment.

1   In Photoshop, choose File > Browse in Bridge or select the Launch Bridge button (Br) in the Application bar. Navigate to the ps04lessons folder and double-click on ps0501_done.psd to open the image. The completed image file appears. You can leave the file open for reference, or choose File > Close to close it now.

The completed selection file.

2   Return to Adobe Bridge by choosing File > Browse in Bridge or selecting the Go to Bridge button in the Options bar. Navigate to the ps04lessons folder and double-click on ps0501.psd to open the image. An image of a car appears.

3   Choose File > Save As. When the Save As dialog box appears, navigate to the ps04lessons folder. In the Name text field, type **ps0501_work**. Choose Photoshop PSD from the Format drop-down menu and press Save. If the Photoshop format options dialog box appears, press OK.

4   Select the Rectangular Marquee tool (⬚), near the top of the Tools panel.

5   Make sure that Snap is checked by choosing View > Snap. If it is checked, it is already active.

6   Position your cursor in the upper-left side of the guide in the car image, and drag a rectangular selection down toward the lower-right corner of the guide. A rectangular selection appears as you drag, and it stays active when you release the mouse.

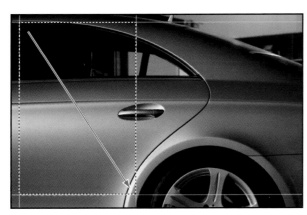

Creating a rectangular selection in the image.

You'll now apply an adjustment layer to lighten just the selected area of the image. You are lightening this region so that a text overlay can be placed over that part of the image.

7   If the Layers panel is not visible, choose Window > Layers and click on the Background layer to make it active.

8   Click on the Adjustments icon (●) at the bottom of the Layers panel to display the Adjustments panel.

7 Click on the Curves button (⟋). The Curves dialog box appears inside of the Adjustments panel, and a new Curves adjustment layer is added to the Layers panel.

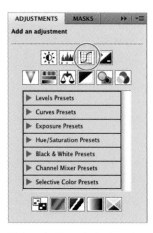

Click on the Curves button to create a new Curves adjustment layer.

8 To ensure consistent results, first click the panel menu (•≡) in the upper–right corner of the Adjustments panel and choose Curves Display Options. In the *Show Amount of:* section, select Light, if that radio button is not already selected. The Light option bases the anchor points of the curve on values based upon light. You would choose Pigment for corrections that are more representative of ink on paper. Click OK to close the Curves Display Options dialog box.

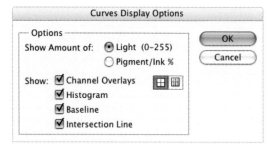

Select Light *in the Curve Display options.*

Curves display the intensity values for RGB images in a range from 0 to 255, with black (zero) at the bottom–left corner. The diagonal line in the middle of the Curves pane represents the tonal values of the image. Because the image is in the Light display mode, the lower–left anchor point of the diagonal line represents the shadow (or darkest) tonal values in the image, and the upper–right anchor point represents the highlight (or lightest) tonal values in the image.

9   Click and drag the lower-left anchor point (shadow) straight up, keeping it flush with the left side of the curve window, until the Output text field reads approximately 192, or type **192** into the Output text field. The rectangular selection in the image is lightened.

Because you used an adjustment layer, you can double-click on the Curves thumbnail in the Layers panel to re-open the Curves panel as often as you like, to readjust the lightness in the rectangular selection.

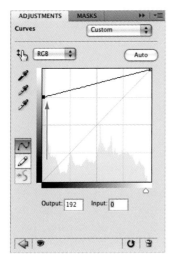 

Make a curve adjustment to   The result.
the selection.

10   Now go back to the Layers panel, click the box to the left of the text layer named poster text; the eye icon (👁) appears, and the layer is now visible. The text appears over the lightened area.

Creating a square selection

In this section, you'll learn how to create a square selection using the Rectangular Marquee tool.

1   Click on the Background thumbnail in the Layers panel to select it.

2   Select the Rectangular Marquee tool (⬚) and position your cursor over the taillight of the car. Click and drag while holding the Shift key. Note that your selection is constrained, creating a square selection. When you have created a square (size doesn't matter), first release the mouse and then the Shift key.

Click and drag while holding the Shift key.

3   With the square selection still active, position your cursor over the selected region of the image. Notice that an arrow with a dashed box appears (▷▫). This indicates that this selection shape can be moved without moving any of the pixel information in the image.

4   Click and drag the selection to another location. Only the selection moves. Reposition the selection over the taillight.

5 Select the Move tool (⊕) and position the cursor over the selected region. Notice that an icon with an arrow and scissors appears (▶✂). This indicates that if you move the selection, you will cut, or move, the pixels with the selection.

6 Click and drag the selection; the selected region of the image moves with the selection.

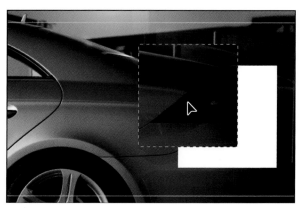

When the Move tool is selected, the pixels are moved with the selection.

7 Select Edit > Undo Move, or use the keyboard shortcut Ctrl+Z (Windows) or Command+Z (Mac OS) to undo your last step.

8 You'll now alter that section of the image. Note that when you edit a region of an image without creating a layer, you are affecting the actual pixels of the image and cannot easily undo your edits after the image has been saved, closed, and reopened.

9 With the square region of the taillight still selected, choose Window > Adjustments to display the Adjustments panel and click the Hue/Saturation button (▦). This displays the Hue/Saturation options within the Adjustments panel. You will now adjust the hue, or color, of this region. Click and drag the Hue slider to change the color of the selected region. Select any color that you like, in this example, the Hue slider is moved to -150.

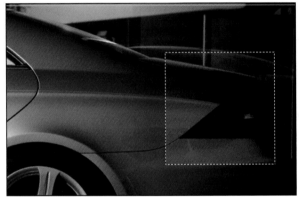

Changing the hue of the   *The result.*
selected region.

10 The new hue is applied to the taillight region as an adjustment layer.

11 Choose File > Save; keep the image open for the next part of this lesson.

Creating a selection from a center point

1 Click and hold on the Rectangular Marquee tool (▢) and select the hidden Elliptical Marquee tool (◯).

2 Limber up your fingers, because this selection technique requires you to hold down two modifier keys as you drag.

3   You'll now draw a circle selection from the center of the image. Place your cursor in the approximate center of the tire, and then hold down the Alt (Windows) or Option (Mac OS) key and the Shift key. Click and drag to pull a circular selection from the center origin point. Release the mouse (before the modifier keys) when you have created a selection that is surrounding the tire. If necessary, you can click and drag the selection while you still have the Elliptical Marquee tool selected.

Hold down Alt/Option when dragging, to create a selection from the center.

While holding down the Alt (Windows) or Option (Mac OS) key and the Shift key, you can also add the space bar to reposition the selection as you are dragging with the Marquee tool. Release the space bar to continue sizing the selection.

4   Whether you need to adjust your selection or not, choose Select > Transform Selection. A bounding box with anchor points appears around your selection. Use the bounding box's anchor points to adjust the size and proportions of the selection. Note that you can scale proportionally by holding down the Shift key when you transform the selection.

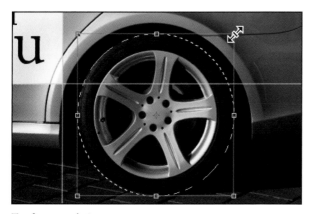

Transform your selection.

5 When you are finished with the transformation, press the check mark (✔) in the upper-right corner of the Options bar to confirm your transformation change, or press the Esc key in the upper-left corner of your keyboard to cancel the selection transformation.

6 Choose File > Save. Keep this file open for the next part of this lesson.

Changing a selection into a layer

You will now move your selection up to a new layer. By moving a selection to its own independent layer, you can have more control over the selected region while leaving the original image data intact.

1 With the tire still selected, click on the Background layer to make it active. Press Ctrl+J (Windows) or Command+J (Mac OS). Think of this as the *Jump my selection to a new layer* keyboard shortcut. Alternatively, to create a new layer for your selection, you can select Layer > New > Layer via Copy. The selection marquee disappears and the selected region is moved and copied to a new layer, named Layer 1.

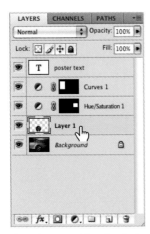

A new layer created from the selection.

2 Now you will apply a filter to this new layer. Choose Filter > Blur >Motion Blur. The Motion Blur dialog box appears.

3   In the Motion Blur dialog box, type **0** (zero) in the Angle text field and **45** in the Distance text field; then press OK. A motion blur is applied to the tire.

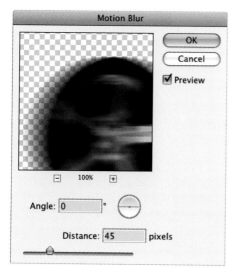

Applying the motion blur.   *The result.*

4   Select the Move tool (✛), move the tire slightly to the right, and press **5**. By pressing 5, you have changed the opacity of this layer to 50 percent.

5   Congratulations! You have finished the marquee selection part of this lesson. Choose File > Save, and then File > Close.

Working with the Magic Wand tool

The Magic Wand makes selections based on tonal similarities; it lets you select a consistently colored area (for example, a blue sky) without having to trace its outline. You control the range it automatically selects by adjusting the tolerance.

1   Choose File > Browse in Bridge or select the Launch Bridge button (Br) in the Application bar to launch Adobe Bridge. Then navigate to the ps04lessons folder and open the image ps0502.psd. An image of a kite appears.

2   Choose File > Save As; the Save As dialog box appears. Navigate to the ps04lessons folder and type **ps0502_work** into the Name text field. Make sure that Photoshop is selected from the Format drop-down menu, and press Save.

3   Select and hold on the Quick Selection tool (✎) to locate and select the hidden Magic Wand tool (✳).

4 In the Options bar, make sure the tolerance is set to 32.

5 Position your cursor over the red portion of the kite and click once. Notice that similar tonal areas that are contiguous (touching) are selected. Place your cursor over different parts of the kite and click to see the different selections that are created. The selections pick up only similar tonal areas that are contiguous, which in this case is generally not the most effective way to make a selection.

6 Choose Select > Deselect, or use the keyboard shortcut Ctrl+D (Windows) or Command+D (Mac OS).

7 Click once in the sky at the top center of the image. The sky becomes selected. Don't worry if the sky is not entirely selected, it is because those areas are outside of the tolerance range of the area that you selected with the Magic Wand tool.

Image with the background selected.

 To see what is included in a selection, position any selection tool over the image. If the icon appears as a hollow arrow with a dotted box next to it, it is over an active selection. If the icon of the tool or crosshair appears, then that area is not part of the active selection.

8 Press Ctrl+0 (zero) (Windows) or Command+0 (zero) (Mac OS) to fit the window to the screen. Then hold down the Shift key and click the area of sky that was left unselected. Those areas are added to the selection of the sky.

9 Choose Select > Inverse. Now the selection has been turned inside out, selecting the kite. Inversing a selection is a helpful technique when solid colors are part of an image, as you can make quick selections instead of focusing on the more diversely colored areas of an image.

If you have control over the environment when you capture your images, it can be helpful to take a picture of an object against a solid background. That way, you can create quick selections using tools like Quick Selection and the Magic Wand.

10 Don't worry if you accidentally deselect a region, as Photoshop remembers your last selection. With the selection of the kite still active, choose Select > Deselect, and the selection is deselected; then choose Select > Reselect to reselect the kite.

11 Now you will sharpen the kite without affecting the sky. Choose Filter > Sharpen > Unsharp Mask. The Unsharp Mask dialog box appears.

12 Drag the Amount slider to the right to about 140, or type **140** into the Amount text field. Type **.8** into the Radius text field and slide the Threshold slider to about 5, or type **5** into the Threshold text field. Read more about unsharp mask in Photoshop Lesson 6, "Creating a Good Image."

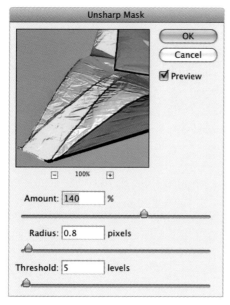

Sharpening the selection only.

13 Click and drag in the preview pane to bring the kite into view. Notice that in the preview pane of the Unsharp Mask dialog box, only the kite is sharpened. Position your cursor over the kite in the preview pane, and then click and hold. This temporarily turns the preview off. Release the mouse to see the Unsharp Mask filter effect applied. Press OK.

14 Choose File > Save. Then choose File > Close to close this file.

The Lasso tool

The Lasso tool is a freeform selection tool. It is great for creating an initial, rough selection, and even better for cleaning up an existing selection. The selection that you create is as accurate as your hand on the mouse or trackpad allows it to be, which is why it lends itself to general cleaning up of selections. The best advice when using this tool is not to worry about being too precise; you can modify the selection, as you will see later in this section.

1   Choose File > Browse in Bridge, or select the Launch Bridge button (Br) in the Application bar, to open Adobe Bridge. Navigate to the ps04lessons folder inside the CS4lessons folder you copied to your computer. Double-click on ps0503.psd to open the image. An image of a building appears.

2   Choose File > Save As. When the Save As dialog box appears, navigate to the ps04lessons folder. In the Name text field, type **ps0503_work**. Choose Photoshop PSD from the Format drop-down menu and click Save.

You will now create an initial selection using the Magic Wand tool similar to the previous exercise, and then clean up that selection using the Lasso tool.

3   Select the Magic Wand tool (⚝) in the Tools panel.

4   Click on the right side of the building in the background of the image to make an initial selection.

Clicking with the Magic Wand tool to create an initial selection.

Adding to and subtracting from selections

The Magic Wand tool has created a selection that encompasses a good portion of the building in the background, but it did not select the windows. You'll now use the Lasso tool to refine that selection to include the areas that the Magic Wand tool missed.

1   Select the Lasso tool (◠) in the Tools panel.

2   Position your cursor over the building in the background. Hold down the Shift key and click and drag around areas that are currently not selected. This makes a new path that overlaps the active selection. As you just discovered, holding down the Shift key adds to the existing selection.

3   Continue circling areas using the Lasso tool while holding down the Shift key to continue adding areas to the existing selection. The goal here is to isolate the background from the building in the foreground.

The original selection.   *Adding to the selection.*

There may be some areas of the image where the initial selection went too far and selected part of the foreground building, which is undesirable. If your selection didn't extend into the building, you can go to the next section, "Using the Quick Selection tool." Otherwise, continue to step 4.

4   To subtract from your selection, hold down the Alt (Windows) or Option (Mac OS) key. This time, you see the Lasso tool with a minus sign next to it.

5   Click and drag from outside the selected area and into the active selection. Release the mouse when you have circled back to your original starting point. The new Lasso selection you made is deleted from the existing selection.

Using the Shift key to add to a selection, and the Alt (Windows) Option (Mac OS) key to delete from a selection, you can edit selections created with any of the selection tools.

6   Keep this image open for the next part of this lesson.

Using the Quick Selection tool

The Quick Selection tool allows you to paint your selection on an image. As you drag, the selection expands outward and finds defined edges of contrast to use as boundaries for the selection.

1   Make sure that ps0503_work.psd is open and that there is no active selection. If you have a selection active, deselect it by choosing Select > Deselect, or pressing Ctrl+D (Windows) or Command+D (Mac OS).

2   Choose View > Fit on Screen to see the entire image in your document window.

3   Choose the Quick Selection tool (🖌) in the Tools panel.

4   Position your cursor over the foreground building. You see a circle with a small crosshair in the center (⊙).

The circle and crosshair will not appear if you have the Caps Lock key depressed.

5   Now, click and drag to paint over the edge of the building in the foreground, making sure that the edge of your brush does not extend into the background building. You can release the mouse and continue painting as the new regions are added to the existing selection. Note that when you paint over the upper-left part of the building in the foreground, the selection may extend into the background; you will fix this later.

Initial selection with the Quick Selection tool.

6   Now you'll delete some of the selection of the background building in the upper-left. If it helps, zoom into the top of the foreground building. Press and hold the Alt (Windows) or Option (Mac OS) key, and paint around the ornate decoration at the top. Note that by holding down the Alt/Option key, you are deleting from the existing selection.

7   If it helps, adjust the Quick Selection brush size by pressing the [(left bracket) repeatedly to reduce the selection size, or the] (right bracket) to increase the selection size.

8   Keep the selection active for the next section.

Understanding the Refine Selection Edge feature

The Refine Selection Edge feature in Adobe Photoshop CS4 allows you to alter the edge of a selection using a choice of selection previews, making it easier to view your edits. In this section, you'll experiment with the varying results of this new feature.

1   With the ps0503_work.psd image still open and the building selection still active, select the Refine Edge button on the Options bar at the top of your screen. The Refine Edge dialog box appears.

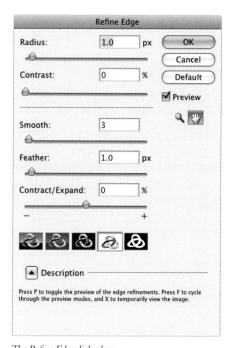

The Refine Edge dialog box.

2   The selected area of the image appears, previewed on a white background. Press the letter **F** on your keyboard to toggle through the different previews. At the bottom of the dialog box, you see the preview buttons highlight as you toggle through them.

Refine Edge with white background.

3   You'll now change some of your edge selection settings. Type **3** in the Smooth text field, **8** in the Feather text field, and **0** in the Contract/Expand text field, then press OK.

Preview your selection in the Refine Edge dialog box.

4   Select the Dodge tool (◉) from the Tools panel. The Dodge tool is used to lighten or darken areas of an image. It is based on a traditional photographer's technique for regulating light exposure in specific areas of an image while creating a print. Be careful with this tool, as the more you paint with the Dodge tool, the lighter it becomes.

5   In the Options bar, select Highlights from the Range drop-down menu. This instructs the Dodge tool to lighten only the highlight areas of the image.

6   With the Dodge tool selected, paint the faces of the lions and the detail of the foreground building to lighten it up.

7   Choose File > Save, and then File > Close to close the file.

Using Quick Mask

Earlier in this lesson, you learned how to add to and subtract from selections. Another method for modifying selections is to use Quick Mask. Rather than using selection tools to modify the selection, you'll use the Paint Brush tool in the Quick Mask mode and paint to modify your selection. This is a type of art therapy for those who are selection-tool-challenged. Note that when creating a mask, by default it is the inverse of a selection; it covers the unselected part of the image and protects it from any editing or manipulations you apply.

In this lesson, you will create a mask using the Quick Mask feature, save the selection, and then copy and paste the selection into another image.

1   To see the file in its completed stage, choose File > Browse in Bridge and navigate to the ps04lessons folder. Locate the file named ps0504_done.psd and double-click to open it in Photoshop. A picture with a duck and penguins appears. You can keep the file open for reference or choose File > Close now.

The completed exercise.

2   Choose File > Browse in Bridge, or select the Launch Bridge button (Br) in the Application bar, to launch Adobe Bridge. Then navigate to the ps04lessons folder and open the image named ps0504.psd; an image of a duck appears.

3   Select the Lasso tool (⌀) and make a quick (and rough) selection around the duck. Make sure that as you click and drag, creating a selection that encompasses the duck, the Lasso tool finishes where it started, creating a closed selection around the duck. Don't worry about the accuracy of this selection, as you are going to paint the rest of the selection using Photoshop's painting tools in the Quick Mask mode.

4   Select the Quick Mask Mode button (⌑) at the bottom of the Tools panel, or use the keyboard shortcut **Q**. Your image is now displayed with a red area (representing the mask) over areas of the image that are not part of the selection.

5 Now you will use the painting tools to refine this selection. Select the Brush tool (✐) in the Tools panel.

Create a rough selection using the Lasso tool.

The selection in the Quick Mask mode.

6 Click the Default Foreground and Background Colors button at the bottom of the Tools panel (▣), or press **D** on your keyboard, to return to the default foreground and background colors of black and white. Painting with black adds to the mask, essentially blocking that area of the image from any changes. Painting with white subtracts from the mask, essentially making that area of the image active and ready for changes.

These tips will help you to make more accurate corrections on the mask:

BRUSH FUNCTION	BRUSH KEYBOARD SHORTCUTS
Make brush size larger	] (right bracket)
Make brush size smaller	[(left bracket)
Make brush harder	Shift+] (right bracket)
Make brush softer	Shift+[(left bracket)
Return to default black and white colors	D
Switch foreground and background colors	X

7 Choose View > Actual Pixels to view the image at 100 percent. Zoom in further if necessary.

8 With black as your foreground color, start painting close to the duck, where there might be some green grass that you inadvertently included in the selection. Keep in mind that the areas where the red mask appears will not be part of the selection.

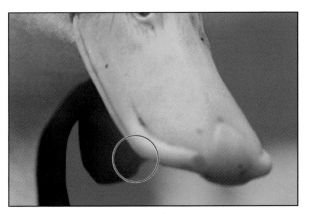

Paint the mask to make a more accurate selection.

9 If you accidentally paint into or select some of the duck, press **X** on your keyboard to swap the foreground and background colors, putting white in the foreground. Start painting with white, and you will see that this eliminates the mask, thereby making the regions that you paint with white part of the selection.

10 Continue painting until the selection is more accurate. When you are satisfied with your work, view the selection by clicking on the Quick Mask Mode button, at the bottom of the Tools panel, again or pressing **Q** on your keyboard. This exits the Quick Mask mode and displays the selection that you have created as a marquee. You can press **Q** to re-enter the Quick Mask mode to fine-tune the selection even further, if necessary. Keep the selection active for the next section.

Saving selections

You spent quite some time editing the selection in the last part of this lesson. It would be a shame to lose that selection by closing your file or clicking somewhere else on your image. In this part of the lesson, you'll learn how to save a selection so that you can close the file, reopen it, and retrieve the selection whenever you like.

1 With your duck selection active, choose Select > Save Selection.

2 Type **duck** in the Name text field and press OK.

3   Choose Window > Channels to see that you have a saved channel (or selection) named duck. Selections that are saved with an image are known as alpha channels. Channels are not supported by all file formats. Only Photoshop, PDF, PICT, Pixar, TIFF, PSD, and Raw formats save alpha channels with the file.

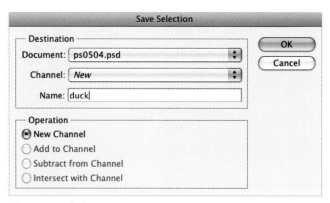

Name your saved selection.   *The Channels panel.*

4   Choose Select > Deselect, or press Ctrl+D (Windows) or Command+D (Mac OS), to deselect the active selection.

5   Once a selection is saved, you can easily reselect it by choosing Select > Load Selection. Select duck and click OK. The duck selection is reactivated.

You can save multiple selections in an image, but take note: your file size will increase each time you save a new selection. When multiple selections are saved, you will need to click on the Channel drop-down menu and choose which saved selection to display.

Copying and pasting a selection

There are many different methods for moving a selection from one image to another. In this lesson, you will simply copy a selection and paste it into another image.

1   Choose Edit > Copy, or use the keyboard shortcut Ctrl+C (Windows) or Command+C (Mac OS).

2   Choose File > Browse in Bridge, or press the Launch Bridge button in the Options bar, and navigate to the ps04lessons folder. Double-click the file named ps0505.psd to open it in Photoshop. A photograph of penguins appears.

3   Choose File >Save As. In the Save As dialog box, navigate to the ps04lessons folder and type **ps0505_work** in the Name text field. Leave the format set to Photoshop and click Save.

4   With the image of the penguins in front, select Edit > Paste, or use the keyboard shortcut Ctrl+V (Windows) or Command+V (Mac OS). The duck selection is placed in the penguin image on its own independent layer, making it easy to reposition.

A new layer is created when the   *The result.*
selection is pasted.

5   Select the Move Tool (✥) and reposition the duck so that it is flush with the bottom of the image.

6   Choose File > Save, then choose File > Close to close the file. Close any other open files without saving.

Using the Pen tool for selections

The Pen tool (◊) is the most accurate of all the selection tools in Photoshop. The selection that it creates is referred to as a path. A path utilizes points and segments to define a border. Paths are not only more accurate than other selection methods, but they are also more economical, as they do not increase file size, unlike saved channel selections. This is because paths don't contain image data; they are simply outlines. In this section, you will learn how to make a basic path, and then use it to make a selection that you can use for adjusting an image's tonal values.

Pen tool terminology

Bézier curve: Originally developed by Pierre Bézier in the 1970s for CAD/CAM operations, the Bézier curve became the underpinning of the entire Adobe PostScript drawing model. The depth and size of a Bézier curve is controlled by fixed points and direction lines.

Anchor points: Anchor points are used to control the shape of a path or object. They are automatically created by the shape tools. You can manually create anchor points by clicking from point to point with the Pen tool.

Direction lines: These are essentially the handles that you use on anchor points to adjust the depth and angle of curved paths.

Closed shape: When a path is created, it becomes a closed shape when the starting point joins the endpoint.

Simple path: A path consists of one or more straight or curved segments. Anchor points mark the endpoints of the path segments. In the next section, you will learn how to control the anchor points.

1   Choose File > Browse in Bridge or click the Launch Bridge button (Br) in the Options bar to launch Adobe Bridge. Then navigate to the ps04lessons folder and open image ps0506.psd.

2   Choose File > Save As. When the Save As dialog box appears, navigate to the ps04lessons folder. In the File name text field, type **ps0506_work**. Choose Photoshop PSD from the Format drop-down menu and press Save. If the Photoshop Format Options dialog box appears, press OK.

This part of the exercise will guide you through the basics of using the Pen tool.

3   Select the Pen tool (◊) from the Tools panel.

4   Position the cursor over the image, and notice that an X appears in the lower-right corner of the tool. This signifies that you are beginning a new path.

5   When the Pen tool is selected, the Options bar displays three path buttons: Shape layers, Paths, and Fill pixels. Click the second icon for Paths.

Select Paths in the Pen tool options.

6   Increase the zoom level by pressing the Ctrl+plus sign (Windows) or Command+plus sign (Mac OS), so that you can view the exercise file in the image window as large as possible. If you zoom too far in, zoom out by using the minus sign with the Ctrl or Command key.

7 Place the pen tip at the first box in Example A, and click once to create the first anchor point of the path. Don't worry if it's not exactly on the corner, as you can adjust the path later.

8 Place the pen tip at the second box on Example A and click once. Another anchor point is created, with a line connecting the first anchor point to the second.

9 Continue clicking on each box in the exercise until you reach the last box on the path. If you're having difficulties seeing the line segments between the points on your path, you can temporarily hide the Exercise layer by clicking on the visibility icon next to that layer.

10 Hold down the Ctrl (Windows) or Command (Mac OS) key, and click on the white background to deactivate the path that was just drawn to prepare for the next path.

In Example A, only straight line segments were used to draw a path; now you'll use curved line segments.

11 Reposition the document in the window so that Example B is visible.

12 With the Pen tool selected, click on the small square (the first anchor point in the path) and drag upwards to create directional handles. Directional handles control where the following path will go. Note that when you create directional handles, you should drag until the length is the same or slightly beyond the arch that you are creating.

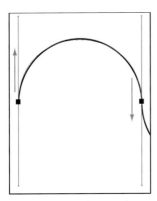

Click and drag with the Pen tool to create directional handles.

13 Click on the second box in Example B, and drag the directional handle downward. Keep dragging until the path closely matches the curve of Example B. Don't worry if it's not exact for this part of the lesson.

14 Click on the third box in Example B, and drag upward to create the next line segment. Continue this process to the end of the Example B diagram.

15 To edit the position of the points on the path, you'll use the Direct Selection tool (⬚). Click and hold on the Selection tool (▶) and select the hidden Direct Selection tool.

16 Position the Direct Selection tool over a path segment (the area between two anchor points) and click once; the directional handles that control that line segment are displayed. Click and drag on any of the directional handles to fine-tune your line segments. You can also click directly on each anchor point to reposition them if necessary.

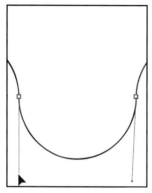

Adjusting the directional handles using the Direct Selection tool.

17 Choose File > Save, then choose File > Close to close the file.

Using the Pen tool to select an area of an image

1 Choose File > Browse in Bridge or click the Launch Bridge button (Br) in the Application bar to launch Adobe Bridge. Then navigate to the ps04lessons folder and open image ps0507.psd.

2 Choose File > Save As. When the Save As dialog box appears, navigate to the ps04lessons folder. In the Name text field, type **ps0507_work**. Choose Photoshop PSD from the Format drop-down menu and press Save. If the Photoshop Format Options dialog box appears, press OK.

3 On the keyboard, hold down the Ctrl (Windows) or Command (Mac OS) key; then press the plus sign once to zoom in at 200 percent, until your zoom percentage is at 200 percent. Position the apple on the left side of the image that is in focus so that you can see the entire apple in the document window.

4 Select the Pen tool (✒), and begin drawing a path around the apple using the skills you learned in the previous exercise by clicking and dragging at the top edge of the apple and dragging a handle to the right.

5   Move the pen tool further along the apple, and click and drag again, dragging out directional handles each time, creating curved line segments that match the shape of the apple.

6   When you get back to the area where you began the path, the Pen tool has a circle next to it, indicating that when you click back on that first anchor point, it will close the path.

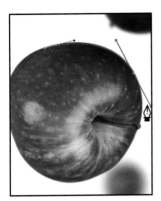 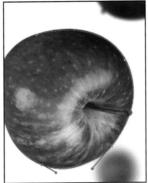

Creating a path around the edge of the apple.

7   Choose Window > Paths. The Paths panel appears. This is where path information is stored. You see one path in the panel, named Work Path.

8   Double-click on the name Work Path in the Paths panel. The Save Path dialog box appears. Type **Apple** in the Name text field and press OK.

The Paths panel with the renamed path.

9   In the Paths panel, click below the name of the path to deselect the path. To reselect the path, simply click on the path name.

10   Now you'll apply an adjustment to this path selection. If the Layers panel is not visible, choose Window > Layers.

11 Click and hold on the Create New Fill or Adjustment Layer button (⬤) at the bottom of the Layers panel and select Hue/Saturation. The Adjustments panel becomes active and the Hue/Saturation adjustment is displayed.

12 Drag the Hue slider to +116 or type the value into the Hue text field. You should see only the apple turn green.

13 A new adjustment layer is created, named Hue/Saturation 1. The pen path you created is visible to the right of the Hue/Saturation adjustment layer thumbnail and acts as a mask, blocking the adjustment from occurring outside of the path.

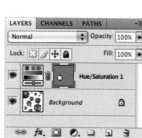

The Hue/Saturation adjustment layer.   Adjustment layer with a vector mask.   The result.

If you want to have multiple paths in the Paths panel, deselect any active path before you begin drawing a new path. If you don't deselect, the new path you create will be added to, and become part of, the currently active path.

14 Choose File > Save, then choose File > Close to close the file.

More Pen tool selection techniques

In the last exercise, you created a curved path. Now you'll create a path with a combination of straight lines and curves.

1 Choose File > Browse in Bridge or select the Launch Bridge button (⬚) in the Options bar to launch Adobe Bridge. Then navigate to the ps04lessons folder and open image ps0508.psd.

2 Choose View > Fit on Screen, or use the keyboard shortcut Ctrl+0 (zero) (Windows) or Command+0 (zero) (Mac OS).

3 With the Pen tool (◊), create the first anchor point at the bottom–left side of the door by clicking once.

4 Staying on the left side of the door, click again at the location that is aligned with the top of the door frame's crossbar.

The second path point.

5 Now, to set up the path for a curve segment around the arc of the door window, place the pen over the last anchor point. When you see a right slash next to the pen cursor, click and drag to pull a Bézier directional handle. Drag until the directional handle is even with the top horizontal bar inside the door window. The purpose of this handle is to set the direction of the curve segment that follows.

The Bézier handle.

6 To form the first curve segment, place the pen cursor at the top of the arc of the door window, and then click, hold, and drag to the right until the curve forms around the left side of the window's arc; then release the mouse button.

The curve and its anchor point.

7 To finish off the curve, place your cursor at the right side of the door, aligned with the top of the doorframe's crossbar. Click and drag straight down to form the remainder of the curve.

The completed curve.

8 Because the next segment is going to be a straight line and not a curve, you'll need to remove the last handle. Position the cursor over the last anchor point; a left slash appears next to the Pen cursor. This indicates that you are positioned over an active anchor point. Click with the Alt (Windows) or Option (Mac OS) key depressed; the handle disappears.

9 Click on the bottom-right side of the door to create a straight line segment.

10 To finish the path, continue to click straight line segments along the bottom of the door. If you need some help, look at the example.

The completed, closed path, selected with the Direct Selection tool.

11 Editing paths requires a different strategy when working with curve segments. With the Direct Selection tool (⟨⟩), select the path in the image to activate it, and then select the anchor point at the top of the door. Two direction handles appear next to the selected anchor point. You also see handles at the bottom of each respective curve segment to the left and the right. These are used for adjusting the curve.

12 Select the end of one of the handles and drag it up and down to see how it affects the curve. Also drag the handle in toward and away from the anchor point. If you need to adjust any part of your path to make it more accurate, take the time to do so now.

13 Double-click on the name Work Path in the Paths panel, and in the Name text field, type **door**. Keep the image open for the next section.

Converting a path to a selection

Paths don't contain image data, so if you want to copy the contents of a path, you need to convert it to a selection.

1 Make sure that the file from the last exercise is still open.

2 Click on the path named Door in the Paths panel to make the path active.

3 At the bottom of the Paths panel, there are five path icons next to the panel trash can:

- **Fill path with foreground color** (○) fills the selected path with the current foreground color.

- **Stroke path with brush** (○) is better used if you first Alt/Option+click on the icon and choose the tool from the drop-down menu that includes the brush you want to stroke with.

- **Load path as a selection** ( ) makes a selection from the active path.

- **Make work path from selection** (⌒) creates a path from an active selection.

- **Create new path** (⊒) is used to start a new blank path when you want to create multiple paths in an image.

4 Choose Load path as a selection to create a selection from the door path.

5 Choose Select > Deselect, or use the keyboard shortcut Ctrl+D (Windows) or Command+D (Mac OS), to deselect the selection.

6 Choose File > Close, without saving the document.

Self study

Take some time to work with the images in this lesson to strengthen your selection skills. For instance, you used ps0503.psd with the Lasso and Quick Selection tools. Try making different selections in the image as well as using the key commands to add and subtract from the selection border. Also experiment with Quick Mask.

Review

Questions

1 Which selection tool is best used when an image has areas of similar color?

2 Which key should you hold down when adding to a selection?

3 What can you do to copy the image data inside a path?

4 Which feature in Photoshop CS4 allows you to edit your selection using different masking options?

Answers

1 The Magic Wand is a good tool to use when you have areas of an image with similar colors. The Magic Wand tool selects similar colors based on the Tolerance setting in the Options bar.

2 Hold down the Shift key to add to a selection. This works with any of the selection tools.

3 To select the pixel data inside of a path, you can activate the path by Ctrl+clicking (Windows) or Command+clicking (Mac OS) on the path in the Paths panel or by clicking the Load Path as Selection button at the bottom of the Paths panel.

4 The Refine Selection dialog box allows you to select the best masking technique and to preview edge selection changes that you are making.

Lesson 5

What you'll learn in this lesson:

- Selecting color
- Using the Brush tool
- Applying transparency
- Using the blend modes
- Retouching images

Painting and Retouching

In this lesson, you get a quick primer in color and color models, and then you will have an opportunity to practice using Photoshop's painting tools, such as the painting, cloning, and healing tools.

Starting up

Before starting, make sure that your tools and panels are consistent by resetting your preferences. See "Resetting the Photoshop workspace" on pages XXV-XXVI.

You will work with several files from the ps05lessons folder in this lesson. Make sure that you have loaded the CS4lessons folder onto your hard drive from the supplied DVD. See "Loading lesson files" on page XXIX.

See Lesson 5 in action!

Use the accompanying video to gain a better understanding of how to use some of the features shown in this lesson. The video tutorial for this lesson can be found on the included DVD.

Setting up your color settings for this lesson

Before you begin selecting random colors for painting, you should have an understanding of color modes and Photoshop's color settings. Let's start with a basic introductory overview of the two main color modes that you will use in this lesson, RGB and CMYK.

Color primer

This lesson is about painting, adding colors, and changing and retouching images. It is important to understand that what you see on the screen is not necessarily what your final viewers will see (print or web). Bright colors tend to become duller when output to a printer, and some colors can't even be reproduced on the monitor or on paper. This is due to the fact that each device—whether it's a monitor, printer, or TV screen—has a different color gamut.

Understanding color gamut

The gamut represents the number of colors that can be represented, detected, or reproduced on a specific device. Although you may not realize it, you have experience with different gamuts already; your eyes can see many more colors than your monitor or a printing press can reproduce.

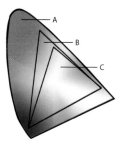

*A. Colors that your eye recognizes. **B.** Colors that your monitor recognizes. **C.** Colors that your printer reproduces.*

In this lesson, you will learn how you can address some of the color limitations that are inherent to working with color that is displayed or output by different devices. A quick introduction to the RGB and CMYK color models will help you to get a better grasp on what you can achieve. Understand that there are entire books on this subject, but you will at least gain enough information to be dangerous after reading this section.

The RGB color model

The RGB (Red, Green, Blue) color model is an additive model in which red, green, and blue are combined in various ways to create other colors.

1   Choose File > Browse, and navigate to the ps05lessons folder. Open the file named ps06rgb.psd. An image with red, green, and blue circles appears. Try to imagine the three color circles as light beams from three flashlights with red, green, and blue colored gels.

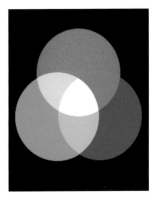

Red, green, blue.

2   Select the Move tool (⊹), and then check the *Auto-Select* checkbox in the Options bar. By checking *Auto-Select*, you can automatically activate a layer by selecting pixel information on that layer. One at a time, click and drag the red, green, and blue circles around on the image.

Notice that white light is generated where the three colors intersect.

3   Now, turn off the visibility of the layers by selecting the eye icon (👁) to the left of each layer name, with the exception of the black layer. It is just like turning off a flashlight; when there is no light, there is no color.

4   Choose File > Close. Choose to not save changes.

The CMYK color model

CMYK (Cyan, Magenta, Yellow, and Black [or Key]—black was once referred to as the *Key* color) is a subtractive color model, meaning that as ink is applied to a piece of paper, these colors absorb light. This color model is based on mixing the CMYK pigments to create other colors.

Ideally, by combining CMY inks together, the color black should result. In reality, the combination of those three pigments creates a dark, muddy color, and so black is added to create a panel with true blacks. CMYK works through light absorption. The colors that are seen are the portion of visible light that is reflected, not absorbed, by the objects on which the light falls.

In CMYK, magenta plus yellow creates red, magenta plus cyan creates blue, and cyan plus yellow creates green.

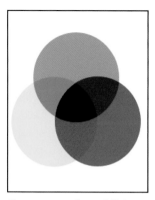

Cyan, magenta, yellow, and black.

1 Choose File > Browse, and navigate to the ps05lessons folder. Open the file named ps06cmyk. An image with cyan, magenta, and yellow circles appears. Think of the colors in this file as being created in ink printed onto paper.

2 With the Move tool (⊹) selected, and the *Auto-Select* checkbox checked, individually click and drag the cyan, magenta, and yellow circles around on the image to see the color combinations that are created with ink pigments of these three colors. Notice that black appears at the intersection of all three, but, as mentioned earlier, it would never reproduce that purely on a printing press.

3 Choose File > Close to close the ps06cmyk image. Do not save your changes.

4 Uncheck the *Auto-Select* checkbox in the Options bar.

Why you will work in the RGB mode

Unless you use an advanced color management system, you should do much of your creative work in the RGB mode. The CMYK mode is limited in its capabilities (fewer menu selections), and if you work in this mode, you have already made some decisions about your final image output that may not be accurate. Follow this short color primer to help you achieve the results that you expect.

In this lesson, you'll use generic profiles for your monitor and output devices. If you want to create a custom monitor profile, follow the instructions in the Photoshop Help menu, under the heading, "Calibrate and profile your monitor."

1 Choose File > Browse, or select the Launch Bridge icon (▣) in the upper-right corner of the Application bar.

2 Navigate to the ps05lessons folder and open the image ps0601.psd. A very colorful image of a woman appears.

A colorful RGB image.

3 Press Ctrl+Y (Windows) or Command+Y (Mac OS); some of the colors become duller. By pressing Ctrl+Y/Command+Y, you have turned on the CMYK Preview. This is a toggle keyboard shortcut, which means you can press Ctrl+Y/Command+Y again to turn the preview off. Note that the text in your title bar indicates whether this preview is active or not. Keep the file open for the next part of this lesson.

Essentially, the preview is visually attempting to simulate what colors would look like if you were to print this image to a printer. Understanding the color settings is important, as the settings you choose affect the colors you use and how they appear in their final destination, whether that is the web, print, or video.

Editing color settings

For this lesson, you will adjust the color settings for Photoshop as if the final destination for this image is in print. Note that if you have any version of Creative Suite 4 installed, you can adjust your color settings suite-wide, using Adobe Bridge. Applying color settings through Adobe Bridge saves you the time and trouble of making sure that all the colors are consistent throughout your production process. If you have a suite installed, follow the steps that are indicated for suite users; if you have Adobe Photoshop installed independently, follow the steps for adjusting Photoshop color settings only.

1   Choose File > Browse, or select the Launch Bridge button (Br) in the upper-right corner of the Application bar. If you do not have the entire Creative Suite 4 installed, leave Adobe Bridge open and skip to step 3.

2   Choose Edit > Creative Suite Color Settings and select North America Prepress 2, if it is not already selected. Press the Apply button. The new color settings are applied throughout the suite applications. Note that the setting you selected is a generic setting created for a printing process that is typical in North America.

3   In Photoshop, choose Edit > Color Settings, even if you have already set them in Adobe Bridge.

4   If North America Prepress 2 is not selected in the Settings drop-down menu, choose it now. Leave the Colors Settings dialog box open.

5   While still in the Color Settings dialog box, press Ctrl+Y (Windows) or Command+Y (Mac OS) to use the toggle shortcut for the CMYK preview. You can tell if you are in the CMYK preview by looking at the title bar of the image window. Notice that CMYK appears in parentheses at the end of the title.

ps0601.psd @ 66.7% (COLOR, RGB/8 /CMYK) ×

The title bar indicates that this image is in the CMYK preview mode.

It is good to get this sneak peak into what your CMYK image will look like, but there is still the issue of having many different kinds of CMYK output devices. You might have one printer that produces excellent results and another that can hardly hold a color. In the next section, you will learn about the different CMYK settings and how they can affect your image.

6 Make sure that the CMYK preview is still on. If not, press Ctrl+Y (Windows) or Command+Y (Mac OS) again. From the CMYK drop-down menu in the Working Spaces section of the Color Settings dialog box, choose U.S. Sheetfed Uncoated v2.

Notice the color change in the image. Photoshop is now displaying the characteristics of the color space for images printed on a sheetfed press. This would be the generic setting you might choose if you were sending this image to a printing press that printed on individual sheets of paper.

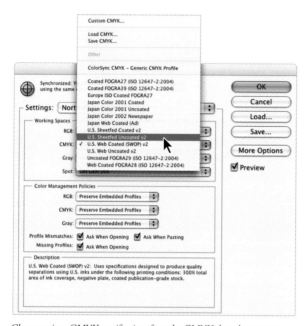

Choose various CMYK specifications from the CMYK drop-down menu.

7 From the CMYK drop-down menu, choose Japan Web Coated (Ad). Notice that the color preview changes again. You might use this selection if you were sending this image overseas to be printed on a large catalog or book press. A web press is a high-volume, high-speed printing press that uses rolls of paper rather than individual sheets.

You do not want to pick a CMYK setting just because it looks good on your screen; you want to choose one based upon a recommendation from a printer, or else you should use the generic settings that Adobe provides. The purpose of selecting an accurate setting is not only to keep your expectations realistic; it also helps you accurately adjust an image to produce the best and most accurate results.

8   From the Settings drop-down menu, choose the North America Prepress 2 setting again, and press OK. Keep the file open for the next part of this lesson.

Keep in mind that if you are using your images for web only, then you can also use the preview feature to view your image on different platforms. To make this change, you would choose View > Proof Setup and choose either Macintosh RGB or Windows RGB from the menu.

Selecting colors

There are many methods that you can use to select colors to paint with in Photoshop. Most methods end up using the Color Picker dialog box. In this section, you will review how to use the Color Picker to choose accurate colors.

1   Select the Set foreground color box at the bottom of the Tools panel. The Color Picker appears. It is tough to represent a 3D color space in 2D, but Photoshop does a pretty good job of interpreting colors in the Color Picker. Using the Color Picker, you can enter values on the right, or use the Hue slider and color field on the left to create a custom color.

2   Now, with the Color Picker open, click and drag the color slider to change the hue of your selected color. The active color is represented as a circle in the color field.

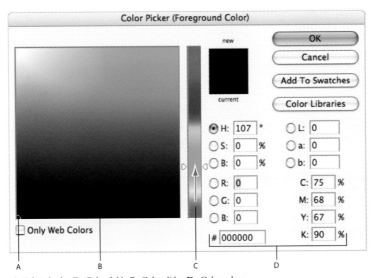

A. Selected color. B. Color field. C. Color slider. D. Color values.

3   Now, click in the color field, and then click and drag your selected color toward the upper-right corner of the color field, making it a brighter, more saturated color. To choose a lighter color, click and drag the selected color to the upper-left corner of the color field. Even though you can select virtually any color using this method, you may not achieve the best results.

4   Press Ctrl+Shift+Y (Windows) or Command+Shift+Y (Mac OS) to see how the CMYK preview affects the colors in the Color Picker. Notice that colors that willnot print well in CMYK show up with in gray (gammut warning) . Press Ctrl+Shift+Y/ Command+Shift+Y again to turn off the CMYK preview.

Perhaps you are creating images for the web and you want to work with web-safe colors only. This is very restrictive, but you can limit your color choices by checking the *Only Web Colors* checkbox in the Color Picker.

5   Check and uncheck the *Only Web Colors* checkbox to see the difference in selectable colors in the color field.

There are also warning icons in the Color Picker to help you choose the best colors for print and the web.

6   Click in the lower-left corner of the color field and drag up toward the upper-right corner. Note that at some point, when you enter into the brighter colors, an Out of gamut for printing warning icon (⚠) appears. This indicates that although you may have selected a very nice color, it is never going to print, based upon your present color settings. Select the Out of gamut warning icon, and Photoshop redirects you to the closest color you can achieve.

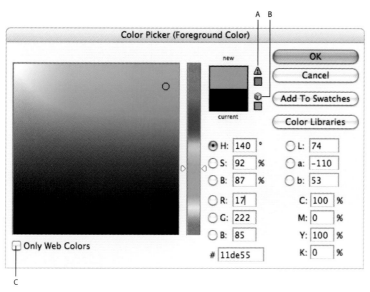

A. Out of gamut warning. *B*. Not a web safe color warning. *C*. Only Web Colors.

7   Click and drag your selected color in the color field until you see the Not a web safe color alert icon (◉) appear. Click on the Not a web safe color icon to be redirected to the closest web-safe color.

8   Position the Color Picker so that you can see part of the ps0601.psd image, then position the cursor over any part of the image. Notice that the cursor turns into the Eyedropper tool (𝒫). Click to select any color from the image.

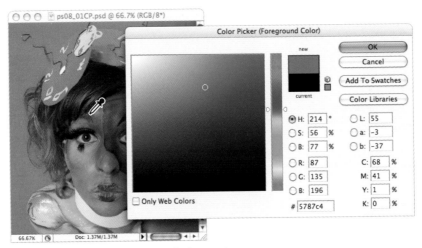

Click outside the Color Picker to sample a color from your image.

9   Press OK in the Color Picker dialog box.

10 Choose File > Close. If asked to save changes, select No.

Starting to paint

Now that you know a little more about color and finding it in Photoshop, you will start to do some painting. You will work on a new blank document to begin with, but once you have the basics of the painting tools down, you'll put your knowledge to work on actual image files.

1   Under the File menu, choose New. The New dialog box appears.

2   Type **painting** in the Name text field. From the preset drop-down menu, choose Default Photoshop Size. Leave all other settings at their defaults and press OK. A new blank document is created; keep it open for the next part of this lesson.

Using the Color panel

Another way to select color is to use the Color panel.

1   If the Color panel is not visible, choose Window > Color.

Place your cursor over the color ramp at the bottom of the panel, then click and drag across the displayed color spectrum. Notice that the RGB sliders adjust to indicate the color combinations creating the active color. If you have a specific color in mind, you can individually drag the sliders or key in numeric values.

Note that the last color you activated appears in the Set Foreground Color box, located in the Color panel, as well as near the bottom of the Tools panel.

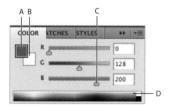

A. Set foreground color.
B. Set background color.
C. Slider. D. Color ramp.

2   Click once on the Set Foreground Color box to open the Color Picker. Type the following values in the RGB text fields on the right side of the Color Picker dialog box: R: **74** G: **150** B: **190**. Press OK.

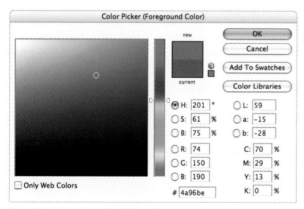

Manually enter values in the Color Picker.

Using the Brush tool

The Brush tool paints using the foreground color. You can control the brush type, size, softness, mode, and opacity with the Brush tool Options.

1 Select the Brush tool (✐) in the Tools panel.

2 Press the arrow next to the brush diameter in the Options bar to open the Brush Preset picker.

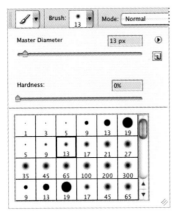

Press the arrow in the Brush Options bar to open the presets.

3 If you are not in the default panel view, click and hold on the panel menu in the upper-right corner of the Brush Preset picker and choose Small Thumbnail View.

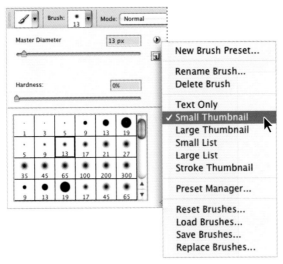

You can use the panel menu to choose different views.

4 Position your cursor over any of the brushes to see a tooltip appear. The tooltip provides a description of the brush, such as soft, airbrush, hard, or chalk, as well as its size in pixels.

5 Locate the brush with the description Soft Round 45 pixels, toward the top of the panel, and double-click on it. The brush is selected and the Brushes Preset picker is closed.

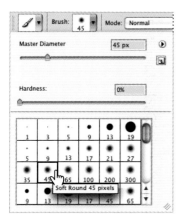

The Brush Preset picker and the Soft Round 45 pixel brush.

6 Position your cursor on the left side of the image window, then click and drag to paint a curved line similar to the example below.

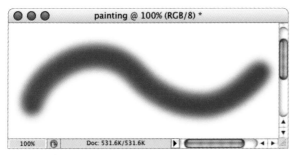

Painted brush stroke.

7 Using the Color panel, click on a different color from the color ramp (no specific color is necessary for this exercise). Then paint another brush stroke that crosses over, or intersects, with the first brush stroke.

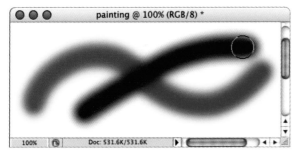

Painting a second brush stroke.

Note that when you paint, the Brush tool cursor displays the diameter of the brush that is selected. To resize the brush, you can return to the Brush Preset picker in the Options bar, but it is more intuitive to resize your brush dynamically, using a keyboard shortcut.

If you have the Caps Lock key selected, your Brush tool cursor appears as a crosshair.

8 Press the] (right bracket) to increase the brush size. Now press the [(left bracket) to decrease the size of the brush. As this blank document is for experimentation only, you can paint after resizing to see the size difference.

9 Choose File > Save to save the file. Keep the file open for the next part of this lesson.

Changing opacity

Changing the level of opacity affects how transparent your brush strokes look over other image information. In this section, you will experiment with different percentages of opacity.

1 With the painting.psd file still open, choose Window > Swatches. The Swatches panel appears, with predetermined colors ready for you to use.

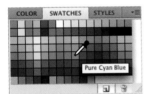

The Swatches panel.

2 Position your cursor over any swatch color and you'll see an eyedropper, along with a tooltip indicating the name of the color. Click on any one of the swatches; it becomes your current foreground color.

3 Now, to change its opacity, go to the Options bar at the top and click on the right-facing arrow next to 100%. A slider appears. Drag the slider to the left to lower the opacity to about 50 percent, and then click on the arrow to collapse the slider. Alternatively, you can type **50** into the opacity text field, if you prefer. Understand that changing the opacity of a color does not affect any of the painting that you have already completed, but it will affect future painting.

Change the opacity of the brush to 50 percent.

You can also change the opacity in Photoshop by holding down the Ctrl (Windows) or Command (Mac OS) key while dragging the cursor in the Opacity percentage value in the Options bar. A double-arrow appears (⇔), allowing you to slide the opacity down or up without even having to reveal the slider.

4 Click and drag with the Brush tool to paint over the canvas. Make sure to overlap existing colors to see how one color interacts with another. Take some time here to experiment with different colors, opacity settings, and brush sizes.

5 Choose File > Save and then File > Close to close the file.

Save time—learn the shortcuts

There are many keyboard shortcuts to help you when painting in Photoshop, most of which are integrated into the exercises in this lesson. Here is a list that will help you save time and work more efficiently:

BRUSH FUNCTION	BRUSH KEYBOARD SHORTCUTS
Open the Brush Preset picker	Right-click (Windows) Ctrl+click (Mac OS)
Increase Brush size	] (right bracket)
Decrease Brush Size	[(left bracket)
Make Brush Harder	Shift+] (right bracket)
Make Brush Softer	Shift+[(left bracket)
Change Opacity	Type a value, such as 55 for 55 percent or 4 for 40 percent.
100% Opacity	Type **0** (zero)

Applying color to an image

You can color anything realistically in Photoshop by using different opacity levels and blending modes. In this part of the lesson, you'll take a grayscale image and tint it with color. Understand that you can also paint color images to change the color of an object, like clothing for a catalog, or just to add interesting tints for mood and effect.

1 Choose File > Browse, or select the Launch Bridge button (Br) in the Application bar, to launch or bring forward Adobe Bridge. Then navigate to the ps05lessons folder and open image ps0602.psd.

2 Double-click on the Zoom tool (🔍) in the Tools panel to change the view to 100 percent. You may need to resize the image window to view more of the image.

 Resize your window automatically by checking the Resize Windows To Fit *checkbox in the Options bar at the top of the Photoshop workspace.*

3 Choose Image > Mode > RGB Color. In order to colorize a grayscale image, it needs to be in a mode that supports color channels.

4 Choose File > Save As; the Save As dialog box appears. Navigate to the ps05lessons folder and type **ps0602_work** into the Name text field. Choose Photoshop from the Format drop-down menu and Press Save.

5 If you do not see the Swatches panel, choose Window > Swatches.

6 Select the Brush tool and Right-click (Windows) or Ctrl+click (Mac OS) on the canvas to open the contextual Brush Preset picker. Slide the Master Diameter to 17 and the Hardness slider to 0. Press Enter (Windows) or Return (Mac OS) to exit.

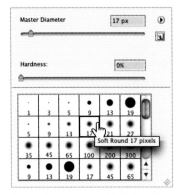

Change the brush size to 17 pixels, and make the brush softer.

7 Using the Opacity slider in the Options bar, change the opacity of the brush to 85 percent, or type **85** into the Opacity text field.

8 Position your cursor over an orange color in the Swatches panel until the tooltip indicates the color is *Pure Yellow Orange*, and then click to select the color.

9 Using the Brush tool, paint over the ceramic vessels at the bottom of the image. Notice that at 85 percent, the color is slightly transparent but still contains some of the image information underneath. You'll now paint these vases more realistically.

Painted vases at 85 percent opacity.

10 Choose File > Revert to return the image to the last saved version. Leave the file open.

Changing blending modes

Opacity is one way to alter the appearance or strength of a brush stroke. Another method is to change the blending mode of the painting tool you are using. The blending mode controls how pixels in the image are affected by painting. There are many modes to select from, and each creates a different result. This is because each blending mode is unique, but also because the blending result is based upon the color you are painting with and the color of the underlying image. In this section, you will colorize the photo by leaving the opacity at 100 percent and changing the blending mode.

1   Make sure that ps0602_work.psd is still open and double-click on the Zoom tool (🔍) in the Tools panel to change your view to 100 percent.

Make sure the Swatches panel is forward and the Brush tool (✐) is selected for this part of the lesson.

2. Choose Image > Mode > RGB Color to put this image back into the RGB mode.

3   Right-click (Windows) or Ctrl+click (Mac OS) anywhere in the document window. This opens the contextual Brush Preset picker.

4   Click on the panel menu of the Brush Preset picker in the upper-right corner and select Small List. When you release the mouse, the brushes appear as a descriptive list.

5   If it is not still active, double-click to select the Soft Round 13 pixels brush from the list of preset brushes.

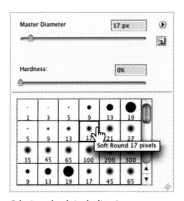

Selecting a brush in the list view.

6   Make sure that you still have the Pure Yellow Orange color selected from your Swatches panel; if not, select it now.

7   In the Options bar, change the opacity to 100 percent, or type **0** (zero). Typing zero when any painting or retouching tool is active is the keyboard shortcut to return to 100 percent opacity.

8   Select Color from the Mode drop-down list. This is where you select various blending modes for your painting tools. Color is close to the bottom of this drop-down menu, so you may have to scroll to see it.

Change the blending mode to Color.

9   Using the Brush tool, paint over the ceramic vessels at the bottom of the image. Notice that the strength or opacity of the color varies according to the tonality of the painted area. This is because using the color blending mode you selected (Color) retains the grayscale information in the image. Where the image is lighter, the application of the orange color is lighter, and where the image is darker, the application of the orange color is darker.

Experiment with different colors to colorize the photo, but avoid painting the stone. Also try using different modes with the same color to see how differently each mode affects the colorization. Some modes may have no effect at all. Experiment all you want with painting at this point. You can choose Ctrl+Z (Windows) or Command+Z (Mac OS) to undo a brush stroke that you do not like, or use Ctrl+Alt+Z (Windows) or Command+Option+Z (Mac OS) to undo again and again.

Ceramic vases painted in the Color mode.

Don't like what you have done in just one area of the image? Select the Eraser tool and hold down Alt (Windows) or Option (Mac OS); then click and drag to erase to the last version saved. You can also change the brush size, opacity, and hardness of the Eraser tool, using the Options bar.

10 Choose File > Save, and leave the file open for the next section.

The Eyedropper tool

The Eyedropper tool is used for sampling color from an image. This color can then be used for painting, or for use with text color. In this section, you will sample a color from another image to colorize the stone building in ps0602.psd.

1 Make sure that ps0602_work.psd is still open, and choose File > Browse, or select the Launch Bridge button (Br) in the Application bar. Navigate to the ps05lessons folder and open the file named ps0603.psd.

2 Click on the Arrange Documents button (▦), in the Application bar, and choose 2 Up from the drop-down menu.

3 Click on the title bar for the ps0602_work.psd image to bring that image forward.

Images tiled vertically.

4   Choose the Eyedropper tool (✐) and position it over the yellow building in the color image. Click once. The color is selected as the foreground color in the Tools panel.

5   Select the Brush tool, then using the Options bar at the top, make sure that Color is selected from the Mode drop-down menu and that the Opacity slider is set at 100 percent.

6   With the Brush tool (✐) selected, paint the stone wall with the color you just sampled. You can experiment at this point and sample other colors for painting. Don't forget that you can always undo what you don't like.

*Colorizing the stone wall
with the Brush tool.*

7   Choose File > Save, then File > Close to close both the ps0602_work.psd and the ps0603.psd files.

Retouching images

There are many techniques you can use to clean up an original image, from using any of the healing tools to that old standby, the Clone tool. In this lesson, you will retouch an image.

1   To view the final image, choose File > Browse or select the Launch Bridge button (Br) in the Application bar to launch Adobe Bridge. Navigate to the ps05lessons folder and open image ps0604_done.psd.

The image after using the retouching tools.

2   You can choose File > Close after viewing this file, or leave it open for reference.

Using the Clone Stamp tool

One of the problems with old photographs is that they most likely contain a large number of defects. These defects can include watermarks, tears, fold marks, and so forth. There are many different ways to fix these defects; one of the most useful is the Clone Stamp tool. The Clone Stamp tool lets you replace pixels in one area of the image by sampling from another area. In this part of the lesson, you'll use the Clone Stamp tool, and you will also have an opportunity to explore the new Clone Source panel.

1 Choose File > Browse or select the Launch Bridge button (Br) in the Application bar to launch Adobe Bridge. Navigate to the ps05lessons folder and open image ps0604.psd.

2 Choose File > Save As; the Save As dialog box appears. Navigate to the ps05lessons folder and type **ps0604_work** into the Name text field. Choose Photoshop from the Format drop-down menu and press Save.

You'll first experiment with the Clone Stamp tool (🖐). Don't worry about what you do to the image at this stage, as you will revert to saved when done.

3 Position your cursor over the nose of the girl in the image and hold down the Alt (Windows) or Option (Mac OS) key. Your cursor turns into a precision crosshair. When you see this crosshair, click with your mouse. You have just defined the source image area for the Clone Stamp tool.

4 Now position the cursor to the right of the girl's face, then click and drag to start painting with the Clone Stamp tool. The source area that you defined is recreated where you are painting. Watch carefully, as you will see a coinciding crosshair indicating the area of the source that you are copying.

The clone source and results.

5 Press the] (right bracket) key to enlarge the Clone Stamp brush. All the keyboard commands you reviewed for the Brush tool work with other painting tools as well.

6 Type **5**. By typing a numeric value when a painting tool is active, you can dynamically change the opacity. Start painting with the Clone Stamp tool again and notice that it is now cloning at a 50 percent opacity.

7 Type **0** (zero) to return to 100 percent opacity.

8 You have completed the experimental exercise using the Clone Stamp tool. Choose File > Revert to go back to the original image.

Repairing fold lines

You will now repair the fold lines in the upper-right corner of the image.

1 Select the Zoom tool from the Tools panel, and if it is not already selected, check the *Resize Windows To Fit* checkbox in the Options bar. By checking this box, the window will automatically resize when you zoom.

2 Click approximately three times in the upper-right corner of the image. There you see fold marks that you will repair using the Clone Stamp tool.

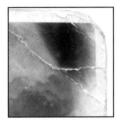

Fold marks that you will repair.

3 Select the Clone Stamp tool (🔲) from the Tools panel.

4 Right-click (Windows) or Ctrl+click (Mac OS) on the image area to open the Brush Preset picker. Double-click on the Soft Round 13 pixels brush to select that brush and close the Brush Preset picker.

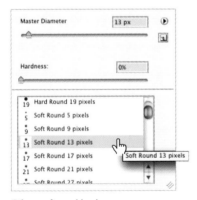

Select a soft round brush.

5 Position your cursor to the left of the fold mark, approximately in the center of the fold. Hold down Alt (Windows) or Option (Mac OS), and click to define that area as the source.

6 Position the Clone Stamp tool over the middle of the fold line itself, and click and release. Depending upon what you are cloning, it is usually wise to apply a clone source in small applications, rather than painting with long brush strokes.

7 Press Shift+[(left bracket) several times to make your brush softer. This way, you can better disguise the edges of your cloning.

8 Continue painting over the fold lines in the upper-left corner. As you paint, you will see crosshairs representing the sampled area. Keep an eye on the crosshairs; you don't want to introduce unwanted areas into the image.

It is not unusual to have to redefine the clone source over and over again. You may have to Alt/Option+click in the areas outside of the fold line repeatedly to find better-matched sources for cloning. You may even find that you Alt/Option+click and then paint, and then Alt/Option+click and paint again, until you conceal the fold mark.

Don't forget some of the selection techniques that you learned in Photoshop Lesson 4, "Making the Best Selections." You can activate the edge of the area to be retouched so that you can keep your clone stamping inside the image area and not cross into the white border.

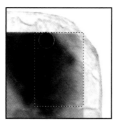

Create selections to help you control the cloning.

With the Clone Stamp tool, it is important to sample tonal areas that are similar to the tonal area you are covering. Otherwise, the retouching will look very obvious.

9 Choose File > Save. Keep this image open for the next part of this lesson.

The History panel

You can use the History panel to jump to previous states in an image. This is an important aid when retouching photos. In this section, you will explore the History panel as it relates to the previous section, and then continue to utilize it as you work forward in Photoshop.

1   Make sure that ps0604_work.psd is still open from the last section.

2   Choose Window > History. The History panel appears. Grab the lower-right corner of the panel and pull it down to expand the panel and reveal all the previous states in History.

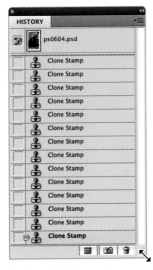

Resizing the History panel.

3   You see many Clone Stamp states, or a listing of any function that you performed while the image was open. As you click on each state, you reveal the image at that point in your work history. You can click back one state at a time, or you can jump to any state in the panel, including the top state, always the name of the file, which is the state of the original image when it was first opened. You can utilize this as a strategy for redoing work that does not meet with your satisfaction.

4   If you need to redo some of the cloning that you did in the previous section, click on a state in the History panel for your starting point, and redo some of your work.

All states in the History panel are deleted when the file is closed.

5   Choose File > Save. Keep this file open for the next part of the lesson.

The Spot Healing Brush

The Spot Healing Brush tool paints with sampled pixels from an image and matches the texture, lighting, transparency, and shading of the pixels that are sampled to the pixels being retouched, or healed. Note that unlike the Clone Stamp tool, the Spot Healing Brush automatically samples from around the retouched area.

1 With the ps0604_work.psd file still open, select View > Fit on Screen, or use the keyboard shortcut Ctrl+0 (zero) (Windows) or Command+0 (zero) (Mac OS).

2 Select the Zoom tool (⌕), then click and drag the lower-right section of the image to zoom into the lower-right corner.

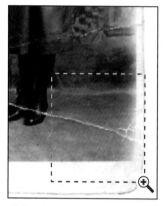

Click and drag with the Zoom tool.

Because you do not have to define a source with the Spot Healing tool, it can be easier to retouch. It is not the absolute answer to every retouching need, but it works well when retouching sections of an image that are not defined and detailed, like blemishes on skin or backgrounds.

3 Select the Spot Healing Brush tool (✐), and then click and release repeatedly over the fold marks in the lower-right corner of the image. The tool initially creates a dark region, indicating the area that is to be retouched, but don't panic, it will blend well when you release the mouse. Now, using the Spot Healing Brush, repair the fold lines. Use the History panel to undo steps, if necessary.

4 Choose File > Save. Keep this file open for the next part of this lesson.

The Healing Brush

The Healing Brush tool also lets you correct imperfections. Like the Clone Stamp tool, you use the Healing Brush tool to paint with pixels you sample from the image, but the Healing Brush tool also matches the texture, lighting, transparency, and shading of the sampled pixels. In this section, you will remove some defects in the girl's dress.

1   Make sure that ps0604_work.psd is still open from the last section, and choose
    View > Fit on Screen.

2   Select the Zoom tool, then click and drag over the bottom area of the girl's dress.

Click and drag to zoom into the dress.

3   Click and hold on the Spot Healing Brush (⟋) in the Tools panel to select the hidden
    tool, the Healing Brush (⟋).

4   Position your cursor over an area near to, but outside, the fold line in the skirt, as you are
    going to define this area as your source. Hold down Alt (Windows) or Option (Mac OS),
    and click to define the source for your Healing Brush tool.

5   Now, paint over the fold line that is closest to the source area you defined.

6   Repeat this process; Alt/Option+click in appropriate source areas near the folds across
    the dress, then paint over the fold lines, using the Healing Brush tool. Don't forget to
    change the size using the left and right brackets, if necessary.

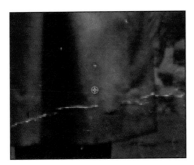

*Define a source and then paint with the
Healing Brush tool.*

7   Choose File > Save, and leave this file open for the next part of this lesson.

Using the Patch tool

You may find that there are large areas of scratches or dust marks that need to be retouched. You can use the Patch tool to replace large amounts of an image with image data that you sample as your source. In this section, you will fix the large dusty area in the upper-left part of the image.

1   With the ps0604_work.psd file still open, choose View Fit on Screen, or use the keyboard shortcut Ctrl+0 (zero) (Windows) or Command+0 (zero) (Mac OS).

2   Select the Zoom tool (🔍), and then click and drag to zoom into the upper-left area of the image.

Click and drag to zoom into the upper-left corner.

3   Hold down on the Healing Brush tool (✐) and select the hidden Patch tool (◇).

4   Click and drag a selection to select a small area with defects. Then click and drag that selection over an area of the image with fewer defects, to use as a source.

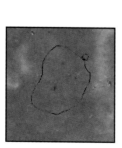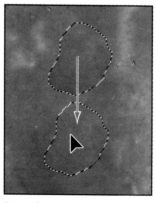

The original. *Drag with the Patch tool.* *The result.*

5 Continue to make selections and patch with the Patch tool to clean up most of the dust marks in the upper-right corner of the image.

6 Choose File > Save. Keep the file open for the next part of this lesson.

Using the Clone Source panel

When using the Clone Source panel, you can set up to five clone sources for the Clone Stamp or Healing Brush tools to use. The sources can be from the same image you are working on or from other open images. Using the Clone Source panel, you can even preview the clone source before painting, and rotate and scale the source. In this section, you will clone the upper-left corner of the ps0604_work.psd image and rotate it to repair the upper-right corner of the image. You will also define a second clone source to add an art deco border around the edge of the image.

1 Make sure that ps0604_work.psd is still open, and choose View > Fit on Screen.

2 Choose Window > Clone Source to open the Clone Source panel. If it helps, press Ctrl+plus sign (Windows) or Command+plus sign (Mac OS) on the upper-left corner.

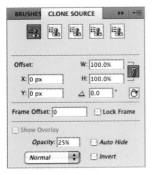

The Clone Source panel.

The Clone Source panel displays five icons, each representing a sampled source. You will start out using the first clone source.

3 Choose the Clone Stamp tool (♨). Verify in the Options bar that the Mode is Normal and Opacity is 100 percent.

4   Click on the first Clone Source icon in the Clone Source panel and position your cursor over the top-left corner of the image. Hold down the Alt (Windows) or Option (Mac OS) key and click to define this corner as the first clone source.

You will now use this corner to replace the damaged corner in the upper right.

Select the first Clone Source icon.   *Alt/Option+click on the upper-left corner.*

5   If you zoomed into the upper-left corner, hold down the spacebar to turn your cursor into the Hand tool (✍), then click and drag to the left. Think of the image as being a piece of paper that you are pushing to the left to see the upper-right corner of the image.

6   When you are positioned over the right corner, check the *Show Overlay* checkbox (if it is unchecked) in the Clone Source panel. A ghosted image of your clone source is displayed.

Check Show Overlay *to see your clone source before cloning.*

7 Now, type **90** in the Rotate text field in the Clone Source panel. The corner is rotated so that you can fit it in as a new corner in the upper-right area of the image.

Use the Clone Source panel to rotate your source.

8 Verify that your brush size is approximately the width of the white border. You can preview the brush size by positioning your cursor over the white border. If you do not see the brush size preview, you may have your Caps Lock key selected. If necessary, make your brush smaller using the [(left bracket), or larger using the] (right bracket) keys repeatedly.

9 Make sure the corner is aligned with the outside of the underlying image (original upper-right corner). Don't worry about aligning with the original inside border.

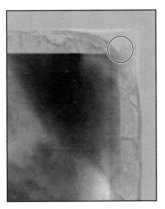 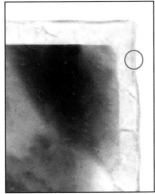

Align the corner before starting to clone.

10 Start painting only the corner with the Clone Stamp tool. Now the corner has been added to the image. Uncheck the *Show Overlay* checkbox to better see your results.

11 Choose File > Save and keep this file open for the next part of this lesson.

Cloning from another source

In this section, you will open an image to clone a decoration, and then apply it to the ps0604_work image.

1 Choose File > Browse, or select the Launch Bridge button (⬚) in the Application bar. When Adobe Bridge appears, navigate to the ps05lessons folder and double-click on the image named ps0605.psd. An image with a decorative border appears.

2 If the Clone Source panel is not visible, choose Window > Clone Source. Make sure that the *Show Overlay* checkbox is unchecked.

3 Select the Clone Stamp tool (⬚) and then click on the second Clone Source icon.

4 Position your cursor over the upper-left corner of the decorative border, and then hold down the Alt (Windows) or Option (Mac OS) key and click to define this area of the image as your second clone source.

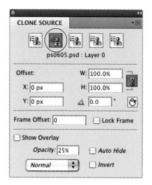 

Define the upper-left corner as the second clone source.

5 Select the third Clone Source icon in the Clone Source panel.

6 Position your cursor over the upper-right corner of the decorative border, then hold down the Alt (Windows) or Option (Mac OS) key and click to define this area of the image as your third clone source.

7 Choose Window > ps0604_work.psd to bring that image to the front.

8 If you cannot see your entire ps0604_work.psd image, choose View > Fit on Screen, or use the keyboard shortcut Ctrl+0 (zero) (Windows) or Command+0 (zero) (Mac OS).

9 To make the clone of the decorative border appear "antique," you will make some modifications to the Clone Stamp tool options. With the Clone Stamp tool selected, go to the Options bar and select Luminosity from the Mode drop-down menu. Type **50** into the Opacity text field.

10 Select the second Clone Source icon, then check the *Show Overlay* checkbox in the Clone Source panel.

11 Position your cursor in the upper-left corner of the ps0604_work.psd image, and you see the preview of the decorative border. When you have the decorative corner positioned roughly in the upper-left corner, start painting. Try to follow the swirls of the design as best you can, but don't worry about being exact. The blending mode and opacity that you set in the Options bar helps to blend this into the original image. Keep in mind that when you paint with a lighter opacity, additional painting adds to the initial opacity. If it helps to see the results, turn off the *Show Overlay* checkbox. Check it back on for the remainder of this lesson.

Paint with the Clone tool.   *The result.*

Now you will clone the third source to the upper-right corner of the image. This time, you can experiment with the position of the decoration on the image.

12 Navigate to the upper-right side of the ps0604_work image and select the third Clone Source icon from the Clone Source panel. You will now use the Clone Source panel to reposition the upper-right corner clone source.

13 Hold down Alt+Shift (Windows) or Option+Shift (Mac OS) and press the left, right, up, or down arrow key on your keyboard to nudge the overlay into a better position. No specific position is required for this lesson; simply find a location that you feel works well.

14 Once you have the clone source in position, start painting. Lightly paint the decoration into the upper-right corner. If you feel your brush is too hard-edged, press Shift+[(left bracket) to make it softer.

15 Choose File > Save. Keep the ps0604_work.psd file open for the next part of this lesson. Choose Window > ps0605.psd to bring that image forward. Then choose File > Close. If asked to save changes, select No.

Self study

Return to the ps0604_work.psd image and use a variety of retouching tools, such the Clone Stamp, Spot Healing, and Healing Brush tools, to fix the rest of the damaged areas in the image. Also use the retouching tools to remove dust.

Use the Clone Source panel to repair the lower-left and lower-right corners of the ps0604_work.psd image.

Review

Questions

1 If you have an image in the grayscale mode and you want to colorize it, what must you do first?

2 What blending mode preserves the underlying grayscale of an image and applies a hue of the selected color? Hint: it is typically used for tinting images.

3 What is the main difference between the way the Clone Stamp and Healing Brush replace information in an image?

4 How many clone sources can be set in the Clone Source panel?

Answers

1 In order to use color, you must choose a color mode that supports color, such as RGB or CMYK. You can change the color mode by selecting the Image > Mode menu.

2 The Color blending mode is used for tinting images.

3 The Clone Stamp makes an exact copy of the sampled area, whereas the Healing Brush makes a copy of the sampled area and matches the texture, lighting, transparency, and shading of the sampled pixels.

4 You can set up to five clone sources in the Clone Source panel.

What you'll learn in this lesson:

- Choosing color settings
- Using the histogram
- Discovering a neutral
- Using curves
- Unsharp masking
- Using Camera Raw

Creating a Good Image

You can create interesting imagery in Photoshop, including compositions, filter effects, and even 3D imagery when using Photoshop CS4 Extended. But it is important to have a great-looking image to serve as the foundation of your work.

Starting up

There are simple steps that you can take to create a brighter, cleaner, more accurate image. In this lesson, you'll learn how to use the Curves controls and how to sharpen your images. You'll learn what a neutral is and how to use it to color correct your images. You'll also have the opportunity to work with a Camera Raw image, using the improved Camera Raw plug-in.

Although the steps may at first seem time-consuming, they go quickly when not accompanied by the "whys and hows" included in this lesson. In fact, the process works almost like magic; a few steps and your image looks great!

Before starting, make sure that your tools and panels are consistent by resetting your preferences. See "Resetting Adobe Photoshop CS4 preferences" on pages XXV-XXVI.

You will work with several files from the ps06lessons folder in this lesson. Make sure that you have loaded the CS4lessons folder onto your hard drive from the supplied DVD. See "Loading lesson files" on page XXIX.

See Lesson 6 in action!

Use the accompanying video to gain a better understanding of how to use some of the features shown in this lesson. The video tutorial for this lesson can be found on the included DVD.

Choosing your color settings

What many Photoshop users do not understand is the importance of knowing where an image is going to be published; whether for print, the web, or even a digital device like a cell phone. You read a little about color settings in Photoshop Lesson 4, "Painting and Retouching," where you discovered some of Photoshop's pre-defined settings. These help adapt the colors and values of an image for different uses. If not set properly, your images may appear very dark, especially in the shadow areas. For this lesson, you will use generic color settings that work well for a typical print image. You are also introduced to settings for other types of output, including the web.

1   Choose Edit > Color Settings in Photoshop CS4. The Color Settings dialog box appears. In this example, the icon in the upper-left corner indicates that Photoshop's Color Settings are not synchronized with the other applications in the Creative Suite. Refer back to Photoshop Lesson 4, "Painting and Retouching," for more information about defining Color Settings using Adobe Bridge.

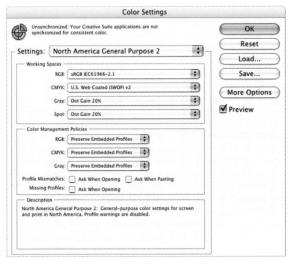

The Color Settings dialog box at its default settings.

2   As a default, North America General Purpose 2 is selected. This setting is good for images that are to be printed on coated paper stock. Coated paper has a coating that allows the paper to be printed without significant ink absorption. If you plan on printing on an uncoated stock, which, due to ink absorption, tends to produce a darker image, choose U.S. Sheetfed Uncoated v2 from the CMYK drop-down menu.

When you see U.S. Web Coated in the CMYK drop-down menu, it is not referring to the web, as in Internet. A web press is used for printing books, catalogs, newspapers, and magazines. It is a high-run, high-speed, printing press that uses rolls of paper rather than individual sheets.

3   For this example, make sure that the default settings of North America General Purpose 2 are selected. Press OK to exit the Color Settings dialog box.

Opening the file

1   Choose File > Browse. When Adobe Bridge is forward, navigate to the ps06lessons folder that you copied onto your hard drive.

2   Locate the image named ps0701.psd and double-click on it to open it in Photoshop. You can also choose to right-click (Windows) or Ctrl+click (Mac OS) and select Open with Adobe Photoshop CS4. An image of a girl appears; because this is not a professional photograph, it offers many issues that need to be addressed, pretty much presenting you with one of your "worst-case scenarios." You will have an opportunity to address issues such as incorrect color, red eye, and retouching in this lesson.

Note the comparison of images: the one on the left is uncorrected, and the one on the right is corrected. You'll correct the image on the left in the next few steps.

The image before correction.   *The image after correction.*

3 Choose File > Save As. The Save As dialog box appears. Navigate to the ps06lessons folder on your hard drive. In the Name text field, type **ps0701_work**, choose Photoshop from the Format drop-down menu, and press Save. Leave the image open.

Why you should work in RGB

In this lesson, you start and stay in the RGB (Red, Green, Blue) color mode. There are two reasons for this: you will that find more tools are available in this mode, and changes to color values in RGB degrade your image less than if you are working in CMYK. If you were sending this image to a commercial printer, you would make sure your color settings were accurate, and then convert your image to CMYK by choosing Image > Mode > CMYK Color.

If you want to see the CMYK preview while working in RGB, press Ctrl+Y (Windows) or Command+Y (Mac OS). This way, you can work in the RGB mode while you see the CMYK preview on your screen. This is a toggle keyboard shortcut, meaning that if you press Ctrl+Y or Command+Y again, the preview is turned off. You may not see a difference in the image, depending upon the range of colors, but the title tab indicates that you are in CMYK preview mode by displaying /CMYK after the title of the image.

Reading a histogram

Understanding image histograms is probably the single most important concept to become familiar with when working with images in Photoshop. A histogram can tell you whether your image has been properly exposed, whether the lighting is correct, and what adjustments will work best to improve your image. You will reference the Histogram panel throughout this lesson.

1 If your Histogram panel is not visible, choose Window > Histogram. The Histogram panel appears.

A histogram shows the tonal values that range from the lightest to the darkest in an image. Histograms can vary in appearance, but typically you want to see a full, rich, mountainous area representing tonal values. See the figures for examples of a histogram with many values, one with very few values, and the images relating to each.

A good histogram and its related image.

A poor histogram and its related image.

Keep an eye on your Histogram panel. Simply doing normal corrections to an image can break up a histogram, giving you an image that starts to look posterized (when a region of an image with a continuous gradation of tone is replaced with several regions of fewer tones.) Avoid breaking up the histogram by learning to use multi-function tools, like the Curves panel, and making changes using adjustment layers, which don't change your original image data.

2 To make sure that the values you read in Photoshop are accurate, select the Eyedropper tool (✐). Notice that the Options bar (across the top of the document window) changes to offer options specific to the Eyedropper tool. Click and hold on the Sample Size drop-down menu and choose 3 by 3 Average. This ensures a representative sample of an area, rather than the value of a single screen pixel.

Set up the Eyedropper tool to sample more pixel information.

Taking care of that nasty red eye

Before making adjustments, spend some time addressing the red eye in this image. Red eye typically occurs when you use a camera with a built-in flash. The light of the flash occurs too fast for the iris of the **eye** to close the pupil, revealing the blood-rich area alongside the iris. There are many cameras that come with features to help you avoid this phenomenon, and most professional photographers don't experience this, as they typically use a flash that is not directly positioned in front of the subject. Also, there is a solution that is built right into Photoshop.

1   With the ps0701_work.psd image open, click and hold down on the Spot Healing Brush tool (✐) and drag down to select the Red Eye tool.

2   Click and drag, creating a marquee around the left eye; when you release the mouse, the red eye is removed. If you missed a section, you can repeat this without damaging the areas that are not part of the red eye.

3   Now, click and drag to surround the right eye, again repeating to add any areas that are not corrected.

4   Choose File > Save, or use the keyboard shortcut Ctrl+S (Windows) or Command+S (Mac OS).

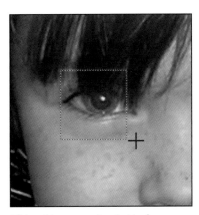

Click and drag, surrounding the iris of an eye, using the Red Eye tool to get rid of the red.

Making the Curve adjustment

You will now address the tonal values of this image. To do this, you will take advantage of the Curves Adjustments panel feature available in the Layers panel.

1   If the Layers panel is not visible, choose Window > Layers. Click and hold on the Create New Fill or Adjustment Layer button (⬤) at the bottom of the Layers panel, select Curves, and release the mouse. The Curves Adjustment options appear.

2 Click on the Switch Panel to Expanded View button (⬚) in the lower-left corner of the Adjustments panel.

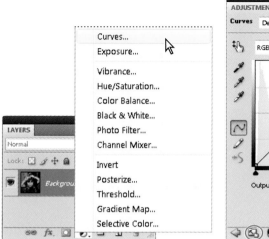

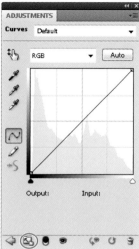

Select the Curves Adjustment.

The Curves dialog box appears.

By using adjustments, you can make changes to an image's tonal values without destroying the original image data. See Chapter 9, "Taking Layers to the Max," for more information about how to use the Adjustments panel. Leave the Curves Adjustments panel open for the next section.

Keep in mind that adjustments work very differently than in previous versions of Photoshop and could possibly be confusing to both new and existing Photoshop users. Read these tips before you proceed any further, and refer back to them if you have any problems following future adjustment steps.

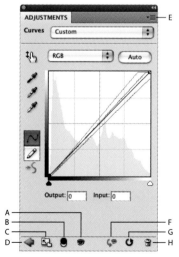

*A. Toggle layer visibility. **B**. Clip to layer below. **C**. Switch panel view. **D**. Return to adjustment list.*
*E. Panel menu. **F**. View previous state. **G**. Reset to defaults. **H**. Delete adjustment layer.*

Once you choose to create an adjustment layer, it appears in the Adjustments panel; an example is the Curves adjustment panel that you just revealed. If you accidently leave the curves adjustment, by selecting another adjustment, or by pressing the Return to Adjustment List button (◀), at the bottom of the Adjustments panel, you see a panel with links to the other adjustments that you can make. If you want to return to the current adjustment, press the Return to Controls for Current Adjustment Layer button (▶).

If you make an error, you can undo one step by pressing Ctrl+Z (Windows) or Command+Z (Mac OS). If you want to return to the defaults for this adjustment, choose the Reset to Adjustment Defaults button (↺) in the lower-right corner of the Adjustments panel.

If you want to eliminate the adjustment layer, choose the Delete this Adjustment Layer button (🗑).

If you exit the Adjustments panel and want to edit an existing adjustment, select the adjustment layer from the Layers panel. When you double-click on the adjustment layer, the adjustment appears ready to edit in the Adjustments panel.

Defining the highlight and shadow

In this section, you'll set the highlight and shadow to predetermined values using the Set White Point and Set Black Point tools available in Curves Adjustments panel. Before you do this, you'll determine what those values should be. This is a critical part of the process, as the default for the white point is 0, meaning that the lightest part of the image will have no value when printed, and any detail in this area will be lost.

Some images can get away with not having tonal values in very bright areas. Typically, reflections from metal, fire, and extremely sunlit areas, as well as reflections off other shiny objects like jewelry, do not have value in those reflective areas.

These are referred to as specular highlights. By leaving them without any value, it helps the rest of the image look balanced, and allows the shine to *pop* out of the image. See the figure below for an example.

This image has specular highlights, which should be left with a value of zero.

Inputting the white and black point values

The process of defining values for the lightest and darkest points in your image is not difficult, but it helps if you know where the image is going to be used. If you have a good relationship with a printer, they can tell you what values work best for their presses, or you can just use the generic values suggested in this book. The values shown in this example are good for typical printing setups and for web display.

1   Double-click on the Set White Point button (✎); the Select Target Highlight Color dialog box appears. Even though you are in RGB, you can set values in any of the color environments displayed in this window. In this example, you'll use CMYK values.

2   Type **5** in the C (Cyan) text field, **3** in the M (Magenta) text field, and **3** in the Y (Yellow) text field. Leave K (Black) at 0. A warning dialog box appears, asking if you would like to save the target values, press Yes.

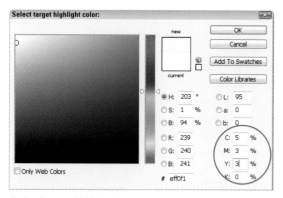

Setting the target highlight color.

3   Now, double-click on the Set Black Point button (✎). The Select Target Shadow Color dialog box appears.

4   Type **65** in the C (Cyan) text field, **53** in the M (Magenta) text field, **51** in the Y (Yellow) text box, and **95** in the K (Black) text field. Press OK. A warning dialog box appears, asking if you would like to save the target values; press Yes.

It is important to note that your printer may be able to achieve a richer black than the one offered here. If you have a relationship with a printer, ask for their maximum black value and enter it here. Otherwise, use these standard values.

5   Now, select the Set White Point button (✐), and then hold down Alt (Windows) or Option (Mac OS) and cross over the image. Notice that the image appears almost posterized: this is the automatic clipping that is visible when you hold down the Alt/Option key. The clipping makes it easier to locate the darkest and lightest areas of an image—an essential task if you are trying to improve an image's tonal values.

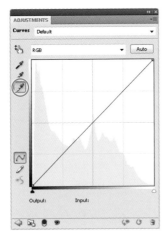

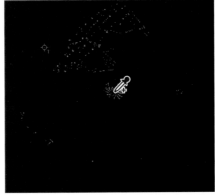

Select the Set White Point button.   *Hold down the Alt/Option key while positioning the cursor over the image.*

The lightest areas of the image are highlighted, but you can turn off the clipping at any time by releasing the Alt/Option key. When in the clipping mode, notice that the white stripes in the piece of peppermint candy, above the child's head, appear to be the lightest part of the image. There are some other areas that are reflections of shiny objects (specular highlights) that should be ignored when defining a highlight. In the next step, you will simply drop a color sampler on the lightest part of this image. This way, you can refer back to it at a later time.

If you can't see at your present zoom level, release the Alt/Option key and zoom closer into the candy, by holding down Ctrl+spacebar (Windows) or Command+spacebar (Mac OS) and clicking and dragging a marquee around the candy. Hold down the spacebar and click and drag to reposition the image, if necessary.

6   With the highlight eyedropper (✐) active continue holding down the Alt/Option key, causing the image to display in the posterized view.

Here is where it might get tricky: add the Shift key to this configuration, your cursor changes into the Color Sampler tool (✎). Click on the lightest area you can find inside the piece of candy. A color sample appears on the image, but no change has yet been made to the image.

Add a color sample to mark the lightest point in the image.

 If necessary, you can reposition the Color Sample by holding down the Shift key and dragging it to a new location.

7 Make sure that the Set White Point eyedropper is still selected, and hold down the Alt/Option key. Click on the lightest area of the candy, which is indicated by the color sampler you just dropped on the image. Then release the Alt/Option key.

The image highlight is adjusted to your newly defined highlight color values.

 If this gives you unexpected results, you might have clicked on the red part of the candy. You can undo by pressing Ctrl+Z (Windows) or Command+Z (Mac OS), and then try clicking on the white area of the candy again. Keep in mind that the color sample that you dropped is only a marker; you do not have to move the sampler to change the highlight.

Now you will set the black, or darkest, part of your image.

8 Before you begin, press Ctrl+0 (Windows) or Command+0 (Mac OS) to make the image fit in the window. You will now try a slight variation of the same method that you used to select the lightest point of the image.

9 Select the Set Black Point eyedropper (✎) on the Adjustments panel, and hold down the Alt/Option key. Now (pay attention, this is where it is different) click on the shadow slider (▲) that appears in the lower-left corner of the Curves Adjustments panel, and drag it toward the right.

When dragging the slider (slowly), notice that clipping appears, indicating (with darker colors) the shadow areas of this image. Notice that the shadow in the lower-right part of her dress appears to be the darkest area of the image. Hold down the Shift key, and click to mark this area with a color sample. Then release the Alt/Option key.

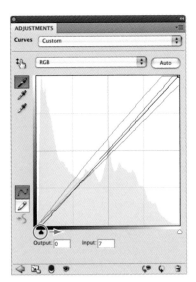

To see the darkest parts of this image, hold down the Alt/Option key and slide the shadow slider to the right.

Depending upon the input device you might have, many areas display as the darkest areas of an image. This is an indication that the input device, whether a scanner or camera, does not have a large dynamic range of tonal values that it can record. You might have to take a logical guess as to what is the darkest part of the image.

10 With the Set Black Point eyedropper still selected, click on the color sample that you dropped on the image. This has now been set as the darkest area of the image, using the values you input earlier in this example.

You should already see a difference in the image—a slight colorcast has been removed and the colors look a little cleaner—but you are not done yet. The next step involves balancing the midtones (middle values) of the image.

11 Leave the Curves Adjustments panel visible for the next exercise.

Adjusting the midtones

In many cases, you need to lighten the midtones (middle values of an image) in order to make details more apparent in an image. In an RGB image, the default for the Curves dialog box is to display the curves based upon light values. It can sometimes be more logical to adjust color based upon actual pigment, or ink.

1   With the Curves Adjustments panel still visible, click and hold on the panel menu (in the upper-right corner of the panel) and select Curves Display Options. The Curves Display Options dialog box appears.

Change the method of interpreting color from light to pigment.

Click on the *Pigment/Ink %* radio button in the Show Amount of: section, then click OK.

2   Now, select the center (midtone area) of the black curve and drag downwards (don't worry about the colored curves, as Photoshop is making an overall change in this window). Move the curve downwards slightly to lighten the image in the midtones. This is the only visual correction that you will make to this image. You want to be careful that you do not adjust too much, as you can lose valuable information.

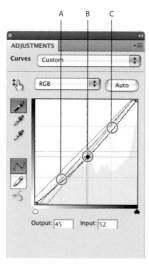

A. *Three-quarter tones.* **B**. *Midtones.*
C. *Quarter tones*

3   Add a little contrast to your image by clicking on the three-quarter tone area of the black curve line (the area between the middle of the curve and the top, as shown in the figure), then clicking and dragging up slightly. Again, this is a visual correction, so don't make too drastic a change.

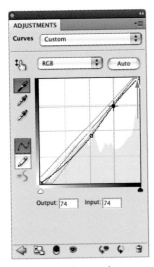
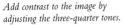

Add contrast to the image by
adjusting the three-quarter tones.

The work image as it appears after making some
curve adjustments.

4   Keep the Curves dialog box open for the next section of this lesson.

You can usually see a color cast by looking at the white and gray areas of an image, but, in some cases, you may not have any gray or white objects in your image. If these are art images, you may not want to neutralize them (for example, orange sunsets on the beach, or nice yellow candlelight images). Use the technique shown in this lesson at your discretion. It helps with a typical image, but it takes practice and experience to correct for every type of image.

Understanding neutral colors

A neutral is essentially anything in the image that is gray: a shade of gray, or even light to dark grays. A gray value is a perfect tool to help you measure color values, as it is composed of equal amounts of red, green, and blue. Knowing this allows you to pick up color inaccuracies by reading values in the Photoshop Info panel, rather than just guessing which colors need to be adjusted.

The first image you see below is definitely not correct, but exactly what is wrong? By looking at the Info panel, you can tell that the RGB values are not equal. In the second image, they are almost exactly equal. By looking at only the RGB values, you can tell that the image on the bottom is much more balanced than the image on the top.

The neutrals in this image are not balanced; as you can tell because the RGB values are not equal in value.

The neutrals in this image are balanced; as you can tell because the RGB values are equal.

Setting the neutral

In this section, you'll balance the neutrals in the image.

1 With the Curves panel still open, set another Color Sampler marker by Shift+clicking on the gray jacket that is visible to the left of the subject. In this image, this is the neutral that you are using as a reference for this example. In your images, you might find a neutral in a shadow on a white shirt, a gray piece of equipment, or a countertop.

Some photographers like to include a gray card (available at photo supply stores) in their images to help them color-balance their images.

2 If the Info panel is not open, choose Window > Info. The Info panel appears.

In the Info panel, you see general information about RGB and CMYK values, as well as pinpoint information about the three Color Sampler markers you have created. You'll only focus on the #3 marker, as the first two were to indicate highlight and shadow.

Notice that to the right of the #3 marker in the Info panel, there are two values separated by a forward slash. You'll focus only on the set of values to the right of the slash. Depending upon where you clicked in the gray shirt, you could have different values. The numbers to the left of the forward slash are the values before you started making adjustments in the Curves panel. The numbers to the right of the forward slash are the new values that you are creating with your curve adjustments.

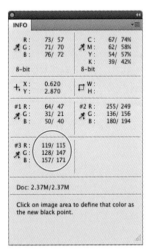

Focus on the values to the right of the forward slash.

3 Select the Set Gray Point button (🖊).

4   Click once on the #3 marker you created. The new color values may not be exactly the same, but they come closer to matching each other's values.

The Info panel after the #3 marker is selected as a gray point.

 If you want more advanced correction, you can enter each of the individual color curves and adjust them separately by dragging the curve up or down, while watching the values change in the Info panel.

5   Press Ctrl+S (Windows) or Command+S (Mac OS) to save your work file.

6   If your Layers panel is not visible, choose Window > Layers. On the Layers panel, click on the visibility eye icon (👁) to the left of the Curves 1 adjustment layer to toggle off and on the curves adjustment you just made. Make sure that the Curves layer's visibility is turned back on before you move on to the next section.

Click on the visibility eye icon to turn off and on the adjustment layer.

7   Choose File > Save. Keep this file open for the next part of this lesson.

Sharpening your image

Now that you have adjusted the tonal values of your image, you'll want to apply some sharpening to the image. In this section, you'll discover how to use unsharp masking. It is a confusing term, but is derived from the traditional (pre-computer) technique used to sharpen images.

To simplify this example, you'll flatten the adjustment layer into the Background layer.

If you are an advanced user, you can avoid flattening by selecting the Background layer, Shift+clicking on the Curves 1 layer, then right-clicking (Windows) or Ctrl+clicking (Mac OS) and choosing Convert to Smart Object. This embeds the selected layers into your Photoshop file, but allows you to view and work with them as one layer. If further editing is needed, you can simply double-click on the Smart Object layer, and the layers open in their own separate document.

1 Choose Flatten image from the Layers panel menu, as shown in the figure.

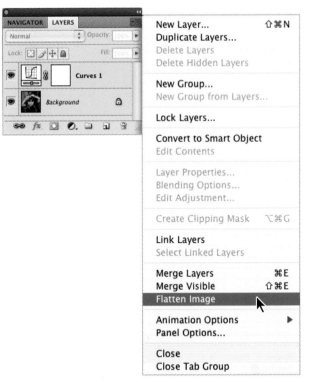

Choose Flatten image from the panel menu.

2   Choose View > Actual pixels. The image may appear very large; you can pan the image by holding down the spacebar and pushing the image around on the screen. Position the image so that you can see an area with detail, such as one of the eyes. Note that you should be in Actual Pixel view when using most filters, or you may not see accurate results on your screen.

 Hold down the spacebar, and click and drag on the image area to adjust the position of the image in the window.

3   Choose Filter > Convert for Smart Filters. (This step is unnecessary if you already converted your layers into a Smart Object.) If an Adobe Photoshop dialog box appears informing you that the layer is being converted into a Smart Object, press OK. Smart Objects allow you to edit filters more freely. An icon (⬚) appears in the lower-right corner of the layer thumbnail, indicating that this is now a Smart Object.

4   Choose Filter > Sharpen > Unsharp Mask. The Unsharp Mask dialog box appears.

You can click and drag inside the preview pane to change the part of the image that appears there.

Unsharp masking defined

Unsharp masking is a traditional film compositing technique used to sharpen edges in an image. The Unsharp Mask filter corrects blurring in the image, and it compensates for blurring that occurs during the resampling and printing process. Applying the Unsharp Mask filter is recommended whether your final destination is in print or online.

The Unsharp Mask filter assesses the brightness levels of adjacent pixels and increases their relative contrast: it lightens the light pixels that are located next to darker pixels, as it darkens those darker pixels. You set the extent and range of lightening and darkening that occurs, using the sliders in the Unsharp Mask dialog box. When sharpening an image, it's important to understand that the effects of the Unsharp Mask filter are far more pronounced on-screen than they appear in high-resolution output, such as a printed piece.

In the Unsharp Mask dialog box, you have the following options:

Amount determines how much the contrast of pixels is increased. Typically an amount of 150 percent or more is applied, but this amount is very reliant on the subject matter. Overdoing Unsharp Mask on a person's face can be rather harsh, so that value can be set lower (150 percent) as compared to an image of a piece of equipment, where fine detail is important (300 percent+).

Radius determines the number of pixels surrounding the edge pixels that are affected by the sharpening. For high-resolution images, a radius between 1 and 2 is recommended. If you are creating oversized posters and billboards, you might try experimenting with larger values.

Threshold determines how different the brightness values between two pixels must be before they are considered edge pixels and thus are sharpened by the filter. To avoid introducing unwanted noise into your image, a minimum Threshold setting of 10 is recommended.

5 Type **150** into the Amount text box. Because this is an image of a child, you can apply a higher amount of sharpening without bringing out unflattering detail.

Click and hold on the Preview pane to turn the preview off and on as you make changes.

6 Type **1** in the Radius text field and **10** in the Threshold text field, and click OK.

Using the Unsharp Mask dialog box.

7 Choose File > Save. Keep the file open for the next part of this lesson.

Because you used the Smart Filter feature, you can turn the visibility of the filter off and on at any time by clicking on the eye icon to the left of Smart Filters in the Layers panel.

Comparing your image with the original

You can use the History panel in Adobe Photoshop for many functions. In this section, you'll use the History panel to compare the original image with your finished file.

1 If the History panel is not visible, choose Window > History.

2 Make sure that you have the final step you performed selected. In this case, it should be the Unsharp Mask filter. If you have some extra steps because you were experimenting with the Smart Filter thumbnail, just click on the Unsharp Mask state in the History panel.

3 Click on the Create New Document from Current State button (⬒) at the bottom of the History panel. A new file is created.

4 Click back on your original image, ps0701_work.psd, and press Ctrl+0 (zero) (Windows) or Command+0 (zero) (Mac OS) to fit the image on your screen.

5 Click on the original snapshot located at the top of the History panel. This returns you to the original state. Click on the Arrange Documents button in the Application bar and select 2 Up to place the images side by side. You should see quite a difference between the images.

If you are having difficulty viewing the images, choose Window > Arrange > Tile.

Comparing your corrected image with the original image.

6 Choose File > Save, and then File > Close to close your ps0701_work files.

7 Choose File > Close for the unsharp mask file created from your History panel. When asked to save the changes, click No.

Congratulations! You have finished the color-correction part of this lesson.

Using the Camera Raw plug-in

In this section, you'll discover how to open and make changes to a Camera Raw file. Camera Raw really deserves more than can be covered in this lesson, but this will give you an introduction, and hopefully get you interested enough to investigate further on your own.

What is a Camera Raw file?

A Camera Raw image file contains the unprocessed data from the image sensor of a digital camera; essentially, it is a digital negative of your image. By working with a Raw file, you have greater control and flexibility, while still maintaining the original image file.

The Raw format is proprietary and differs from one camera manufacturer to another, and sometimes even between cameras made by the same manufacturer. This differentiation can lead to many issues, mostly that you also need the camera's proprietary software to open the Raw file, unless, of course, you are using Photoshop CS4's Camera Raw plug-in. The Camera Raw plug-in supports more than 150 camera manufacturers, and allows you to open other types of files into the Camera Raw plug-in, including TIFFs and JPEGs. If you are not sure whether your camera is supported by the Camera Raw plug-in, go to *adobe.com* and type **Support Camera Raw cameras** in the Search text box.

1   Choose File > Browse to launch Adobe Bridge, if it is not already open. You can also select the Launch Bridge button (Br) in the Application bar to launch Adobe Bridge.

2   Navigate to the ps06lessons folder, inside the CS4lessons folder on your hard drive. Select the image named ps0702.CR2. This is a Camera Raw file from a Canon Rebel digital camera. Note that each manufacturer has its own extensions; the CR2 extension is unique to Canon cameras.

3 Double-click on the ps0702.CR2 file to automatically launch and open the file in Photoshop's Camera Raw plug-in.

The Camera Raw plug-in automatically launches when a Raw file is opened.

If you attempt to open a Raw file that is not recognized by the Camera RAW plug-in, you may need to update your plug-in. Go to adobe.com to download the latest version.

When the Camera Raw plug-in opens, you see a Control panel across the top, as well as additional tabbed panels on the right. See the table for definitions of each button in the Control panel.

ICON	TOOL NAME	USE
🔍	Zoom tool (Z)	Increases or decreases the magnification level of a Camera Raw preview.
✋	Hand tool (H)	Allows you to reposition a Raw image, when magnified, in the preview pane.
🖊	White Balance tool (I)	Balances colors in a Raw image when you click on a neutral gray area in the image.
🖊	Color Sampler tool (S)	Reads image data and leave markers on the Raw image.
🔲	Crop tool (C)	Crops a Raw image right in the preview pane.
📐	Straighten tool (A)	Realigns an image.
🖌	Spot Removal tool (B)	Heals or clones a Raw image in the preview pane.
👁	Red-Eye Removal (E)	Removes red eye from a Raw image.
🖌	Adjustment Brush (K)	Paints adjustments of color, brightness, contrast, and more.
▮	Graduated Filter (G)	Replicates the effect of a conventional graduated filter, one that is composed of a single sheet of glass, plastic, or gel that is half color graduating to a half clear section.
☰	Open preferences dialog box (Ctrl+K, Command+K)	Changes preferences, such as where XMP files are saved.
↺	Rotate image 90 degrees counterclockwise (L)	Rotates an image 90 degrees counter-clockwise.
↻	Rotate image 90 degrees clockwise (R)	Rotates an image 90 degrees clockwise.

You'll have an opportunity to use several of these tools in the next lesson. Before starting, have a look at the panels on the right, and learn a bit about how they are used.

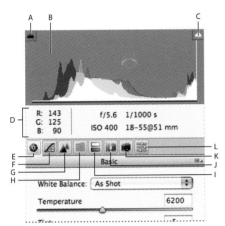

A. Shadow Clipping Warning button. B. Histogram. C. Highlight Clipping Warning button. D. Info.
E. Basic panel. F. Tone Curve panel. G. Detail. H. HSL/Grayscale. I. Split Toning. J. Lens Correction.
K. Camera Calibration. L. Presets.

A. Shadow Clipping Warning button: Indicates if an image is underexposed, with large areas of shadow being clipped. Clipped shadows appear as a solid dark area if not corrected using the exposure controls.

B. Histogram: Shows you where image data resides on the tone curve.

C. Highlight Clipping Warning button: Indicates if an image is overexposed, with large areas of highlight being clipped. A clipped highlight appears as a solid white area if not corrected using the exposure controls.

D. Info: Displays the RGB readings that enable you to check your colors and balance.

E. Basic panel: Contains the main controls, such as White Balance, Exposure, and Fill Light, among others.

F. Tone Curve panel: Adjusts the tone curve. The Point tab must be brought to the front (by clicking on it) to activate point-by-point controls.

G. Detail: Adjusts Sharpening and Noise Reduction.

H. HSL/Grayscale: Allows you to create grayscale images with total control over individual colors and brightness.

I. Split Toning
Introduces additional color tones into image highlights and shadows.

J. Lens Correction
Corrects for lens problems, including fringing and vignetting.

K. Camera Calibration
With the Camera Calibration tab, you can shoot a Macbeth color reference chart (available from camera suppliers). Then you can set Color Samplers on the reference chart, and use the sliders to balance the RGB values shown in the Info section. Settings can be saved by selecting the Presets tab and clicking on the New Preset button in the lower-right corner, or by choosing Save Settings from the panel menu.

L. Presets
Stores settings for future use in the Presets tab.

Using Camera Raw controls

In this section, you'll use a few of the controls you just reviewed.

1 Make sure that the Camera image is back to its original settings by holding down the Alt (Windows) or Option (Mac OS) key and clicking on Reset, located at the bottom-right corner. The Cancel button becomes Reset when you hold down the Alt or Option key.

2 The first thing you are going to do with this image is balance the color. You can do this with the White Balance controls. In this instance, you'll keep it simple by selecting the White Balance tool (✐) from the Control panel.

A good neutral to balance from is the light gray section of the name tag. With the White Balance tool selected, click on the white part of the name tag. The image is balanced, using that section of the image as a reference.

With the White Balance tool selected, click on the name tag.

You'll now adjust some of the other settings available in the Basic tab, to make the image more colorful while still maintaining good color balance.

The image looks a bit underexposed; the girl's face is somewhat dark. You'll bring out more detail in the girl's face with the Brightness slider. By using a combination of the Brightness and Recovery sliders, you can bring out additional detail without overexposing the highlights.

3   Click on the Exposure slider and drag to the left until you reach the −0.35 mark, or type **−.35** in the Exposure text field.

4   Click on the Brightness slider in the Basic tab and drag to the right to about the +120 mark, or type **120** into the Brightness text field.

5   Recover some of the lost highlights by clicking and dragging the Recovery slider right, to the 60 mark, or by typing **60** in the Recovery text field.

Whenever the original image has a high luminance (brightness) range, a highlight recovery in Camera Raw can help extend the range of the processed image. By adjusting the Exposure down and the Brightness up, you can maintain highlight detail that would otherwise be lost.

6   Increase the contrast in the image by clicking and dragging the contrast slider right, to the 60 mark, or by typing **60** into the Contrast text field.

Increase the richness of color by using the Vibrance slider. Do not increase it too much if you plan on printing the image, as oversaturated, rich colors do not generally convert well to CMYK.

7   Drag the Vibrance slider right, over to the 25 mark, or type **25** into the Vibrance text field.

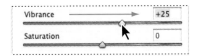

Drag the Vibrance slider to the right.

8 Select the Crop tool (⌗) from the Control panel, and click and drag to select an image area that is a little closer to the girl's face.

Cropping an image in the Camera Raw Plug-in.

Now you'll save your settings.

9 Click on the Presets tab. Press the Save Preset button (⊒) in the lower-right corner of the Presets panel. Type the name **Canon_outdoor** and press OK.

10 Keep the Camera Raw Plug-in window open for the next step.

Saving a DNG file

Next, you will save your image as a DNG file. A DNG file is essentially a digital negative file that maintains all the corrections you have made, in addition to the original unprocessed Raw image.

Adobe created the DNG format to provide a standard for Raw files. As mentioned previously, camera vendors have their own proprietary Raw formats and their own extensions and proprietary software to open and edit them. The DNG format was developed to provide a standard maximum-resolution format that all camera vendors would eventually support directly in their cameras. Right now, DNG provides you with the opportunity to save your original Camera Raw files in a format that you should be able to open for many years to come. Note that you can reopen the DNG over and over again, making additional changes without degrading the original image.

1   Press the Save Image button in the lower-left corner of the Camera Raw dialog box. The Save Options dialog box appears.

2   Leave the Destination set to Save in Same Location, then click on the arrow to the right of the second drop-down menu in the File Naming section and choose 2 Digit Serial Number. This will automatically number your files, starting with the original document name followed by 01.

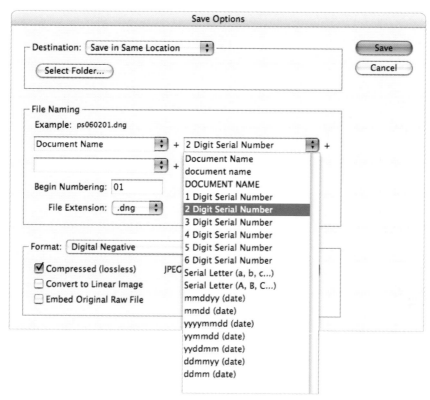

The Camera Raw Save Options dialog box.

3   Press Save. You are returned to the Camera Raw dialog box.

4   Click the Open Image button. The adjusted and cropped image is opened in Photoshop. You can continue working on this file. If you save the file now, you will see the standard Photoshop Save As dialog box. Note that whatever you save is a copy of the original Camera Raw file—your DNG file remains intact.

Reopening a DNG file

You'll now use Bridge to access your saved DNG file.

1   Access Bridge by choosing File > Browse, or by selecting the Launch Bridge button (Br) in the upper-left corner of the Photoshop window.

2   If you are not still in the ps06lessons folder, navigate to it now. Double-click on the file you have created, ps070201.dng.

Note that the file reopens in the Camera Raw plug-in dialog box and that you can undo and redo settings, as the original has remained intact.

Congratulations! You have completed the lesson on Camera Raw images.

Self study

In this section, you can try this exercise on your own.

In this section, you'll learn how to take advantage of the Smart Objects and Smart Filters features using a technique that includes painting on the Filter effects mask thumbnail.

1   Choose File > Browse and locate the file named ps0703.psd, located in the ps06lessons folder.

2   Alt (Windows) or Option (Mac OS) double-click on the Background layer to turn it into a layer (Layer 0).

3   Select Filter > Convert for Smart Filters, and press OK if a Photoshop dialog box appears. Then choose Filter > Blur > Gaussian Blur. Again, press OK if an Adobe Photoshop dialog box appears. The Gaussian Blur dialog box appears. Use the slider at the bottom of the dialog box to apply a blur to the image. Move the slider until you can easily see the results; there's no exact number that you should set for this exercise, but make sure it is set at an amount high enough that you can see the results easily. Press OK when done. After you apply the Blur filter, a Smart Filter layer appears with a Filter effects mask thumbnail.

4   Select the Filter effects mask to activate it. This is the large white square to the left of Smart Filters in the Layers panel.

5   Choose the Brush tool (✎) from the Tools panel, and press D on your keyboard. This changes your foreground and background colors to the default colors of black and white.

6   If black is not set as your foreground color, press X to swap the foreground and background colors. Using the Paintbrush tool, paint over the image; note that where you paint with black, the blur disappears. Press X to swap the colors so that white is now the foreground color, then paint over areas where the blur is not visible, to restore it. While painting, try various values: for instance, if you type **5**, you are painting with a 50 percent opacity; if you type **46**, you paint with a 46 percent opacity. Type **0** to return to 100 percent opacity. This is a technique that is worth experimenting with—try other filters on your own to explore painting on Filter effect masks to hide or reveal the effect of each filter.

Review

Questions

1 Name an example of how a color sampler can be used.

2 What color mode is typically used for color-correcting an image?

3 What is a neutral? How can you use it to color-correct an image?

4 How can you tell if an image has been corrected in Adobe Photoshop?

5 What is a DNG file?

Answers

1 It is common for the Color Sampler tool to be used inside the Curves panel, where it can be used to mark white, black, or gray points on the image. Using a Color Sampler makes it much easier to read the data from one particular point of the image from the Info panel.

2 There are many theories as to which color mode is the best working environment for color correction. Unless you are in a color-calibrated environment (using LAB), RGB should be the mode you choose to work in for color correction.

3 A neutral is a gray, or a shade of gray. You can often find a gray area in an image that can be used as a measuring tool to see if your colors are balanced. Some photographers like to introduce their own gray card in order to have a neutral against which to balance. They then crop the gray card out of the image when they are finished correcting the color balance.

4 By viewing the Histogram panel, you can tell if an image's tone curve has been adjusted. Even if you make simple curve adjustments, some degradation will occur in the tonal values of the image.

5 The DNG (Digital Negative) format is a non-proprietary, publicly documented, and widely supported format for storing raw camera data. The DNG format was developed to provide a standard format that all camera vendors would eventually support. You may also use DNG as an intermediate format for storing images that were originally captured using a proprietary camera raw format.

Lesson 1

What you'll learn in this lesson:

* Exploring Dreamweaver's primary features

* Introducing new features in CS4

* Understanding how web sites and web pages work

* Coding HTML/XHTML: the basics

Dreamweaver CS4 Jumpstart

Whether you are a novice web designer or an experienced developer, Dreamweaver is a comprehensive tool you can use for site design, layout, and management. In this lesson, you'll take a tour of Dreamweaver's key features and get a better understanding of how web pages work.

Starting up

Before starting, make sure that your tools and panels are consistent by resetting your workspace. See "Resetting the Dreamweaver workspace" on page XXVII.

You will work with several files from the dw01lessons folder in this lesson. Make sure that you have loaded the CS4lessons folder onto your hard drive from he supplied DVD. See "Loading lesson files" on page XXIX.

Note: If you want to get started creating a page, jump ahead to "Tag structure and attributes". Otherwise, the next few pages provide you with an overview of key capabilities and features of Dreamweaver CS4.

See Lesson 1 in action!

Use the accompanying video to gain a better understanding of how to use some of the features shown in this lesson. The video tutorial for this lesson can be found on the included DVD.

What is Dreamweaver?

Dreamweaver is an excellent coding and development tool for new and experienced users alike, and it has quickly become the preferred web site creation and management program, providing a creative environment for designers. Whether you design web sites, develop mobile phone content, or script complex server-side applications, Dreamweaver has something to offer.

Design and layout tools

Dreamweaver's many icon-driven menus and detailed panels make it easy to insert and format text, images, and media (such as video files and Flash movies). This means that you can create great-looking and functional web pages without knowing a single line of code—Dreamweaver takes care of building the code behind the scenes for you. Dreamweaver does not create graphics from scratch; instead, it is fully integrated with Adobe Photoshop CS4, so you can import and adjust graphics from within the application.

The Insert panel features objects in several categories that let you easily add images, web forms, and media to your page.

Site management and File Transfer Protocol

Dreamweaver has everything you need for complete site management, including built-in file transfer protocol (FTP) capabilities between a server and your local machine, reusable objects (such as page templates and library items), and several safety mechanisms (such as link checkers and site reports) so that you can ensure that your site works well and looks good. If you're designing your pages with Cascading Style Sheets (CSS), the Browser Compatibility Check and CSS Advisor features will help you to locate and troubleshoot any potential display issues that may occur across different web browsers.

Coding environment and text editor

Dreamweaver lets you work in a code-only view of your document that acts as a powerful text editor. Edit HTML code directly and switch views to see the results of your code as you work. Features such as color-coding, indentation, and visual aids make Dreamweaver a perfect text editing or coding environment for web designers of any level.

For more experienced developers, Dreamweaver also supports popular coding and scripting languages, such as JavaScript, and several server-side languages, including ColdFusion, PHP, and ASP.NET. Specialized insert menus and code panels help you to build pages and applications in the language of your choice.

Code view is a full-featured text editor that color-codes tags and scripts for editing that's easier to decipher.

Scripting languages, such as those used to build interactive web pages or e-commerce sites, fall into two categories: client-side and server-side. Client-side languages (such as JavaScript) run in your browser, while server-side languages (such as ColdFusion) require special software installed on the server to run.

Who uses Dreamweaver?

Dreamweaver's popularity is a result of its diversity. Its ability to take a site from conception through to launch—and maintenance afterward—makes it a preferred tool among industry professionals, businesses, and educational institutions. However, it remains easy and accessible enough for novice designers to get up-and-running quickly. It's not unusual to see Dreamweaver utilized for personal projects or by small businesses and media professionals, such as photographers and painters, to maintain a web presence.

What's new in Dreamweaver CS4?

In this lesson, you'll look at some of the newest features in Dreamweaver CS4, if you are using Dreamweaver for the first time or new to web design, keep in mind that some of these features are geared to intermediate or advanced users. You may choose to skip this section and go directly "An overview of the features" later in this lesson.

CS4 introduces many innovative design and coding features as well as improvements to Dreamweaver's flagship features. Because Dreamweaver is part of the industry-standard Adobe Creative Suite, it has been engineered to work as seamlessly as possible with files from other CS4 applications, offering native support for Photoshop files and the ability to edit placed images directly in Adobe Photoshop CS4.

New user interface

When you launch Dreamweaver CS4, one of the first things you'll notice is that it now features a user interface that is consistent with the rest of the applications in the Creative Suite. A highlight of this new interface is the workspace configurator, which allows you to easily choose the most efficient workspace for the job at hand.

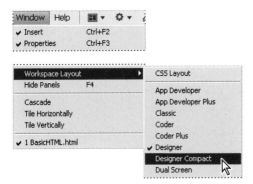

Choose the workspace that matches your tasks—or create your own.

Dreamweaver has included some common workspaces for you, but you can also choose to create your own custom workspaces. Among the included workspaces is the new compact mode for your panels, which lets you conserve monitor space by collapsing your panels onto the right side of the screen and expand them only when needed.

Live View

Experience tells you that visual web editors often display differently from the browsers they're emulating. As script-driven interactivity gains popularity, the need to accurately design the different states of your page (including menus, panels, and interface elements) has become increasingly important. The static nature of Design view in Dreamweaver might no longer meet users' advanced needs.

Dreamweaver's new Live View mode uses the WebKit rendering engine (which is also the basis for the Safari web browser and Adobe AIR) to give you a more accurate preview of your page, usually just as a browser would render it. In addition, you can interact with your page directly within Dreamweaver, viewing all the various states it may require in context.

Live View enables you to interact with your pages.

When you select Live Code while in Live View mode, you can see, in real time, how visually changing your page affects the code behind the scenes. You can preview your code as classes are added and removed using JavaScript, as dynamic content is inserted using Spry, and much more.

It's one thing, however, to preview these states, and another to effectively work with them. The Freeze JavaScript button (or the F6 key) *freezes* your page in a particular state (for example, with a menu locked open and a hover effect in place). You can then edit those interactively displayed elements directly in Dreamweaver, without having to use the Preview in Browser feature (F12) and your favorite web browser.

Related files

Web-based projects are becoming more complex than ever before, and you often find that even a single page is composed of a variety of assets. These assets can include Cascading Style Sheets (CSS), external JavaScript files, or even server-side includes. Dreamweaver CS4 has a new feature that will help you be much more effective at designing and managing sites and applications with multiple assets.

The Related Files bar now runs across the top of your document window, just below the document tabs. The bar shows you all the various files that combine to create your finished page. Switch between these files using the Related Files bar without losing the visual preview of their parent page. Design view (or Live View) always shows the parent file, but you can now edit any of the related files without losing their important visual context.

The Related Files bar shows you the various files that are part of your finished page.

Code Navigator

Using the new Code Navigator, you can easily jump to any of the related files (including the specific rules within) that combine to create the final display of a selected element. It is no longer necessary to look through multiple style sheets to find a specific rule. It's now just a context menu-click away in Dreamweaver. With the Code Navigator, when you hover over a CSS rule you are able to see the properties and values and click on them to navigate to that specific code. As with related files, you can do this without losing the visual context that's so important to creating interactive experiences.

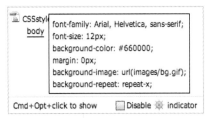

The Code Navigator allows you to easily jump to any of your related files.

CSS improvements

The rebuilt Property Inspector reduces the risk of making mistakes when adding HTML and CSS for text. In earlier versions, Dreamweaver would sometimes add HTML to the page, and sometimes create CSS styles, depending on which buttons you clicked in the Property Inspector. This often led to a long, undesired list of styles with ambiguous names, such as Style1, Style2, and so on. In Dreamweaver CS4, the two functions—adding HTML and creating styles—are divided into two different views of the Property Inspector.

The reconfigured Property Inspector eliminates confusion when using HTML and CSS.

HTML data sets

Dreamweaver's new HTML data set feature lets you convert a regular HTML file to a small database system. For instance, you can create an HTML table with rows and columns of data, and use Dreamweaver to import that table into another web page (using JavaScript and Spry). Then you can present that data in a variety of different ways, such as a "Master/Detail" page that lets a user view a master summary of rows from the table, click an item in the list, and instantly see all the details for that table row.

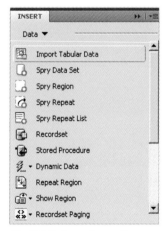

The HTML data set feature allows you to import and present data in different ways.

Photoshop smart objects

For this version, Dreamweaver supports a key, long-standing feature of the other Creative Suite programs—smart objects. Dreamweaver CS4 offers support for Photoshop smart objects, meaning you can drag a PSD file into a web page within Dreamweaver, optimize the image for the web, and even resize it. If you later update the original PSD file, a red arrow appears on the image in Dreamweaver, indicating that the source file has changed. You can then click the Update from Original button in the Property Inspector, and a new version of the image is created.

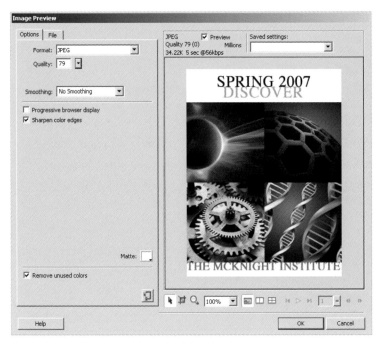

Smart objects provide easier optimizing and updating of graphics.

Other new features

Adobe AIR authoring support

Adobe AIR is a cross-platform system that lets developers combine HTML, AJAX, Adobe Flash, and Flex technologies to deploy Rich Internet Applications (RIAs) on the desktop. Because it fully supports Adobe AIR, Dreamweaver allows developers to use familiar tools to build their applications and easily deliver a single application installer that works across multiple operating systems.

Subversion

Dreamweaver now includes Subversion, a version control system similar to CVS and Visual Sourcesafe (VSS). Subversion is typically used by companies to maintain a team environment on larger projects that require changes to be logged, and versions to be controlled. Previously in Dreamweaver, if you wanted to maintain versions, you would have to do the work yourself—maintaining folders and copies of previous versions. With Subversion, all files are kept on the Subversion server. Changes are tracked so that you can restore your project to any previous state.

An overview of features

This book is dedicated to exploring, learning, and putting to use all that Dreamweaver has to offer. This section looks at some of the application's key features.

Three different points of view: When you edit a document, Dreamweaver lets you see your work in one of three views: the Design, Split, or Code view. Dreamweaver's easy-to-use Design view lets you build visually and see everything come to life as you create your pages. More experienced web designers and coders can use the Code view to edit a document's HTML code and scripts directly, enhanced with easy-to-read color-coding and visual aids.

For those who like something in between, the Split view provides a split-pane Design and Code view all at once. You can easily change views at any time with a single click in the Document toolbar.

The Split view lets you edit your page visually while seeing the code being created behind the scenes.

Built-in FTP: You can easily upload and download files to and from your web server using the Files panel's drag-and-drop interface, or use the Get/Put button at any time to post pages you're currently working on. There's no need for separate software. Dreamweaver also provides Check In/Check Out functionality and synchronization features for easy management.

Page and code object Insert panels: You can find intuitive icons for most common web page elements in a categorized Insert panel, from which you can add elements to your page with a single click. You can use additional panels to fine-tune any page element to ensure that you see exactly what you want. Included in the default Insert panel are tools for formatting text, building forms, and creating layouts. Customize a Favorites tab with your most-used icons.

The Insert panel is divided into several categories geared toward specific tasks.

Customizable workspace layouts: You can save combinations and positions of panels and toolbars for easy recall at any time. Save multiple workspace layouts for different users, or create different workspaces for specific tasks, such as coding or designing page layouts.

You can customize the Favorites panel with icons from any of the other Insert panel categories.

Powerful visual aids: Take advantage of the precision you're accustomed to in other design programs through Dreamweaver's guides, rulers, measuring tools, and customizable positioning grid. Dreamweaver's Design-Time style sheets let you customize the look of your page exclusively for the editing process, making layout quicker and easier without permanently altering the page's appearance.

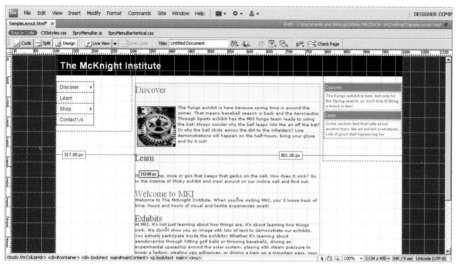

Rulers, a document grid, and guides help you to size and position page items with precision.

CSS panel: Take advantage of the vast design and formatting options that CSS provides through Dreamweaver's full-featured CSS panel, which lets you create, edit, and manage styles on-the-fly from a single panel.

How web sites work

Before embarking on the task of building web pages (and in turn, a web site), it's a good idea to know the basics of how web sites work, how your users view them, and what you need to know to make sure your web site looks and works its best.

A simple flow chart

What happens when you type in a web site address? Most people don't even think about it; they just type in a URL, and a web site appears in a flash. They likely don't realize how many things are going on behind the scenes to make sure that pages gets delivered to their computers so that they can do their shopping, check their e-mail, or research a project.

When you type in a URL or IP address, you are connecting to a remote computer (referred to as a server) and downloading the documents, images, and resources necessary to reconstruct the pages you will view at that site. Web pages aren't delivered as a finished product; your web browser (Internet Explorer, Firefox, Safari, and so on) is responsible for reconstructing and formatting the pages based on the HTML code included in the pages. HTML (Hypertext Markup Language) is a simple, tag-based language that instructs your browser how and where to insert and format pictures, text, and media files. Web pages are written in HTML, and Dreamweaver builds HTML for you behind the scenes as you construct your page in the Design view.

An Internet Service Provider (ISP) enables you to connect to the Internet. Some well-known ISPs include America Online and Earthlink. You view web pages over an Internet connection using a browser, such as Internet Explorer, Firefox, or Safari. A browser can decipher and display web pages and their content, including images, text, and video.

Domain names and IP addresses

When you type in a web site address, you usually enter the web site's domain name (such as *eBay.com*). The web site owner purchased this domain name and uses it to mask an IP address, which is a numerical address used to locate and dial up the pages and files associated with a specific web site.

So how does the web know what domains match what IP address (and in turn, which web sites)? It uses a Domain Name Service (DNS) server, which makes connections between domain names and IP addresses.

Servers and web hosts

A DNS server is responsible for matching a domain name with its companion IP address. Think of the DNS server as the operator at the phone company who connects calls through a massive switchboard. DNS servers are typically maintained by either the web host or the registrar from which the domain was purchased. Once the match is made, the request from your user is routed to the appropriate server and folder where your web site resides. When the request reaches the correct account, the server directs it to the first page of the web site, which is typically named index.html, default.html, or whatever the server is set up to recognize as a default starting page.

A server is a machine very much like your desktop PC, but it's capable of handling traffic from thousands of users (often at the same time!), and it maintains a constant connection to the Internet so that your web site is available 24 hours a day. Servers are typically maintained by web hosts, companies that charge a fee to host and serve your web site to the public. A single server can sometimes host hundreds of web sites. Web hosting services are available from a variety of providers, including well-known Internet service companies, such as Yahoo!, and large, dedicated hosting companies, such as GoDaddy. It is also common for a large company to maintain its own servers and web sites on its premises.

The role of web browsers

A web browser is an application that downloads and displays HTML pages. Every time you request a page by clicking a link or typing in a web site address, you are requesting an HTML page and any files it includes. The browser's job is to reconstruct and display that page based on the instructions in the HTML code, which guides the layout and formatting of the text, images, and other assets used in the page. The HTML code works like a set of assembly instructions for the browser to use.

An introduction to HTML

HTML is what makes the Web work; web pages are built using HTML code, which in turn is read and used by your web browser to lay out and format text, images, and video on your page. As you design and lay out web pages in Design view, Dreamweaver writes the code behind the scenes that is necessary to display and format your page in a web browser.

Contrary to what you may think, HTML is not a programming language, but rather a simple text-based markup language. HTML is not proprietary to Dreamweaver—you can create and edit HTML in any text editor, even simple applications such as Windows Notepad and Mac OS X's TextEdit. Dreamweaver's job is to give you a visual way to create web pages without having to code by hand. If you like to work with code, however, Dreamweaver's Code view, discussed earlier, is a fully featured text editor with color-coding and formatting tools that make it far easier to write and read HTML and other languages.

Tag structure and attributes

HTML uses tags, or bracketed keywords, that you can use to place or format content. Many tags require a closing tag, which is the keyword preceded by a forward slash (/).

1   Choose File > Open. When the Open dialog box appears, navigate to the dw01lessons folder. Select BasicHTML.html and press Open.

2   Select the Split button (⬚) in the Document toolbar to see the layout as well as the code that makes up the page.

Take a look at line 10 (indicated at the left edge of the Code panel). The text *My Bold Title* is inside a Strong tag, which is simply the word *strong* contained within angled brackets. Any words or characters inside these tags are formatted in bold, and appear as shown in the Design view.

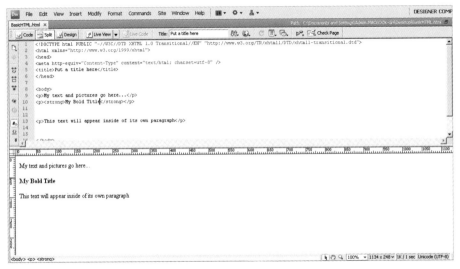

A look at the code reveals the tags used to format text in your page.

Tags can also accept CSS rules that specify additional information for how the tag should display the content. CSS rules can take a number of different values, such as a size, a color, or a direction in which to align something. Take a look at the line that reads *This text will appear inside of its own paragraph*. This line is enclosed in a *p* (paragraph) tag, which separates it from the other text by a line above and below. You can add a class rule to this to align the text in whichever direction you want.

3   Highlight the entire line that reads *This text will appear inside of its own paragraph* at the bottom of the Design view.

4   With the CSS button selected in the Property Inspector, locate the paragraph align buttons. Press the Align Center button (≡).

5   In the New CSS Rule dialog box, type **.center** into the Selector Name field, and
press OK.

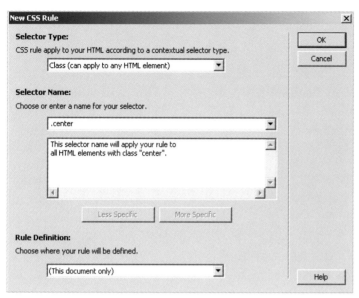

Name a newly created style in the New CSS Rule dialog box.

6   The text is now centered. Take a look at the Code view, and notice that the .center rule
has been added to the opening *<p>* tag.

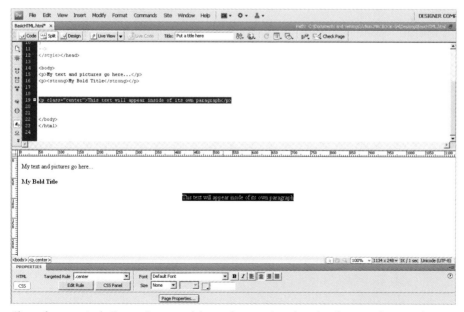

Align or format text in the Property Inspector, and then see the appropriate rules and attributes created in your code.

For more information on formatting text with CSS rules, please see Dreamweaver Lesson 3, "Adding Text and Images."

7   Choose File > Save to save your work, then choose File > Close.

The structure of an HTML document

Although you use many HTML tags to format text, certain tags are devoted to establishing structures, such as lists, tables, or, most importantly, the HTML documents themselves. The HTML tag is the most fundamental tag. It is used to specify the beginning and end of HTML in a document:

```
<html></html>
```

Inside the main HTML tags are two tags that define the key areas of your web page: the head and the body. The head of your page contains items that are not visible to your user, but are important nonetheless, such as search engine keywords, page descriptions, and links to outside scripts or style sheets. You create the head of the document inside the HTML tags using the *<head>* tag:

```
<html>
<head></head>
</html>
```

The body of your page is where all the visible elements of your page are contained. Here is where you place and format text, images, and other media. You define the body of the page using the *<body>* tag:

```
<html>
<head></head>
<body>

My text and pictures go here...

</body>
</html>
```

Whenever you create a new HTML document in Dreamweaver, this framework is created automatically before you add anything to the page. Any visual elements you add to the page are added, using the appropriate HTML code inside the *<body>* tags.

Placing images in HTML

You use some tags in HTML to place items, such as pictures or media files, inside a web page. The *<img>* tag is the most common example; its job is to place and format an image on the page. To place an image and see the resulting code, follow these steps:

1   Choose File > Open. When the Open dialog box appears, navigate to the dw01lessons folder. Select the Images.html file and press Open to edit the file.

2   Click the Split button (⊞) in the Document toolbar so that you're viewing both the layout and the code for your page. In the Design view portion of the Split view, click below the line of text to place your cursor underneath it. This is where you'll place a new image.

Enter the Split view before you insert the image onto your page.

3 From the Common category in the Insert panel on the right side of the screen, click on the Images element (▣) and choose Image. When the Select Image Source dialog box appears, select the file named gears.jpg, located in the images folder within the dw01lessons folder.

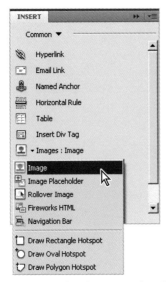

Choose Image from the Common tab on the Insert bar.

4 Press OK (Windows) or Choose (Mac OS); when the Image Tag Accessibility Attributes dialog box appears, type the words **Gears Image** in the Alternate text field, and press OK to place the image.

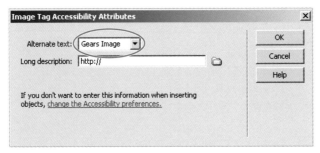

Attach alternate text to your image.

The Image Tag Accessibility Attributes dialog box appears when you add images, to provide additional information for users with special needs (such as the visually impaired). You should always provide each image with alternative text, but you can disable this panel by choosing Edit > Preferences (Windows) or Dreamweaver > Preferences (Mac OS). In the Accessibility category, uncheck the Images option.

5   The code shows that the HTML *<img>* tag has been used to place the image. Click once on the image in the document window to select it. The Property Inspector at the bottom of the page displays and sets the properties for the image.

6   In the Border box of the Property Inspector, type **3** to set a three-pixel border around the image, then press Enter (Windows) or Return (Mac OS). Click on the background of the page to deselect and note the appearance of the border. The *<img>* tag now contains the border attribute, which is set to a value of 3, just the way you typed it in the Property Inspector.

As you change or add options to a selected image, Dreamweaver changes code behind the scenes.

7   Choose File > Save to save your work, then choose File > Close.

Note that in HTML, images and media are not embedded, but placed. This means that the tags point to files in their exact locations relative to the page. The tags count on those files always being where they're supposed to be in order to display them. This is why HTML pages are typically very lightweight in terms of file size.

Colors in HTML

In Dreamweaver's various panels and in your code, each color is referred to by a six-character code preceded by a pound sign. This code is called hexadecimal code, and is the system that HTML pages use to identify and use colors. You can reproduce almost any color using a unique hexadecimal code. For example, you represent dark red in HTML as #CC0000.

The first, middle, and last two digits of the hexadecimal code correspond to values in the RGB spectrum. For instance, white, which is represented in RGB as R:255 G:255 B:255, is represented in HTML as #FFFFFF (255|255|255). Choosing colors is easy, thanks to a handy Swatches panel, which you can find in many places throughout the work area.

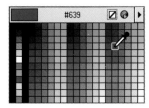

The Swatches panel makes it easy to work with colors.

The color pickers in Adobe Photoshop and Illustrator also display and accept hexadecimal codes, making it easy to copy and paste colors between these applications and Dreamweaver.

Case sensitivity and whitespace rules

HTML is a flexible language that has very few rules regarding its own appearance. Based on how strictly you want to write it, HTML can be either very specific about whether tags are written in upper- or lowercase (called case sensitivity), or not specific at all. To see how HTML treats whitespace, follow these steps.

1 Choose File > Open. When the Open dialog box appears, navigate to the dw01lessons folder. Select the Whitespace.html file, then press Open.

2 If your file is not in Split view, press the Split button (⊞) in the Document toolbar, so that you can view both the layout and the code. Notice three seemingly identical tags beneath line 9 in your code:

All these tags are valid, even though they have very different case structures.

All three tags use a completely different case structure, but all are valid and are treated in the same way. Take a look at the text that reads *This is one sentence. This is another.* The code shows a lot of space between the two lines, but the Design view shows no space at all. This is because both whitespace and line returns between two pieces of text or tags are not recognized.

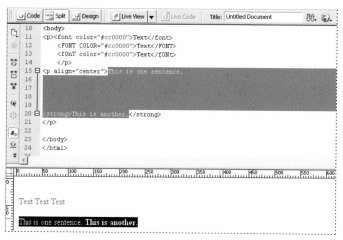

Despite the large amount of space between the two sentences, they appear side-by-side in the Design view.

3   To create a line return, or a new paragraph, you need to enter the necessary HTML tags. In the Design view at the bottom, position your cursor after the first sentence, then press Shift+Enter (Windows) or Shift+Return (Mac OS) twice. This creates two line returns—you can see that each line return is created in your code by a *
* (break) tag. When rendered in the browser, the *
* tag adds blank lines between the sentences, however the sentences are technically within the same paragraph.

To create a line return, hold down the Shift key while pressing the Enter or Return key.

4   To create a new paragraph, position your cursor before the phrase, *This is another*, and press Enter (Windows) or Return (Mac OS). The text is separated by a line above and below, and is wrapped inside a set of *<p>* (paragraph) tags.

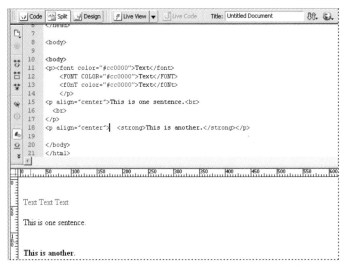

Dreamweaver creates a new paragraph each time you press the Enter or Return key.

Other than a standard single space (such as the ones used between words), several consecutive spaces created by the spacebar are ignored, and are displayed as only one space in Design view and in a browser.

5   Choose File > Save to save your work then choose File > Close.

Tag hierarchy

HTML tags follow a certain order of weight, or hierarchy, to make sure that everything displays as it should. The tag at the top of the hierarchy is the *<html>* tag, and every other tag you create is contained within it. Tags such as the *<body>* tag always hold smaller tags, such as the *<p>* (paragraph), *<img>* (image), and *<strong>* (bold) tags. In addition, structural tags (such as those that create paragraphs, lists, and tables) hold more weight than formatting tags such as *<strong>* (bold) and *<em>* (italic). Take this line of code for example:

```
<strong><p>Big bold paragraph</p></strong>
```

Although code such as this may work in certain browsers, it isn't recommended, because the *<strong>* tag technically holds less weight than the *<p>* tag. The following code represents a safer and more proper way to include the bold type:

```
<p><strong>Big bold paragraph</strong></p>
```

Dreamweaver generally does a great job of keeping tags properly nested, or contained within each other. When you choose to manipulate the code by hand, you should always keep good coding techniques in mind.

XHTML 1.0 Transitional

The latest recommended version of HTML is XHTML 1.0, a stricter version of HTML that makes the language more compatible with newer platforms, such as mobile phones and handheld devices, which require code to be perfectly formed. XHTML combines elements of HTML and XML, a language used to describe data. XML, or Extensible Markup Language, has become a popular method of exchanging information among seemingly unrelated applications, platforms, and systems. By default, Dreamweaver creates new web pages using the XHTML 1.0 Transitional standard.

What's the difference?

Although tags and attributes remain the same, the structure of the language changes with XHTML, becoming stricter. Whereas HTML was very forgiving of sloppy coding practices such as overlapping or unclosed tags, XHTML requires all tags to be closed and properly nested. HTML doesn't care which case you use when constructing tags, but in XHTML, all tags must be lowercase.

For example, a *
* (break) tag, which normally doesn't require a closing tag, now must be closed. You can write tags to *self-close* by using a forward slash—making sure there is a space between the (*br*) and the forward slash—and then closing the bracket like so:

```
<br />
```

The result is a well-formed language that takes advantage of newer browsers and device platforms, while remaining compatible with older browsers. Working with XHTML in Dreamweaver requires nothing more than selecting XHTML 1.0 Transitional as the Document Type (DocType) when creating a new page.

Explorations in code

Although this book occasionally refers to the code for examples, hand-coding is not a primary goal of the included lessons. The best way to learn how code represents the layouts you are building visually is to switch to the Code view and explore what's happening behind the scenes.

It's important to remember that every button, panel, and menu in Dreamweaver represents some type of HTML tag, attribute, or value; very rarely will you learn something that is unrelated or proprietary to Dreamweaver alone. Think of the Dreamweaver workspace as a pretty face on the HTML language.

A look at the Welcome Screen

A common fixture in most CS4 applications is the Welcome Screen, which is a launching pad for new and recent documents. In Dreamweaver, the Welcome Screen appears when the application launches or when no documents are open. From the Welcome Screen, you can create new pages, create a new site definition, open a recent document, or use one of Dreamweaver's many starter pages or layouts.

The Welcome Screen appears when you launch the application, or when no documents are open.

Here's what you'll find on the Welcome Screen:

Open a Recent Item: A list of the last few documents you worked on appears in the leftmost column, or you can browse to open a different file using the Open button (📁) at the bottom.

Create New: In addition to HTML pages, you can choose from a variety of new document formats, such as CSS, JavaScript, and XML. Dreamweaver is not just a web page-building tool, but also a superior text editor, making it ideal for creating many non-HTML files. You can also define a new Dreamweaver site using the link at the bottom, or choose the More folder for even more new file options.

Create from Samples: If you're not up to creating a design from scratch, or if you need a little inspiration, Dreamweaver features several starter files, ranging from complete page designs to stripped-down starter layouts. Starter page designs are categorized into several themes, from Health and Fitness to Entertainment, giving you plenty of options for getting started quickly and in style. Basic starter pages include many useful and common layout structures for e-commerce, photo display, and utility forms.

Creating, opening, and saving documents

The lessons throughout this book require that you create, save, and open existing files. You can accomplish most file-related tasks from the File menu at the top, or from the Start page that appears when you launch Dreamweaver.

Creating new documents

Dreamweaver creates text files, commonly in the form of HTML files (or web pages). It can also create files in a variety of text-based languages, including CSS, XML, JavaScript, and even Flash ActionScript.

You can create blank files that you build from the ground up, or get started with a variety of layout templates and themes. You can create new documents from the File menu or from the Welcome Screen.

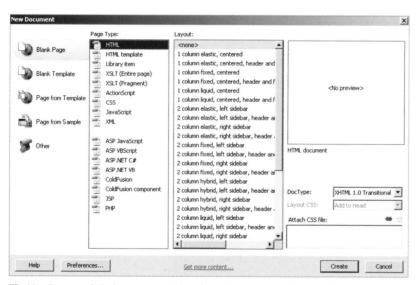

The New Document dialog box gives you a choice of new files in a variety of formats and templates.

1   To create a new document, choose File > New. The New Document dialog box appears.

2   Select Blank Page and under the Page Type column, choose HTML. Under Layout, choose <none> to start a new blank document. Leave the DocType drop-down menu at its default. Press Create.

3   Choose File > Save or File > Save As to start the process of saving your document.

4   When prompted, choose a location for your file and assign it a name. Note that you must save HTML files with an .html extension, or they will not be interpreted properly in a browser. This rule applies for files of any type (such as .xml, .css, and .cfm).

Opening a recently opened document

To open a document you've worked on recently, Choose File > Open Recent or, from the Welcome Screen, select a document under the Open a Recent Item column.

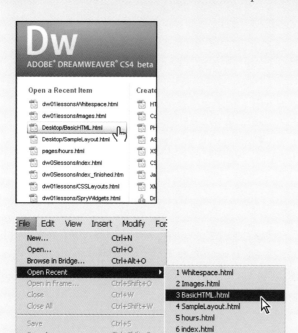

Choose a file from the Welcome Screen or choose File > Open Recent to select a recently opened file.

Now that you've seen what Dreamweaver can do, it's time to put what you've learned into practice. Move to the next lesson so that you can begin building your first Dreamweaver site!

Self study

Explore the ready-to-use CSS layouts available in Dreamweaver by choosing File > New, then selecting HTML from the Page Type column. Browse the options listed in the Layout column and open a few layouts. Identify some that you'd like to use as a starting point for any future project.

Review

Questions

1 From what two locations in Dreamweaver can a new document be created?

2 In what three views does Dreamweaver allow you to view and edit documents?

3 True or False: When a web page is requested, it is delivered to a user's browser as a completed, flat file ready for viewing.

Answers

1 From the Welcome Screen or by choosing File > New.

2 Design, Split, and Code views.

3 False. Files are delivered individually; the browser uses HTML code to assemble the resources together to display a finished page.

What you'll learn in this lesson:

- Creating a site definition
- Establishing local root and remote folders
- Adding and defining pages
- Selecting, viewing, and organizing files with the Files panel
- Uploading and downloading files to and from your remote server

Setting Up a New Site

Dreamweaver's strength lies in its powerful site creation and management tools. You can use the software to create everything from individual pages to complete web sites. The pages you create within your site can share similar topics, a cohesive design, or a common purpose. And, once your Dreamweaver site is complete, you can efficiently manage and distribute it from within the program.

Starting up

Before starting, make sure that your tools and panels are consistent by resetting your workspace. See "Resetting the Dreamweaver workspace" on page XXVII.

You will work with several files from the dw02lessons folder in this lesson. Make sure that you have loaded the CS4lessons folder onto your hard drive from the supplied DVD. See "Loading lesson files" on page XXIX.

See Lesson 2 in action!

Use the accompanying video to gain a better understanding of how to use some of the features shown in this lesson. The video tutorial for this lesson can be found on the included DVD.

Creating a new site

In Dreamweaver, the term *site* refers to the local and remote storage locations where the files that make up a web site are stored. A site can also include a testing server location for processing dynamic pages. To take full advantage of Dreamweaver's features, you should always start by creating a site.

The easiest way to create a new site in Dreamweaver is to use the Site Definition wizard. Choose Site > New Site, and the wizard appears.

You can also use the Manage Sites dialog box to create a new site. This and other functions of the Manage Sites dialog box are discussed later in this book.

In this lesson, you begin by using the Site Definition wizard to accomplish the following tasks:

* Define the site

* Name the site

* Define the local root folder

* Set up a remote folder

* Explore advanced settings

* Save the site

By default, the Site Definition wizard opens with the Basic tab selected. The options available here will help guide you through the essentials of defining your site. The Advanced tab allows you to set up local, remote, and testing servers directly.

The first screen you see in the Basic tab of the Site Definition wizard allows you to name your site. Avoid using spaces (use underscores instead), periods, slashes, or any other punctuation in your site name, as doing so will likely cause the server to misdirect your files.

To create a new site:

1   Launch Dreamweaver CS4, if it is not already open, then choose Site > New Site. First, you have to name the site. In the Name field, type **museum_site**.

2   If you are working directly on a web server (instead of locally), you can also enter the HTTP address of your server in this window. Because you'll be working locally in this lesson, entering an HTTP address isn't necessary, so leave the HTTP Address field blank and press Next.

The HTTP address can be input into the site definition.

3　You can use Dreamweaver to build web applications using any of five server technologies: ColdFusion, ASP.NET, ASP, JSP, or PHP. Each technology corresponds to a document type in Dreamweaver. Because you won't be using any of these server-scripting environments for this lesson, leave the radio button next to *No, I do not want to use a server technology* selected, then press Next to proceed to the next screen in the wizard.

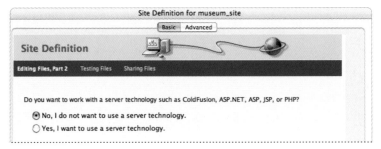

You can build your site using different server technologies.

At this point, you need to set up a local root folder, which is where Dreamweaver stores the files with which you're currently working. The local root folder definition screen allows you to enter information regarding where you'll be working with your files during development.

4　In this lesson, you'll be working locally and uploading to the server when you're ready, so click the first of the two radio buttons listed, labeled *Edit local copies on my machine*. Dreamweaver asks where you want to store your files locally. You can either create a folder on your hard drive and build your site from scratch, or use a pre-existing folder of content that you've already created for this site. You'll use the second option for this lesson.

To ensure that the links you set up on your computer will work when you upload the site to a web server, it is essential that you store all the site's resources in one main folder on your hard drive, then identify it within Dreamweaver. This is because the links will only work properly if all of the site's elements remain in the same relative location on the web server as with your hard drive.

5   Click on the folder icon (📁) to the right of this field to navigate to your prebuilt files.

6   Navigate to your desktop and locate the museum_files folder inside the dw02lessons folder you copied to your desktop earlier.

7   Click Open to open this folder, then press Select (Windows) or Choose (Mac OS) to choose this as your local root folder. The field now shows the path to your newly defined local root folder. Press Next.

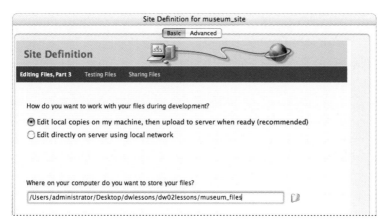

Define the path to your local root folder.

8   In most cases, the remote folder is the location on the computer where your web server is running. This is where you'll upload and store your files for deployment to the Web. When you set up a remote folder, you have to choose a method for Dreamweaver to upload and download files to this server. The drop-down menu on this screen offers you a list of access options. Choose FTP (the most commonly used method) from the drop-down menu.

9 Additional fields for FTP address, folder location, login, and password appear. These fields are required to gain FTP access to a server.

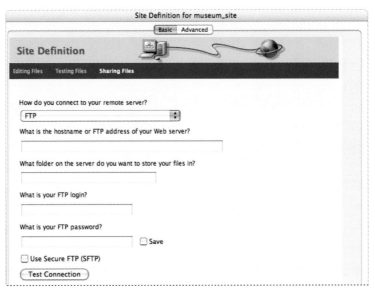

Set up access to your remote folder.

10 You do not have to define your remote folder at this stage. Dreamweaver allows you to define your remote folder at a later time, such as when you're ready to upload. In this lesson, you'll work locally now and define your remote folder using the Files panel later. From the drop-down menu, choose None for the remote connection choice. Press Next.

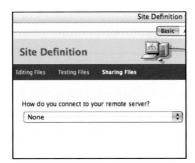

Choose None to define your remote folder later.

11 The final screen in the Basic tab of the Site Definition wizard is a summary of all the settings you just selected. Check that your local information, including the site name and the location of your local root folder (museum_files), is correct. If it isn't, press the Back button to bring you back to the screen containing the error.

Note that the Remote Server and Testing Server options reflect that you'll set them up later.

The Summary screen shows the site definition choices you've made.

You've now completed the site definition process, using the Basic interface of the Site Definition wizard. Don't close the wizard yet, though, as you'll now explore the options found under the Advanced tab.

Advanced site-creation options

Don't ignore the Advanced tab of the Site Definition window, as it offers access to many settings that aren't available in the Site Definition wizard.

The Advanced tab also offers access to all the settings options available in the wizard's Basic tab, so you can go straight to the Advanced tab to create a site when you gain more experience with Dreamweaver.

To create a new site, using Advanced options:

1   Click the Advanced tab in the Site Definition dialog box.

2   From the categories on the left, choose Local Info.

3   Note that the Site Name and Local Root Folder fields are populated by the information you entered using the wizard.

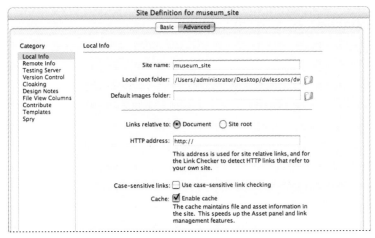

The information you entered using the wizard is reflected here.

The information you set in the Local Info window identifies the site files in Dreamweaver and enables the software's site management features. One of the more important Local Info settings is case-sensitive link checking.

The case-sensitive link checking feature ensures that your links will work on a Unix server, where links are case-sensitive. If you're using a Windows or Mac server, this doesn't matter as much, but it is a good idea to follow the strict naming and linking conventions of a Unix system in case you ever move your site to a different server.

4   Click the checkbox next to Use case-sensitive link checking.

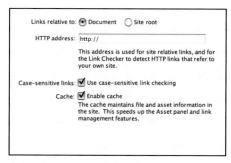

Activate the case-sensitive link checking option.

The remaining categories to the left of the Advanced tab of the Site Definition window help to define your site's production, collaboration, and deployment capabilities. They include the following:

Remote Info is necessary to upload the site files to the web server. Contact your server administrator to determine which method to use for your site.

Testing Servers act like public servers in order to test dynamic pages and connections to the database.

Version Control gives you access to Subversion, a system similar to CVS (Concurrent Versions System) and Visual Sourcesafe (VSS) that logs changes and controls document versions.

Cloaking allows you to specify file types or specific files that you do not want uploaded to the server.

Design Notes is a collaboration tool that keeps notes regarding the development of the page or site.

File View Columns is an organizational tool. If you want to share the custom columns with others, you must enable Design Notes as well.

Contribute is a separate application that enables users with basic word processing and web browser skills and little or no HTML knowledge to create and maintain web pages.

Templates can be automatically updated with rewritten document paths using this option.

Spry is a JavaScript library for web designers. It allows designers to build pages that provide a richer experience for their users.

Additional category options found in the Advanced tab.

At this point, you are finished defining your settings, so press OK; Dreamweaver creates a site with the settings you have defined. Note that the Files panel on the right side of your screen displays your local root folder and all its enclosed content files.

The Files panel shows all the files in your local root folder.

You are now ready to build pages for your web site.

Adding pages

Dreamweaver contains many features to assist you in building pages for your site. With these features, you can define properties for those pages, including titles, background colors or images, and default text and link colors.

It's important to consider that users will view your pages with different browsers on different platforms (and in different languages). Fortunately, Dreamweaver also includes tools that allow you to create and test pages to ensure compatibility with most users.

To add a page to your site:

1   Choose File > New. The New Document dialog box opens.

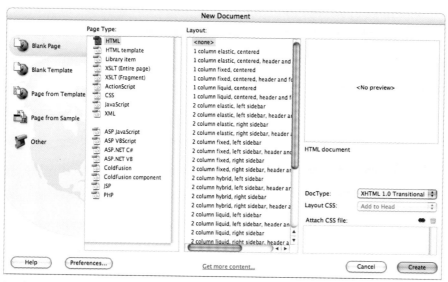

Use the New Document dialog box to add a page to your site.

2   You can create a new page using a predesigned layout, or start with a blank page and build a layout of your own. In this exercise, you'll start with a blank page. Click on the Blank Page category on the left side of the New Document dialog box.

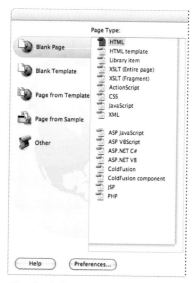

Select the Blank Page *category on the left side of the New Document dialog box.*

3 In the Page Type column, you can select the type of page you want to create (for example, HTML, ColdFusion, and so on). Select HTML.

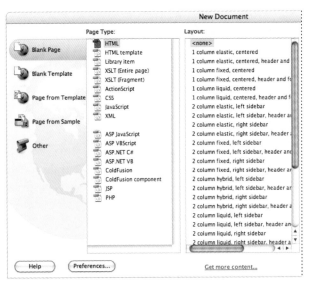

Choose the type of page you want to create (HTML).

In the Layout column, you can choose to base your page on a prebuilt design (created using Cascading Style Sheets [CSS], which are discussed in detail later in this book). These predesigned layouts fall into one of four categories:

Fixed columns do not resize based on the user's browser settings. They are measured in pixels.

Elastic columns adapt to the user's text settings, but not when the browser window is resized. These columns are measured in ems (a traditional typography measurement).

Liquid columns resize if the user resizes the browser window, but not if the user changes the text settings.

Hybrid columns combine any of the other three options (for example, three-column hybrid).

4   Click on <none> in the Layout column to build the page without using a
prebuilt layout.

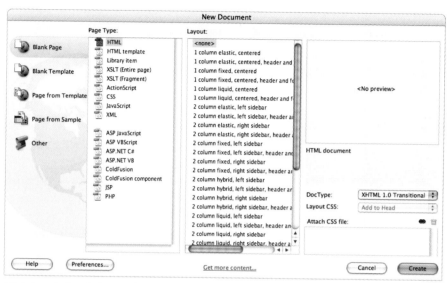

Select <none> from the Layout column.

5   Leave the DocType setting at XHTML 1.0 Transitional. The DocType drop-down menu
defines the document type and compliance with different versions of HTML. XHTML
1.0 Transitional is the default setting and is suitable in most cases.

Choose XHTML 1.0 Transitional as your DocType.

*The Layout CSS and Attach CSS settings are irrelevant here, as you didn't choose a CSS-based
layout for this page.*

6 Press Create to create a new, blank HTML page.

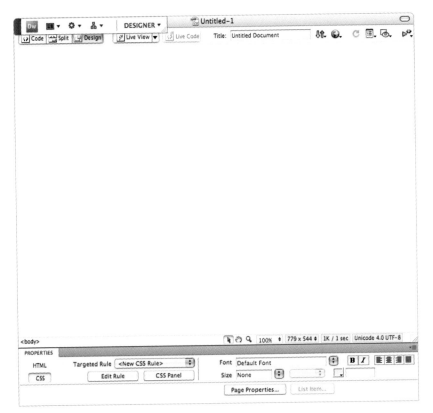

Your new, blank HTML page.

Saving a page to your site

You should get accustomed to saving pages to your local root folder early and often. It is very important that you store all your site's resources in one main folder on your hard drive so that the links you set on your computer will work when your site is uploaded to a server.

1 Choose File > Save.

2 In the Save As dialog box, navigate to your desktop, and locate the museum_files folder (your local root folder, as defined earlier).

3   In the Name field, name your file **index.html**.

The Internet standard for naming your home page, or the first page users see when they access your site, is index.html. The only time you should not name your home page index.html is if your server administrator requests another name, such as home.html or default.html.

4   Leave the Save As Type field set to All Documents (Windows only), and select None from the Unicode Normalization Form drop-down menu.

5   Click Save to save the page in your local root folder.

Use the Save As dialog box to save your new page in your site.

Defining page properties

Now that you've created a page in Dreamweaver, you'll use the Page Properties dialog box to specify its layout and formatting properties. You use this dialog box to define page properties for each new page you create, and to modify the settings for pages you've already created.

1   Use the Page Properties dialog box to set page titles, background colors and images, text and link colors, and other basic properties of every web page. To access the Page Properties dialog box, choose Modify > Page Properties, or use the keyboard shortcut Ctrl+J (Windows) or Command+J (Mac OS). The Page Properties dialog box appears, with the Appearance (CSS) category selected by default.

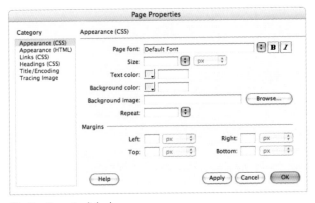

The Page Properties dialog box.

Settings found in the Appearance (CSS) category will automatically create a Cascading Style Sheet that defines the appearance of your page. Using a CSS to define these page properties adds flexibility to your design, as styling can be changed more easily, and more universally, than if your defaults are defined using HTML code.

2   The Page font and Size fields define the default appearance of text on your page. For now, leave these settings at their defaults. You'll be styling type with CSS in later lessons in this book.

3   The Text color option allows you to set a default color in which to render type. To set a text color, click on the color swatch next to Text; the Swatches panel appears. You can choose your default text color by clicking on the appropriate swatch from the Swatches panel. Try this by clicking on any color swatch, and press Apply to apply your desired default text color.

You can also type the hexadecimal notation for your desired color into the text field. Type the hex code **666666** in the text field to specify a dark gray as the default text color.

You'll see the effects of this change later in this lesson, when you add text to your page using the Files panel.

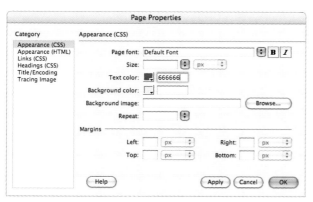

Set a default text color using the Swatches panel.

4   Use the Background color option to choose a background color for your page. If you also choose a background image, the color will appear while the image downloads, at which time the image will then cover the color. If there are transparent areas in the background image, the background color will show through. To choose a background color, click on the color swatch next to the Background text field; the Swatches panel appears. You can choose your background color by clicking on the appropriate swatch from the Swatches panel. Try this by clicking on any color swatch, then press Apply to see the results.

You can also choose the background color by typing the hexadecimal notation for your desired color into the Background field. Type the hex code **d7d7d7** in the Background text field, then press Apply to specify a light gray as the background color.

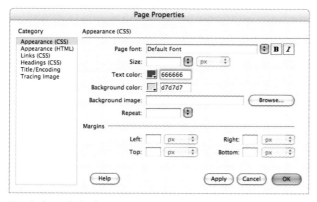

Set a background color for your page.

5 The Background image field allows you to set a background image for your page. Dreamweaver mimics a browser's behavior by repeating, or tiling, the background image to fill the window. To choose a background image, click the Browse button next to the Background image text field. The Select Image Source dialog box appears.

6 Navigate to the museum_files folder within dw02lessons and select background.gif for your page background; then press OK (Windows) or Choose (Mac OS).

7 Leave the Repeat setting at its default, which automatically tiles the background image both horizontally and vertically as needed to fill the page background.

8 Click the Apply button to see the image as the background of your page.

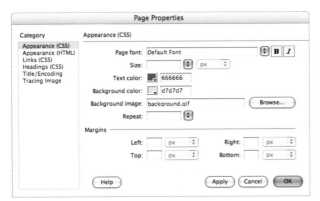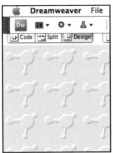

Choose a background image for your page (background.gif).

 You can also type the path to your background image into the Background image text field.

9 By default, Dreamweaver places your text and images in close proximity to the top and left edges of the page. To build in some extra room between your page edges and the content on them, use the Margin settings in the Page Properties dialog box. In the Left margin field, type **25** to place your content 25 pixels from the left edge of the page. In the Top margin field, type **25** to place your content 25 pixels from the top edge of the page.

The Appearance (HTML) category in the Page Properties dialog box contains many of the same settings you just defined. Setting default page attributes with HTML code, however, does not automatically create a Cascading Style Sheet, and is therefore less flexible than using CSS.

The Links (CSS) category allows you to define the appearance of linked text within your document. For more information on creating hyperlinks, see Lesson 3, "Adding Text and Images."

10 Click on the Link's category on the left-hand side and leave the Link font and Size settings at their defaults (same as page font). This ensures that your hyperlinks will display in the same typeface and size as the rest of the text on your page.

11 Set the colors for your different link types in the following fields:

Link Color: Type **83432** for the default link color applied to linked text on your web page.

Visited links: Type **666666** for the color applied to linked text after a user has clicked on it.

Rollover links: Type **CC4300** for the color applied to linked text when a user rolls over it.

Active links: Type **CC6500** for the color applied when the user clicks on linked text.

12 Because you're using CSS formatting, you can choose whether or not (and/or when) you want your links to be underlined. (This is not possible with HTML formatting.) Choose the default setting of Always Underline in the Underline Style drop-down menu.

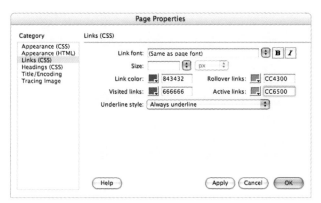

Choose default colors for links, visited links, and active links.

You can also select the desired link color from the Swatches panel.

The Headings (CSS) category allows you to define the font, style, size, and color of heading text within your document.

13 Leave the settings in the Headings category at their defaults for now. You'll be using CSS to style your heading text later in this book.

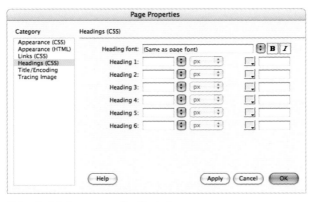

Define the default appearance of heading text on your page.

14 Click on the Title/Encoding category to the left of the Page Properties dialog box to expose more settings:

- Type **Museum Home** in the Title text field. This sets the title that appears in the title bar of most browser windows. It's also the default title used when a user bookmarks your page.

- Leave the Document Type (DTD) set to XHTML 1.0 Transitional. This makes the HTML document XHTML-compliant.

- Choose Unicode 4.0 (UTF-8) from the Encoding drop-down menu. This specifies the encoding used for characters in your document.

- Make sure the Unicode Normalization Form is set to None and that Include Unicode Signature (BOM) is unchecked. Both settings are unnecessary for this lesson.

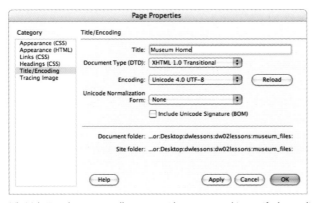

The Title/Encoding category allows you to title your page and/or specify the encoding used.

The Reload button simply converts the existing document to the encoding you've chosen. It's not necessary to click this button now.

15 Click on the Tracing Image category in the left part of the Page Properties dialog box. A tracing image is a JPEG, GIF, or PNG image that you create in a separate graphics application, such as Adobe Photoshop or Fireworks. It is placed in the background of your page for you to use as a guide to recreate a desired page design.

16 Press the Browse button next to the Tracing image field. You can also type the path to your image directly into this text field.

17 In the Select Image Source dialog box, navigate to your dw02lessons folder, and inside the museum_files folder, select the file named tracing.gif; then press OK (Windows) or Choose (Mac OS).

18 Set the transparency of the tracing image to 50 percent by sliding the Transparency slider to the left.

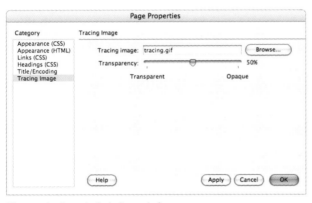

Place a tracing image in the background of your page.

19 Press Apply to see the results.

20 When activated, the tracing image replaces any background image and/or color you've added to your page, but only in the document window. Tracing images are never visible when you view your page in a browser. Highlight the path in the Tracing image text field and press the Delete key.

21 Press the Apply button to remove the tracing image and redisplay your background image.

22 Press OK to close the Page Properties dialog box.

23 Choose File > Save. Now that you've finished setting up your page properties, you'll examine your page in Dreamweaver's three different work view modes.

Work views

In this book's lessons, you'll do most of your work in the Design view, as you're taking advantage of Dreamweaver's visual page layout features. You can, however, easily access the HTML code being written as you work in the Design view, and use it to edit your pages through Dreamweaver's other work views. You'll switch views, using the Document toolbar.

The Document toolbar.

1 In the Document toolbar, press the Design View button (⊞), if it is not currently selected. Design View is a fully editable, visual representation of your page, similar to what the viewer would see in a browser.

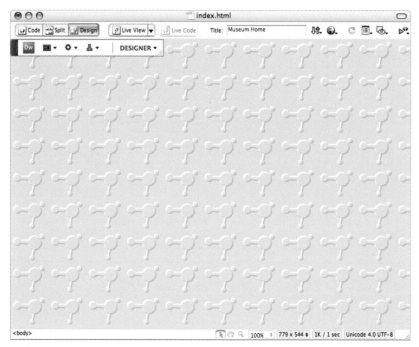

With Design view, you see your page as the viewer will see it.

2   Click on the Code View button (⬚) to switch to the Code view. Your page is now
displayed in a hand-coding environment used for writing and editing HTML and other
types of code, including JavaScript, PHP, and ColdFusion.

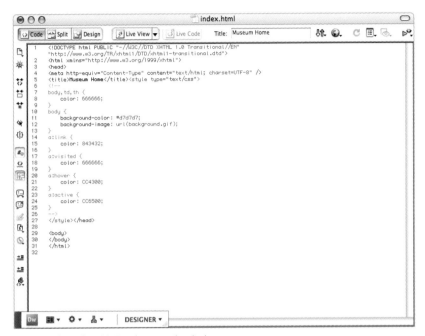

Code view shows the HTML code generated to display your page.

3   Click on the Split View button (▦) to split the document window between the Code and Design views. This view is a great learning tool, as it displays and highlights the HTML code generated when you make a change visually in Design mode, and vice versa.

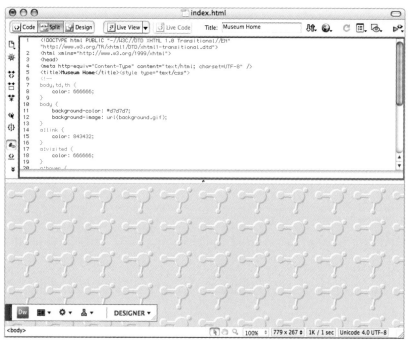

Use Split view to display your page in both modes at once.

4   Switch back to the Design view to continue this lesson.

A look at the Files panel

One of the benefits of working with local files stored in one centralized folder on your hard drive is that they are easy to manage. Dreamweaver provides the Files panel to help you manage files locally and transfer them to and from a remote server. The Files panel maintains a parallel structure between local and remote sites, copying and removing files when needed to ensure synchronicity between the two.

The default workspace in Dreamweaver displays the Files panel in the panel grouping to the right of the document window.

When you chose to use the museum_site folder as your local root folder earlier in this lesson, Dreamweaver set up a connection to those local files through the Files panel. You should now be able to see the entire contents of this folder in the Files panel. If not, choose Window > Workspace Layout > Designer to reset the workspace.

You have access to the complete contents of your local root folder in the Files panel.

Viewing local files

You can view local files and folders within the Files panel, whether they're associated with a Dreamweaver site or not.

1   Click on the drop-down menu in the upper-left part of the Files panel, and choose Desktop (Windows) or Computer > Desktop folder (Mac OS) to view the current contents of your Desktop folder.

2   Choose Local Disk (C:) (Windows) or Macintosh HD (Mac OS) from this menu to access the contents of your hard drive.

3   Choose CD Drive (D:) (Windows) from this menu to view the contents of an inserted CD. On a Mac, the CD icon and the name of the CD appears in the menu.

4   Choose museum_site to return to your local root folder view.

Selecting and editing files

You can select, open, and drag HTML pages, graphics, text, and other files listed in the Files panel to the document window for placement.

1 If it's not already open, double-click on the index.html file, located in the Files panel. The page opens for editing.

2 Click and drag the space.jpg image file from the Files panel to the index.html document window. (If an Image Tag Accessibility Attributes window appears, press OK to close it.) The image is added to the open page.

If you have Fireworks installed on your computer, you can double-click on the space.jpg image file to open it in Fireworks for editing and optimizing.

3 Double-click on the exhibit_3.txt file in the Files panel to open it directly in Dreamweaver.

4 Choose Edit > Select All to select all the text in this file.

5 Choose Edit > Copy to copy the text to the clipboard.

6 Click on the index.html tab of the document window to return to the index page. Click on your page to the right of the image to place an insertion cursor.

7 Choose Edit > Paste. The text is added to the open page, beneath the image.

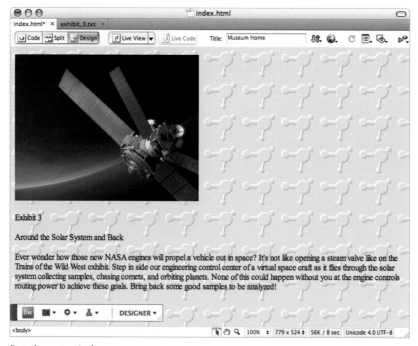

Paste the new text in the page.

Files panel options

The Files panel also offers additional controls for displaying and transferring files. Many of these controls are located in a toolbar at the top of the panel.

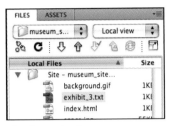

The Files panel toolbar.

1   Click on the Connect to remote host button (⚡) to connect to your remote site at any time. If you haven't specified a remote server yet, the Site Definition wizard opens and prompts you to do so. Close this window to continue.

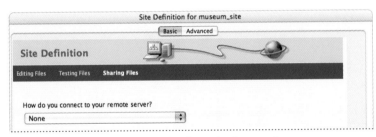

Use the Connect to remote host button on the Files panel toolbar as an alternate way to access the Site Definition wizard.

2   Click on the Refresh button (C) to refresh Dreamweaver's connection to your local root folder and any remote directories. You should use this button periodically to make sure Dreamweaver recognizes added files.

3   Click on the Get File(s) button (⬇) to copy selected files from your remote server to the local root folder. Because you haven't defined a remote server, Dreamweaver prompts you to do so now. Press No to continue.

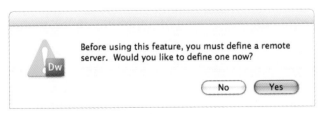

Press No to define your remote server later.

4   Click on the Put File(s) button (↑) to copy selected files from your local root folder to the remote server. Because you haven't defined a remote server, Dreamweaver prompts you to do so now. Press No to continue.

5   Click on the Check Out File(s) button (✓) to transfer a copy of the file from the remote server to your local root folder, and mark the file as checked out on the server. This option is available only if you've enabled the Check In and Check Out option in the Site Definition dialog box.

6   Click on the Check In button (🔒) to transfer a copy of the file from your local root folder to the remote server, and make the file available to others for editing. This option is available only if you've enabled the Check In and Check Out option in the Site Definition dialog box.

This option must be selected in order to check files in and out of your server.

7   Note the Synchronize button (🔄) which allows you to synchronize files between your local and remote sites. This feature is not available unless you have defined and have a live connection to a remote server.

Changing the Files panel view

When working with a Dreamweaver site, you can reconfigure the Files panel by changing what appears in it (such as local or remote sites) or by expanding and collapsing the panel.

Site views

With the Files panel collapsed (the default), you use the Site View drop-down menu to change what's visible in the panel.

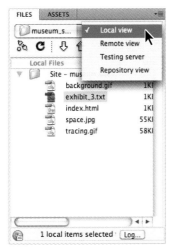

The Files panel in collapsed mode.

1   Choose Local View to display only the contents of your local root folder.

2   Choose Remote View to display only the contents of the remote server.

3   Choose Testing Server to display the content of a local server used for trying out pages prior to upload.

4   Choose Repository View to display the contents of an SVN repository and manage your files directly through Subversion.

Expanding and collapsing

The Files panel is collapsed and docked within the panel group by default. You can expand the Files panel to give you a better view of local and remote sites. When the Files panel is expanded, the contents of the local root folder are on one side, and either the remote or the testing server is on the other.

1 With the Files panel collapsed, click on the Expand to show local and remote sites button (⊞) to enlarge and reconfigure the panel.

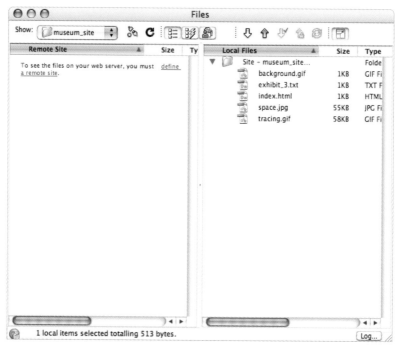

The Files panel, in expanded mode.

 If you expand the Files panel while it's docked (Windows only), you won't be able to work in the document window, as the Files panel fills that space. Collapse the Files panel to restore access to the document window.

2 The toolbar at the top of the expanded Files panel mimics the toolbar when the panel is collapsed, with a slightly different configuration. The view buttons in the center of the toolbar allow you to switch the view displayed on the left side of the panel. By default, the Site Files button (⊞) is pushed, which lists the contents of the remote site on the left side of the panel. Press the Testing Server button (⊞) to switch this view to a list of files on the testing server, if you've defined one.

3 Press the Repository Files button (⊞) to view an existing SVN repository and manage your files directly through Subversion.

4 All the other buttons in this toolbar represent the same control options available when the Files panel is collapsed. With the Files panel expanded, press the Collapse button (⊞) to reduce the panel to its default state.

Choose File > Close. You have completed this lesson. Now that you've learned the basics of creating sites, setting page properties, and managing site files, you'll use these skills in Dreamweaver Lesson 3, "Adding Text and Images."

Self study

Using your new knowledge of site creation techniques in Dreamweaver, try some of the following tasks to build on your experience:

1   Choose Site > New Site to invoke the Site Definition wizard, and use it to create a new local site called Practice_Site. Click on the Advanced tab, and use the Local Info settings to define the folder practice_files, located in the dw02lessons folder on your desktop, as your local root folder. (Remote/testing server access is not required for this exercise.) Then explore the other categories in the Advanced tab, noting how you can use them to change your site definition in various ways.

2   Use the File > New command to create a new, blank HTML page, and save it to your Practice_Site. Then choose Modify > Page Properties to access the Page Properties dialog box, and experiment with the background, link, margin, and title options available. Finally, switch to the Code and Design view in the document window to view the code generated by your experimentation.

3   Ensure that the Files panel is collapsed and docked, and refresh its contents. Switch back to the Design view and drag and drop the tubes.jpg image from the Files panel to add it to your page. Then double-click on the text file sticky.txt to open it directly in Dreamweaver. Copy and paste the text from the text file into the document window, next to the image. Save the page as your home page for this site, and close the document window.

Review

Questions

1   What characters should you avoid using when naming your site, and why?

2   How is the local root folder essential to the creation of your site?

3   Why is it advisable to set case-sensitive link checking when you're creating a site definition?

4   What happens if you've chosen both a background color and a background image for a page within your site?

5   Where can you view, select, open, and copy files to and from your local root folder, and to and from remote and/or testing servers?

Answers

1   Avoid using spaces (use underscores instead), periods, slashes, or any other unnecessary punctuation in your site name, as doing so will likely cause the server to misdirect your files.

2   It's essential that you store all your site's resources in your local root folder to ensure that the links you set on your computer will work when your site is uploaded to a server. This is because all the elements of your site must remain in the same relative location on the web server as they are on your hard drive, for your links to work properly.

3   You should use case-sensitive link checking because you want to ensure that your links will work on a Unix server, where links are case-sensitive. If you're using a Windows or Mac OS server, this doesn't matter as much, but it's a good practice to follow the strict naming and linking conventions of a Unix system in case you ever move your site to a different server.

4   If you've added both a background color and a background image for your page, the color will appear while the image downloads, at which time the image will then cover the color. If there are transparent areas in the background image, the background color will show through.

5   Dreamweaver provides the Files panel to help you not only manage files locally, but also transfer them to and from a remote server. You can view, select, open, and copy files to and from your local root folder and to and from remote and/or testing servers in this panel.

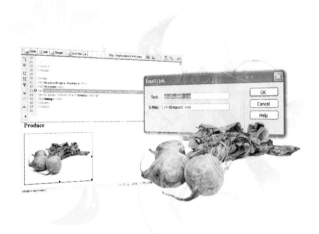

**What you'll learn
in this lesson:**

- Previewing pages
- Adding text
- Understanding styles
- Creating hyperlinks
- Creating lists
- Inserting and editing images

Adding Text and Images

Text and images are the building blocks of most web sites. In this lesson, you'll learn how to add text and images to web pages to create an immersive and interactive experience for your visitors.

Starting up

Before starting, make sure that your tools and panels are consistent by resetting your workspace. See "Resetting the Dreamweaver workspace" on page XXVII.

You will work with several files from the dw03lessons folder in this lesson. Make sure that you have loaded the CS4lessons folder onto your hard drive from the supplied DVD. See "Loading lesson files" on page XXIX.

Before you begin, you need to create a site definition that points to the dw03lessons folder from the included DVD that contains resources you need for these lessons. Go to Site > New Site, and name the site **dw03lessons**, or, for details on creating a site definition, refer to Dreamweaver Lesson 2, "Setting Up a New Site."

See Lesson 3 in action!

Use the accompanying video to gain a better understanding of how to use some of the features shown in this lesson. The video tutorial for this lesson can be found on the included DVD.

Typography and images on the web

Without text and images, most web sites would be pretty sparse. Dreamweaver CS4 offers some convenient features for placing images and formatting text. In this lesson, you'll be building a web site with some photos and text for the front page of a fictional store.

Adding text

You should already have created a new site, using the dw03lessons folder as your root. In this section, you'll be adding a headline and formatting the text on the events.html page.

1   If it's not already open, launch Dreamweaver CS4.

2   Make sure your dw03lessons site is open in the Files panel. If not, open it now.

3   Double-click on the events.html file in your Files panel to open it in the design view. Without any formatting, the text seems random and lacks purpose. First, you'll add a headline to give the first paragraph some context.

4   Click to place your cursor in front of the word *There's* in the first paragraph. Type **OrganicUtopia Events** and press Enter (Windows) or Return (Mac OS) to create a line break.

5   Click and drag to highlight the phrase you just typed. You will now format your text using the Property Inspector. Located at the bottom of the screen, the Property Inspector allows you to format your text using a combination of HTML and CSS. HTML stands for Hypertext Markup Language, and CSS stands for Cascading Styles Sheets. You will learn much more about the use of HTML and CSS in the next lesson; however, you will need to have a basic understanding of these two languages in order to use the Property Inspector to format your text.

6   In the Property Inspector, click on the HTML button on the left side to see your HTML formatting options. Choose Heading 1 from the Format drop-down menu. The text gets larger and becomes bold. By default, the style of any HTML text formatted as Heading 1 is generic: the color is black and the font-family is Times New Roman.

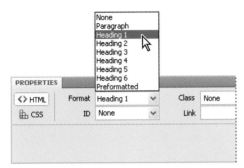

Use the Format drop-down menu in the Property Inspector to make the selected text a level-1 heading.

Although you are working in Dreamweaver's Design view, you have actually changed the HTML code for this page. Elements such as text are wrapped in opening and closing tags, and everything between these two tags is controlled by the properties of the tags. The text *OrganicUtopia Events* originally had an opening and closing tag defining it as a paragraph. The code looked like this:

```
<p>OrganicUtopia Events</p>
```

The first *<p>* is the opening tag for a paragraph element, and the second *</p>* is the closing tag for a paragraph. You then selected the text and formatted the text as a Heading 1 element, and so the HTML code changed to this:

```
<h1>OrganicUtopia Events</h1>
```

So now, the text OrganicUtopia Events is wrapped in an *<h1>* tag. Headings are important structural elements in HTML. The largest heading is H1, and the subsequent headings become smaller with H2, H3, and so on. For the next step, you will format this text in order to change the font style of this heading to Arial; however, you will not be using HTML to accomplish this, but rather CSS.

7   Click anywhere inside the heading OrganicUtopia Events; you do not need to have it selected. In the Property Inspector, click on the CSS button to access the formatting options. Choose Arial, Helvetica, sans-serif from the Font drop-down menu.

The CSS section of the Property Inspector allows you to change the font.

The New CSS Rule dialog box appears.

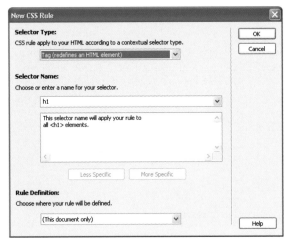

The New CSS Rule dialog box appears the first time you style text.

8   From the Selector Type drop-down menu, click on the drop-down menu and choose Tag. In the second field marked *Selector Name*, the selector h1 has been chosen for you. Dreamweaver does this because you placed your cursor inside the text formatted as H1. Press OK. Your heading is now styled in Arial.

Dreamweaver allows you to format text in a way that is similar to desktop publishing and word processing applications, but there are important differences to keep in mind. When you chose the styling, Arial, Helvetica, and sans-serif, they were listed together as one option in the Font drop-down menu. When a web page is rendered in a browser, it uses the fonts installed on the user's computer. Assigning multiple fonts allows you to control which font is used if the person viewing your page doesn't have a specific font installed. In this case, if the user doesn't have Arial, Helvetica displays instead. Sans-serif is included as the last option in case the user doesn't have Arial or Helvetica. A generic font family is listed at the end of all the options in the Font drop-down menu.

You will now change the text color using the Property Inspector.

9   Highlight *OrganicUtopia Events* and click on the Text Color button to the right of the Size drop-down menu. When the Swatches panel appears, hover over the color swatches. At the top of the Swatches panel, a different hexadecimal color value appears for each color. When you locate the value labeled #9C3, click once to apply the color.

10   Choose File > Save. Keep this file open for the next part of this lesson.

An introduction to styles

You have styled the first element on your page by first formatting text as a Heading 1 in HTML, and then you changed the font, size, and color using CSS. It's important to realize that every change you make in the Design view creates or modifies code. In the next exercise, you'll begin to explore the HTML and CSS code behind the Design view. To help put this exercise in context, a little background on HTML and CSS is in order.

The HTML language has been around since the dawn of the web. It's easiest to think of HTML as the structure behind the pages that are rendered in your web browser. An HTML page at its most basic is a collection of text, images, and sometimes multimedia such as Flash or video files. The different sections of a web page, such as a paragraph, a heading, or a list, are all *elements*. Another way to define an element in HTML is as a set of tags such as the *<h1>* tag used in the last exercise.

CSS is also a language, but it has not been around as long as HTML. In many ways, CSS was created in order to fill in some of the shortcomings of HTML. CSS is a simple language that works in combination with HTML to apply style to the content in web pages, such as text, images, tables, and form elements. CSS creates rules, or style instructions, that the HTML elements on your page follow. The most important thing to remember is that HTML and CSS are two separate languages but they are very closely aligned and work together very well.

In the last exercise, you were introduced to this interplay between HTML and CSS. There was an HTML element for the Heading 1 formatting. In the code it looks like this:

```
<h1>Organic Utopia Events</h1>
```

That was the HTML element. The CSS *rule* that defines the appearance of the *<h1>* element looks like this:

```
h1

{
font-family: Arial, Helvetica, sans-serif;
color: #9C3;
}
```

CSS has a different syntax than HTML. In HTML, tags are defined by angled brackets, and you have opening tags, *<h1>*, and closing tags, *</h1>*. In CSS code, brackets are not used. In the CSS code above, the h1 is referred to as the *selector* because it is selecting the HTML element and then changing the appearance. Because you've established that HTML and CSS are two separate languages and have different syntax, it's important that you see where this code lives in your web page. You will do this by changing Dreamweaver's workspace.

1   Click on the Split button (⊞) in the Document toolbar to open up the Split view. The Split view allows you to see your code and the design of your page simultaneously.

2   Click quickly three times in the paragraph beneath OrganicUtopia Events in the Design view. In the Code view the text is highlighted between the opening and closing paragraph tags. As noted above, this is referred to as the paragraph element. On the line below is an h2 element.

A paragraph highlighted in the Split view.

You will now change the font size of your paragraphs.

3   Choose 18 from the Size drop-down menu in the Property Inspector. The New CSS Rule dialog box appears again. This dialog box appears because it is the first time you have attempted to style a paragraph. After you define the properties, all text formatted as a paragraph will appear the same.

4   From the Selector Type drop-down menu, choose Tag. Because there are different categories of CSS rules, Dreamweaver wants to know which one you would like to use. You will stick with Tag for now (as you did in the last exercise). In the second field marked *Selector Name*, the selector p has been chosen for you because your cursor was inside a paragraph. Press OK to apply the changes; in this case, the font size is set to 18 pixels. Now let's look at the CSS code that is defining this font size.

5   Within the Code view of the split screen is all the HTML and CSS code that defines the appearance of this page. On the right side of the Code view, scroll up by clicking on the up arrow or by clicking the scroll bar and dragging upwards. Toward the top of the page, you are looking for a few lines of code that look like this:

```
<style type="text/css">
<!--

h1

{
font-family: Arial, Helvetica, sans-serif;
color: #9C3;
}

p   {
font-size:18px;
}

-->

</style>
```

Between the two *<style>* tags are all the CSS rules you have created up to this point. Previously, you learned that CSS has a different syntax than HTML: because all the CSS rules are actually contained within an opening *<style>* tag and a closing *</style>* tag, they are allowed to have a different syntax. Additionally, the style tag itself is nested inside of an opening and closing *<head>* tag. In the world of HTML, nothing contained within head tags is rendered on a web browser's screen. You will explore this further in the next chapter, but this is referred to as an internal style sheet.

You will now see that changes made in Dreamweaver's Code view apply to the Design view as well.

6   In the Code view, locate the line *font-size:18px* in the rule for p, and select the value 18 by clicking and dragging over it. Type **14** to change the value. Although you made a change in the Code view, it has not yet been automatically updated in your Design view. You need to refresh your page in order to see the changes apply in the Design view.

7   In the Property Inspector, press the Refresh button to apply the changes; your paragraph text becomes smaller.

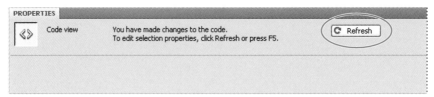

Changes made in the Code view are reflected in the Design view after pressing the Refresh button.

On the web, font sizes are specified differently than they are in print. The numerical choices in the Size drop-down menu refer to pixels instead of points. Also, the xx-small through larger options may seem oddly generic if you are accustomed to the precision of print layout. Because web pages are displayed on a variety of monitors and browsers, relative measurements can be a useful way for designers to plan ahead for inevitable discrepancies in the rendering of pages.

8   Click inside the first paragraph in the Design view. You will now change the color of the paragraph slightly to a dark gray rather than the default pure black. In the Property Inspector, click on the color swatch and in the top-left corner, locate the dark gray swatch, which is hexadecimal color #666. Click on the swatch to apply the color. Notice that not only does the appearance in the Design view change, but in your Code view a new line of CSS has also been created (color: #666;).

Working in the Split view can be a great way to learn about hand-coding without diving in headfirst. Even if you're not quite comfortable editing code, keeping an eye on the code that Dreamweaver writes for you can give you a better understanding of how things like CSS affect your web pages.

9   Click on the Design view tab to return to Design view.

10 Choose File > Save. Keep this file open for the next part of this lesson.

Previewing pages in a web browser

Viewing your pages in the Design view is helpful, but visitors to your site will be using a web browser to access your site. In Dreamweaver Lesson 1, "Dreamweaver CS4 Jumpstart," you learned how browsers use HTML code to render a page. Unfortunately, not every browser renders HTML code in exactly the same way, so it's important to test-drive your pages in a number of different browsers to check for inconsistencies and basic functionality.

Next, you'll use Dreamweaver's Preview in Browser feature to see how the OrganicUtopia site looks in a web browser.

1   With events.html open in Dreamweaver, choose File > Preview in Browser and select a browser from the available options. This list varies, depending on the browsers you have installed on your hard drive.

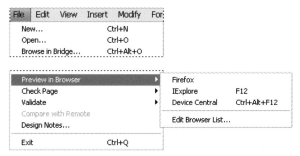

Preview in Browser allows you to see how a selected browser would render your page.

The options found under File > Preview in Browser can be customized by choosing File > Preview in Browser > Edit Browser List.

2   When events.html opens in the browser of your choice, look for differences between the Design view preview and the version rendered by your browser. At this stage there shouldn't be anything too surprising, but there may be subtle differences in spacing and font weight. Close your web browser.

There is another method to preview your pages using the Live View feature, which is new to Dreamweaver CS4. Live View allows you to preview your page without having to leave the Dreamweaver workspace.

3   Press the Live View button located to the right of the Design View button. You will not see a dramatic shift, but your text will be slightly closer to the left edge of the window. Select the first heading in the window and try to delete it; you will be unable to, because Live View is a non-editable workspace.

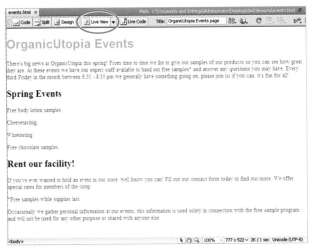

When Live View is enabled, Dreamweaver simulates a web browser.

4   Click on Live View again to deactivate this view. While Live View is a useful addition to Dreamweaver, it does not replace the need to preview your page in a browser. Web pages might be rendered differently depending on your visitor's browser, and so a good habit to get into is checking your page occasionally as you make changes to your design. As you become more skilled at styling your pages with CSS, you'll learn how to compensate for some of these discrepancies in web browser display.

Understanding hyperlinks

When people visit a web site, they usually expect to see more than one page. Imagine trying to shop for a new book by your favorite author on a site that consisted of nothing more than a single order form with every book offered by a retailer like *Amazon.com*. This might seem absurd, but without hyperlinks you wouldn't have much choice.

Hyperlinks make the web a truly interactive environment. They allow the user to freely navigate throughout a web site, or jump from one site to another. There are a number of ways to create links in Dreamweaver, but before you get started, you should be aware of some fundamentals.

Links rely on directory paths to locate files. A directory path is simply a description of a file's location that can be understood by a computer. A classic, real-world example is an address. If you wanted to send a letter to your friend Sally in Florida, you would have to specify the state, city, street, and house where Sally can be found. If Sally lived at 123 Palm Street in Orlando, the path would be:

Florida/Orlando/123 Palm Street/Sally

This simply means that inside Florida, inside Orlando, in the house numbered 123 on a street named Palm Street, you can find a person named Sally. Hyperlinks follow the same logic:

www.somewebsitesomewhere.com/photos/mydog.jpg

This URL address is a link to a JPEG image named mydog.jpg, which is inside a folder named photos on a web site named somewebsitesomewhere.com.

Creating hyperlinks

Later in this lesson, you'll be creating a gallery page to showcase some of the sample products mentioned in the main paragraph. Before you work on that page, you'll link it to the home page by creating a hyperlink.

1   In the Property Inspector, click on the HTML button to access the HTML properties.

2   In the first paragraph, highlight the word *products* in the second sentence.

3   In the Property Inspector, type **products.html** in the Link text field. Press Enter (Windows) or Return (Mac OS). The highlighted word *products* automatically becomes underlined. It is important to note that we have created this page for you and it is currently inside your site folder, you are simply linking to it.

*Type **products.html** into the Link text field in the Property Inspector.*

4   Choose File > Save and then File > Preview in Browser.

5   Click on the new *products* link. The products page appears in your browser window. This is because a previously existing page named products.html was located in this folder.

Now visitors can easily navigate to the products page, but what happens when they want to go back to the events page? It looks like you'll need another link.

6   Return to Dreamweaver and double-click on products.html in the Files panel. Click to the right of the word *Produce* and press Enter (Windows) or Return (Mac OS) to create a new line. Choose Insert > Hyperlink to open the Hyperlink dialog box.

The Hyperlink dialog box is one of the many ways to create a link in Dreamweaver. It offers all the options found in the Property Inspector, with a few additions.

7   Type **Events** in the Text field.

The Hyperlink dialog box is one of the many ways to create links in Dreamweaver.

8   Click on the Browse button to the right of the Link text field to open the Select File
dialog box. The dw03lessons folder you defined as the root for this site should be selected
for you by default. If not, locate it on your hard drive. Select events.html and press OK
(Windows) or Choose (Mac OS).

9   Press OK in the Hyperlink dialog box. A link to events.html has been created for you,
using the text entered into the Text field in the Hyperlink dialog box. Choose File >
Save and keep this file open for the next part of this lesson.

Relative versus absolute hyperlinks

After reading about the fundamentals of hyperlinks and directory paths a few pages ago, you
may have been surprised by the simplicity of linking events.html and products.html. Instead
of entering a long directory path in the Link text fields, you merely typed the name of the
file. This kind of link is called a *relative* link. Let's go back to the address example to see how
this works.

Remember Sally from Orlando? Imagine you were already standing on Palm Street, where she
lives. If you called her for directions to her house, she probably wouldn't begin by telling you
how to get to Florida. At this point, all you need is a house number. Relative links work the
same way. Because events.html and products.html both reside in the dw03lessons folder, you
don't need to tell the browser where to find this folder.

Now you'll create an absolute link that will allow visitors to access the Adobe web site to learn
more about Dreamweaver CS4.

1   Click on the events.html tab above the Document toolbar to bring the page forward.
Scroll down to the bottom of the page if necessary. Create a new line at the bottom
of the page after text that reads (Occasionally we gather...), and type **This page was
created with Adobe Dreamweaver**.

2   Highlight the words *Adobe Dreamweaver* and in the Common section of the Insert panel
on the right side of the screen, click on the Hyperlink icon to open the Hyperlink
dialog box.

*The Hyperlink icon in the Insert panel
is another convenient way to create links.*

3   The Hyperlink dialog box opens. Notice that Adobe Dreamweaver has been entered
into the Text field for you. In the Link field, type the text **http://www.adobe.com/
products/dreamweaver/index.html**. Make sure to include the colon and the
appropriate number of forward slashes.

The absolute link http://www.adobe.com/products/dreamweaver/index.html instructs
the browser to find a web site named adobe.com on the World Wide Web. Then the
browser looks for a file named index.html inside a folder named dreamweaver inside a
folder named products.

4   Choose _blank from the Target drop-down menu. Choosing the _blank option will
cause the hyperlink to the Adobe web site to open in a new, blank browser window.

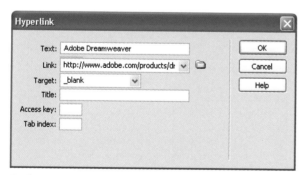

Set the target window for the hyperlink to open in a blank browser window or tab.

5   Press OK to close the Hyperlink dialog box. Choose File > Save, then File > Preview in
Browser, or press the Preview/Debug in Browser button (●) in the Document toolbar.

6   Click on the *Adobe Dreamweaver* text. Unlike the Events and Products links you created earlier, this link causes your browser to open a new tab or window, and it is pointing to an external web page on the Internet.

Linking to an e-mail address

Absolute and relative links can be used to access web pages, but it's also possible to link to an e-mail address. Instead of opening a new web page, an e-mail link opens up the default mail program on a visitor's computer and populates the address field with the address you specify when creating the link. As you may imagine, this kind of link can work differently depending on how your visitors have configured their computers.

In the last part of this lesson, you gave the visitor a link to some information on Dreamweaver. Now you'll link them to an e-mail address where they can get some information on learning Dreamweaver from the folks who wrote this book.

1   Place your cursor at the end of the last line, then hold down your Shift key and press Enter (Windows) or Return (Mac OS). Instead of creating a new paragraph, this creates a line break, or a soft return, and the text begins immediately below the previous line. Type **Contact info@aquent.com for classes on using Adobe Dreamweaver CS4**.

2   Highlight the text *info@aquent.com* and click the Email Link button (🖾) in the Insert panel.

3   The Email Link dialog box opens with both fields automatically populated. Press OK. You may preview this page in your browser if you choose, however be aware that if you click on the link, your email client will begin to launch.

The Email Link dialog box allows you to link to an e-mail address.

Creating lists

Bulleted lists may be familiar to you if you have worked with word processing or desktop publishing applications. Lists are a helpful way to present information to a reader without the formal constraints of a paragraph. They are especially important on the web. Studies indicate that people typically skim web pages instead of reading them from beginning to end. Creating lists will make it easier for your visitors to get the most from your web site without sifting through many paragraphs of text.

1   On the events.html page, click and drag to highlight the four lines below *Spring Events:*.

2   Click the Unordered List button (≣) in the Property Inspector. The highlighted text becomes indented, and a bullet point is placed at the beginning of each line.

Use the Unordered List button in the Property Inspector to create a bulleted list.

3   Click the Ordered List button (≣) to the right of the Unordered List button. The bullets change to sequential numbers. Like most things in Dreamweaver, additional options are available for lists.

4   Choose Format > List > Properties to open the List Properties dialog box. Choose Bulleted List from the List type drop-down menu. The Numbered List and Bulleted List options in the List type drop-down menu allow you to switch between ordered and unordered lists.

5   From the Style drop-down menu, choose Square. This changes the default circular bullets to square bullets. Press OK to exit the List Properties dialog box.

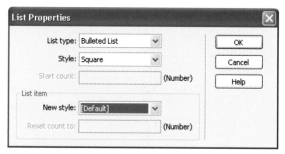

Change the bullet style to square in the List Properties dialog box.

You may have noticed that the four lines of text in your list have lost their style. They are slightly larger than your paragraphs and colored the default black instead of the dark gray you applied earlier. This is because you have added a list element to your HTML page, and while the appearance of paragraphs has been defined using CSS, the appearance of lists has not. You will now create a new CSS rule for the appearance of a list.

6   With all four lines still highlighted, click on the CSS button in the Property Inspector. Click on the arrow to the right of the Size field. Choose 14 from the Size drop-down menu in the Property Inspector. The New CSS Rule dialog box appears. This dialog box appears because it is the first time you have attempted to style an unordered list. After you define the properties, all text formatted as an unordered list will appear the same.

7   From the Selector Type drop-down menu, choose Tag. In the second field marked *Selector Name*, the selector *ul* has been chosen for you; *ul* is the HTML tag for an unordered list. If *ul* is not chosen for you, type **ul** inside this text field. Press OK to apply the changes; in this case the font size is set to 14 pixels. Now you need to change the color of the unordered list to match the color of your paragraph.

8   In the Property Inspector, click on the color swatch and in the top-left corner locate the dark gray swatch, which is hexadecimal color #666. Click on the swatch to apply the color.

9   Choose File > Save. Leave this file open for the next part of this lesson.

Using the Text Insert panel

There are a number of ways to format text in Dreamweaver. One method you haven't explored yet is the Text Insert panel. Because most of the options available in the Text Insert panel are also available in the Property Inspector, you may find it more convenient to use the Property Inspector for common tasks. However, you should be aware of the Character menu located in the Text Insert panel. One of the most common items in the Character menu used on the web is the copyright symbol, ©. You will now insert a copyright notification at the bottom of your Events page.

1   Click to the left of the sentence *This page was created with Adobe Dreamweaver* and type **2008**.

2   Click before the text 2008 to insert your cursor.

3   Click on the menu at the top of the Insert panel and choose Text. Scroll all the way to the bottom of the resulting list and click on Characters to open a menu. Choose the copyright symbol from the list to add it to the beginning of the line.

The copyright symbol can be inserted from the Character menu.

4   Highlight the last two lines on your page, beginning with the newly inserted copyright symbol and ending with *Adobe Dreamweaver CS4.* You are going to set these two lines apart from the rest of the page by italicizing them. Layout considerations such as headers and footers will be discussed throughout the following lessons in this book, but for now you can use the Text options in the Insert panel to italicize these two lines.

5   Scroll to the top of the Text options in the Insert panel and click the Italic option.

You could have also used the Italic button in the Property Inspector. Additionally, you could have also selected the text and chosen Insert > HTML > Text Objects to accomplish the same thing.

6   Choose File > Save.

Inserting images

Images are an essential part of most web pages. Just as lists make content friendlier and more accessible, images help to give your visitors the rich, immersive experience that they've come to expect on the web.

Image resolution

While it is possible to resize images with Dreamweaver, it's generally not a good idea. Specifying the width and height of an image in the Property Inspector changes the display size of the image, but it does not resample the image the way a graphic processing application like Photoshop does. The difference may not seem immediately apparent, as a properly resized image may appear identical to an improperly resized image. Unfortunately, visitors to your web site will be the first to notice an oversight in resizing your images.

If you've ever downloaded a large file from the web, you've probably had the experience of waiting impatiently while a progress bar inches its way across the screen like a glacier. This may be an exaggeration, but the fact is that every time you access a page on the Internet, you are downloading all the contents of that page. Images always significantly increase the size of an HTML file, so it's important to properly resize them before including them on your site.

Image formats

The two most common image formats on the web are JPEG and GIF. While an exhaustive description of how each of these formats compresses data is beyond the scope of this book (not to mention most people's attention span), a general overview can help you avoid some common pitfalls.

The JPEG format was created by a committee named the Joint Photographic Experts Group. Its express purpose is to compress photographic images. Specifically, it uses lossy compression to reduce the size of a file. This means that it selectively discards information. When you save a JPEG, you decide how much information you are willing to sacrifice by selecting a quality level. A high-quality image preserves more information and results in a larger file size. A low-quality image discards more information, but produces a smaller file size. The goal is to reduce file size as much as possible without creating distortion and artifacts.

Because JPEGs were designed to handle photographic images, they can significantly reduce the size of images containing gradients and soft edges, without producing noticeable degradation. However, reproducing sharp edges and solid areas of color often requires a higher quality setting.

The GIF format was created by CompuServe. GIF is an acronym for Graphics Interchange Format. Unlike the JPEG format, GIFs do not use lossy compression. Instead, GIFs rely on a maximum of 256 colors to reduce the size of images. This means that images with a limited number of colors can be reproduced without degradation. Logos, illustrations, and line drawings are well-suited to this format. Unlike JPEGs, GIFs excel at reproducing sharp edges and solid areas of color. However, because photographic elements such as gradients and soft edges require a large number of colors to appear convincing, GIF images containing these elements look choppy and posterized.

Creating a simple gallery page

Now that you have a better understanding of the types of images that are appropriate for using on your web site, it's time to build the products page that you linked to earlier in this lesson.

1   Double-click on products.html in the Files panel. Place your cursor after the word *Produce* and press Enter (Windows) or Return (Mac OS) to create a new line.

2   Choose Insert > Image. The Select Image Source dialog box appears. Navigate to the dw03lessons folder that you chose as your root folder at the beginning of the lesson and open the images folder. Select beets.jpg and press OK (Windows) or Choose (Mac OS).

3   When the Image Tag Accessibility Attributes dialog box appears, type **Beets** in the Alternate text field. Press OK.

The Alternate text field in the Image Tag Accessibility Attributes dialog box corresponds to the Alt attribute of an <img> tag. Including a description of the inserted image in this field is not technically necessary, but it is good practice. It provides information about the images to visually impaired visitors using screen readers. Also, Alt text is displayed in place of images on some handheld devices and browsers with images disabled.

4   Click on the Split button (⊞) in the Document toolbar to view the code that was written by Dreamweaver when you inserted beets.jpg. An *<img>* tag was created, with four attributes. The src attribute is a relative link to the .jpg file in your images folder. The alt attribute is the alternate text you specified in the last step. The width and height attributes are simply the width and height of the image, and these have automatically been added by Dreamweaver. Press the Design button to return to this view.

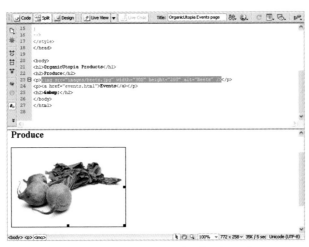

Dreamweaver creates an <img> tag with a number of attributes when you insert an image.

5   Double-click on the images folder in the Files panel to reveal its contents. Click to the right of the beets image and press Enter (Windows) or Return (Mac OS) to create a new line. Click and drag cucumbers.jpg below the beets image in the Design view. When the Image Tag Accessibility Attributes dialog box appears, type **Cucumbers** into the Alternate text field. Press OK.

6   In the Property Inspector, type **5** into the Border text field and press Enter (Windows) or Return (Mac OS). A border attribute is added to the new *<img>* tag in the Code view and a black, 5-pixel-wide border appears in the Design view.

7   Click on the beets image in the Design view and type **5** in the Border text field in the Property Inspector to give this image a matching border.

Adding a border attribute to an <img> tag with the Property Inspector is a quick way to create a border, but it doesn't give you as much control or flexibility as a CSS-generated border. In Dreamweaver Lesson 4, "Styling Your Pages with CSS," you'll learn about the advantages of style sheets.

8   Click to the right of the cucumber image to place your cursor, and press Enter (Windows) or Return (Mac OS) to create a new line. To add the last image, you'll use the Insert panel. Click the menu at the top of the Insert panel and choose Common from the list. Click on the Images:Image option, and the Select Image Source dialog box appears.

9   Navigate to the images folder if necessary, select the eggplants.jpg image, and press OK (Windows) or Choose (Mac OS).

*Choose Image from the Images drop-down menu
in the Common section of the Insert panel.*

10 Type **Eggplants** in the Alternate text field of the Image Tag Accessibility Attributes dialog box, then press OK.

11 In the Property Inspector, type **5** into the Border text field and press Enter (Windows) or Return (Mac OS).

12 Choose File > Save and leave products.html open for the next part of this lesson.

Linking images

Often, gallery pages on the web contain small thumbnail images that are linked to larger, high-resolution images. Like many web conventions, there are practical reasons for this format. Because all the images on a gallery page must be downloaded by visitors in order to view the page, small images are necessary to keep the page from taking too long to load. Additionally, a user's screen isn't large enough to accommodate multiple large pictures at one time. Giving your visitor a way to preview which pictures they would like to see at a larger scale makes the page more usable and more interactive.

1   In products.html, click on the beets.jpg image to select it. In the Property Inspector, type
     images/beets_large.jpg into the Link text field. Press Enter (Windows) or Return
     (Mac OS). The 5-pixel border around the image turns blue. This border indicates that the
     image is a link.

2   Click on the cucumber.jpg image to select it. For this image, you'll use Dreamweaver's
     Point to File feature to create a link. In the Property Inspector, locate the Point to
     File icon (⊕) next to the Link text field. Click and drag this icon into the Files panel.
     A blue arrow with a target at the end follows your cursor. As you hover over items in
     the Files panel, they become highlighted. Release the mouse while hovering over the
     cucumbers_large.jpg file.

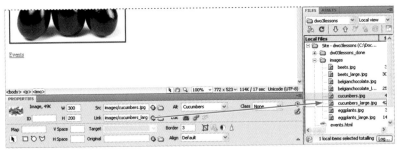

With the Point to File feature, you can simply click and drag to create a link.

3   Select the eggplants.jpg image and use the Point to File icon to link it to
     eggplants_large.jpg.

4   Choose File > Save, and then File > Preview in Browser. Click on the thumbnails to
     see the large versions of each image. You'll have to use your browser's back button to get
     back to the products page, as you didn't select _blank from the target drop-down menu
     in the Property Inspector.

Using image placeholders

Often, you will want to start building web pages before you have all the final content available.
This happens regularly in professional situations where different people may be responsible for
preparing images, writing copy, and creating the site. Next, you'll build a second section in the
products.html page that will eventually include a collection of chocolate pictures.

1   In Dreamweaver, on the products.html page, place your cursor to the right of the
     eggplants.jpg image, and press Enter (Windows) or Return (Mac OS) to create a
     new line.

2   Type **Chocolate**, then press the HTML button in the Property Inspector and choose
     Heading 2 from the Format drop-down menu. Press Enter/Return to create a line below
     the Chocolate heading.

3   Choose Insert > Image Objects > Image Placeholder. When the Image Placeholder dialog box appears, type **belgianchocolate** in the Name text field, **300** in the Width text field, and **200** in the Height text field. Leave the Color set to the default and the Alternative text field blank. Press OK to exit the dialog box.

A gray box with the name belgianchocolate appears. This box is simply an *<img>* tag with an empty src attribute. If you are new to web design, it's important to note that placeholders are not required, they are useful in allowing you to visualize a page when you don't have images available. Now you'll insert an image into the placeholder by setting the src attribute in the Property Inspector.

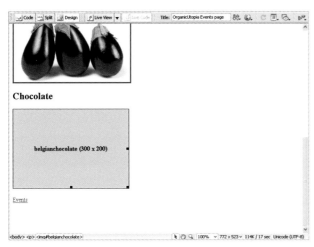

The belgianchocolate image placeholder.

4   With the belgianchocolate image placeholder selected, click and drag the Point to File icon to the right and locate the belgianchocolate.jpg image. The belgianchocolate JPEG replaces the gray box.

5   In the Property Inspector, type **5** into the Border text field and use the Src Point to File icon (⊙) to link belgianchocolate.jpg to belgianchocolate_large.jpg. Choose File > Save and leave this file open for the next part of this lesson.

Editing images

Although it's best to make adjustments to your images using a professional graphics-editing program like Adobe Photoshop, sometimes that's not an option. Dreamweaver offers a number of editing options, including an Edit link that allows you to quickly open a selected image in the graphics editor of your choice.

The Edit button can be customized in the File Types/Editors section of the Preferences dialog box. You can use this section to add or subtract programs from the list of available editors, and set programs as the primary choice for handling specific file extensions.

Adjusting brightness and contrast

Now you'll use Dreamweaver's Brightness and Contrast button to lighten up the eggplants image on your products page.

1   Click on the eggplants.jpg image in products.html to select it, then click on the Brightness and Contrast button (◐) in the Property Inspector.

Select the Brightness and Contrast button in the Property Inspector.

A warning dialog box appears, indicating that you are about to make permanent changes to the selected image. Press OK.

2   When the Brightness/Contrast dialog box appears, drag the Brightness slider to 20 or type **20** in the text field to the right of the slider.

3   Drag the Contrast slider to 10 or type **10** in the text field to the right of the slider.

4   Click the *Preview* checkbox in the lower-right corner to see the original photo. Click the *Preview* checkbox again to see the changes. Press OK.

While changing the brightness and contrast is very convenient in Dreamweaver, you should be sure you are not performing the corrections on the original, as these changes are destructive.

Resizing images

Next, you'll see how Dreamweaver allows you to quickly optimize images; you'll change the size and quality of the belgianchocolate.jpg image. But before you make any permanent changes, you'll duplicate this image in the Files panel. It's good practice to save copies of your image files before making permanent changes. Later, you'll use this backup copy to undo your changes.

1   In the Files panel, click on the belgianchocolate.jpg file to select it. From the Files panel menu, select Edit > Duplicate. A new file named Copy of belgianchocolate.jpg appears in the list of files inside the images folder.

2   Click on the belgianchocolate.jpg image in the Document window to make sure it is selected, then click the Edit Image Settings button (♂) in the Property Inspector. The Image Preview dialog box opens; it offers many of the features included in the Adobe Photoshop CS4 Save for Web & Devices dialog box.

3   Make sure that the Options tab in the top-left corner is selected. Click on the black arrow to the right of the Quality text field and drag the slider down to 30 percent. The belgianchocolate.jpg image in the preview window becomes pixelated. As discussed earlier, a lower JPEG quality setting reduces file size at the cost of image clarity, and so this is not a good setting.

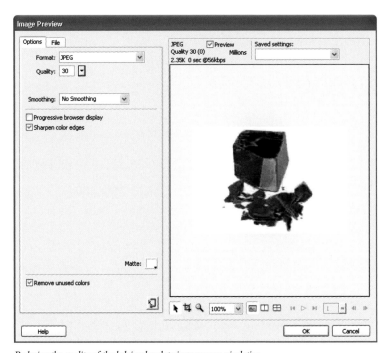

Reducing the quality of the belgianchocolate image causes pixelation.

4   Drag the quality slider back up to 70 percent and click the File tab in the top-left corner of the dialog box.

5   In the Scale section, drag the % slider to 60 percent. The belgianchocolate.jpg image in the preview window shrinks; its new dimensions are reflected in the W and H text fields.

6   Press OK to exit the Image Preview dialog box. The belgianchocolate.jpg image is reduced to 60 percent of its original size.

The belgianchocolate image has been resized and permanently altered.

 Similar to the brightness and contrast features, be careful when resizing images in Dreamweaver. In the workflow of this exercise, if you were to save this file, the source image would have been permanently resized.

Updating images

Assuming you have a backup copy of an image, it is possible to swap one image for another. To swap out the image, you'll simply change the src attribute, using the Property Inspector. But first, it's a good idea to rename the duplicate image to get rid of the spaces in the filename.

1   Right-click (Windows) or Ctrl+click (Mac OS) the file named Copy of belgianchocolate.jpg in the Files panel and choose Edit > Rename. Type **belgianchocolate_copy.jpg** and press Enter (Windows) or Return (Mac OS).

 Although filenames including spaces usually work just fine on your home computer, many web servers aren't designed to handle them. To prevent broken links, it is a common practice to use the underscore or hyphen characters in place of spaces when naming files for the web.

2   Click on the belgianchocolate.jpg image in the Design view to select it. In the Property Inspector, highlight the text that reads *images/belgianchocolate.jpg* in the Src text field.

3   Click and drag the Point to File icon to the belgianchocolate_copy.jpg image you just renamed. The resized belgianchocolate.jpg image is replaced with the copy you made earlier.

4   Choose File > Save.

Self study

To practice styling text with the Property Inspector, create styles for the text in events.html. If you're feeling bold, try copying the CSS styles from the Code view.

To make the thumbnail links in products.html open in a new window, set their target attributes to _blank in the Property Inspector.

Try adding your own photos to the products page. Remember to be careful when resizing them!

Review

Questions

1   Of the two most common image formats used on the web, which is better suited for saving a logo?

2   If an inserted image is too small, can you make it larger by increasing its size in the Property Inspector?

3   How do you insert a copyright symbol (©) in Dreamweaver?

Answers

1   Because logos usually contain a lot of hard edges and solid areas of color, the GIF format is the most appropriate choice.

2   Yes, it is possible to increase the display size of an image; however, doing so reduces image quality.

3   Use the Characters drop-down menu in the Text tab of the Insert bar.

Lesson 4

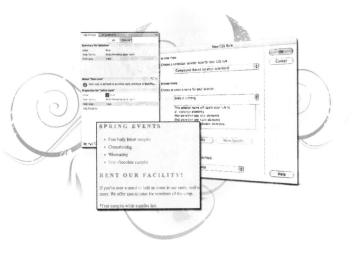

What you'll learn in this lesson:

- Introducing Cascading Style Sheets (CSS)
- Comparing CSS and *<font>* tags
- Using the CSS Styles panel
- Creating Class and Tag styles

Styling Your Pages with CSS

Many years ago, creating a beautiful web page required a lot of work, using the limited capabilities of HTML tags. The introduction of Cascading Style Sheets changed the way pages are created, giving designers an extraordinary amount of control over page formatting, as well as the ability to freely position content anywhere on a page. In this lesson, you'll learn how to take your pages further with Cascading Style Sheets.

Starting up

Before starting, make sure that your tools and panels are consistent by resetting your workspace. See "Resetting the Dreamweaver workspace" on page XXVII.

You will work with several files from the dw04lessons folder in this lesson. Make sure that you have loaded the CS4lessons folder onto your hard drive from the supplied DVD. See "Loading lesson files" on page XXIX.

Before you begin, you need to create a site definition that points to the dw04lessons folder from the included DVD that contains resources you need for these lessons. Go to Site > New Site, or, for details on creating a site definition, refer to Dreamweaver Lesson 2, "Setting Up a New Site."

See Lesson 4 in action!

Use the accompanying video to gain a better understanding of how to use some of the features shown in this lesson. The video tutorial for this lesson can be found on the included DVD.

What are Cascading Style Sheets?

In the last chapter you had a brief introduction to Cascading Style Sheets (CSS); now you will dive in a bit deeper. CSS is a simple language that works alongside HTML to apply formatting to content in web pages, such as text, images, tables, and form elements. Developed by the World Wide Web Consortium (W3C), CSS creates rules, or style instructions, that elements on your page follow. There are three locations for CSS: (1) directly within the *<head>* section of an HTML document, (2) inline (the CSS is located side by side with your HTML tags), or (3) an external file that can be linked to any number of HTML pages. If you completed Dreamweaver Lesson 3, you have had experience with the first option.

A style sheet is a collection of CSS rules; typically, rules that belong to a specific project, theme, or section are grouped together, but you can group rules in any way you want. You can place style sheets directly within your page using the *<style>* tag or in an external .css file that is linked to your document with the *<link>* tag. A single page or set of pages can use several style sheets at once.

You can apply CSS rules selectively to any number of elements on a page, or use them to modify the appearance of an existing HTML tag. Whenever or wherever you apply a rule, that rule remains linked to its original definition in the style sheet, so any changes you make to the rule automatically carry over to all items to which the rule has been applied.

Each CSS rule is composed of one or more properties, such as color, style, and font size, which dictate how an item is formatted when the rule is applied. A single CSS rule can include several properties, just as a single style sheet can include multiple CSS rules. Dreamweaver's CSS Styles panel lets you easily view and modify any of these properties and change the appearance of your page in real time.

This sample rule is composed of three properties that control the color, typeface, and size of any text to which it's applied. In the simplest example, the CSS rules define the appearance of an H1 or heading element:

```
H1 {
    color: red;
    font-family: Arial,Helvetica,Sans-serif;
    font-size: 28px;
}
```

Here is the result of the preceding code snippet:

CSS-styled text shown in the Design view.

CSS rules can affect properties as simple as typeface, size, and color; and as complex as positioning and visibility. Dreamweaver uses CSS as the primary method of styling page text and elements, and its detailed CSS Styles panel makes it possible to create and manage styles at any point during a project.

A little bit of ancient history: when *<font>* tags roamed the Earth

Before CSS came along, you styled text on a page using the *<font>* tag in HTML; you could wrap this limited but easy-to-use tag around any paragraph, phrase, or tidbit of text to apply color, or set the font size and typeface. Although it worked well enough most of the time, the *<font>* tag was a one-shot deal. Once applied, that tag's job was done and you had to use a new *<font>* tag to style additional text, even if the color, size, and typeface values were exactly the same. You will now open an HTML document in which the list is styled using the *<font>* tag.

1   In your Files panel, locate and double-click the HTML file named FontTagList.html to open it in the document window.

2   Press the Code View button (⊞) in the Document toolbar at the top of the document window. Notice that the *<font>* tag is used to style the items in the bulleted list.

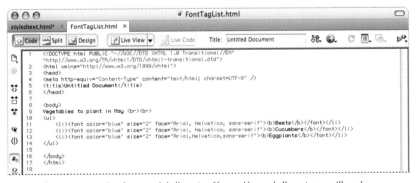

Here, a <font> tag is used to format each bullet point. If you add more bullet points, you'll need to use more <font> tags to keep the style of those bullets consistent with the others.

As you can see, there's a lot of repetition in this code.

3   Press the Design View button (⊞) on the Document toolbar. Position your cursor at the end of the last bulleted item, press Enter (Windows) or Return (Mac OS) to add a new bullet point, and type **Peppers**. You see that the text reverts to the default typeface, size, and color. You would have to add a new *<font>* tag with the same attributes as the others to get it to match. If you wanted to change an attribute such as the color for all the bullet points, you would have to adjust each tag separately. In early versions of Dreamweaver, there were actually ways to perform global changes using HTML; however, these were sometimes tricky to control, and CSS offers a better solution in any case.

Vegetables to plant in May

- Beets
- Cucumbers
- Eggplants
- Peppers

You may lose the formatting between bullet points when using <font> tags.

4   Choose File > Save to save your work, then choose File > Close.

The dawn of CSS

CSS introduces a new level of control and flexibility beyond the *<font>* tags in HTML. A significant benefit of CSS is the ability to apply consistent formatting of elements across one or all pages in a web site. In the following exercises you will learn a few different ways to create CSS rules that affect the style of your text. The first method you will explore involves creating tag- or element-based style rules. If you completed Dreamweaver Lesson 3, you saw this method used to format text. This type of rule alters the appearance of an existing HTML tag, so the tag and any content that appears within it always appear formatted in a specific way. Instead of having to add a *<font>* tag around the contents of each new bullet point in a list, it would be easier for you to tell the HTML tags used to create lists, that bullet point items should always be formatted a certain way.

1   Locate and double-click the file named CSSList.html from the Files panel to open it.

2   Press the Design View button (⊞) in the Document toolbar if necessary. The list that appears onscreen, unlike the one you saw in the previous example, is formatted without the use of *<font>* tags, and uses only CSS.

3   Position your cursor after the last bulleted item and press the Enter (Windows) or Return (Mac OS) key to create a new bullet point. Type in **Peppers**. The new text matches the bullet points above it.

4   Press Enter/Return again to add a fifth bullet point, and type **Okra**.

No matter how many bullet points you add, the formatting is applied automatically every time.

5   Select Split view at the top of the document window so that you can see both code and design:

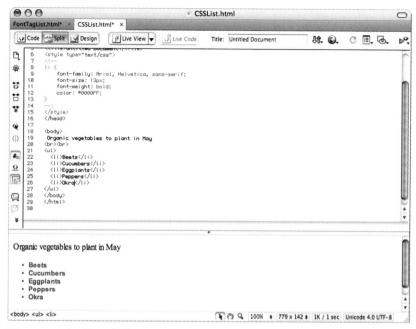

Tags are not used to format this list.

What you'll notice is the absence of any formatting tags like the *<font>* tags you saw in the last exercise. In this example you have several list items; however, all the styling information, such as the font-family, size, font-weight, and color, is being defined in one place: the CSS rule for the *<li>* tag.

6   If necessary, scroll to the top of the page and you'll see the code that makes this possible:

```
<style type="text/css">
<!--
li {

    font-family: Arial, Helvetica, sans-serif;
    font-size: 13px;
    font-weight: bold;
    color: #0000FF;
}
-->
</style>
```

The formatting rules for color, weight, size, and typeface are assigned directly to the *<li>* tag, which creates new bullet points in an HTML list. It's almost like a dress code for all *<li>* tags; they know that when they are used on the page, they must look a certain way. Best of all, if you need to modify their appearance, you don't have to go through every *<li>* tag in your document and modify *<font>* tags or attributes; just make your changes to that single style rule at the top of the page. You will get a chance to do this shortly; however, let's take a step back and look at how CSS is controlled in Dreamweaver.

7   Choose File > Save to save your work, then choose File > Close.

How do you create CSS rules in Dreamweaver?

In this exercise you will take a tour of Dreamweaver's CSS controls. If you haven't worked with CSS before, this is a chance to learn a bit more about how it works. If you have worked with CSS previously, this section will help you understand the Dreamweaver interface and how it applies to familiar concepts. Regardless of your comfort level with CSS, you won't be making any changes, merely getting familiar with features that you will be using in later exercises.

You work with CSS rules in a few ways in Dreamweaver:

Using the CSS Styles panel

You can use Dreamweaver's CSS Styles panel to create new rules and/or style sheets that you can place directly within one or more pages in your site. You can easily modify rules directly from the CSS Styles panel. Furthermore, you can selectively apply rules from several places, including the Style or Class menu on the Property Inspector, or the tag selector at the bottom of the document window.

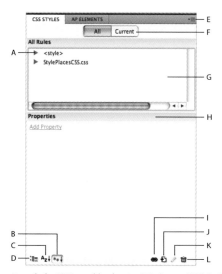

Launch the CSS panel by choosing Window > CSS Styles. **A**. *Internal Style Sheet.* **B**. *Show Only Set Properties.* **C**. *Show List View.* **D**. *Show Category View.* **E**. *CSS panel menu.* **F**. *Switch to Current Selection Mode.* **G**. *Rules pane.* **H**. *Properties pane.* **I**. *Attach Style Sheet.* **J**. *New CSS Rule.* **K**. *Edit Style Sheet.* **L**. *Delete Embedded Style Sheet.*

1   Choose Window > CSS Styles to open the CSS Styles panel. You'll now free up some screen space by closing the Insert panel: double-click the Insert tab to collapse this panel.

2   Double-click the StylePlaces.html document in your Files panel to open it.

3   Click in the first line, *Hi there! I'm styled with an INLINE style!*

4   Press the Current button in the CSS Styles panel. A summary pane lists the CSS properties for the current selection. Take a few moments to read through this panel and absorb the summary. Don't worry too much about each detail; you'll have plenty of time to familiarize yourself with this panel. It hopefully makes sense that the properties of the first paragraph are the color blue, the font-family Arial, and the font size of 14 pixels.

Press the Current button to view the rules for a selection.

5   Click on the second paragraph and notice that the color property changes to red. Click on the third paragraph and notice that the color property changes to green. The current selection always lists the properties of the selected text.

6   Press the All button in the CSS Styles panel to return to this view.

Directly from the Property Inspector

Whenever you format text directly on your page using the Property Inspector, Dreamweaver saves your settings as a new, named rule in your document. You can then reapply the rule as many times as you need to by using the Property Inspector or tag selector. Rules that Dreamweaver creates appear in your CSS panel, where you can easily modify or rename them.

1   Click in the second paragraph, *Hi there! I'm styled with an embedded, or INTERNAL style sheet!*

2   In the Property Inspector at the bottom of the screen, press the HTML button, if necessary. This paragraph is styled using a CSS class named red. You'll learn more about classes and how to create and modify them shortly.

3   Press the CSS button in the Property Inspector. You can see the properties of this rule here in the Inspector, and you can also create and modify them here as you did in the previous lesson.

CSS styles are automatically created when you format text with the Property Inspector.

4   Compare the Property Inspector with the CSS Styles panel for a moment: they are displaying the exact same information (as long as you are in the Current mode of the CSS Styles panel).

In the Code view

CSS rules can also be created and modified directly in the Code view. Editing CSS in Dreamweaver's Code view offers a great degree of control and is often called *hand-coding.* Many coders and designers prefer hand-coding because of this control. However, this precise control also has its downsides. For example, when you work in the Code view the potential for error increases dramatically, and misspellings or an incomplete knowledge of CSS syntax can easily break a page.

1   Click in the second paragraph if you are not currently inside it. Press the Code View button to view your page in Code view. If you haven't worked with code previously, see if you can locate the second paragraph. On the left side of the screen, notice the line numbers running from top to bottom; when working with code, each line has its own number, making it easy to refer to and locate objects.

2   On line 24, click and drag just the text, *Hi there! I'm styled with an embedded, or INTERNAL style sheet!* Do not highlight the tags, just the text.

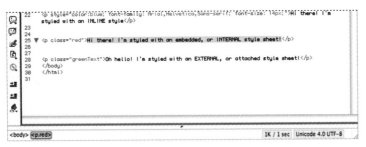

Click and drag the text in Code View to select it.

3   Press the Design view button (⊞) to see the second paragraph highlighted.

Working with the Code Navigator

New to Dreamweaver CS4 is the Code Navigator, which serves a dual purpose. The Code Navigator allows you to view the CSS properties directly in the Design view through a small pop-up window. Additionally, it allows you to click on a property and edit it directly in the Split view.

1   Press Ctrl+Alt (Windows) or Command+Option (Mac OS) and click on the third paragraph. A small window appears, listing the properties of the CSS rule applying to this paragraph. The window lists the name of the style sheet, as well as the rule *.greentext*.

2   Place your cursor over the *.greentext* class, and the properties appear in a yellow pop-up window. This feature allows you to quickly view the properties without needing to move to the CSS Styles panel or go into Code view.

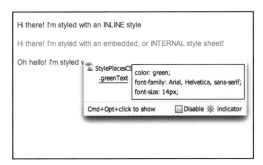

The Code Navigator displays the CSS rules applied to a paragraph.

3   Press the Design view button (▦) to return to the design view.

Understanding Style Sheets

The term "Cascading" in Cascading Style Sheets alludes to the fact that styles can live in three different places, each of which has its strengths and weaknesses. You've actually been working with all three types of styles in the last exercise. The first line is being defined with an inline style, the second with an internal style sheet, and the third with an external style sheet.

Inline style sheets

An inline style is a set of CSS properties defined directly in an HTML tag using the style attribute. These are slightly less common because you can't reuse them, which somewhat defeats the purpose of using style sheets in the first place.

1   Click three times rapidly to select the first paragraph.

2   Press the Split view button (▦), and notice that your selected text is nested inside a paragraph or *<p>* element; however, the CSS style rules for color, font-family, and font-size are contained directly inside the opening paragraph tag. This is called an inline style because the CSS rules are not separated from the HTML.

Although inline styles are part of the CSS language, they are not often used. They present many of the same problems as the older *<font>* tags in HTML. They only apply to one tag at a time and are not easily reusable. So when are they used? Inline styles are useful when an internal or external style sheet may not be available; a good example of this is HTML-based e-mail.

```
20
21    <body>
22    <p style="color:blue; font-family: Arial,Helvetica,Sans-serif; font-size: 14px;">Hi there! I'm
      styled with an INLINE style</p>
23
24
25    <p class="red">Hi there! I'm styled with an embedded, or INTERNAL style sheet!</p>
26
27
28    <p class="greenText">Oh hello! I'm styled with an EXTERNAL, or attached style sheet!</p>
29    </body>
30    </html>
31
```

An inline style places the CSS rules inside an opening paragraph tag.

Internal versus external style sheets

Internal style sheets are CSS rules that are contained directly within a document, using the *<style>* tag. The entire style sheet is contained within the opening and closing *<style>* tags. External style sheets are style rules saved in a separate document with the extension ".css". One of the fundamental differences between internal and external style sheets is that with internal style sheets, the CSS rules apply only to the HTML in a single document. For example, if you had a ten-page web site and could only use internal style sheets, you would essentially have ten styles sheets: one per page. If you made a change on one page and then needed to make the other pages look the same, you would have to either copy or redefine internal styles from page to page, not an enjoyable prospect. External style sheets, by contrast, have CSS rules located in one single document. You can attach .css files, or external style sheets, to an unlimited number of HTML pages. This method is extremely flexible: if a style rule such as the font-color for a paragraph is changed in the external style sheet, all paragraphs in the site are instantly modified, whether it be 2 pages, 10 pages or 100 pages.

In Dreamweaver, when you create a new style, the default behavior is to use an internal style sheet. In many ways, a web browser doesn't care which type of style sheet you use; it renders the page exactly the same. There are certain situations when an internal style sheet makes more sense than an external style sheet and vice-versa. You will explore this in more detail in later exercises, but first you need to know how to determine whether a style is internal or external.

1   In the CSS Styles panel, click on the All button. In the top half of the screen you will see a listing for *<style>* and one for StylePlacesCSS.css. The first line is the internal style sheet, and the second is for the external style sheet.

2 If necessary, click on the arrow to the left of the plus sign (Windows) or the arrow (Mac OS) to the left of the *<style>* option, and it expands to show you the rule for the class red. Click on the arrow to the left of StylePlacesCSS.css to expand this and see the rule for the class .greentext. You may have noticed that the listing for the inline style is not here; only rules for internal and external style sheets are visible in All mode.

In the last exercise, you used the Code Navigator to view the CSS rules applied to a paragraph. You can also use the Code Navigator to quickly determine where the CSS rules are located.

3 Click inside the second paragraph and Ctrl+Alt+click (Windows) or Command+Option+click (Mac OS) to open the Code Navigator. The window reads StylePlaces.html and the class *.red* is indented below it. If a style is located inside an HTML document, as it is in this case, it must be an internal style.

The Code Navigator has located the origin of this CSS rule to be in StylePlaces.html.

4 Place your cursor over the *.red* class, and all the properties appear; this is a quick way to determine the properties.

5 Click on the *.red* rule, and Dreamweaver's Split view opens, sending you directly to the internal style. An experienced hand-coder might use this to directly edit the rule, although you will not be making any changes at this point. Now you will look at the external style sheet again using the Code Navigator.

6 Ctrl+Alt+click (Windows) or Command+Option+click (Mac OS) in the third paragraph to open the Code Navigator.

7 This time, the Code Navigator window lists StylePlacesCSS.css first. If a style is located inside a .css document, as it is in this case, it is an external style. Place your cursor over the *.greentext* class, and all the properties appear.

8 Click on the *.greentext* class, and in the Split view, the external style sheet StylePlacesCSS.css appears. Doing this actually opens the external style sheet, which is a separate document. To return to the original HTML document, press the Source Code button.

Clicking on the Source Code button switches you from the external style sheet back to the original HTML file.

9 Choose File > Save All. Close this document for now. Choosing *Save All* saves not just the HTML document but the external stylesheet at the same time.

Understanding why they're called Cascading

You have defined style sheets and determined that there are three categories of styles. Additionally, you have seen that an HTML document such as the one from the last exercise can contain all three types. Now you'll begin to explore when you might use one type over the other. A good way to look at this is to ask the question, Which one of the style types is strongest? Consider the following situation: you have a paragraph, or more accurately a *<p>* tag, in your document and you have the style types (inline, internal, and external). Each one defines the *<p>* tag but they all use different properties, so which one wins? The answer is that the inline style is the strongest because it is closer to the HTML source. The internal style sheet is the next strongest because it is one step farther away from the HTML source, as it is located in the head section of the HTML document. Finally there is the external style sheet, which is a separate document and technically the least strongest because it is farthest away from the actual source.

Creating and modifying styles

You will now get a chance to begin working more deeply with CSS. In this exercise, you'll be picking up where you left off in the last chapter with the events page for the OrganicUtopia web site. In that chapter you covered the creation of new CSS rules; however, you essentially worked with just one category of CSS rules, the element or tag-based rules. In all instances from the last chapter, you defined the properties for a tag, such as *<h1>*, *<p>*, and *<ul>* (unordered lists). You will now explore how to create classes and IDs. First, a brief review of the styles you used in the last chapter tag styles.

A tag style assigns rules directly to a specific HTML tag to alter its appearance. You can attach tag styles to any tag from the *<body>* tag down; as a matter of fact, when you modify page properties (Modify > Page Properties) to change default text formatting and background color, you are using a tag style assigned to the *<body>* tag.

The most basic tag styles are very straightforward. For instance, when you create a rule definition for the *<p>* (paragraph) tag, all paragraphs appear the same. The limitations begin when you want to customize one specific paragraph to appear different from the others. You will explore some solutions to this dilemma; for now, keep in mind that tag styles are a great way to ensure consistency across multiple elements and pages where specific tags are used, such as lists, tables, and paragraphs.

1   Double-click the events.html file in the Files panel to open it. This page has already had its Heading 1, paragraph, and list styled. You will now style the Heading 2.

2   In the Design view, click inside the heading *Spring Events*. This is already formatted as a Heading 2 for you.

3   Click on the CSS button in the left side of the Property Inspector; this allows you to define the properties of the Heading.

4   Choose 18 from the Size drop-down menu on the Property Inspector, and the New CSS Rule dialog box appears. From the Choose a contextual selector type for your CSS rule drop-down menu, choose Tag. In the second field marked *Selector Name*, the selector h2 has been chosen for you. Dreamweaver does this because you placed your cursor inside the text formatted as h2. Press OK. Now you can add additional properties, and Dreamweaver adds them to the definition of the h2 tag.

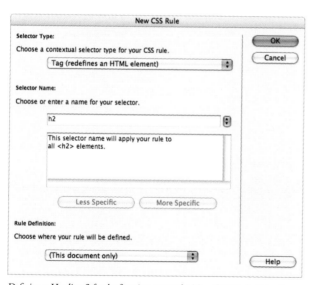

Defining a Heading 2 for the first time causes the New CSS Rule dialog box to appear.

5   In the Property Inspector, click on the color swatch to choose a color for your text from the Swatches panel that appears. Select a dark green. The color #390, located in the top row, is used in this example. Your heading now changes to green. You have just styled the font-size and color of the *<h2>* tag. At this point, all text formatted as h2 appears this way. You will now format the last heading in the page in order to see this.

6   Click inside the text, *Rent our facility*. In the Property Inspector, click on the HTML button. You need to toggle into this view because you now want to change the HTML formatting not the CSS.

7   In the Property Inspector, note that the Format for this text is currently set to None. From the Format drop-down menu, choose Heading 2 to see your text change.

Formatting text as a Heading 2 assumes the properties of the CSS rule.

What you have seen in this exercise is an example of HTML and CSS working together with a tag style. In this case, all text tagged in the HTML as a Heading 2 or *<h2>* is defined by the CSS rule as green and 18 pixels. At this point you may be itching to create more complex layouts; if you understand the fundamentals of styling tags, it will pay off as you move to the next level of CSS.

Creating a class style with the Property Inspector

In the last exercise, you created a new CSS rule by defining the properties of the *<h2>* tag. Now you will create another CSS rule, this time using a class. In CSS, class styles have unique names and are not associated with any specific HTML tag. A CSS class can have a specific style that can be applied to one or more elements in your web site. So you might create a class called *holidayText*, for example, and the properties of this class might just be a single rule defining the font-color. Once the class is created, this text could then be applied to a table, paragraph, heading, or form element simultaneously. So on Halloween, if you change the property of the font-color to orange, all text that is defined by the *holidayText* class is orange, and on Valentine's Day, if you change the property of the font-color to red, it all changes to red.

In this exercise, you will create a class using the Property Inspector for the copyright text at the bottom of the page in order to distinguish it from the rest of the page.

1   Click at the end of the paragraph reading *Occasionally we gather personal information at our events* and drag all the way down to the bottom of the page to select the copyright paragraph. Press the CSS button in the Property Inspector if necessary; note that this text has a size of 14 pixels and a dark grey color. This is because these are paragraphs and the CSS rules for paragraphs have these properties. You will now format all this text with a different size and font, and then add a background color.

2 In the Property Inspector, click on the drop-down menu for Size and change the size from 14 pixels to 10 pixels. The New CSS Rule dialog box appears. The default choice for Selector Type is *Class*, which is what you would like to use. Classes, unlike the Tag styles you have been using, must be named; additionally, you must name the class, as Dreamweaver does not do it for you.

Previous versions of Dreamweaver automatically assigned generic names to new classes, such as .style1, .style2, and so on. In addition to the New CSS Rule dialog box, this is perhaps one of the most substantial changes in Dreamweaver CS4 when it comes to styles: users are now required to name CSS classes. Although this may seem to be an extra step, it is a good one. By being forced to assign names to styles, users are more aware of the code they are generating and make their web pages easier to maintain.

3 In the Selector Name field, type **copyright**. As you type, notice that Dreamweaver adds the text, *This selector name will apply your rule to all HTML elements with class "copyright"*. This is Dreamweaver's way of helping you understand how your new class can be applied.

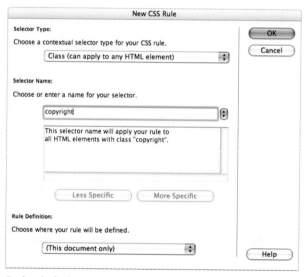

Set the rules for the new copyright class.

4 Press OK. You now see the text formatted at 10 pixels. Once the class is created, you can add other properties.

5 Click once in the first line of the copyright text. Notice in the Property Inspector that in the Targeted Rule section, the menu is set for .copyright. This is important, as it confirms that you are modifying the class, not the paragraph. In the Property Inspector, choose Verdana, Geneva, sans-serif from the Font menu to add this property to the copyright class. Now you'll add a new line of text and apply the copyright class to it.

6 Place your cursor at the end of the last line of the paragraph and press Enter (Windows) or Return (Mac OS) to add a new line. Type the following text: **All images on this website are the copyright of Bob Underwood.** Notice that the text is using the paragraph style; you need to instruct Dreamweaver to use the copyright class for this line.

7 From the Targeted Rule drop-down menu of the Property Inspector, choose copyright in the Apply Class section, The copyright class is now applied to this paragraph as well.

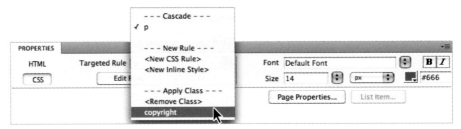

Use the Targeted Rule menu in the Property Inspector to apply an existing class to an element.

Creating and modifying styles in the CSS Styles panel

Using the Property Inspector is a quick and easy way to create and apply styles and make some basic formatting choices; however, the number of style choices in the Property Inspector is very limited. To take advantage of the full power of CSS, you will begin to dive into the CSS Styles panel. In this exercise, you'll explore some of the powerful options that CSS has at its disposal. The first thing you'll do is change the background color of your page by adding a new style to the body tag.

1 At the top of the CSS Styles panel, make sure the All tab is active, and locate *<style>* underneath; if it is not currently expanded, click on the arrow to see the list of current rules in your document. You will now add a new rule for the body tag in order to change the background color.

2 Click on the New CSS Rule icon (⊛) at the bottom of the CSS Styles panel. This displays the same dialog box you are accustomed to working with, just accessed from a different location. From the Choose a contextual selector type for your CSS rule drop-down menu, choose Tag. Previously, you have accepted the automatic choices in the Selector Name section, but in this case, you need to instruct Dreamweaver that you would like to create a new rule for the body tag.

3 From the Choose or enter a name for your selector drop-down menu, select body. Press OK. The CSS Rule Definition dialog box appears. This dialog box gives you access to the numerous styling options available in CSS.

CSS Rule definition for body

Category	Type
Type	
Background	Font-family:
Block	
Box	Font-size: ▢ px ▢ Font-weight:
Border	
List	Font-style: ▢ Font-variant:
Positioning	
Extensions	Line-height: ▢ px ▢ Font-transform:

Font-decoration: ☐ underline   Color: ▢
☐ overline
☐ line-through
☐ blink
☐ none

Help   Apply   Cancel   OK

Creating a new rule for the body tag launches the CSS Rule Definition dialog box.

4 In the left Category column, select Background to access the Background properties. In the field for Background-color, type in the following hexadecimal number: **#E0F0E4**. The background color does not apply automatically. Press the Apply button in the bottom-right corner to preview the new background color.

5 Press OK to confirm the background color. You will now change the background color for the copyright class at the bottom of the page.

6 In the list of rules in the CSS Styles panel, double-click the *.copyright* class to edit these properties.

Double-clicking a style in the style window opens the CSS Rule Definition dialog box.

7 In the CSS Rule Definition dialog box that appears, click on the Background Category, click on the Background-color swatch, and choose white (#FFF) from the list. Press OK. The two copyright paragraphs at the bottom of the page are styled with white backgrounds. The gap between the two paragraphs reveals the background color because these separate paragraphs, and are both block elements. The gap is somewhat visually unappealing and is something you will be fixing a bit later in the lesson.

Advanced text formatting with CSS

Text on the web is necessarily limited due to the fact that designers cannot assume that fonts they choose in Dreamweaver will be available to the user. There is a small set of fonts that designers can use that are essentially guaranteed to be on all users' systems. Given this limitation, you can use some of the properties in CSS to give your text a distinctive look. In this exercise you will work with the line spacing of your paragraphs and lists, and the letter spacing of your headings.

1 In the CSS panel, double-click on the rule for p (paragraph) to open the CSS Rule Definition dialog box. You will now override the default line-height for your paragraphs. If you have a print background, you may be familiar with leading, which is the amount of space between the lines in a paragraph. Line-height is the same thing as leading.

2 In the Line-height field, type **20**; the value is automatically set for pixels. Press Apply, and you will see the space between your paragraph lines increase. Extra line-height can often make your text more readable, so it is great that you have this option in CSS. However, a problem may arise if you change the font-size. For example, setting the fixed value of 20 pixels looks good with 14-pixel type, but what if you were to later change the font-size of your paragraph? The 20-pixel line-height would look strange. A more flexible way to assign line-height is to use a percentage.

3 From Line-height drop-down menu to the right of the text field, choose percent (%). Change the value from 20 to **120**, and press Apply, you won't actually see a dramatic difference because the end result is similar, but by assigning line-height to 120 percent, your initial font-size isn't as important. There will always be the height of the line plus 20 percent extra, no matter what the font-size is. Press OK.

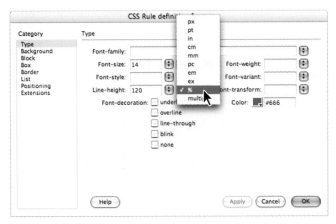

Changing the line-height value of a paragraph to a percentage is more flexible than using pixels.

Notice that the list under Spring Events did not change. This is because the line-height property applies solely to paragraphs, not lists. If you want to make this list appear the same, you could always apply the same value of line-height. However, you will add extra space between the lines to make the list stand out from the rest of the page.

4   In the CSS Styles panel, double-click on the *ul* rule. The CSS Rule Definition dialog box appears. In the field for line-height, type **150**; then from the drop-down menu to the right, select percentage. Press OK, and you now have extra space between your list items. Now you'll style your Heading 2 element.

5   In the CSS Styles panel, double-click the *h2* rule. In the Text-transform section, click on the menu, and from the list, choose uppercase. Press Apply, and you will see your two headings, *Spring Events* and *Rent Our Facility!,* transform to uppercase. This helps your headings stand out and is a lot faster than retyping these headings by hand. Now you'll add some space between all the letters.

Transforming your text to uppercase is just a style; in the HTML, your original text still has the standard formatting. One of the few times this might be an issue is if your web page is being viewed without a style sheet; many cell phones and PDAs do not fully support style sheets (or use them at all), and so your text would appear lowercase as it is in the HTML.

6   Select the Block category in the CSS Rule Definition dialog box. Block styles generally control the way text is displayed in the browser. In the field for Letter-spacing, type **5**; then choose px from the drop-down menu to the right. Press Apply, and the two headings are extended. Each letter pair has 5 pixels of space between them. Press OK. When used well, letter-spacing can make your headings more readable and unique.

> **SPRING EVENTS**
>
> - Free body lotion samples
> - Cheesetasting.
> - Winetasting
> - Free chocolate samples
>
> **RENT OUR FACILITY!**
>
> If you've ever wanted to hold an event in our store, well n
> more. We offer special rates for members of the coop.
>
> *Free samples while supplies last.

Adding letter-spacing and uppercasing to your headings can make them stand out.

Fine-tuning page appearance with contextual and pseudo-class selectors

Earlier in the lesson, you learned that you need more control over your CSS. For example, you will now look at a solution for the following problem. Look at the Spring Events list on your page: lines 1 and 4 both begin with the word Free. Let's say you wanted to emphasize this word slightly to attract your user's attention. You could simply bold the word, but what if you not only wanted to bold it, but change the color as well. It would be possible to create a class to do this, but there is another option that has some useful benefits, with the daunting name of *contextual selectors.*

(To make things even more difficult, Dreamweaver actually refers to contextual selectors, which is the official CSS term for them, as *compound selectors*.) Despite the terminology, they are very powerful and important to understand.

Contextual selectors apply formatting to tags and classes when they appear in a specific combination. For instance, you usually have rules for the *<p>* (paragraph) and *<strong>* (strong) tag, but then you might have another set of rules for *<strong>* tags inside *<p>* tags. For instance, you can designate that any text inside a *<strong>* tag must be red, unless it is used within a *<p>* tag, in which case it should be blue. This breathes new life into your tag styles by multiplying the number of times you can use them in conjunction with each other.

1   In the first line of the Spring Events list, select the word *Free*. Click on the HTML button in the Property Inspector, then press the Bold button. Using the example from above, let's say that simply bolding this wasn't enough and you wanted to add some color.

2   Press on the CSS button in the Property Inspector; then click on the menu for Targeted Rule and choose <New CSS Rule>. You must do this; otherwise, when you choose a color, you will target the whole list, which is not what you want.

3   Click on the color swatch in the Property Inspector and choose the dark green swatch in the top row, #030. The New CSS Rule dialog box appears.

4   From the Choose a contextual selector type for your css rule drop-down menu, choose Compound (based on your selection). In the Selector Name field, the text, *body ul li strong*, appears. This may look strange at first, but it's actually very logical if you read it from left to right. The body tag is the ancestor, or parent, of the ul tag, which is the parent of the li tag, which is the parent of the strong tag. In other words, your style will only apply to strong tags, which are nested in a list item (which is nested in the unordered list, and so on).

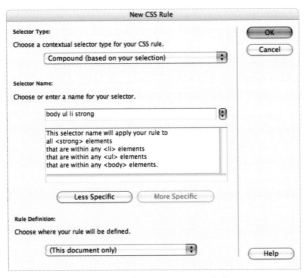

Set the Selector Type to Compound to create a contextual selector.

In the official specification of CSS, the concept of ancestor and parent elements is an important one. In fact, the concept is taken even further, in the example above, where the ul tag is referred to as the child of the body element because it is the direct descendant of the body element. There are even sibling elements!

In many ways, including the body element in this rule is overkill. Technically speaking, body is the ancestor of all tags in a document, as it nests virtually everything else, and so you can actually remove it and make your code a little easier to read.

5   Below the Selector Name section, click on the Less Specific button, and the list of rules is shortened to *ul li strong*; this has no effect on the behavior of the rule. Press OK. The word Free is now bolded and dark green. Deselect the text to see the final result. The rule is in place, and anything that is bolded inside a list will have this appearance. You can see this now by bolding the word Free in the fourth line of the list.

6   Press the HTML button in the Property Inspector. Select the word Free in the fourth line and then press the Bold button in the Property Inspector. The word takes on the same appearance. Bolding anything else in the list causes it to have the same appearance, while bolding anything not in a list has only the default effect.

Styling hyperlinks

You're slowly beginning to pull together a page with a color theme to it, even if there is no layout *per se*. A frequently asked question when people are learning to create web pages is how to style the hyperlinks on a page. This can be accomplished with CSS, although there are some precautions. Since the early days of CSS, the default style for unvisited hyperlinks has been a bright blue with an underline for unvisited hyperlinks and a purple color with an underline for visited hyperlinks. An argument is sometimes made that users might be confused by hyperlinks that do not fit this mold. On the other hand, many designers like being able to color their hyperlinks to match the rest of their page. Regardless of the debate, it's important to understand how to do this.

Technically speaking, hyperlinks live in a category called *pseudo-class*. A pseudo-class selector affects a part or state of a selected tag or class. A state often refers to an item's appearance in response to something happening, such as the mouse pointer rolling over it. One of the most common pseudo-class selectors is applied to the *<a>* tag, which is used to create hyperlinks. You'll now create a pseudo-class selector to affect the appearance of hyperlinks on the events. html page in different states:

1   Choose New from the CSS Styles panel menu to create a new rule. The New CSS Rule dialog box appears.

2   From the Choose a contextual selector type for your CSS rule drop-down menu, choose Compound. In the Selector Name section, click to open the drop-down menu to the right of the selector field. You may have different selectors appearing at the top of your menu; this is because Dreamweaver is attempting to create a compound rule, but in fact you are only interested in the last four options, which are a:link, a:visited, a:hover, and a:active. Choose a:link, which affects the appearance of a hyperlink when it hasn't yet been visited. Press OK.

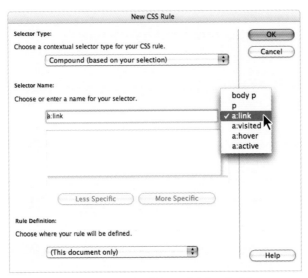

Set the Selector type to Compound and choose a:link from the Selector menu.

3   The CSS Rule Definition dialog box appears. Under the Type category, click the color swatch next to Color and choose the green shade you used in the previous exercise (#030). Press OK, and the products link in the first paragraph as well as the two links at the bottom of the page are now green instead of blue. Now you'll set the style for hover links, or a:hover.

4   Once again, choose New from the CSS Styles panel menu and the New CSS Rule dialog box opens. You will leave the state for the visited link alone for now. In this case, the default purple is fine. You will now change the state for a:hover, which defines the color of a hyperlink when a user places their cursor over it.

5   From the Choose a contextual selector type for your CSS rule drop-down menu, choose Compound. In the Selector Name section, choose a:hover from the drop-down menu, then press OK.

6   From the Type category, click the color swatch next to Color and select the bright orange approximately in the center of the Swatches panel (#C60). In the Text-decoration section, mark the last checkbox labeled *none*. This removes the underline from the hyperlink for the hover state only. Press OK.

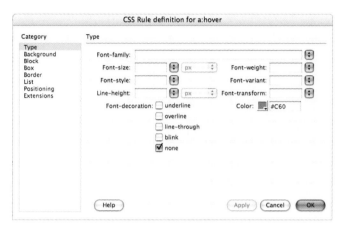

Set properties for a:hover, or the appearance of hyperlinks when the mouse pointer rolls over them.

You can preview the appearance of the hyperlinks by opening your page in a browser.

7   Choose File > Save; then choose File > Preview in Browser and choose a browser from the list to launch it. Place your cursor over the products link, but don't click it. This is the hover link. Click on the products link to bring you to the products page, and then click back to the events page by clicking the Events link at the bottom of the page. The products link is now purple because the browser understands you have visited it.

You will leave off styling the a:active link for now. Setting the a:active property defines the way a link appears when it is being clicked on by a user. Close the web browser.

Div tags and CSS IDs

Your page is coming along nicely on the style front, as you have used quite a bit of CSS, but looking at your page, it's fair to say that it is still lacking a cohesive style. All your various headings and paragraphs, as well as your list, are floating about on the page, and with the exception of the copyright text at the bottom of the page, it's difficult at a single glance to get a sense of where one section ends and another begins. It's time to add more structure to your page through the use of the *<div>* tag and more control of your CSS with IDs.

Let's look at the structure first. It would be nice to gather the text on the bottom of your page, starting with the line, *Occasionally we gather…*, and then the two paragraphs below, and put it all into a single section. You could then take this new section and style it separately from the rest of the page. This is possible with the *<div>* tag. In this exercise, you will begin by creating a footer ID.

1   Click and drag to select all the text from the line, *Occasionally we gather...*, down to the bottom of the page. You will be grouping these three paragraphs together.

2   Double-click on the Insert tab to open it; if the drop-down menu is not set to Common, do so now. In the Common section, press the Insert Div Tag (▤) button, and the Insert Div Tag dialog box opens. In the Insert section, the default choice is *Wrap around selection*; this is exactly what you want to do, so leave this option as is.

Press the Insert Div Tag button in the Common section of the Insert panel.

A *<div>* tag by itself doesn't do anything until some CSS properties are attached to it. In other words, unlike other HTML tags, which often have a default visual effect in the browser (think of headings), the *<div>* tag has no effect on your rendered page unless you specifically instruct it to. You will now get to do this.

3   In the field labeled ID, type **footer**. Just like classes, IDs should have good, descriptive names to help identify them. You'll now apply a background color of white to the entire block of text you selected. Notice that there is a field for class as well. Classes and IDs are very similar. The difference between them is that classes can be used multiple times on different elements on a page, whereas an ID can only be used once. In this case, an ID is appropriate because there is only one footer on this page.

4   Click the New CSS Rule button. You needn't change anything here; you are creating an ID with the name footer. The footer name is preceded by the pound sign (#). This is the main difference between ID names and class names. If this were a class named footer, it would be named *.footer*. Press OK, and the CSS Rule Definition dialog box appears.

5 Select the Background category, then click on the Background-color swatch. Choose the pure white swatch (#FFF) and press OK. Press OK to close the Insert Div Tag dialog box. In Dreamweaver's Design view, a box has appeared around the text and there is now a white background unifying the footer text.

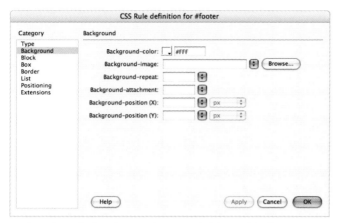

Set the Background-color to #FFF in the CSS Rule definition dialog box.

If you haven't guessed by now, these are the beginning steps toward page layout with CSS. A footer is a common element on most pages, and there are a few other obvious ones as well: headers, sidebars, and navigation bars to name a few. You'll begin working with these page structures more deeply in upcoming lessons, but first you'll need to have some more control of the CSS rules that you've been working with this lesson.

Internal versus external style sheets

Now that you've seen how to modify a few items in a single page at once, you can only imagine how powerful a style sheet shared by every page in your web site can be. When you create new CSS rules, you have the opportunity to define them in the current document or in a new CSS file. A collection of rules stored in a separate .css file is referred to as an *external style sheet*. You can attach external style sheets to any number of pages in a site so that they all share the same style rules.

So far, you've created internal, or embedded, styles. This means you wrote the style rules directly into the page using the *<style>* tag. Although you can format a page with an internal style sheet, this method is not very portable. To apply the same rules in another page, you have to copy and paste the internal style sheet from one page to another. This can create inconsistency among pages if the same rule is updated in one page and not the other.

To utilize the true power of style sheets, you can create an external style sheet that any and all pages on your site can share. When you change an external style, pages linked to that style sheet are updated. This is especially handy when working with sites containing many pages and sections.

You can create external style sheets in the following ways:

- Move rules from an internal style sheet into a new CSS file.

- Define styles in a page in a new document using the New CSS Rule panel.

- Create a new CSS document from the Start page or File menu.

Now you will export internal styles from your events.html page into a separate CSS file so that other pages may share them.

1   With the events.html document open, expand the style sheet shown in the CSS Styles panel so that you can see all the rules you have created. If you have limited screenspace, double-click on the Insert panel to collapse it.

2   Click on the *<style>* tag at the top of the panel and then scroll down if necessary to locate the last rule. Shift+click the last rule in the panel so that all the rules are selected. In the upper-right corner, press the CSS Styles panel menu button (-≡) and choose Move CSS Rules.

Select all rules in your style sheet and then choose Move CSS Rules.

3   The Move CSS Rules dialog box appears, asking if you want to move the styles to an existing or a new style sheet. Select A New Style Sheet and press OK.

4   A Save Style Sheet dialog box appears, asking you to choose a name and location for the new file that is about to be created. Name it **mystyles,** navigate to the root folder of your site (dw04lessons folder), and choose Save.

5   Your CSS Styles panel now shows a new style sheet: mystyles.css. The internal style sheet (shown as *<style>*) is still in your document, but it contains no rules. Click the plus sign (Windows) or arrow (Mac OS) to the left of mystyles.css to expand it and reveal all the rules it contains. There should be no surprises there; the same rules that were in your internal style sheet are now in an external one.

Attaching an external style sheet to your page

Dreamweaver automatically made the new external style sheet available to the current page by attaching it. However, you will have to point other pages to this style sheet in order for them to use it. You can accomplish this with the Attach Style Sheet command in the CSS Styles panel.

1   Double-click on the products.html file from the Files panel. This page contains event information with no formatting applied.

2   At the bottom of the CSS Styles panel, click the Attach Style Sheet icon (●). The Attach Style Sheet panel appears.

3   Next to File/URL, click the Browse button to locate a style sheet file to attach. In the dw04lessons folder, select the mystyles.css file from the Select Style Sheet dialog box and press OK (Windows) or Choose (Mac OS). Press OK to close the Attach External Style Sheet dialog box.

Adding an external style sheet.

The page refreshes with the styles defined in the external style sheet. You can also see that the CSS Styles panel shows that mystyles.css and all its rules are now available for use and editing.

Modifying attached style sheets

Because an attached style sheet appears in your CSS Styles panel, you can modify any of its rules just as you would with an internal style sheet. If you modify an external style in one page, the changes apply across other pages that share that style sheet. You'll take one step closer to layout now by modifying the body property in order to add some margins to your page.

1   In the CSS Styles panel, click on the plus sign (Windows) or arrow (Mac OS) to the left of mystyles.css and double-click on the body rule. The CSS Rule Definition dialog box opens.

2   Click on the Box category and deselect the checkbox labeled *Same for all* in the Margin column.

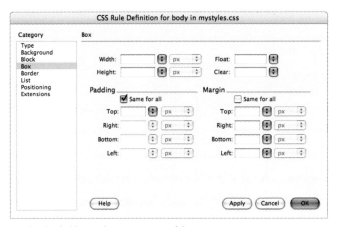

Deselect the checkbox in the Margin section of the Box category.

Because CSS is based on a box model, it views every tag as a container. Because the *<body>* tag is the largest container, if you modify its margins, it affects all the content on the page. You'll specifically be changing the left and right margins to create a more centered layout.

3   In the Margin field labeled Right, type **15**, and choose % from the drop-down menu.

4   In the Margin field labeled Left, type **15**, and choose % from the menu. Press OK, and your content shifts toward the center.

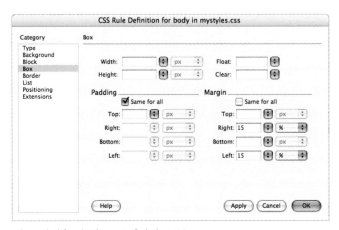

Change the left and right margin for body to 15 percent.

5   Choose File > Save All, and then preview your page in the browser. You are able to navigate between the products page and the events page using the hyperlinks in each document. Shorten the width of your browser, and notice that the content adjusts accordingly. There will always be 15 percent space to the left of content in the browser window and 15 percent to the right, thereby centering your content. Open the events.html file in your web browser to see how this page appearance is now being controlled by the external style sheet. When done, close the browser.

Creating a new .css file (external style sheet)

Although it's easy to export styles to a new .css file, you can also create styles in a new .css file from the beginning. The New CSS Rule dialog box gives you this option whenever you create a new rule. By creating styles in an external .css file, you can avoid the extra step of exporting them later, and make the style sheet available to other pages immediately.

1   In the Files panel, double-click on the event1.html file.

2   From the CSS Styles panel menu, choose New; the New CSS Rule dialog box appears.

3   Set the Selector Type as Tag, and choose body from the Tag drop-down menu if it is not automatically selected. At the bottom of the screen, click on the Rule Definition menu and choose (New Style Sheet File); then press OK.

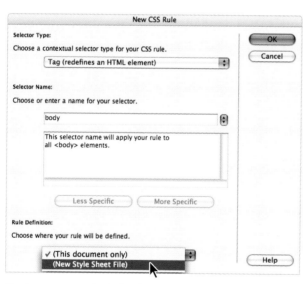

Creating a new external style sheet from scratch.

4   You are prompted to name and save the new .css file. Name it **morestyles.css** and save it in the root folder of your site.

5   When the CSS Rule Definition dialog box appears, choose the Background category. Set the background color to light yellow, #FFFFCC. Press OK to create the rule.

Your page's background color should be yellow, and the CSS Styles panel reflects that the style was created in a new external style sheet. Now you can attach this style sheet to any other page in your site.

6   Choose File > Save All.

Congratulations! You have finished Dreamweaver Lesson 4, "Styling Your Pages with CSS."

CSS FYI

Inheritance

When you nest one rule inside another, the nested rule inherits properties from the rule in which it's contained. For instance, if you define a font-size and font-family for all <p> tags, it carries over to a class style used within the paragraph that doesn't specify values for either property. It automatically inherits the font-size and font-family from the <p> tag selector.

CSS rule weight

What happens if two classes of the same name exist in the same page? It is possible to have two identically named styles, either in the same style sheet or between internal and external style sheets used by the same page. Along the same lines, it is possible to have two rules that both apply to the same tag. If either of these cases exists, how do you know which rule is followed?

You know which rule is followed based on two factors: weight and placement. If two selectors are the same weight (for instance, two tag selectors for the body tag), then the last defined rule takes precedence.

If a rule of the same name is defined in both an internal and external style sheet in your document, the rule from the last defined style sheet takes precedence. For instance, if an external style sheet is attached to the page anywhere after the internal style sheet, the rule in the attached stylesheet wins.

Self study

Create a new document and add some unique content, such as text or images, to it. Afterwards, use the CSS Styles panel to define at least one tag style, two class styles, and one contextual selector (advanced) in a new, external .css file. Create a second document and attach your new external style sheet to it, using the Attach Style Sheet command from the CSS Styles panel. Add content to this page, and style it using the style rules already available from your external style sheet. If desired, make changes to the rules from either document, and watch how both documents are affected by any modifications made to the external style sheet.

Adobe Device Central

The widespread use of Internet-ready devices, such as mobile phones and PDAs, makes it more necessary than ever to adapt your work for multiple sizes and platforms. Dreamweaver CS3 is now integrated with Adobe Device Central, which displays and simulates the appearance of HTML content in a variety of mobile, PDA, and handheld device skins and environments. Building your pages using the best practices of CSS will help optimize your pages for the small screens of mobile device.

To preview a page in Device Central:

1   With your finished events.html file open, choose File > Preview in Browser > Device Central. Device Central, which is a separate application, launches.

2   The Device Central application shows the page in the default mobile device. The first time you open Device Central, a list of device profiles is pulled from the Adobe web site. To see how this page will look in a mobile phone or PDA, double-click a device name from the list in the. We used the Motorola M702iS listing.

3   Choose File > Close (Windows) or Device Central > Quit (Mac OS) to exit Device Central and return to Dreamweaver. Choose File > Close to close the file.

Review

Questions
1   What are the three types of selectors that can be chosen when creating a new CSS rule?

2   In what three places can styles be defined?

3   True or false: A style sheet is composed of several CSS rules and their properties.

Answers
1   Tag, Class, and Advanced (which includes contextual and pseudo-class selectors).

2   Inline (written directly into a tag), embedded (inside a specific page using the *<style>* tag), or external (inside a separate .css file).

3   True. A style sheet can contain many CSS rules and their properties.

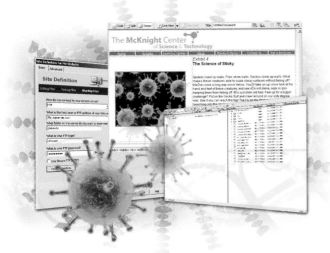

What you'll learn in this lesson:

- Uploading and managing files

- Optimizing pages for performance and search engines

- Using Site Reports

- Using the CSS Advisor & Browser Compatibility Check

Managing Your Web Site:
Reports, Optimization, and Maintenance

When it's time to release your web site to the world, you'll want to take some last steps to make sure your site works at, and looks, its best. Dreamweaver has a powerful set of reports, link checkers, and problem-solving tools to locate and fix any potential issues before final upload. When you're ready, the built-in FTP and synchronization features of the Files panel will get you up and running.

Starting up

Before starting, make sure that your tools and panels are consistent by resetting your workspace. See "Resetting the Dreamweaver workspace" on page XXVII.

You will work with several files from the dw05lessons folder in this lesson. Make sure that you have loaded the CS4lessons folder onto your hard drive from the supplied DVD. See "Loading lesson files" on page XXIX.

Before you begin, you need to create a site definition that points to the dw05lessons folder from the included DVD that contains resources you need for these lessons. Go to Site > New Site, or, for details on creating a site definition, refer to Dreamweaver Lesson 2, "Setting Up a New Site."

See Lesson 5 in action!

Use the accompanying video to gain a better understanding of how to use some of the features shown in this lesson. The video tutorial for this lesson can be found on the included DVD.

Working with the Files panel

You've already used the Files panel throughout this book to locate and open files within your site projects. In addition to serving as a useful file browser, the Files panel also serves as a full-featured file transfer application and synchronization tool. From the Files panel, you can upload your site to a web server, synchronize local and remote files, and manage files and notes between multiple designers.

Creating a remote connection

The Files panel uploads, retrieves, and synchronizes files between your local site and a web server. Typically, this is done using File Transfer Protocol (FTP), which connects to and allows interaction between your local machine and a web server. Before you can transfer files, you'll first need to establish a remote connection to the web server that stores your web site files. You will not be able to proceed with this portion of the lesson if you do not have FTP information available for a web server. If you do not have this information or do not have a connection to the Internet, you may skip to the "Testing Site Integrity" exercise in this lesson and proceed from there.

To get started, make sure you have the following:

- **The FTP address of the web server and specific directory.** This would be provided by your web-hosting provider as part of your account details, or from your company or organization's IT department. A typical FTP address looks like *ftp.mysite.com.*

- **A user login and password for access to the server.** Most web servers require a user login and password for access. This information should be available from your web-hosting provider as part of your account details, or from your organization's IT department.

- **The specific directory to which your files should be uploaded.** In many cases, this is the main directory or folder that appears when you connect to your web server. However, in certain cases, you'll need to upload files to a specific directory other than the main directory.

- **The web address (URL) or IP address where you can view your uploaded files on the server.** Sample addresses would be *www.mysite.com/*, *www.mysite.com/2007/*, or *http://100.0.0.1.*

1   To begin creating a remote connection, choose Site > Manage Sites. The Manage Sites dialog box appears.

2   Select the Lesson 5 site definition (you set this up at the beginning of the lesson) and click Edit. If you haven't created a site definition for this lesson, make sure you do so now, as discussed in Dreamweaver Lesson 2, "Setting Up a New Site."

3   The Site Definition dialog box appears. If necessary, click the Basic tab at the top to view the dialog box in Basic mode. Press the Edit button and the Site Definition window appears. Click the Basic tab, if necessary, and rename your site **My Website**. Press the Next button at the bottom until you advance to the Sharing Files panel.

4   Locate the drop-down menu below *How do you connect to your remote server?*, and choose FTP. Several fields appear below the drop-down menu, where you can fill in your information.

5   Enter your specific FTP information in the text fields, as shown in the example figure. In this example, the folder was defined; however, this is optional.

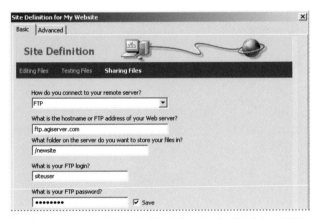

Sample remote connection information. Your information should include an FTP address, login, and password, with a possible folder name.

6   Click the Test Connection button at the bottom of the panel to verify that Dreamweaver can connect to your server. If the information you've provided is valid, a dialog box appears, confirming that Dreamweaver has successfully connected to your web server.

A dialog box lets you know if your connection was successful. If you receive an FTP error, double-check your FTP information, and make any necessary corrections.

7   Press the Next button at the bottom of the panel to advance to the Sharing Files, Part 2 panel. Press Next again to accept the default settings in this panel. When the Summary appears, Press Done to exit the dialog box and save your new connection information.

8   Press Done in the Manage Sites dialog box, as you're now finished editing the site definition.

If you receive an FTP error dialog box, verify the FTP address, login, password, and directory; make any necessary corrections. You will need a live Internet connection to perform this test!

Certain servers may require a passive FTP connection to connect successfully. If you are certain your FTP information is correct, but experience a long delay or failure when connecting, check the Use Passive FTP *checkbox in the Advanced tab, Remote Info category, and try again.*

Viewing files on a remote web server

Once you've established a connection to your web server, you can expand the Files panel for a split view that displays both your remote and local files. You can easily drag and drop between both sides to upload or download files and update existing files.

1 If necessary, choose Window > Files to open the Files panel. Click the Expand button (⊞) at the top of the Files panel to ungroup and expand it to full view.

2 Locate and click the Connect button (⚡) above the left-hand column at the top of the panel. Dreamweaver attempts to connect to your remote server, and, if successful, displays all its files on the left side of the Files panel.

It's important to note that web servers can be configured in many different ways, and you may need to edit your site settings again once you have made a successful connection (in particular, the folder information). A discussion of the different ways that web servers might be configured is outside the scope of this book; if you have specific questions regarding your site, you should contact an IT professional or your web-hosting company.

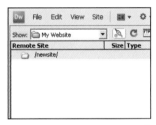

Click the Connect button to view files on your remote server in the left column of the Files panel.

Transferring files to and from a remote server with Get and Put

The built-in FTP and file transfer functionality of the Files panel makes it a snap to place files on your remote server or download files onto your local machine. This can be accomplished using the Get and Put buttons, or by dragging and dropping files between the Remote and Local file listings in the Files panel. Please note again, this exercise involves publishing your sample documents to a remote server, and therefore publishing them to the Internet; be very careful not to overwrite any pre-existing files that may be crucial to your web site.

1   Make sure you've connected to the remote server as described in the previous exercise, and that you can see your remote files in the left-hand column of the Files panel.

2   Select the index.html file from the local file listing on the right side of your Files panel, and press the Put button (⬆) at the top of the panel. Choose *No* when asked if you would like to include dependent files.

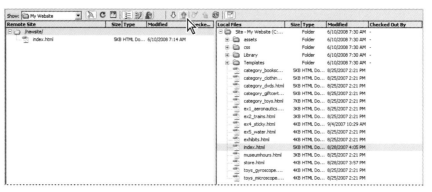

Select a file and click the Put button to upload it to the remote server.

When you transfer a document between a local and remote folder, a window may open, offering you the option of transferring the document's dependent files. Dependent files are images, external style sheets, and other files referenced in your document that a browser loads when it loads the document. For the purposes of this exercise, it will be unnecessary to transfer dependent files.

Alternatively, you can click and drag a file from the right (local) column to the left (remote) column.

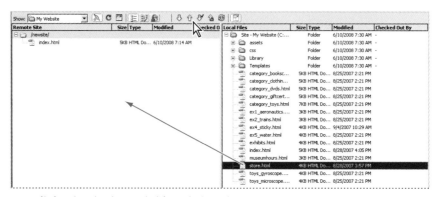

Drag a file from the right column to the left to upload it to the remote server.

To get (download) a file from the remote server:

1   Make sure you've connected to the remote server as described in the previous exercise, and that you can see your remote files in the left-hand column of the Files panel.

2   Select a file from the remote file listing on the left side of your Files panel, and press the Get button (⊕) at the top of the panel.

Alternatively, you can click and drag a file from the left (remote) column to the right (local) column. Note that a dialog box may appear, asking if you'd like to overwrite your local copy if the file already exists in your local file listing.

You can update the local or remote file listing at any time by clicking the Refresh button (⟳) at the top of the Files panel.

Using Check In/Check Out and Design Notes

If you're collaborating with others on a project, you'll want to set up an environment where everyone can edit files independently without overlapping or overwriting someone else's work. For these situations, the Check In/Out and Design Notes features can help you to manage workflow and communicate with others on a Dreamweaver site project.

Check In and Check Out

Dreamweaver's Check In/Check Out feature is a way of letting others know that you are working on a file and don't want it disturbed. When Check In/Check Out is enabled, a document that you're editing becomes locked on the remote server to prevent others from modifying the same file at the same time. If you attempt to open a file that's been checked out by another user, you see a warning that lets you know that the file is in use and who is currently working with it. Check In/Check Out doesn't require any additional software to run, and other Dreamweaver users can check out files if they also have Check In/Check Out enabled in their site definition.

The Check In/Check Out system does not work with a testing server. To transfer files to and from a testing server (if one is set up), use the standard Get and Put commands.

1   Choose Site > Manage Sites. Select the Dreamweaver site that you want to enable Check In/Check Out for and choose Edit.

2   In Basic View, press the Next button until you reach the Sharing Files, Part 2 section and then select *Yes, enable check in and check out*. A new section appears in the window. If you want to make sure a file is properly checked out when you open it, make sure the checkbox next to the *Dreamweaver should check it out* option is checked. If you want to work with a read-only copy, select I want to view a read-only copy.

Type your name and email. This information will appear to other users who attempt to retrieve a file that you have checked out (as long as they are using Dreamweaver). Press Next and then press Done to exit.

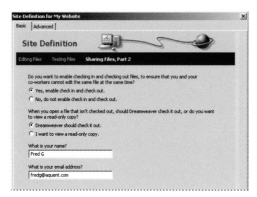

Enable check in/check out in the Site Definition panel to manage workflow between several users.

How does Check In/Check Out work?

Dreamweaver creates a lock (LCK) file for every document that is checked out; this basic text file contains the name and e-mail address of the user who has checked out the file. LCK files are written to both the remote server and local folder using the same name as the active file. When files are checked back in, the LCK files are deleted from both the remote server and local folder.

Although LCK files are not visible in the Files panel, they work behind the scenes to let Dreamweaver know what's checked out and what isn't. Checked-out files appear on both the local and remote file listings with a check mark next to them. Note that a colleague not using Dreamweaver can potentially overwrite a file that's checked out—however, LCK files are visible in applications other than Dreamweaver, and their appearance alone can help avoid any overwriting issues.

A user will be allowed to override your lock and switch checkout status to themselves. Make sure you establish rules with others about how to share and manage locked files.

Checking files in and out

When you check a file out, you are downloading it from the remote server to your local root folder, and placing a lock on the remote copy. Both your local copy and the remote copy appear with check marks next to them, which indicates that the file is currently checked out for editing. When you check a file back in, you are uploading the modified version to the remote server, and removing any locks currently on it.

1   Launch the Files panel and click the Expand button to expand it so that you can see both your local and remote files listed.

2   Select the file in your local folder that you want to check out, and use the Check Out button (🖉) at the top of the panel. Note that Dreamweaver overwrites your local copy of the file, as it needs to get the remote file from the server. The local and remote versions of the file appear with check marks next to them in the Files panel.

3   Open the checked file from your Local Files panel for editing. Make any necessary changes to the file, then save and close it.

4   From the Files panel, select the file again in the local Files panel and check it back in, using the Check In button (🔒) at the top of the panel. The file is uploaded to—and unlocked on—the remote server.

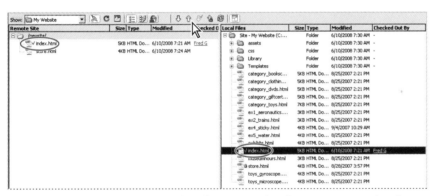

Check files out before modifying them so that others won't accidentally overwrite your work at the same time.

When you transfer a document between a local and remote folder, a window may open offering you the option of transferring the document's dependent files. Dependent files are images, external style sheets, and other files referenced in your document that a browser loads when it loads the document. For this exercise, it won't be necessary for you to transfer dependent files.

Your local copy becomes read-only, and appears with a padlock next to it. Next time you open the file for editing, Dreamweaver will automatically check out and get the latest copy from the server.

5   Collapse the Files panel to return it to the dock.

Using Design Notes

Design Notes store additional information about a file or media object in your Dreamweaver site. These notes can be for your own use, or they can be shared with others using the same root folder. Design Notes can be set to appear automatically when the file is opened, making it easy to display up-to-date information to others working on the same site. All Design Notes are stored as separate files in a _notes folder inside of your site's root directory.

What can be put in Design Notes?

Design Notes can contain any information that is important to the file or project; you can store design instructions, updates about the project, or contact information for project managers and supervisors. You can also store sensitive information that you ideally would not want in the file itself, such as the name of the last designer to work on the file or the location of important assets. You can even set the status of the file to indicate what stage of the revision the file is in.

1   To create a Design Note, under the Files panel, open a file from the current site.

2   Choose File > Design Notes. The Design Notes dialog box appears.

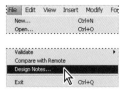

With a file open, select File > Design Notes to add or modify existing Design Notes for that specific file.

3   Type a message in the Notes field. To insert the current date stamp, click the Calendar button (▦) above the Notes field. If you want the note displayed when the file is next opened, check *Show when file is opened*.

4   Use the Status menu to set the document status; this can be useful in letting other collaborators know the revision stage of the current document.

5   Press OK to create the Design Note.

    To view a Design Note, choose File > Design Notes when a file is open in the document window. As mentioned earlier, you can also choose to have Design Notes automatically appear when the file is first opened.

Design Notes can also be created or viewed directly from the Files panel; right-click (Windows) or Ctrl+click (Mac OS) a document in the files list and choose Design Notes from the contextual menu.

Sharing Design Notes

By default, Design Notes are stored only in the local site folder, and are not automatically copied to the remote server. However, you can share Design Notes with other collaborators by having Dreamweaver automatically upload and update them on the remote server.

1   Choose Site > Manage Sites. Select your site from the Sites panel and choose Edit.

2   In Advanced view, choose Design Notes from the left.

3   Under the Design Notes panel, check *Upload Design Notes for sharing*. Design Notes are now copied and updated on the remote server so that other users can share them.

4   Choose OK to update the site definition, then press Done to close the Manage Sites dialog box.

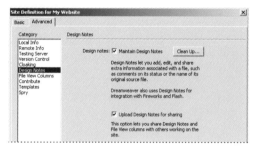

Set up Design Notes for sharing so that other Dreamweaver users can see and modify Design Notes on the remote server.

Displaying Design Notes in the Files panel

A convenient way to view and access Design Notes is by enabling the Design Notes column in the Files panel. An icon that can be used to open and edit Design Notes accompanies documents that have an associated Design Note. This feature also allows you to see all available Design Notes at a glance.

1   Choose Site > Manage Sites. Select your site from the Sites panel and choose Edit. In Advanced view, choose File View Columns from the left.

2   Under File View Columns, select the Notes item from the list and check *Show under the Options group*.

3   Choose OK to update the site definition, then press Done to close the Manage Sites dialog box. A Notes column appears in the Files panel; a Notes icon (💬) is displayed next to each file that currently is associated with a Design Note.

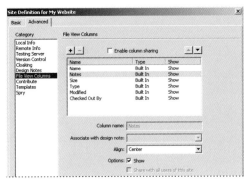

Use the Site Definition panel's File View Columns category to show Design Notes in both the local and remote file listings.

Testing site integrity

Catching potential issues on a page before your visitors do is key to ensuring success from the start. Broken links, display issues, or unreadable pages can make the difference between a great first impression and a poor one. To look for and address problems before you publish your site, Dreamweaver provides many useful tools that can point out potential hazards and, in some cases, help you find the solution.

Using Check Links

The Check Links feature detects any broken links between pages in your local site and will identify orphaned files that are not linked to or used by any document within the site.

1   From the Files panel, double-click and open the index.html document.

2   Choose File > Check Page > Links.

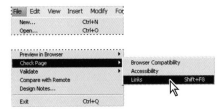

Choose File > Check Page > Links to check for broken links in the current document.

3   The Link Checker panel appears; you see one listing here. A link to the exhibits.html page is misspelled; you need to fix the error.

4   Click on the link name under the Broken Links column. The link name becomes editable.

5   Click on the folder icon to the far right. A Select File dialog box appears. Select the file **exhibits.html** and then press Choose. In the Link Checker tab, press Enter (Windows) or Return (Mac OS), and the broken link disappears.

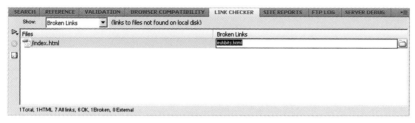

Retype the link or browse for the correct file using the folder icon to the right.

6   Close the Link Checker panel by right-clicking (Windows) Ctrl+clicking (Mac OS) on the panel and choosing Close Tab Group. Save and close the current document.

Checking links sitewide

Check Links can be used on a single document, multiple documents (through the Files panel), or an entire local site at once.

1   Choose Site > Check Links Sitewide.

2   The Link Checker panel appears; by default, any broken links are displayed. You should see roughly 12 links here, all referencing the same incorrect link to category_books_cds.html.

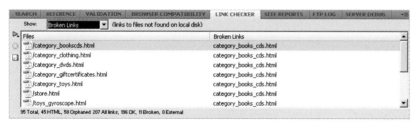

Choose Site > Check Links Sitewide to check for broken links throughout the current local site. The Link Checker panel opens and displays any broken links found.

3   To view external links, choose External Links from the Show drop-down menu at the top of the panel.

External links are displayed but aren't validated by Dreamweaver. The Link Checker can only validate links between local documents and files.

4   To view orphaned files, choose Orphaned Files from the Show drop-down menu at the top of the panel. Orphaned files are files that are not currently being linked to in your site. You will not be doing anything with these files at this moment.

5   Choose Broken Links from the Show drop-down menu to return to the broken links report. Click on the first of the broken links shown to edit it. Type **category_bookscds.html** to correct the link, and then press Enter (Windows) or Return (Mac OS).

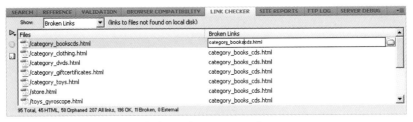

Adjust a link directly from the Link Checker panel to correct it sitewide.

6   A dialog box appears, asking if you'd like to make the same correction throughout the entire current local site. Press Yes.

Viewing Link Checker results

If and when the Link Checker returns results, you can jump to any problem document to view and fix any issues. The Link Checker panel's Show menu (located at the top of the panel) toggles between three different Link Checker reports: Broken Links, Orphaned Files, and External Links.

Broken Links lists links that point to files not found within the local site. To jump to a page that contains a broken link, double-click the filename shown in the left column of the Link Checker panel. To correct a link directly from the Link Checker panel, click the link shown under the Broken Links column of the panel to edit it. Type in the proper page name or use the folder to browse to the proper file. If you edit a broken link this way, Dreamweaver can apply the same correction throughout other pages on your site.

Orphaned Files are any pages, images, or media files not linked to, referenced, or used by any files in your site. This report can be useful in identifying unused files that can be cleaned up from the local site, or pages that should be linked to (like a site map) but were overlooked.

External Links lists any links to outside web sites, pages, or files; and like the Broken Links panel, allows you to directly edit them or jump to the page that contains them. It's important to note, however, that Dreamweaver does not validate external links—you will still be responsible for double-checking these links on your own. You'll also notice that e-mail (mailto:) links are included in this list.

Generating site reports

Dreamweaver's site reports feature is an indispensable asset for detecting potential design and accessibility issues before publishing your site to the web. Reports can be generated in several categories to give you a virtual picture of health, and the opportunity to locate and fix minor or major issues across an entire Dreamweaver site. These issues can include missing alternate text or titles, CSS issues, and recommendations for better accessibility practices, based on the W3C's Web Consortium Accessibility Guidelines (WCAG).

Reports can be generated for a single page, selected documents, or the entire current local site. Any results open and display in the Results panel, where you can see a list of issues and the pages on which they are located.

1   To run a site report, choose Site > Reports. The Reports dialog box opens, displaying two categories of reports: Workflow and HTML.

  It is not necessary to have a document open in order to run sitewide reports.

  Workflow reports display information about Design Notes, check in and check out operations, and recently modified files. HTML reports display potential design, accessibility, and display issues, based on best practices and W3C/WCAG accessibility guidelines.

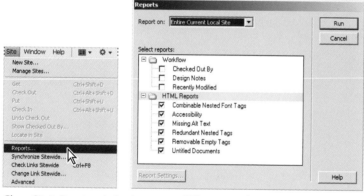

Choose Site > Reports, and select the reports you'd like to run in the Site Reports dialog box.

2   In the Reports panel, check all the reports under the HTML category. At the top of the panel, select Entire Current Local Site from the Report on drop-down menu.

3   Click Run in the top-right corner of the Reports panel. The Results panel appears, displaying any potential issues. Note that depending on the size of your site and number of issues found, it may take a few moments for all results to display.

4   Leave the Results panel open; you'll learn how to read and address issues in the next exercise.

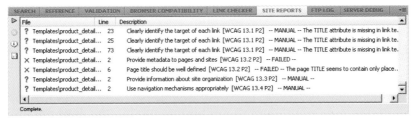

The Results panel displays issues found across your entire current local site.

Understanding report results

At first glance, you may be overwhelmed at the amount of information returned by site reports. Keep in mind that many of the listings returned are recommendations or possible issues that should be looked into. Learning to read these site reports a little more closely will enable you to decide which items are crucial to your site's performance, requiring immediate action. Listings are displayed with three distinct icons.

ICON	NAME	USE
?	Question Mark	These listings suggest possible accessibility issues that should be investigated. Many of these issues have a reference to a specific W3C/WCAG guideline.
✗	Red X	These listings indicate a failure to meet a certain guideline or requirement. Possible listings could include missing header information, deprecated HTML markup, or page titles that are not defined properly.
⚠	Warning Sign	Warnings indicate missing information that may be potentially detrimental to a site's performance, such as missing ALT text for images.

Addressing a listed item

After you've sifted through the report results, you'll want to use the Results panel to address items listed in the Site Reports tab.

1   Go to the Site Reports tab on the Results panel. Click the Description column header to sort the results. Scroll to the very bottom of the page until you see several listings accompanied by warning signs.

2   Find the listing for the store.html document, and click the More Info button (Φ) on the left edge of the Results panel for a detailed description, and recommended course of action. The Description dialog box shows that an image on this page is missing the ALT attribute and alternate text.

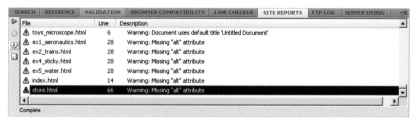

Select a listing and click the Info button to display a detailed description about the issue found.

3   Press OK to exit the Description dialog box and return to the Site Reports tab of the Results panel. Double-click the store.html listing to open the page for editing. The line where the issue begins should appear highlighted in Split view.

4   Select the large image in the middle of the page (giftcardpromo.jpg), and, in the Property Inspector, type **MKI Gift Cards are now available!** in the Alt field and press Enter (Windows) or Return (Mac OS).

Select the problem image and enter text in the Alt field to rectify the problem.

5   Save and close the page, and close the Results panel.

 A full listing of accessibility guidelines, or WCAG, for web page designers and developers is available at the World Wide Web Consortium (W3C) web site at W3.org.

Saving reports

In a case such as this when you have numerous warnings or suggestions, you might want to save them for future reference. Reports can be saved as XML for import into databases, existing template files, and archival files. You can sort report results using the Results panel before saving them.

1   If necessary, choose Window > Results > Site Reports to open the Site Reports tab.

2   Click on any column header to sort reports by type, page name, line number, and description.

3   Click the Save Report button (▣) on the left edge of the Results panel. When the Save Report dialog box appears, assign the report a name, and choose a location for the file.

4   Save and close the page, and close the Results panel.

The Browser Compatibility Check

When you format page content or create layouts with CSS, you'll want to be certain that your pages appear consistently across a variety of browsers. Some combinations of HTML and CSS can unearth some nasty display bugs in specific browsers. In fact, some browsers may not support certain CSS properties at all. To seek out and fix any potential CSS display problems, you'll use Dreamweaver's new Browser Compatibility Check (BCC) reports in conjunction with the CSS Advisor.

The CSS Advisor

A new addition to the reporting tools in Dreamweaver CS4 is the CSS Advisor, which provides descriptions and solutions for CSS problems found during the BCC. Located in the lower-right corner of the Browser Compatibility Check panel, the CSS Advisor provides a direct link to the CSS Advisor section of Adobe's web site to find a fix for any CSS issues found and displayed in the Results panel.

1   To use the CSS Advisor, from the Files panel, locate and open the ex5_water.html document for editing.

2   Choose File > Check Page > Browser Compatibility.

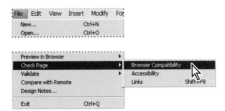

Choose File > Check Page > Browser Compatibility to run the BCC for this document.

3   The Results panel opens and displays any errors or issues in the Browser Compatibility Check tab. Items returned indicate any potential CSS display issues; each result is accompanied by a confidence rating icon that tells you how likely it is that the problem will occur. This page should return one error.

4   Because the error listed is within the external style sheet you will need to open it and run the check again. Click on the styles.css button at the top of your document and choose File > Check Page > Browser Compatibility. The errors found refer to a CSS property *filter* which would affect the rendering of this page in a number of different browsers. If you navigate through the styles.css style sheet you can locate the property on line 26.

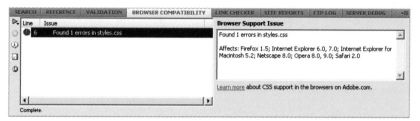

The Browser Compatibility Check tab on the Results panel displays a single error and description.

5   By default, the BCC checks for issues in the following browsers: Firefox 1.5; Internet Explorer (Windows) 6.0 and 7.0; Internet Explorer (Macintosh) 5.2; Netscape Navigator 8.0; Opera 8.0 and 9.0; and Safari 2.0. You can modify the target browsers and versions by choosing Settings from the green Run button (▸) on the BCC panel.

Optimizing pages for launch

Although page optimization is discussed at this point in the book, it is by no means an afterthought. A big part of preparing a site for success involves making it accessible to users with special needs, such as those who are visually impaired, or preparing it for indexing by various search engines. In addition to clean design and well-written content, pages can be optimized through the use of keywords, descriptions, and often-overlooked tag attributes, such as alternate text (alt) for images and a page's Title area. Combined, these pieces of information facilitate site usability and visibility in several essential ways.

Search engine visibility and Search Engine Optimization

A big part of a web site's success stems from its visibility. Visibility comes through good advertising, networking with other sites, and, above all, proper indexing and listings on the Web's major search engines. Search engines can be a key to generating business and visits to your site, but only if your web site can be easily found. Major search engines such as Google (which powers AOL, MySpace, and Netscape searches), Yahoo! (which powers AltaVista and others), and LiveSearch (formerly MSN Search) use a variety of factors to index and generate listings for web sites. Many of these factors start at home, or more appropriately, on your home page.

Titling your documents with the *<title>* tag

Each document's head area contains a *<title>* tag, which Dreamweaver automatically inserts with any new HTML/XHTML document. At its most basic, the *<title>* tag sets a display title for a page that appears at the top of the browser window. You can modify the *<title>* tag contents using the Title text field that sits at the top of your document window. By default, each new document is issued the default title of Untitled Document. The *<title>* tag and its contents, however, can be a powerful and effective way to assist search engines in indexing your page.

What makes a good title?

A good document title ideally should include keywords that describe your site's main service, locale, and category of business or information. In addition to the obvious—your company's name—think about the categories you would want your site to appear under on a web directory or as the result of a web search. For instance, the McKnight Institute would ideally want users looking for science museums or exhibits in the Philadelphia, Pennsylvania, area to find them first. A possible title could be: The McKnight Institute: Science Museum, Educational Exhibits and Attractions, Philadelphia, Pennsylvania.

This title contains several important keywords that describe the Institute's offerings, and features the Institute's name and location. In addition, re-shuffling these phrases and words produces several other search terms that could be beneficial to the Institute, such as:

- Science Exhibits
- Philadelphia Museum
- Pennsylvania Attractions

Avoid the rookie mistake of including only your company name in the document title. Remember, web searchers who haven't used your business before will only search by terms that apply to the service they are seeking (for example, wedding photographers, Washington, D.C.). Even the most recognized names on the web, such as eBay and Amazon, include generic search terms in their page titles.

To add a title to your web page:

1   From the Files panel, select and open the index.html document to open it for editing.

2   Locate the Title text field at the top of the document window. It currently displays the default title of Untitled Document. Select its contents and type **The McKnight Institute: Science Museum, Educational Exhibits and Attractions, Philadelphia, Pennsylvania** and press Enter (Windows) or Return (Mac OS).

*Add a well-constructed title to the index.html page
to make it more search-engine and bookmark friendly.*

3   Choose File > Save to save the document, and then choose File > Preview in Browser > [Default browser] to open the document in your system's primary browser.

4   Note the title that now appears in the bar at the top of the browser window. Close the browser window and return to Dreamweaver.

*The most basic purpose of the <title> tag is to display a title at the top of the browser window.
If used properly, it can also be used as a powerful hook for search engines.*

While there is technically no limit to title length, the W3C's Web Consortium Accessibility Guide recommends that page titles be a maximum of 64 characters to be considered 'well-defined.' Titles exceeding this length may generate warnings in the Site Reports Results panel. Longer titles may also appear truncated (cut off) when displayed in some browser windows.

Bookmark-ability: another benefit of the <*title*> tag

It's common for users to bookmark a site or specific page they've found so that they can easily return to it. Every browser has a bookmark feature, which allows users to mark and display favorite sites in an organized list; sometimes, favorite sites are listed in a Bookmarks bar in the browser window.

The document title determines the text that appears with a bookmark, so it's important to consider this when creating a good document title. Using a vague or non-descriptive title (or even worse, the default Untitled Document text) can make it impossible for a user to remember which bookmark is yours. A good title appears as a descriptive bookmark in a browser's Favorites list or Bookmarks bar.

Adding meta keywords and descriptions

While Search Engine Optimization (SEO) is a broad topic that's far beyond the scope of this book, good SEO methods begin at the design level. Search engines use a variety of factors to rank and list web pages. Keywords and descriptions can help specify the search terms that are associated with your site and how it's listed. The HTML <*meta*> tag enables you to associate any page with a specific list of search terms, as well as a brief description of the page or the web site itself. Like the <*title*> tag, <*meta*> tags are placed in the <*head*> section of a page, and can be added from the Common Insert bar on the right side of your workspace.

1   If it's not already open, open the index.html document for editing.

2   From the Common Insert bar, choose the Keywords button from the Head tags group.

3   When the Keywords field appears in the Property Inspector, add a comma-separated list of search keywords that you'd like associated with this page, or the site in general. While there is no general consensus on the limit of how many keywords you can use, common sense says that you should be able to categorize your site in roughly 20 keywords or fewer. For example, type **The McKnight Institute, science museum, technology exhibits, attractions, family attractions, philadelphia, pennsylvania museums**. Press Return (Windows) or Enter (Mac OS) to add the keywords.

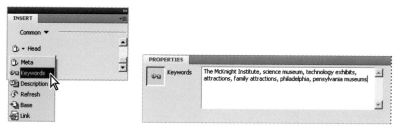

From the Common category of the Insert bar, choose the Keywords object from the Head tags group and enter a list of keywords in the resulting dialog box.

4   Now you'll add a description that a search engine can use to summarize your page when creating a listing for it. Choose the Description button from the Head tags group on the Common Insert bar.

5   When the Description dialog box appears, type in a brief descriptive paragraph (fewer than 250 characters, including spaces). For example, type **The McKnight Center is a family-oriented education center and museum that explores the history of technology and scientific discovery through hands-on exhibits and events**. Press OK.

Add a short description that search engines can use to display a caption for your site listing.

6   Choose File > Save, then choose File > Close to close the file.

Describing images with alternate text

Each image placed in your page can feature alternate text, which describes that image and also acts as a placeholder in its absence. Alternate text is added with the alt attribute of the *<img>* tag, and, for each image, alternate text can be specified using the Alt field located on the Property Inspector. In the past, alternate text was used as a placeholder for an image that failed to load, or for larger images downloading through slow dial-up connections.

With increased download speeds and the widespread availability of high-speed Internet access, this usage of the Alt attribute has been given a lower priority because of two more popular uses: accessibility and search engine visibility. Accessibility is an important part of web page design, and refers to a page or collective web site's usability by people with disabilities. Alternate text provides a way for disability assistants such as voice browsers, screen readers, and other specialized browsers to interpret and describe images and graphics included on a page. Visually impaired users frequently make use of screen readers to 'speak' the contents of a web page out loud.

Search engines such as Google Images make use of alternate text to provide information about image listings. The more accurate and concise the description, the more likely it is that users will find what they are looking for on your site. Also, well-indexed images are another hook that allows users to find your site—for example, a user searching for an image of a scientific nature may discover many of the images on the MKI site through an image search.

1   To add alt text to your page, first locate and open the ex4_sticky.html page from the Files panel.

2   Select the single image located in the middle of the page (stick.jpg). If necessary, choose Window > Properties to open the Property Inspector.

3   On the Property Inspector, locate the Alt text field. Type the words **The Science of Sticky Exhibit at MKI**, and press Return (Windows) or Enter (Mac OS). Leave the image selected.

Add alternate text for a selected image using the Alt field located on the Property Inspector.

4 Switch to Code view by clicking the Code button in the upper-left corner of the document window. Note the highlighted section of code, which should include an *<img>* tag. The tag will appear with an alt attribute with your new text set as its value.

The newly added alternate text, shown in Code view. Alternate text is added using the <img> tag's alt attribute.

5 Click the Design button at the top of the document window to return to Design view, and choose File > Save to save your page.

Rather than manually searching for missing titles or alternate text, use Dreamweaver's site reports, as shown earlier in this lesson, to generate listings of instances of missing alternate text throughout your site.

6 Choose File > Close to close the file.

Launching your site

Before launching your site for the public—and to ensure that your site works at, and looks, its best—take a moment to go over this pre-flight checklist.

Site Launch Checklist

☐ Enter FTP or upload information and test your FTP connection.

☐ Check links sitewide and repair missing or broken links and images.

☐ Run site reports and address crucial issues. Put special emphasis on:

☐ Missing document titles

☐ Missing alt text

☐ Invalid markup that may cause display issues

☐ Open the homepage (index.html, and so on) and navigate through your site, using menus, links in copy, and linked images to check page flow. Do this in several browsers, and, if possible, on both Windows and Macintosh platforms.

☐ View your home page and major section pages in a web browser in the three most common screen resolutions: 640x480, 800x600, and 1024x768.

Uploading your site

At this point, if you have been following along without having access to a remote FTP server, you will now require one to continue this lesson.

1   If you're ready to upload your site to the remote web server, make sure that the Files panel is open (Window > Files).

2   Click the Expand button (⊡) at the top of the Files panel to display it in two-column expanded view.

3   Click the Connect button (⅊) above the left (remote view) column to connect to your remote web server.

You need to have created a valid connection, as described earlier in the lesson.

Once a successful connection is made, the remote files (if any) display in the left-hand column.

4   In the right column, click and select the Folder icon at the very top of the file listing. This should be the root folder, and displays the current site definition title (Site Dreamweaver Lesson 5, for example).

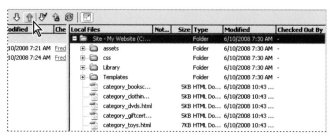

Select the root folder of your local site and click the Put button to upload the entire site to the web server.

5   Click the Put button at the top of the Files panel to copy the entire current local site and all included files to the current directory on the remote server. A dialog box appears with the message, *Are you sure you wish to put the entire site?*

6   Press OK to begin copying the files to the remote server. A progress bar continues to
    display until all files have been successfully copied.

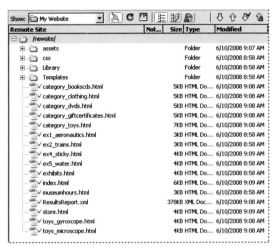

*The entire web site has been successfully uploaded to the server, and
displays in the remote view on the left.*

7   Collapse the Files panel to return it to the dock.

Getting help and using the reference guides

Whether you are seeking a solution to a Dreamweaver-specific problem, or looking up the
appropriate CSS rule to format a page item, you can use Dreamweaver's built-in Help system
and integrated reference guides. In addition, the Help menu provides direct links to many
online resources and Adobe support areas where you can seek help from Adobe professionals
and the Dreamweaver user community.

1   To access the Help system, choose Help > Dreamweaver Help. The Adobe Help Viewer
    panel appears.

2   Enter a search term at the top of the panel, or browse by topic on the left-hand side of
    the panel.

3   For more help options and a searchable knowledge base, choose Help > Dreamweaver
    Support Center. For the Dreamweaver support forums, choose Help > Adobe
    Online Forums.

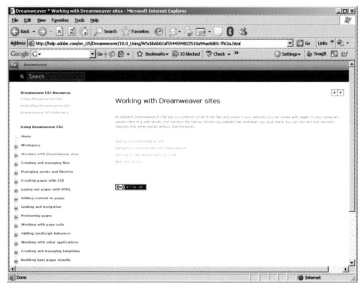

The Help menu.

The Reference panel

Dreamweaver's Reference panel is like a full library of technical books, including reference
guides for HTML, CSS, JavaScript, and Dreamweaver-friendly, server-side languages such as
ColdFusion and JSP.

1   To open the Reference panel, choose Help > Reference.

2   From the menu at the top left corner of the panel, select the *Usablenet Accessibility
    Reference* from the Book menu.

3   Click on the Rule menu and a list of various guidelines to help you make your web
    sites more accessible is listed. Choosing any topic reveals detailed information in the
    window below.

Suggested next steps

Congratulations on launching your first Dreamweaver site project! There's nothing more exciting than having your hard work on the web, and available for the world to see. The important thing to remember is that your web site should not be static; part of maintaining a successful web site requires continuously evolving it to meet the needs of your viewers, and keeping the content fresh and new.

Whether your site is for business, pleasure, or self-promotion, be sure to solicit feedback from friends, family, and colleagues after you've launched. Alert a small and trusted group about the launch by sending out an e-mail, mailing a postcard, or posting a notice on a blog (sometimes this is referred to as the 'beta' stage). Feedback and constructive criticism (a little praise is okay, too) are the best ways to objectively know what needs improvement. You'll probably receive more feedback and suggestions than you can handle, so focus on points that are common across multiple users, and address any major issues before making a more public launch (for instance, to your entire client base).

Focus on focus groups

Focus groups are an excellent way to get non-biased feedback on a major new site or product launch, and they have been a regular practice in product marketing and research for years. A focus group is composed of a group of individuals who are brought together to analyze, try out, and comment on a specific product—in this case, your web site—for the purpose of obtaining feedback and testing the product's effectiveness.

Groups can be guided through certain portions or processes on the site, or may be encouraged to navigate it on their own. Afterwards, they are polled with specific questions about their experience, and the results are put together to form a picture of the site's usability, effectiveness, and impact. This may include questions such as the following:

- Did you feel the web site was easy to navigate? On a scale from 1 to 10, how would you rate the difficulty level in locating specific pages or topics?

- Did the design, including graphics and color themes, effectively help communicate the web site's offerings?

- On a scale from 1 to 10, how would you rate the quality of the written content on the site?

Focus groups are often interactive, encouraging participants to talk with each other and share their opinions. In some cases, a moderator may be used to regulate group discussions, and hand out questionnaires. Participants can be composed of a focused demographic group (for instance, 25- to 35-year-old technology professionals), or they can represent a diverse professional and demographic range.

Focus groups are reasonable for any size company to organize—even if it's just you and five friends—and are a highly effective way to find out what's currently working and what's not. Give it a try; you may find the results encouraging, surprising, or even slightly discouraging. The trick is to use this feedback wisely toward the main purpose of making a better web site, and you'll be glad you did.

Web site design resources

There is a vast amount of information, and many tutorial-based web sites, covering topics from web page standards to advanced CSS design. Here is a small sampling of some useful sites that can help you take your skills and knowledge further. Use these in conjunction with Dreamweaver's built-in reference guides and Adobe's online support forums:

W3C (World Wide Web Consortium) – *www.w3.org*

W3Schools – *www.w3schools.com*

A List Apart – *http://alistapart.com/*

Adobe's Dreamweaver Developer Center – *www.adobe.com/devnet/dreamweaver/*

CSS Zengarden – *www.csszengarden.com/*

maxdesign – *http://css.maxdesign.com.au/*

CSSplay – *www.cssplay.co.uk/www*

Self study

1   Import a site from a previous lesson from this book or import your own site, and run a site report for broken links, orphaned files, and so on.

2   Investigate Dreamweaver's CSS Advisor by examining various files from this lesson and previous lessons. Using the CSS Advisor is a great way to learn more about CSS and browser compatibility issues.

Review

Questions

1 What does FTP stand for, and what is it used for?

2 What three purposes do document titles serve, and why are they important?

3 What are three possible pre-flight checklist items you need to address before launching a web site?

Answers

1 File Transfer Protocol. FTP is used to connect to and transfer files between your local machine and a web server.

2 Document titles display a title at the top of the browser window, display in a user's bookmarks bar, and are an important hook for search engines.

3 **a**. Enter and test your FTP connection information in the Site Definition panel.

b. Run site reports to rectify any potential design or accessibility issues, such as missing alternate text for images or empty document titles.

c. Run the Link Checker sitewide to check for broken links between pages or incorrect image references.

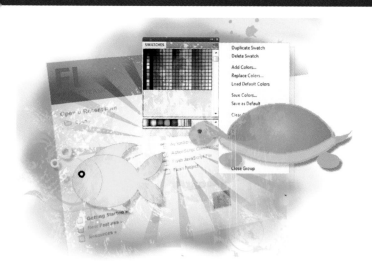

What you'll learn in this lesson:

- Using Flash's key features and capabilities

- Exploring the Flash Player

- Saving and opening documents

- Examining the Flash workspace

- Understanding illustration and animation essentials

Flash CS4 Jumpstart

This lesson takes you through the basics you'll need to get up-and-running with Flash CS4 Professional.

Starting up

In this lesson, you will set up a new Flash document and work with several prepared files to explore Flash's tools and features.

Before starting, make sure that your tools and panels are consistent by resetting your workspace. See "Resetting the Flash workspace" on page XXVII.

You will work with several files from the fl01lessons folder in this lesson. Make sure that you have loaded the CS4lessons folder onto your hard drive from the supplied DVD. See "Loading lesson files" on page XXIX.

See Lesson 1 in action!

Use the accompanying video to gain a better understanding of how to use some of the features shown in this lesson. The video tutorial for this lesson can be found on the included DVD.

What is Flash?

You may have heard about Flash and seen it on eye-catching web sites, online games, and banner advertisements. But did you know that you can use Flash for more than creating animated graphics? With Flash CS4 Professional, you can also manipulate video and sound, and even connect to databases to build web-based applications, such as shopping carts, or display news feeds of continuously updated information.

There are four key feature areas in Flash CS4 Professional:

Drawing environment. Flash features a complete set of drawing tools to handle intricate illustration and typography. Like its cousin, Adobe Illustrator CS4, Flash is a native vector-drawing application where you'll create rich, detailed, and scalable digital illustrations. Flash now supports Illustrator and Photoshop files in their native file formats, .ai and .psd, making it easy to work with your favorite applications. All the content you create in Flash or these other programs can be brought to life through animation and interactivity.

Animation. Flash creates lightweight animation that incorporates images, sound, and video, and can be quickly downloaded through the web. It has become a favorite—and essential—tool among web designers and developers who want to take their creativity to a whole new level. Flash animation is featured on web sites, CD-ROMs, and interactive games, and has become very popular for developing interactive, web-based advertisements. Flash's compact files make it the ideal application for creating animated content, games, and applications for mobile phones and PDAs.

Flash supports traditional frame-by-frame animation as well as its own method of animation, known as tweening. With tweening, you specify an object to animate, create starting and ending frames, and Flash automatically creates the frames in between (hence *tween*) to create slick motion, color, and transformation effects. You'll design your own Flash animations in Flash Lesson 3, "Creating Basic Animation."

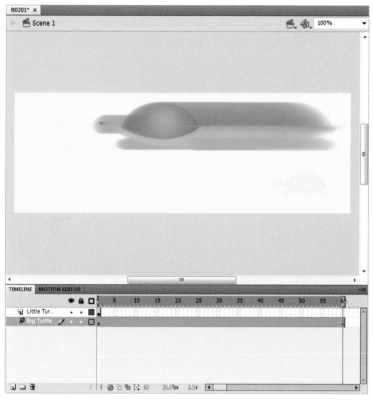

Flash's animation tweening generates slick animation between starting and ending frames.

Layout. The Flash Stage gives you the flexibility to create extraordinary web site layouts without the design restrictions that are typical of HTML-based web pages. You can position content anywhere on the Flash Stage with flexibility and precision, taking your layouts far beyond the limitations of static web pages. Flash movies can also include any typefaces you choose, allowing you to use fancy typography and unusual fonts freely on your web pages, which is typically difficult outside of Flash.

Programming. Hidden beneath the beauty of Flash CS4 Professional is the brain of ActionScript, a powerful, built-in scripting language that extends your capabilities beyond simple design and animation. With basic ActionScript, you can control movie playback or give functionality to buttons. If you venture deeper, ActionScript can turn Flash into a full-fledged, application-building environment to create shopping carts, music players, games, and mobile phone applications.

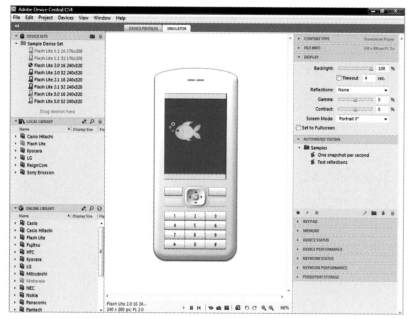

Flash can develop lightweight games for phones, PDAs, and other consumer devices.

About Flash Player

The Flash Player is a standalone application found most often as a plug-in to such popular browsers as Internet Explorer, Safari, and Firefox. The Flash Player is required to play compressed Flash movies (.swf files), much like a movie projector is needed to play film reels.

The Flash Player is much more than just a playback machine, however. It reads instructions written in ActionScript to add rich interactivity to your movies.

As of this writing, the Flash Player is installed on more than 99 percent of Internet-enabled computers, so a majority of your online audience is already equipped to view your Flash creations. For users who do not have Flash Player installed, it is available as a free download from the Adobe web site, *adobe.com*.

Flash Player 10, including both a standalone application and browser plug-in, is automatically installed with the Flash CS4 Professional application.

Flash file types

You'll work with two types of files in Flash: .fla and .swf. Each one has a very specific purpose in the process of creating your Flash movie.

When you create and save a new document, Flash generates an .fla (Flash authoring) document. These are the working documents you'll use to design, edit, and store resources such as graphics, images, sound, and video. Additionally, each .fla document stores its own unique settings for final publishing. Because they are intended for designing and editing, .fla files can't be viewed with the Flash Player—they're used as the foundation to publish your final movie files in the .swf file format.

Shockwave Flash, or .swf, files are completed, compressed movie files exported from the Flash CS4 Professional application. These files, created from your original .fla authoring files, are the only format the Flash Player can display and play. Although you can import .swf files into the Flash CS4 Professional application, you cannot edit them; you will need to reopen the original .fla files to make changes or additions.

Now that you know what you're going to be working with, it's time to get your first Flash document started and begin exploring the Flash CS4 Professional workspace.

Creating a new document

Before you can draw or animate, you need to create a new document, or more specifically, an .fla file where all your work takes place. You can create and open documents from the Welcome Screen or from the File menu at the top of the screen.

The Welcome Screen is the launch pad for creating and opening files, including handy, built-in sample templates for common document types, such as advertising banners and graphics for cell phones. The Welcome Screen appears when Flash is first launched or when no documents are open in the application.

The Welcome Screen is the launch pad for new documents, including many templates for common projects.

1 To create a new .fla document using the Welcome Screen, open Flash CS4 Professional. If the application is already open, close any files that are currently open using File > Close All.

2 From the Create New column in the middle of the Welcome Screen, select Flash File (ActionScript 3.0). Your workspace, including the Stage, Timeline, and Tools panel, appears.

Alternatively, you can create a new .fla document using the File menu. If you already created a new document using the Welcome Screen, this is not necessary.

3 Choose File > New. The New Document dialog box appears.

4 Select Flash File (ActionScript 3.0), and press OK to create the new document. Your workspace appears.

Setting up your new document

Now that you've created your new Flash file, take a moment to specify some important settings for it. These settings, or properties, will prepare your document before you get to work.

1   Choose Modify > Document or use the keyboard shortcut Ctrl+J (Windows) or Command+J (Mac OS) to open the Document Properties dialog box.

2   In the Width and Height fields, type **500** and **300**, respectively, to set the size of your movie. These dimensions set the width and height of the Stage, measured in pixels. The size of the Stage is identical to the size of your final movie, so make sure the size accommodates the design you want to create.

3   Click on the Background Color swatch (▭) and the Swatches panel appears. This lets you choose the color of your Stage and, in turn, the background color for your final movie (.swf file) when it's published. If necessary, set the background color to white (#FFFFFF).

4   Type **30** in the Frame rate field to set your movie's frame rate to 30 fps (frames per second). The frame rate determines the playback speed and performance of your movie.

The Match to Printer option sets your new document to match the paper size of your default system printer. This option is typically set to Default, requiring you to specify the width and height, or use the default Dimensions settings stored in Flash.

5   From the Ruler units drop-down menu, choose Pixels, if it is not already selected, to define the unit of measurement used throughout your Flash movie, including rulers, panels, and dialog boxes.

6   Press OK to exit the Document Properties dialog box and apply these settings. Leave the new document open. You'll save it in the next part of this lesson.

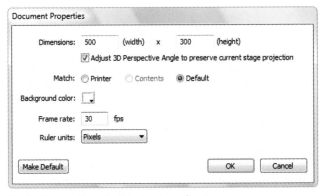

Use the Document Properties dialog box to specify settings.

If you are new to designing for the web, the concept of pixels may feel a bit alien to you. It helps to remember that there are generally 72 pixels in one inch for size calculation. If you prefer, you can use the Document Properties dialog box at any time to change the Ruler units for your file to a different unit of measurement.

Saving your Flash document

Your new document should be saved before starting any work or adding any content. By default, the application saves documents in Flash CS4 (.fla) format.

1 Choose File > Save.

2 In the Save As dialog box that appears, type fl0201_work.fla into the Name text field. Navigate to the fl01lessons folder, and press Save. Choose File > Close to close the document.

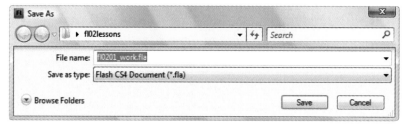

Use the Save dialog box to choose a name and location for your new file.

 Always include the .fla extension at the end of your filename to make it easy to identify the file format.

To share your work with designers using earlier versions of Flash, you can choose to save your document in Flash CS3 format. Flash CS4 Professional format files will not open in previous versions of Flash, unless you set the format to Flash CS3 when saving the file. Flash CS4 Professional can open files created in older versions of Flash.

Get started with sample templates

Flash includes a variety of sample templates to streamline the process of setting up common Flash projects. Creating files from these templates will pre-configure options such as document size and ActionScript version. Choose File > New > Template to view Flash's included templates.

In the Advertising section, templates include common banner sizes. Be aware that creating files from these templates sets the Flash player and ActionScript versions extremely conservatively for maximum compatibility. If you were planning on using the latest and greatest techniques and features in your project, this may be constricting.

The Handset and Devices categories automatically set document size to the appropriate resolution for the selected device. These templates also use appropriate versions of Flash Lite.

The Photo Slideshow category with its included Modern Photo Slideshow template is a quick and easy way to create a photo slideshow. Simply repopulate the file with your own photos. All the appropriate ActionScript has been written for you.

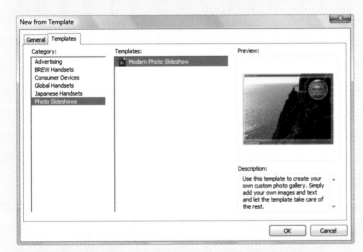

The Modern Photo Slideshow is one of the many useful templates available from the New from Template dialog box.

Opening documents

Knowing how to open documents is as important as knowing how to save them. In addition to files created in Flash CS4 Professional, such as those included with this book, you can open documents created in previous versions of Flash. The steps are simple.

1   Choose File > Open. Use the Open dialog box to locate the fl0201_work.fla file you previously saved into the fl01lessons folder.

2   Select the fl0201_work.fla file, then press Open. Leave this file open. You will be using it in the next exercise.

Don't confuse the Open command with the Import options also found in the File menu. To access files created in other applications, such as Photoshop or Illustrator, you must use the Import menu.

If you want to reopen a document on which you have recently worked, there's a shortcut. To list the last ten documents you've opened, and to reopen one, choose File > Open Recent, then select the file you need.

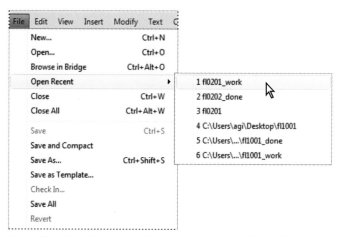

Choose File > Open Recent to access the last ten documents opened in Flash.

You can also open files using the Open button ( ) at the bottom of the Open Recent Items column on the Welcome Screen. Above this icon, you'll see the last eight documents you worked on; this is a useful alternative to the Open Recent menu option.

The Flash workspace

Now that you know how to create, save, and open Flash documents, you're ready to get familiar with the workspace where you'll spend your time creating Flash content.

The Stage and work area

After you create a Flash document, the center of your screen, called the *Stage*, is where the action happens. The Stage is the visible area of your movie, where you place graphics and build animations. By default, the Flash Stage appears white, but, as you saw earlier, you can change this from the Document Properties dialog box using the Modify > Document command.

The gray area surrounding the Stage is the *work area*; artwork you place or create here is not included in your final movie. Think of this area as the *backstage*; for instance, you can animate a character to enter from the work area onto the Stage. The work area is also a good place to store objects that are not ready to appear in your movie. The Stage reflects the actual size of the movie you create when it is published.

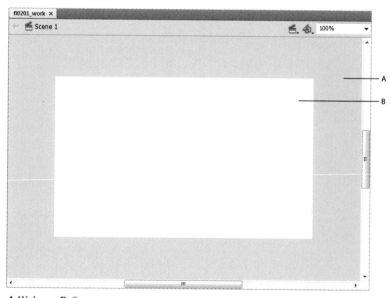

A. Work area. *B. Stage.*

The Flash Tools panel

The Flash Tools panel includes everything you need to create, select, or edit graphics on the Stage. You can use the double arrows at the top of the Tools panel to collapse the panel icon-only view, or to expand the panel and see all of the tools.

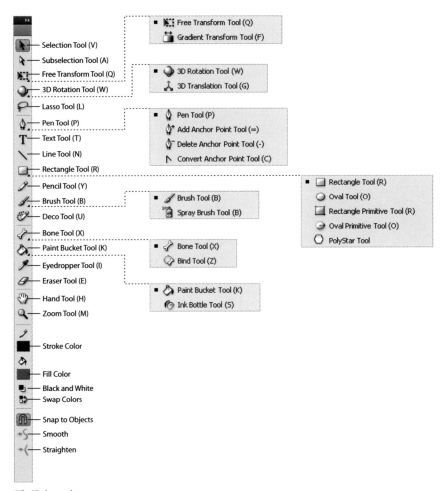

The Tools panel.

Selection tools

ICON	TOOL NAME	USE	WHERE IT'S COVERED
➤	Selection	Moves selections or layers.	Lessons 1
⬉	Subselection	Selects and moves points on a path.	Lesson 2
⬚	Free Transform	Resizes, rotates, and skews objects.	Lesson 3
◯	Lasso	Makes selections.	Lesson 2
⟳	3D Rotation	Rotates objects in 3D space	Not referenced in this book

Drawing and Text tools

ICON	TOOL NAME	USE	WHERE IT'S COVERED
✒	Pen	Draws a vector path.	Lesson 2
T	Text	Creates a text box.	Lesson 2
╲	Line	Draws straight lines.	Lesson 2
▢	Shapes	Draws vector shapes.	Lesson 2
✐	Pencil	Draws freehand paths.	Lesson 2
⟋	Brush	Draws freehand filled areas.	Not referenced in this book
✣	Deco	Creates patterns using symbols	Lesson 3

Color tools

ICON	TOOL NAME	USE	WHERE IT'S COVERED
⬗	Ink Bottle	Applies or modifies strokes.	Lessons 2
⬖	Paint Bucket	Applies or modifies fills.	Lessons 2
⟋	Eyedropper	Samples colors and styles.	Lessons 2
▱	Eraser	Erases artwork.	Not referenced in this book
✦	Bone	Creates Inverse Kinematic objects	Not referenced in this book

Navigation tools

ICON	TOOL NAME	USE	WHERE IT'S COVERED
🖐	Hand	Navigates the page.	Lesson 1
🔍	Zoom	Increases or decreases the relative size of the view.	Lesson 1

Stroke and fill color selectors

ICON	TOOL NAME	USE	WHERE IT'S COVERED
✏	Stroke Color	Selects stroke (outline) color	Lesson 2
🖌	Fill Color	Selects fill (inside) color	Lesson 2
🗗	Default Stroke/Fill	Sets stroke and fill to default colors: black and white.	Lesson 2
🔁	Swap Colors	Swaps stroke and fill colors	Lesson 2
⊘	No Color	Sets selected color to none	Lesson 2

Tool options

ICON	TOOL NAME	USE	WHERE IT'S COVERED
🧲	Snap to Objects	Enables snapping between objects on the Stage.	Not referenced in this book

The Property Inspector

The Property Inspector appears on the right side of your Flash workspace. Grouped with the Library panel, it displays properties and options for objects selected on the Stage, and also allows you to modify them. The Property Inspector is contextual, and so the information it displays is specific to the tool or object you select.

The Property Inspector is an essential part of the Flash workflow; it can display and set an object's properties, including width, height, position, and fill color. Let's take a look at the Property Inspector in action.

1   If the fl0201_work.fla file is not still open from the last exercise, choose File > Open to reopen it from inside the fl01lessons folder. Select the Rectangle tool (□) from the Tools panel.

2   At the bottom of the Tools panel, click the Fill Color swatch (⌂). When the Swatches panel appears, choose a yellow shade from the right side of the Swatches panel.

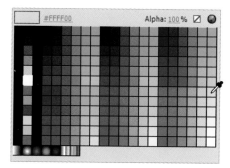

Choose fill and stroke colors using the swatches at the bottom of the Tools panel.

3   Move your cursor to the center of the Stage. Click and hold, then drag to draw a new rectangle. Release the mouse button after you have created a rectangle at the center of the Stage.

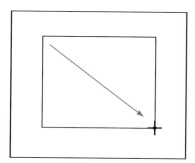

To draw shapes on the Stage, select a Shape tool, then click and drag.

4   Choose the Selection tool (\) from the top of the Tools panel, and double-click the fill of the new shape to select it. Notice that the Property Inspector on the right side of the workspace now displays the selected shape's width (W) and height (H) in pixels. Above the width and height, the object's X and Y positions on the Stage are also displayed.

5   Click the underlined number next to W: to highlight the current value, then type **250** to set the rectangle's width. Press Enter (Windows) or Return (Mac OS). Use this same method to set the height to 150.

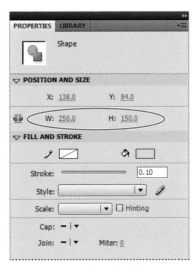

You can set properties for a selected shape using the Property Inspector.

6   Choose the Text tool (T) from the Tools panel. Click above the new rectangle you created and type the phrase **Flash CS4**. Notice that the Property Inspector now displays text options such as font and size.

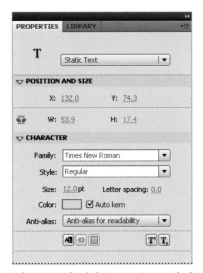

When text is selected, the Property Inspector displays relevant options such as font and size.

7 Click and drag inside the new text box to select all the text. In the Property Inspector, locate the Family drop-down menu and choose Arial (or, if that's unavailable, Verdana). Click on the Size and set the type size to 45.

8 In the Property Inspector, click the Color swatch and choose a blue shade from the Swatches panel that appears to change the color of your type. In this exercise, the color #000099 was used.

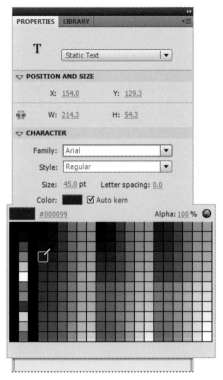

Select and format type directly from the Property Inspector.

9   Choose File > Save to save your work, then choose File > Close.

In addition to text and graphics, the Property Inspector also works with the Timeline, allowing you to set options and view information for specific frames. You will use this essential tool throughout the lessons to modify objects on the Stage, and frames in the Timeline.

The Property Inspector shows options for an active tool or information about a selected object, even frames on the Timeline.

Panels and panel groups

The Flash workspace is extremely flexible. It is organized into a series of panels, many of which you'll become quite familiar with, including the Library panel, Property Inspector, and Timeline. You're free to arrange any of these panels however you like. You can also open panels that are not available in the default workspace and arrange, group, and resize them to suit your needs.

Panels can be freely repositioned, resized, and grouped.

Eventually you'll want to take control of your workspace and customize it to your preference, but for now, the flexibility of the workspace might be more confusing than advantageous. If you mistakenly drag panels around and start losing them, you can always reset your panels to their default positions by choosing Window > Workspace > Essentials. If you're migrating to Flash CS4 from an earlier version, you may also be interested in the Classic option found in this menu. For the sake of consistency, this book uses the default CS4 workspace.

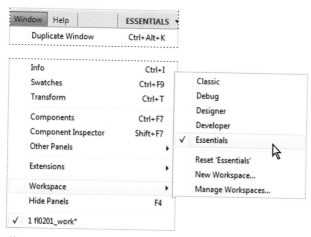

Choose Window > Workspace > Essentials to reset your workspace to the Flash CS4 defaults.

It's also important to note that each panel features a panel menu that can be accessed from the button in the top-right corner. This menu contains options that may or may not be available inside the panel. Sometimes this menu is superfluous; sometimes it's integral. Just remember to keep it in the back of your mind. It's usually the first place to look if you can't find an option that you're looking for.

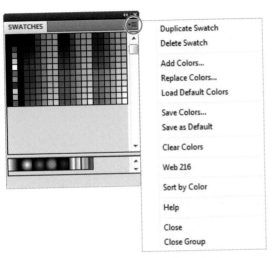

Panel menus are accessed using the button in the top-right corner.

The Timeline

The Flash Timeline is the heart of the action, where you create animations and sequence graphics with sound, video, and controls. The Timeline comprises frames, each one representing a point in time, just like a historical timeline. Graphics and animations are placed at specific points, or keyframes, along the Timeline to create sequences, slide shows, or movies. You can place ActionScript on individual keyframes to control playback and add interactivity, or place sounds along the Timeline to add sound effects, music, and dialogue.

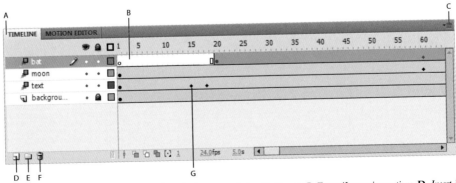

A. Click and drag to undock the Timeline from the document window. B. Frames. C. Frame/Layer view options. D. Insert Layer. E. Insert Layer Folder. F. Delete Layer. G. Keyframe.

The Timeline also comprises layers; layers behave like transparent pieces of film stacked on top of one another. Each animation and piece of artwork can be placed on its own individual layer, which helps you organize and manage your work. If you've worked with other Adobe CS4 applications, such as Illustrator, Photoshop, or InDesign, you may already be familiar with the power and flexibility of layers. Like all panels, the Timeline has a panel menu. Most of the options included in the Timeline's panel menu relate to customizing its display. Here you can adjust the size of layers and frames and turn on Preview mode to display the objects included on each layer as a thumbnail in the Timeline.

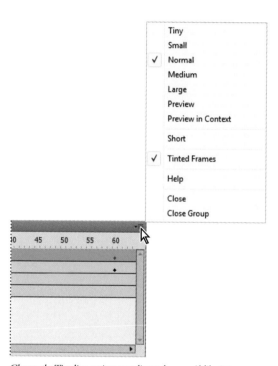

Change the Timeline settings according to how you'd like it to appear.

In this exercise, you'll explore a Timeline with multiple keyframes, animations, and layers to see how a typical Flash document looks.

1   Choose File > Open, and select the fl0203.fla document inside the fl01lessons folder. Press Open to open it for editing.

2   Examine the Timeline below the Stage. You'll see that it contains a layer, with a layer folder above it. Layer folders can contain layers and are used to organize the Timeline when layers start to add up. Click the arrow to the left of the Gears layer folder to expand it and reveal its contents. The three indented layers under the Gears name are the layers that are inside the folder.

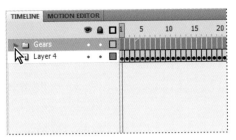
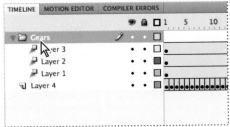

Click the arrow to the left of a layer folder to expand it.

3   Each of the three layers contains a separate animation that is marked at the beginning and end with a keyframe. Keyframes are special frames that are created along the Timeline where you want to introduce or remove a graphic, start or end an animation, or trigger something to happen with ActionScript. A blue background on frames indicates a Motion tween animation. Press Enter (Windows) or Return (Mac OS) to play the Timeline.

4   Look at Layer 4 in the Timeline, which contains several consecutive keyframes. Click once on each keyframe to jump to that frame and see what it displays at that specific point in time.

5   To shuttle through the Timeline, grab the playhead at the top (indicated by the red marker), and drag it in either direction.

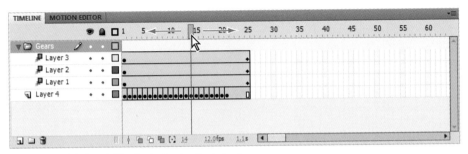

Shuttle back and forth in the Timeline by dragging the playhead.

6   Choose File > Close to close the current document. If prompted to save any changes, press Don't Save.

Tabbing between open documents

When you have more than one document open at a time, each document displays its own tab at the top of the document window. Click on a document's tab to switch to it and bring it forward for editing. To close the active document, you can choose File > Close, or use the small *x* that appears at the top of the document's tab. To close all open documents at once, choose File > Close All.

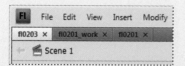

Tab easily between multiple documents at a time.

The Swatches panel

You'll see the swatch icon (☐) quite a few times in Flash—it opens the Swatches panel, which is used to set colors for backgrounds, fills, outlines, and type. You can choose from 256 web-safe colors and seven preset gradients, or create your own. You will learn how to add your own custom colors and gradients to the Swatches panel in Flash Lesson 2, "Getting Started with the Drawing Tools."

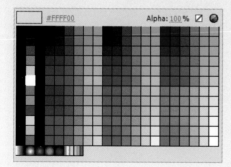

The Flash CS4 Swatches panel.

The six-character code at the top of the Swatches panel is a hexadecimal code, the standard color-coding system for the web. As you choose colors from the Swatches panel, you'll see the hexadecimal value for the selected color displayed at the top. The Color Picker in Adobe CS4 applications such as Illustrator and Photoshop also features hexadecimal values, so you can easily match colors between applications by copying and pasting the code shown.

Practicing with the Flash tools

Now that you've had a tour of the Flash tools and workspace, it's time to take them for a test drive. In the following exercises, you'll complete the illustration shown in fl0202_fish.fla while getting the feel for the selection, drawing, and transformation tools. You'll also use Flash tweening to create your first animation.

The drawing and selection tools in action

Your first steps will be to create and modify shapes and freehand artwork with the drawing tools, and then fine-tune your work with the selection tools. The selection tools work as a team with the drawing tools to position and modify shapes, illustrations, and type.

1   If you haven't done so already, open the fl0202.fla file located in the fl01lessons folder.

2   Choose File > Save As; the Save As dialog box appears. In the Name text field, type **fl0202_work.fla**, then navigate to the fl01lessons folder and press Save.

3   Choose the Selection tool (**k**) in the Tools panel. This versatile tool can select, move, and manipulate objects directly on the Stage.

4   On the Stage, click once on the fin above the fish's body to select it. Click and drag it downward until it joins with the body. Release the mouse button.

Use the Selection tool to select and move objects on the Stage.

5   You need to make a copy of this fin to use on the bottom of the fish. The easiest way is to clone it, or to drag a copy from the original. To do this, click the top fin once to select it, then, while holding the Alt (Windows) or Option (Mac OS) key, click and drag a copy away from the original fin.

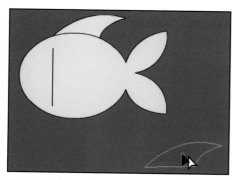

Hold down Alt (Windows) or Option (Mac OS) and drag an object to clone it.

6   Because the new copy will serve as the bottom fin, you'll need to flip it around so it's pointed in the proper direction. Click once to select the new fin copy, and choose Modify > Transform > Flip Vertical. This Transform menu command flips the fin so it's pointed in the right direction.

The Transform menu features commands that flip, skew, and rotate a selected object.

7   Still using the Selection tool, click and drag the new fin copy to the bottom of the fish's body, and leave it selected.

8   The new fin is almost there, but it's a bit big. There are several places within Flash where you can resize an object, including the Transform panel; choose Window > Transform to open it.

9   With the new fin selected, type **60** in the horizontal and vertical Scale fields at the top of the panel and press Enter or Return to commit the change. The fin is reduced to 60 percent of its original size.

The Transform panel precisely resizes objects by a set percentage.

Notice the Constrain button (⊶) (Windows) or the Constrain checkbox (Mac OS) next to the Transform panel's Width and Height scale text fields. When you check this box, you can enter a size in only one field and Flash automatically resizes the selected object proportionally.

10 To add an eye to your fish, select the Oval tool (○) from the Tools panel. You may need to click and hold on the Rectangle tool (□) to access this tool. At the bottom of the Tools panel, click on the Fill color swatch and choose black as the fill color.

11 The Oval tool lets you manipulate shapes even further; here, you'll add an inner radius to ovals to create ring-style shapes. In the Property Inspector, type **50** in the Inner radius text field and press Enter or Return.

12 Select Layer 1 in the Timeline by clicking on the name, and click and drag on the left side of the fish to draw a small oval, which will serve as the fish's eye. Make sure to position your oval before de-selecting it to avoid removing color from the fish below.

To create perfect circles, hold down the Shift key while drawing ovals.

Use the Oval tool with an inner radius to add an eye to your fish.

Congratulations! You've designed your first graphic object in Flash. However, this fish is rather basic.

Using gradient and color tools

Now you'll add some depth and more vibrant color to your fish, using the gradient colors and artistic stroke styles.

1   Choose the Selection tool (↖) from the Tools panel, and click once inside the body of the fish; a dotted pattern indicates the fill area is selected.

2   To change the body's color, click on the Fill color swatch at the bottom of the Tools panel. In the resulting Swatches panel, choose the orange/yellow gradient located at the bottom of the panel to apply it to the selected area. Deselect the fish by choosing Edit > Deselect All or by clicking offstage in the gray work area.

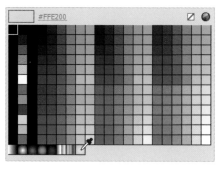
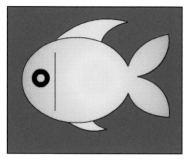

Give your fish more depth by filling it with a gradient from your Swatches panel.

3 The Eyedropper tool (✐) enables you to sample a color from one object and transfer it to another. You'll use it to apply the body color to the fish's fins. Using the Selection tool (↖), hold down the Shift key and click once on each fin so that both are selected at the same time. Select the Eyedropper tool from the Tools panel. Click once on the body of the fish to sample the new color and apply it to the selected fins.

4 Choose Edit > Deselect All to deselect all items on the Stage. In the Tools panel, click and hold the Paint Bucket tool (⬥) and select the Ink Bottle tool (⬥) from the menu that appears. The Ink Bottle tool lets you change an object's stroke color. You'll use the Property Inspector to set a stroke color and style to apply.

5 In the Property Inspector, click the Stroke color swatch and type **#FF6600** (orange) into the hexadecimal field at the top-left corner of the Swatches panel that appears. Press Enter or Return to set this color.

6 Click on the Style menu that appears below the color swatches. Choose the ragged style from the drop-down menu.

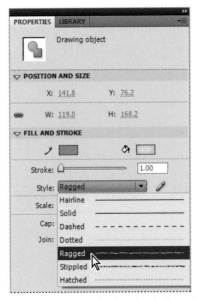

Choose a stroke color and style and apply them using the Ink Bottle tool.

7 Click on the edge of the fish body to apply the new stroke color and style. Click on the edge of the remaining two fins and the gill line to apply the same color and stroke style to all three. Choose Edit > Deselect All to deselect any active items on the Stage.

8 Choose the Selection tool from the top of the Tools panel. Move the pointer slightly to the right of the gill line without touching it; a small curve appears below your pointer. Click and drag slightly to the right to bend the gill line into a curve.

The Selection tool can bend straight lines or distort shapes.

9 Click and hold the Rectangle tool (▢) in the Tools panel and select the Oval tool (⊖). Click the Fill color swatch at the bottom of the Tools panel, and choose a light blue color. Click the Stroke color swatch and set your stroke color to No color (☑).

10 While holding down the Shift key, draw several ovals in front of the fish to create bubbles.

11 Choose File > Save to save your work.

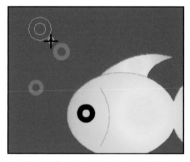

Use the Oval Primitive tool to draw bubbles in front of your fish.

12 Choose File > Open, select the fl0202_done.fla file in the fl01lessons folder, and press Open to open it. Compare your work against the completed file fl0202_done.fla. Choose File > Close All to close all currently open documents.

You're off to a good start with the drawing tools. You will work with these tools in more depth in Flash Lesson 2, "Getting Started with the Drawing Tools."

Animation in action

Flash is known for powerful, yet easy-to-use animation that you create directly in the Timeline. The Timeline displays content over periods of time, represented on the Timeline in frames. Each frame can be set as a keyframe, where items can be placed and animation can start or end.

Flash can generate animation with little more than a starting point and ending point; this method is known as tweening. You tell Flash where you want an object to start and stop its animation, and it figures out the frames in between. To apply the same animation behavior to more than one object on the Stage, you'll use the new Copy Motion and Paste Motion features.

1   Choose File > Open and, when prompted, select the fl0201.fla file in the fl01lessons folder. Press Open. Two tortoises appear on the Stage. In the next steps you'll animate the big turtle crossing the stage.

2   Using the Selection tool (ᴋ), click on the big turtle. Notice that the Big Turtle layer in the Timeline is highlighted in blue, along with the 60 frames included in the Big Turtle layer. Right-click (Windows) or Ctrl+click (Mac OS) on the big turtle and choose Create Motion Tween from the context menu.

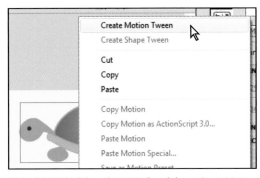

Right-click/Ctrl+click on the Big Turtle and choose Create Motion Tween from the context menu.

Motion tweens allow you to easily create animations by simply adjusting an object's properties at different points on the Timeline. Flash takes care of all the heavy lifting.

3   Click and drag the playhead to frame 60.

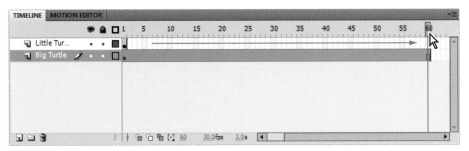

Drag the playhead to frame 60.

4   Click and drag the big turtle to the left side of the stage (just before the head reaches the edge). When you release the mouse, you will see a green motion spline appear between his old location and his new one.

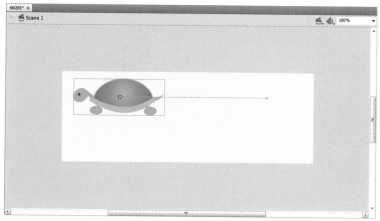

The big turtle repositioned.

5   Press Enter or Return to preview your first animation. It feels good, doesn't it?

Getting help

If at any point you can't find a specific command, want to know how a tool works, or want to learn how to complete a certain task, you can always consult the Flash Help menu. The Help menu launches the Help viewer (an all-in-one glossary, troubleshooter, and reference manual), and also provides links to key Adobe forums and support centers.

The Flash Help viewer is a good source for quick answers.

1   Choose Help > Flash Help.

2   When the panel appears, use the categorized list on the left, or type in a search term to get help on a specific topic or keyword.

Support forums

Adobe's Flash forums can be a rich source of answers, ideas, and tips from experts and other avid Flash users. You can search for answers to common questions or post your own topics and questions.

1   Choose Help > Flash Developer Center. The Support forum launches in your system's default browser.

2   In the search field in the upper-right corner, enter terms you want to explore, then press the Search button.

3   To post topics, questions, or replies, click the Your Account link at the top of the page to log in with your Adobe ID.

You must register to post questions or replies to Adobe's Flash forums.

Moving forward

In the next chapter, you'll put pen to paper (or mouse to Stage, rather) to get your creativity flowing with the Flash drawing tools. Now that you've become familiar with the workspace, things should be just a bit easier. Don't hesitate to reference this chapter again to refresh your memory.

Self study

Create and save a new document in the fl01lessons folder. Use the Property Inspector to set dimensions, background color, and frame rate. Experiment with the drawing tools you've learned so far, to create artwork on the Stage, and use the Selection tool to move and adjust the artwork as needed.

To get a feel for the workspace, experiment with different panel setups and positions. The Workspace menu (Window > Workspace) features some presets that show how you can maximize the space in your work area.

Try animating the little turtle in fl0201.fla. Experiment with animating other properties using the Property Inspector.

Review

Questions

1 From what two locations can you open a document that was previously open?

2 What panel allows you to view information about a selected object, or set options for an active tool?

3 What method does Flash use to automatically create animation from a starting and ending point?

Answers

1 From File > Open Recent, or the Open a Recent Item column on the Welcome Screen.

2 The Property Inspector.

3 Tweening.

Lesson 2

What you'll learn in this lesson:

- Working with shapes
- Using the Pencil tool
- Using the Line tool
- Using the Pen tool
- Importing and outlining a reference graphic.

Getting Started with the Drawing Tools

In addition to being a stellar animation and new media-publishing tool, Flash is also a full-featured vector illustration program that enables you to create attractive graphics and digital illustrations for use in your movies. If you use industry-standard applications such as Photoshop or Illustrator, you'll find many similarities as well as some powerful tools that are unique to Flash.

Starting up

Before starting, make sure that your tools and panels are consistent by resetting your workspace. See "Resetting the Flash workspace" on page XXVII.

You will work with several files from the fl02lessons folder in this lesson. Make sure that you have loaded the CS4lessons folder onto your hard drive from the supplied DVD. See "Loading lesson files" on page XXIX.

See Lesson 2 in action!

Use the accompanying video to gain a better understanding of how to use some of the features shown in this lesson. The video tutorial for this lesson can be found on the included DVD.

Drawing in Flash

Adobe Flash CS4 Professional has more powerful tools and features than ever to help you create shapes and lines. Whatever you create with the drawing tools can then be animated using the Timeline. In this lesson, you will experiment with two different drawing models that you can use to create artwork in Flash: the Merge Drawing mode and the Object Drawing model.

Using the Merge Drawing model

The default model is the Merge Drawing mode. At first, this model may be difficult for new users to grasp, especially those already familiar with the drawing tools in Adobe Illustrator. In this lesson, however, you'll see how the Merge Drawing mode offers some unique benefits over traditional drawing tools. To view the finished project, choose File > Open within Flash CS4. In the Open dialog box, navigate to the fl02lessons folder and select the file, fl0302_done.fla, then press Open. Keep this file open for reference or choose File > Close to close the file.

The finished project.

Creating artwork in Merged Drawing mode

In Merge Drawing mode, shapes can be easily torn apart like clay—strokes can be separated from fills (and vice versa) and you can create partial selections to break up your shapes even further. Most importantly, two shapes drawn in this mode will automatically merge when they overlap, making it easy to create complex combined shapes. Mergeable artwork is easily distinguishable on the Stage by its stippled (dotted) appearance.

You'll first get familiar with how this unique model behaves before diving into a more complex drawing lesson.

1 Launch Flash CS4 Professional, if it is not already open.

2 Choose File > Open and navigate to the fl02lessons folder that you copied onto your computer. Select and open the file named fl0301.fla. You'll start your artwork off with a basic shape drawn in Merge Drawing mode. First, you'll need to make sure you're in the right drawing mode.

3 Select the Oval tool (○) from the Flash Tools panel. This tool is grouped with the other shape tools, and you may need to click and hold down the mouse button on currently selected shape tool to select it.

4 At the bottom of the Flash Tools panel, locate the Object Drawing button (○) and make sure it's *not* selected. This button controls whether or not you're drawing in Merge or Object Drawing mode. On Windows systems, it appears with a white border around it, if selected; on Mac OS systems, the button appears shaded.

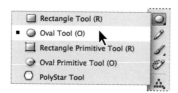

Click and hold down your mouse button to reveal more shape tools under the Rectangle tool.

5 Next, you'll choose your fill (inside) and stroke (outline) colors. At the bottom of the Flash Tools panel, locate the color swatch marked with a pencil icon (⌀) and click it. The Swatches panel appears—select black as your stroke color. Below it, click the color swatch marked with a paint bucket icon (⌀)—from the Swatches panel, select a light orange for your fill color. Click the Reset button at the bottom of the Property Inspector.

6 Click and drag in the middle of your Stage to draw an oval—once you're satisfied with the size and shape, release the mouse button. Switch to your Selection tool (▶) at the top of the Tools panel; this tool allows you to select, move, and manipulate items on the Stage.

7 Click once on the fill (inside) area of your shape and the fill becomes selected without the stroke (outline). Double-click the fill, and both the stroke and fill become selected. You can now move or manipulate the shape as one whole object. Deselect the shape by clicking on the Stage.

8 Off to the upper-left corner, click and drag to create a marquee (selection area), and release it once it partially overlaps your new shape. You'll notice that the shape becomes partially selected; you can now use the Selection tool (Ⓚ) to click and drag the selected portion away from the rest.

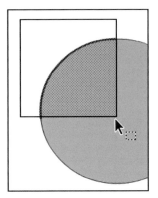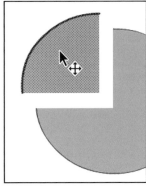

You can partially select mergeable shapes and pull them apart, which can create some interesting shape variations.

9 Next, you'll draw a new shape that overlaps the current one. Reselect the Oval tool (○) from the Tools panel on the right. You can leave your current color settings the same. Click and drag to draw a new shape that partially overlaps the first. Once again, switch to the Selection tool.

10 Double-click the fill of the new shape to select it, and pull it away from the existing one. You'll notice that the new shape has taken a piece out of the old one where the two overlapped!

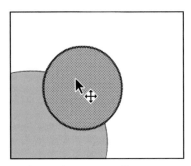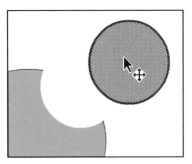

Overlapping shapes automatically merge, causing one to "knock" the other out when removed.

11 Choose File > Save As. In the Save As dialog box, navigate to the fl02lessons folder, then type **fl0301_work.fla** into the Name text field. Press Save.

Working with Drawing Objects

In contrast to artwork created in Merge Drawing mode (referred to simply as *shapes*), Object Drawing mode provides more rigid control over artwork created on the Stage. Much like drawing shapes in Illustrator CS4, shapes drawn in this mode group their stroke and fill together to avoid separation, and so partial selections are prevented. Drawing Objects give you the ability to stack and arrange shapes within a single layer, providing a lot of layering control.

1   Select a green shade from the Fill color swatch on the Tools panel. Click and hold your mouse button on the Oval tool (○) to reveal the other shape tools, and select the Polystar tool (○).

2   Locate the Object Drawing button (○) at the bottom of the Tools panel, and click to select it. The button should be pressed in at this point, indicating that Object Drawing mode is enabled.

3   Click and drag to draw a new polygon on the Stage. You'll notice the shape appears inside a bounding box. Switch to the Selection tool (▸) and choose Edit > Deselect All.

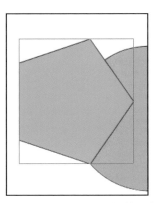

Drawing Objects appear inside of bounding boxes, and their strokes and fills can't be separated.

4   If you click once on the fill or stroke of the shape, the bounding box around the entire shape appears selected. Click and drag to draw a selection area (marquee) around part of the polygon, and you'll see that partial selections also result in the entire shape becoming selected.

5 Double-click the fill of the shape—you'll be brought inside the Drawing Object to edit its contents. Interestingly enough, the contents of the Drawing Object are simply the same, mergeable shapes you worked with in the last lesson. You can think of a Drawing Object as a container around a mergeable shape that keeps its parts grouped together.

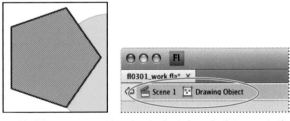

Double-clicking a Drawing Object doesn't select it, but rather brings you inside to edit its contents.

6 Exit the Drawing Object by double-clicking on the Stage. Once again, return to the Tools panel and select the Polystar tool (○). Click and drag to draw another shape on the Stage that overlaps the first.

7 Choose the Selection tool and select the new shape. Pull it slightly away from the original shape—you'll notice the two shapes did not merge as they would with mergeable shapes. Leave the new shape selected and make sure that it still slightly overlaps the first polystar.

8 Next, you'll see how Drawing Objects can be meticulously stacked and arranged, even on the same Timeline layer. With the new shape selected, choose Modify > Arrange > Send to Back. The new shape is pushed behind the first. The Arrange menu allows you to restack Drawing Objects, groups, and symbols. Symbols are covered in more detail in Chapter 4, "Using Symbols and the Library."

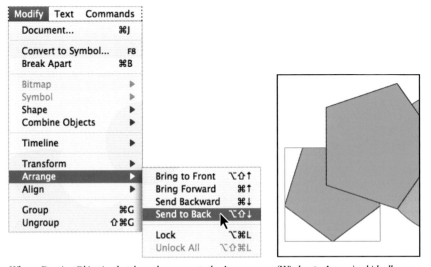

When a Drawing Object is selected, you have access to the Arrange menu (Window > Arrange), which allows you to change that shape's stacking order relative to other Drawing Objects on the Stage.

9   Choose File > Save, then choose File > Close.

Mergeable shapes always fall below Drawing Objects, groups, or symbols on the Stage. To have a mergeable shape appear above other items, you need to place it on its own layer and move that layer to the top of the stack.

You can also exit a Drawing Object's Edit mode using the links shown above the Stage. Click on the Scene 1 link to return to the main Timeline, and you should no longer see the words Drawing Object appear to its right.

Putting it all together

Now that you have a feel for how the two drawing modes work, you'll complete a piece of artwork using your new skills and become familiar with additional drawing tools.

1   Choose File > Open and navigate to the fl02lessons folder. Select and open the file named fl0302.fla.

2   Choose File > Save As. In the Save As dialog box, navigate to the fl02lessons folder, then type **fl0302_work.fla** into the Name text field. Press Save.

3   On the Stage, you see a single oval—switch to the Selection tool (ꜝ) and click once on the oval to select it. A bounding box appears, indicating that this is a Drawing Object. A look at the Property Inspector confirms this, as it should read Drawing Object at the top.

4   In order to dissect this shape further, you'll need to break it back down to a mergeable shape like the ones you created earlier. Make sure the shape is selected, and choose Modify > Break Apart. The shape now appears with a dotted pattern that indicates it is mergeable artwork.

The Break Apart command allows you to break any artwork down to its next most basic form.

5 To create the mouth of your fish, click and drag with your Selection tool to create a partial selection that overlaps the left edge of the oval. Delete the selected portion by using the Backspace (Windows) or Delete (Mac OS) key. With mergeable shapes, you can delete partial selections to dissect shapes in unusual ways.

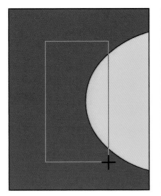

Create a partial selection around the oval where you'll form the mouth of your fish.

6 With the Selection tool active, move your cursor close to the open-ended stroke at the top of the oval. When an L-shaped angle icon (↖⌐) appears below your pointer, click and drag the anchor point down and to the left as shown below.

7 Continue using the Selection tool to click and drag the bottom anchor point up to meet the first anchor point as shown below.

The Selection tool can pull open-ended paths to reshape an object.

8 Choose File > Save to save your file.

Paths on mergeable shapes automatically join when Snap to Objects is enabled. Snap to Objects can be enabled using View > Snapping > Snap to Objects, or by using the Snap to Objects button ( ) at the bottom of the Tools panel.

Using the Line tool

Most illustration programs have a line tool, and while it's not the most creative tool in the box, you can use Flash's Selection tool to make it more useful. In the following steps, you'll form the tail of your fish using a few simple moves.

1   Select the Line tool (\ ) from the Tools panel. Make sure that Object Drawing mode is disabled (if necessary, deselect the Object Drawing button ( ) at the bottom of the Tools panel). Select Solid from the style menu on the Preoperties panel to set a solid line.

2   Move your crosshair cursor close to the right edge of the oval, and click and drag to draw an upward diagonal line. Starting where your first line leaves off, click and drag to draw a second line that meets the oval again below where the first line began.

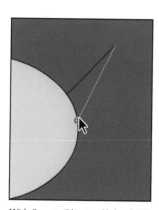

With Snap to Object enabled and Object Drawing disabled, diagonal lines automatically join if drawn close enough together.

3   Where the last line meets the oval, click and drag to draw a diagonal line moving downward. As you did in step 2, click and drag where the line leaves off to draw a second line that meets the oval again. These steps should have formed a spiky *tail* that you'll fine-tune in the next steps.

4   To change this from a spiky tail to a rounded, more appropriate one, you'll use the Selection tool. Choose the Selection tool ( ), and move your cursor toward the middle of the first diagonal line you created. Once you are close enough, a curved icon appears ( ) below your pointer. Click and drag upward to bend the line into a curve. As you can see, the Selection tool can also bend or reshape straight lines and curves.

5   Repeat step 4 for each of the three remaining lines until the tail is formed.

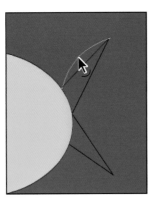

The Selection tool can be used to easily reshape lines and curves.

6   Next you'll need to fill the two sides of your new tail. By default, shapes drawn with path-centric tools such as the Line, Pen, and Pencil tools do not automatically fill. To fill these shapes, click and hold the Ink Bottle tool (♦), if necessary, to locate and choose the Paint Bucket tool (♦) from the Tools panel.

The Paint Bucket tool allows you to add fills where none exist, or to change the color of an existing fill.

7   Click on the Fill color swatch at the bottom of the Tools panel. Choose the light orange color marked #FFCC00. (You can also type this in the text field at the top of the Swatches panel to select the specified color.) Click inside of the tail fins to fill them with the selected color.

Add fills to empty paths using the Paint Bucket tool.

8   Switch back to the Line tool, and click and drag to draw two close, parallel, vertical lines in the middle of the oval. You will use these to form the gills for your fish.

9   Switch to the Selection tool (↖), and use the technique shown in steps 4 and 5 to bend each line into a slight curve in the same direction.

Use the same technique you used to create the tail to bend out some gills for your fish.

10   With the Selection tool active, click and select each of the two overlapping lines that separate the tail from the fish body. Press Backspace (Windows) or Delete (Mac OS) to clear the lines away.

11   Choose File > Save to save your file.

You can easily switch from any tool to the Selection tool by pressing the V key, without having to go over to the Tools panel.

What the hex is a hexadecimal code?

You may have noticed that each color you choose (including colors referenced in these lessons) is marked with a hexadecimal code, a 6-character code preceded by a pound (#) sign. A hexadecimal code is a binary representation of an RGB color, used to indicate colors within web-specific languages and applications (such as HTML, Dreamweaver, and Fireworks).

Each byte, or pair of two digits, represents the red, green, and blue values for that color, respectively, from 00 to FF (in decimal notation, the values 0 to 255). For example, white in standard RGB values is notated as 255,255,255—in hexadecimal notation, #FFFFFF.

While it's not at all necessary (and somewhat impossible) to memorize the hexadecimal values for every popular color, becoming comfortable with this notation will help you work your way through Flash's color panels as well as those of other applications.

A helpful hint: the Photoshop and Illustrator color pickers also display a hexadecimal code for any color selected, making it easy to match colors between applications.

Using the Pen tool

For precision illustration tasks, you will most likely want to use the Pen tool. The Pen tool allows for point-to-point drawing, and precise control over curves and lines in between. You can even add or remove points to fine-tune your work. If you've used the Pen tool in Illustrator CS4, you'll already be familiar with the Pen tool and its related tools.

You'll use the Pen tool to create fins for your new fish in the following steps.

1 Select the Pen tool (◊) from the Tools panel. In the Property Inspector or Tools panel, set your stroke color to black (#000000).

2 In the space above your oval, click and release the mouse pointer on the Stage to create a new point. Move your pointer to the left of the point you just created, and click and release again to create a second point. This point is joined to the first by a new path (line).

3 Position your cursor above and to the right of your last point. Click and hold down your mouse button, and then drag to the right. This forms a curve between your new point and the last one. Once you've gotten the curve just right, release the mouse button.

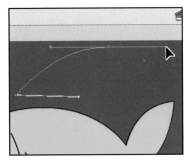

Creating precision lines and curves using the Pen tool.

You can create curves from any new point by holding down the mouse button and dragging in the direction you want to form the curve. (Be sure not to release the mouse button first!)

4 Next, you'll close up the shape. The next time you create a point, however, the Pen tool will attempt to draw a curve in the same direction as the last. To reset the last point drawn so that you can control the curve, click on the last point you created.

5 Move your pointer over the first point you created, and you should see a small loop appear below the pen cursor. Click and hold down your mouse button; drag to the right to form the final curve, and release the mouse to complete the shape.

6 As with other path-based tools, shapes created with the Pen tool do not automatically fill. To fill the new shape, choose the Paint Bucket tool (⬧) from the Tools panel. From the Fill color swatch in the Tools panel, choose the orange labeled #FFCC00.

7 Click once inside your new shape to fill it with the currently active fill color.

8 Now you'll move the fin into place and connect it with the rest of the body. Choose the Selection tool (▶), and double-click the fill of the fin to select the entire shape. Drag it into place at the top of the oval, slightly overlapping it. Click the Stage to deselect the shape; when you deselect the shape, the two become merged.

Move your new fin into place above the fish body.

9 The fin should now be merged with the oval. Use the Selection tool and click once to select the portion of the stroke that overlaps onto the oval. Only that portion should become selected. Press Backspace (Windows) or Delete (Mac OS) to clear away the selected stroke.

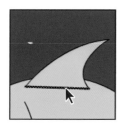 

Intersecting strokes in mergeable artwork become segmented and can be individually selected and removed.

By default, strokes that overlap between two merged shapes become segmented, and individual portions can be selected and removed.

10 Choose File > Save to save your file.

Using the Add and Delete Anchor Point tools

You can add or remove points along existing paths with the Add and Delete Anchor Point tools. These tools are found under the Pen tool and enable you to further fine-tune your illustrations. You'll add a bottom fin to your fish by manipulating the existing oval shape that forms its body.

1   Choose the Subselection tool (⟨k⟩) from the Tools panel. Click on the edge of the oval; this reveals the points and paths that form this shape. From here, you can manipulate, add, or remove points along this path.

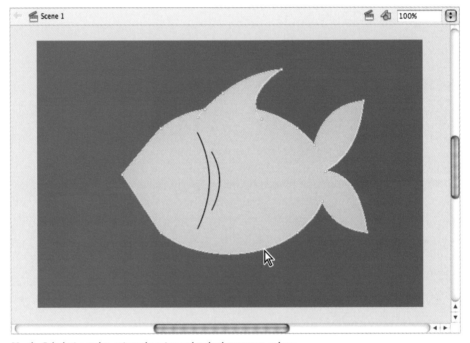

Use the Subselection tool to activate the points and paths that compose a shape.

2   Click and hold down your mouse pointer on the Pen tool—this reveals the Add, Delete, and Convert Anchor Point tools. Choose the Add Anchor Point tool (◊⁺).

3   At the bottom center of the oval, you'll notice a single anchor point. Using the Add
     Anchor Point tool, click once to the left and once to the right of that point to add two
     new anchor points.

     If you add the anchor point(s) in the wrong place, or add too many, choose the Delete
     Anchor Point tool ($\Diamond$) and click on any point to remove it.

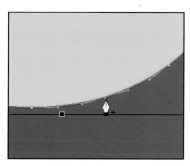

*Use the Add Anchor Point tool to add two
additional points surrounding the bottom point.*

4   Choose the Subselection tool and, if necessary, click on the outline of your oval to
     reactivate the points and paths. Click the point at the very bottom of the oval to activate
     it—the point now appears solid instead of hollow.

5   Click and drag the point down and to the right, which extends that portion of the oval
     into a fin-like shape.

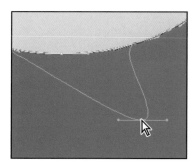

*With more points in place, you can easily pull out
and extend a fin from the existing shape.*

6   Choose File > Save to save your file, and leave the file open.

Using the Combine Objects menu

If you need to create more complex combinations of shapes, you can use the Combine Objects menu, found at Modify > Combine Objects. This menu enables you to create punches, crops, or intersections between overlapping shapes, and even lets you convert mergeable artwork into Drawing Objects.

Before you can perform any Combine Objects menu commands on a piece of artwork, it first must be converted to a Drawing Object. To do this, you'll use the Union command to convert your fish from mergeable artwork to a Drawing Object.

1   Select the entire fish by choosing Edit > Select All. You can also use the Selection tool (⬥) to draw a selection area around the artwork if you prefer.

2   Choose Modify > Combine Objects > Union. This command converts the selected artwork to a Drawing Object, and a bounding box appears around your fish and its parts. Choose Edit > Deselect All.

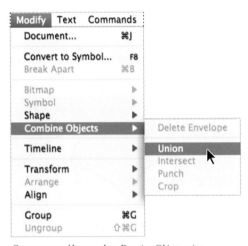

Convert mergeable artwork to Drawing Objects using
Modify > Combine Objects > Union.

3   Select the Polystar tool (◯), and enable Object Drawing mode by selecting the button at the bottom of the Tools panel. From the Property Inspector, press the Options button. This opens the Tool Settings dialog box for the Polystar tool.

4   In the Tool Settings dialog box, type 3 for the number of sides, and press OK to exit the dialog box. On the Stage, while holding your Shift key (to constrain the angle), click and drag to draw a right-pointing triangle.

If the new triangle appears unfilled, select any fill color from the Tools panel, and use the Paint Bucket tool to fill it.

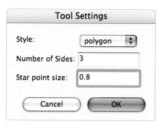
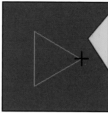

Use the Polystar tool to set and draw a triangle shape that you'll punch from the fish below.

5   With the shape still selected, choose the Free Transform tool (⬚) from the Tools panel. A bounding box with handles appears—grab the top middle handle and drag it downward to scale the shape down vertically.

Choose the Selection tool and move the shape so that it overlaps the fish on the left where a mouth should be.

6   Choose Edit > Select All so that the new shape and your fish both appear selected. Choose Modify > Combine Objects > Punch. The new shape is knocked out from your fish, leaving behind a mouth-like opening.

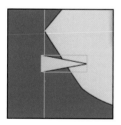

Use Modify > Combine Objects > Punch to subtract one shape from another.

7   Select the Oval tool from the Tools panel. Make sure you have a fill color selected (any color will do). With the Shift key held down, click and drag to draw a small, perfect circle. (To match the figure shown in this example, use your Property Inspector to set the circle to a width and height of 50.) Switch to your Selection tool and position the circle on top of your fish above the mouth you created.

8 Choose Edit > Select All. With both the circle and fish selected, choose Modify > Combine Objects > Punch. This punches the circle into the body of the fish, making space for an eye.

Use the Punch command to create a space for your fish's eye.

9 Choose File > Save to save your file.

The Combine Objects menu

There are several commands available at Modify Combine Objects, not all of which you may use right away. Here's an overview of what each menu command does so that you can decide for yourself when and whether to use them.

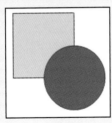 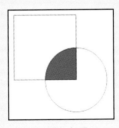 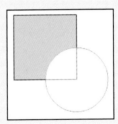 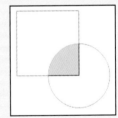

From left to right: Original shapes, Intersect, Punch, Crop.

Union: Converts mergeable shapes into Drawing Objects. You can group several shapes into a single Drawing Object. In addition, shapes that are part of an Intersect, Punch, or Crop operation must all be Drawing Objects.

Intersect: Leaves behind only the overlapping area of two shapes.

Punch: Knocks out the top shape from the bottom shape.

Crop: Crops the bottom shape to conform to the top shape.

Using the Primitive tools (Smart Shapes)

Introduced in Flash CS3, the Rectangle and Oval Primitive tools provide you with a powerful way to create common variations on these basic shapes. From rounded or scalloped rectangles, to double-radius ovals, these smart shapes are especially powerful, because you can continue to modify them long after they've been created.

Using the Oval Primitive tool

Your new fish needs an eye, and the best tool for the job is the Oval Primitive tool, which allows you to create complex variations on ovals and circles.

1 Select the Oval Primitive tool (⊝) from the Tools panel. This tool can be found underneath the existing shape tools. From the Tools panel, choose black (#000000) for your fill color, and set the stroke to None (☑).

2 Choose View > Snapping, and select Snap to Objects to temporarily disable object snapping. While holding your Shift key (to constrain width and height), click and drag to draw a small circle on the Stage. Switch to your Selection tool (▶), and position the circle above the spot where the eye should appear on your fish (a hole should appear there from the last exercise).

Use the W and H values on the Property Inspector to set the new circle's size to **45** by **45**.

3 In the Property Inspector, locate the three sliders at the bottom marked Start Angle, End Angle, and Inner Radius. Click and drag the Inner Radius slider toward the right, and you'll see that it forms a knockout in the center of the circle. Set the Inner Radius to suit your artwork (the figure and sample file use a value of around 49).

You can also enter a precise value in the text field to the right of the slider.

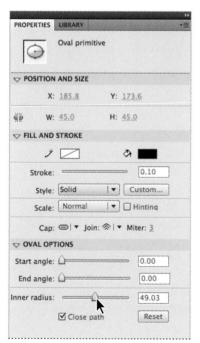 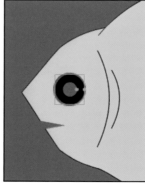

Use the Inner Radius slider to punch a center into an oval primitive.

4   Locate the Start Angle and End Angle sliders in the Property Inspector. Click and drag the Start Angle slider until its value reads somewhere between 40 and 45. You'll notice that as you increase the angle, the circle forms a *C* shape—this slider tells the circle to begin its circumference (shape) at a different angle, resulting in a partial shape!

5   You'll now perform the same action for the End Angle. Grab the End Angle slider and drag it to the right until the value reads about 330. The circle now ends at a different location as well. As you can see, this can be very powerful in any situation where you need to create wedges or partial circle shapes without the need for complex punch or knockout commands.

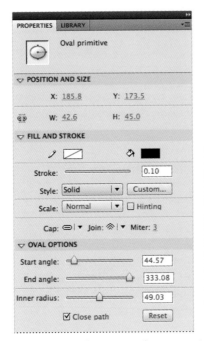
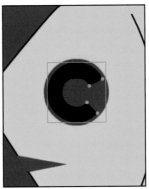

Use the sliders to affect your smart shape at any point. You can even deselect and return to the shape later on to edit its settings.

6   Choose View > Snapping > Snap to Objects to re-enable object snapping.

Oval Primative shapes

For each oval primitive shape drawn, you'll see a discrete handle (it looks like an anchor point) on its right side. As an alternative to the Start and End Angle sliders, you can click and drag this handle in a clockwise or counter-clockwise motion to manually alter the start or end angle of the shape.

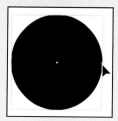 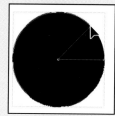 

The Rectangle Primitive tool

The close cousin of the Oval Primitive tool is the Rectangle Primitive tool, which gives you control over corner radii on rectangles and squares. Like the Oval Primitive tool, you can easily set values for a new primitive shape, and return to edit it at any time.

It's time to give your fish a way to speak its mind, so you'll create a basic word balloon using the power of the primitive.

1　Choose the Rectangle Primitive tool (□) from the shape tools group on the Tools panel. From the Tools panel or the Property Inspector, set a fill color of white (#FFFFFF) and a stroke color of black (#000000).

2　Click and drag to draw a rectangle to the upper left of your fish. It's okay if it goes off the Stage into the pasteboard. If you'd like to match the sample file, use the Property Inspector to set the rectangle's size to **200** pixels wide by **130** pixels high.

3   In the Property Inspector, locate the Rectangle Options section; you'll see four text fields and a slider. Here is where you set the corner radius for all or each of your rectangle's corners. By default, the four corners are locked together and use the same value.

Click and drag the slider to the right until the corner values read about 40—you see the corners of the rectangle begin to round out.

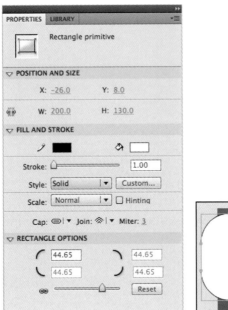 

Add a corner radius to the rectangle primitive using the slider in the Property Inspector.

 To give each corner a unique value, click the chain link icon to the left of the slider to unlock the four corners. You can then type in a different value for each corner in its respective text field.

4   Next, you'll modify the corner radius using a slightly different technique. Instead of using the slider in the Property Inspector, you can grab the points adjacent to any corner and drag them to reshape the corner radius.

5   Switch to the Selection tool (⬉), then click and drag the point in the upper-right corner of your rectangle to the left and right. As you can see, this modifies the corners of your rectangle—move slightly to the right to reduce the corner radius.

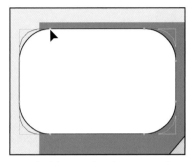

Using the Selection tool can be a more tactile way to modify corners.

6   Choose File > Save to save your work.

You'll now add the stem to make this a true word balloon—however, you may have noticed that primitive shapes behave unlike any other shape you've used so far. While they appear to look and function much like Drawing Objects, they actually can't be modified in the way that Drawing Objects can.

Neither the Selection nor Subselection tool will allow you to modify them in the way you've been able to do with Drawing Objects and mergeable artwork. To accomplish this, you need to break the shape down to artwork that you can manipulate freely. Keep in mind, however, that doing this is a one-way street: You can't convert a shape or Drawing Object back into a primitive once it's been broken apart.

7   If it's not already active, switch to the Selection tool (⬉) and click once to select the rectangle primitive.

8 You'll now break this out of a primitive down to artwork you can manipulate further. Choose Modify > Break Apart, and the shape now appears with the dotted pattern that indicates it is now a mergeable shape. Keep in mind that you cannot go back.

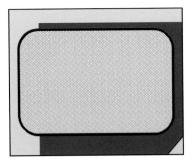

Use Modify > Break Apart to convert the primitive shape to a mergeable shape.

Choose the Subselection tool (↖) from the Tools panel and click once on the edge of the shape to reveal its points and paths.

9 Switch to the Add Anchor Point tool (♦⁺). In the lower-right corner of the rectangle, click to create two new consecutive anchor points before the corner.

10 Switch to the Subselection tool, again, then click on the second point (the one closest to the corner) and drag it down and to the right to form the stem of your word balloon.

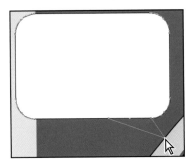

Form a stem by pulling out the second of the two new points you created.

11 With the shape still selected, choose Modify > Combine Objects > Union to convert the shape to a Drawing Object, which you can easily move and stack later on.

12 Choose File > Save to save your work.

Adding text to your artwork

Flash allows you to create and style text to include in your movies, which can also be incorporated into animations or rendered in 3D. In addition, text is one of a few objects in Flash that can have filters applied to enhance its appearance.

You'll use the Text tool to add and style some cool text inside of your fish's word balloon.

1 Select the Text tool (T) from the Tools panel. Click once within your word balloon to create a new text box. The box appears with a blinking cursor inside.

2 Type the words **Go Fish!** inside the text box. Click and drag within the box so that both words appear selected.

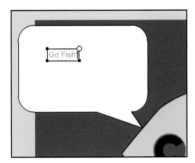

Use the Text tool to add some text to your word balloon.

3 In the Property Inspector, locate the CHARACTER options, which include menus for Family, Color, and Size. Choose Arial Black (or equivalent) from the Family menu to change the typeface. Move your cursor above the Size value, and drag to the right to increase the type size to 45 points. Click the Color swatch and set the type color to black (#000000).

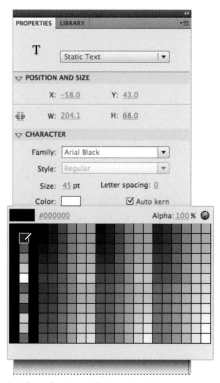

Specify typeface, size, and color options for your new text from the Property Inspector.

4   To force your text to two lines, or to force any text to work within a confined width, you'll resize the text box to a fixed width. To do this, leave your Text tool active, and move your cursor to the top-right corner of your text box. Click and drag to down to size the width of the box until the text is forced to two lines.

This forces any further text that you add to the text box to wrap.

You can easily resize text boxes by dragging any of the four corners. This forces text to wrap within the text area.

5   Click and drag inside of the text box to select all the text inside. Locate the PARAGRAPH options in the Property Inspector, and expand it by clicking on its title bar. You see options for Format (alignment), spacing, and more.

6   Under the Format section, press the Align Center button (≣) to center the selected text within your text box. Under Spacing, locate and move your pointer above the line spacing value (second slider). Click and drag to the left to reduce the line spacing to −20px.

7   If you'd like, experiment with some of the other values under the PARAGRAPH options to modify the appearance and position of your text.

Choose File > Save to save your file.

Adding filters

To enhance the appearance of text, you can add popular live filters such as drop shadows, blurs, glows, and more. Filters can also be applied to other objects in your movie, such as button and movie clip symbols (covered later in this book). For now, you'll add some basic filters to make your text stand out.

1   Switch to the Selection tool (↖), and click once on your text box to select it.

Pressing the V key while editing text simply types a v in the text box; it doesn't switch to the Selection tool as anticipated. To exit a text box, use the Esc (escape) key, and then press the V key to jump to the Selection tool.

2 At the bottom of the Property Inspector, locate and expand the FILTERS section. (Try collapsing the Paragraph options to give your filter options more space.)

3 In the lower-left corner of the FILTERS section, press the Add Filter button (⤴) to add a new filter. A menu appears, showing you the various filters you can apply to your text. Select the Drop Shadow filter.

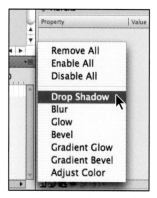

Apply filters to selected text from the FILTERS
section of the Property Inspector.

4 Options appear for the new Drop Shadow filter, which you can fine-tune. To start, click and drag left above the Strength value to reduce the strength (opacity) to 30 percent.

5 Click and drag to the right above the Distance value to increase the distance to 10 pixels. Under the Quality setting, select High.

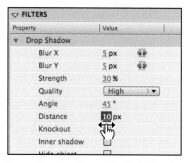

Set specific options for your filter, including color,
strength, and distance.

6 Choose File > Save to save your file.

Working with colors

Flash offers a lot of options for creating, saving, and working with colors and gradients. In addition, the panels and workspace make it easy to choose and apply colors from virtually anywhere, or to save color sets that you can share between multiple Flash documents and projects.

Getting set up

1   First you'll want to make sure that the Color and Swatches panels are visible. Choose Window > Color, and then Window > Swatches to open these two panels. Click and drag the Color panel on top of the Swatches panel, until you see a light blue border on all four sides—the two become grouped together, making it easier to spot and move them around.

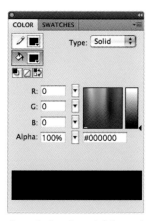

Group the Swatches and Color panels together by dragging one over the other.

2   Drag the new panel group by its title bar to the top of the Property Inspector and Library panel on the right-hand side, releasing the mouse when you see a light blue line. The two panels should now appear docked in the panel group above the Property Inspector and Library panel.

Creating gradients

A gradient is a gradual blend between two or more colors, and is often used for complex color transitions or to imply lighting effects. You can create and save gradients and apply them to fills or strokes within your artwork.

Flash supports *linear* gradients and *radial* gradients. Both types can include any number of colors.

Linear gradients blend in a uniform manner and, as the name implies, in a straight line going in any direction or angle.

Radial gradients blend in a circular manner, either from the inside out or the outside in (depending on your perspective, of course).

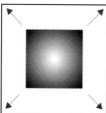

On the left, a linear gradient; on the right, a radial gradient.

Your fish is almost complete, so it's time to bring it to life with some dynamic and exciting colors.

1 Choose your Selection tool (↖), and click once on your fish to select it. Choose Modify > Break Apart to separate the fish and its parts, and then choose Edit > Deselect All. Click once on the body of the fish, and click on the Fill color selector on the Color panel.

2 Locate the Type drop-down menu at the top-right corner of the Color panel. This allows you to choose a solid color or gradient for the currently active color. Choose Radial to set a radial gradient to your fill. The fish displays the default black-to-white gradient.

Choose Radial to switch your shape's fill to a radial gradient.

3 At the bottom of the Color panel, you see the color ramp, which now appears with two color stops (sliders), one for each color that forms your gradient. You'll need to assign a new color to each stop.

4 Double-click the right slider, and the Swatches panel appears. Choose the dark orange color marked #CC6600.

Double-click the left slider, and from the Swatches panel, choose the light orange color marked #FF9900.

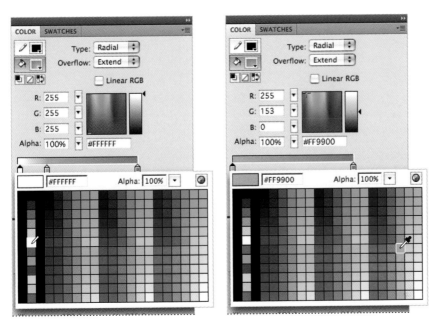

Set a unique value for each color stop on your gradient.

5 The position and distance between the two sliders determines the blend point. Moving one slider closer to the other changes the balance between the two colors.

Click and drag the left slider slightly toward the middle—this makes the lighter orange more prominent than the dark orange.

6 To add colors to your gradient, you'll add more color stops. Add a new color stop by clicking on the far left edge of the color ramp. A new stop should appear below the color ramp. Double-click the stop, and choose white (#FFFFFF) from the Swatches panel.

Now, you'll save this gradient for use later on.

7 Locate and open the Color panel menu (•≡) in the upper-right corner of the panel. Choose Add Swatch to add your new gradient swatch to the existing swatch presets.

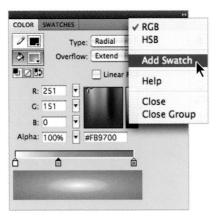

Save your new gradient as a preset that you can recall later on from the Swatches panel.

8 Choose File > Save to save your file.

Using opacity with gradient colors

A cool feature in Flash is the ability to set a unique opacity level for each individual color in a gradient. This can create some interesting effects, and add cool lighting-style effects to your illustrations. In this next exercise, you'll create and color some underwater bubbles using this interesting effect.

1 Choose the Oval tool (○) from the Tools panel. If it's not already enabled, activate Object Drawing mode by pressing the button at the bottom of the Tools panel.

2 From the bottom of the Tools panel, choose white (#FFFFFF) for your stroke color, and choose the black-to-white radial gradient preset for your fill color.

3 While holding the Shift key down (to constrain proportions), click and drag to draw a small circle to the left of your fish. Leave the circle selected.

4 If it's not already open, choose Window > Color to open the Color panel. Click the Fill button so that the gradient fill appears in the color ramp at the bottom of the panel.

5   Double-click the black color stop to open the Swatches panel, and choose white (#FFFFFF).

6   With the stop still active, locate the Alpha slider; this sets the opacity of the selected color in the current gradient. Click and drag the slider downward until the value reads 0 percent. This produces an interesting light flare effect inside the bubble.

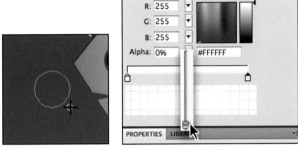

Draw a new oval, and use the Color panel to reduce the opacity of one of your oval's gradient colors.

7   Choose File > Save to save your file.

Creating custom colors

As you may have discovered, creating and saving a solid color swatch is nearly identical to creating and saving a gradient swatch. In this case, you'll set specific RGB values to create a color that you can apply to your artwork, as well as add to your existing swatches.

1   Choose the Selection tool (★) and click once on your fish to select it. The Color panel should reflect the current stroke and fill color.

2   Click the Stroke button (✎ ■) so that the Color panel displays the current stroke color. The Type menu should read Solid, and the current color should be black (#000000).

3   Locate the R, G, and B text fields on the Color panel, and type **250**, **100**, and **16**, respectively. This creates a dark orange color that is immediately applied to the stroke.

4   Open the Color panel menu from the icon located in the upper-right corner, and select Add Swatch to add your new color to the Swatches panel.

5   Choose File > Save to save your file.

Saving a custom color set

Once you've added new color swatches, you'll want to save that set for use with other projects and documents. If you've ever created and saved custom color swatches in applications like Photoshop or Illustrator, you'll find that saving color sets in Flash is very similar.

1 If it's not already open or visible, choose Window > Swatches to open the Swatches panel. Press the panel menu button (⁃≡) in the upper-right corner of the Swatches panel.

2 From the panel menu, choose Save Colors.

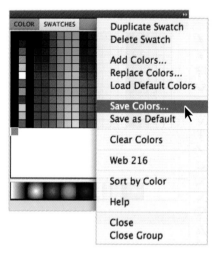

Save the current swatches as a new color set that you can recall at any time.

3 From the dialog box that appears, choose your Save location (for this lesson, you can choose the fl02lessons folder), and name the new file **fl03colors.clr.**

4 Press Save to save the color set into the selected folder. The color set appears in your destination folder as a single .clr (Flash Color Set) file.

You can also choose to save your swatches in .act (Adobe Color Table) format, which allows you to exchange it with Adobe applications such as Photoshop and Fireworks. You can even load .act color tables exported from Fireworks back into Flash if you'd like!

Organizing and layering graphics

As you build more complex graphics on the Stage, you'll want to position and layer them as needed to make your movie work for you. Flash gives you a lot of control over your Stage through a robust layer structure that you may already be accustomed to using in other Adobe design applications.

Working with layers

On a single layer, you have a great deal of flexibility to arrange Drawing Objects and grouped graphics—however, as your artwork becomes more complex, you'll want the power of layers to stack and arrange your artwork. In addition to controlling stacking order, layers let you hide specific graphics from view, and even lock those items from accidentally being edited or deleted.

You can think of layers as clear pieces of film that you can place graphics on and stack together; each layer sits above another, allowing you reveal the items below, but also to control which items appear above or below another. Each layer and its contents can be isolated in view, toggled out of view, or locked to prevent editing.

In the next steps, you'll separate the graphics you've created so far onto individual layers for more control.

1   To start, you'll make sure that each set of graphics you want to assign to a layer is grouped or converted to a Drawing Object. This will make them easier to move and distribute.

Verify that your word balloon (leave the text separate) is a Drawing Object by selecting it and viewing its info in the Property Inspector. If not, use Modify > Combine Objects > Union to convert it to a Drawing Object.

2   Select your fish and its eye together—convert them to a single Drawing Object by choosing Modify > Combine Objects > Union.

3   Choose Edit > Select All so that all items on your Stage become selected. Right-click (Windows) or Ctrl+click (Mac OS) on any of the selected items—a contextual menu appears.

Use Distribute to Layers to separate multiple objects
at once to their own layers on the Timeline.

4   At the bottom of the menu, locate and select Distribute To Layers. All the items on your Stage are placed onto several new layers, which appear on the Timeline panel at the bottom.

The layers are named generically (Layer 2, Layer 3, and so on). To fix this, you'll identify which graphics belong to which layers and rename them appropriately.

5   Choose Edit > Deselect All. First, click on the fish on the Stage to select it, and look at the Timeline panel below. The layer that becomes selected is the one to which it belongs. Double-click directly on the layer's name to edit it, and type in the name **Fish**.

6   Repeat step 4 for the bubble and word balloon, naming them **Bubble** and **Word Balloon**, respectively. If you have an empty layer named Layer 1 left behind, select it and use the Delete Layer icon (🗑) below the Timeline to delete it.

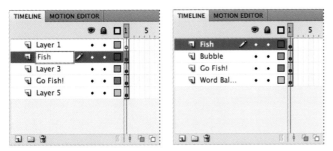

Double-click a layer's name to edit it. Rename your layers clearly so you know exactly what's on each one.

7   Choose File > Save to save your file.

Arranging, locking, and hiding layers

Once you've arranged your artwork on individual layers, you can easily control which layers are visible (or invisible) and editable, and easily rearrange the order and appearance of items in your movie.

1   Locate the layer titled Go Fish, which contains the text you created earlier. Click to select it.

2   Click and drag upwards on the layer—you see a black beam follow your cursor within the layers. This indicates where the layer will be moved when you release the mouse.

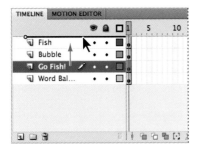

When dragging layers, follow the black beam to determine where your layer will be placed.

3 Drag the layer all the way up and release it at the top of the layer stack to move the text to the top.

4 Use the same technique shown in step 2 to reorder your layers from top to bottom, as follows: Go Fish, Word Balloon, Fish, Bubble.

5 Locate the two column headers above your layers—one appears with an visibility icon (👁) and one appears with a padlock icon (🔒), which means that it is locked. Under the padlock column, click on the Text, Word Balloon, and Bubble layers to lock those layers (a padlock icon should appear on the layer). Leave the Fish layer unlocked.

6 Click the Go Fish layer below the visibility column—a red X appears and the text disappears. Toggle the layer's visibility back on again by clicking the red X.

Click under the padlock or eye icon to lock, hide, and show specific layers.

To lock all layers except for the one you're targeting, hold down the Alt key (Windows) or Option key (Mac OS) and click on the target layer below the padlock column. All layers except for the one you clicked will lock. This also works for visibility!

Creating layer folders

As you accumulate more layers on the Timeline, it makes sense to try and group them logically so that you can easily view, lock, and hide related layers with a few clicks. You can create layer folders on the Timeline that can group several related layers together, making it easy to collapse, hide, and lock them as needed.

1 Click to select the Go Fish layer, which should currently be the topmost layer on the Timeline.

2 Locate the New Layer Folder button (📁) below the layer stack, and click it once to create a new folder above the current layer.

3 Double-click the Folder title, and type **Word Balloon Parts** as the new name.

4 Click and drag the Go Fish layer up below the folder and to the right and release it—it should now appear indented below the folder, indicating it is now inside the new folder. (Follow the bar—it should appear indented below the layer folder before you release the mouse button.)

Move layers into your new layer folder.

5 Repeat step 4 with the Word Balloon layer to add it to the new layer folder. If necessary, rearrange the two layers within the folder so that the text appears above the Word Balloon.

6 Collapse the layer folder and hide its included layers by clicking the arrow that appears to the left of the folder name. The Word Balloon and Go Fish layers temporarily disappear from view on the Timeline.

Collapse or expand a layer (and its contents) by using the arrow shown to the left of its title.

7 Choose File > Save to save your file.

You can now lock or hide all layers under that folder at once by clicking the layer folder under the Padlock and Visibility columns, respectively. To access individual layers again, simply expand the layer folder.

 Layer folders can be created several levels deep, allowing you a lot of organizational control when you need it. To create a nested layer folder, select any layer inside of a layer folder and click the New Layer Folder button below the Timeline.

Transforming graphics

Once you've created artwork on the Stage, Flash gives you a lot of options for scaling, rotating, skewing, and tweaking graphics and colors. Transforming existing graphics is as much a part of illustration as building them, so in the next steps you'll explore the various tools and panels at your disposal.

The Transform menu and Free Transform tool

The Modify menu at the top of your screen features a Transform menu, which provides shortcuts to many common transformation tasks as well as helpful dialog boxes. You'll use this menu in the next exercise to tweak the size and rotation of your fish.

1   Choose the Selection tool (⬧), and click once on the fish to select it (make sure its layer is unlocked).

2   Choose Modify > Transform > Scale and Rotate. This opens the Scale and Rotate dialog box, where you can enter values for Scale (in percentage) and rotation (in degrees).

Choose Modify > Transform > Scale and Rotate to open the Scale and Rotate dialog box.

3   Type **75** for the Scale value, and **25** for the rotation value; then press OK to exit the dialog box.

4 Your fish now appears smaller and rotated slightly upward. To fine-tune, you'll use the Free Transform tool, which offers a more tactile (but less precise) way of scaling and rotating your artwork.

Rotate the fish.

5 Leave the fish selected, and choose the Free Transform tool (✥) from the Tools panel. The fish now appears inside a black bounding box with eight handles.

6 Move your mouse pointer over the top-right handle of the bounding box until you see a double-arrow icon appear. While holding down the Shift key, click and drag the corner handle down and to the left to resize your fish slightly smaller.

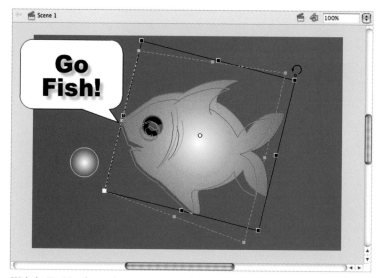

With the Free Transform tool, you can use corner handles to rotate or resize your artwork.

7 Move your cursor just above the same handle until you see the rotating arrow icon (↻). Once this icon appears, click and drag in a clockwise or counter-clockwise motion to adjust the rotation of your graphics to your liking.

8 Choose File > Save to save your file.

Getting the (transformation) point

What is that mysterious white dot that appears in the middle of your artwork when you use the Free Transform tool? That's your transformation point, which determines the point on a graphic from which scaling and rotation is set.

If you'd like to rotate a graphic around a different point than the center, for instance, you can move the transformation point to a different location within your graphic.

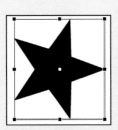  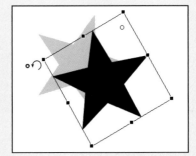

To do this, select your graphic with the Free Transform tool, locate the point, and click and drag it to a different part of your graphic.

The Transform panel

An alternative to the Free Transform tool and Transform menus is the Transform panel, which offers many of the same features plus some additional options for skewing and transforming graphics in the 3D plane.

1 If necessary, unlock the Bubble layer for editing. Use the Selection tool (▸) to select the bubble graphic.

2 Select Edit > Copy and then Edit > Paste in Center to make a copy of the bubble. Repeat this to make a third bubble. Arrange the three bubbles vertically to the left of your fish's mouth.

3 Select the bottommost bubble. Choose Window > Transform to open the Transform panel. Locate the horizontal and vertical scale values at the top. Click the *Constrain* checkbox directly to the right, which will keep the horizontal and vertical values locked together.

4 Click and drag left over the horizontal value until the overall scale of the bubble is reduced to around 50 percent.

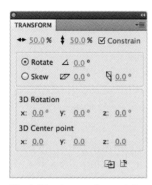

Use the Transform panel to precisely scale an object.

5 Select the next bubble above the last, and repeat the same technique from step 4 to reduce this bubble to 75 percent. This time, however, click and select the *Skew* radio button. Click and drag the horizontal (left) skew value until it reads –20 degrees. This adds a slight leftward tilt to the bubble.

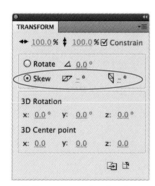

Add skewing to an object by selecting it and using the Skew values on the Transform panel.

6 Select the top bubble, and click to select the Skew radio button. Click and drag the horizontal (left) skew value until it reads 15 degrees. Close the Transform panel.

To remove all the transformation values from an object, select it and click the Remove Transform button ( ) at the bottom of the Transform panel.

Transforming gradients

If you use gradients to fill or stroke graphics in your movie, you can precisely position, scale, and modify them using the Gradient Transform tool. Because your fish and bubbles both use gradient fills, you'll finalize your artwork with a little gradient tweaking.

1   Using the Selection tool (⬆), click on the body of your fish to select it.

2   Click on the fish body once to select it—you should see the orange gradient you created earlier in the lesson displayed in the Property Inspector as the active fill color. From the Tools panel, click and hold down your pointer on the Free Transform tool (⬚) to select the Gradient Transform tool (⬚).

3   A circular bounding box appears around your fish. Move your cursor over the center point of the bounding box until a four-way arrow appears. You can click and drag this point to shift the center point of the gradient. Click and drag the point up and to the left—this helps to imply a light source coming from the upper left.

Move the point shown in a Gradient Transform bounding box to shift a gradient's center point.

4   Locate the scale handle in the lower-right corner of the bounding box. Click and drag it inwards to scale the gradient down inside the fish. This increases the presence of the darkest color that makes up your fill.

Scale down a gradient using the handle shown. This also changes the perceived balance of colors.

5   Choose File > Save to save your file.

For linear gradients, the rotate handle allows you to change the direction of the gradient. This also works for radial gradients if the center point is offset from the middle.

Self study

Using the technique shown in the last exercise, shift the gradient points for your three bubbles to match the fish.

Review

Questions

1 Name two primary differences between mergeable shapes and Drawing Objects.

2 Which tool would you choose to manipulate individual points that make up a shape or path?

3 What three advantages does isolating artwork on a layer offer?

Answers

1 Drawing Objects can be arranged, whereas mergeable shapes cannot. Mergeable shapes can be partially selected, whereas Drawing Objects cannot.

2 The Subselection tool.

3 The ability to control stacking order, turn visibility on or off, and lock contents for editing.

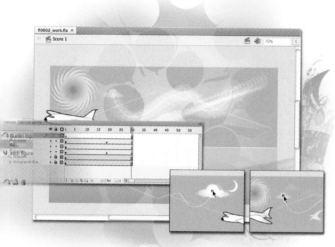

What you'll learn in this lesson:

- Using the Timeline
- Understanding the difference between frames and keyframes
- Setting up frame-by-frame animation
- Taking advantage of tweening
- Using motion guides
- Testing your movie

Creating Basic Animation

Adobe Flash is widely regarded as the tool of choice for animation for the web. With its ability to manipulate graphics in a variety of ways, the possibilities are endless when it comes to creating exciting, eye-catching animations for your projects.

Flash CS4 features significant new changes to the animation engine that are certain to make it more intuitive for new and experienced users alike.

Starting up

Before starting, make sure that your tools and panels are consistent by resetting your workspace. See "Resetting the Flash workspace" on page XXVII.

You will work with several files from the fl03lessons folder in this lesson. Make sure that you have loaded the CS4lessons folder onto your hard drive from the supplied DVD. See "Loading lesson files" on page XXVII.

See Lesson 3 in action!

Use the accompanying video to gain a better understanding of how to use some of the features shown in this lesson. The video tutorial for this lesson can be found on the included DVD.

The project

To see a completed example of the animated web banner you'll be creating, launch Flash and open the fl0601_done.fla file. Close the Flash Player and return to Flash CS4 Professional when you're done.

Introducing keyframes and the Timeline

One of the most important panels in the Flash workspace is the Timeline, which is where graphics, text, and media are sequenced and animation is created. The Timeline allows you to have items appear, disappear, or change appearance and position at different points in time.

The Timeline consists of three main components: layers, frames, and keyframes.

Layers

Layers enable you to stack and organize your graphics, media, and animations separately from one another, thereby giving you greater control over your project elements. If you've used other design applications such as Adobe Photoshop or Illustrator, it's likely that you've worked with layers before.

Flash also utilizes special types of layers for tasks such as tweening (animation), masking, and Inverse Kinematics, which you'll explore in this chapter and the next.

Frames and keyframes

On the Flash Timeline, time is represented by frames, which are displayed as small boxes across each layer of the Timeline. Time is subdivided into frames based on your frame rate. In a document set to the default frame rate of 24 fps (frames per second), every 24 frames on your Timeline represent one second of playback in your movie.

The playhead, shown as a vertical red beam, passes each frame when a movie plays back, much like movie film passing in front of a projector bulb.

When you decide you want to place a graphic, play a sound, or start an animation at a specific point along the Timeline, you must first create a keyframe. Keyframes are created to mark significant points along the Timeline where content can be placed. A keyframe can extend across the Timeline as long as you need it to keep its contents in view. By default, each new layer on the Timeline contains a single keyframe at frame 1.

The best way to understand the Timeline is to dive right in and work with it. In this next exercise, you'll sequence some items across the Timeline and work with layers to get started.

1   Choose File > Open, and locate and select the lesson file named fl0601.fla located in the fl03lessons folder. Choose Open to open the file.

Examine the Stage, and you see an airplane graphic along with two pieces of text that read *Takeoff* and *Landing*. In addition to the background layer and diagram layer (which you'll use as a visual aid later on), each of these items sits on its own named layer.

Note the frame ruler at the top of the Timeline, which marks frame numbers in 5-frame increments.

2   Choose File > Save As. In the Save As dialog box, navigate to the fl03lessons folder and type **fl0601_work.fla** in the Name text field. Press Save.

3   Let's get a feel for sequencing items across the Timeline. Click directly on the Timeline on the Airplane layer at frame 15 to select that frame (it should appear highlighted in blue).

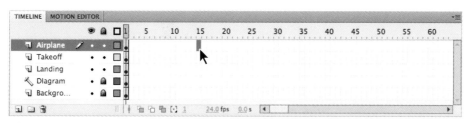

Select a frame directly on the layer to insert a keyframe at that position.

4   Right-click (Windows) or Ctrl+click (Mac OS) and choose Insert Keyframe to insert a new keyframe at this frame. The new keyframe appears with a border and bullet.

Insert a new keyframe.

Notice that the airplane on the previous keyframe (frame 1) has been duplicated on the new keyframe—you can now reposition this airplane on the Stage. However, you first need to extend the Background and Diagram layers so you can use them for reference.

5   Select frame 30 on the Background layer. Right-click (Windows) or Ctrl+click (Mac OS), and choose Insert Frame from the contextual menu that appears. This extends the Background layer up until frame 30.

Repeat step 5 for the Diagram layer so that it also extends up until frame 30.

Here, you added frames on the Diagram and Background layer to extend them up until frame 30.

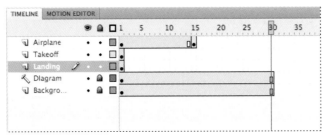

Add frames after a keyframe to extend it further along the Timeline.

6   Click on the Airplane layer and select keyframe 15. Using the Selection tool (*k*), grab the airplane that appears selected on the Stage, and drag it to the top-middle of the Stage. Use the Diagram layer as a reference.

7   Select frame 30 on the Airplane layer. Right-click (Windows) or Ctrl+click (Mac OS) on the selected frame, and select Insert Keyframe to add a keyframe at this position. Once again, the airplane from the previous keyframe is duplicated on this new keyframe.

8   Click on the Airplane layer and select keyframe 30. Using the Selection tool, grab the airplane that appears selected on the Stage, and drag it to the left edge of the Stage just above the ground. Again, use the dotted line and airplane images on the Diagram layer as a reference.

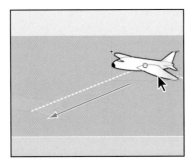

Move the airplane along the Stage.

9   Click on frame 1 of any Layer to bring your playhead back to the beginning of the movie. Press Enter (Windows) or Return (Mac OS) to play back your Timeline so far.

10 On the Landing layer, the text sits in the correct position but appears way too early in the movie (It shouldn't appear until frame 30, where the plane actually *lands*). Rather than create a new keyframe, you simply move the existing one by dragging it to a new location along the Timeline.

Click on the keyframe at frame 1 of the Landing layer to select it. Move your pointer over the frame again until a small white box appears below your cursor. Click, hold down your mouse button, drag the keyframe right, and release it at frame 30.

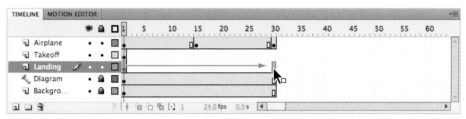

You can click and drag a selected keyframe to reposition on the Timeline.

11 The last finishing touch is to ensure that the Takeoff text hangs out on the Timeline just a bit longer. You'll use the same technique you used to extend the Background and Diagram layers.

Click and select frame 15 on the Takeoff layer. Right-click (Windows) or Ctrl+click (Mac OS) on the selected frame, and choose Insert Frame to add a frame and extend the first keyframe up to frame 15.

12 Press Enter (Windows) or Return (Mac OS) to play your Timeline back. The airplane should appear in three different positions, and the text should appear and disappear at different points.

13 Choose File > Save to save your movie, then choose File > Close to close the file.

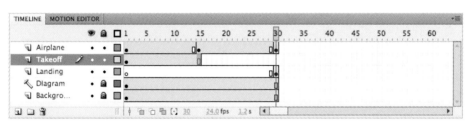

The final Timeline as it should appear in your file.

Keyframes can also be created using the F6 shortcut key, or by right-clicking (Windows) or Ctrl+clicking (Mac OS) directly on a frame and choosing Insert Keyframe from the contextual menu that appears.

Building animation: Enter the tween

Flash's strength lies in its ability to create automatically generated animations, or *tweens*, making it easy and intuitive to get things moving on your Stage. You simply need to let Flash know where an object needs to start, and where it needs to end, and Flash draws the frames in-between, saving you the painstaking work of creating dozens of frames by hand and moving or manipulating the artwork in small steps.

There are two types of tweens you can create on the Timeline: motion tweens and shape tweens. In the following steps, you'll focus on getting objects moving with motion tweens and the new animation engine in Flash CS4.

New: Tween layers and automatic keyframing

The animation engine in Flash CS4 has been completely redesigned to make creating animation easier and more intuitive for new and existing Flash users. Now, the process of manually creating keyframes has been eliminated in favor of the *tween span,* a single sequence of frames that can include any number of movements and tweens on a single object.

Within a single tween span, you only need to move or modify an object at a certain point in time, and Flash automatically creates keyframes to mark those movements where they occur on the Timeline. A layer that contains one or more tween spans is called a *tween layer.*

New Term: Motion Tween

A motion tween is an automatic animation performed on a symbol instance that can incorporate changes in position, scale, size, color effects, and filters. To create a motion tween, you right-click (Windows) or Ctrl+click (Mac OS) a keyframe that contains a single symbol instance and choose Create Motion Tween from the contextual menu that appears.

It's time to dive right in and get things moving on your Stage:

1 Choose File > Open and select the fl0602.fla file from this lesson's folder.

You'll notice some familiar graphics from the last exercise—except this time you'll get things moving with some fluid animation.

2 Choose File > Save As. In the Save As dialog box, navigate to the fl03lessons folder and type **fl0602_work.fla** in the Name text field. Press Save.

3   Let's begin with the Airplane layer—you'll want to move the airplane as you did in the previous exercise, but have it animate its movement from place to place. Right-click (Windows) or Ctrl+click (Mac OS) on the first frame of this layer and choose Create Motion Tween. A 24-frame tween span is created on this layer.

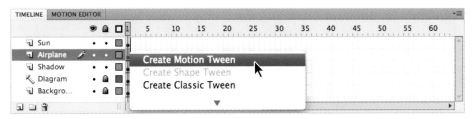

Right-click (Windows) or Ctrl+click (Mac OS) on a keyframe to create a motion tween.

4   To create animation, you simply need to move the playhead to a position on the Timeline and change the appearance or position of the graphic at that point in time. In this case, the goal is to get the airplane to the middle position at frame 15. To do this, click and drag the playhead to the frame 15 marker. Using the Selection tool ( ), click and drag the airplane graphic to the middle position (use the diagram layer as a reference). Notice that a black dot marks an automatically created keyframe at this position.

5   You'll see a line appear on the Stage that outlines the motion of the airplane—this is referred to as a motion path. Click to select frame 1 on the Timeline ruler to return your playhead to the beginning of the movie, and press Enter (Windows) or Return (Mac OS) to play back your Timeline—you should see your airplane glide from one place to another!

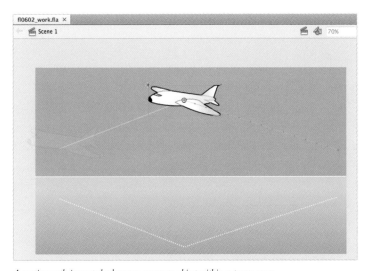

A motion path is created when you move an object within a tween span.

6   The next step is to get your airplane from the middle position to its final position on the left. To create an even number of frames for each movement, you're going to need to extend the tween span a bit. Move your mouse pointer over the last frame of the tween span (directly over the layer itself) until you see a double-arrow icon (◄|►). Click and drag to the right to stretch the span until it ends at frame 30.

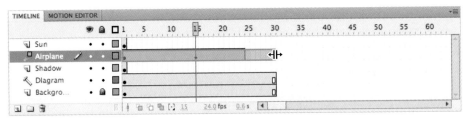

Extend or trim a tween span by clicking and dragging the last frame of the tween span.

You may notice that keyframe 15 moved slightly when you adjusted the length of the tween span. Keyframes shift as you readjust the length of a tween span, and this is okay to leave as is.

7   On the frame ruler at the top, click on frame 30 to jump the playhead to this position. Select the airplane, being careful not to click on the small circle in the center and drag it to the left side of the Stage to the landing position (use the diagram layer as a reference). Another keyframe is created at this position in the tween span to mark the change.

8   Press Enter (Windows) or Return (Mac OS) to play back the Timeline, and you see your airplane glide from place to place.

9   Choose File > Save. Leave the file open.

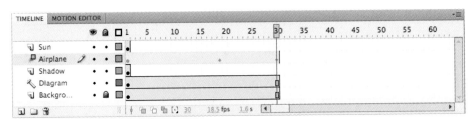

The finished Timeline.

The Tween Rules

It most certainly does, but in this case, it refers to some rules that apply when creating motion tweens and tween spans on the Timeline.

- The length of any new tween span, by default, matches the frame rate of your movie. A movie at the default 24 fps frame rate will create 24-frame tween spans, and a movie at 30 fps will create 30-frame tween spans.

- To be included in a tween span, a graphic, text, or imported bitmap image must be converted to a symbol first. If you attempt to create a motion tween on a non-symbol, Flash will prompt you to convert the item to a symbol on the spot.

- Only one symbol or graphic can be tweened at a time. If you attempt to apply a motion tween to a layer with several objects, it will prompt you to convert the graphics to a single symbol.

- Tween spans can include changes to position, size/scale, color effects, and filters (for movie clips and buttons). To morph the shape of an object, you'll use shape tweens (discussed later in this chapter).

Tweening multiple objects

To tween multiple graphics simultaneously, you simply need to place each one on its own individual layer. Each animated item will always need to have a dedicated tween span and tween layer. In this exercise you'll add layers to animate the shadow and text elements to complete the scene.

1   Select the first keyframe of the Shadow layer. Right-click (Windows) or Ctrl+click (Mac OS) on this keyframe and choose Create Motion Tween from the menu that appears. A tween span is created on this layer, and the shadow graphic is ready to be tweened.

2   Click on the Timeline ruler and drag the playhead to frame 15. At this frame, use the Selection tool (▶) to select and move the shadow so it sits below your airplane.

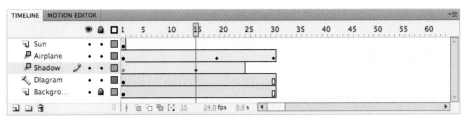

Create a tween span on the Shadow layer, and reposition the shadow on frame 15.

3   Move your mouse pointer over the last frame of the new tween span, and click and drag it to extend it to frame 30 (it should be as long as the airplane layer's tween span).

4 Click and drag the playhead to frame 30. On this frame, select the shadow once again and position it so it sits below the airplane in its landing position.

5 Press Enter (Windows) or Return (Mac OS) to play back your animation, and you should see the shadow move in tandem with your airplane!

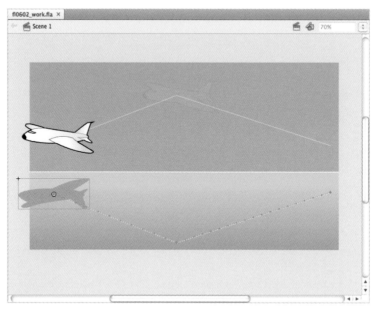

Reposition your shadow to match the movement of the airplane above.

6 Choose File > Save to save your work. Leave the file open.

 A tween layer won't allow you to place or draw additional graphics on it once it's been created. You will get a warning dialog box if you attempt to add content to an existing tween layer.

Previewing animation with Test Movie

Pressing Enter (Windows) or Return (Mac OS) (referred to as Live Preview) is a quick way of seeing your animation as you build it, but the performance of your animation is based on many factors, including frame rate, the complexity of Stage graphics, and the number of simultaneous animations running on the Stage at once.

To get a more accurate picture of your animation as your end user will see it, use the Control menu's Test Movie command. This command temporarily publishes your movie and displays it as your user will see it in the Flash Player.

1   With the current file open, choose Control > Test Movie.

2   The Flash Player opens, and displays and plays your movie. At this point, you can only stop the movie by using the Control menu. Choose Control > Stop.

You may have noticed that your diagram layer never shows in the final, published movie. The Diagram layer is a special type of layer called a Guide, whose contents are used strictly for visual reference and don't publish to your final movie. You can convert any standard layer to a Guide layer.

Generally, performance will be better in the Flash Player as you're viewing a flattened and optimized version of your movie.

3   Close the Flash Player window and return to your file.

You can use Ctrl+Enter (Windows) or Command+Return (Mac OS) as a shortcut instead of Control > Test Movie. This shortcut key combination will be used several times throughout the lesson.

Moving and transforming tween paths

Once a tween has been created, you may decide that the entire animation needs to be repositioned or shifted. Thanks to the new motion paths that appear on the Stage, this task has become easier than ever.

1   Click the Shadow layer in the Timeline, locate the motion path that your shadow graphic follows along the bottom of the Stage.

2   Using the Selection tool (↖), click once on the motion path to select it in its entirety.

3 Click anywhere on the motion path and then drag it straight down—this moves the path and the entire animation along with it. Move it down until the bottom of the motion path touches the bottom of the Stage. (Note: you can disregard the positioning shown on the Diagram layer at this point.)

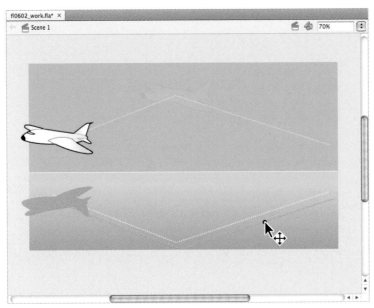

Click and drag a motion path to move it and the animated objects that follow it.

4 Leave the path selected, and choose the Free Transform tool (✳) from the Tools panel. A bounding box with eight handles appears around the motion path. You can transform the motion path just as you would a graphic to change its scaling or rotation.

5 Grab the bottom middle handle and pull it upwards slightly to change the vertical scaling of the path. You may notice that while the scaling of the path changes, the actual shadow does not!

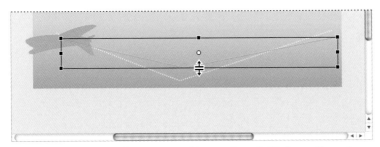

You can transform a motion path just as you would a piece of artwork. This has no effect on the animated object that follows it, however.

6 Press Enter (Windows) or Return (Mac OS) to play back your modified animation.

7 Choose File > Save to save your file.

Incorporating color effects and scaling

The cool thing about motion tweens is that you can have several properties of your graphic all animate at once, even within the same tween span. In addition to position, you can tween opacity (transparency), color tints, scaling, and rotation of an object to create more complex animation behavior.

For your airplane shadow, you'll want to manipulate the size and opacity of the shadow as the plane flies at different heights from the ground.

1   Select frame 19 of the Shadow layer. This brings you to the part of the tween span where the shadow appears in the middle of the Stage. Because the plane is at a higher altitude, the shadow should appear lighter and smaller.

2   Choose the Selection tool (↖), then select the shadow directly on the Stage at frame 19, and locate the Color Effect options under the Property Inspector panel on the right. If necessary, click on the arrow to the left of Color Effect to display the Style menu below it.

3   From the Style menu, choose Alpha, which controls the transparency of your symbol instance. Use the slider to set the Alpha back to 50 percent. Leave the shadow selected.

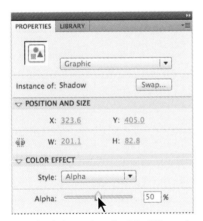
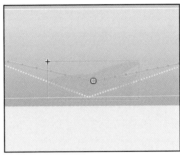

Select the shadow and use the Color Effects options to set its Alpha (transparency) to 50 percent.

4   Next, you'll reduce the size of your shadow slightly, as the airplane is higher off the ground. Choose Modify > Transform > Scale and Rotate. This opens the Scale and Rotate dialog box. Set the scale value to **60** percent, and press OK.

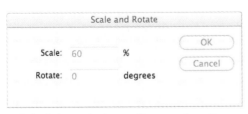
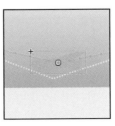

Scale the shadow graphic down to 60 percent at frame 19.

5   Drag the playhead to the beginning of the Timeline, and press Enter (Windows) or Return (Mac OS) to play back your animation—notice that the Alpha and scaling effects have been added to your tween!

However, also notice that the size and Alpha of the shadow don't return to their original values when the animation reaches frame 30. You'll fine-tune this in the next lesson.

6   Choose File > Save to save your movie.

New: Introducing the Motion Editor

Docked behind the Timeline panel is the Motion Editor, a powerful new panel that enables you to fine-tune and modify animation with precision. The Motion Editor displays all properties of a selected tween span in a graph-like format where you can adjust individual properties (such as position and Alpha) in a tactile, precise way.

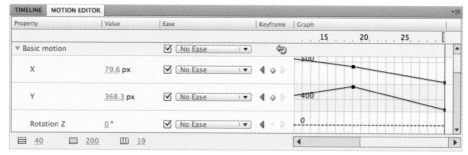

The Motion Editor is a powerful new addition that allows you to see and adjust every aspect of your animation in a graph-like format.

Previous Flash users will find this to be a welcome addition, but if this is your first time animating in Flash, you'll also enjoy the flexibility that comes with the new Motion Editor.

Let's take a look at the Motion Editor, and see how it works:

1   Click the Motion Editor tab to bring it forward. The Motion Editor appears docked behind the Timeline panel at the bottom of your workspace.

2   Before you can use or view properties in the Motion Editor, you'll first need to select a tweened object on the Stage. Click on the Shadow graphic on the Stage to select it and view its animation properties in the Motion Editor.

3   Each row across represents a different property that is either being tweened or can be tweened if desired. Use the vertical scroll bar on the right side of the Motion Editor to scroll down and see more properties.

You should see that every property you've tweened for your Shadow graphic, such as x position, y position, and Alpha, all have lines running across. These lines represent the value of each property at different points along the Timeline. As the line goes higher, so does the value.

4 Within the Basic Motion category click on the X property to expand it, this expands the row to full height. Click on the X property again to collapse it to it's original height. This expands that row to full height. You can also make more room for the Motion Editor by dragging the divider in between the bottom of the Stage and the top of the Motion Editor/Timeline panels.

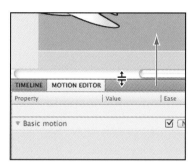

Click between the Motion Editor and the Stage to expand its height.

5 Scroll down and take a look at the Skew X and Skew Y properties. These rows display dashed lines, which indicate that there is no value for these properties. (You haven't applied any skewing to your graphic.)

6 Leave the Motion Editor open for the next exercise.

Modifying the animation using the Motion Editor

Let's go ahead and put the Motion Editor to use by modifying the animation you created earlier.

You'll remember that the Alpha and scale values of your shadow didn't switch back even as the airplane returned to the ground in frame 30. You'll need to adjust these values to change later in the animation, and the Motion Editor will help you do that.

1 If the Motion Editor is not already visible, click its tab above the Timeline to bring it forward. Note: If you accidentally collapsed the panel, you can reopen it by choosing Window > Motion Editor.

2 Using the Selection tool (↖), click to select the Shadow graphic on the Stage to reveal its properties in the Motion Editor. Scroll down if necessary and locate the Alpha/Alpha amount row nested inside the Color Effect category.

3 If, necessary, expand the Alpha amount row by clicking on it. Use the horizontal scroll bar to scroll across, and watch as the line starts at 100 percent (top), dips down at frame 19 to 50 percent, and remains there. A dashed line appears from that point on. You'll need to add a keyframe along this line to change its value at a different point in time.

4 Scroll right until you reach the end of the Alpha amount line (frame 30). Right-click (Windows) or Ctrl+click (Mac OS) on the very end of the line, and select Add Keyframe from the small contextual menu that appears.

This creates a draggable point on the line at frame 30. From here, you can either drag the point up or down to change the Alpha value, or specify an exact value on the left.

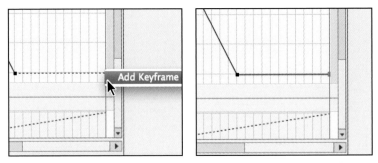

Right-click (Windows) or Ctrl+click (Mac OS) at any point along a value line to add keyframes that you can use to adjust values.

5 Leave the point selected, and on the left side of the row, locate the Alpha amount value. Click and drag on the value until it reads 100 percent. You should see the point (keyframe) you created move to the top position on the right and the shadow on the Stage become opaque.

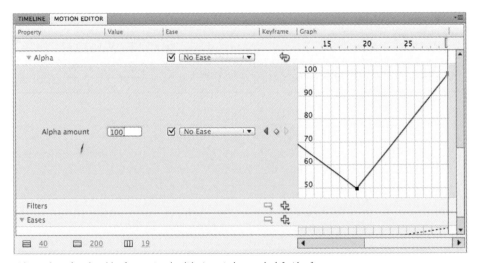

Adjust values of a selected keyframe using the slider/type-in box on the left side of a row.

To expand the height of the current row for a larger view, click on the row anywhere within the gray area on the left side of the Motion Editor.

6   Directly above the Alpha row, locate the Scale X and Scale Y rows, which affect horizontal and vertical scaling (respectively). You animated these properties when you scaled down the shadow earlier. Once again, scroll to the end of the row so that the end of the value line is visible.

7   At the end of the Scale X line, right-click (Windows) or Ctrl+click (Mac OS) directly on the line and choose Add Keyframe from the contextual menu that appears.

Another way that you can create additional points along the value line is by holding down Ctrl (Windows) or Command (Mac OS) and clicking directly on the line. Add the Alt (Windows)/ Option (Mac OS) key to this combo to remove an existing point.

8   Click and drag the new point (keyframe) straight up until the value on the left reads 60 percent. The value is shown on the left side of the Motion Editor directly to the right of where it reads Scale X. As you change this value, you will also see the plane shadow scale.

9   Repeat steps 7 and 8 for the Scale Y value, also returning its value to 60 percent at the end of the line (frame 30).

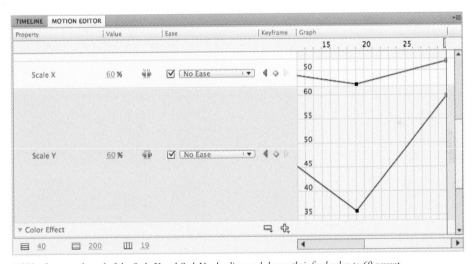

Add keyframes to the end of the Scale X and Scale Y value lines and change their final value to 60 percent.

10 Press Ctrl+Enter (Windows) or Command+Return (Mac OS) to preview the animation with the new adjustments you've made. You should see the shadow animate back to full opacity and its original size as the animation reaches its completion. Close the Flash Player once you've viewed your movie.

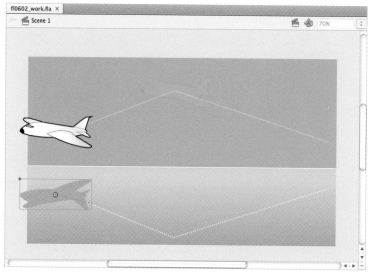

The airplane's shadow now returns to full size and opacity by frame 30.

11 Choose File > Save, and leave this file open.

The Motion Editor displays a frame ruler and playhead at the top just like the Timeline, so you can easily preview your changes as you go, without the need to switch back to the Timeline panel.

Making moves: Navigating the Timeline

Now that you are working across several frames and tween spans across the Timeline, you'll want to be able to navigate the Timeline and view animation sequences in a number of ways.

Here are a few short tips for navigating the Timeline that you'll find useful:

- **Preview an animation** by pressing Enter (Windows) or Return (Mac OS) to start playback of the Timeline and view an entire animation sequence.

- **Move frame-by-frame through the Timeline** by using the , (comma) and . (period) keys.

- **Move in any direction at any speed** by clicking and dragging the playhead back and forth across the frame ruler. This is referred to as *scrubbing*.

- **Rewind and jump to the beginning of the Timeline** by choosing Control > Rewind or pressing Shift+, (comma).

Tweening rotation

If you need to incorporate one or more full rotations in a tween, you'll find that rotation has its own special option in the Property Inspector. Rotations may need to occur more than once (for instance, three full revolutions)—behavior that Flash can't figure out from a graphic's position alone.

In the following steps, you'll add a tween to the Sun graphic on your Stage, and rotate it using the Property Inspector's rotation menu.

1 Bring the Timeline panel forward by clicking its tab below the Stage, or by choosing Window > Timeline. Select keyframe 1 of the Sun layer on the Timeline.

2 Right-click (Windows) or Ctrl+click (Mac OS) on the keyframe and choose Create Motion Tween from the contextual menu that appears. The layer is converted to a tween layer and a new tween span is created.

3 Just as you did with the other tween layers earlier, move your pointer over the last frame of the tween span, and then click and drag it to the right until it ends at frame 30.

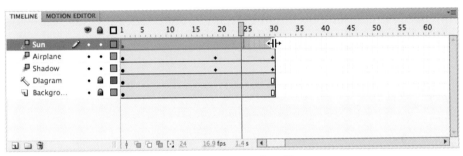

Add a motion tween to the Sun layer, and expand the tween span to frame 30.

4 Leave the frame selected, and locate (and if necessary, expand) the Rotation options in the Property Inspector on the right of your workspace.

5 Place your cursor over the 0 in the Rotate property and then click and drag to set the rotate count to 3 times. This sets the number of revolutions the sun will complete during the course of the tween span.

6   Under the Rotate value, click on the Direction drop-down menu. This allows you to choose the direction (clockwise or counter-clockwise) of the revolutions. Select CW for clockwise if it's not already selected.

Set the rotations to 3 on the Property Inspector.
If necessary, set the direction to CW (clockwise).

7   To put the finishing touches on your animation scene, select the Sun layer, and then click and drag it directly below the Airplane layer.

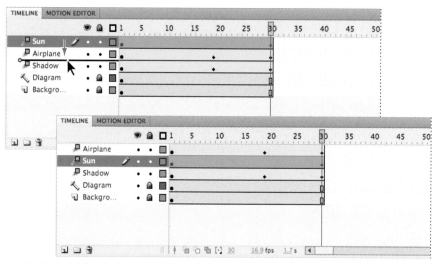

Drag the Sun layer below the Airplane layer to complete the scene.

Press Enter (Windows) or Return (Mac OS) to play back your movie, and you'll see the sun rotate three times clockwise! Experiment with different numbers of revolutions to increase the perceived speed of the rotation.

Remember, increasing revolutions without increasing the length of the tween span will result in faster rotation.

8 Choose File > Save to save your file.

New Feature: Rotation

The Rotation options now feature the ability to add a specific amount of degrees to the number of full rotations you've chosen. For instance, you can set three rotations and 45 degrees if you'd like! Previous versions of Flash only accepted whole number rotation values.

Controlling animation paths

You may have noticed how all the tweens you've created so far move in a straight line. While this may work in certain situations, there will certainly be a time when you want an animated object to follow a curved or unusual path.

To accomplish this, you can manipulate the motion path that your animated object follows. This motion path behaves much like any other path, and can be curved or manipulated using the Selection tool.

1 Select the Airplane layer in the Timeline. Choose the Selection tool (⬉), and move your pointer over the right half of the airplane's motion path (animation path). You should see a curved line appear below your cursor (⬉) when you get close enough to the line.

2 Click and drag up to bend the line into an upward curve, as shown in the figure below.

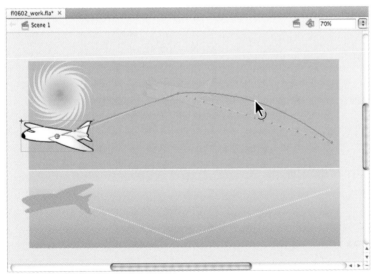

Click and drag over the middle of a line to bend it into a curve.

3 Move your pointer over the second half of the motion path (where the plane begins to fly down again) until the same curved icon appears below your cursor. Click and drag down to bend the line into a downward curve.

4   Press Enter (Windows) or Return (Mac OS) to play back your animation, and you'll see your airplane follow the new curve of the motion path.

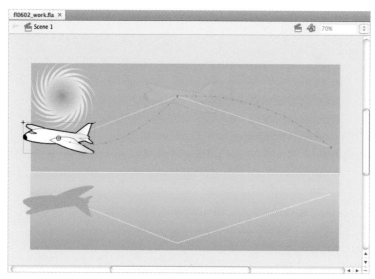

The airplane now follows the newly adjusted motion path.

5   Choose File > Save to save your file.

Where did Motion Guide layers go?

Experienced Flash users may notice the absence of the Add Motion Guide icon below the Timeline. Major changes in the animation engine, as well as the addition of motion paths in Flash, have essentially removed the need for Motion Guide layers.

What happens to my existing Flash files that use Motion Guide layers?

The good news is that Flash CS4 will continue to support Motion Guide layers from previously created documents. You will be able to modify motion guides paths, and any tweens using them are treated as *classic* tweens (discussed later in this chapter).

How do I create a motion guide if I still want to?

Interestingly enough, despite the removal of the Add Motion Guide button, it is still possible to create a Motion Guide layer, but in a very non-obvious way. The Flash CS4 team thought enough to include a discreet way to create motion guides using standard guide layers.

Because traditional motion guides only work with classic (old-school) tweens, they are discussed in detail later in this lesson under "Legacy techniques: Creating classic tweens."

Morphing graphics and colors with shape tweens

So far, the tweens you've created have involved moving, scaling, or rotating symbol instances across the Stage. However, you may want to create some cool animations by having an object change its shape or color.

For these tasks, you'll explore shape tweens, which allow you to animate changes in shape and color between two graphics. You can also create cool *morphing* effects by having one object gradually transform into another.

Shape tween basics

The good news for experienced Flash users is that the process of creating a shape tween has not changed. For new users, shape tweens differ in some important ways from the motion tweens you learned about earlier in the chapter.

Some major differences are:

- Unlike motion tweens, shape tweens can't work with symbol instances. You can only use mergeable artwork or drawing objects. Primitive shapes can be used, but they must be broken down first.

- Shape tweens require the creation of two keyframes to contain the starting and ending shapes of the tween.

- Shape tweens do not have motion paths, so their motion, if any, is always linear (they move in a straight line).

- The Motion Editor can't be used to adjust shape tweens.

In this section, you'll create a shape tween to transform a moon into a bird in your animation scene.

1   Make sure the Timeline panel is visible by clicking its tab below the Stage, or by choosing Window > Timeline.

2   Select the Airplane layer and click the New Layer icon (⊒) below the Timeline to create a new layer; rename it Shape Morph. At this time, lock your other layers so you don't accidentally disturb their contents.

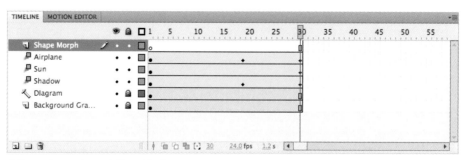

Add a new layer and name it Shape Morph.

To lock all layers except for the one you want to work on, hold down the Alt (Windows)/Option (Mac OS) key and click the dot below the padlock icon on the layer you'd like to use. All other layers except for the selected one automatically lock.

3   Click and drag the playhead to the beginning of the timeline at frame 1. Bring the Library panel forward by clicking its tab—you'll find it docked behind the Property Inspector on the right. In the Library panel, locate the Moon graphic symbol, and drag an instance of it to the upper-right corner of the Stage. It is automatically placed on the new layer you just created.

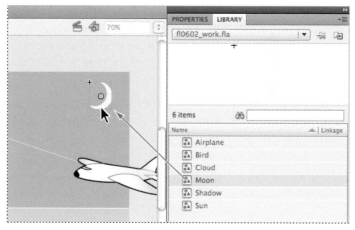

Drag an instance of the Moon graphic to the Stage.

You won't be able to drag a symbol to a locked layer, so if you're having difficulty, make sure that you have that Shape Morph layer selected on the Timeline, and that it is unlocked.

4   Because shape tweens can't work with symbol instances, you'll need to break this symbol back down to basic artwork again to use it in your shape tween. Use the Selection tool to select the new symbol instance, and choose Modify > Break Apart to break it down to non-symbol artwork.

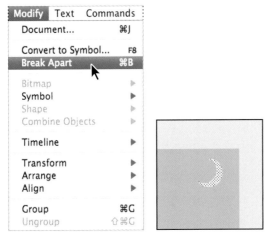

Choose Modify > Break Apart to break a symbol instance apart and prepare it for shape tweening.

5   Next, you'll need to add a second keyframe that will contain a new shape that your moon will transform into. Click and select frame 30 on the Shape Morph layer. Right-click (Windows) or Ctrl+click (Mac OS) on the selected frame and choose Insert Blank Keyframe to add a new empty keyframe at this position.

The only difference between inserting a keyframe or a blank keyframe is whether or not Flash copies the contents of the previous keyframe to the new one. For a shape tween, you generally aren't reusing the shape from the starting keyframe, so adding a blank keyframe is a better choice.

6   Click to select the new keyframe (30). Locate the Bird graphic symbol in your Library panel, and drag an instance of it to the middle of the Stage slightly above the ground.

7 Once again, choose Modify > Break Apart to break the symbol instance down to basic artwork. Now that you have two unique shapes on keyframes 1 and 30, you're ready to create a shape tween to have one transform into another.

Place and break apart the Bird graphic
to prepare it for shape tweening.

8 Click to select keyframe 1. Right-click (Windows) or Ctrl+Click (Mac OS) on the keyframe and choose Create Shape Tween from the contextual menu that appears. A green shaded area and an arrow appear between the two keyframes, letting you know that the shape tween has been successfully created.

9 Press Enter (Windows) or Return (Mac OS) to play back your animation, and watch as the first shape gradually morphs into the second!

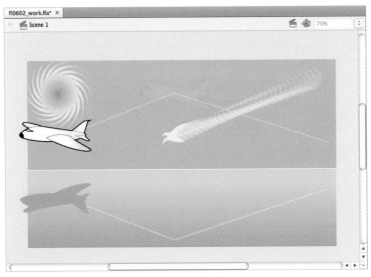

Your completed shape tween, shown in Onion Skin view.

10 Choose File > Save to save your file.

If your tween displays a dashed line instead of an arrow, be sure to check that both pieces of artwork have been broken out of their symbol form. If either piece of artwork still exists as a graphic symbol, the shape tween can't be properly created.

Getting in shape: Making the most of shape tweens

Shape tweening is part technique, part luck of the draw. Every pair of shapes will yield a unique result, but in some cases the transition between two shapes may not be what you expect. In some cases, the transition may not be pretty at all. To get the best results from your shape tweens, here are some general pointers to consider:

1 Try using solid, whole shapes. For instance, if you have a face and two eyes, avoid trying to morph all three in a single shape tween. Consider breaking each element out onto its own layer for best results.

2 Try and keep the number of starting and ending shapes the same. Two shapes to two shapes, as opposed to two shapes to three shapes, will yield cleaner results.

3 If your starting shape includes a stroke, try to include one on the ending shape as well.

Legacy techniques: Creating classic tweens

In previous versions of Flash, the process of creating motion tweens was very different. In fact, it was much more like creating shape tweens, whereby a set of keyframes had to be manually created to mark the beginning and end of a motion tween.

While it's highly recommended that you use the new tween model, there may be cases where you need to create or modify a *classic* motion tween within an older Flash file. The next lesson illustrates this technique for just those times.

1 Press the insert layer button (⊒) below the Timeline to add a new layer. Name this new layer Classic Tween.

2 From the Library panel on the right, locate and drag an instance of the Cloud graphic symbol to the first keyframe of the new layer. Use the Selection tool (⬂) to position it in the upper-right corner of the Stage.

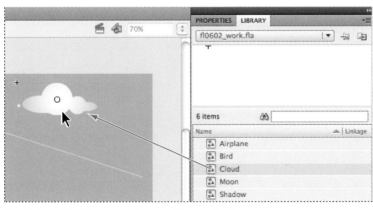

Drag instance of the Cloud graphic from your Library to the Stage.

3   Classic motion tweens require a starting and ending keyframe, so you'll need to create the ending keyframe further down on this layer. Select frame 30 of this layer, and press the F6 shortcut key to create a new keyframe at this position.

4   The cloud from keyframe 1 has been duplicated onto this new keyframe—you'll change the position of this copy to mark where the cloud should go during the course of the animation. Click and drag the cloud instance on keyframe 30 straight to the left so it sits beside the sun.

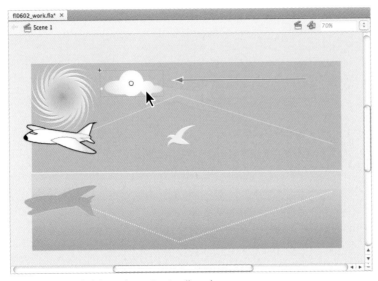

Move the cloud to the left to indicate where it will travel to.

5   Now it's time to finalize the tween. Click and select keyframe 1. Right-click (Windows) or Ctrl+click (Mac OS) on the keyframe and choose Create Classic Tween from the contextual menu that appears. A purple, shaded area and arrow should appear in between the two keyframes, indicating the tween has been successfully created.

6   Choose Control > Test Movie to preview your animation. The cloud moves to the left across the Stage!

7   Close the Flash Player, and choose File > Save to save your work.

Motion tween rules

As with tween layers and tween spans, classic motion tweens have some rules that need to be followed to ensure that they are created properly.

- Motion tweens require a starting and ending keyframe.
- Classic tweens can only use symbol instances.
- Both keyframes require an instance of the same symbol; you can't tween between two different symbol instances.
- Only one object can be tweened at a time on a single layer.

Adding color effects and scaling to a classic tween

When using classic tweens, you can animate several properties at once, just as you did with the airplane's shadow earlier in the chapter. By making changes to the starting or ending instance of the cloud, you can incorporate transparency, scaling, and other properties in the tween along with the existing motion.

1 If it's not visible, bring the Property Inspector forward by clicking its tab on the right side, or by choosing Window > Properties.

2 Click keyframe 30 directly on the Classic Tween layer to select it. The cloud on this keyframe should also appear selected on the Stage. Click once more on the cloud so it's active in the Property Inspector on the right.

3 Under the Property Inspector's Color Effect options, locate and click on the Style menu and select Alpha. When the Alpha slider appears, click and drag it to the left to set the Alpha value to 50 percent.

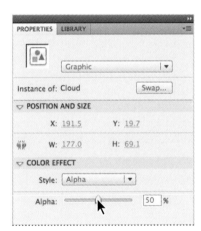 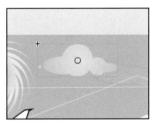

Select the cloud on frame 30 and use the Color options on the Property Inspector to set its Alpha to 50 percent.

4 Leave the cloud selected, and choose Modify > Transform > Scale and Rotate. In the Scale and Rotate dialog box that appears, type **50%** for the Scale value, and press OK to apply the new value.

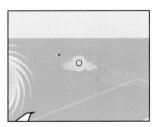

The cloud shown after color effects and scaling have been applied.

5   Press Enter (Windows) or Return (Mac OS) to play back your Timeline, and watch as the cloud fades and shrinks as it moves across the sky.

6   Choose File > Save to save your file.

There is a big difference between selecting a keyframe and selecting the contents of a keyframe. If an object on the Stage appears selected, but you don't see its options in the Property Inspector, click once more on the object to make it active. This is sometimes referred to as focusing *an object.*

Unlike tween spans, classic tweens will not prevent you from adding other objects to the same layer. While this will not generate a warning, adding something to a layer that contains a classic tween will likely break the tween.

(Re)creating motion guides for classic tweens

Experienced Flash designers may have already noticed the apparent removal of the Add Motion Guide button below the Timeline, and, in turn, the ability to create Motion Guide layers. A technique still exists for creating *classic* motion guides when and if necessary. In the following steps, you'll change the path of animation for your classic tween using good, old-fashioned motion guides.

1   Click and select your Classic Tween layer on the Timeline.

2   Click the Add Layer button (◻) below the Timeline to create a new layer above the Classic Tween layer, and rename it Motion Guide. You'll use standard drawing tools, such as the Pencil tool, to create a random path that your cloud can follow.

3   Select the Pencil tool (✎) from the Tools panel, and make sure that you have a stroke color selected. In addition, make sure that Object Drawing is *not* enabled. The button at the bottom of the Tools panel, (◯), should be popped out.

4   On the new layer, use the Pencil tool to draw a single interesting path that starts about where the cloud begins, and ends about where it ends on the left side of the Stage. This path is what your classic tween will follow in just a few moments.

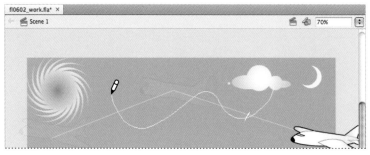

Use the Pencil tool to draw a path on the new layer you created.

5   The trick to making sure the classic tween will follow this path is to first convert this layer to a Guide layer. Right-click (Windows) or Ctrl+click (Mac OS) on the title area of the Motion Guide layer, and choose Guide from the contextual menu that appears. The layer icon is replaced by a T-square icon (✎), indicating that this is now a Guide layer.

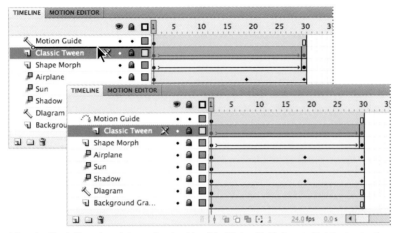

Move the Classic Tween layer below and to the right of the Motion Guide layer to bind the two together.

6   Next, select the Classic Tween layer, and carefully drag it up and to the right below the Motion Guide layer until it appears indented underneath it. This lets the Classic Tween layer know to follow whatever path it finds on the Motion Guide layer above it.

7   To get your cloud following the path, you'll need to snap the cloud instances at the beginning and end keyframes of the classic tween layer to the beginning and end of the path, respectively. Choose the Selection tool (🡤), click on keyframe 1 of the classic tween layer, and drag the cloud on this keyframe over the beginning of the path you created until the center snaps in place.

Snap the cloud instances on keyframes 1 and 30 to the beginning and end of the path, respectively.

Select keyframe 30 of the classic tween layer, and click and drag the cloud on this keyframe to the end of the path until it again snaps in place.

For symbol instances to properly snap in place to a path acting as a motion guide, make sure Snap To Objects is enabled. Choose View > Snapping > Snap To Objects to make sure it is checked.

8 Press Enter (Windows) or Return (Mac OS) to preview your animation—your cloud should now follow the path you created on the Motion Guide layer.

9 Choose File > Save to save your file.

Troubleshooting Motion Guides

Motion guides can be a bit tricky the first few times around. If your animation is not following the motion guide you created, use the following points to troubleshoot your animation:

- Make sure that both the starting and ending instance are snapped directly onto the path you created. If either instance is not seated properly on the motion guide, it will not work. Think of it as putting a train on the tracks.

- Make sure your motion path is NOT a drawing object, group, or symbol. Animations can only follow paths drawn in Merged Drawing mode. A telltale sign that you may not be using the right type of artwork is if your path appears inside a bounding box.

- Avoid using unusual stroke styles, such as dashes, dots, or ragged strokes. These occasionally cause unpredictable behavior if used on a motion path.

Adjusting animation with onion skinning

One of Flash's most useful visual aids is the Onion Skin, which allows you to view all frames of an animation at once on the Stage. This helps you make crucial decisions, such as how far to move or scale an object during the course of an animation. It also helps you see how your animation works alongside of other items on the Stage as the Timeline plays back.

Onion skinning can be enabled for a single layer or multiple layers at once; simply unlock a layer if you want to view it as onion skins, or lock it if you don't.

In the following steps, you'll see how you can adjust your existing tweens in Onion Skin view.

1 On the Timeline, lock all layers except for your Shadow, Shape Morph, and Classic Tween layers. If necessary, click and drag the playhead to the end of your Timeline to frame 30.

2   At the bottom of the Timeline, locate the cluster of five small buttons, and click the second from the left, (⬛), to enable Onion Skin view. Two brackets appear on the frame ruler at the top of the Timeline. These brackets allow you to select the range of frames that you'd like to view in Onion Skin mode.

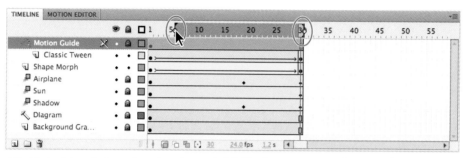

Adjust the brackets on the frame ruler to choose how much of the Timeline you want to reveal in Onion Skin mode.

3   Click and drag the left bracket to position it at the very beginning of the Timeline (frame 1). With the playhead at frame 30, the right bracket is at the end of the Timeline. You should now see all frames of animation on the unlocked layers.

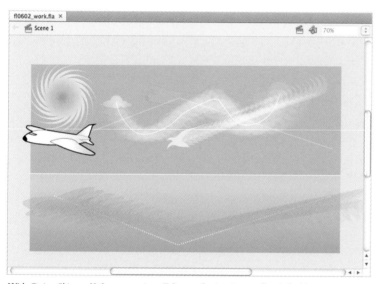

With Onion Skin enabled, you can view all frames of animation on all unlocked layers.

4   On the Shape Morph layer, select the moon shape and drag it slightly downward, click anywhere in the background and you will see the frames in between adjust automatically. Use the angle of the frames in between until you get the shape morph moving in a straight line from right to left.

5   On the Shadow layer, grab the starting shadow symbol instance on the right side of the Stage and drag it down slightly. You see the trajectory of the tween change, and the motion path readjusts as well.

Adjust animation in Onion Skin view to reveal how frames will be redrawn in a tween.

6   Use the same technique to adjust the starting and ending position of your Cloud graphic on the Classic Tween layer. Try relocating the cloud to the opposite side of the Stage by moving the starting and ending instances individually, and watch how the frames redraw in between.

If the full-color frames in Onion Skin are difficult to look at, try Onion Skin Outlines. Click the button directly to the right of Onion Skin (third from the left in the button cluster below the Timeline); this displays all frames in an outline view that's easier to see in certain situations.

7   Choose File > Save to save your file, and choose File > Close to close the file.

Self study

Add a new layer to your lesson file, and drag an additional airplane from the Library panel to the new layer. Create a tween that incorporates changes to position, color and size. Add a second layer, and draw a shape that you'd like to morph. Create a second shape on a new keyframe at the end of that layer, and create a shape tween between the two shapes.

Review

Questions

1 What three types of tweens can be created in Flash?

2 What are two reasons why you would create a keyframe on a layer along the Timeline?

3 How many objects can be tweened at the same time on a single layer?

Answers

1 Motion tweens, shape tweens, and classic tweens.

2 To have an object appear at that point in time, or to start an animation sequence (tween).

3 One.

What you'll learn in this lesson:

- Publishing to the web and CD

- Customizing Publish Settings

- Creating a standalone, full-screen projector

- Exporting to video

Delivering Your Final Movie

Although Flash is commonly thought of as a web design and development program, it's also a full-featured multimedia authoring tool. With Flash CS4 Professional, you can publish content for distribution to the web, CDs, DVDs, and video.

Starting up

Before starting, make sure that your tools and panels are consistent by resetting your preferences. See "Resetting the Flash workspace" on page XXVII.

You will work with several files from the fl04lessons folder in this lesson. Make sure that you have loaded the CS4lessons folder onto your hard drive from the supplied DVD. See "Loading lesson files" on page XXIX.

See Lesson 4 in action!

Use the accompanying video to gain a better understanding of how to use some of the features shown in this lesson. The video tutorial for this lesson can be found on the included DVD.

The project

In this lesson, you won't be creating a movie or even a piece of one. Instead, you'll be publishing existing movies to the web and CD-ROM. You will also learn how to customize Publish settings to adapt Flash content for a variety of applications and, finally, you will create a Flash projector file to deploy your Flash movies as standalone files.

The publishing process

By now you should be very familiar with the Test Movie command. As you learned in previous lessons, the command generates an SWF file so that you can preview how your animation looks and how its interactive elements behave. Although Test Movie works very well as a preview and you can embed the resulting SWF directly into a web page, the Publish command gives you a much wider range of options. By default, the Publish command creates an HTML page with your SWF file embedded into it for display. It is important to remember that when you publish a file, you have to target a version of the Flash player to publish to. So, if you prefer, you can alter your Publish settings to convert the FLA file to a GIF, JPEG, PNG, or QuickTime file. When combined with your SWF file, this option allows your Flash file to be displayed by viewers who have the targeted Flash player, and the image file to be displayed by viewers who lack the correct version of the player. This alternative publishing format also includes the HTML needed to display the images in a viewer's browser window.

Publishing to the web

For the best possible user experience, a Flash file must be embedded into a web page. If you are familiar with an HTML authoring program such as Adobe Dreamweaver, you could export an SWF file and then embed it into a page manually. An easier approach, however, is to use Flash's Publish command, which does all the work for you by creating an SWF file, an HTML file that has your SWF file embedded into it, and a JavaScript file that allows your Flash movie to automatically play in browsers that would normally block Flash content. Once you have the SWF, HTML, and JavaScript files, you can easily upload them to your web site.

Publishing a file is simple. With your FLA file open, select File > Publish. Flash then creates HTML, SWF, and JavaScript files, and saves them to the directory that contains the FLA file.

Customizing the Publish settings

The default settings are fine for many situations, but you can customize the Publish settings for better results. Give it a try:

1 From the fl04lessons folder, open the file named fl1501.fla, which is an animated footer for a web site.

2 Choose File > Publish Settings to open the Publish Settings dialog box. The dialog box is initially composed of three tabs: Formats, which lets you choose the publish format; Flash, which contains settings for the FLA file you're publishing; and HTML, which enables you to customize the associated HTML file. By default, Flash is already set to publish a Flash movie and embed it in an HTML page. If you choose another format in the Formats tab, additional tabs related to that format appear. For now, keep the default Format settings.

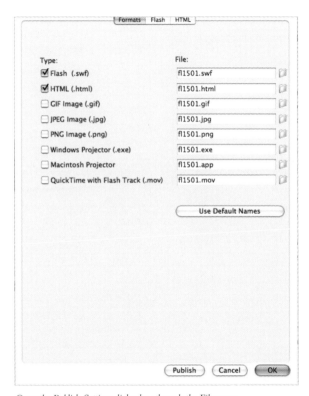

Open the Publish Settings dialog box through the File menu.

3   Click the Flash tab. The settings here control how the Flash movie you publish is created. They are grouped into three general sections: SWF file options, image options, and audio options. Make sure that Player is set to Flash Player 9, and ActionScript is set to ActionScript 2.0. By default, the Flash Player version is set to the most recent version available. In addition, Flash automatically sets the ActionScript version to match the choice you make when you choose ActionScript 2.0 or 3.0 when first creating a document.

4   In the Advanced section, click to turn on the *Protect from import* checkbox and in the SWF Settings section, click to turn off the *Include hidden layers* checkbox. The *Protect from import* option prevents a user from downloading your Flash movie and reimporting it into Flash to reuse. Deselecting the *Include hidden layers* option ensures that layers that are hidden are not included in the published file.

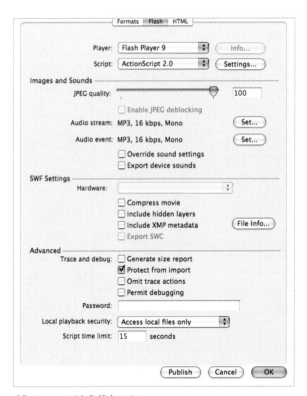

Adjust your movie's Publish settings.

You can set three additional options for the Flash file export. Omit Trace Action and Permit Debugging are specifically geared toward working with ActionScript, while Generate Size Report creates a text file that breaks down the size of each scene and symbol in your movie.

5   Raise the JPEG Quality slider to 100 to ensure the least amount of compression on the bitmap images in your movie.

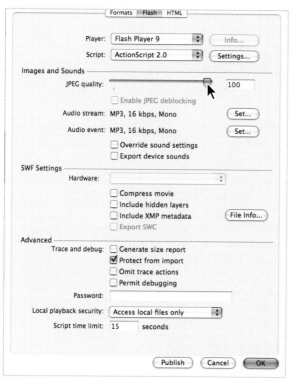

Drag the JPEG quality slider to 100.

Although the example file does not use any audio effects, the Images and Sounds section of the Flash tab enables you to set a movie's audio quality. By clicking on the Set buttons to the right of Audio stream and Audio event, you can open up dialog boxes that control how those types of audio objects are compressed. The default MP3 setting is very efficient in most situations.

6   Click the HTML tab to view the options for the HTML file that you are publishing.
By default, Template is set to display Flash only. Click the Info button to the right of the
Template drop-down menu to view the description of the current template. For Flash
Only, the Info pop-up explains that this template is intended as a container for your Flash
movie, and that the publish operation creates a file named AC_OETags.js, which is an
external JavaScript file that the HTML page needs to display the Flash content correctly.
Close the pop-up after you have reviewed the description.

Review the descriptions on the HTML tab.

7   Make sure the *Detect Flash Version* checkbox is selected. This configures your document to
detect the user's version of Flash Player and sends the user to an alternative HTML page
if the targeted player isn't present.

8   Select Percent from the Dimensions drop-down menu. The Dimensions menu sets
the display size of the Flash movie in your HTML page. Make sure Width and Height
are both set to 100 percent to ensure that the movie scales to fit the size of the
browser window.

9 In the Playback options area, make sure the *Display Menu* checkbox is selected. The playback options control how the Flash movie behaves when loaded into the browser. With *Display Menu* on, the user can display a context menu by right-clicking (Windows) or Ctrl+clicking (Mac OS) on the Flash movie in the browser.

Because the example movie uses a nested movie clip symbol, the HTML tab's Paused at Start and Loop Playback options would have no effect; they target the main Timeline only. Device Fonts is a Windows-only solution that substitutes system fonts for fonts used in the Flash movie that are not loaded on the user's computer.

10 Choose Best from the Quality drop-down menu to ensure that the Flash movie displays at its highest possible quality setting. Be aware that this setting has a downside: the processing time needed to achieve Best quality is longer than for lower settings.

11 Leave Window Mode, HTML Alignment, and Scale at the default settings. Window Mode controls the appearance of the box in which the SWF file appears; you can use it to create an SWF file with a transparent background. HTML Alignment controls the position of the SWF file window in the web page. Window Mode controls the appearance of the box in which the SWF file appears; you can use it to create an SWF file with a transparent background. Apply Scale only if you changed the SWF file's original dimensions.

12 Next to Flash Alignment options, set Horizontal to Center and Vertical to Top, which places the SWF file in the upper-middle portion of the browser window.

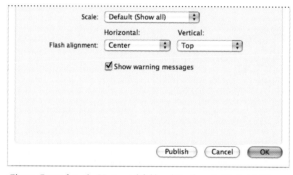

Choose Center from the Horizontal field and Top from the Vertical field.

13 Press OK to keep these settings. They are saved when you save the Flash document.

To publish the file with your new settings, you can choose File > Publish while the file is open, or you can publish directly from the Publish Settings panel by clicking its Publish button.

CD-ROM delivery

The web is not your only option for delivering your Flash content. You can distribute it offline, as well as through CDs and DVDs, by creating projector files. A projector file is a standalone executable Flash document that can be downloaded or delivered on a CD or DVD. Projector files are often used to deliver games and presentations that are deployed locally on the viewer's computer and not through the Internet. Because the Flash Player is included in the projector, users can display the Flash content without a web browser.

Creating a standalone projector

Like publishing to the web, the process of publishing an FLA file to a projector file starts in the Publish Settings panel. The difference is what you set in the Formats tab.

1   Open the fl1502.fla file from the fl04lessons folder. This file contains the beginning stages of a game called Dodge 'Em that you will publish as an executable projector file.

2   Choose File > Publish Settings.

3   In the Formats tab of the Publish Settings panel, turn off the *Flash* and *HTML* checkboxes. Turn on the checkbox next to *Windows Projector* (Windows) or *Macintosh Projector* (Mac OS). Unlike Flash and HTML files, there are no editable options for the Projector format.

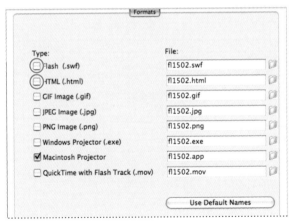

Deselect the Flash and HTML checkboxes and choose either Windows Projector or Macintosh Projector.

The File fields to the right of each output type allow you to specify a name for your file and an output location. By default, the output name and location are the same as that of your Flash FLA file.

4   Click the Publish button in the Publish Settings panel to produce a standalone Flash projector. Press OK.

If the Publish Settings panel is closed, you can publish a file by choosing File > Publish or pressing Shift+F12.

5   Minimize Flash, and, from your desktop, navigate to the fl04lessons folder. Double-click on the fl1502.exe (Windows) or fl1502.app (Mac OS) file to launch it. The Dodge 'Em game that you just published should open and play inside a window on your desktop. The window is the same size as the Stage was in Flash. Close the file and return to Flash.

Make a full-screen projector

The projector's ability to deliver standalone Flash movies makes it an ideal choice for delivering content, such as interactive portfolios, marketing materials, and presentations. However, watching a presentation on-screen surrounded by all the other icons and applications that may be running on your desktop can be distracting. With a little ActionScript, you can set a Flash projector file to launch as a full-screen application.

1   If the fl1502.fla file is not already open, open it now. Select the first frame of the Actions layer in the Timeline.

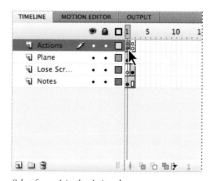

Select frame 1 in the Actions layer.

2   Choose Window > Actions to open the Actions panel.

3 The first line of code is a *stop( )* action to stop the movement of the playhead at frame 1. Place your cursor at the end of the first line, after the semicolon, and press the Enter (Windows) or Return (Mac OS) key.

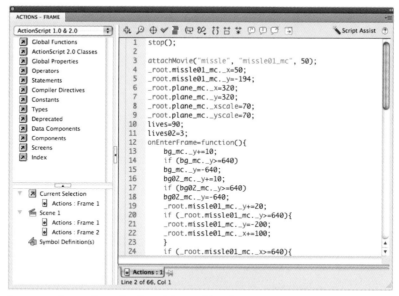

Insert a space between the stop( ) action and the rest of the code.

4 With your cursor now on line 2, type in the following line of code:

```
fscommand("fullscreen", true);
```

Fscommand is an ActionScript function that enables the SWF movie to communicate with the container that is holding it, whether that container is a web browser or the standalone Flash Player, as it is here. The command tells the Flash Player to display at the full-screen resolution of the viewer's monitor, thus ensuring an immersive experience.

The ActionScript function fscommand allows an SWF movie to communicate with its container application.

5 Close the Actions panel. Save your file using File > Save, then publish it using File > Publish.

6 Minimize Flash, and, from your desktop, navigate to the fl04lessons folder and double-click on the Flash Projector file to open it. The file should now appear at the full-screen resolution.

If your Flash movie is not sized proportionally to the viewer's screen resolution, the fscommand reveals the area outside the Stage to make up for the different ratio.

7 Close the file, return to Flash, and close the project.

The fscommand folder

CD-ROM developers can take advantage of the fscommand folder to have Flash launch other applications. For example, you could use Flash to create an installer application or an interactive form. For security reasons, Flash cannot connect and run applications on your local hard drive. Instead, you must create a folder named fscommand and place your executable files there. The fscommand folder must be in the same directory as your Flash projector file.

Using Export Movie

You can extend your range of output formats by using the Export Movie command. In addition to creating SWF files, Export Movie can export the content of the main Timeline to AVI and QuickTime video formats, or as a sequence of still images for editing in applications like Photoshop, Premiere, and After Effects. In addition to the extended options you have for saving in different formats, the main difference between the Export command and the Publish command that you have worked with previously is that the Publish settings are stored in your FLA file when you save your document, while export options are not.

1 In the fl04lessons folder, open the file named fl1503.fla, which is a variation of the animated web site footer you worked with in the first exercise. The main difference is that here the animation takes place on the main Timeline instead of in a nested movie clip. This is a very important distinction when exporting Flash content to other formats, as the majority of the exportable formats lack interactivity and simply display the content of the main Timeline as it appears in Flash.

2 Choose File > Export > Export Movie.

This exercise covers exporting the entire movie from the Timeline. If you would rather export only a single frame, select that frame, and then choose File > Export > Export Image.

3 In the resulting dialog box, choose the fl04lessons folder in the Save As drop-down menu, if it is not already listed there.

4   Select QuickTime (.mov) in the Save as type drop-down menu. This creates a standalone QuickTime movie that can be played using the free QuickTime player, converted for display on such mobile devices as PSPs and iPods, or imported into video editing or motions graphics programs, such as Adobe Premiere or After Effects. Press Save. The QuickTime Export Settings dialog box appears.

5   In the QuickTime Export Settings dialog box, ensure that the *Maintain Aspect Ratio* checkbox below the Render boxes is unchecked.

Below the Render height field in the QuickTime Export Settings dialog box, you'll see the second, Ignore Stage Color checkbox. This generates a QuickTime movie with an alpha channel that you can then import into a video editing or motion graphics program, such as Adobe Premiere or After Effects.

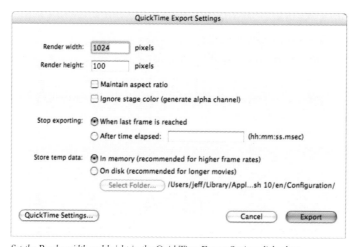

Set the Render width and height in the QuickTime Export Settings dialog box.

6   Leave the *Stop Exporting* and *Store Temp Date* radio buttons unchanged. They allow you to specify how much of your movie is rendered to video and whether you want to use either your system's memory or hard drive space during the rendering process. The defaults work fine for this animation. Press Export. Flash builds your QuickTime movie.

You may receive a message informing you that Flash has finished building your movie. Press OK.

7   Minimize Flash and navigate to the fl04lessons folder. Double-click on your QuickTime movie to play it, and view the animation you have just exported.

8   Choose File > Save, then File > Close.

An overview of FTP

FTP is an acronym for the phrase File Transfer Protocol. These are the set of rules that allow different computers to connect to each other over the web. Once you have created and published your Flash movie, you need to upload it to a web server in order to allow people to view it online. Whether this web server is one that you maintain yourself, one set up for you by your company's IT department, or space you rent from a web host, the publishing process is basically the same. While there are standalone FTP applications that allow you to connect to a web server, Adobe's industry-leading web design application, Dreamweaver, comes complete with an internal FTP engine that integrates very well with Flash content. The basic steps to follow when uploading Flash content for the Internet are:

1   Create a Flash movie and publish it to your local hard drive.

2   Upload your Flash movie to your web server, along with any secondary content (HTML and JavaScript files) created by the publishing process. Your web hosting service or IT department can provide you with information on where to upload your files, as well as the login and password information you need to connect.

3   If you want to make any changes to the movie, edit the file you published to your local hard drive, not the version on the web server.

4   Re-upload the edited version of your Flash movie to the web server, including any secondary content you may have modified.

Using Adobe Device Central in Flash

Adobe Device Central is a tool available within many of Adobe's CS4 applications. It is a simulation platform that is useful for developing content for mobile devices. It allows you to preview how Flash content looks and functions on a variety of mobile devices. You can access Device Central when you start a project, or later in the development cycle. You use Device Central by targeting one of the Flash Lite players in the Publish Settings dialog box. Flash Lite is Adobe's standalone application for playing Flash content on mobile devices. In this exercise you'll explore the steps used when creating content for mobile devices using Device Central.

1   Choose File > Open. Navigate to the fl04lessons folder and select the file named LampPost.fla. Press Open.

This Flash file was designed to play on the type of small screen found on a mobile phone or PDA. You must now direct the file to play in the Flash Lite player.

2   Choose File > Publish Settings to target the Flash Lite player as your publishing environment.

3 In the Publish Settings dialog box, click the Flash tab to make it active, then select Flash Lite 2.1 from the Version or Player drop-down menu. Leave all other settings unchanged. Press OK to close the Publish Settings dialog box.

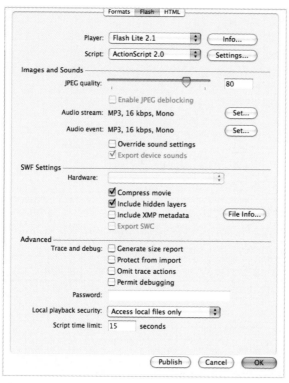

The Publish Settings dialog box controls the options for your published SWF files.

4 Choose Control > Test Movie to preview your Flash file. With Flash Lite set as your player, the movie opens in Adobe Device Central.

When you test the Flash movie, you will receive an error message in the Output panel that states, "WARNING: This movie uses features that are not supported in the Flash Lite 2.1 Player." This message is caused by an image created in Adobe Illustrator that was embedded in this file using an older version of Flash. You can ignore this warning message; it does not prevent you from previewing the file using Adobe Device Central.

5   From the list of available devices on the top-left side of the window, double-click any of the Flash Lite samples to preview your Flash animation on a cellphone. The list of available devices is based on the version of the Flash Lite Player that you selected in step 3. Device names that are dimmed are not available using the selected version of the Flash Lite Player.

Adobe Device Central previews your Flash movie on a variety of phones and mobile devices.

Using Device Central, you can choose the mobile device on which you want to preview your Flash file by choosing one from the list of available devices on the left side of the window. The device emulator is located in the center of your screen and it allows you to see your project. If your project uses ActionScript, you can also interact with it. On the right side of the interface, controls are available for evaluating the display and performance settings based upon the device you have selected.

6   In Adobe Device Central, select File > Return to Flash to return to the Flash authoring environment. You can continue to develop your Flash file and switch back to Device Central whenever you want to preview your changes.

Some ActionScript is not supported by Flash Lite. If you are using ActionScript in your Flash movie that is not supported by Flash Lite, you will be notified of this in the Output panel when you test your movie.

Self study

Open the LampPost.fla file in the fl04lessons folder and add the *fscommand* to the Actions layer so that the file can display full screen. Publish the file as a Flash projector.

Open the masthead.fla file in the fl04lessons folder, and publish it as a Flash movie embedded in an HTML document. Experiment with different JPEG quality settings to see the effects on the resulting SWF file's size.

Review

Questions

1   What is the advantage of using the Publish command instead of the Test Movie command?

2   Why would you want to export a QuickTime Movie or AVI file?

3   When using the standalone Flash projector, where must you store any executable applications that you want Flash to launch?

Answers

1   The Publish command can create a playable SWF file and automatically embed it into an HTML page. The Publish command also offers a wide range of exportable formats in addition to standard .swf creation.

2   To display your Flash animation on video devices such as iPods and PSPs, as well as to import into a video editing or motion graphics program.

3   Inside a folder named fscommand, which must be in the same directory as your Flash projector application.

- Working in the Fireworks interface
- Creating and editing bitmap and vector images
- Adding text, color, and layers
- Using slices for interactivity
- Optimizing graphics for the Web

Adobe Fireworks Jumpstart

Fireworks is a unique hybrid of vector and bitmap graphics programs. It provides a user-friendly environment for prototyping web sites and user interfaces, and creating and optimizing images for the Web. And because it's part of Adobe's Creative Suite, Fireworks also offers time-saving integration with Photoshop, Illustrator, Dreamweaver, and Flash.

Starting up

Before starting, make sure that your tools and panels are consistent by resetting your workspace. See "Resetting the Fireworks workspace" on page XXVII.

You will work with several files from the fw01lessons folder in this lesson. Make sure that you have loaded the CS4lessons folder onto your hard drive from the supplied DVD. See "Loading lesson files" on page XXIX.

See Lesson 1 in action!

Use the accompanying video to gain a better understanding of how to use some of the features shown in this lesson. Visit digitalclassroombooks.com to view the sample tutorial for this lesson.

About Fireworks

Adobe Fireworks is a versatile graphics program that combines features found in image-editing, vector-drawing, and Web-optimizing applications. Instead of jumping from one program to another to create graphics for your web site, Fireworks lets you use one program from start to finish.

Work with vector and bitmap objects

Fireworks includes tools for working with both vector and bitmap graphics. You can draw an object and then use a wide array of tools, effects, and commands to enhance it. If you've created a graphic in another program, Fireworks also imports and edits graphics in JPEG, GIF, PNG, PSD, and many other file formats.

Make graphics interactive

In Fireworks, you can add interactive areas to a Web graphic using slices. Slices divide an image into exportable areas, to which you can apply rollovers and other interactive behaviors.

Optimize and export graphics

The optimization features of Fireworks help you find the right balance between file size and visual quality for your graphics. Once you've optimized your graphics, you can export them in a number of different file formats, including JPEG, GIF, animated GIF, and HTML tables containing sliced images.

Vector and bitmap graphics

Graphics on your computer are displayed in either *vector* or *bitmap* format. It's important that you understand the difference between the two file types, because Fireworks is capable of opening and editing both formats.

About vector graphics

Vector graphics are drawn objects that use anchor points, lines, and vectors, or mathematical equations that contain color and position information. They are defined by a series of points that describe the outline of the graphic. The color of the graphic is composed of the color of its outline (or *stroke*) and the color of its interior (or *fill*).

Vector graphics are also described as resolution-independent. This means that a graphic's appearance doesn't change when you move, resize, or reshape it.

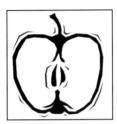

Vector graphics feature crisp edges and flat areas of color.

About bitmap graphics

As you may already know, your computer screen is a large grid of pixels. Bitmap graphics are composed of dots (or *pixels*) arranged inside this grid. In a bitmap graphic, the image is defined by the location and color value of each pixel in the grid. When viewed at a certain distance, the dots create the illusion of continuous tone, as in a mosaic.

Bitmap graphics are resolution-dependent, which means that the image data is restricted to a grid of a certain, specified size. Enlarging or transforming a bitmap graphic changes the pixels in the grid, which can make the edges of the image appear jagged.

Bitmap graphics feature gradations in tone and softer edges.

The Start page

When you start Fireworks without opening a document, the Fireworks Start page appears in the work environment. The Start page gives you quick access to Fireworks tutorials, recent files, and Fireworks Exchange, where you can add new capabilities to some Fireworks features.

1 Disable the Start page by clicking the *Don't Show Again* checkbox when the Start page opens. Fireworks lets you re-access the Start page if you want to later. Press OK.

2 Close the Start page. You'll be creating a new document using the File > New menu command.

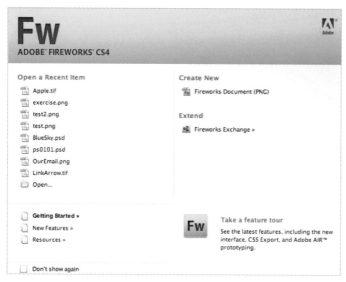

The Start page appears by default when Fireworks is first opened.

Creating a new Fireworks document

As with most computer applications, your first step is to create a new document.

New documents in Fireworks default to its native file format, Portable Network Graphic (PNG). This means that regardless of the optimization and export settings you select, the original Fireworks PNG file is preserved to allow easy editing later.

1 Select File > New. The New Document dialog box opens.

2 In the New Document dialog box, type **800** in the Width text field, **600** in the Height
   text field, and make sure that both drop-down menus are set to Pixels. Measurements are
   usually expressed in pixels in Fireworks, as you're designing for a pixel-based monitor.

Use the New Document dialog box to set up your file.

3 Set the Resolution, or number of pixels per inch in your bitmap grid, to 72. Most
   computer monitors can only display graphics at between 72 and 100 pixels per inch.

4 Leave the Canvas Color, or the background color, as Transparent. You could also have
   used the Custom color swatch to select a custom canvas color.

5 Press OK to accept your new document settings.

Workspace basics

You create and manipulate your files using various elements, such as panels, bars, and windows.
Any arrangement of these elements is called a *workspace*. The workspaces of the different
applications in the Adobe Creative Suite share the same basic appearance, so that you can easily
move between the applications.

Fireworks workspace overview

When you open a new document in Fireworks, the document window appears in the center of the screen, and displays the file you're working on. Document windows can be tabbed and, in certain cases, grouped and docked.

The document window displays the file you're working on in the center of the screen.

The Fireworks workspace includes the Tools panel, Property Inspector, Application bar, and other panels.

- The Application bar, across the top of your screen, contains a workspace button for switching workspaces, menus, and other application controls.

The Application bar contains menus and other application controls.

- The Property Inspector, at the bottom of the document window, initially displays document properties. It's context-sensitive, however, and changes depending on which tool you've chosen, or what you've selected in the document.

The Property Inspector is context-sensitive and displays content relative to what you've selected.

- The Tools panel, on the left side of the screen, contains Bitmap, Vector, and Web tool groups. These tools are used for creating and editing elements of your graphic. Related tools are grouped, or nested.

The Tools panel contains tools for creating and editing elements of your graphic.

Other Fireworks panels

Panels are floating windows that let you work with layers, paths, and colors, and otherwise edit the appearance or behavior of a selected object. Although they are docked to the right side of the workspace by default, each panel is draggable, and so you can group panels into your own custom arrangements.

Panels let you edit the appearance or behavior of a selected object.

Working with bitmaps

Creating bitmaps

As mentioned earlier in this lesson, bitmap graphics are composed of small squares called *pixels*, which fit together like the tiles of a mosaic to create an image. Some examples of bitmap graphics are photographs captured with your digital camera, or graphics created in paint programs. They are sometimes referred to as *raster,* or *pixel-based*, images.

In Fireworks, you can create bitmap images by drawing and painting with bitmap tools, by converting vector objects to bitmap images, or by opening or importing images.

Bitmap images cannot be converted to vector objects.

Importing a bitmap

In this exercise, you'll import a JPEG file to use as a header graphic for a web page. Fireworks imports and edits graphics in JPEG, GIF, PNG, PSD, and many other file formats.

1   With your Fireworks document open, select File > Import. The Import File dialog box opens.

2   Navigate to the fw01lessons folder within the CS4lessons folder, and select the file BlueSky.jpg.

3   Press Open. The corner-shaped, import cursor indicates that the file is ready to be placed in your Fireworks document.

4   Double-click in the upper-left corner of your canvas to place the image at its original size.

You can also drag the import cursor to draw a rectangle that scales the image to fit.

Bitmap images are imported using the File > Import command.

Cropping a bitmap

The imported image fills your canvas, but you'll want to crop its dimensions for use as a web page header.

1 From the Tools panel, choose the Crop tool (⌗).

2 Choose View > Rulers, if you do not see the rulers in the document window. Position your cursor on the left edge of the canvas, at the 200-pixel mark on the vertical ruler.

3 Drag down to the 300-pixel mark on the vertical ruler, and across to the right edge of your canvas. You should end up with a crop selection box that is 800 pixels wide and 100 pixels high.

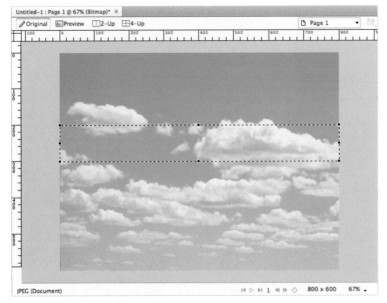

Images can be cropped with the Crop tool.

4   Double-click inside the bounding box or press Enter to crop the selection.

To cancel a crop selection, press Esc.

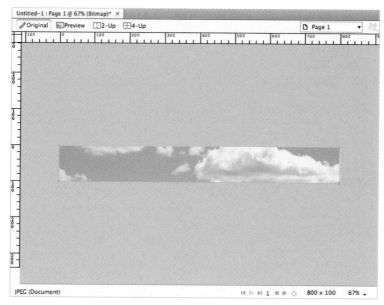

Double-click inside the bounding box to accept your crop.

Applying a filter

Next you'll use a filter to lighten a portion of the image and complete the bitmap portion of your header graphic.

1   From the Tools panel, choose the Rectangular Marquee tool (⬚).

2   Drag a rectangle over the bottom half of your header graphic. A flashing selection outline appears over the area, identifying those pixels as being currently selected for editing.

A selection flashes when the pixels inside are ready for editing.

3   Select Filters > Adjust Color > Hue/Saturation. The Hue/Saturation dialog box appears.

4   In the Hue/Saturation dialog box, slide the Lightness slider to 50, and click the *Preview* checkbox to see the results of the lightening in your image.

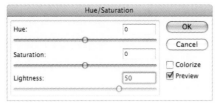

Set a Lightness value in the Hue/Saturation dialog box.

5   Press OK to accept the Hue/Saturation filter setting.

Press OK to accept your filter setting.

6   Choose File > Save, and save this file as Header.png in the fw01lessons folder. Now you'll work with the vector tools to add a navigation bar to your header.

Working with vector objects

As mentioned previously, a vector graphic's shape is defined by a path, and by the anchor points that are plotted along it. A vector graphic's stroke color follows the path, and its fill occupies the area inside the path.

Vector object shapes include basic shapes, free-form shapes, and Auto Shapes, or object groups that have special controls for adjusting them. You can use a variety of tools in Fireworks to draw and edit vector objects.

Drawing and editing basic shapes

You use the basic shape tools to draw rectangles, ellipses, and polygons.

Fireworks features both basic and auto shape tools.

Drawing a rectangle

The Rectangle tool draws rectangles as grouped objects. To move a rectangle corner point independently, you need to ungroup the rectangle or use the Subselection tool (⤳).

1   From the Tools panel, select the Rectangle tool (□).

If you can't see the Rectangle tool in the Tools panel, click and hold on the tool to choose it from the list that appears.

2   Move the pointer to the canvas, positioning it on the left side of the lightened area of your header. The cursor changes to a plus sign (+), indicating that you can draw the rectangle.

3   Click and drag diagonally from upper left to lower right, creating a rectangle that is 750 pixels wide and 25 pixels high, and leaving a small margin of the lightened sky around it.

The rectangle automatically fills with the default fill color (black). Leave the fill at its default; you'll change it later in this exercise.

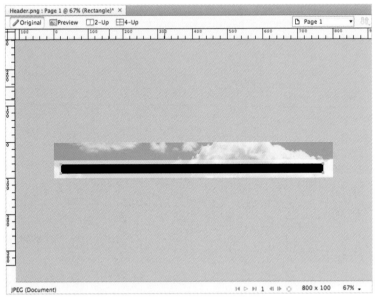

Leave the rectangle's fill at its default color (black).

While holding down the mouse button, press and hold the spacebar to adjust the position of a basic shape as you draw it. Release the spacebar to continue drawing the object.

Resizing a rectangle

If you have difficulty drawing your rectangle at the correct size by dragging, you can do one of the following:

- Enter new width (W) or height (H) values in the Property Inspector or the Info panel.

- In the Select section of the Tools panel, select the Scale tool and drag a corner transform handle.

- Select Modify > Transform > Scale and drag a corner transform handle, or select Modify > Transform > Numeric Transform and enter new dimensions.

- Drag a corner point on the rectangle.

Auto Shapes

Auto Shapes, unlike other object groups, have diamond-shaped control points in addition to the object group handles. Dragging a control point alters only its associated visual property. Most control points have tool tips that describe how they affect the Auto Shape.

Auto Shape tools create shapes in preset orientations. For example, the Arrow tool draws arrows horizontally.

Use the Auto Shape tools to create shapes with preset orientations.

The Auto Shape tools

Arrow: Simple arrows of any proportions, and straight or bent lines.

Arrow Line: Straight, thin arrow lines providing quick access to common arrowheads (simply click either end of the line).

Beveled Rectangle: Rectangles with beveled corners.

Chamfer Rectangle: Rectangles with chamfers (corners that are rounded inside the rectangle).

Connector Line: Three-segment connector lines, such as those used to connect the elements of a flowchart or organizational chart.

Doughnut: Filled rings.

L-Shape: Right-angled corner shapes.

Measure Tool: Simple arrow lines that indicate dimensions for key design elements in pixels or inches.

Pie: Pie charts.

Rounded Rectangle: Rectangles with rounded corners.

Smart Polygon: Equilateral polygons with 3 to 25 sides.

Spiral: Open spirals.

Star: Stars with any number of points from 3 to 25.

Working with text

Now you'll add some text to serve as navigation links for your header bar.

Fireworks provides many features typically reserved for desktop publishing applications, including the ability to use a variety of fonts at different sizes as well as kerning, spacing, color, and leading controls.

Create and move text blocks

Text entered into a Fireworks document appears inside a text block (a rectangle with handles). Text blocks are either auto-sizing or fixed-width blocks.

- An auto-sizing text block expands horizontally as you enter type, and shrinks when you remove text. When you click on the canvas with the Text tool and start typing, auto-sizing text blocks are created by default.

- Fixed-width text blocks are created by default when you drag to draw a text block using the Text tool. They allow you to control the width of wrapped text.

When the text pointer is active within a text block, a hollow circle or hollow square appears in the upper-right corner of the text block. The circle indicates an auto-sizing text block; the square indicates a fixed-width text block. Double-click the corner to change from one text block to the other.

1   Select the Text tool (T).

2   In the Property Inspector, set the following:

- Arial Bold for the font and style.

- 12 points for the font size.

- White for the font color. Click the color swatch and choose white from the color palette.

Use the Property Inspector to set the attributes of the type you'll enter.

3   Create a fixed-width text block by dragging to draw a text block inside the navigation bar. Leave a small margin, but extend the text block at least halfway across the navigation bar.

To move the text block while you drag to create it, hold down the mouse button, press and hold down the spacebar, and drag the text block to another location.

4   Type the following navigation links, with five spaces between each: **Home**, **About Us**, **Products**, **Services**, **Contact Us**.

5   Click once in the document window with the Zoom tool (⊙) to confirm that you've typed correctly.

Type the navigation links as shown.

6   If you choose, you can select text within the text block and reformat it.

Formatting and editing text

The quickest method of editing text in Fireworks is to use the Property Inspector. As an alternative to the Property Inspector, you can also use commands in the Text menu.

1 Do one of the following to select the text you want to change:

   - Click a text block with the Pointer tool (↖) or Subselection tool (↘) to select the entire block. To select multiple blocks simultaneously, hold down Shift as you select each block.

   - Double-click a text block with the Pointer or Subselection tool, and then highlight a range of text.

   - Click inside a text block with the Text tool, and then highlight a range of text.

2 Change or reformat the text.

3 To exit the text block, do one of the following:

   - Click outside the text block.

   - Select another tool in the Tools panel.

   - Press Esc on your keyboard.

4 Select File > Save to save your file.

Applying color

Fireworks has a wide variety of features for creating, selecting, and applying colors. You'll now use some of these features to add color to your navigation bar and text links.

Apply a sampled color

1 With the Pointer tool (↖), click the (black) navigation bar to select it.

2 Select the Eyedropper tool (⌁) from the Tools panel.

3 Click in the blue sky at the top of your header graphic to sample that color.

4 The blue sky color is applied to the navigation bar.

The Eyedropper tool allows you to sample color from your image.

You can also apply color to image elements in other ways.

Apply a swatch color to text

1 With the Text tool, drag to select all your text links.

2 Click the Fill Color box icon (◈☐) in the Tools panel to make it active.

3 Select Window > Swatches.

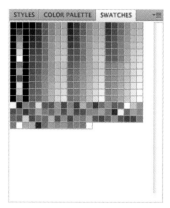

Use the Swatches panel to apply color to your text.

4 Click on a dark-blue swatch (of your choice) to apply the color to the fill of your text.

Using the Color Mixer

If you choose, you can use the Color Mixer by choosing Window > Color Mixer to view and change your current stroke and fill colors.

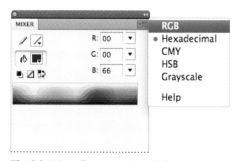

The Color Mixer allows you to view and change your current stroke and fill colors.

By default, the Color Mixer identifies RGB colors as hexadecimal, displaying hexadecimal color values for red (R), green (G), and blue (B) color components. Hexadecimal RGB values are calculated based on a range of values from 00 to FF.

You can select alternative color models from the Color Mixer panel menu. Although CMYK is a color model option, graphics exported directly from Fireworks are not typically intended for printing.

Using Layers

In Fireworks, you use layers to separate your document into discrete planes, as if the elements were created on separate acetate overlays. A document can be made up of many layers, each in turn containing sublayers or objects. As a point of reference, Fireworks layers resemble layer sets in Adobe Photoshop.

The Layers panel

Each element in a Fireworks document resides on a layer. You can either create layers before you begin adding elements or add layers as needed. The canvas is below all layers and is not technically a layer.

Each element in a Fireworks document resides on a layer.

The Layers panel displays the current state of all layers in your image. The name of an active layer is always highlighted. The stacking order is the order in which objects appear in the document and determines how objects on one layer overlap objects on another. Fireworks places the most recently created layer on the top of the stack. You can easily rearrange the order of layers and of objects within layers.

Activate a layer

When you draw, paste, or import an object in your document, it is automatically placed at the top of the active layer.

To activate a layer, do one of the following:

* Click a layer name in the Layers panel.
* Select an object on a layer.

Organizing layers

In a Fireworks document, you organize layers and objects by naming them and rearranging their stacking order in the Layers panel.

Moving layers and objects in the Layers panel changes the order in which objects appear on the canvas. Objects at the top of a layer appear above other objects in that layer on the canvas. Objects on the topmost layer appear in front of objects on lower layers.

Naming layer objects

1 Double-click the Bitmap object in the Layers panel.

2 Type the new name, **Photo**, for the object and press Enter.

3 Repeat the process to rename the Home layer to Links.

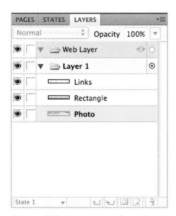

It's a good idea to name your layers descriptively.

Moving a layer object

1   Click the Photo object in the Layers panel. Drag it above the Nav Bar object, releasing it when you see a double line appear between the Links and Nav Bar objects.

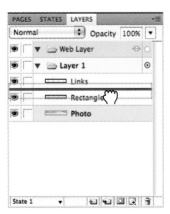

Dragging layers changes the order in which objects appear on the canvas.

2   The Nav Bar object disappears from your image, as it's now obscured by the Photo object.

Protecting layer objects

Locking an individual object protects it by preventing it from being selected or edited. A padlock icon (🔒) indicates a locked item. You can also protect objects and layers by hiding them.

1   Lock the Links object by clicking the square in the column immediately to the left of the object name.

2   Lock the Photo object by clicking the square in the column immediately to the left of the object name.

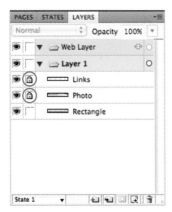

Objects on locked layers can't be selected.

3   Click with the Pointer tool ( ), noting that neither of these objects can now be selected.

Show or hide objects and layers

Hiding an individual object protects it by preventing it from being viewed, selected, or edited. A visibility icon ( ) indicates a visible item.

1   Hide the Links object by clicking the square in the far-left column next to the object name. The missing visibility icon indicates that the object is invisible.

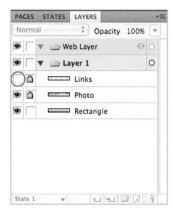

A missing visibility icon indicates an invisible layer.

2   Show the Links object again by clicking the square in the far-left column next to the object name. The visibility icon indicates that the object is now visible.

Merging objects in the Layers panel

To clean up your Layers panel, you can merge objects. Objects and bitmaps to be merged do not have to be adjacent in the Layers panel or reside on the same layer.

Merging down results in all selected vector and bitmap objects becoming flattened into the bitmap object that lies beneath. Vector objects and bitmap objects cannot be edited separately once merged.

1   Unlock the Links and Photo objects in the Layers panel, and click to select the Links object and only the Links object.

Shift+click or Ctrl+click to select multiple objects.

2   To merge the Links and Photo objects, do one of the following:

• Select Merge Down from the Layers panel menu.

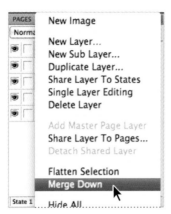

Merging down results in all selected vector and bitmap objects becoming flattened.

• Select Modify > Merge Down.

• Right-click (Windows) or Ctrl+click (Mac OS) the selected layer and select Merge Down.

Deleting a layer object

Because you won't be using it after all, you'll now delete the Rectangle object.

1   Click the Rectangle object to activate it.

2   Click the Delete Selection button (🗑) at the bottom of the Layers panel.

Unwanted layers are deleted using the Delete Selection button.

About the Web layer

The Web layer appears by default as the top layer in every Fireworks document. It contains Web objects, such as slices, used for adding interactivity to exported documents.

You can't delete, duplicate, move, or rename the Web layer. You also can't merge objects that live on the Web layer.

Creating slices for interactivity

Slices are Web objects that are created using HTML code, and are an essential part of creating interactivity in a Fireworks document.

Slicing carves up a document into smaller pieces and exports each piece as a separate file. When it's exported, Fireworks creates the HTML code that will reassemble the graphic in a Web browser.

Although it's also used for optimizing and updating, the biggest advantage of slicing is that it adds interactivity so that images can respond to user actions.

Create rectangular slices

You can create rectangular slices by drawing with the Slice tool.

1   Select the Slice tool (✐).

2   Drag to draw a slice object over the Home portion of your header graphic. Be sure to make it cover the entire (lightened) area from top to bottom.

3   Repeat the process for the About Us, Products, Services, and Contact Us link areas.

Slicing adds interactivity so that images can respond to user actions.

To adjust the position of a slice as you drag to draw it, hold down the mouse button, press and hold down the spacebar, and then drag the slice to another location on the canvas. Release the spacebar to continue drawing the slice.

Resizing one or more slices

You can edit the slice guides (lines extending from the slice object) to define the boundaries of the split image files that are created when the document is exported.

1   Position the Pointer tool (▶) or Subselection tool (▷) over a slice guide. The pointer changes to the guide movement pointer.

Drag a slice's guides to resize it.

2   Drag the slice guide to the desired location. The slices and all adjacent slices are resized. Working with slices can be compared to using a table in a word-processing application. When you drag a slice guide to resize a slice, all adjacent rectangular slices are also resized. You can also use the Property Inspector to resize and transform slices.

If multiple slice objects are aligned along a single slice guide, you can drag that slice guide to resize all the slice objects simultaneously.

View and select slices

You can control the visibility of slices in your document by using the Layers panel and the Tools panel. When you turn slice visibility off for the whole document, slice guides are also hidden. The Web layer displays all the Web objects in the document.

1   Select Window > Layers.

2   Expand the Web layer by clicking the triangle.

The Web layer displays all the Web objects in a document.

3   Click a slice name to select it.

Naming slices

1   Double-click the bottommost slice in the Web layer.

2   Type the new name, **Home**, for the slice and press Enter.

3   Repeat the process to rename the About, Products, Services, and Contact slices.

It's a good idea to name your slices descriptively.

Show and hide slices

Hiding a slice simply makes the slice invisible in the Fireworks PNG file. Hidden slice objects can, however, be exported in the HTML file.

1   Click the visibility icon (👁) next to the Home slice in the Layers panel to hide it.

Hiding a slice makes it invisible.

2   To show the Home slice again, click in the visibility column next to the Home slice in the Layers panel.

3   To hide or show slice guides in any document view, select View > Slice Guides.

Making slices interactive

Fireworks provides you with two ways to make slices interactive:

*   For simple interactivity, you can use the drag-and-drop rollover method.

*   For more complicated interactivity, you can use the Behaviors panel.

About rollovers

In a rollover, when the mouse pointer rolls over one graphic, that action triggers the display of another graphic. In Fireworks, the trigger is always a Web object (that is, a slice).

The simplest rollover swaps an image in State 1 with an image directly below it in State 2. You can also build more complicated rollovers in Fireworks.

Adding simple interactivity to slices

Because it's the fastest and most efficient way to create rollover effects, you'll use the drag-and-drop rollover method. This method allows you to determine what happens when the pointer passes over a slice. The end result is commonly called a *rollover image*.

When a slice is selected, a round circle with crosshairs appears in the center of the slice. This is called a *behavior handle*.

The drag-and-drop method is the most efficient way to create rollover effects.

Dragging the behavior handle from a trigger slice and dropping it onto a target slice allows you to quickly create rollover effects. When you select a trigger Web object created by using a behavior handle or the Behaviors panel, all its behavior relationships are displayed. By default, a blue behavior line represents a rollover interaction.

   The trigger and target can be the same slice.

Create and attach a simple rollover

A simple rollover swaps in the state directly under the top state and involves only one slice.

1 With the Pointer tool (**k**), select the slice you named Home earlier.

2 Click on the crosshairs in the middle of the slice, and drag to the left to link the slice to itself. The Swap Image dialog box opens.

The trigger for a rollover and its target can be the same slice.

3 In the Swap Image dialog box, make sure that the slice is set to swap with State 2, which will become your rollover state.

4 Repeat step 3 for each of your remaining slices.

5 Access the States panel by selecting Window > States. The default State 1 should be selected.

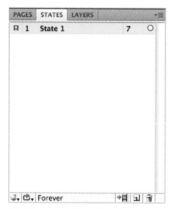

The States panel shows the rollover states for your document.

6   In the States panel menu, choose Duplicate State, and press OK in the Duplicate State dialog box. State 2 appears as your rollover state. Make sure State 2 is selected before moving on to the next step.

Choose Duplicate State to duplicate State 1.

7   In the Layers panel, select the Bitmap layer.

8   Select Filters > Adjust Color > Hue/Saturation, and slide the Hue slider to 70. This is the color that each slice button will change to when the pointer rolls over it. Press OK to accept this setting.

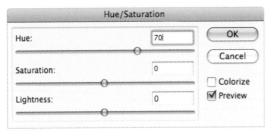

Use Hue/Saturation to change the appearance of your rollover state.

9   Click the Preview tab at the top of the document window, or select File > Preview in Browser to test the rollover.

Test your rollover using the Preview tab.

You've now finished creating your header graphic, including an interactive navigation bar. But in order to use it on a web page (or on multiple web pages), you must first optimize and export this graphic correctly.

Optimizing and exporting

Getting your graphics out of Fireworks is a two-step process. Before exporting, you have to optimize your graphics, which involves restricting the file size so that they download quickly, while keeping them looking as good as possible.

You can take advantage of the Export Wizard to be guided through the optimization and export process. This wizard recommends settings, and shows you the Image Preview to help with optimization.

The Image Preview can also be used independently of the wizard.

Using the Export Wizard

The Export Wizard guides you through the optimization and export process step by step.

1   Select File > Export Wizard. The Export Wizard dialog box opens.

The Export Wizard guides you through optimization and export.

2   Choose to select an export format. If desired, you can also choose to add a Target export file size in this dialog box. Press Continue.

3   Choose *JavaScript rollover* as the intended export for frames in your document, and press Continue.

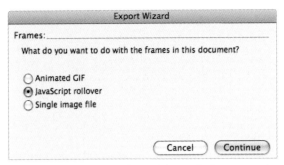

Choose JavaScript rollover *as the intended export for frames in your document.*

4   The Analysis Results window opens, recommending different export formats for your graphic, based on its content and potential usage. Press Exit to close the wizard.

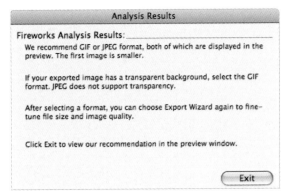

The Analysis Results window recommends different export formats.

5   The Image Preview window opens with recommended export options.

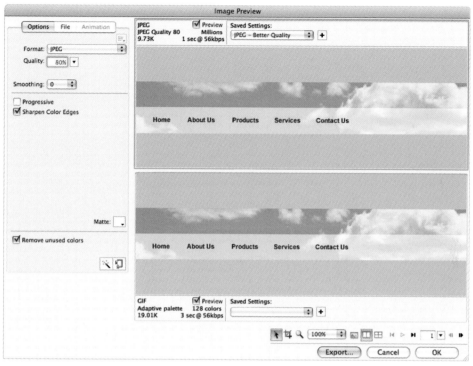

Image Preview displays the document or graphic exactly as it will be exported.

Using the Image Preview

You can open the Image Preview either through the Export Wizard or from the File menu, by choosing File > Image Preview.

The preview area displays the document or graphic exactly as it is exported and estimates file size and download time with the current export settings.

When you export animated GIFs or JavaScript rollovers, the estimated file size represents the total size across all states.

To increase redraw speed of the Image Preview, deselect Preview.

Changing the preview area

If you can't clearly judge the quality of the image(s) in the Preview window, do one of the following:

- To zoom in, press the Zoom button (🔍) and click in the preview. Alt+click (Windows) or Opt+click (Mac OS) the button in the preview to zoom out.

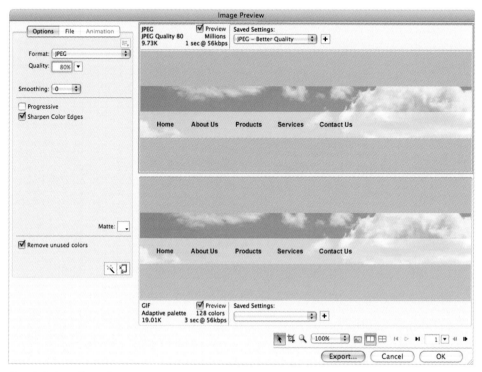

Zoom in to change the preview area.

- To pan around the image, click the Pointer button (⊼) at the bottom of the dialog box and drag in the preview. Alternately, you can hold down the spacebar when the Zoom pointer is active and drag in the preview.

- To divide the preview area to compare settings, click a split-view button (⊓). Each preview window can display a preview of the graphic with different export settings.

Click a split-view button to divide the preview area.

When you zoom or pan while multiple views are open, all views zoom and pan simultaneously.

Setting export options

You can change the settings to reduce file size without sacrificing quality.

1 In the Options panel on the left side of the Image Preview window, choose the JPEG Format at 80 percent quality. The JPEG format was recommended by the Export Wizard, and works well here because there's no transparency or animation in this graphic.

2 Leave the other settings at their defaults, and examine the download information being displayed at the top of the Image Preview window. By exporting this graphic as a JPEG, you'll reduce the file size to 9.73K, and it will only take 1 second to download from the Web using a 56 Kbps modem.

Use these settings to optimize your graphic as a JPEG.

3 Make sure there's no noticeable loss of quality in the JPEG portion of the Image Preview, as this is often a byproduct of reducing the file size.

4 Click the JPEG portion of the Image Preview once to make sure it is the format that will be exported.

Exporting using Image Preview

1   Press Export. The Export dialog box opens.

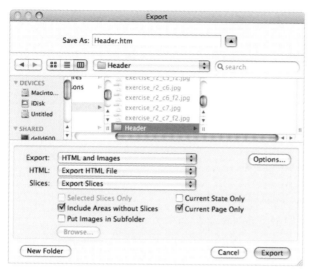

Export directly from Image Preview using the Export dialog box.

2   In the Export dialog box, do the following:

- Choose to Export HTML and Images to include your slices and rollovers.

- Choose to Export HTML File in the HTML category.

- For Slices, choose to Export Slices.

- Leave the other settings at their defaults, and choose to save your files to the fw01lessons folder within the CS4lessons folder.

3   Press Export.

All the files necessary for you to import this rollover graphic into a web page are exported, including all slices and rollover images, as well as the HTML code that houses and assembles it into a single image.

To have more control over this process, you can use workspace tools such as the Optimize panel, the preview buttons in the document window, and the Export dialog box.

Optimizing in the workspace

Fireworks provides optimization and export features in the workspace itself that give you control over how files are exported. You can use preset optimization options, or you can customize the optimization by choosing specific options such as file type and the color palette used.

The Optimize panel contains the most useful controls for optimizing. By default, the panel shows settings that refer to the active selection (a slice or the whole document).

The Optimize panel shows settings for the active document.

The preview buttons in the document window show how the exported graphic would appear with the current optimization settings.

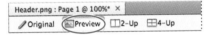

Click on the preview buttons to see how the exported graphic will appear.

You can optimize the whole document in the same format, or select individual slices or areas of a JPEG and select different optimization settings for each.

Choose a file type

Customize the optimization by selecting a specific file type from the Export File Format pop-up menu in the Optimize panel and then setting format-specific options, such as color depth, dither, and quality. You can save the settings as a new preset.

GIF

Graphics Interchange Format (GIF) is a popular Web graphic format that is ideal for cartoons, logos, images with transparent areas, and animations. Images with areas of solid color compress best when exported as GIF files. GIF files contain a maximum of 256 colors.

JPEG

Developed by the Joint Photographic Experts Group (JPEG) specifically for photographic or high-color images. JPEG supports millions of colors (24-bit). The JPEG format is best for scanned photographs, images using textures, images with gradient color transitions, and any images that require more than 256 colors.

PNG

Portable Network Graphic (PNG) is a versatile Web graphic format that can support up to 32-bit color, contain transparency or an alpha channel, and be progressive. However, not all Web browsers can view PNG images. Although PNG is the native file format for Fireworks, Fireworks PNG files contain additional application-specific information that is not stored in an exported PNG file or in files created in other applications.

WBMP

Wireless Bitmap (WBMP) is a graphic format created for mobile computing devices such as cell phones and PDAs. This format is used on Wireless Application Protocol (WAP) pages. Because WBMP is a 1-bit format, only two colors are visible: black and white.

TIFF

Tagged Image File Format (TIFF) is a graphic format used for storing bitmap images. TIFF files are most commonly used in print publishing. Many multimedia applications also accept imported TIFF files.

BMP

The Microsoft Windows graphic file format. Many applications can import BMP images.

PICT

Developed by Apple Computer and most commonly used on Macintosh operating systems. Most Mac applications are capable of importing PICT images.

Saving optimization settings

By default, Fireworks remembers the last optimization settings you used after saving or exporting a file. You can then easily apply these settings to new documents.

Saved optimization settings appear at the bottom of the Settings pop-up menu in the Optimize panel and in the Property Inspector. When you save a preset, the file is saved in the Export Settings folder in the Fireworks configuration folder on your hard drive.

To save optimization settings:

1   From the Optimize panel Options menu, select Save Settings.

Select Save Settings to save optimization settings.

2   Type a name for the optimization preset and press OK.

Exporting a single image

If you've opened an existing image in Fireworks, you can save it rather than export it.

1   In the Optimize panel, select a file format and set format-specific options.

2   Select File > Export.

3   Select a location to export the image file to.

4   Enter a filename with no extension. An extension is added during export based on the file type.

5   From the Export pop-up menu, select Images Only.

6   Press Save.

Export a sliced document

As you've seen, when you export a sliced Fireworks document, an HTML file and all associated images are exported. The HTML file can then be viewed in a web browser or imported into other applications for further editing.

You can also choose to export only selected slices from your graphic.

Exporting selected slices

1 Shift+click to select multiple slices.

2 Select File > Export.

3 Select a location in which to store the exported files, such as a folder within your local web site.

4 From the Export pop-up menu, select HTML and Images.

5 Enter a filename with no extension. An extension is added during export based on the file type.

If you are exporting multiple slices, Fireworks uses the name you enter as the root name for all exported graphics.

6 From the Slices pop-up menu, select Export Slices.

Use settings in the Export dialog box to define which slices are exported.

7 To export only the slices you selected before export, choose *Selected Slices Only*, and ensure that the *Include Areas without Slices* option is not selected.

8 Press Save.

Results of exporting

When you export HTML from Fireworks, it produces the following:

- If the document contains interactive elements, all the HTML code necessary to reassemble sliced images and any JavaScript code. The HTML code automatically contains links to the exported image.

- One or more image files, based on how many slices are in your document and how many states you include in rollovers.

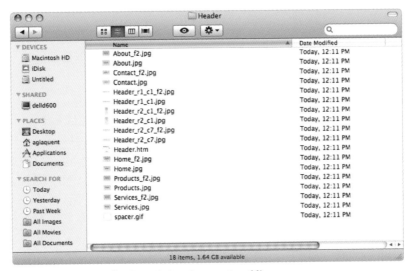

When you export HTML from Fireworks, it produces a variety of files.

- A file called spacer.gif, if necessary. The spacer.gif file is a transparent, 1-pixel-by-1-pixel GIF image that Fireworks uses to fix spacing problems when sliced images are reassembled in the HTML code. You can choose whether Fireworks exports a spacer.

- If you export or copy HTML to Dreamweaver, notes files may be created that make the integration between the two programs easier. These files have an .mno extension.

Congratulations! You have now completed your introduction to Adobe Fireworks. You can use the knowledge gained from creating a web page header graphic, complete with vector and bitmap elements, slices, and rollover interactivity, to inform your future use of Fireworks.

Self study

Try some of the following tasks to build on your experience with Fireworks:

1   Create a new file, and choose File > Import to import a bitmap image into the workspace. Use the selection tools to select a portion of the graphic, and apply a filter to that selection, leaving the other pixels untouched.

2   Create a new file, and draw a pie chart using the Pie Auto Shape tool. Use the other drawing tools to edit the dimensions of the pie's slices, and then experiment with applying color and text to the slices.

3   Use the Optimize panel in the workspace to optimize one of the graphics you've created, choosing the appropriate export settings for the content of the graphic. Save your optimization settings for future use with a similar graphic.

Review

Questions

1   How do vector graphics differ from bitmap graphics?

2   What is the default format for all new Fireworks files?

3   How can you tell whether a text block is auto-sizing or fixed-width?

4   What is the difference between the Web layer and other layers in your document?

5   When is it best to optimize a graphic as a JPEG, and what images are best exported as GIFs?

Answers

1   Vector graphics are drawn objects that use anchor points, lines, and vectors, or mathematical equations that contain color and position information. Bitmap graphics are composed of dots (or pixels) arranged inside a grid, and the image is defined by the location and color value of each pixel in the grid.

2   New documents in Fireworks default to its native file format, Portable Network Graphic (PNG). This means that regardless of the optimization and export settings you select, the original Fireworks PNG file is preserved to allow easy editing later.

3   When the text pointer is active within a text block, a hollow circle or hollow square appears in the upper right corner of the text block. The circle indicates an auto-sizing text block; the square indicates a fixed-width text block. Double-click the corner to change from one text block to the other.

4   The Web layer appears by default as the top layer in every Fireworks document. It contains Web objects, such as slices, used for adding interactivity to exported documents. You can't delete, duplicate, move, or rename the Web layer. You also can't merge objects that live on the Web layer.

5   The JPEG format is best for scanned photographs, images using textures, images with gradient color transitions, and any images that require more than 256 colors. Images with areas of solid color compress best when exported as GIF files, because they contain a maximum of 256 colors.

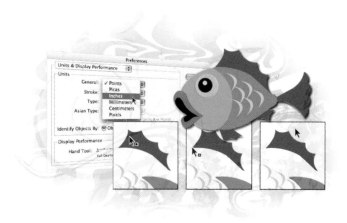

What you'll learn in this lesson:

- Creating shapes
- Selecting objects using the selection tools
- Transforming shapes
- Using layers to organize artwork

Illustrator CS4 Essentials

Illustrator can be used to create many types of artwork. In this lesson, you will use the shape tools, work with basic selection techniques, and assemble some artwork using object stacking order. Along the way, you will learn some helpful tips for creating artwork on your own.

Starting up

Before starting, make sure that your tools and panels are consistent by resetting your workspace. See "Resetting Adobe Illustrator CS4 Preferences" on page XXVII.

You will work with several files from the ai01lessons folder in this lesson. Make sure that you have loaded the CS4lessons folder onto your hard drive from the supplied DVD. See "Loading lesson files" on page XXIX.

Use the accompanying video to gain a better understanding of how to use some of the features shown in this lesson. The video tutorial for this lesson can be found on the included DVD.

Using the shape tools

Making shapes is an important part of using Adobe Illustrator. In Lesson 4, "Working with the Drawing Tools," you learn how to make your own custom shapes and lines using the Pen tool, but many times you will work with shapes that are ready-to-go, right off the Tools panel.

Though it may seem simple if you have used Illustrator before, transferring a shape from the Tools panel to the artboard can be a little confusing for new users. To start this lesson, you'll create a new blank document; think of it as a piece of scratch paper that you can use for shape practice. You will put a number of shapes on this new document throughout the exercise; feel free to delete or reposition them as you move on to make room for new ones. You won't use this document in any other lessons.

1   In Illustrator, choose File > New; the New Document dialog box appears.

2   If they are not already selected, choose Print from the New Document Profile drop-down menu and Inches from the Units drop-down menu. When you change the units to inches, the New Document Profile setting changes to [Custom].

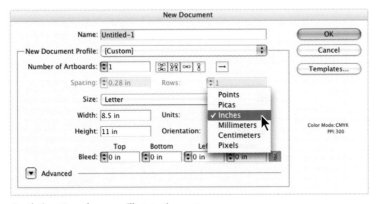

Specify the settings of your new Illustrator document.

3   Press OK. A new blank document appears.

4   Select the Rectangle tool (□) from the Tools panel. Click and drag anywhere on the artboard. By clicking and dragging, you determine the placement and size of the rectangle. Typically, you would pull from the upper-left corner diagonally to the lower-right corner.

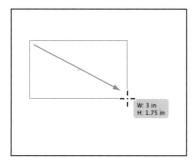

Click and drag from the upper-left to the lower-right corner.

5   It is essential that you save your files often after you start working. Choose File > Save As to save this file. The Save As dialog box appears.

6   Type **ai0301_work.ai** into the File name (Windows) or Save As (Mac OS) text field, navigate to the ai01lessons folder within the CS4lessons folder that you dragged onto your desktop, then press Save.

7   When the Illustrator Options dialog box appears, leave the version set to Illustrator CS4 and press OK. The file is saved.

If you are not able to save in the ai01lessons folder, the folder may be locked. See the tip on page 4 for instructions to unlock your lessons folder.

Repositioning and visually resizing the rectangle

Now that you have your first shape on the page, perhaps you want to relocate it or alter its shape or size.

1 Choose the Selection tool (k) from the Tools panel. A bounding box with eight handles appears around the rectangle you just drew. If you do not see the eight handles, make sure you have the rectangle selected by clicking on it once. If the bounding box is still not visible, choose View > Show Bounding Box. The bounding box is a feature that can be turned on or off and that allows you to transform a shape without switching away from the Selection tool.

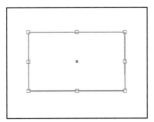

The bounding box provides handles to help transform shapes.

2 Using the Selection tool, click inside the rectangle and drag it to another location on the page (do not click on the handles, as that resizes the shape).

If you click inside a shape and it becomes unselected, it probably has no fill. Fill and stroke are discussed in Lesson 4, "Adding Color." By pressing the letter D, you revert back to the default white fill and black stroke, and you can easily select the shape.

3 Hover over the bottom-middle handle until the cursor becomes a vertical arrow and the word *path* appears. Click and drag. When you click on a middle handle and drag, you adjust the size of the selected handle's side only.

4 Click on a corner handle and drag. When you click on a corner handle, you adjust both the sides connected to the corner point.

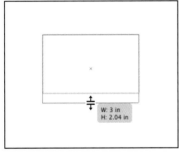
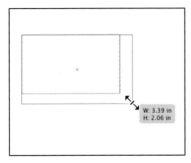

Click and drag a middle point.   *Click and drag a corner point.*

5   Choose File > Save to save your work.

Finding or changing the shape's dimensions using the Transform panel

What if you need to know a shape's dimensions, or need it to be an exact size? This is when you should refer to the Transform panel.

1   Make sure the rectangle is still selected and open the Transform panel by choosing Window > Transform. The Transform panel appears. The values displayed are for the selected item, which in this case is the rectangle.

The Transform panel displays information about the rectangle's location and size. Here is something to keep in mind: the values (except for the X and Y values, which refer to the selected reference point) displayed in the Transform panel refer to the rectangle's bounding box. By default, the reference point is the center of the shape.

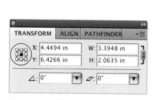
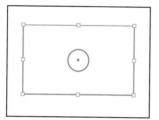

The center reference point.   The reference point locator.

2   Click on the upper-left corner of the reference point locator to see that the X and Y values change, reflecting the shape's position based upon the upper-left corner as the reference point. Because you created your rectangle without given parameters, its values are different from those displayed in the figure below.

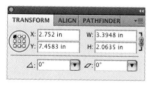

The X and Y coordinates change depending
on the reference point selected.

3   Choose View > Show Rulers to display the rulers, or use the keyboard shortcut Ctrl+R (Windows) or Command+R (Mac OS).

The default ruler origin of zero is located in the lower-left corner of the artboard. This can be confusing if you are accustomed to the rulers in page layout applications, which start at zero in the upper-left corner of the page.

4   In the Transform panel, type **2** into the X text field and press the Tab key to move the cursor to the Y text field. Type **10** into the Y text field. Make sure the Constrain Width and Height proportions button (⬤) is not selected, then type **1** into the W (Width) text field and **1** into the H (Height) text field. The rectangle is now positioned and sized according to these values.

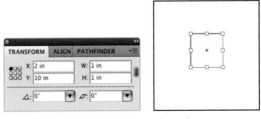

Manually enter values.   The result.

5   Choose File > Save to save your work.

Rotating and shearing using the Transform panel

You can also use the Transform panel to enter exact rotation and shear values for the shapes on the artboard.

1   With the shape still selected, type **25** into the Rotate text field at the bottom of the Transform panel and press Enter (Windows) or Return (Mac OS). The square rotates 25 degrees counterclockwise and the dimensions in the Transform panel are updated.

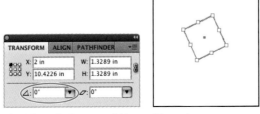

Type 25 into the Rotate text field.   The result.

2   Click and hold on the arrow to the right of the Shear text field and choose 30° from the drop-down menu. Illustrator shears the shape by 30 degrees.

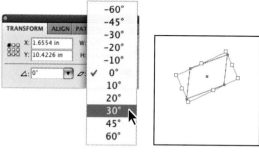

Type a value into the Shear text field.   The result.

3   Choose File > Save.

Constraining a shape

You have created a shape visually and then used the Transform feature to make the rectangle a square. You can also use keyboard commands to create the shape that you want right from the Tools panel.

1   Select the Rectangle tool (□) from the Tools panel.

2   Hold down the Shift key and click and drag on an empty area on the artboard. Note that the shape tool is constrained to create a square. In order for the finished product to remain a square (and not become a rectangle), you must release the mouse before you release the Shift key. Now try this with the Ellipse tool.

3   The Ellipse tool (○) is hidden beneath the Rectangle tool. Click and hold on the Rectangle tool in the Tools panel to reveal and select the Ellipse tool.

Select the hidden Ellipse tool.

4 Hold down the Shift key, click on an empty area of the artboard, and drag to create a circle. Remember to release the mouse before you release the Shift key to keep the shape a circle.

5 Choose File > Save. Keep this file open for the next part of the lesson.

Entering exact dimensions

You can also modify a shape's properties and dimensions through the shape tool's dialog box. You'll do that now using the Ellipse tool.

Before you start, you should know where to set the units of measurement. Even after indicating that you want the rulers to use inches, you may still have values recognized in points.

1 Choose Edit > Preferences > Units & Display Performance (Windows) or Illustrator > Preferences > Units & Display Performance (Mac OS). The Preferences dialog box appears.

2 Select Inches from the General drop-down menu, if it is not already selected. Leave all other measurements the same and press OK.

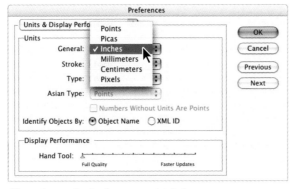

Change the general units of measurements to inches.

3 Using the Ellipse tool (○), click once on the artboard. The Ellipse dialog box appears.

If the Ellipse dialog box does not appear, you may have inadvertently clicked and dragged. Even a slight drag instructs Illustrator to create a tiny shape rather than open the dialog box. If this happens, press Ctrl+Z (Windows) or Command+Z (Mac OS) and click on the artboard again.

4   Type **4** into the Width text field, then click on the word *Height*. When you do this, the measurement is matched to the value that you entered into the Width text field. Press OK.

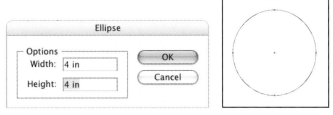

Click on Height to match the value in the Width text field.

You can use this same method to change shape options.

5   Hidden beneath the Ellipse tool in the Tools panel are a number of other shape tools. Click and hold the Ellipse tool to see the other options. Select the Star tool (☆) and click once on a blank area of the artboard. The Star dialog box appears.

6   Set the star's Radius 1 to **1.5** inches and its Radius 2 to **2** inches; then type **15** in the Points text field. Press OK.

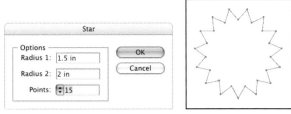

Enter star values.   *The result.*

7   Choose File > Save, then File > Close. You won't be working with this file anymore.

You will now create a logo using some of these basic shapes as well as additional fundamental features.

Selecting artwork

In this part of the lesson, you will receive a quick primer on the selection tools and techniques in Adobe Illustrator. As the old saying goes, you have to select it to affect it. You need to know how to select objects in order to reposition, color, transform, and apply effects to them.

Helpful keyboard shortcuts for selections

FUNCTION	WINDOWS	MAC OS
Switch to last-used selection tool	Ctrl	Command
Switch between Direct Selection tool and Group Selection tool	Alt	Option
Add to a selection	Shift+click	Shift+click
Subtract from a selection	Shift+click	Shift+click
Change pointer to cross hair for selected tools	Caps Lock	Caps Lock

The selection tools

While there are several selection tools in Adobe Illustrator, the two main tools are the Selection tool and the Direct Selection tool. You will have an opportunity to experiment with selections in this part of the lesson.

1   Choose File > Open and navigate to the ai01lessons folder. Select the file named ai0302.ai and press Open. A file opens with a completed fish illustration on the top and the individual components of that fish at the bottom. The top fish artwork is locked and not accessible; use this for reference as you follow the exercise.

2   Choose File > Save As. The Save As dialog box appears.

3   Type **ai0302_work.ai** into the Name text field and press OK. When the Illustration Options dialog box appears, press OK.

4   Choose the Selection tool (▸) from the Tools panel and pass the cursor over the shape pieces at the bottom of the artwork. As you pass over the objects, notice that the cursor changes to reflect where there are selectable objects. Do not click to select any of these objects just yet.

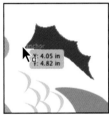

Selectable object.   *Anchor point.*   *No selectable object.*

5   Click on the large red fin; the entire fin is selected. If you do not see the bounding box appear around the fin, choose View > Show Bounding Box.

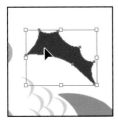

The entire shape is selected and has a bounding box surrounding it.

6   Click and drag to reposition the fin anywhere on the page. When you use the Selection tool, you select an entire object or group.

7   Choose the Direct Selection tool (⇘) from the Tools panel. Using this tool allows you to select individual points or path segments of an object.

8   Without clicking on the selected large fin, reposition the cursor over one of the tips of the fin to see how the cursor changes to indicate that there is a selectable anchor beneath the cursor. A light-gray box giving the x- and y-coordinates of the anchor point also appears. Click when you see the arrow with the small white square.

Cursor changes to show the selectable item.   *Individual anchor point selected.*

9   Notice that only the anchor point that you clicked on is solid; all the other anchor points are hollow and not active.

10 Click on the solid anchor point and drag upward to reposition the anchor point and change the shape of the fin. By using the Direct Selection tool, you can alter the shape of an object.

Click and drag with the Direct Selection tool to alter a shape.

11 Press Ctrl+Z (Windows) or Command+Z (Mac OS) to undo the last step, or choose Edit > Undo Move.

12 Choose File > Save. Keep this file open for the next part of this lesson.

Grouping the scales

You will now turn the individual scales in the artwork into a group that you can move and modify as a collective unit.

1 Activate the Selection tool (➤). Click on one of the pale orange scales, then add to the selection by holding down the Shift key and clicking on one of the other five scales.

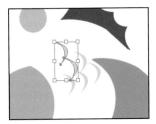

Shift+click to add to the selection.

2 With the two scales selected, choose Object > Group or use the keyboard shortcut Ctrl+G (Windows) or Command+G (Mac OS). The two scales are grouped together. When you select one with the Selection tool, the other is also selected.

3 Shift+click a third scale to add to the selection, then Shift+click the remaining scales. All the scales are now selected.

4 Press Ctrl+G (Windows) or Command+G (Mac OS) to group all the six scales together.

5 Choose Select > Deselect, or press Shift+Ctrl+A (Windows) or Shift+Command+A (Mac OS), to deselect the scales.

6 Using the Selection tool, click on one of the first scales you selected. The scales act as a collective group now, and all the scales are selected.

7   Press Shift+Ctrl (Windows) or Command+A (Mac OS) to deselect everything again.

You will now use the Group Selection tool to select individual items in a group.

8   Click and hold down on the Direct Selection tool (↖) in the Tools panel and choose the hidden Group Selection tool (↖).

9   Click once on the top-most scale of the group; only the one scale is selected.

10   Now click on the same scale again and the second scale that you grouped back in step 1 also becomes selected.

11   Click on the same scale a third time and the entire last group of items becomes selected. By using the Group Selection tool, you can select individual items and even groups within groups.

12   With all the scales selected, click and drag the scales on top of the fish's orange body.

Click and drag to reposition the scales.

13   Now switch back to the Selection tool to reposition the rest of the separate components together to complete the fish. The positioning guides help you to best position and arrange the different pieces into one fish.

The completed fish.

14   Choose File > Save, then File > Close to close the document. You won't be working with this file anymore.

Isolation mode

Isolation mode is an Illustrator mode in which you can select and edit individual components or sub-layers of a grouped object. There are four ways to enter into isolation mode:

- Double-click a group using the Selection tool (▶).

- Click the Isolate Selected Group button (▦) in the Control panel.

- Right-click (Windows) or Ctrl+click (Mac OS) a group and choose Isolate Selected Group.

- Select a group in the Layers panel and choose Enter Isolation Mode from the Layers panel menu (▾≡).

Using shape and transform tools to create artwork

You will add to the basics that you have discovered to complete some different fish artwork.

1   Choose File > Open and navigate to the ai01lessons folder. Double-click on ai0303_done.ai to open the file in Adobe Illustrator. Artwork of two swimming fish appears.

You can leave this file open for reference or choose File > Close.

2   Choose File > Open, navigate to the ai01lessons folder, and double-click on the ai0303.ai file. A document with four guides in the center of the page opens.

3   Choose File > Save As. The Save As dialog box appears.

4   Type **ai0303_work.ai** into the Save As text field and navigate to the ai01lessons folder you saved on your hard drive; then press Save.

5   When the Illustrator Options dialog box appears, press OK.

Using the transform tools

There are several transform tools. Though each performs a different task, they are essentially used in the same manner.

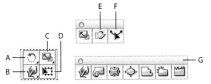

A. Rotate. B. Warp tools. C. Scale. D. Free Transform.
E. Shear. F. Reshape. G. Additional Warp tools.

You used the Transform panel to rotate and shear earlier in this lesson. You will now use the transform tools to make changes by entering exact values.

1   Click and hold on the Star tool (☆) in the Tools panel to reveal the hidden tools. Select the Rounded Rectangle tool (▢).

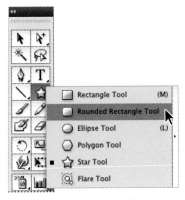

Select the Rounded Rectangle tool.

2   Click and drag to create a square with rounded corners of any size.

3 Activate the Selection tool (▶) and, using the bounding box's anchors, click and drag until the rounded rectangle fits the dimensions of the guides located in the center of the document.

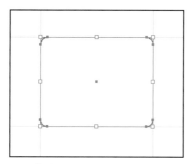

Manually drag anchors to fit the rectangle inside the guides.

Adding a fill color

You will now fill the rounded rectangle with a color.

1 Make sure the rounded rectangle is still selected. If it is not selected, click on it using the Selection tool (▶).

2 Locate the Control panel at the top of your workspace and click on the Fill box on the left side of the Control panel. Color swatches appear, from which you can choose a color. Pass your cursor over the swatches, and each color's name appears in a tooltip. Select the color named *CMYK Blue*. If the tooltip does not appear, select the color you see highlighted in the figure below. Illustrator colors the shape blue.

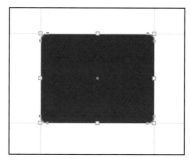

Select CMYK Blue for the fill.   *The result.*

3 Lock the selected rectangle by pressing Ctrl+2 (Windows) or Command+2 (Mac OS), or by choosing Object > Lock > Selection. This makes it impossible to select the rectangle unless you unlock it. This feature is extremely helpful when you start creating more complicated artwork.

Modifying a shape

You will now use the shape tools to create and add light rays to the illustration.

1   From the list of hidden shape tools beneath the Rounded Rectangle tool in the Tools panel, select the Polygon tool (○) and click once on the artboard. The Polygon dialog box appears.

2   Leave the radius as it is; type **3** into the Sides text field and press OK. A triangle is drawn.

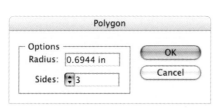

Change the amount of sides.   *The result.*

3   Choose the Selection tool (▸), and click and drag the top center anchor of the bounding box upward, to stretch the triangle.

4   Elongate the triangle more by clicking on the lower-right corner of the bounding box, pulling down, and dragging the anchor to the left.

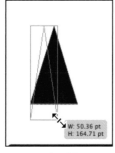

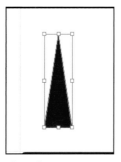

Click and drag upward.   *Drag inward and down.*   *The result.*

By clicking and dragging the anchor, you visually resize the shape.

Entering a shape size in the Transform panel

For the purpose of this illustration, you will use the Transform panel to make sure that the triangle is sized correctly.

1   If it is not visible, choose Window > Transform to open the Transform panel.

2   With the triangle still selected, type **.5** in the W (Width) text field, and type **2** into the H (Height) text field. Press Enter (Windows) or Return (Mac OS).

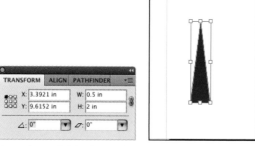

Enter values in the Transform panel.   *The result.*

3   Press **D**; the triangle's color reverts to the default white fill and black stroke colors.

4   Click once on the Stroke box in the Control panel at the top of the Illustrator work area and select None from the Stroke swatches drop-down menu. The triangle is not visible at this time (as it is white on a white background), but you can still see its anchor points.

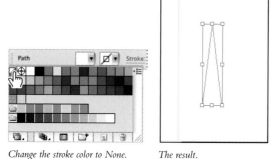

Change the stroke color to None.   *The result.*

Viewing in Outline view

By default, previews of Adobe Illustrator artwork are in color. There will be times, however, when you create shapes that are white, or possibly have no fill or stroke color. Finding these items on your white artboard after you deselect them can be difficult. This is where Outline view can help.

1   With the Selection tool (*****), click somewhere on the artboard to deselect the triangle. Unless your triangle crosses over the rectangle you created earlier, you can no longer see the shape.

2   Choose View > Outline, or press Ctrl+Y (Windows) or Command+Y (Mac OS).
     Outline view displays artwork so that only its outlines (or paths) are visible. Viewing
     artwork without fill and stroke attributes speeds up the time it takes Illustrator to redraw
     the screen when working with complex artwork; it is also helpful when you need to
     locate hidden shapes.

3   With the Selection tool, click on one of the triangle's sides and reposition it so its tip
     touches the center (indicated by an x) of the rectangle.

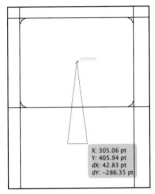

*The triangle and rectangle arranged in
the Outline view.*

4   Choose View > Preview, or press Ctrl+Y (Windows) or Command+Y (Mac OS) once
     more. The color attributes are visible again.

Rotating the shape

You will now create a series of triangle shapes and rotate them 360 degrees, creating what will
look like rays of light.

1   Make sure the triangle is selected.

2   Select the Rotate tool (○) from the Tools panel. The Rotate tool allows you to visually
     rotate objects, as well as enter specific rotation angles. In this example, you will enter
     values so that the triangles are evenly spaced.

3   Alt+click (Windows) or Option+click (Mac OS) the tip of the triangle aligned with the
     rectangle's center. When you have a Rotate tool selected and you Alt+click (Windows)
     or Option+click (Mac OS) on the artboard, you define the reference point from which
     the selected shape is rotated. Doing this also displays the Rotate dialog box, in which you
     can enter an exact value for the angle.

4 Type **18** into the Angle text field and press Copy. This rotates a copy of your triangle 18 degrees and keeps the original triangle intact. The value of 18 degrees evenly divides into 360 degrees, which will make the distribution of these rays even when you circle back to the starting point.

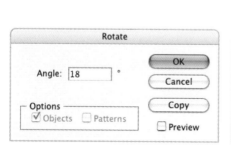

Enter rotate values and press Copy.　　　　　*A rotated copy is created.*

5 Press Ctrl+D (Windows) or Command+D (Mac OS) to repeat the transformation. The triangle shape copies, and rotates again.

6 Continue to press Ctrl+D (Windows) or Command+D (Mac OS) until you reach the original triangle.

The triangle after being rotated.

Changing the color of the triangles

You will now select the triangles and change their opacity.

1 Switch to the Selection tool (🔧) and select any one of the white triangles.

2 Choose Select > Same > Fill Color and all the white triangles become selected. The Select > Same feature can be helpful when selecting objects that share a common feature, including fill color, stroke color, stroke point size, and more.

3   Choose Object > Group. Grouping these shapes together makes it easier to select them later.

4   Type **50** into the Opacity text field in the Control panel and press Enter (Windows) or Return (Mac OS) to change the opacity of the white triangles to 50 percent.

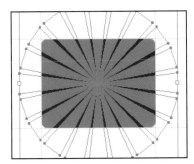

Select the triangles and change the opacity to 50 percent.

5   Choose File > Save to save your work.

Using layers when building an illustration

Layers have many uses in Adobe Illustrator. In this lesson, you will find out how to use layers to lock and temporarily hide artwork that you don't want to inadvertently select while you work on other things.

1   Open the Layers panel by pressing the Layers button (⬦) in the dock on the right side of the workspace. Notice that when you start to work in Illustrator, you begin with a layer named Layer 1. All the artwork that you have created throughout this lesson is added as a sub-layer to this layer. You will now lock a sub-layer and create a new layer onto which you can put additional artwork.

2   Click on the Toggles lock (a small empty box) to the left of Layer 1 in the Layers panel. A padlock icon (🔒) appears, indicating that this layer is locked. You cannot select or change any items on this layer.

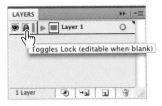

The Toggles lock area of the Layers panel.

> *Earlier in this lesson, you selected and locked the rectangle using the Object > Lock menu item. That method works well for individual items, especially if you don't typically work with layers. Locking a layer is different, as it locks all items on the layer at once.*

3   To unlock the layer, click on the padlock icon. The layer unlocks.

4   Relock Layer 1 by clicking on the Toggles lock square again.

Creating a new blank layer

You will now create a new blank layer onto which you can paste artwork.

1   Alt+click (Windows) or Option+click (Mac OS) the Create New Layer button (▣) at the bottom of the Layers panel. The Layer Options dialog box appears. By holding down the Alt/Option key, you can name the layer before its creation.

2   Type **Fish** into the Name text field and press OK. A new empty layer appears on top of the original (Layer 1) displayed in the Layers panel. You are now ready to copy and paste artwork from another Illustrator file into this one.

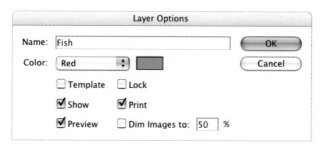

Name the new layer.

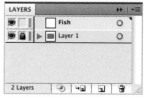

The layer in the Layers panel.

Cutting and pasting objects

You will now open another document and cut and paste artwork from one Illustrator file to another.

1   Choose File > Open. In the Open dialog box, navigate to the ai01lessons folder and double-click on the file named ai0304.ai. Artwork of two fish appears.

The fish artwork.

2   Use the Selection tool (k) to click once on the larger of the two fish, then Shift+click on the second fish to add it to the selection.

3   Choose Edit > Cut, or press Ctrl+X (Windows) or Command+X (Mac OS), to cut the fish.

4   Return to the work file by choosing Window > ai0303_work.ai. Choose Edit > Paste, or press Ctrl+V (Windows) or Command+V (Mac OS), to paste the fish onto the artboard. The fish are pasted onto the Fish layer, which is the active layer.

5   Press Shift+Ctrl+A (Windows) or Shift+Command+A (Mac OS), or click on a blank area of the artboard, to deselect the fish.

6 Activate the Selection tool; click on the smaller of the two fish and drag it to a spot on top of the larger fish. Notice that the smaller fish disappears behind the larger fish. The order in which artwork appears is based on the order in which artwork is created. Newer artwork is placed higher in the object stacking order, which can be changed using the Arrange feature.

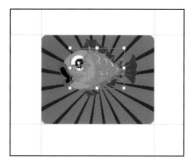

The smaller fish falls behind the larger fish in the stacking order.

7 With the smaller fish still selected, choose Object > Arrange > Bring to Front.

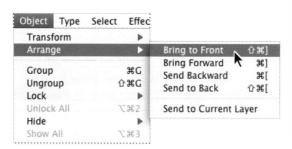

Choose to bring the small fish to the front.   *The result.*

8 Select the smaller fish and reposition it so that it slightly overlaps the bottom of the larger fish.

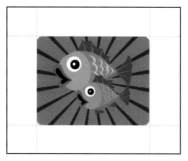

Reposition the smaller fish to overlap the larger fish slightly.

9 Choose File > Save. Keep this file open for the next part of this lesson, but close ai0304. ai. When asked if you'd like to save the changes made to the document, choose No (Windows) or Don't Save (Mac OS).

Creating bubbles

You will now create a bubble, and then clone it several times to finish the illustration.

1 Click and hold down on the last-used shape tool (the Polygon tool) in the Tools panel and select the hidden Ellipse tool (○).

2 Click once on the artboard to display the Ellipse dialog box.

3 Type .5 into the Width text field, then click on the word *Height*. This enters the **.5** value into the height text field as well. Press OK. A small circle is created.

4 Click the Fill color swatch in the Control panel and choose the color CMYK Cyan from the drop-down swatches menu.

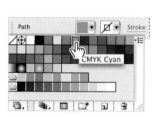

Change the fill color to CMYK Cyan.   *The result.*

5 If the Stroke is not set to none (☑), choose the Stroke box in the Control panel and choose None from the drop-down swatches menu.

Now you will create a smaller circle to use as a reflection in the circle you already created.

6 With the Ellipse tool still active, click once on the artboard.

7 In the resulting Ellipse dialog box, type **.1** into the Width text field then click on the word *Height* to match values. Press OK.

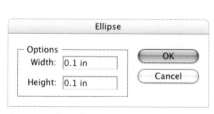
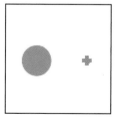

Create a smaller circle.   *The result.*

8 Use the Fill box in the Control panel to select White for the small circle's fill.

9 Activate the Selection tool (⬉), then click and drag the smaller circle on top of the larger cyan (blue) circle. Position it anywhere you want on the circle, as long as it looks like a light reflection on the bubble.

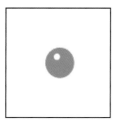

*Position the smaller white circle
on top of the cyan circle.*

10 Shift+click the larger and smaller circles to select them both. Choose Object > Group, or press Ctrl+G (Windows) or Command+G (Mac OS), to group the circles.

11 Choose File > Save to save your work.

Cloning the bubble group

You will now clone, or duplicate, the bubble several times.

1 Make sure the bubble group is selected.

2 Hover your cursor over the bubble and hold down the Alt (Windows) or Option (Mac OS) key. Note that the icon becomes a double cursor (⬉⬉).

3 While holding down on the Alt/Option key, click and drag to the right. Notice that as you drag, the original group of circles remains intact and you create a second group. Release the mouse when you are off to the right and the cloned bubble no longer touches the original.

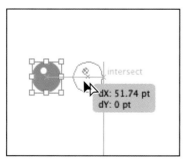

*Hold down the Alt (Windows) or Option (Mac OS)
key, then click and drag.*

4   Press Ctrl+D (Windows) or Command+D (Mac OS) to repeat the duplication. Illustrator remembers the distance and angle of the last movement. You can also perform this function by selecting Object > Transform > Transform Again.

5   Press Ctrl+D (Windows) or Command+D (Mac OS) once more to create a total of four circle groups.

If you hold down the Shift key while cloning, you can constrain the cloned objects to move on a straight path, or a 45- or 90-degree angle.

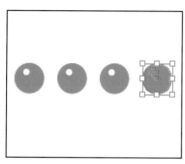

Clone the circle group three times.

6   Choose File > Save to save your work. Keep the file open for the next part of the lesson.

Repeating a resize transform

You will now use the Transform Again keyboard shortcut to transform the bubbles so they are varying sizes.

1   Select the second bubble. You will leave the original bubble at its present size.

2   Hold down the Shift key (to constrain the proportions as you resize), and click and drag a corner anchor point to resize the bubble only slightly. An exact amount is not important for this. Once you resize, do not perform any other actions, such as repositioning. The resizing has to be the last action that you performed for the Transform Again feature to work properly.

3   Select the third bubble group and press Ctrl+D (Windows) or Command+D (Mac OS). This applies the same transformation to the third bubble. With the same bubble still selected, press Ctrl +D (Windows) or Command+D (Mac OS) again and the resize transformation is applied, making it even smaller.

4   Select the last (fourth) bubble and press Ctrl+D (Windows) or Command+D (Mac OS) three times, making this the smallest bubble.

The bubbles after they have been transformed into differently sized bubbles.

Remember that the Transform Again feature (Ctrl+D [Windows] or Command+D [Mac OS]) repeats the most recent transformation, including positioning, that you performed. If you resize and then move an object, the repositioning, not the resizing, is repeated. If this occurs, press Ctrl+Z (Windows) or Command+Z (Mac OS) until you return to the point where all the bubbles are the same size. Then restart at step 1.

5   Using the Selection tool (▸), click and drag each bubble down and position them around the fish, on top of the rectangle. No exact position is necessary.

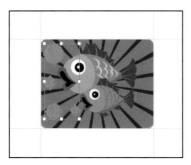

Click and drag the bubbles to reposition them in the artwork.

6   Choose File > Save to save your work. Keep the file open for the next part of the lesson.

Moving objects from one layer to another

You will now move the bubbles onto Layer 1, under the rays of light.

1   Select one of the bubble groups, then Shift+click the remaining three so that all four bubble groups are selected.

2   If the Layers panel is not visible, open it by clicking the Layers button (◉) in the dock or by choosing Windows > Layers.

A colored dot appears to the right of the Fish layer in the Layers panel. This colored dot is called the selection indicator. If Illustrator's settings are at their defaults, the indicator is red, matching the layer selection color.

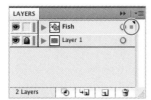

When something on a layer is selected, the selection indicator appears.

3   Click the padlock icon (🔒) to the left of Layer 1 to unlock the layer.

4   Click and drag the selection indicator from the Fish layer down to Layer 1. The bubbles are now on Layer 1 instead of on the Fish layer.

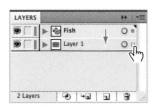

Click and drag the selection indicator to the layer beneath.

5   Click on any one of the triangles that you used to create the rays of light. Because they were grouped earlier, selecting one selects the entire group.

6   Choose Object > Arrange > Bring to Front; the triangles are now on top of the bubbles, but not on top of the fish. This is because the Fish layer is higher in the stacking order than anything on Layer 1.

7   Choose File > Save, then File > Close.

Congratulations! You have completed Illustrator Lesson 2, "Illustrator CS4 Essentials."

Self study

Practice will help you to create the shapes that you want. To practice on your own, open the file named ai0305.ai and create the shapes that are locked on the base layer.

Review

Questions

1 Which selection tool allows you to select an individual anchor point or path segment?

2 What key modifier do you hold down to constrain a shape to equal width and height values?

3 What are two methods of inputting exact height and width values for shapes?

Answers

1 The Direct Selection tool allows you to select an individual anchor point or path segment.

2 Constrain a shape's proportions by pressing the Shift key while dragging the shape.

3 You can enter values for shapes by doing either of the following:

   a. Select a shape tool and click once on the artboard. This opens the shape options dialog box, in which you can enter width and height values.

   b. After a shape has been created, choose Window > Transform and enter values into the Width and Height text fields.

Lesson 2

What you'll learn in this lesson:

- Using the Appearance panel
- Applying and adjusting fills and strokes
- Using the Live Paint Bucket tool
- Creating and applying a gradient
- Creating and updating a pattern swatch

Adding Color

Adobe Illustrator CS4 provides a number of methods to help add color to your artwork. In this lesson, you discover how to enhance your artwork with color, gradients, and patterns.

Starting up

Before starting, make sure that your tools and panels are consistent by resetting your workspace. See "Resetting Adobe Illustrator CS4 Preferences" on page XXVII.

You will work with several files from the ai02lessons folder in this lesson. Make sure that you have loaded the CS4lessons folder onto your hard drive from the supplied DVD. See "Loading lesson files" on page XXIX.

See Lesson 2 in action!

Use the accompanying video to gain a better understanding of how to use some of the features shown in this lesson. The video tutorial for this lesson can be found on the included DVD.

Basics of the Appearance panel

The Appearance panel in Illustrator allows you to adjust an object's fill and stroke, in addition to any effects that have been applied to the object. The Appearance panel is also an indispensable tool for determining the structure of an object. Fills and strokes are shown in the order that they are applied to an object, the same way that other effects are ordered chronologically. As your Illustrator artwork increases in complexity, the Appearance panel becomes more important, as it makes the process of editing and adjusting your document much easier. Let's explore the Appearance panel.

1   With Adobe Illustrator CS4 open, select the Go to Bridge button (⏵Br) in the Control panel.

2   Once Bridge opens, navigate to the ai02lessons folder and open the ai0401.ai file by double-clicking on it.

3   The file opens in Illustrator. Activate the Selection tool (➤) in the Tools panel and select the orange oval behind the *ATOMIC REGION* text by clicking to the left or the right of the letters.

4   Open the Appearance panel by choosing Window > Appearance or by pressing the Appearance button (◉) in the dock on the right side of your workspace.

The Appearance panel displays the attributes of the currently selected object. In this example, the object that is selected is filled with an orange color, has no stroke, and has two effects applied to it. Without the Appearance panel, it would take you a while to determine the attributes of this object.

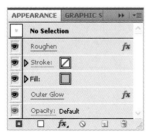

The Appearance panel shows you all the attributes associated with the selected object on your page.

5   In the Appearance panel, select the Stroke listing. Upon clicking the listing, a stroke color swatches panel and a Stroke Weight drop-down menu and slider appear, built directly into the panel.

6   Choose 3 pt from the Stroke Weigh drop-down menu. This applies a 3-point stroke to the orange background object.

7   Press the arrow next to the Stroke Color drop-down menu and choose White from the Swatches panel that appears.

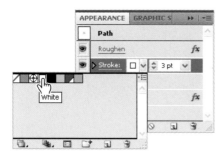

The Stroke Color option in the Control panel makes it easy to apply a color to the stroke of a selected object.

Now that you have applied a white stroke to your object, the Appearance panel updates to reflect this change.

8   Choose File > Save As. In the Save As dialog box, navigate to the ai02lessons folder and type **ai0401_work.ai** in the Name (Windows) or Save As (Mac OS) text field. Choose Adobe Illustrator from the Save as type (Windows) or Format (Mac OS) drop-down menu and press Save. When the Illustrator Options dialog box appears, press OK. Keep the file open for the next part of the lesson.

Fills and strokes

In Illustrator, an object has two basic attributes: a fill and a stroke. Fills and strokes can be customized with solid colors, tints of a color, patterns, or gradients. You can further customize strokes so that their weight is any size you want. In the following steps, you'll make some adjustments to the fill and stroke of the type at the top of the page.

1   Using the Selection tool (▸), select the *ATOMIC REGION* text frame.

2   In the Control panel, click and hold on the Stroke Color swatch, choose purple from the Stroke Swatches panel that appears. The purple is applied to the stroke of the selected text.

3   Change the weight of the selected text's stroke to 5 points by choosing 5 pt from the Stroke Weight drop-down menu in the Control panel, or by typing **5 pt** into the Stroke Weight text field.

4   Click the Fill color swatch in the Control panel. When the Fill Swatches panel appears, choose the tan color. This changes the selected type's fill color to tan.

To make the heading type really stand out, you will add a few effects to it.

5   Choose Effect > Brush Strokes > Spatter. In the resulting Effects dialog box, set the Spray Radius to **5** and the Smoothness to **3** by typing these values in their respective text fields or by dragging the sliders for each setting. Press OK.

6   Choose Effect > Warp > Bulge. In the Warp Options dialog box, type **11** in the Bend text field to set the bend to 11 percent, and press OK.

The headline type, after applying a fill, stroke, and some other effects.

If you look in your Appearance panel, you see that the Spatter and Warp: Bulge effects have been added to your type to create a more dynamic look.

Saving swatches

Adobe Illustrator CS4 contains a Swatches panel that allows you to store colors for multiple uses in your document. You can create colors using several different methods in Illustrator, and by adding them to the Swatches panel, you can store them for frequent and consistent use. Storing a swatch of a color that you plan to reuse guarantees that the color is exactly the same each time it is used. Let's create a new swatch for your document.

1   Click on the artboard (the white area surrounding the page) to deselect any objects in your document. You can also use the keyboard shortcut, Shift+Ctrl+A (Windows) or Shift+Command+A (Mac OS).

2   Click the Fill color swatch in the Control panel; the swatch expands to reveal the Fill Swatches panel. Press the panel menu button (⋅≡) in the upper-right corner of the panel and choose New Swatch.

If the New Swatch option is grayed out, select a swatch in the Swatches panel first.

Choose New Swatch from the panel menu to define a new swatch color.

3   In the resulting New Swatch dialog box, pick a slate gray color by dragging the sliders at the bottom of the dialog box until you achieve the desired color. In this example, the combination of CMYK, C=30, M=25, Y=18, K=75, was used.

Notice that as you adjust the colors at the bottom of the New Swatch dialog box, the name changes to reflect the color values that you have chosen. This is the default behavior in Illustrator, but you aren't limited to this naming convention. To choose your own name, simply highlight the CMYK values in the Swatch Name text field and type **Slate Gray**. Press OK.

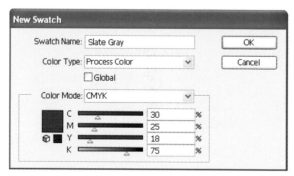

Create a custom color that will always appear in the Swatches panel of this document.

The swatch that you created is now available whenever you open this document, and can be applied to any additional objects that you create in the future.

4   Select the Type tool (T), then drag to select the *Tour Dates* text. You can also select the entire line by triple-clicking anywhere within the line of text.

5   Click the Fill color swatch in the Control panel and select the Slate Gray swatch that you created in step 3.

6   Use the keyboard shortcut Shift+Ctrl+A (Windows) or Shift+Command+A (Mac OS) to deselect all objects in the document.

7   Choose File > Save to save the document.

Reusing swatches

When you create swatches in an Illustrator document, those swatches are available only in that document by default. However, users commonly repurpose those swatches in other Illustrator documents. For example, maybe you created a poster like the one in this lesson, but then need to create a brochure that will be sent out to prospective customers. Instead of recreating all those swatches for the brochure, you can choose Save Swatch Library as AI from the Swatches panel menu, which creates a new file containing all the swatches in your current document. To reuse the swatches in another document, simply choose Open Swatch Library > Other Library from the Swatches panel menu. Now all those swatches are available to apply to objects in your new document.

There is also an option called Save Swatch Library as ASE (Adobe Swatch Exchange) in the Swatches panel menu. This performs a very similar task to Save Swatch Library as AI, except that the ASE format is interchangeable with other CS4 applications. These swatch libraries can be opened within Adobe Photoshop and Adobe InDesign, making it very easy to share colors between multiple applications. Unfortunately, any swatch patterns that have been added to the swatch library will not be accessible inside programs other than Illustrator.

Global colors

Simplifying your color and swatch options even further is an additional option available within each swatch that makes changing colors that have been used within your document a simple, hassle-free process. This option is the *Global* checkbox, found within the Swatch Options of each color. What makes this checkbox so useful is that every object that has a global swatch applied updates dynamically when that swatch is modified. Let's see how global colors can save you time when working in Illustrator.

1   Choose the Selection tool (➤) from the Tools panel, then press the Swatches button (▦) in the dock on the right side of your workspace to open the Swatches panel.

Notice that there is one swatch in the Swatches panel that looks slightly different from the rest of the swatches, in that it contains a small, white triangle in its lower-right corner. This icon indicates that this swatch is a global color.

The white triangle icon on a swatch represents a global color.

2   Double-click on the global swatch to display the Swatch Options dialog box. You'll notice that the *Global* checkbox is checked, indicating that this color is a global color. Any object in the document that has this color applied to it updates when the swatch is modified.

3   Turn on the Preview option by clicking in the *Preview* checkbox. This allows you to see any changes to your file as you try out options in the Swatches panel.

4   Adjust the CMYK values of the swatch to create a darker purple color. For this example, you set the values to: C=72 M=87 Y=20 K=22. As you adjust the values, notice that all the purple elements in the document update immediately to reflect the new color. Press OK and choose File > Save.

Swatch Options	
Swatch Name: C=72 M=87 Y=20 K=22	OK
Color Type: Process Color	Cancel
☑ Global	
Color Mode: CMYK	☑ Preview
C	72 %
M	87 %
Y	20 %
K	22 %

By turning on the Preview checkbox, you can see any changes to objects that have been colored using the global swatch.

You've just experienced the power of global swatches, a great feature that you can use in your day-to-day Illustrator work. If you apply a non-global color to several objects on your page, the process of updating those objects is much more cumbersome than if you use a global swatch.

Saving a set of colors as a group

When working in Illustrator, you'll often end up with quite a few swatches in your Swatches panel. As you experiment with colors and make adjustments, the number of swatches can increase to a point that makes it difficult to find a particular color. Fortunately, Illustrator simplifies the process of locating specific swatches by allowing you to create color groups to organize swatches into logical categories. Let's organize the swatches in the Swatches panel into color groups.

1   In the Swatches panel, hold down the Ctrl key (Windows) or the Command key (Mac OS) and select the six color swatches that follow the registration swatch (▦) in the Swatches panel to highlight them.

2   Press the New Color Group button (▣) at the bottom of the panel. The New Color Group dialog box appears.

3   In the New Color Group dialog box, type **Atomic Region Colors** in the Name text field. Press OK.

The New Color Group dialog box allows you to name the group that contains your swatches.

4   Choose File > Save to save your work. Keep the file open.

After creating the new color group, you can see that the swatches you selected in step 2 have been moved inside a color group. This is indicated by a small folder icon to the left of the swatches, which are grouped together inside a slim, white border. You can still select and apply each swatch as you did before, but now the colors are organized logically. If you hover your cursor over the color group folder icon, *Atomic Region Colors* appears in a tooltip.

If you do not see the tooltip as you hover over the color group folder icon, press Ctrl+K (Windows) or Command+K (Mac OS) to open the General Preferences. Make sure the Show Tool Tips checkbox is turned on and press OK.

Using the Color Guide panel

The Color Guide, which made its debut in Illustrator CS3, provides you with inspiration as you apply color to your artwork. The Color Guide panel suggests harmonious colors based on the color that is active in the Tools panel. You can change the suggested colors by changing the harmony rule, which is the method by which the Color Guide panel makes its color suggestions. Let's see how you can use the Color Guide panel to add a group of colors to your Swatches panel.

1   Open the Color panel by pressing the Color button (🖌) in the dock on the right side of the workspace, or choose Window > Color.

2   With the Fill icon (🔳) selected, click in the red area of the CMYK Spectrum at the bottom of the Color panel to choose a red color as a base to work with.

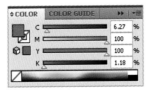

By clicking on the CMYK Spectrum at the bottom of the Color panel, you can set a new color as the base color.

3   To the right of the tab at the top of the Color panel is a tab that says Color Guide. Click on the Color Guide tab to reveal the Color Guide panel.

Notice that the color that you chose in step 2 is located in the upper-left corner of the Color Guide panel and is set as the base color. Next, you'll change the harmony rule, which dictates what colors the Color Guide suggests as harmonious colors with the base color.

4   From the Harmony Rules drop-down menu in the Color Guide panel, take a look at the different color schemes that the Color Guide suggests for each option. Choose High Contrast 2.

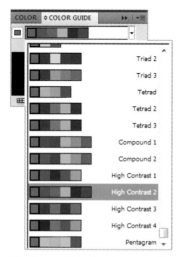

The Harmony Rules drop-down menu allows you to choose different schemes that Illustrator uses to suggest harmonious colors relative to the base color.

5   Click the Save color group to Swatches panel button (⊡) in the lower-right corner of the Color Guide panel to save the color scheme as a separate group in the Swatches panel.

As you are working in the Color Guide panel, you may notice that there are many swatches that appear in the large area of the Color Guide panel. These swatches are variations of the colors that appear in the Color Harmony menu at the top of the panel. You can add any of these swatches to the Swatches panel by dragging the swatch from the Color Guide panel to the Swatches panel.

6   Press the Swatches button (▦) in the dock to open the Swatches panel and see that the new color group from the Color Guide panel has been added to the Swatches panel. You'll use this color group later in this lesson.

7   Choose File > Save to save your work. Keep the file open.

Coloring objects

When working in Illustrator, the standard method of applying color to objects has always been to select an object with either the Selection or Direct Selection tool, then click on a color or swatch to change the color of the object. Illustrator also provides some advanced methods that allow you to apply color to objects more efficiently. In the following steps, you'll use the Live Paint feature to apply color to objects in Illustrator that would normally require you to perform various Pathfinder operations. You'll then make adjustments to the colors of a Live Paint object using a feature called Live Color.

Live Paint

With Live Paint, you can apply color to an object that has been converted into a Live Paint group. A Live Paint group is broken down into components in which objects overlap each other. Once an object is a Live Paint group, you can easily apply colors to different areas of that group. Let's begin!

1   Using the Selection tool (▲), click on the atom graphic to select it. You can see that this graphic is a group of several separate items.

2   Click on the Live Paint Bucket tool (⌗) in the Tools panel, or press **K** on your keyboard.

3   In the Swatches panel, click on the red swatch that is inside the color group that you added to the Swatches panel from the Color Guide.

4   Your cursor now looks like this (⌗), and if you hover your cursor over the selected atom graphic, the atom's paths are highlighted, and text reading, *Click to make a Live Paint Group,* appears to the right of the cursor. Click on the graphic to do just this.

5   Now when you hover your cursor over the atom graphic that has been converted to a Live Paint group, you see that different regions of the graphic become highlighted. If you click on an area, Illustrator colors it with the currently selected colors. Fill one of the rings with the red swatch that is currently selected, but only part of the ring. You want to create the illusion of the ring going around the sphere in the middle of the graphic.

You may want to zoom in on the atom graphic to make it easier to apply color to the smaller areas of the graphic. Zoom in to the graphic using the Zoom tool (🔍) in the Tools panel.

6   Use the right arrow key on your keyboard to toggle over to the first green color in the middle swatch above your cursor and apply that color to a different ring.

The three swatches that appear above your Live Paint Bucket cursor represent the previous, current, and next swatches within the current color group in the Swatches panel. It may help to understand this if you have the Swatches panel open as you key through the swatches. With the Swatches panel open, you can see how the active color changes in the Swatches panel, which also correlates to the swatches shown above your cursor.

7 Continue applying colors until all the rings have a different color, then select an orange color from the Swatches panel and apply the color to the sphere in the middle of the graphic.

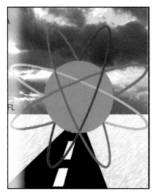

The atom graphic after applying color using the Live Paint Bucket tool.

8 Use the keyboard shortcut Ctrl+Shift+A (Windows) or Command+Shift+A (Mac OS) to deselect the atom graphic and see your work more clearly.

If you want to adjust colors using the Live Paint Bucket tool, hold down the Alt (Windows) or Option (Mac OS) key to pick a color that is already applied to your graphic instead of searching for the correct swatch in the Swatches panel.

9 Choose File > Save to save your work.

Live Color

The Live Color feature in Illustrator CS4 allows you to edit existing color groups and reassign or reduce colors in your document. This is a great feature that allows you to globally adjust several colors at once within your artwork. In the following steps, you'll adjust the atom's colors.

1 Using the Selection tool (⬈), select the atom graphic.

2 Press the Recolor Artwork button (⬤) in the Control panel to open the Live Color dialog box.

3 Click the Edit button (near the top of the Live Color dialog box) to edit the active colors of the selected object.

4 Select the Atomic Region Colors color group from the Color Groups list on the right side of the Live Color dialog box. This applies the Atomic Region Colors to the selected object. Notice how the colors change.

On the left side of the Live Color dialog box is a color wheel that displays the current active colors from the chosen color group. Each color is represented by a marker on the color wheel.

5 Click on and drag the largest marker—representing the color group's base color—in the color group. Experiment by spinning the colors around on the color wheel and dragging the markers toward and away from the center of the color wheel. Once you have a combination of colors that you like, press OK.

6 A dialog box may appear, asking if you want to save the changes to the color group named *Atomic Region Colors*. Choose No. This applies the colors that you chose from the color wheel to the selected atom graphic without changing the appearance of the saved color group.

7 Press Shift+Ctrl+A (Windows) or Shift+Command+A (Mac OS) to deselect the atom. Choose File > Save to save your work. Keep the file open.

Using Live Color, you were able to adjust multiple colors at a time while still retaining their relationship to each other. Live Color gives you great flexibility when you need to alter the appearance of multiple objects in your artwork.

Creating a gradient swatch

Earlier in this lesson, you learned how to create and edit swatches in your artwork. Now you will learn how to add and edit a gradient swatch to apply to the atom artwork in your document. Let's begin.

1 Press the Gradient button (▣) in the dock on the right side of the workspace, or choose Window > Gradient, to open the Gradient panel.

Press the Gradient panel menu button (•≡) and choose Show Options to display the entire Gradient panel with all its options.

2 Click once on the gradient slider in the middle of the Gradient panel to activate it. Once activated, two gradient stops appear below the gradient slider. Double-click on the black gradient stop to activate it.

3 Choose one of the orange swatches to apply it to the color stop. You should now have a white-to-orange gradient in the Gradient panel. If you don't, double-click the other color stop and apply the white swatch to it.

Transparent color stops

Illustrator includes the ability for gradient color stops to be transparent. To try this, double-click on one of the color stops in the active gradient and set its opacity level at the top of the Swatches panel.

4   From the Type drop-down menu in the Gradient panel, change the gradient type
    to Radial.

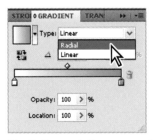

The Gradient panel allows you to specify
all the attributes of your gradient.

5   Switch to the Swatches panel. To make the white-to-orange gradient a swatch, press
    the New Swatch button (⬌) at the bottom of the Swatches panel. In the resulting New
    Swatch dialog box, name the gradient Orange Gradient and press OK. The gradient has
    been added to the Swatches panel.

    Now that you've created a new gradient swatch, you can apply it to the center portion of
    the atom graphic in your artwork. Remember that this atom graphic is still a Live Paint
    object. In the next steps, you'll use the Live Paint Selection tool to select all the elements
    that make up the center portion of the atom graphic.

6   Select the Live Paint Selection tool (⬌) from the Tools panel.

7   Click on one of the sections that make up the sphere in the center of the atom graphic
    and choose Select > Same > Fill Color from the menu at the top of the screen. This
    selects all the sections that make up that area of the graphic.

8   Click on the Orange Gradient swatch in the Swatches panel to apply it to the selected
    elements. This applies the gradient to each individual element within the selection.

    After creating a gradient swatch, you may need to alter the gradient or perhaps the colors
    used within the gradient swatch. This is easily accomplished in Illustrator.

9   Press Shift+Ctrl+A (Windows) or Shift+Command+A (Mac OS) to deselect the sphere,
    then select the Orange Gradient swatch in the Swatches panel.

10 In the Gradient panel, replace the orange color with a color of your choosing.

11 In order to see both panels at the same time, click the Expand Panels button (◂◂) at the top-right corner of the dock. Hold down the Alt (Windows) or Option (Mac OS) key, and click and drag the Gradient Fill icon in the Gradient panel and drop it on top of the existing Orange Gradient swatch in the Swatches panel. This replaces the old gradient swatch with the new one, but keeps the same name.

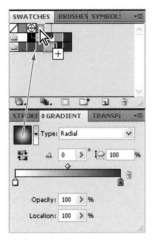

Replace the gradient in the Swatches panel with the new gradient in the Gradient panel.

Notice that when you replace the old gradient swatch with the new one, all objects in your artwork that were based on the original gradient swatch update to reflect the appearance of the new gradient swatch. If you want to change the name of your swatch, double-click it in the Swatches panel and type in a new name.

Creating a pattern swatch

Adobe Illustrator CS4 allows you to fill objects with patterns that repeat automatically. Patterns can be used in several ways and can be scaled and rotated as needed. In this example, you'll create a pattern that will appear over the cloud area of your artwork.

1 Using the Type tool, highlight the word *atomic* at the top of your artwork. Press Ctrl+C (Windows) or Command+C (Mac OS) to copy the selected text.

2 Press Ctrl+Shift+A (Windows) or Command+Shift+A (Mac OS) to deselect the type. Click somewhere on the artboard of your document to create a new line of text and press Ctrl+V (Windows) or Command+V (Mac OS), or choose Edit > Paste, to paste the word in the new location.

Notice that the pasted text only retains the general appearance of the copied text; no extra effects are included.

3   Double-click on the Scale tool (⬚) in the Tools panel. In the resulting Scale dialog box, set the Uniform Scale to 40 percent and make sure that the *Scale Strokes & Effects* checkbox is checked. Press OK.

4   Switch to the Selection tool (▸) and drag the frame containing the word *atomic* into the Swatches panel to add it as a pattern swatch. Delete the text from the artboard.

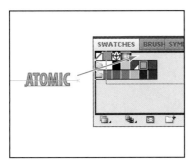

Illustrator makes the process of creating a pattern swatch very easy by simply dragging your item into the Swatches panel.

Now you need to create an object to fill with your pattern swatch.

5   Using the Rectangle tool (□), which may be hidden beneath another shape tool, draw a rectangle around the top portion of your artwork, from the horizon to the top of the document.

6   With the rectangle still selected, make sure the Fill box at the bottom of the Tools panel is in the foreground. Click on the atomic swatch that you just dragged to the Swatches panel.

The word *atomic* now fills the rectangle in a repeating pattern. Notice that the instances of the word *atomic* have no spaces between them, causing the pattern to look like one long word that is difficult to read. When you create a pattern, the outermost bounds of the object that you use as a pattern become the repeating pattern. Let's fix this to make it more readable.

7   Press Shift+Ctrl+A (Windows) or Shift+Command+A (Mac OS) to deselect the rectangle. Drag the pattern swatch from the Swatches panel to the artboard of your document. The text that was used to create the swatch appears on the artboard exactly as it was originally.

8   Using the Rectangle tool, draw a rectangle around the word *atomic*, making sure that the fill and stroke of the rectangle are set to none. Make the rectangle slightly larger than the text, especially on the sides of the word. Send the rectangle behind the type by choosing Object > Arrange > Send to Back from the menu.

9   Activate the Selection tool, and Shift+click the rectangle and the text to select both. In the Control panel, click the Horizontal Align Center (≜) and the Vertical Align Center (◦) buttons to align the two objects to each other.

Align the rectangle and the text.

10   With the type and the rectangle still selected, hold down the Alt (Windows) or Option (Mac OS) key and drag the objects on top of the original pattern swatch in the Swatches panel to replace the old pattern swatch with the new one. Notice that the pattern instantly updates in the rectangle that contained the pattern fill.

Now you will transform only the pattern fill inside the rectangle to change how the pattern fills the object.

11   Use the Selection tool to select the rectangle containing the pattern fill, and double-click on the Scale tool (▨) to open the Scale dialog box. Turn the *Preview* and *Patterns* checkboxes on and the *Objects* checkbox off, and experiment with different scaling values to see the effects they have on your pattern. This example uses 60 percent. Press OK.

12   With the rectangle still selected, double-click on the Rotate tool (○) to open the Rotate dialog box. Once again, turn the *Preview* and *Patterns* checkboxes on and the *Objects* checkbox off, and experiment with different rotation values. This example uses 30 degrees.

13   With the rectangle still selected, press Ctrl+[(Windows) or Command+[(Mac OS) several times until the rectangle appears behind all the objects in the artwork except for the sky.

14   As a finishing touch, open the Transparency panel from the dock by pressing the Transparency button (◉), and choose Darken from the blending mode drop-down menu.

15   Choose File > Save to save your work, then choose File > Close.

If you want to move your pattern around inside your shape to get the ideal tile pattern, hold down the tilde key (~). It's the key just under the Escape key at the top left corner of the keyboard. Take the Selection tool and click on the art that has the pattern fill. Then hold down the tilde key and click and drag inside the shape. Then let go of the mouse. The shape will not have moved at all, but the pattern will be in a different location. The same thing can be done with the keyboard arrow keys. Click on the shape with the Selection tool and then hold down the down arrow key. The pattern will move down.

Spot colors

When designing a product that will be reproduced on a printing press, some decisions need to be made regarding what colors will be used in the document. So far in this lesson, you have created all your swatches based on the CMYK color space. CMYK colors—Cyan, Magenta, Yellow, and Black—are referred to in the printing industry as *process colors*. Using these four inks printed in succession, it is possible to create a wide range of colors on a printed piece. Photographs, for example, are printed using process colors. However, process colors do have limitations. Certain colors are simply not achievable using CMYK due to the somewhat limited gamut of the CMYK color space. To more accurately achieve a specific color on a printed piece, spot colors come in handy.

Spot colors are colored inks that are specifically mixed to produce a desired color. The most common spot colors in the printing industry are made by a company called Pantone, Inc. *Pantone* and *spot color* are used almost synonymously in the printing industry, as Pantone colors are the primary inks used to specify spot colors for a printing job.

Spot colors can be used in many ways, but the primary reasons for using a spot color are:

* When color matching is critical. If a company logo is required to appear in the exact same color each time it is printed, a spot color may be used to reproduce the color consistently. In this example, adding a spot color to an existing process color job increases the costs of the project.

* To save money, instead of printing a product, such as a business card, using four process colors, you may choose to print the card in two spot colors or one spot color and black to reduce the cost of the printed product.

* To produce very rich, vibrant colors. These may be colors that process printing cannot recreate. This type of print job is often very expensive to produce.

In the following exercise, you will finish a business card that was started by using the atom logo from the poster you created earlier. You will then load Pantone colors into Illustrator CS4 that will be used to colorize the atom logo and some other elements within the business card.

1   Choose File > Browse in Bridge or press the Go to Bridge button (▸Br) in the menu bar.

2   Navigate to the ai02lessons folder within Bridge and open the file ai0402.ai by double-clicking on it.

3   Back in Illustrator, choose File > Save As. In the Save As dialog box, navigate to the ai02lessons folder and type **ai0402_work.ai** in the File name field. Choose Adobe Illustrator from the Save as type drop-down menu and choose Save. Press OK when the Illustrator Options dialog box appears.

4 Open the completed poster file (ai0401_done.ai) using the same method outlined in steps 2 and 3.

5 Using the Selection tool (▶), select the atom logo in the poster file and choose Edit > Copy. Close the poster file. If asked if you want to save changes to the file, choose No (Windows) or Don't Save (Mac OS).

6 With the business card file open, choose Edit > Paste.

The atom logo is clearly way too big for your business card, so let's scale it down to fit a little better.

7 Double-click on the Scale tool (◱) in the Tools panel to open the Scale dialog box. Select the *Uniform* radio button and type **20** in the Scale text field. To see the change in scaling before you apply it, ensure that the *Preview* checkbox is checked. Press OK.

8 Using the Selection tool, position the atom logo beneath the *Atomic Region* text on the business card.

9 Choose File > Save to save your work.

Loading Pantone colors

Now you will load some Pantone colors into your document to color the card's elements.

1 In the application bar, choose Window > Swatch Libraries > Color Books > PANTONE solid coated. This opens a new panel on your screen that lists all the colors in the PANTONE solid coated library.

2 From the panel menu of the PANTONE solid coated panel, choose Small List View to make it easier to identify the swatches; then, from the same panel menu, choose Show Find Field.

Change the view of and add a find field to the Pantone solid coated panel.

3   In the Find field of the PANTONE solid coated panel, type **7409**. Illustrator highlights the color in the panel that matches the number that you entered. Select the highlighted number and drag it into your Swatches panel to add it to your list of swatches. Repeat this step for color 512, and then close the PANTONE solid coated panel.

Notice that the icons you dragged into the Swatches panel have a different icon from the rest (⬚). The white, lower-right corner with the black dot indicates that the swatches are spot colors.

4   Using the Selection tool (▸), select the text box containing the text on the right side of the business card. Click on the Fill button in the Control panel and choose the swatch named 7409 from the swatches. The text fills with the 7409 color.

Do the same to the yellow oval graphic behind the Atomic Region text.

5   Use the Selection tool to select the *Atomic Region* text, and change the stroke by clicking on the stroke button in the Control panel and selecting the purple 512 color. Change the text's fill by clicking on the Fill button in the Control panel and selecting the same purple 512 color that you applied to the stroke.

6   Click on the Color button in the dock to open the Color panel. Reduce the fill's tint value by dragging the tint slider at the top of the panel to 60 percent to create a contrast between the text's fill and stroke.

Drag the tint slider of the Color panel to change the value of the Pantone color in the fill of the text.

Applying spot colors to the logo

You will now apply spot colors to the atom logo. To do this, you will use the Live Color feature to remap the colors in the atom logo to a Pantone color. First, you will create a new color group that contains the two Pantone colors in your job.

1   Make sure that nothing is selected in your document by clicking on a white area outside the business card or by using the keyboard shortcut Shift+Ctrl+A (Windows) or Shift+Command+A (Mac OS).

2   Open the Swatches panel from the dock. Select both Pantone colors—7409 and 512—by holding down the Shift key while clicking on them. Press the New Color Group button (▣) at the bottom of the Swatches panel.

3   In the resulting New Color Group dialog box, type **Pantone group** in the Name text field and press OK.

4   Activate the Selection tool (⬉) and select the atom logo. Select the Recolor Artwork button (◉) in the Control panel.

5   In the Recolor Artwork dialog box, press the Assign button to activate that portion of the dialog box. Click on Pantone group in the Color Groups section on the right side of the Recolor Artwork dialog box.

6   In the Colors drop-down menu to the left of the Color Groups list, change the value from Auto to 1 to tell Illustrator to remap all the colors in the logo to one color.

7   Press OK. If asked if you would like to save the changes to the color group, choose No.

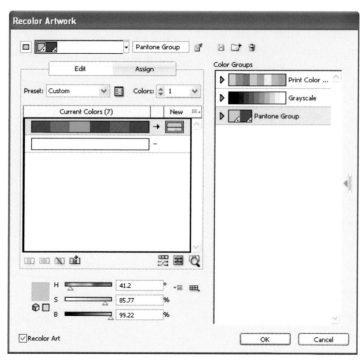

The Recolor Artwork dialog box allows you to remap a group of colors to a different group of colors in the selected artwork.

You can now see that all the colors that were in the atom logo have been remapped to one Pantone color on the business card.

8   To finish the business card, draw a rectangle the size of the business card using the Rectangle tool (▭). Click and drag from the upper-left corner of the document to the lower-right corner. Fill the rectangle with the Pantone 512 purple color by clicking on the Fill button in the Control panel and choosing the Pantone 512 swatch. If your color is still using the 60 percent tint that was previously set in the Color panel, change it back to 100 percent.

9   Choose Object > Arrange > Send to Back to put the purple rectangle behind the text, creating a purple background for the business card.

10 Choose File > Save to save your work, then File > Close.

Congratulations! You have completed Lesson 4, "Adding Color."

Self study

In this lesson, you were introduced to several great new features of Adobe Illustrator CS4, as well as some features that aren't so new, but deserve further investigation nonetheless.

The Appearance panel is a highly underused feature of Adobe Illustrator; practice on your own by exploring the capabilities harnessed within the Appearance panel. Start by drawing a line with the Line Segment tool then expanding the weight of the stroke. Add another stroke to it from within the Appearance panel, setting it to a different weight and color; you'll see that you can apply more than one stroke to a single object!

Explore Live Paint and Live Color in more detail. See Lesson 5, "Working with the Drawing Tools," for information about converting a picture into a vector-based piece of art using the Live Trace feature and then coloring it using Live Paint. Furthermore, you can experiment with Color Groups and the Recolor Artwork dialog box to change how your artwork is colorized in Illustrator.

You've worked with the Color Guide and its color harmony rules, which allow you to look at variations of the selected color group. Go to *kuler.adobe.com* to check out different color themes that people have created to share with other users. You can even post your own themes to this web site. Even better: you can download these themes to your computer and import them into the Creative Suite applications to apply to objects within your documents.

Review

Questions

1 What does the appearance of this swatch icon (●) in the Swatches panel indicate?

2 Where in Adobe Illustrator CS4 would you look to identify the attributes of a selected object?

3 True or false: You can share swatches that you created in Adobe Illustrator CS4 with other Adobe CS4 programs.

4 When you see this swatch icon (▨) in the Swatches panel, what does it indicate?

5 How do you edit a pattern swatch?

Answers

1 This swatch icon (◉) indicates that the color is a spot color.

2 You can locate the attributes of a selected object in the Appearance panel.

3 True. You can choose the Save Swatch Library as ASE command from the panel menu of the Swatches panel. This saves all your swatches as a separate Swatch Library file (.ase) that can be imported into other CS4 applications.

4 This swatch icon (▨) indicates that the color is a global color.

5 To edit a pattern swatch, drag the swatch icon from the Swatches panel onto your Illustrator artboard. Make the necessary changes, then select the pattern art and drag it back into the Swatches panel. If you want to replace the old pattern swatch, simply hold down the Alt (Windows) or Option (Mac OS) key on your keyboard as you drag the pattern artwork on top of the old pattern swatch in the Swatches panel.

Drawing straight lines

The first skill you need to master when working with the Pen tool is creating a straight line. To do this, you make corner anchor points with the Pen tool. Straight lines are automatically generated as a result.

1   In Illustrator, choose File > Open. When the Open dialog box appears, navigate to the ai03lessons folder and select the ai0501.ai file. Press OK. This is a practice file containing several different line templates that you will work through in the following exercises.

2   Choose File > Save As. In the Save As dialog box, navigate to the ai03lessons folder and type **ai0501_work.ai** into the Name text field; then press Save. In the resulting Illustrator Options dialog box, press OK to accept the default settings.

3   In the Control panel at the top of the workspace, select None (☒) from the Fill color drop-down menu. Select the color black from the Stroke color drop-down menu and select 2 pt from the Stroke Weight drop-down menu.

4   Select the Pen tool (✎) from the Tools panel and locate the template labeled Exercise 1 on the artboard. Click and release your left mouse button while hovering over label 1. This starts the line by creating the first anchor point.

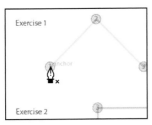

Use the Pen tool to create the first anchor point.

5   Move your cursor to the part of the line labeled 2, and click and release your mouse. The second point of the line is created. The Pen tool automatically draws a straight line between the two points you have established.

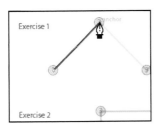

Create the second anchor point.

6   Continue to click and release to complete the line through labels 3, 4, 5, 6, and 7. Notice how the Pen tool automatically continues the line to include each new anchor point that you designate.

7   After you have set a final anchor point at label 7, press and hold Ctrl (Windows) or Command (Mac OS) and click on any empty area of the page. This deselects and ends the line. If you don't deselect and end the line, the Pen tool continues to link the line you just created to any anchor points that you create from here on.

8   Position the cursor over label 1 of Exercise 2. Click and release the left mouse button to create the first anchor point of the new line.

9   Position the cursor over label 2. Hold down the Shift key, then click and release to create the second point of the line; the Pen tool automatically connects the two points with a straight line. Because you were holding the Shift key when the second point was created, Illustrator automatically draws a perfectly horizontal line.

10 Position the cursor over label 3. Again hold the Shift key and click and release the left mouse button to set a third anchor point. This time, the line created is a perfect vertical line.

11 Continue holding down the Shift key while clicking at labels 4, 5, and 6. Doing this draws the line between points 4 and 5 at a perfect 135-degree angle, as the Shift key constrains the angle to 45-degree increments.

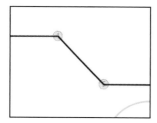

Pressing Shift while clicking allows you to create
90- and 45-degree angles with the Pen tool.

12 With a final anchor point at label 6, hold down the Ctrl key (Windows) or Command key (Mac OS) and click on the artboard to deselect and end the line.

13 Choose File > Save to save your work.

Drawing curved lines

Straight lines can only take you so far; more organic and complex compositions require you to use curved lines to render subjects. You will now complete Exercise 3.

1 Position your cursor over label 1 at the beginning of the curved line. Click and, without releasing the mouse, drag your cursor up slightly above the hump of the line to create your first anchor point. As you drag your cursor up, it looks like you are dragging a line away from the point. You are, in fact, creating a direction handle for the anchor point.

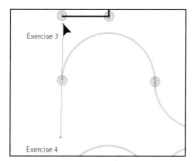

Dragging while clicking with the Pen tool allows you to create direction handles.

What are direction handles?

When you select or create a smooth point, you can see the direction handles of that point. Direction handles control the angle and length of curves. Direction handles comprise two parts: direction lines and the direction points at the ends of the lines. An anchor point can have zero, one, or two direction handles, depending on the kind of point it is. Direction handles serve as a kind of road map for the line, controlling how the lines approach and leave each anchor point. If the exiting handle is downward-facing, the line leaves the anchor point and goes down. Similarly, the line faces upwards if the direction handle is pointing upwards.

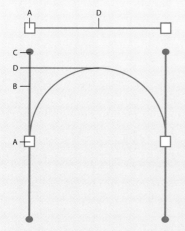

A. Anchor point. B. Direction Line. C. Direction Handle. D. Line Segment.

2   Place your cursor over label 2, located at the end of the first curve in Exercise 3. Click and drag straight down to create the second anchor point. Continue to drag the mouse until you form the curve in the template. As you drag your cursor down, you will notice that a curve is being formed between the two anchor points in real time. As long as you do not release the mouse button, you can reshape this line by dragging the mouse in different directions.

If you need to modify any of the previous points, choose Edit > Undo or use the keyboard shortcut, Ctrl + Z (Windows) or Command + Z (Mac OS). Do not worry if the curves do not follow the template perfectly, they can be adjusted in future steps.

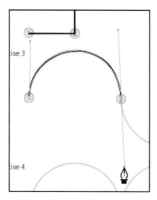

Dragging while creating the second anchor point allows you to curve the path.

3   Place your cursor over label 3, located at the end of the second curve. Click and drag up to create the third anchor point of the line. Continue to drag the mouse until you form the curve indicated by the template. Again, as long as you do not release the mouse button, you can reshape this line depending on the direction in which you drag the mouse.

4   Place your cursor over label 4, located at the end of the second curve. As in step 3, click and drag down to create the fourth and final anchor point of the line. Continue to drag the mouse until you form the curve indicated by the template.

5   As in the previous exercise, after you have created your final anchor point at label 4, hold down Ctrl (Windows) or Command (Mac OS) and click on the artboard.

6   If necessary, use the Direct Select tool (⬞) to reposition the handles and points so the curves follow the path more closely, then choose File > Save to save your work.

Drawing hinged curves

In the previous exercise, you created S-curves, lines curved in the opposite direction from the previous one. In this exercise, you will create hinged curves, lines that curve in the same direction; in this case, they will all curve up like a scallop. You will now complete Exercise 4.

1   Position your cursor over label 1 at the beginning of the curved line in Exercise 4. As you did in the previous exercise, click and drag your cursor up slightly above the hump of the line to create your first anchor point.

2   Place your cursor over label 2, located at the end of the first curve. Click and drag straight down to create the second anchor point. Continue to drag the mouse until you form the curve in the template.

3   Press and hold the Alt (Windows) or Option (Mac OS) key on the keyboard. This temporarily changes the Pen tool into the Convert Anchor Point tool, which is a separate tool in the Pen tool grouping. Among other things (covered later in this chapter), this tool is used to edit direction handles. Position the Convert Anchor Point tool over the direction point for the exiting direction line, and click and drag this point so that it points upward. The two direction lines now form a V.

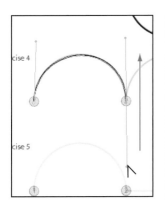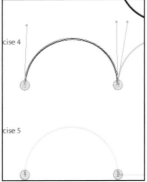

Move the direction handle to change the direction of the next path.

Direction handles control the curvature of the lines in a path. Because the exiting direction handle created in step 3 is pointing down, the line will want to go down. To draw the hinged curve, you must change the angle of this direction handle so that it points upward.

4   Place your cursor over label 3, located at the end of the second curve. Click and drag straight down to create the third anchor point. Continue to drag the mouse until you form the curve in the template.

5 Again, press and hold Alt (Windows) or Option (Mac OS) to temporarily switch the Pen tool to the Convert Anchor Point tool. Once again, position the Convert Anchor Point tool over the direction point for the exiting direction line, and click and drag this point so that it points upward and the direction lines form a V.

6 Repeat step 4 for the final curve at label 4. After you have created this final anchor point, hold down the Ctrl (Windows) or Command (Mac OS) key and click on the artboard.

7 Choose File > Save to save your work.

Drawing curved lines to straight lines

While some compositions you create in Adobe Illustrator are composed of only straight or curved lines, most are probably some combination of the two. The following two exercises cover how to draw straight and curved lines together as part of the same path. You will now complete Exercise 5.

1 Position your cursor over label 1 at the beginning of the curved line in Exercise 5. Hold the Shift key, and click and drag your cursor up slightly above the hump of the line to create your first anchor point. As you drag your cursor upwards, your movement is constrained to a perfectly vertical line. Release the mouse before releasing the Shift key.

2 Place your cursor over label 2, located at the end of the first curve. Again, while holding the Shift key, click and drag straight down to create the second anchor point. Continue to drag the mouse until you form the curve in the template.

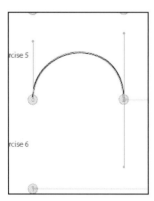

Create another curved path.

Direction handles control the curvature of the lines in a path. Because the exiting direction handle created in step 2 is pointing down, the line will want to go down. If you drag the direction point so that the line points up as in the previous exercise, it will want to curve up. To form a straight line, however, you want to remove this directional handle entirely, thus converting the anchor point into a corner point.

3   Position your cursor over the anchor point you created in step 2. The Pen tool cursor changes, giving you the ability to convert the anchor point you just created.

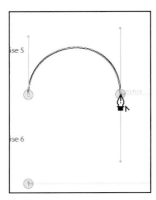

The Pen tool cursor changes, allowing you to modify the anchor point.

4   While hovering over the anchor point, click the mouse. This collapses the anchor's outgoing direction handle, allowing you to create a straight line.

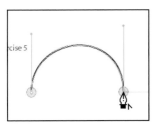

Collapse the direction handle.

5   Place the cursor over label 3. Hold the Shift key on the keyboard, and click at label 3 to create a straight line to finish the path.

6   After you have created your final anchor point at label 3, hold down Ctrl (Windows) or Command (Mac OS) and click on the artboard to deselect and end the line.

7   Choose File > Save to save your work.

Drawing straight lines to curved lines

Now, you will work from the opposite direction and connect straight lines to curved lines. Practice with Exercise 6.

1   Locate the template labeled Exercise 6. Hold the Pen tool over the start of the line (labeled 1). The cursor changes (✎₊), indicating that you will start a new line. Click and release your left mouse button while hovering over label 1. This starts the line by creating the first anchor point.

2   Place the cursor over label 2. Hold the Shift key and click at label 2 to create a perfectly straight line between points 1 and 2 on the path.

3   Position your cursor over the anchor point you created in step 2. The Pen tool cursor changes (✎₊), indicating that you can change the direction of the direction handle.

4   While hovering over the anchor point, click and drag upwards in the direction of the curve you want to draw. This creates a new direction handle.

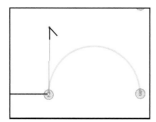

Change the direction of the direction handle.

5   Position the Pen tool over label 3. Click and drag down to create the curve seen in the template.

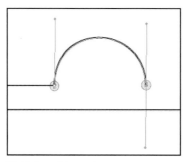

Finish the path by creating a curve.

6   After you have created your final anchor point at label 3, hold down the Ctrl (Windows) or Command (Mac OS) key and click on the artboard to deselect and end the line.

7   Choose File > Save, then choose File > Close.

Tracing images

Illustrator is often used to convert artwork that has been scanned or rendered in a pixel-based painting program, like Adobe Photoshop, into crisp vector line art.

Placing an image as a template

1 Create a new Illustrator document by choosing File > New. In the New Document dialog box, type **ai0502** in the Name text field. Choose Print from the New Document Profile drop-down menu. Choose Letter from the Size drop-down menu, if it is not already selected. Press OK.

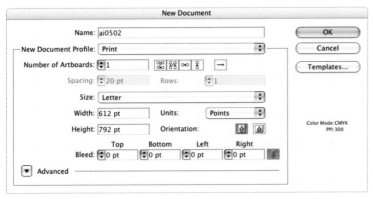

The New Document dialog box.

2 Choose File > Save As. In the Save As dialog box, navigate to the ai03lessons folder, then type **ai0502_work.ai** in the Name text field. Press Save.

3 The Illustrator Options dialog box appears. Leave all settings at their defaults and press OK.

4 Choose File > Place. In the Place dialog box, navigate to the ai03lessons folder and select the ai0502.tif file. Select the *Template* checkbox at the bottom of the Place dialog box to import the selected artwork as a template layer. Press Place. A faint outline of a truck appears in your document.

5 Click anywhere on the artboard to deselect the template. In the Control panel, choose None (▱) from the Fill Color drop-down menu and choose the color black from the Stroke Color drop-down menu. Choose 2 pt from the Stroke Weight drop-down menu.

6 Select the Pen tool (◊) from the Tools panel. Position the cursor near label 1, then click and release to create the first anchor point of the path along the tracing template for the truck. If necessary, increase the magnification to see the template more clearly.

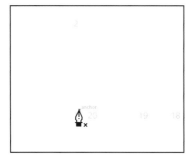

Create the first anchor point of the truck.

7 Press and hold the Shift key and click along the truck outline near label 2. This creates a second anchor point, and Illustrator automatically draws a straight line between them.

8 Press and hold the Shift key, and click at label 3 to continue tracing the truck's outline.

9 Continue to hold down the Shift key, and click along the truck body at labels 4, 5, 6, and 7.

10 The line between labels 7 and 8 is diagonal, so release the Shift key and click at label 8.

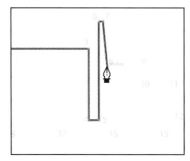

Continue outlining the truck.

11 Again press and hold the Shift key, and click at labels 9 and 10.

12 Release the Shift key on the keyboard and click at label 11. Up to this point, the exercise has dealt entirely with creating straight lines and corner points; for the line between labels 11 and 12, you need to create a curved line.

13 Because the point created at label 11 is a corner point, the Pen tool automatically attempts to create a straight line between this anchor and the next one. You can override this tendency by converting the anchor point you just created, as you did in a previous exercise. Hover the Pen tool over the anchor point created at label 11, and look for the Convert Anchor Point symbol (Ν) to appear next to the tool. Click and drag with the tool in the direction of the curve to create a new directional handle.

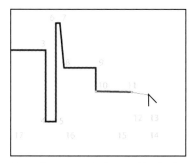

As you drag to create the directional handle, the cursor has the appearance of an arrowhead without a stem.

14 Click with the Pen tool at label 12 to create a smooth point and complete the line.

15 Hold the Shift key on the keyboard, and click labels 13, 14, then 15.

16 The half circle between labels 15 and 16 presents the same challenge that you faced previously. Again, hover the Pen tool over the anchor point you just created. While holding the Shift key, click and drag upward to create a constrained directional handle.

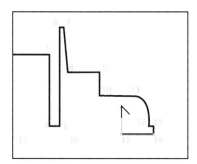

Move the direction handle up to start another curve.

17 At label 16, click and drag the cursor down to create a new smooth point and continue the line.

18 Position the cursor over the anchor point that you just created at label 16, and click on it when you see the Convert Anchor Point symbol (Ν) appear next to the Pen tool. Hold down the Shift key and click at label 17.

19 Repeat steps 16 to 18 until you reach the anchor point numbered 20. After you have collapsed the anchor point at label 20, position your cursor over label 1. A circle appears next to the Pen tool (✏.), indicating that this action will close the path you have just drawn. Click on the anchor point to complete the line and close the path.

20 Choose File > Save, then choose File > Close.

Other drawing tools

While the Pen tool is definitely the most versatile drawing tool in the application, there are several other drawing tools that exist to fulfill specific functions.

Using the Line Segment and Arc tools

As the tool names imply, the Line Segment and Arc tools create line segments and arcs. As you learned in the previous exercises, the Pen tool can also create lines and arcs; however, unlike line segments and arcs that can be created with the Pen tool, each new line or arc is separate and unique from the previous one.

1 Choose File > Open. In the Open dialog box, navigate to the ai03lessons folder and select the ai0503.ai file. Press Open.

This is a practice file containing several different line templates that you will work through in the following exercises. Choose File > Save As. In the Save As dialog box, navigate to the ai03lessons folder, and type **ai0503_work.ai** in the Name text field. Press Save.

2 In the Control panel, choose None (▨) from the Fill Color drop-down menu and choose the color black from the Stroke Color drop-down menu. Choose 2 pt from the Stroke Weight drop-down menu.

3 Select the Line Segment tool (\) from the Tools panel on the left, and locate the template labeled Exercise 1. Hold the Line Segment tool over the start of the first line (labeled 1). Click and drag with your mouse from label 1 to label 2 to create a line segment.

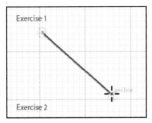

Using the Line Segment tool.

4 Position the cursor over label 3. While holding the Shift key, click and drag the mouse from label 3 to label 4. The Shift key is used to constrain the Line Segment tool to perfectly horizontal, vertical, or diagonal (45-degree) lines.

5   Position the cursor over label 5. While holding the Shift key, click and drag the mouse from label 5 to label 6.

6   Press and hold the Line Segment tool to view the hidden tools. Select the Arc tool (⌒) and locate the template labeled Exercise 2. Hold the Arc tool over the start of the first line (labeled 1). Click and drag with your mouse from label 1 to label 2. This creates an arc.

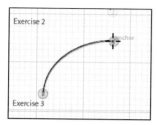

Create an arc path.

7   Position the cursor over label 3. While holding the Shift key, click and drag the mouse from label 3 to label 4. The Shift key constrains the created arc.

8   Position the cursor over label 5. Click and drag to label 6. Continue pressing down the mouse button, and notice that the arc is very similar to the others you have previously created. While still holding the mouse button, press **F** on the keyboard and release it to reverse the direction of the arc.

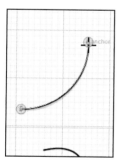

*Press F while creating an arc
to reverse the curve's direction.*

While drawing an arc, press the up and down arrow keys on the keyboard to change the angle of the arc.

9   Choose File > Save to save your work.

Using the Pencil, Smooth, and Path Eraser tools

While the Pen tool exists for precise line work, the Pencil tool creates freeform lines. In addition to being able to draw lines, the Pencil tool can also be used to refine existing lines. You will now complete Exercise 3.

1   Select the Pencil tool (✐) from the Tools panel and locate the template labeled Exercise 3. Hold the Pencil tool over the start of the first line (labeled 1). Click and drag with your mouse from label 1 to label 2 to replicate the looping line shown in the template.

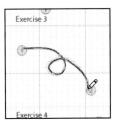

Create a line using the Pencil tool.

2   Choose the Selection tool (▸) and highlight the line between labels 3 and 4. Select the Pencil tool, then click and drag along the guideline between labels 3 and 4. The line adjusts to fit the new path you have created.

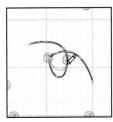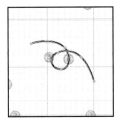

Select, then redraw a part of the path.

3   Choose the Selection tool again and highlight the line between labels 5 and 6. Press and hold the Pencil tool in the Tools panel, and choose the Smooth tool (✐).

4   Beginning at label 6, click and drag the Smooth tool back and forth across the jagged part of the line to label 7. This smooths out the jagged line. Depending upon the magnification at which you are viewing the page, you may have to repeat this process several times to match the example. When viewing the page at a higher magnification level, you will need more passes across the artwork with the Smooth tool.

 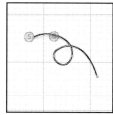

Smooth the path using the Smooth tool.

5   With the Selection tool, highlight the line between labels 7 and 8. Press and hold the Smooth tool in the Tools panel and choose the Path Eraser tool (✐).

6   Beginning at label 7, click and drag the Path Eraser tool back and forth across the selected line to erase it. Be sure to thoroughly overlap the line or you may leave stray segments intact.

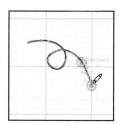 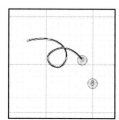

Using the Path Eraser tool, erase the path between labels 7 and 8.

7   Choose File > Save to save your work.

Using the Eraser tool

Introduced in Illustrator CS3, the Eraser tool was a welcome addition to the application's wide range of drawing and editing tools. It can erase vector objects in much the same fashion as a real-world eraser. This opens the door to the creation of a wide range of organic shapes in a very intuitive way.

1 Using the Selection tool (↖), highlight the black circle in Exercise 4, then choose the Eraser tool (✐) in the Tools panel.

2 Click and drag from label 1 to label 2 in a pattern similar to the one in the template to the left of it. The Eraser tool bisects the circle, forming two separate shapes. Be certain to start outside the shape before clicking and dragging.

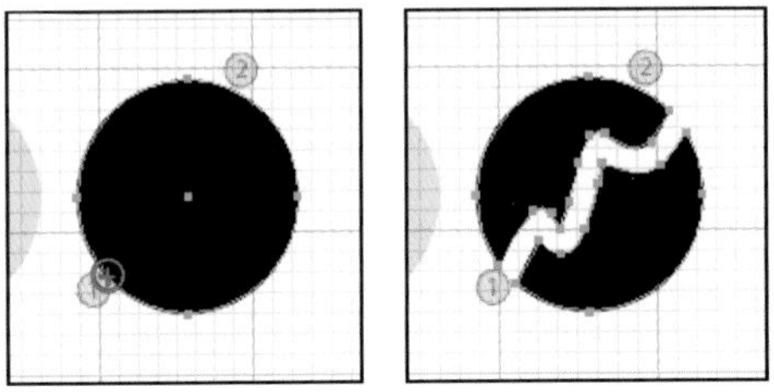

Use the Eraser tool to bisect the circle.

3 Choose the Selection tool and highlight the black line located between labels 3 and 4. Choose the Eraser tool and drag over the line between labels 3 and 4 to sever it.

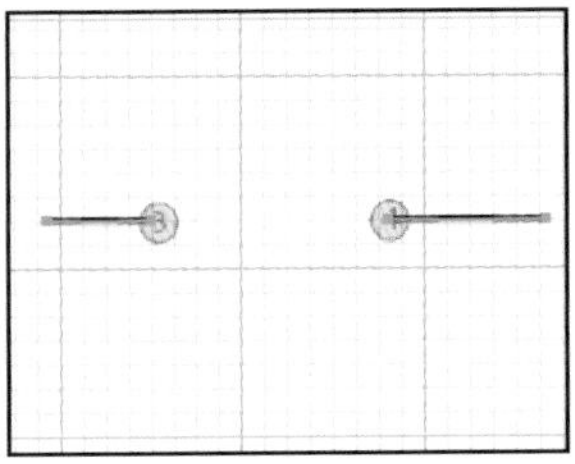

Use the Eraser tool to remove a section of the path.

4 Choose File > Save to save your work.

Editing existing paths

In addition to creating lines and shapes, the tools in Illustrator provide the ability to modify paths that you have already created. The two main ways to do this are by adding or removing anchor points to a path, and converting anchor points from smooth to corner points, or vice versa.

Adding and removing points

The best way to modify paths in your artwork is to add or remove anchor points from an existing path. Both the Pen tool and the Control panel can be used to modify the anchor points. You will now complete Exercise 5.

1   Using the Selection tool (), select the first path in Exercise 5 to highlight it, then choose the Pen tool () from the Tools panel.

2   Place the Pen tool over the portion of the path at label 1. The new cursor () indicates that clicking with the Pen tool will create an anchor point on the line segment. Click on the line segment to create a new anchor point.

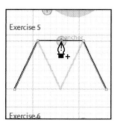

Create a new anchor point.

3   The anchor point that was just created is automatically highlighted. Use the arrow keys on your keyboard to move this anchor point into position to match the template.

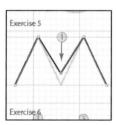

Move the anchor point using the
arrow keys on the keyboard.

4   Now you'll move to the next template. Choose the Direct Selection tool () from the Tools panel, and draw a selection marquee around the anchor point at label 2 to highlight it.

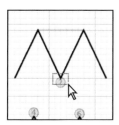

Select the anchor point.

5   Press the Remove Selected Anchor Points button () in the Control panel to remove the highlighted anchor point from the line and make it match the template.

When the path is selected, you can also use the Pen tool to remove an anchor point. The only disadvantage to using the Pen tool to remove anchor points is that it cannot remove points from the beginning or end of a line.

6   Choose File > Save to save your work.

Refining a curve

You will now complete Exercise 5.

1   Locate the third and final path in Exercise 5. Using the Direct Selection tool (⬚), draw a selection marquee around the anchor point at label 3.

2   Press the Convert Selected Anchor Point to Corner button (⬚) in the Control panel to change the smooth point into a corner point. This changes the curvature of the preceding line segment.

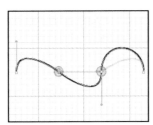

The curve changes.

3   With the line still selected, click and hold the Pen tool (◊) in the Tools panel, then select the Convert Anchor Point tool (Ν).

4   Select the anchor point at label 4 to convert it from a smooth point to a corner point.

If you want to convert a corner point to a smooth point, you can do so either from the Control panel or by clicking and dragging on a corner point with the Convert Anchor Point tool.

5   Press Ctrl+Shift+A (Windows) or Command+Shift+A (Mac OS) to deselect everything on the artboard. Choose File > Save to save your work.

Cutting and joining paths

One of Illustrator's very helpful features is the ability to cut and join paths. Paths can be cut either at anchor points or line segments, but they may only be joined by connecting two adjacent anchor points, called end points. You will now complete Exercise 6.

1   Locate Exercise 6. Select the Direct Selection tool (⬉) from the Tools panel, and draw a selection marquee around the anchor point at label 1.

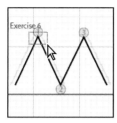

Draw a marquee around the anchor point.

2   Press the Cut Path at Selected Anchor Points button (⬚) in the Control panel to sever the path at this point. Repeat this step for the anchor point at label 2.

3   Press and hold the Eraser tool (⬚) in the Tools panel to reveal and select the Scissors tool (✂). Click on the anchor point at label 3. This tool performs the same function as the Cut Path at Selected Anchor Point button in the Control panel.

If you miss the anchor point even by a little, the Scissors tool displays an error message and you have to try again.

4   Choose the Selection tool (▶) in the Tools panel, and use it to move the individual line segments apart to the positions of the blue lines in the template.

5   Select the Direct Selection tool and draw a selection marquee around the two end points located at label 4. These end points are not connected.

6   Press the Connect Selected End Points button (⬚) in the Control panel. When the Join dialog box appears, choose the default Corner option and press OK. This merges the two anchor points into one.

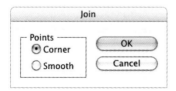

Choose Corner points in the Join dialog box.

7   Shift+click to select the two end points located at label 5, and select Object > Path > Join. When the Join dialog box appears, select Corner and press OK.

8   Select the two end points located at label 6 by clicking and dragging to create a marquees containing both points, then right-click (Windows) or Ctrl+click (Mac OS) on the page and choose Join from the contextual menu. In the Join dialog box, select Corner and press OK.

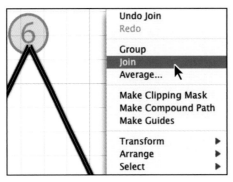

Right-click or Ctrl+click and choose Join from the contextual menu.

9   Select the two end points located at labels 7 and 8 by drawing a selection marquee using the Direct Selection tool.

10 Press the Connect Selected End Points button ( ) in the Control panel. A line connecting the two selected end points is created.

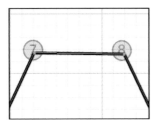

The two end points are connected.

11 Choose File > Save, then choose File > Close.

Working with Live Trace

There are times when it may be inefficient to draw complex illustrations by hand if a suitable raster version exists. At times like this, it may be better to simply scan the original artwork and use the Live Trace feature in Illustrator to have the application convert it into vector art for you.

Using the tracing presets

The Live Trace feature in Illustrator comes complete with various presets for rendering a wide variety of artwork into vector form.

1   Choose File > Open. In the Open dialog box, navigate to the ai03lessons folder and select the ai0504.ai file. This is a practice file containing an embedded JPEG graphic that you will modify in the following exercises.

Choose File > Save As. In the Save As dialog box, navigate to the ai03lessons folder and type **ai0504_work.ai** in the Name text field. Press Save.

2   Choose the Selection tool (☛) from the Tools panel and select the butterfly image. Locate the Live Trace button in the Control panel at the top of the workspace.

3   Press the arrow next to the Live Trace button and select Hand Drawn Sketch. This option renders the entire drawing as lines and is not suitable for this image, as it would eliminate the wide range of line weights used in the original drawing.

The Live Trace Preset Options.

4   Select the Inked Drawing preset from the Preset drop-down menu to have the program retrace the image with new settings. This is better, but several of the spots on the bottom wings vanish and the lines don't seem to match up with each other.

The image shown using the Inked Drawing preset.

5   With the image still selected, select the Comic Art preset from the Live Trace drop-down menu to have the program retrace the image with new settings. This preset seems to more closely match the artwork than the two previous choices.

The image shown using the Comic Art Live Trace preset.

Even the best of presets are guesses for what will probably work well with the provided type of artwork. For more control over the conversion, you can tweak the preset in the Tracing Options dialog box. Working with the Tracing Options dialog box is covered in the next section.

6   Choose File > Save to save your work.

Understanding tracing options

While the Tracing presets often produce acceptable results, the Tracing Options dialog box allows you to determine the specific settings for the tracing of a particular object.

1   With the traced image of the butterfly still selected, press the Tracing Options button (⊞) next to the Preset drop-down menu in the Control panel to open the Tracing Options dialog box.

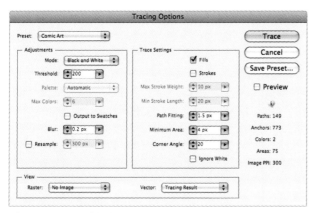

The Tracing Options dialog box.

2   The Tracing Options dialog box is divided into four different sections: Preset, Adjustments, Trace Settings, and View.

Preset: This drop-down menu is used to select which preset's options to display in the dialog box.

Adjustments: This controls the options that govern what happens to an image before the tracing operation is performed, as well as how colors are handled after the operation.

ADJUSTMENT	USE
Mode	Specifies a color mode for the tracing result. The choices in this menu are Color, Black & White, or Grayscale.
Threshold	Specifies a value for generating a black-and-white tracing result from the original image. All pixels lighter than the Threshold value are converted to white, while all pixels darker than the Threshold value are converted to black. (This option is available only when Mode is set to Black and White.)
Palette	Specifies a panel for generating a color or grayscale tracing from the original image. (This option is available only when Mode is set to Color or Grayscale.) To let Illustrator determine the colors in the tracing, select Automatic. To use a custom panel for the tracing, select a swatch library name. The swatch library must be open in order for it to appear in the panel menu.

ADJUSTMENT	USE
Max Colors	Active only when the Color or Grayscale option is selected in the mode menu and when the Palette menu is set to automatic. The Max Colors menu is used to specify the maximum number of colors that will be rendered in the tracing result.
Output To Swatches	Creates a new swatch in the Swatches panel for each color in the tracing result.
Blur	Blurs the original image before generating the tracing result. Select this option to reduce small artifacts and smooth jagged edges in the tracing result.
Resample	Resamples the original image to the specified resolution before generating the tracing result. This option is useful for speeding up the tracing process for large images but can yield degraded results.

Trace Settings: This controls the setting for the tracing operation.

SETTING	USE
Fills	Creates filled regions in the tracing result.
Strokes	Creates stroked paths in the tracing result.
Max Stroke Weight	Specifies the maximum width of features in the original image that can be stroked. Features larger than the maximum width become outlined areas in the tracing result.
Min Stroke Length	Specifies the minimum length of features in the original image that can be stroked. Features smaller than the minimum length are omitted from the tracing result.
Path Fitting	Controls the distance between the traced shape and the original pixel shape. Lower values create a path that is closer to the original pixel shapes, while higher values create looser-fitting paths.
Minimum Area	Specifies the smallest feature in the original image that will be traced. The value for this property is based on the overall area of the objects being traced.
Corner Angle	Controls the sharpness of a turn in the original image that is considered a corner anchor point in the tracing result. For more information on the difference between a corner anchor point and a smooth anchor point, you should review the sections on working with anchor points and drawing with the Pen tool earlier in this lesson.

View: This controls how the original bitmap image and vector result are displayed on the artboard.

3   In the Tracing Options dialog box, press the arrow next to the Threshold text field and change the value to 50. This changes the black and white balance of the traced image and makes the spots on the lower part of the wing more distinct.

4   Highlight the value in the Path Fitting text field and type **.5 px**.

5   Changing any setting in the dialog box, as you have done here, creates a custom tracing preset. To save this preset for later use, press the Save Preset button.

6   In the Save Tracing Preset dialog box, type **Modified Comic** into the Name text field and press OK. Press Trace to trace the butterfly image.

7   Choose File > Save to save your work.

Expanding Live Traced artwork

You may have noticed by now that even though you can change the tracing setting of the image, you don't have access to the anchor points that make up the new vector artwork. This is because the tracing is a type of intermediate stage between the original raster graphic and the fully editable vector artwork that Illustrator typically creates. To make the live traced artwork fully editable requires that you expand it.

1   With the traced image of the butterfly still selected, press the Expand button in the Control panel. The paths that make up the traced artwork are now fully editable.

2   When the original bitmap was traced, the white background became a shape. This can cause a problem, as you probably don't want a white frame around your vector artwork. Choose the Direct Selection tool (k) from the Tools panel and click the artboard to deselect all objects, then click to select the white area behind the butterfly.

The white shape is selected.

3   Press the Backspace (Windows) or Delete (Mac OS) key on the keyboard to remove the white from the artboard, leaving only the butterfly tracing itself.

4   Choose File > Save to save your work.

    Another way to avoid including white objects when you trace bitmap objects is to choose the Ignore White checkbox in the Live Trace settings window at the time you start the Live Trace.

Working with Live Paint

Traditionally Illustrator required a closed path in order to fill an area with color. Live Paint turns this working method on its head and gives the Illustrator artist the ability to fill color into any area created by overlapping lines or shapes.

Creating a Live Paint group

The Live Paint tools, the Live Paint Bucket tool, and the Live Paint Selection tool can only affect objects that are part of a Live Paint group.

1 Choose the Selection tool (➤) from the Tools panel and select the expanded image of the butterfly. Choose Object > Live Paint > Make to convert the artwork into a Live Paint group.

When you have a Live Paint group selected, a small symbol that looks like a snowflake or a star appears in each marker of the bounding box that surrounds it.

2 Choose File > Save to save your work.

Setting Gap Detection options

Earlier in this lesson, you learned that the areas that can receive color must be defined by overlapping lines. This isn't always the case though; it is possible to tell the program that two lines are close enough together to constitute an enclosed area. To do this, you must work with the Gap Detection options.

1 Choose Object > Live Paint > Gap Options.

2 In the Gap Options dialog box, make sure the *Gap Detection* checkbox is selected, and choose Medium Gaps from the Paint stops at drop-down menu. This allows paint to fill any area that has less than a 6-pt opening.

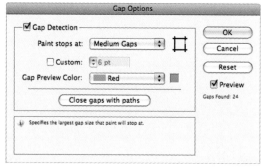

The Gap Options dialog box.

A progress bar may appear, temporarily freezing the screen while the dialogs setting are updated on your Live Paint group.

3   Press OK to close the dialog box.

4   Using the Selection tool (↖), click an empty area of the artboard to deselect the butterfly.

5   Choose File > Save to save your work.

Using the Live Paint Bucket tool

The Live Paint Bucket tool is used to fill enclosed areas with color. When combined with the Live Paint group's Gap Options, the Live Paint Bucket tool fills any area composed of overlapping paths or semi-overlapping paths with the currently selected fill color. The tool's options can also be set so that it can apply the active fill, the stroke color, or both.

1   Choose the Live Paint Bucket tool (⌗) in the Tools panel. Press the Swatches button (▦) in the dock on the right side of the workspace to open the Swatches panel. One of the color groups in the Swatches panel is called *Grape blow Pop*. Select the third color in this group, a lavender, as your fill color.

2   Hover the cursor over the first open area of the left wing. The area highlights red, indicating that it can be filled with the Live Paint Bucket tool. Click on the area to fill it with the current fill color.

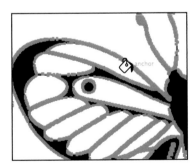

Fill the area with color using the Live Paint feature.

3   Fill in the rest of the top wings with the same color.

4   Press the right arrow key on the keyboard to select the next color swatch in the swatch group. Fill the remaining white area of the wings with the darker purple.

Fill the remaining areas.

Double-click on the Live Paint Bucket tool to open the Tool Options dialog box. In this dialog box, you can adjust the tool's highlighting options, as well as whether the tool can color fill, strokes, or both.

5   Choose File > Save to save your work.

Using the Live Paint Selection tool

The Live Paint Selection tool is used to select areas in a Live Paint group and assign colors to them.

1   Choose the Live Paint Selection tool (⬚) from the Tools panel.

2   Select the black circle on the top-left wing to select it, then hold the Shift key on the keyboard and select the right black circle.

Select both circles.

3 Choose the white color swatch from the Fill Color drop-down menu in the Control panel to fill the circle with the new color.

4 Choose File > Save, and choose File > Close to close the file.

Congratulations! You have completed Illustrator Lesson 4, "Working with the Drawing Tools."

Self study

Create a basic composition by overlapping two simple shapes within a frame. Convert the three objects (the two shapes and the frame) into a Live Paint group. Make multiple copies of this Live Paint group and then, using only black-and-white, create different color variations for these compositions with the Live Paint Bucket tool.

Another good exercise is to scan in a variety of images, black-and-white and color, and test the various Live Trace presets.

Review

Questions

1 When drawing with the Pen tool, how does creating the first point of a straight line differ from creating the first point of a curved line?

2 How do you import a bitmap image that you want to trace in Illustrator?

3 How can you set a Live Paint group to treat areas that do not have overlapping paths as areas that can be filled with color?

Answers

1 To create the first point for a straight line, you must click and release the Pen tool. When creating a curved line, you should click and drag the Pen tool in the direction of the curve you want to create.

2 Use the File > Place command and check the *Template* option in the Place dialog box. While the Template option is not required, it is helpful for tracing scanned artwork.

3 By turning on Gap Detection (Object > Live Paint > Gap Detection), you can fill areas that do not have overlapping paths.

Lesson 1

What you'll learn in this lesson:

- Understanding the InDesign workspace
- Working with panels and tools
- Navigating through InDesign documents
- Flowing text
- Using Styles to format text and objects

InDesign CS4 Essential Skills

This lesson helps to get you started with InDesign right away, covering the essential skills necessary for creating and editing documents. In this lesson, you will discover essential skills for working efficiently with InDesign documents. You'll start by understanding how to navigate within an InDesign document; you'll then place graphics and add formatting to text, creating a finished newsletter.

Starting up

Before starting, make sure that your tools and panels are consistent by resetting your preferences. See "Resetting the InDesign workspace and preferences" on page XXVII.

You will work with several files from the id01lessons folder in this lesson. Make sure that you have copied the id01lessons folder onto your hard drive from the Digital Classroom DVD. See "Loading lesson files" on page XXIX. If you are new to InDesign, it may be easier to follow the lesson if the id01lessons folder is placed on your desktop.

See Lesson 1 in action!

Use the accompanying video to gain a better understanding of how to use some of the features shown in this lesson. The video tutorial for this lesson can be found on the included DVD.

InDesign tools

InDesign uses tools for creating or modifying everything that appears in your document. You'll also use tools for navigating around the document. Tools are all located in the Tools panel, located along the left side of your screen.

Many tools have related tools available for selection by clicking and holding on the tool that is displayed. You can identify the tools that offer additional functionality by the small arrow in the lower-right corner of these tools. You can also right-click (Windows) or Ctrl-click (MacOS) to access hidden tools without waiting.

If you place your cursor over any tool in the Tools panel without clicking, a tooltip appears, displaying the tool's name and keyboard shortcut. You can use the keyboard shortcut to access a tool instead of clicking it.

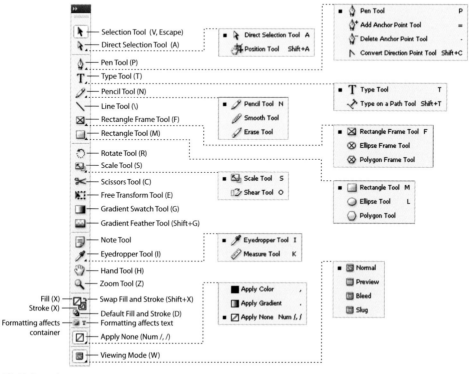

The Tools panel.

The InDesign workspace

InDesign documents are displayed in the center of the work area, while panels that let you control objects or perform specific tasks are displayed along the right side of the workspace in the panel docking area. InDesign has many panels that are critical to the editing and design work you perform. InDesign includes various workspaces that provide easy access to the panels and tools you'll use for specific tasks. Let's take a closer look at the InDesign workspace, including the document window and panels.

The document window

InDesign pages are displayed within a black border. Anything positioned within this area appears when the page is finished. The area outside of the black border is referred to as the pasteboard. Anything that is placed completely outside this black border on the pasteboard is generally not visible when the final document is distributed.

You can use the pasteboard to temporarily hold elements while designing your project. You can move design elements such as images from the pasteboard to the page, trying different layout variations. The pasteboard can also be useful for placing notes to colleagues—or even yourself—regarding the project. To get a better understanding of the InDesign workspace, you'll open up the completed project, reset the workspace, and look at the work area.

1. Choose File > Open. In the Open dialog box, navigate to the id01lessons folder and select the id01_done.indd file. Press Open.

2. Choose Window > Workspace > Typography. Panels containing controls that help you work with type are now displayed.

You can also use the dedicated Workspace switcher, located in the Application bar above the Control panel. The Workspace switcher displays the name of the current workspace and can also be used to change between workspaces or to reset the current workspace. The selected workspace controls which panels display and which menu items are available. Fewer or more panels and menu choices are available based upon the selected workspace.

3   Choose Window > Workspace > Reset Typography to reset the InDesign panels to their default positions for the Typography workspace. This ensures that your panels are in position, making them easier to locate during this lesson.

A. The document window. B. The page border (black lines). C. Bleed guides. D. Margin guides. E. Column guides. F. The pasteboard.

Using guides

Non-printing guides help you align content on your page and create an organized layout. Margin guides define the space around the edge of your document—a space you generally want to keep free from objects. White space around the edge of your documents creates good design, and also eliminates the risk of content being cut off if your document is printed and trimmed to a specific size at a printing plant. Margin guides are displayed in magenta by default, immediately inside the page border. By default they display one-half inch inside of the page edge, but can be adjusted as you will learn in InDesign Lesson 2, "Building Documents with Master Pages."

Individual page guides can also be added manually by dragging them from the rulers onto the page. Both page guides and margin guides are useful, but they can also be distracting when you want to see the elements of your page design. In this case, you can hide the guides.

1   Choose View > Grids & Guides > Hide Guides, or use the keyboard shortcut Ctrl+;
    (Windows) or Command+; (Mac OS), to hide all the guides in the open document.

2   Choose View > Grids & Guides > Show Guides, or use the keyboard shortcut Ctrl+;
    (Windows) or Command+; (Mac OS), to show all the guides in the open document.

    You can show or hide guides by toggling back and forth using these options.

Viewing modes

You can also use viewing modes to hide guides and other items that will not display when the
final document is printed or distributed.

Just as you can hide guides, you can also have InDesign hide content that is positioned on the
pasteboard. The viewing modes option lets you choose whether all content and guides display,
or whether InDesign displays only content that is positioned on the page and will print. Next
you'll explore the various viewing modes.

1   At the bottom of the Tools panel, click and hold the Mode button (▣), and choose
    Preview from the available modes. Notice that the entire pasteboard displays as gray and
    all elements located on the pasteboard are hidden.

2   Click and hold the Mode button again and choose Bleed from the menu. This shows the
    allowable bleed area that was specified when the document was created. Bleed is an area
    outside of the page that is intentionally used by designers so that any inaccuracies in the
    cutting, trimming, and binding process do not create a visible white space along the edge
    of an object that is intended to print all the way to the edge of a document. This mode
    is useful when you need to make sure that all the elements on your page extend to a
    specific bleed value.

3   Click and hold the Mode button again and return to Normal.

*You can also use the shortcut key W to toggle between Preview and Normal modes in InDesign or you
can use the Screen Mode button in the Application bar. Keep in mind that keyboard shortcuts do not
work if you are using the Type tool and working with text inside a text frame.*

Working with panels

Now that you understand the different parts of the workspace, you can begin working with
the interface to learn more about the different panels. You can access panels by clicking
on their name in the panel docking area, or choose the panel you want to access from the
Window menu.

The Tools panel

The Tools panel is located on the left side of your screen and contains all the tools necessary to draw, add, or edit type, and edit items in your document. The Tools panel appears as a single-column attached to the left side of your screen. You can modify the appearance and location of the Tools panel to accommodate your needs.

1   Click on the double-arrow icon at the top of the Tools panel. The Tools panel changes from a single column to a double column. If you click again, it changes to a horizontal layout, and then back to a single column.

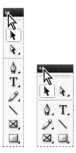

Clicking on the double arrow icon at the top of the Tools panel changes its appearance.

2   Click the gray bar at the top of the Tools panel, and while holding down on the mouse, drag the panel to the right, into the document area. Release the mouse button when over the document area. The Tools panel is repositioned at the location where you released the mouse. You can position the panel anywhere on your display, or return it to the docking area on the side of the workspace.

3   Click the gray bar at the top of the Tools panel and drag the panel to the right so that it is positioned just to the left of the panels. A blue, vertical bar appears. Release the mouse button and the Tools panel is docked to the right of your screen.

Managing panels

InDesign contains panels that help you create the layout and design you desire. The various workspaces include several panels that are docked at the right side of the document window. The available panels change based upon the selected workspace. When the panels display only their name, they are in collapsed mode. Collapsed mode saves screen space by allowing you quick access to many panels, and only displaying the full panel options when you need them.

1   Press the double-arrow icon (◀◀) at the top-right corner of all the docked panels along the right side of the document window. Notice how all the docked panels expand to reveal their options.

2   Press the double-arrow icon again to collapse the dock and return the panels to their previous state.

3   Press the Pages button in the dock. This reveals the entire contents of the Pages panel. By clicking a panel button, only the individual panel expands.

4   Press the Pages button again, and the panel closes and is displayed only as a button.

5   Click and drag the Pages button, moving it to the far left side of the document window. When a vertical bar appears, release the mouse button. The Pages panel is docked to the left side of the document window.

You can place panels anywhere on your workspace, including over the document or on either side of the work area. You may customize panels in any way that makes it easier for you to work. Don't worry if you make a mess, as you can always return to the default layout of the panels by choosing Window > Workspace > Reset.

Working with the Control panel

The Control panel appears across the top of the workspace. The panel is contextual, so the content of the panel changes depending on what tool you are using and what object you have selected.

1   Choose the Selection tool (↖) in the Tools panel. The Control panel changes based upon the tool being used and the items selected in the layout.

2   Using the Selection tool, click the headline, *Fending off the winter blues*, positioned at the top of the page. The Control panel now displays information about this text frame.

3   Double-click the same headline. By double-clicking the text frame, the Selection tool switches to the Text tool. The Control panel now displays information relating to the text.

The Control panel displays information about objects in your layout. The information displayed changes based upon the tool used for selection and the object selected.

Saving your workspace

Once you have selected the panels that you need, and positioned them in the locations that let you work most efficiently, you can save the location and panels being used as a workspace.

Once you have saved a workspace, you can quickly access the exact panels displayed and their location by returning to the default setup of that workspace.

1   Click the Workspace switcher drop-down menu located in the Application bar to the left of the Help search window. From the workspace drop-down menu, choose New Workspace.

2   In the New Workspace window, type **My Workspace** in the Name field, then press OK.

Saving your workspace allows you to easily restore the panel positions.

You've now saved the locations of your panels.

3   From the Workspace menu, click the drop-down menu and choose Typography. Note how the panel locations revert to their default location.

4   Click the Workspace switcher menu and choose My Workspace. Alternatively, choose Window > Workspace > My Workspace. All the panels are restored to the workspace that you saved earlier in this project.

InDesign allows you to create and save multiple workspaces. Workspaces are not document specific, which allows them to be used in any document. Before proceeding to the next section, reset your workspace to the default Typography workspace using the Workspace switcher drop-down menu. This allows the panels to match the descriptions used in the remainder of this lesson.

Navigating through an InDesign document

In this exercise, you'll continue working with the id01_done.indd file, which is the completed newsletter that you opened at the beginning of the lesson. You'll explore the tools used to navigate to different pages in an InDesign document, and learn how to change the document's magnification to see more or less of the details in the document layout.

Using the Pages panel

The Pages panel provides a quick overview of what is displayed on each page of an InDesign document. You can use it to navigate between document pages, rearrange pages, and also add or remove pages.

1　Press the Pages button (🗗) in the dock at the right of the workspace to display the Pages panel. The bottom-left of the Pages panel indicates that there are four pages displayed in three spreads within this document.

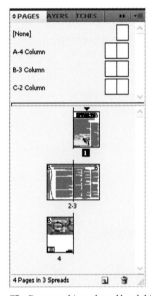

The Pages panel is used to add and delete pages as well as navigate between pages within your InDesign documents.

2　Double-click page 2 in the Pages panel to display page 2 of the document. The left page of the inside spread, which is page 2, appears in the document window.

3　Double-click page 4 in the Pages panel to display page 4 of your document.

If you are unable to see all the pages displayed in the Pages panel, you can make the panel larger by clicking and dragging on the bottom-right corner of the panel to enlarge it. Additionally, InDesign allows you to scroll through the pages in the Pages panel by using the scroll bar in the document window or the scroll wheel on your mouse, or you can click and hold to the side of the page thumbnails and drag up or down to navigate through the pages.

Changing the magnification of your document

So far, you've been viewing this document at the magnification level that was used when the document was last saved. You may find it necessary to get a closer look at parts of your document to check things such as alignment, spacing of type, or position of objects. Here you'll find that InDesign provides tools that make it easy to change the magnification and inspect components of the document.

1   In the Pages panel, double-click on the page 1 icon to display the first page of the document.

2   Select the Zoom tool (🔍). Using the Zoom tool, click and hold in the upper-left corner of the Spinnews logo at the top of the page, then drag down to the lower-right corner of the logo. Release the mouse once you have reached the lower-right corner of the logo. The area you have outlined with the Zoom tool is magnified.

Click and drag to increase the magnification of a specific area.

3   You may find that you enlarged the document too much or not enough. To fine-tune the magnification, click with the Zoom tool to increase the magnification incrementally. Or, if you zoomed in too close, decrease the magnification by pressing and holding the Alt (Windows) or Option (Mac OS) key while clicking with the Zoom tool.

You can quickly increase or decrease the magnification of the document by using the keyboard shortcut Ctrl+plus sign (Windows) or Command+plus sign (Mac OS) to zoom in on a document, or Ctrl+minus sign (Windows) or Command+minus sign (Mac OS) to zoom out. If you have an object selected or your cursor is inserted within a text frame, the page will center on the selected object or cursor when changing the magnification.

4   Select the Hand tool (✋) from the Tools panel, then click and hold down on your page. Notice that the page magnification changes and a red frame appears, indicating which portion of the document will be visible when you have finished scrolling.

5 Arrange the page so that the logo is in the center of your display. Use the Hand tool to move the page within the document window, allowing you to focus on specific areas of the layout.

6 Reposition the red frame so that the entire border of the image is visible, then release the mouse. The zoom returns to its original level, focused on the portion of the page you identified.

You can also access the Hand tool without selecting it from the Tools panel. Press and hold the space bar on your keyboard and your cursor changes to the Hand tool. If you have the Type tool selected, press the Alt (Windows) or Option (Mac OS) key to access the Hand tool.

7 To make your page fit the document window, choose View > Fit Page in Window or press Ctrl+0 (Windows) or Command+0 (Mac OS). The currently selected page is displayed inside the document window.

8 Choose File > Close to close the document. If asked to save, choose No (Windows) or Don't Save (Mac OS).

Working with type

Now that you've had an overview of the InDesign workspace, you'll move into some of the tools that are used for working with type. InDesign provides complete control over the formatting and placement of type on a page and allows you to save formatting attributes so that you can work efficiently and your documents can maintain a consistent appearance. In this section, you'll add the finishing touches to a document, completing the layout by applying formatting to text.

Entering and formatting type

Most text used in an InDesign layout is positioned inside a frame. Frames are containers that hold text or graphics within a layout. InDesign has three types of frames: text, graphic, and unassigned. In this exercise, you'll be working with text frames.

1 Choose File > Open. In the Open dialog box, navigate to the id01lessons folder and select the id01.indd file. Press Open. You will use this project file for the remainder of the lesson.

2 Choose File > Save As. In the Save As dialog box, navigate to the id01lessons folder, or use another folder if you prefer. In the Name field, type **id01_work.indd**, then press Save. This allows you to work without altering the original file.

3 If necessary, press the Pages button (⊞) in the docking area along the right side of the workspace. The Pages panel opens. In the Pages panel, double-click on page 1 to center the page in the workspace.

4   In the Tools panel, select the Type tool (T). You will use the Type tool to create a new text frame. Position your cursor along the left side of the page, where the left margin guide and the first horizontal guide meet. Click and hold down, then drag down and to the right, to the location where the right margin and the second horizontal guide meet. Release the mouse button. A new text frame is created, and a cursor blinks in the top-left corner of the new frame you have created.

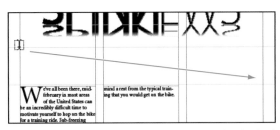

Use the Type tool to create a new text frame. Most text needs to be placed within a frame.

5   Type **Fending off the winter blues with cross-training**. The text appears in the default font and size. Keep the cursor within this text frame, and keep the Type tool selected.

6   In the panel docking area along the right side of the workspace, press the Paragraph Styles button (📑) to open the Paragraph Styles panel. Click to select the Heading style from the list of available styles in the Paragraph Styles panel. The Heading style is applied to the paragraph, which includes all the text within this frame.

Apply the paragraph style to the text.

7   The top line of the sentence is much longer than the bottom line. To balance the lines, press the panel menu button (-≡) in the Control panel and choose Balance Ragged Lines from the submenu. InDesign automatically balances the lines within the frame.

Apply the Balance Ragged Lines command to the headline.

You can also press the Return key while holding the Shift key to create a line break that does not cause a new paragraph to be created. This is referred to as soft return.

Placing and formatting type

You can add text to an InDesign document by typing text into the InDesign page, or by importing the text from an external file, such as a Microsoft Word document or an Excel spreadsheet. InDesign also lets you import ASCII, Rich Text, and InDesign Tagged Text files.

1   If necessary, press the Pages button (⊞) in the dock to open the Pages panel. Double-click on page 2 in the Pages panel. If the pages panel is covering your work area, click the double arrows in the upper-right corner of the panel to reduce it to a button, or you may keep it open if your monitor is large enough to display the panel and the page together.

2   Continuing to use the Type tool (T), click inside the empty text frame that covers the center and right columns, under the headline *Caring for Those Wheels.* The cursor is inserted in this frame, where you will import the text for the body of the story, which was created using word processing software such as Microsoft Word.

3   Choose File > Place. The Place dialog box opens. In the Place dialog box, make certain that Show Import Options is not selected and that Replace Selected items is selected. These options are explained in more detail later in the book.

     Locate and open the id01lessons folder and choose the file Wheels.txt; then press Open. The text from this file is placed inside the frame where the cursor is located.

4   Place the cursor at the start of the story. Click the Paragraph Styles button to display the Paragraph Styles panel. You will apply a paragraph style to format the text you imported. Click the paragraph style Body, and the first paragraph is formatted using the Body style. Paragraph styles apply formatting to the paragraph where the cursor is located. You will now apply formatting to multiple paragraphs by selecting them and repeating the process.

5 Use the keyboard shortcut Ctrl+A (Windows) or Command+A (Mac OS) to select all the type within the current frame. From the Paragraph Styles panel, choose Body. All the selected paragraphs are now formatted using the Body style.

6 Choose Edit > Deselect All to deselect the type.

Flowing type

Stories often continue from one page or column to another. You will set up links between text frames to allow a story to flow into multiple columns.

1 In the lower-left corner of the document area, click the page number drop-down menu and select page 3 to navigate to this page. You can also use this menu to navigate to different pages in your document.

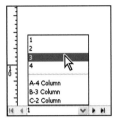

Use the page drop-down menu to navigate between pages.

2 Using the Type tool (T), click inside the first frame on the left side of the page underneath the headline *Race Calendar*.

3 Choose File > Place. In the Place dialog box, navigate to the id01lessons folder. Select the file Calendar.txt and press Open to place the text from the file into your InDesign layout.

4 Activate the Selection tool (↖) from the Tools panel, then, if necessary, click to select the text frame where you imported the text. You can tell the frame is selected by the small, square handles that appear on each corner of the frame, and also in the middle of each side of the frame.

In the upper-left corner of the text frame, slightly below the corner handle, is a small square. This is the In Port, and it is used to describe whether this frame is the continuation of a text flow from another frame. Simply put, does the text start somewhere else, or does it start in this frame? Because the In Port is empty, you can tell that the text starts in this frame. If the In Port contains an arrow, you would know that the text continues from another location.

The lower-right corner of the frame contains an Out Port. This port currently displays a red plus sign, indicating that there is more text in the story than fits within the frame. You can address overset text in a number of ways:

- Delete text

- Reduce the size of the text

- Make the frame larger

- Link the text to another frame

In this case, you will link the text to another frame.

The newly placed text on the page is overset.

5 Using the Selection tool, click once on the red plus sign on lower-right corner of the text frame. The cursor changes appearance to indicate that you are about to link the text to a new location, and displays some of the text that will be linked. The next area you click will be the continuation of the story, so be careful to only click where you want the text to continue.

6 Move your cursor to the center of the middle column. Notice that the cursor changes to show a linked chain. Click to link the first and second frames together. Now you will link the second frame to the third frame.

Linking text from one frame to another.

7 Click the red plus sign on the lower-right corner of the second frame, then click inside the frame located along the right side of the page. The frames in the second and third columns are now linked together.

8 Choose File > Save to save your work.

Using styles

Earlier you worked with paragraph styles to format type. As you saw, these provided a method of applying consistent formatting to the text. Similarly, styles let you easily and repetitively format smaller groups of text along with entire frames and even tables. You'll review the process of applying paragraph styles, then move into other types of styles that can be applied. Later, in InDesign Lesson 4, "Working with Styles," you will work with styles in more detail.

Applying paragraph styles

As you've seen, paragraph styles apply formatting to an entire paragraph of text, and you are not able to apply paragraph styles to an individual word within a paragraph—unless it is the only word in the paragraph, as in this example.

1   Select the Type tool (T) from the Tools panel and click anywhere inside the word *January* located in the first line of the frame on the left side of page 3.

2   In the Paragraph Styles panel, choose Calendar Month to apply the correct formatting to the word *January*. Repeat the process to format the word *February*, and then format *March* by applying the Calendar Month Paragraph Style.

3   Using the Type tool, click and drag to select the text located between the *January* and *February* headings, then click the Calendar Event style in the Paragraph Styles panel. Repeat this process to select all the text between *February* and *March*, and also all the March events.

Format the text using the Calendar Event style from the Paragraph Styles panel.

Notice that the Calendar Event style applied several attributes to the events in a single click, styling the date bold, the name red, and the web address in italic. The Calendar Event style includes several styles that are grouped together into a nested style. A nested style automatically applies several formatting attributes to text within a paragraph. You will learn more about nested styles in InDesign Lesson 4, "Working with Styles."

Applying character styles

Character styles can be applied to individual words or characters. They are useful when applying common formatting attributes such as bold and italic. Character styles are the foundation for the nested styles that you applied to the event listings in the previous section. Here you will apply a character style to individual words.

1   Double-click on page 2 in the Pages panel to display page 2 within the workspace.

2   Using the Zoom tool (Q), increase the magnification so you can easily see the first paragraph of text, which starts with the text *Your wheels.*

3   Select the Type tool (T) from the Tools panel and select the word *wheels* at the top of the first paragraph. You can select the text either by clicking and dragging or by double-clicking on it.

Double-clicking on a word selects the word, triple-clicking selects the line, and quadruple-clicking (that's four clicks) selects the paragraph.

4   Press the Character Styles button (A) in the dock on the right side of the workspace to open the Character Styles panel. Choose Italic from the Character Styles panel to apply the Italic style to the selected word.

 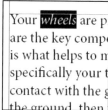

The Character style applies to a word rather than a whole paragraph.

Apply styles using Find/Change

Character Styles make it easy to automate the process of formatting text. In the current story, you want every instance of the word *wheels* to be italicized. Finding each of them individually would be very time-consuming, so let's speed up the process a bit using the Find/Change capabilities and character styles.

1 Using the Type tool (T), right-click (Windows) or Ctrl+click (Mac OS) anywhere within the text frame on page 2. Choose Find/Change from the contextual menu that appears. The Find/Change window opens.

Contextual menus are quick ways to access commands that apply to the part of the document in which you are working. The available commands change based upon the location of the cursor, the tool you are using, and the object selected.

2 In the Find/Change window, working in the Text tab, type **wheels** in the Find what text field and choose Story from the Search drop-down menu. This forces InDesign to search all of the text within the current story.

3 In the Change Format section at the bottom of the window, press the Specify attributes to change button (⚐). The Change Format Settings window opens.

Be careful to not select the Specify attributes to find button, which is an identical button located above the Specify attributes to change button.

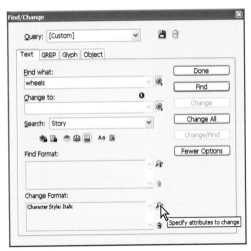

Press the Specify attributes to change button.

4 In the Change Format Settings dialog box, choose Italic from the Character Style menu and press OK. This will change the format of all text that is found, applying the Italic style to the found text.

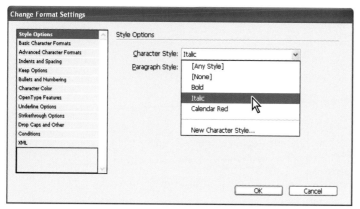

Choose Italic from the Character Style drop-down menu.

5 Press the Change All button. A window appears indicating that the text has been replaced with the specified style. Press OK, then press Done to close the Find/Change dialog box.

InDesign will notify you of how many replacements are made when using the Find/Change option.

Applying object styles

Object styles let you apply formatting to entire objects such as text frames, picture frames, or lines. You can use object styles to quickly and consistently apply color to the fill or stroke (border) of an object, or apply effects such as a drop shadow.

In this next section, you'll place some text into a text frame and then apply an object style to the frame so that the entire frame is formatted.

1 Double-click on page 1 in the Pages panel. You may need to zoom out a bit to see the full page. You can quickly change the page magnification by choosing a percentage from the magnification drop-down menu located in the top of the workspace.

2 Choose the Hand tool ( ) from the Tools panel, then drag from the right to the left until you are able to see the text frame in the pasteboard, located to the right of the page.

3 Select the Type tool (T) from the Tools panel, and click to insert the cursor inside the text frame on the pasteboard.

4 Choose File > Place. In the Place dialog box, navigate to the id01lessons folder and select the file Sidebar.txt. Press Open.

5 Choose the Selection tool (⬆) from the Tools panel and confirm that the text frame is selected. If necessary, click the frame to select it.

6 Choose Window > Object Styles to open the Object Styles panel. In the Object Styles panel, choose Sidebar from the list. The entire frame, including the text, is formatted. Object styles allow you to apply background colors, effects, and nested styles to a frame in a single click. This makes it possible to quickly apply repetitive formatting, and keep your document design consistent.

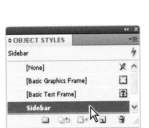

Object styles format entire objects, including text.

7 Using the Selection tool, click in the middle of the frame and drag it to the column on the right side of the first page, aligning the right and bottom edge of the frame with the right and bottom margin guides.

Working with graphics

Graphics are an integral part of page design, and InDesign puts you in control of cropping, sizing, borders, and effects that control the appearance of images you place into your layout. You can import a wide variety of graphic types into your layouts, including .pdf, .tif, .jpg, and .eps. You can place native Creative Suite files such as Photoshop (.psd), Illustrator (.ai), and InDesign (.indd) into your InDesign layout.

Placing graphics

Graphics are placed inside of a frame when you import them into your layout. As you discovered when you imported text, you can create the frame first, and then import the text. Alternatively, you can define the frame at the same time you import the image, or you can let InDesign create a frame for you.

1   Double-click on page 4 in the Pages panel to display page 4 of the document, then choose Edit > Deselect All so that no other objects are selected in the layout. If Deselect All is not available, then no objects are selected.

2   Choose File > Place. In the Place dialog box, navigate to the id01lessons folder and select the file cyclist.psd; then press Open. Because no frame has been selected, InDesign displays a loaded cursor indicating that the image is ready to be placed in the document.

3   Click once in the upper-left corner of the workspace where the red bleed guides intersect, outside of the page area. This places the image at its full size.

4   If the upper-left corner of the image is not correctly positioned at the intersection of the bleed guides, use the Selection tool (⬉) to click and drag the image to the correct position. Next you will resize the image to cover the top half of the layout and extend (bleed) off the edges.

5   Press and hold Shift+Ctrl (Windows) or Shift+Command (Mac OS), then click and hold the lower-right handle of the frame. After pausing for a brief moment, continue to hold the keyboard keys and drag down and to the right until the image extends off the page and the right edge aligns with the bleed line. You have scaled the frame and image proportionately.

Generally you should limit scaling to within 20 percent of the original size of an image so that it remains clear when printed or distributed. Increasing the scaling too much will cause many images to become pixilated or bitmapped, and they will appear to be unclear and of poor quality when printed or converted to PDF.

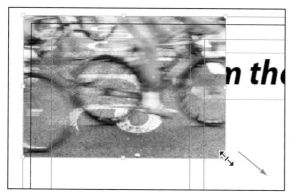

Scaling the image and the frame proportionately.

6   Continuing to use the Selection tool, click and drag upwards on the middle handle located along the bottom of the frame. Drag up until the bottom edge of the frame snaps to the guide located in the middle of the page.

Moving the handles of a frame using the Selection tool changes the size of the frame and adjusts how much of the image is displayed. Using the Shift+Ctrl (Windows) or Shift+Command (Mac OS) modifier keys allows you to scale the image and the frame together.

7   To reveal the text that is beneath the image, position the Selection tool on the image and right-click (Windows) or Ctrl+click (Mac OS); then choose Arrange > Send to Back. The image is placed behind the text.

Positioning graphics within a frame

You may need to crop or scale images that are placed in your layout. Here you will explore some visual tools that help with the positioning and scaling of graphics.

1   Navigate to page 1 by using the page drop-down menu or the Pages panel.

2   Choose the Selection tool (➤), then click to select the graphic frame at the bottom-left corner of page 1. The frame spans the left and center columns. InDesign displays empty graphic frames with an X inside the frame.

3   Choose File > Place. In the Place dialog box, navigate to the id01lessons folder and select the snowshoe.psd image. Press Open. The image is placed inside the selected frame, and is larger than the frame. Next you will determine the size of the image and adjust it to fit within the frame.

4   Choose the Direct Selection tool (➤) in the Tools panel and click to select the snowshoe image. The edges of the image are displayed with a light-brown border, showing the actual size of the graphic within the frame.

5   Select the Hand tool (✋) from the Tools panel. Click and hold the document. As you noticed earlier in this lesson, the page magnification changes and a red frame appears when using the Hand tool.

6 Reposition the red frame so that the entire border of the image is visible, then release the mouse. The zoom returns to its original level, focused on the portion of the page you identified.

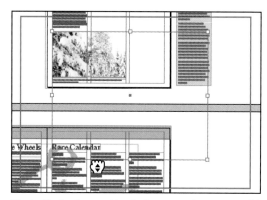

Use the Hand tool to reposition the document so the entire area of the snowshoe image is visible.

7 Choose the Direct Selection tool (🔖), then press and hold Shift. Click and hold the handle in the bottom-right corner of the image; after waiting one moment, continue to hold down the mouse and drag the handle up and to the left, reducing the size of the image. The Shift key maintain the proportions of the image while it is scaled. Reduce the size of the image until its width is slightly larger than the width of the frame, then release the mouse button.

8 Position the cursor in the middle of the frame and notice that the cursor changes to a hand. Click and drag to reposition the graphic within the frame, adjusting the position until the graphic is positioned in a location where you are happy with it.

The Direct Selection tool changes to a hand icon inside of image frames, and is used for repositioning images within their frame. While the icon is identical to the Hand tool, it does not have the same functionality and the two tools are used to perform different tasks.

The cropped image.

With the Direct Selection tool active, click with the mouse on an image and wait for a moment. After pausing, begin moving the image. You get a dynamic preview of the image as you are moving it, which is extremely useful when positioning a graphic within a frame. Pausing before repositioning the image is referred to as patient user mode, and provides benefits when cropping or resizing images.

9   Use the keyboard shortcut Ctrl+0 (Windows) or Command+0 (Mac OS) to fit page 1 within the document window.

10   Choose File > Save to save your work.

Applying text wrap

You can control the position of text relative to graphics and other objects. In some cases you may want text to be placed on top of an image, while in other cases you may want text to wrap around the shape of an image or object. You'll continue to work on the first page of the brochure by applying text wrap to an image.

1   Using the Selection tool (⬉), select the snowshoe image at the bottom of the page. This image is covering part of the text along the bottom part of the first column. You'll enable text wrap on the image to force the text away from the image.

2   Click the Text Wrap button in the panel docking area to open the Text Wrap panel.

3   Press the Wrap around bounding box button (⬛) at the top of the Text Wrap panel to apply the text wrap to the selected image. The text wrap forces the text to flow into the second column, making all the text visible.

*The Wrap around bounding box button in the Text Wrap panel
wraps the text around the bounding box of the frame or shape of an object.*

4   To get a better understanding of how the text wrap is being applied to the text surrounding the graphic frame, use the Selection tool to move the snowshoe image up and down on page 1. As you move the image, you can see how the text moves around the frame. When you're finished, move the image back to its original location.

5   Press the two arrows in the upper-right corner of the Text Wrap panel to close it.

Understanding layers

Layers help you organize the images and text in your layout. Layers are like transparent sheets of cellophane lying on top of each other. If you put an object on a layer that is below another layer, you can see the object as long as there aren't any objects directly above it, regardless of how many layers are on top of it. Layers can also be used to create different versions of projects, or different variations of projects, such as those versions being sent to different audiences or created in different languages.

Layers also allow you to place text and graphics on separate layers, making it easy to proofread text without looking at graphics. Here you'll see how layers can be used in this manner:

1   Navigate to page 2 using the Pages panel, then choose View > Fit Spread in Window to display the entire spread in the workspace. This command displays pages 2 and 3 together.

2   Press the Layers button () in the panel docking area to open the Layers panel.

The Layers panel.

If you have closed a panel instead of placing it in the docking area, you can access it from the Window menu. For example, you can choose Window > Pages. The list of available panels is also determined by the current workspace. To access all panels, choose the Advanced workspace.

3   In the Layers panel there are three layers: Text, Graphics, and Background content. Press the visibility icon (👁) next to the Text layer. The content becomes hidden when you disable its visibility, and all the text is temporarily hidden because the text has been placed on this layer. Press the visibility icon again to show the contents of the Text layer.

4   Turn the visibility of the Graphics and Background Content layers on and off to see the items that are on each of these layers.

InDesign layers are document-wide. When you create a layer, it is available on every page in the document, including the master pages. When you hide or show a layer, you are making an adjustment that impacts all pages in the document.

5   In the Pages panel, double-click page 1.

6   Using the Selection tool (♦), select the snowshoe image at the bottom of the page. In the Layers panel, notice the blue square (■) located to the right of the Text layer. This indicates that the currently selected object is located on the text layer.

7   In the Layers panel, click and drag the blue square to the Graphics layer. The object is moved to this layer, and the edge of the frame containing the snowshoe graphic is now red, the color of the Graphics layer.

Move the image from the Text layer to the Graphics layer.

8   Click the visibility icon (👁) of the Graphics layer to hide the contents of the layer, confirming that the snowshoe image has moved to this layer. Click the visibility icon again to make the layer visible.

9   Click the square immediately to the left of the Graphics layer to lock this layer. Locking the layer prevents you or others from modifying any contents on a layer.

Locking a layer prevents any changes to objects on the layer.

10 Choose the Selection tool and click on the spinnews logo at the top of page 1. You cannot currently select it because the layer is locked.

11 Unlock the layer by clicking on the padlock icon (⌷) immediately to the left of the Graphics layer, then select the spinnews logo using the Selection tool. You can now select the image. Now that the layer is unlocked, it can be selected and moved. If you accidentally select the wrong object, choose Edit > Deselect All or if you accidentally move an object, choose Edit > Undo to return it to the original location.

Locking a layer prevents all items on that layer from being selected. You can use this to organize your layout as you construct your documents. For example, you can create a layer that contains all the guides for your document. This provides another method of hiding and showing your guides quickly.

Applying effects

You can use InDesign to apply special effects to images or objects in your layout. These effects can save you time, as you do not need to use another program, like Photoshop, to achieve some common effects. Effects allow you to alter the appearance and transparency of objects and images without destroying the original. You can remove or alter effects after they have been applied, and the original object or image is not modified. Some of the common effects you can apply using InDesign include Drop shadow, Bevel and Emboss, and Feathering. Next you will apply an effect to an object in this newsletter.

1 Navigate to page 2 by using either the page drop-down menu in the lower-left corner of the workspace or the Pages panel.

2 Using the Selection tool (↖), select the blue border in the upper-left corner of the page. The border spans pages 2 and 3. As you discovered earlier, if the object were placed on a locked layer, you would first need to unlock the layer before the object can be selected and edited. This object should not be on a locked layer, so you should be able to select it without difficulty.

3 Press the Effects button (*fx*) in the panel docking area or choose Windows > Effects to open the Effects panel. Remember, if you've changed workspaces, some of the panel buttons may not be available. You may need to choose the Advanced workspace to see all the panels, such as the Effects panel.

4 Confirm that Object is highlighted in the Effects panel. Press the Add an object effect to the selected target button (*fx*) at the bottom of the panel. Choose Bevel and Emboss from the menu. If you want to see what this effect will do to the selected object, click the Preview check box to enable a preview of the effect.

You can apply an effect independently to an entire object or only to the stroke or fill of the selected object.

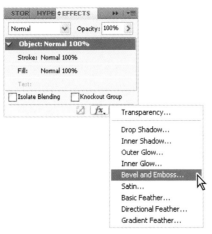

The fx button at the bottom of the Effects panel allows you to choose which effects to apply to selected objects.

5 In the Effects dialog box, leave the settings at the defaults and press OK.

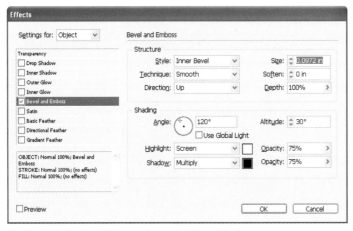

Use the default Bevel and Emboss settings in the Effects dialog box.

6   Switch to the Preview viewing mode using the viewing mode button in the Application bar at the top of the workspace. You can also press the keyboard shortcut W to switch the viewing mode, or access the same viewing mode controls at the bottom of the tools palette. All three options let you switch to the Preview viewing mode, which provides you with a preview of the final project without displaying any of the non-printing elements.

7   Choose File > Save, then choose File > Close to close the file.

Congratulations! You have completed the lesson.

Resources for additional help

In-product help

InDesign includes help documentation directly within the application itself. Choose Help > InDesign Help, and InDesign launches the Adobe Help Viewer, which allows you to search by topic.

On-line help

Adobe makes the documentation for InDesign available on the Web in the form of Livedocs at *http://livedocs.adobe.com/en_US/InDesign/5.0/index.html*. The Livedocs help tends to be more current, as it is updated regularly. The documentation that shipped with the software was likely written months before the software was in its final format, so it may not be as complete or current as the on-line help. In addition, Livedocs provides you with the ability to add comments to topics that you view, and even receive an e-mail when someone else adds a comment to the topic. You can also download many of the help files in PDF format for printing or future reference.

Forums

Adobe on-line forums are an excellent resource for finding solutions to questions you have about InDesign or how InDesign integrates with other applications. Adobe forums are contributed to by a community of beginning, intermediate, and advanced users who may be looking for the same answer as you, or who have already discovered solutions and answers to questions and are willing to share their solutions with other users.

Conferences, seminars, and training

The authors of this book regularly speak at conferences and seminars, and deliver instructor-led training sessions. You can learn more at *agitraining.com*.

Self study

Place some of your own graphics into the newsletter that you just created, then practice cropping and repositioning the graphics within their frames. Move objects to other layers and create your own layer to further refine the organization of the file.

This lesson has given you an overview of the essential capabilities available in the latest version of InDesign. For more in-depth instructions on how to perform many of these tasks in detail, read and work through the other lessons in this book.

Review

Questions

1 What does a red plus sign in the lower-right corner of a text frame indicate?

2 What tool is used to reposition an image inside of a frame?

3 How can you ensure that if you reposition the panels in InDesign to your liking, you could always bring them back to that state?

4 If you cannot see panels that you need to use, how can you display these panels?

Answers

1 There is more text in the frame than can be displayed within the current frame. This is called overset text. You can fix this by linking the text to another frame, editing the text so that it fits within the existing frame, or enlarging the size of the frame.

2 The Direct Selection tool is used for manipulating images within a frame.

3 Save a custom workspace by choosing Window > Workspace > New Workspace.

4 When the workspace is changed, the list of available panels also changes. Use the Advanced workspace to view all the panels. All panels can also be found under the Window menu. Simply choose the panel you want to use from the list and it will display.

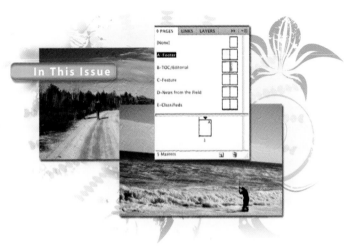

What you'll learn in this lesson:

- Creating and saving custom page sizes
- Creating guides
- Adding sections and page numbering
- Applying master pages to document pages
- Copying and linking master pages between documents

Building Documents with Master Pages

Master pages serve as the foundation for most InDesign documents. You can use master pages to maintain consistency throughout your document and work more efficiently.

Starting up

Before starting, make sure that your tools and panels are consistent by resetting your preferences. See "Resetting the InDesign workspace and preferences" on page XXVII.

You will work with several files from the id02lessons folder in this lesson. Make sure that you have copied the id02lessons folder onto your hard drive from the Digital Classroom DVD. See "Loading lesson files" on page XXIX. This lesson may be easier to follow if the id02lessons folder is on your desktop.

See Lesson 2 in action!

Use the accompanying video to gain a better understanding of how to use some of the features shown in this lesson. The video tutorial for this lesson can be found on the included DVD.

The project

In this lesson, you will create a magazine. You will use master pages to create layout templates for each section in the magazine, including running headers, which run across the top of the page, and running footers, which run across the bottom of the page. Master pages give the publication a consistent look and feel.

Planning your document

Before you start creating a document using InDesign, you need some important information: the final size of the document after it is finished, also known as the *trim size*; how the pages will be held together, also known as the *binding*; and whether the document has images or graphics that extend to the edge of the document—this is known as *bleed*. Once you have this information, you can create the templates for your document pages.

Creating custom page sizes

For this lesson, you will create a custom-sized magazine with colors that extend to the edge of the page. You'll start by creating a new document, and saving the custom size as a preset, which you can use to create subsequent issues of the magazine.

Creating a new custom-sized document

This document will be measured using inches, so you'll start by setting your units of measurement to inches, and then you'll create the custom document size.

1   Choose Edit > Preferences > Units & Increments (Windows), or InDesign > Preferences > Units & Increments (Mac OS). When the Preferences dialog box appears, choose Inches from the Vertical and Horizontal drop-down menus in the Ruler Units section. Press OK.

Changing the unit of measurement when no documents are open causes InDesign to use these settings for all new documents you create.

When working in a document, you can switch the unit of measurement by right-clicking (Windows) or Ctrl+clicking (Mac OS) on the vertical or horizontal ruler.

2   Choose File > New > Document, or press Ctrl+N (Windows) or Command+N (Mac OS), to create a new document.

---

3 In the New Document dialog box, confirm that the Facing Pages check box is selected. In the Page Size section, type **8.125** for the Width and **10.625** for the Height.

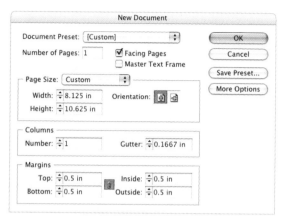

Setting the size of the new document.

4 In the Margins section, make sure that the Make all settings the same button (⊛) is not selected. Type **.5** in the Top, Inside, and Outside margin text fields, and **.75** in the Bottom text field.

5 If the Bleed and Slug section is not visible, press the More Options button on the left side of the dialog box. In the Bleed and Slug section, make sure that the Make all settings the same button is not selected, and then type **.125** in the Bleed Top, Bottom, and Outside margin text fields and **0** for the inside value. Because this is a magazine, it won't bleed into the spine of the page, where the pages are bound together.

6 Press the Save Presets button in the upper-right corner of the New Document dialog box. This allows you to save the custom settings you have just entered.

Type **Newsletter** in the Save Preset As text field, and then press OK. In the New Document dialog box, the Newsletter preset is listed in the preset drop-down menu. This preset is available the next time you need to create a document with similar specifications.

Press OK to leave the New Document dialog box and start creating your document. A new, untitled document is created with the dimensions you entered.

7 Choose File > Save As. In the Save As dialog box, navigate to the id02lessons folder and type **id02_work.indd** in the File name text field. Press Save.

InDesign does include an automatic save feature that can help you recover your document if there is a computer or software problem that causes the program to close unexpectedly, but it is still a good idea to save your work often.

You formatted some items with styles in InDesign Lesson 1. Here you will import the styles from another InDesign document, and so you will not need to create them from scratch. In Lesson 4, "Working with Styles," you will discover how to create and define new styles.

8 Choose Window > Workspace > [Advanced]. Press the Paragraph Styles button (¶) in the panel docking area in the right side of the workspace to open the Paragraph Styles panel. Press the panel menu button (-≡) in the upper-right corner of the Paragraph Styles panel, and from the panel menu, choose Load All Text Styles. The Open a File dialog box appears.

9 In the Open a File dialog box, navigate to the id02lessons folder and select the file named id02styles.indd. Press Open. The Load Styles dialog box appears.

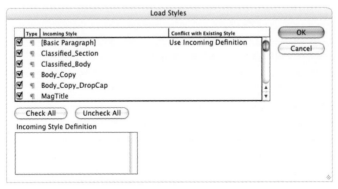

Loading styles lets you import and use styles created in another document.

10 In the Load Styles dialog box, press the Check All button, located in the bottom-left corner, and then press OK. All the paragraph and character styles from this publication are imported into your document.

11 Choose File > Save to save your work. Keep this file open for the next part of the lesson.

Creating and formatting master pages

Master pages serve as a template upon which all document pages are created. They provide the framework for the design of pages. Different master pages may be created for various sections of a magazine or a catalog, ensuring that all pages of these sections maintain a consistent appearance.

The document you are creating currently contains only one document page and one master page. You will add more document pages to complete the magazine, and more master pages to create consistent style and formatting. You will add a master page for the various sections of your magazine. Each of these sections has a different layout, with a different number of columns, margins, and headers. By creating the master pages before working on the document, you will be able to quickly create pages with a consistent design for the magazine.

1 Press the Pages button (⌘) in the panel docking area, or press the keyboard shortcut F12 (Windows) or Command+F12 (Mac OS), to open the Pages panel. Double-click the A-Master label in the top portion of the Pages panel.

The A-Master page is displayed and centered within your workspace. Keep the A-Master page selected in the Pages panel.

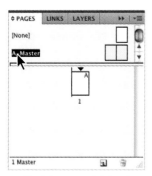

Double-clicking a page label in the Pages panel centers the page in the workspace.

2 In the Pages panel, press the panel menu button (▾≡) and select Master Options for A-Master. The Master Options dialog box appears, allowing you to rename your master page.

3 In the Name field of the Master Options dialog box, type **Footer**. Leave all other settings unchanged, and then press OK. This changes the name from A-Master to A-Footer. You will now add a footer that runs across the bottom of this master page, and then apply it to document pages.

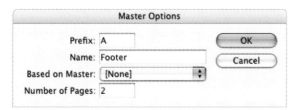

Change the name of a master page using the Master Options dialog box.

Formatting master pages

For this publication, the A-Footer page will also serve as the foundation for the other master pages. Although master pages can be used independent of one another, for this publication you will define that all items appearing on A-Footer will appear on all other master pages. This allows you to create a consistent footer across every page, and the other master pages will have unique header information, which is unique for each section of the magazine.

Adding automatic page numbering

You can have InDesign automatically apply a page number to pages within a document. If you reposition pages, they are renumbered, and you control the style and appearance of the page numbers.

1 In the Pages panel, double-click the left page icon for the A-Footer master page. This fits the left side of your A-Footer master page in the window. To keep the page numbers a consistent distance from the bottom edge of your page, you will create a guide.

2 Move your Selection tool (▸) onto the horizontal ruler running across the top of the page. Ctrl+click (Windows) or Command+click (Mac OS) and drag down from the ruler to create a horizontal ruler guide. Continue dragging until the ruler guide is positioned at 10.25 inches. You can determine the location of the guide in the Control panel, as the position updates as you drag the guide.

Pressing and holding the Ctrl or Command key while dragging causes the guide to go across the entire spread, rather than only one page.

If the page rulers aren't visible, choose View > Show Rulers or press Ctrl+R (Windows) or Command+R (Mac OS).

3 Select the Type tool (T) from the Tools panel. Position the Type tool so the intersecting horizontal and vertical lines near the bottom of the tool is positioned at the bottom-left corner of the margin guides, where the left margin guide and the bottom margin guide intersect. Click and drag down and to the right, creating a text frame that extends from the bottom margin guide down to the guide you created in the previous step and to the 1 inch position. You can see the position of the frame being created in the Control panel and in the horizontal ruler located at the top of the page.

*Creating a frame on the master page
for the automatic page number.*

4 Choose Type > Insert Special Character > Markers > Current Page Number to automatically have InDesign enter the page number on all pages to which this master page is applied. If you prefer to use keyboard commands, you can press Shift+Alt+Ctrl+N (Windows) or Shift+Option+Command+N (Mac OS) to have an automatic page number inserted. The letter *A* is inserted into the text frame. This letter serves as a placeholder for the actual page numbers, and displays as an A because the current page on which you are working is master page *A*.

The Special Characters menu can also be accessed by right-clicking (Windows) or Ctrl+clicking (Mac OS) anywhere in the workspace. If you are working with type, the Special Characters option is available from the contextual menu.

5 Using the Type tool, select the letter *A* that you inserted into the text frame. From the Character Formatting Controls in the Control panel, choose Myriad Pro Bold from the font drop-down menu, and choose 12pt from the font size drop-down menu. Press the Paragraph Formatting Controls button in the Control panel, and then press the Align away from Spine button (≡). This aligns the text to the opposite edge of the binding of the publication.

6 Choose Object > Text Frame Options or press Ctrl+B (Windows) or Command+B (Mac OS). The Text Frame Options dialog box appears. In the General tab, locate the Vertical Justification section and choose Bottom from the Align drop-down menu. Press OK. The baseline of the text aligns to the bottom of the text frame.

Now you will place a copy of the automatic page number on the opposite page.

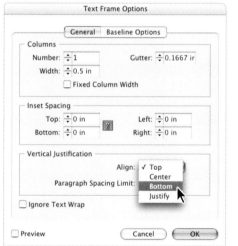
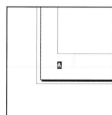

Using the Text Frame Options dialog box to vertically justify text.

7 Choose the Selection tool (★) and make certain the text frame containing the footer is selected. Choose Edit > Copy to copy the frame.

8 Double-click on the right-hand page of the A-Footer master in the Pages panel. Choose Edit > Paste to place the copied text frame into the right-hand page.

9 Use the Selection tool to reposition the text frame so that the top of the frame is aligned to the bottom margin, and the right edge of the frame aligns to the right margin.

Notice that the page number automatically changes to align to the right side of the text frame because you selected the Align away from Spine option.

Using text variables

Use text variables to insert dynamic text that changes contextually. InDesign includes several pre-defined text variables including Chapter Number, File Name, Output Date, and Running Header. You can also edit any of these variables, or create new variables.

Defining new text variables

You will create variable text for your magazine title and page footers.

1   Choose Type > Text Variables > Define. The Text Variables dialog box appears.

2   Select Running Header from the Text Variables section of the dialog box and press the New button on the right side of the dialog box. The New Text Variable dialog box appears.

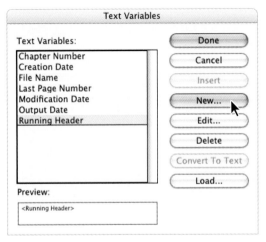

Defining the settings for text variables.

3   In the New Text Variable dialog box, type **Magazine Title** in the Name text field. Leave the Type field as Running Header (Paragraph Style). From the Style drop-down menu, choose the MagTitle paragraph style. In the Options section, select the Change Case check box, and then select the Title Case radio button below it. Press OK.

A new Magazine Title variable appears in the Text Variables dialog box.

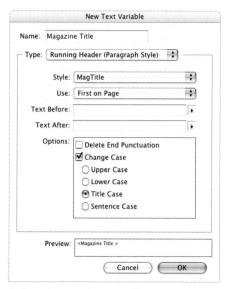

Defining the settings for text variables.

4   Repeat steps 1 and 2 to create another text variable. Name this text variable *Magazine Issue* and select the MagIssue paragraph style from the Style drop-down menu. All the other settings should match the settings used in step 3. The variables for Magazine Title and Magazine Issue are now available in the Text Variables dialog box. Press Done to save these new variables.

Creating page footers

Now you will use the variables you have created to build the footers. Later, you'll discover how InDesign can automatically populate these variables.

1   In the Pages panel, double-click the left page icon of the A–Footer master page.

2   Select the Type tool (T) from the Tools panel. Position the cursor at the bottom-right corner of the page, where the bottom and right margin guides meet. Click and drag down and to the left until the bottom of the frame reaches the bottom ruler guide and the left edge of the frame is approximately at the center of the page. A guide appears once the cursor has reached the center of the page.

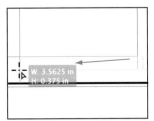

Creating a text frame for the magazine title.

3   In the Control panel, press the Character Formatting Controls button (**A**), and then set the font to Minion Pro Italic, the size to 12pt, and the leading (ⓐ) to Auto. Press the Paragraph Formatting Controls button (¶) and press the Align toward Spine button (≣).

4   Choose Type > Text Variables > Insert Variable > Magazine Title. The variable text <magazine Title> is placed into the frame. Press the space bar to separate this variable from the next variable that you will enter.

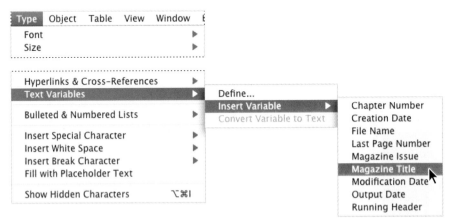

Inserting variable text.

5 In the Control panel, press the Character Formatting Controls button and change the font to Minion Pro Regular. Choose Type > Text Variable > Insert Variable > Magazine Issue. The variable text <magazine Issue> is placed into the frame.

6 Choose the Selection tool (➤) from the Tools panel and make sure the text frame is selected. Choose Object > Text Frame Options. In the Text Frame Options dialog box, select Bottom from the Align drop-down menu located in the Vertical Justification section in the General Tab. This causes the text to align to the bottom of the text frame. Press OK. You will now duplicate this box, moving the duplicate to the facing page.

7 Continuing to use the Selection tool, press and hold the Alt key (Windows) or Option key (Mac OS). While holding this key, click and drag the box you created to the page on the right side of the layout. The box duplicates as you drag it because of the key you are pressing.

8 Position the duplicate frame so that the left edge aligns with the left margin guide, and the bottom of the duplicate frame remains aligned to the ruler guide you created.

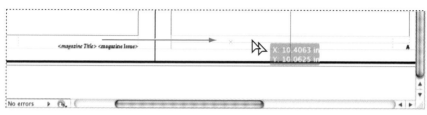

Position the duplicate text frame along the ruler guide, aligning the left edge with the left margin guide.

9 Choose the Type tool and click in the duplicated text frame. Press Ctrl+A (Windows) or Command+A (Mac OS) to select the type, and then press the Delete key.

10 Continuing to work in the same text frame, type **aquent.com.**

11 Choose File > Save to save your work.

Basing master pages on other master pages

You can create additional master pages, and these pages can use the formatting and layout that you've already created for the A-Footer master page. In the next exercise, you'll import master pages that have already been created in another document. You'll then apply the A-Footer master page to these master pages that you import.

To create your own master pages, choose the New Master command from the Pages panel menu.

1   If necessary, open the Pages panel by pressing the Pages button (⊞) in the dock. In the Pages panel, press the panel menu button (·≡) and choose Load Master Pages. The Open a File dialog box appears.

2   In the Open a File dialog box, navigate to the id02lessons folder and select the file called id0201styles.indd. Press Open. Four new master pages are added to your document. These pages correspond to the various sections of the magazine. Next, you'll apply the A-Footer master page you created earlier to these new master pages.

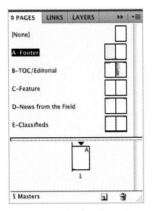

The Pages panel reflects the newly added master pages.

3   Double-click on the name B-TOC/Editorial master page in the Pages panel. By clicking the name instead of the icon, you can view the entire spread.

4   In the Pages panel menu, choose Master Options for B-TOC/Editorial. This opens the Master Options dialog box.

5   In the Master Options dialog box, click the Based on Master drop-down menu and choose A-Footer. Press OK.

Notice that the B-TOC/Editorial master page now includes the footer you created. In the Pages panel, the page icons for B-TOC/Editorial display the letter A, indicating that these master pages are based on the master page A you created.

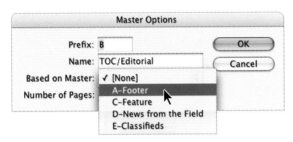
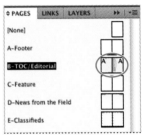

Base the page on the A-Footer master page.

The A indicates that a page is linked to this master.

6   In the Pages panel, click and drag the A-Footer master page onto the C-Feature master page. By dragging and dropping one master page icon onto another, you are applying the master page formatting to the destination page.

Drag the master page by its name instead of its icon to select the entire spread.

7   Drag and drop the A-Footer master page on top of the remaining master pages.

Overriding master page items

Master page items that appear on other pages are locked. The master page items are locked whether you apply a master page to another master page, or to a document page. This prevents you from accidentally modifying master page items that are intended to remain consistent on every page.

In the next exercise, you'll unlock some of the master page items that have been applied to another page, allowing you to selectively delete the footer information.

1   In the Pages panel, double-click the left B-TOC/Editorial master page. Notice that the text frames' edges appear as dotted lines. This indicates that these items are part of a master page that has been applied to this page. These items are locked and cannot be edited.

2   Choose the Selection tool (k) from the Tools panel. Place the cursor over the footer and click. Clicking the footer does not select the item, because it is attached to a master page. In order to modify these items, you must first break the link to the master page.

3   Continuing to use the Selection tool, press the Shift+Ctrl keys (Windows) or Shift+Command keys (Mac OS) and click the text frames containing the page number and footer. Use these modifier keys to select master page items. Press Delete to remove these frames from this page.

4   Choose File > Save to save your work.

Using Shift+Control+click (Windows) or Shift+Command+click (Mac OS) to select and change a master page item is referred to as a local override. The master page remains applied, and only the items you select are modified. To override all master page items on a page, choose Override All Master Page Items from the Pages panel menu (-≡).

Adding placeholder frames to master pages

Creating text and image frames on master pages makes it easier to develop consistent layouts. You can also use frame-fitting options to control how images are sized after they are placed.

1 Select the Type tool (T) from the Tools panel and create a text frame on the In This Issue page. The position and dimensions of the box are not important; you'll be setting these in the next step.

2 Choose the Selection tool (↖) from the Tools panel and make sure the text frame you drew in the last step is selected. In the Control panel, set the reference point (▦)to top left and type **2.9583"** for X and **1.4028"** for Y to set the location of the frame. Then type **4.6667"** for W and **3.6607"** for H to set the size.

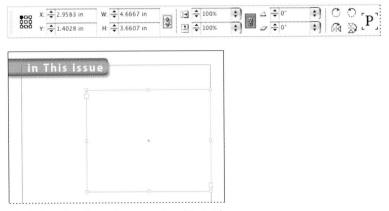

Use the Control panel to set the exact location of the text frame.

3 Now you'll add a number of image frames on the left side of the page. Select the Rectangle Frame tool (⊠) from the Tools panel and draw a small rectangle to the left of the text frame you created in the previous step. You'll use the Control panel to set the exact position and dimensions of this frame.

4 Choose the Selection tool from the Tools panel and make sure the frame you created in the last step is selected. In the Control panel, make sure the reference point (▦) is set to top-left and type the following values to set the dimensions and position: X: **-.125"** Y: **1.4028"** W: **2.3929"** H: **1.625"**.

You have created an image frame that is aligned to the top of the text frame and bleeds off the left side of the page. Next you will define how images placed in this frame will be sized.

5 Using the Selection tool, click to select the image frame you just created. From the menu bar at the top of the workspace, choose Object > Fitting > Frame Fitting Options.

In the Frame Fitting Options dialog box, choose Fill Frame Proportionally from the Fitting drop-down menu in the Fitting on Empty Frame section. Press OK.

You'll now duplicate the empty frame.

Frame Fitting Options

Crop Amount

Top: 0 in   Left: 0 in
Bottom: 0 in   Right: 0 in

Alignment

Reference Point:

Fitting on Empty Frame

Fitting: ✓ None
          Fit Content to Frame
          Fit Content Proportionally
          Fill Frame Proportionally

☑ Preview   Cancel   OK

Choose Fill Frame Proportionally in the Frame Fitting Options dialog box to control how images placed in this frame will be sized.

6 With the image frame still selected, choose Edit > Step and Repeat. This allows you to duplicate an object multiple times, placing each duplicate in a specific location.

7 In the Step and Repeat dialog box, type **3** in the Repeat Count text field, type **0** in the Horizontal Offset text field, and type **2.0625"** in the Vertical Offset text field. Press OK. This creates three copies of the frame, and spaces them 2.0625 inches apart from each other.

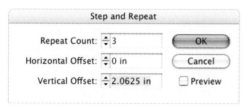

Step and Repeat

Repeat Count: 3   OK

Horizontal Offset: 0 in   Cancel

Vertical Offset: 2.0625 in   ☐ Preview

Create three duplicates of the text frame using Step and Repeat.

8 Choose File > Save to save your file, and keep it open for the next part of the lesson.

Locking Master Items and setting text wrap

In the first lesson, you discovered how to wrap text around an object on a document page. Here you will wrap text around a shape on a master page.

1   Double-click the right page of the B-TOC/Editorial master page in the Pages panel. Using the Selection tool (✦), select the oval shape on the left side of the page and right-click (Windows) or Ctrl+click (Mac OS) on the shape. In the contextual menu, deselect Allow Master Item Overrides. This prohibits designers from making changes to this master page object once it is part of a document page.

Deselect the Allow Master Item Overrides option to keep this item from being modified on a document page.

2   Choose Window > Text Wrap. This opens the Text Wrap panel. From the panel, select the *Wrap around object shape* option (▣) and set the Top Offset to .25 inches, causing the text to wrap around the oval with ¼-inch distance between the text and the oval.

Use the Text Wrap panel to push text away from a frame or object. Here the text wraps above the image, offset by ¼ inch.

3   Close the Text Wrap panel.

Adding layout pages

Now that you have created and formatted all the master pages, you can start to lay out the document pages of the magazine. You'll begin by adding pages to the file.

When you create simple designs for one-time use, it may be easier to not create master pages. For longer documents or any documents that will repeat in a similar way, you should create master pages, as the time invested in defining the design saves time in the long run.

1 Choose Layout > Pages > Add Page, or use the keyboard shortcut Shift+Control+P (Windows) or Shift+Command+P (Mac OS), to add a page to the end of the document. Two pages are now displayed as icons in the Pages panel.

Next you'll insert the pages that will contain the Table of Contents and editorial content.

Adding a page to the document using the Layout menu.

2 In the Pages panel, Alt+click (Windows) or Option+click (Mac OS) on the Create new page button (◻) at the bottom of the Pages panel. This opens the Insert Pages dialog box.

3 In the Insert Pages dialog box, type **2** in the Pages text field, and from the Insert drop-down menu select After Page and type **1** in the text field. Select B-TOC/Editorial from the Master drop-down menu, and then press OK.

This causes two pages to be added after page 1, and the new pages use the B-TOC/ Editorial master page.

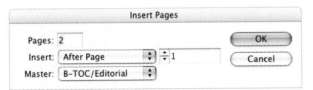

Adding multiple pages to the document. The new pages are based on a specific master page.

This inserts two pages between pages 1 and 2, and applies the B-TOC/Editorial master page to those new pages. This issue of the magazine will be 12 pages. You will now add the additional pages, but because they won't all be in the same section, you'll insert them without a master page assignment.

4 In the Pages panel, Alt+click (Windows) or Option+click (Mac OS) the Create new page button (▯) at the bottom of the panel. The Insert Pages dialog box appears.

5 In the Insert Pages dialog box, type **9** in the Pages text field. Select After Page in the drop-down menu next to Insert, and type **4** in the text field. Choose None from the Master drop-down menu. This inserts nine blank pages into your file after page 4. You now have 13 pages in the document. Because the document is only 12 pages, you'll practice deleting a page.

6 Select page 4 by double-clicking the page icon in the Pages panel. This highlights the page icon in the Pages panel and navigates to this page.

7 Press the Delete selected pages button (🗑) at the bottom of the Pages panel. This deletes page 4 and leaves you with the 12 pages you need for this issue.

8 Choose File > Save to save your work. Keep it open for the next exercise.

Setting numbering and section options

Now you have all the pages you need to set up the numbering and sections. Because you are using InDesign's automatic page numbering, the cover is considered to be page 1 in the document. You actually want page 1 of the magazine to be the third page of the file, with the first two pages considered to be the cover and inside front cover. Using numbering and sections options, you will change the document's sections to reflect your desired numbering sequence.

1   In the Pages panel, double-click the section start icon, located above the first page in the Pages panel. This opens the Numbering & Section Options dialog box.

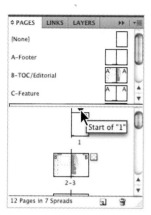

Double-click the section start icon in the Pages panel.

2   In the Numbering & Section Options dialog box, select I, II, III, IV from the Style drop-down menu in the Page Numbering section, and then press OK.

This change adjusts the document's numbering to Roman numerals. You will now create a new section on the third page and have the new section start with page 1.

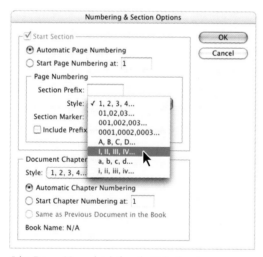

Select Roman Numeral style from the Styles drop-down menu.

3 In the Pages panel, double-click page III to select it. Press the panel menu button (‑≡) in the Pages panel and select Numbering & Section Options. Select the Start Page Numbering at radio button and type **1** in the text field. In the Page Numbering section, select 1, 2, 3, 4 from the Style drop-down list and press OK.

This starts a new section on the third page of the document. The new section starts using the page number 1.

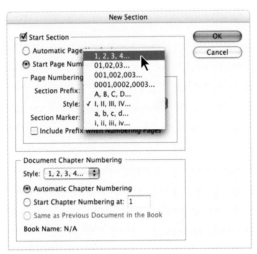

Use Numbering and Section Options to set the numbering for the new section of the magazine.

Placing formatted text

Now that the numbering and section options have been adjusted, you'll add some content to the editorial page. In this case, you'll import text from a document. The text uses placeholder copy and includes pre-formatted styles. You'll then complete the editorial page by adding a picture of the editor.

1 In the Pages panel, double-click the third page of the document. This is the page you set to page 1 in the previous exercise.

2 Select the Type tool (T) from the Tools panel and draw a small text frame on the right side of the page. The exact size and location isn't important; you'll use the Control panel to specify these values.

3 Choose the Selection tool (↖) from the Tools panel and make sure the text frame is selected. In the Control panel at the top of the workspace, make sure the reference point is set to top left. Type **11.0833"** in the X text field and **3"** in the Y text field. Also type **4.6667"** in the W text field and **6.875"** in the H text field.

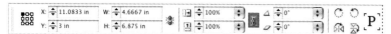

Set the size of the text frame after you create it.

4 With the text frame still selected, choose File > Place. Navigate to the id02lessons folder and select the file Editorial.doc. At the bottom of the Place dialog box, make sure Show Import Options and Replace Selected Item are both checked. Press Open. The Microsoft Word Import Options dialog box appears.

5 In the Microsoft Word Import Options dialog box, make sure the Preserve Styles and Formatting from Text and Tables radio button is selected. Leave all other settings unchanged, and then press OK. The Word document is placed into the text frame and all styles from the Word document are automatically mapped to the InDesign paragraph styles because the styles in each application have been identically named.

Use the Import Options to adjust the styles when importing a Microsoft Word document.

6 Because the editor probably won't get a new picture with each issue of the magazine, it makes sense to place this photo on the master page. Double click on the right-hand page of the B-TOC/Editorial master page. Choose File > Place. In the Place dialog box, navigate to the id02lessons folder and select the file editor.jpg. Uncheck Show Import Options and also uncheck Replace Selected Item. Press Open to import this image. The cursor changes to a loaded cursor, indicating it has an image to place.

7 Move the loaded cursor to the top-right portion of the page, below the *From the Editor* text. Click once to place the photo. Choose the Selection tool from the Tools panel, and then drag the photo until the right side snaps to the right margin. If necessary, use the arrow keys to nudge the photo into place.

Place the editor's photo on the master page beneath the From the Editor text.

8 Choose File > Save to save your work.

Creating the classified page

Local goods and services are often advertised on a classified page located in the back of a magazine. Because most of the space is sold by number of words, characters, or column depth, these layouts typically involve narrow columns to pack as many ads as possible into the space. In this case, a four-column layout with an appropriate header has already been created for you. Next, you'll apply the master page and then add the classified text.

1 In the Pages panel, double-click page 9. Press the Pages panel menu button (‑≡), and choose Apply Master to Pages. The Apply Master dialog box appears.

2 From the Apply Master drop-down menu, choose the master page E-Classifieds. The To Pages text field should reflect the current page number. If necessary, type **9** in this field. Press OK. The header, footer, and four-column layout of the E-Classifieds master page are applied to page 9.

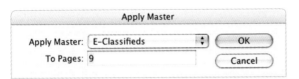

Use the Apply Master option to apply a master page to page 9 of the document.

3 To import the text into the page, choose File > Place. Navigate to the id02lessons folder and select the file named Classifieds.rtf. At the bottom of the Place dialog box, check Show Import Options, and leave Replace Selected Item unchecked. Press Open.

4 In the RTF Import Options dialog box, make sure the *Preserve Styles and Formatting from Text and Tables* radio button is selected. Leave all the other settings at their defaults and press OK.

InDesign remembers the last settings used in the Import Options dialog box. Settings you make will impact similar files you import until you change the import options.

5   On page 9, move the cursor to the upper-left corner of the first column. When the cursor nears the top of the column text frame, the arrow turns from black to white. Press and hold the Shift key, and click to place the text.

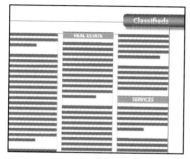

Press and hold the Shift key to automatically flow the text as it is placed in the document.

6   Choose File > Save to save your work.

Adding images and text to the master frames

Earlier in this lesson, you added image and text frames to a master page. Next you will add content to these frames on the document pages.

1   Double-click the table of contents page icon in the Pages panel, which is now labeled with the Roman numeral II. The image and text frames you added earlier have dotted borders, indicating that these frames are linked to a master page and cannot be selected.

2   Choose File > Place. In the Place dialog box, navigate to the id02lessons folder and locate the TOC images folder. Double-click the folder and select the file photo1.jpg. At the bottom of the Place dialog box, uncheck Show Import Options and Replace Selected Item. Press Open.

3   Move your cursor over the top image frame on the left side of the page and click to place the image. The image is placed inside the frame and automatically resized. This is because when you created this image frame on the master page, you applied fitting options to the frame. These options control how InDesign sizes and positions images placed into the empty frame.

After placing images and text in frames originally drawn on the master page, the frame is overridden which means it can now be selected but it still retains all of the properties from the master page and will still update if a change is made to the master page. Properties that you change on a document page do no update if a change is made to the master page.

4 Repeat steps 2 and 3, placing the remaining images from the TOC images folder into the layout.

Now you'll finish the TOC/Editorial spread by adding the Table of Contents to the text frame on the right side of the page.

5 Choose File > Place. In the Place dialog box, navigate to the id02lessons folder. Select the TOC.rtf file. Make sure that Show Import Options and Replace Selected Item are still unchecked. Press Open.

6 Move your cursor over the text box on the right side of the table of contents page, and click to place the text into the layout.

Just like the Editorial and Classified sections, the TOC.rtf file is pre-formatted. In the next section of this exercise, you'll apply the remaining master pages and witness how InDesign updates the content in the footer of each page.

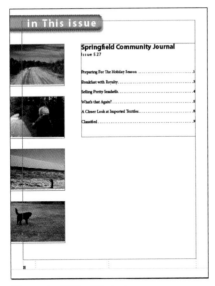

The completed Table of Contents.

Applying master pages to multiple pages

Next you'll complete your work on this magazine by assigning master pages to the remaining pages in the magazine. The editorial content for this publication may not be complete, but you'll get the design ready for the final text to be placed as soon as it is ready.

1   In the Pages panel, press the panel menu button (·≣) and choose Apply Master to Pages. In the Apply Master dialog box, choose C-Feature from the Apply Master drop-down menu.

2   In the To Pages text field, type **2-4**. Be sure to add the hyphen (-) between the 2 and 4. Press OK. The C-Feature master page is applied to pages 2 to 4.

3   Press the Pages panel menu button again and choose Apply Master to Pages. In the resulting Apply Master dialog box, choose D-News from the Apply Master drop-down menu and type **5-8** in the To Pages text field. Press OK.

Scroll through the document pages. The text variables inserted in the footer have been automatically populated with the magazine title and issue. The master pages and text variables provide a convenient way to save time and maintain consistency throughout your design.

4   Choose File > Save to save your work.

Congratulations! You have finished this lesson.

Self study

Create a newsletter for your friends or family. Include a number of sections such as a page with profiles of people, stories relating to events or travels, favorite quotes, top ten lists, and photo galleries. Think about which of these sections share common elements, and design master pages to create a consistent design across these sections. Use headers, footers, guides, text frames, and picture frames on your master pages. If you find yourself repeating steps on multiple pages, consider how you can use features like master pages and text variables to streamline your design process.

Review

Questions

1 Do automatic page numbers always start with page 1?

2 If you want to modify content on a page that is linked to a master page, how do you select this locked content?

3 How can you access styles created in other InDesign documents?

Answers

1 No, you can start page numbering with any page number using the Numbering and Sections dialog box to specify where automatic page numbers start and end.

2 Using the Selection tool (⭢), Shift+Control+click (Windows) or Shift+Command+click (Mac OS) on content that is linked to a master page to break the link.

3 Use the Load Styles command found in the various style panels, to import styles created in other documents.

What you'll learn in this lesson:

- Creating and entering text
- Formatting and styling text
- Editing text in the Story Editor
- Customizing the dictionary
- Applying styles

Working with Text and Type

This lesson covers the essential capabilities for importing, formatting, and flowing text using InDesign CS4.

Starting up

Before starting, make sure that your tools and panels are consistent by resetting your preferences. See "Resetting the InDesign workspace and preferences" on page 3. It is important to use the Typography workspace for this lesson, as described on page XXVII.

You will work with several files from the id03lessons folder in this lesson. Make sure that you have copied the id03lessons folder onto your hard drive from the Digital Classroom DVD. See "Loading lesson files" on page XXIX. This lesson may be easier to follow if the id03lessons folder is on your desktop.

See Lesson 3 in action!

Use the accompanying video to gain a better understanding of how to use some of the features shown in this lesson. The video tutorial for this lesson can be found on the included DVD.

The project

You will explore InDesign's text controls by entering and flowing type into the layout for a fictitious magazine, *Tech*. You will explore a variety of text formatting tools. You will also create styles to easily format the text.

To view the finished project before starting, choose File > Open, navigate to the id03lessons folder, select id0301_done.indd, and then press Open. You can keep the lesson open for reference, or close it by choosing File > Close.

Adding text to your document

Text is almost always contained within a frame. You can use the Type tool, frame tools, or shape tools to draw a frame, then click in the frame using the Type tool to add text. You can also add text that was created using other programs, such as Microsoft Word.

Creating a frame is usually the starting point for adding text to a layout. You'll use the most efficient way to define a new text frame: clicking and dragging with the Type tool.

Creating a text frame

You will start by creating a new text frame and entering text.

1   Choose File > Open. In the Open dialog box, navigate to the id03lessons folder, select the file id0301.indd, then press Open. The document opens to the first page.

     The lower-left section of page 1 has a listing of the stories featured in this issue. You will make a text frame above this box and enter the text, *Inside this issue*.

If the document does not open to page 1, open the Pages panel and double-click on page 1.

2   Choose the Type tool (T) from the Tools panel. Position the cursor directly above the list of stories, then click and drag with the Type tool to define a text frame. Try to make the new frame approximately the same width as the existing text frame below it.

Click and drag with the Type tool to define a frame.

3   Type **Inside this issue:** into the text frame.

If you need to reposition the text frame, choose the Selection tool (↖) from the Tools panel, then click and drag the frame to move it, or use the frame handles to adjust the size of the frame.

When using the Selection tool, you can activate the Type tool (T) by double-clicking on any text frame.

4   Choose File > Save As. In the Save As dialog box, navigate to the id03lessons folder and type **id0301_work.indd** in the Name text field. Press Save.

Changing character attributes

The Control panel at the top of the workspace can be used to adjust the formatting of the text. At the far left of the Control panel there are two buttons: the Character Formatting Controls button (**A**), and, below that, the Paragraph Formatting Controls button (¶).

You can use these buttons to toggle between Paragraph and Character Formatting controls. For this exercise, you will use the Control panel.

You can also use the Character and Paragraph panels to access many of the same controls. Choose Type > Character, or Type > Paragraph.

Changing font and type styles

You'll start by making some basic adjustments to text using the Control panel.

1   Make sure you have the Type tool (T) selected, then click and drag the *Inside this issue:* text to highlight it.

Type must be selected with the Type tool to make most text edits. You can select the frame with the Selection tool and press the Formatting Affects Text button (T) at the bottom of the Tools panel. This works well if you are changing the overall formatting of text.

2 In the Control panel at the top of the workspace, make sure the Character Formatting Controls icon (A) is selected.

The Character Formatting Controls.

3 Press the arrow to the right of the font name to see the drop-down menu listing all the fonts that InDesign is able to access. InDesign has a WYSIWYG (what you see is what you get) font menu, which shows the word *SAMPLE* displayed in the different fonts. Pick any font you'd like, just to see the font change.

The WYSIWYG font menu.

You will now change the text to a different font. Instead of scrolling up and down the list to find a font you already know the name of, you can type it in the font name text field to get to the font more quickly.

4 In the Font drop-down menu in the Control panel, select the text in the Font text field and begin typing **Adobe Garamond Pro**. As soon as you get to the *G* in Garamond, the font name in the list changes; once Adobe Garamond Pro is displayed, press Enter (Windows) or Return (Mac OS). The text is formatted with the new font.

You will now change the type style to bold.

When text is selected, you can sample the appearance of different fonts by clicking to place the cursor in the Font drop-down menu in the Control panel. With the cursor positioned in the font name text field, use the up and down arrows on the keyboard to preview the selected text using different fonts.

5 With the text still selected, locate the Font Style drop-down menu, under the menu where you changed the font in the previous step. Choose Bold from the Font Style drop-down menu. Your type now appears as bold Adobe Garamond Pro. Keep the text selected.

You can use this drop-down menu to set the style of the font, such as bold, italic, or black. InDesign requires that the font style be installed before it will display the style option in the menu. For example, if you have Arial, but you don't have Arial Bold, Bold will not appear in the Font Style drop-down menu, after selecting Arial. This avoids possible problems when printing.

Changing the type style to bold.

Adjusting size

Next you will adjust the size of the selected text.

1 In the Control panel, select the font size (T) and replace it by typing 20 and then pressing Enter (Windows) or Return (Mac OS). The font size increases to 20 points.

2 Choose File > Save to save your work.

Adjusting line spacing

The space between lines of text is known as *leading*. Before computers were used to set type, original letter presses used bars of lead to separate the lines of type, and so the term leading remains, even though it is now only an adjustment made with a click of the mouse.

You will adjust the leading for the list of stories located below the text you were working with in the previous exercise.

1 Using the Type tool (T), click to insert the cursor in the frame listing the stories in this issue. Choose Edit > Select All to select all the text in the frame.

2   In the Control panel, set the Leading (⫴) to 16 by selecting the existing value and typing **16**. Press Enter (Windows) or Return (Mac OS) to set the leading. Keep the text selected.

If you had wanted to set the leading to one of the pre-set choices, you could select these from the drop-down menu.

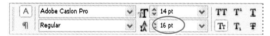

Changing the leading.

Adjusting character spacing: kerning and tracking

You can adjust the space between a group of characters, known as *tracking*, or the space between any pair of characters, known as *kerning*.

1   In the Tracking value (⟨AV⟩) in the Control panel, type **10**, and then press Enter (Windows) or Return (Mac OS) to increase the tracking.

Tracking is measured using a fraction of an em space. A full em space is the width of the letter M of a particular font in a particular size—simply put, an em space varies depending upon the size and font you are using. In this case, the value 10 represents 10/1000ths of an em space.

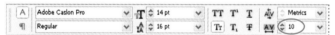

Changing the tracking.

Next you will use the word *Tech* to serve as a logo for the start of the High Tech Corner section. You will kern the letters closer together, and then use baseline shift to further adjust some of the letters.

2   Using the Type tool (T), click between the e and the c in the word *Tech* in the same block of text where you are currently working. The kerning value (⟨AV⟩) just above the Tracking value displays 0. Select the 0 in the Kerning value and then type **–120**, being certain to include the minus symbol to indicate a negative value. Press Enter (Windows) or Return (Mac OS) to set the kerning.

Changing the kerning.

Using a baseline shift

Text sits upon a line that is usually invisible, known as the *baseline*. Baseline shift allows you to change the vertical position of individual characters. This can be useful for fractions or symbols such as trademark or copyright symbols. Here you will use baseline shift to style the text.

1   Select the letters *e* and *c* of the word *Tech* and change their size to 10 using the Font Size drop-down menu in the Control panel.

2   Select only the letter *e* and in the Baseline Shift value (A↕) in the Control panel type **6 pt**, and then press Enter (Windows) or Return (Mac OS). The *e* is shifted upwards, six points off the baseline.

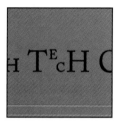

Apply the baseline shift to the letter.

3   Choose File > Save to save your work.

Changing paragraph attributes

You have modified several character attributes that applied only to selected text. Now you will work with paragraph attributes, including text alignment, spacing, and tabs. You will make these adjustments using the paragraph controls section of the Control panel.

Horizontally aligning text

Text generally aligns to the left of a text frame. You can change the alignment so that text aligns to the right side of the frame, is centered, or aligns along both sides of the frame, or have InDesign adjust the alignment depending upon whether the text is on the left or right side of a publication.

1   Press the Pages button (📄) to open the Pages panel. Double-click page 2 to navigate to it, and center this page in the workspace.

2   On page 2, click anywhere in the line of text that reads *Average Cell Phone Usage*. You don't need to highlight the line of text, but simply place the cursor in this line.

3 In the Control panel, press the Paragraph Formatting Controls button (¶) to access the paragraph portion of the Control panel.

The paragraph formatting controls.

4 Press the Align Center button (≣) to align the text to the center of the page. The text is now centered. Keep the cursor in this text.

Changing the spacing before and after paragraphs

Adding space before or after paragraphs makes each paragraph stand out, making a clear transition between ideas or sections.

Next you will adjust all the city names to appear slightly lower than the top line. You will start by placing some extra space after the text *Average Cell Phone Usage.*

1 In the Control panel, locate the Space After text field (.≣), type **.0625**, and then press Enter (Windows) or Return (Mac OS).

2 Choose File > Save to save your work.

Using tabs

Tabs, or tab stops, are often used to align text. Tabs align words based on where you insert a tab by pressing the Tab key on the keyboard. If you have seen a restaurant menu with prices aligned on the right side and a series of periods separating the menu item from the price, you've seen how tabs can be used. Similarly, if you you've looked at a Table of Contents at the start of a book, you've seen how tabs can be used to align the page numbers and separate them from the contents. In this exercise, you will use tabs to separate the city name from the average hours of cellular phone usage.

1 Using the Type tool (T), select all the text in the *Average Cell Phone Usage* text frame by clicking in the text frame and choosing Edit > Select All. When this text was entered, a tab was placed between the city name and the hours.

2 Choose Type > Show Hidden Characters to see the tab, represented by an arrow. Choose Type > Hide Hidden Characters to hide these non-printing characters from view.

3 Choose Type > Tabs to open the Tabs panel. The Tabs panel appears aligned to the top of the selected text frame.

If the Tabs panel is not aligned to the top of the text frame, use the Zoom tool (🔍) to adjust the magnification so that the top of the text frame is visible. After adjusting the magnification, reselect the Type tool, click within the text frame, and select the text. In the right-hand corner of the Tabs panel, click the Position Panel above Text Frame button (🔒). If you move the Tabs panel, press the Position Panel above Text Frame button; the Tabs panel realigns to your text frame. The Position Panel above Text Frame button will position the Tabs panel over the text frame if the entire width of the frame is visible in the display.

Understanding the Tabs panel

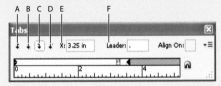

*A. Left-Justified Tab. **B**. Center-Justified Tab. **C**. Right-Justified Tab.*
D. Align to Decimal (or Other Specified Character) Tab.
*E. X text field. **F**. Leader text field.*

There are four ways to align tabs within the Tabs panel. Located at the top left are the Left-Justified Tab (↓), Center-Justified Tab (↓), Right-Justified Tab (↓), and Align to Decimal (or Other Specified Character) Tab (↓) buttons.

Next to the tab button is the X text field. This value represents where the tab sits relative to the ruler. The Leader text field allows you to insert a period, for example, to have leader dots between your tabbed items, as you would find in a Table of Contents or a menu. The Align On text field allows you to set the tab to align on a special character, such as a decimal point for currency or a colon for time. You can also insert and move tabs visually, by clicking to insert them directly above the ruler. The triangles on the left and right sides of the ruler also control the left, right, and first line indents for the active paragraph where the cursor is inserted.

Creating hanging indents

A hanging indent is created when the first line of the paragraph starts at the left margin, but the second and subsequent lines are indented. This is called hanging indentation because the first line hangs out over the rest of the paragraph. To make a hanging indent, make your First line indent a negative value, and the Left indent a positive value.

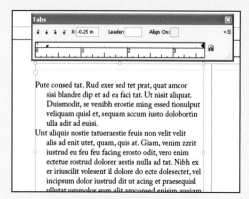

An example of a hanging indent.

4 In the Tabs panel, press the Right-Justified Tab button (↓), then click in the space above the ruler toward the right edge of the tab area. In the selected text, the time values now align to the right of the frame at the location where you placed the tab.

5 With the tab stop you entered in the previous step still selected above the ruler, highlight the X value in the Tabs panel and type **3.25**. Press Enter (Windows) or Return (Mac OS) to set this as the new location for this tab stop. The text is repositioned to this location.

6 With the tab stop still selected in the ruler, type a period into the Leader text field, and then press Enter (Windows) or Return (Mac OS). A series of periods now connect the cities with the time values.

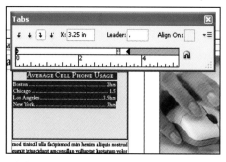

Add leader dots to the listing.

7 Close the Tabs panel, and then choose File > Save to save your work.

Adding rules above or below paragraphs

Rules are lines that you can place above or below a paragraph. You can use rules to separate paragraphs or call attention to headlines. Rules move with the text, and so the rule and the associated text move together. You will add a rule below the words *Average Cell Phone Usage*.

1   Using the Type tool (T), click anywhere inside the text *Average Cell Phone Usage*.

2   Press the panel menu button (-≡) located at the far right side of the Control panel and choose Paragraph Rules from the drop-down menu.

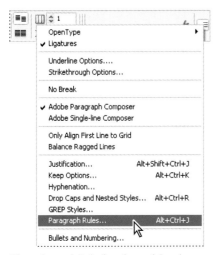

Choose Paragraph Rules from the panel drop-down menu in the Control panel.

3   In the Paragraph Rules dialog box, choose Rule Below from the drop-down menu and select the Rule On check box to enable the rule. Select the Preview check box in the lower-left corner of the dialog box to see the rule applied. Keep the dialog box open.

The line appears and is automatically aligned to the baseline of the text. Next you will examine the offset value, allowing you to move the text vertically.

4   In the Offset text field, make sure the offset value is set to 0.0625. This shifts the line below the baseline. You can use the offset value to move the rule up or down by entering negative or positive values.

5 If necessary, choose Text from the Width drop-down menu so that the line appears only beneath the selected text. Press OK.

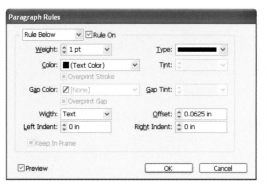
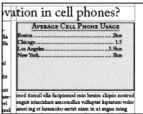

The Paragraph Rules dialog box with the correct settings.

Changing text color

You can change the color of text to make it stand out or appear more visually appealing. When changing text color, you can adjust either the fill or stroke of the text.

1 Using the Type tool (T), select the words *Average Cell Phone Usage*.

2 Press the Swatches button (▦) in the panel docking area to open the Swatches panel. You can also access the Swatches panel by choosing Window > Swatches.

3 In the top-left corner of the Swatches panel, make certain the fill icon (T) is in the foreground. If not, click to select it so that color adjustments affect the fill of the selected object.

The Fill and Stroke controls in the Swatches panel.

4   With the words *Average Cell Phone Usage* still selected, locate the color Blue in the Swatches panel, and then click to select it. The color of the text is changed, as is the rule below the text. The rule changes because the rule was defined to be the same color as the text.

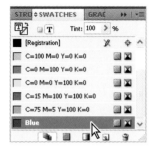

Select the blue swatch in the Swatches panel.

5   Choose File > Save to save your work.

Creating drop caps

Drop caps, or initial caps, help to draw a reader's attention to the start of a story. You will create a drop cap for the beginning of a story on the second page of the magazine.

1   Using the Type tool (T), click anywhere in the first paragraph of the story on page 2. You do not need to highlight the text.

2   In the Paragraph Formatting Controls area of the Control panel (¶), locate the Drop Cap Number of Lines text field (🔤) and change the value to 3. Press Enter (Windows) or Return (Mac OS) to commit the change.

The character *I* now appears as a three-line drop cap.

3   Press the panel menu button (•≡) in the Control panel and choose Drop Caps and Nested Styles.

4 When the Drop Caps and Nested Styles dialog box appears, select the *Preview* check box on the right side to view the changes as they are made. Notice that the *I* is not aligned to the side of the text box. Select the *Align Left Edge* check box to align the *I* to the text box, then press OK. The drop-capped *I* is now aligned against the text frame on the left side.

The drop cap's left edge is aligned to the edge of the text box.

Checking and correcting spelling

Checking spelling is an important part of creating a professional-looking document, and InDesign has several capabilities that can help correct typographical errors or help you identify spelling mistakes.

The Dynamic Spelling and Autocorrect options alert you to misspelled words and can automatically change them for you. In this exercise, you will take a closer look at some of these options, including the ability to find and change words across an entire document or group of documents.

Finding and changing text and text attributes

Let's say you want to change the name *Tech Magazine* in the top folio of each page to be bold. Instead of making the change on each page, you can use Find/Change to modify the formatting of every instance of the word or phrase.

As you learned in InDesign Lesson 2, you could also use a master page to adjust an object with a consistent location on many pages. So there are many time-saving ways to create and modify your layout.

1 Choose the Zoom tool (Q) from the Tools panel and increase the magnification on the top of page 2 so that the words *Tech Magazine* are clearly visible. After the words are visible, switch to the Type tool.

You can also press and hold Ctrl+spacebar (Windows) or Command+spacebar (Mac OS) to temporarily activate the Zoom tool while working with the Type tool.

2   Choose Edit > Find/Change to open the Find/Change dialog box. In the Find/Change dialog box, type **Tech Magazine** in the Find what text field. Next you'll identify the changes to make to this text.

Using Find/Change.

3   In the Change Format text field at the bottom of the Find/Change dialog box, press the Specify Attributes to Change button (⚘). The Change Format Settings dialog box appears.

4   On the left side of the dialog box, choose Basic Character Formats. Select Bold from the Font Style drop-down menu, then press OK. This changes text that meets the Find criteria to bold.

You can also have InDesign search for text based upon style attributes. For example, you could have InDesign locate all text that uses a certain font, style, or color, and have it changed to another style.

5   In the Find/Change dialog box, make sure the Search drop-down menu is set to Document so that the entire document is searched. While you can have InDesign search smaller, more refined areas of a document, here you want to search the entire document.

6   Press Change All. A dialog box appears indicating that the search is complete and that four replacements were made.

7   Press OK to accept the changes, then press Done. All four instances of the words *Tech Magazine* are now bold. If desired, you can scroll or use the Pages panel to navigate to the other pages to confirm the changes.

8   Choose File > Save to save your work.

Checking spelling

InDesign can help you locate misspelled words, repeated words, uncapitalized words, and uncapitalized sentences.

1   Select the Type tool (T) from the Tools panel, then click anywhere in the *What is the next inovation in Cell phones?* headline at the top of page 2.

   The word innovation is intentionally misspelled to help you gain an understanding of the spelling features available within InDesign.

2   Choose Edit > Spelling > Check Spelling. The Check Spelling dialog box appears.

3   Select Story from the Search drop-down menu at the bottom of the dialog box so that only this text frame is searched. A story is a text frame and any linked text frames.

4   *Inovation* is displayed at the top of the dialog box, and listed as not being in the dictionary. The correct spelling of innovation appears in the Suggested Corrections field. Select the correct spelling, innovation, then press Change.

Checking and correcting spelling.

The Start button is available once again, indicating that InDesign has searched the entire story, and that all errors have been corrected.

5   Press Done.

Adding words to the dictionary

You can provide InDesign with a list of common terms, proper names, or industry-specific terms that should be ignored when checking spelling. You can add these words to your dictionary so that InDesign does not indicate that these words are misspelled.

1 In the Pages panel, double-click on page 2 to center the page in the workspace. Using the Type tool (T), insert the cursor at the start of the first paragraph on the top of page 2.

2 Choose Edit > Spelling > Check Spelling.

In the Not in Dictionary section, *Blippa* appears. This is the name of a new product that appears throughout this document.

3 Press Add to place *Blippa* in your user dictionary, and then press Done.

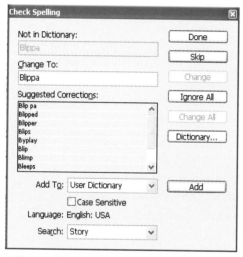

Adding a word to the dictionary.

You can add or remove words from your user dictionary by choosing Edit > Spelling > Dictionary. You can add or remove individual words, or use the Import option to import a list of words to add to the dictionary.

4 Choose File > Save to save your work.

Centralized user dictionary

You can also create a central user dictionary to share with colleagues.

To create and share a dictionary, choose Edit > Preferences > Dictionary (Windows), or InDesign > Preferences > Dictionary (Mac OS). Press the New User Dictionary button (⊒). When the New User Dictionary dialog box appears, name the new dictionary. The location and name of the new dictionary file appear listed under the Language drop-down menu.

After adding your commonly used words to the new dictionary, access the new dictionary file on another user's InDesign program using the Add User Dictionary button (⊕) in their Preferences > Dictionary dialog box.

Checking spelling as you type

Another way to avoid spelling errors is to use InDesign's Dynamic Spelling option, which checks spelling as you type. Words not found in the InDesign dictionaries are marked with a red underline in your layout, as is common in word processing applications such as Microsoft Word.

1   Press the Pages button (⊕) in the dock to open the Pages panel. Locate page 3 and double-click the page 3 icon to center the page in the workspace.

2   Using the Type tool (T), click inside the text frame containing the headline *When is the best time to update equpment?*

3   Choose Edit > Spelling > Dynamic Spelling to activate the Dynamic Spelling feature. A red line appears under the word *equpment*. This may take a moment to occur, as InDesign will review the entire document once Dynamic Spelling is enabled.

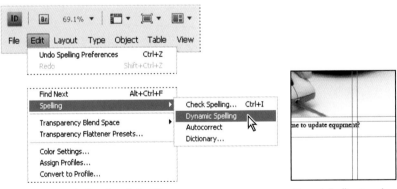

Accessing Dynamic Spelling through the Edit menu.　　　　*Dynamic Spelling turned on.*

4 Right-click (Windows) or Ctrl+click (Mac OS) the word *equpment*. A list of suggested corrections appears in the contextual menu. Choose the word *equipment* from the list, and the misspelled word is corrected.

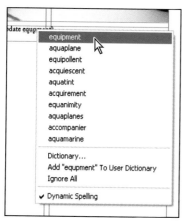

Replacing a word using Dynamic Spelling.

5 Disable Dynamic Spelling by choosing Edit > Spelling > Dynamic Spelling.

Automatically correcting spelling

You can use the Autocorrect feature to correct commonly misspelled words as you type. For example, if you type **hte** when you intend to type **the**, you can have InDesign automatically correct this error as you enter text while typing. You will now enable Autocorrect and add a word to the list of those that are automatically corrected.

1 Using the Pages panel, navigate to page 2 by double-clicking the page 2 icon.

2 Choose Edit > Preferences > Autocorrect (Windows), or InDesign > Preferences > Autocorrect (Mac OS).

3   When the Preferences dialog box appears, select the Enable Autocorrect check box, if it is not already selected.

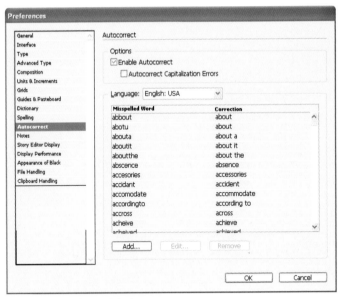

The Autocorrect Preferences dialog box.

4   Press the Add button at the bottom of the dialog box to add your own word to be automatically corrected.

5   In the Add to Autocorrect List dialog box, type **useage** in the Misspelled Word text field, and **usage** in the Correction text field.

This provides InDesign with the incorrect spelling that should be changed and the correct spelling that should be used instead.

Entering a word into Autocorrect.

6   Press OK, then press OK again to close the Preferences dialog box.

7   In the *Average Cell Phone Usage* text frame on page 2, highlight the word *Usage* and delete it from the text frame. You will now re-type this word, intentionally spelling it incorrectly.

8   Type **Useage**, then press the spacebar. The Autocorrect feature corrects the misspelled word. Press the Backspace key to delete the extra space.

Editing text using the Story Editor

In some projects, a story might be spread across several pages. You may find yourself moving from one page to another to edit text, which can distract you from the editing process. When stories are placed across multiple pages, you can use the Story Editor to more easily view all text in one location.

The Story Editor also displays text that does not fit into existing frames, known as *overset text*. Overset text is indicated by a red plus sign that appears at the bottom-right corner of a frame when there is more text than fits into the frame.

1   Using the Type tool (T), click anywhere inside the text frame on page 5 containing the story.

2   Choose Edit > Edit in Story Editor to open the Story Editor window. This allows you to view the entire story across several pages.

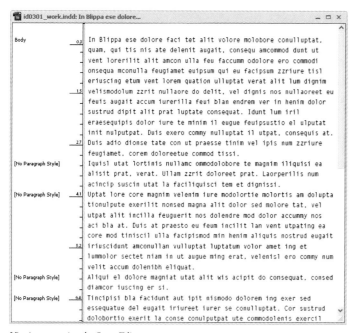

Viewing text using the Story Editor.

3 Use the scroll bar on the right side of the window to navigate to the bottom of the story. The Story Editor allows you to view the overset text.

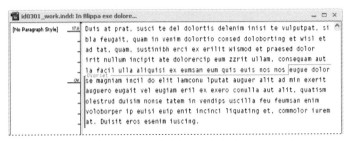

The Story Editor identifies overset text, which does not fit in the current text frames.

4 Highlight from the word eugue to the end of the document and delete the overset text; then close the Story Editor.

In addition to deleting the text, you can also address overset text in a number of ways: For one, make edits to the existing text, creating space for the overset text to move into the existing frames. You can also create more space for the text, either by expanding the existing frames or by linking the text to a new frame, or reduce the size, leading, or tracking of the current text to allow for more text to fit in the same area.

5 Notice that the red plus sign at the end of the text frame has disappeared.

6 Choose File > Save to save your work.

Drag-and-drop text editing

When editing text, it can be faster to use your mouse to relocate text instead of using the menu commands to cut, copy, and paste text. Use drag-and-drop text editing to highlight words or characters, then drag them to a different location. You can use this option in both the Story Editor and in Layout view, although you need to enable it in Layout view, as it is turned off by default.

1 Choose Edit > Preferences > Type (Windows), or InDesign > Preferences > Type (Mac OS).

2   When the Type Preferences dialog box appears, in the Drag and Drop Text Editing section, select the Enable in Layout view check box, and then press OK.

Turning on the Drag and Drop Text Editing option.

3   Click and drag to select the words *cell phone*, without the *s*, in the headline on page 5. With the text selected, click and drag the highlighted words so that they are placed before the word *innovation*. Release the mouse to relocate these words.

4   Delete the word *in* and also the letter *s*. The question mark now follows the word *innovation*.

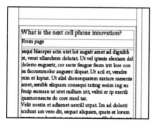

The final text after editing.

5   Choose File > Save to save your work.

Special characters and glyphs

Symbols such as those used for dollars, cents, bullets, copyrights, and registered trademarks can be difficult to insert if you don't remember the appropriate keystrokes.

You can use InDesign's Glyphs panel to see all the characters, known as *glyphs*, within every font. You will work with the Glyphs panel to add a trademark symbol to the words *Tech Magazine*, and you will then use the Find/Change feature to add the symbol to all instances of the name throughout the layout.

1   Choose the Zoom tool (🔍) from the Tools panel and increase the magnification so you can clearly see the words *Tech Magazine* in the top text frame on page 5.

2   Choose the Type tool (T) from the Tools panel and click after the word *Magazine* to insert the cursor.

3   Choose Type > Glyphs to open the Glyphs panel. From the Show drop-down menu, choose Symbols and scroll down until you see the trademark glyph (™).

4   In the Glyphs panel, double-click the trademark symbol to place it after the word *Magazine*.

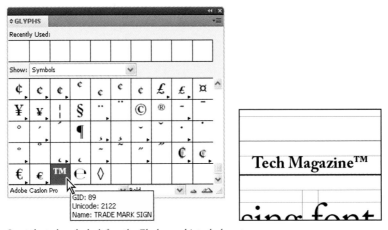

Insert the trademark glyph from the Glyphs panel into the layout.

5   Using the Type tool, highlight the word *Magazine* along with the trademark glyph you just inserted.

6   Choose Edit > Copy to copy these characters.

7   Choose Edit > Find/Change to open the Find/Change dialog box.

8 In the Find what text field, type **Magazine**.

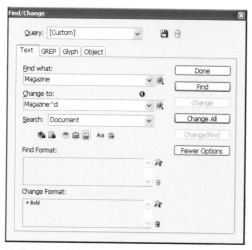

Finding the word Magazine, and changing it to include the trademark symbol.

9 Click inside the Change to text field and choose Edit > Paste. The notation for the symbol is pasted.

10 Press Change All. A dialog box appears indicating that the search is complete and the changes have been made. Press OK.

11 Press Done. All instances of the words *Tech Magazine* now include a trademark symbol.

12 Delete the extra trademark symbol from the Tech Magazine text on page 5, then choose File > Save to save your work.

Using the Glyphs panel and glyph sets

The Glyphs panel also allows you to create a set of commonly used glyphs, making it easy to access the special characters and symbols you use most frequently.

1 In the Glyphs panel, press the panel menu button (·≡), then choose New Glyph Set. In the New Glyph Set dialog box, type Adobe Caslon Pro in the Name text field. Leave the Insert Order drop-down menu at its default, then press OK.

Creating a new glyph set.

2 In the Glyphs panel, select the trademark symbol, if it is not selected. Press the panel menu button and choose Add to Glyph Set; then choose Adobe Caslon Pro from the menu that appears.

3   In the Glyphs panel, click the Show drop-down menu, and choose Adobe Caslon
    Pro from the top of the list. You can add as many glyphs as you like to this glyph set.
    InDesign allows you to add different glyphs from different fonts to a set. You should
    add only those glyphs from one font to each set so that you know you are inserting the
    correct version of a glyph.

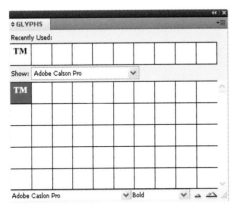

A custom glyph set.

4   Close the Glyphs panel.

Text frame options

InDesign includes options for formatting text frames. These options control the vertical
alignment of type, the distance text is inset from the edge of the frame, and the number of
columns inside the frame. Some of these options are accessible only within the Text Frame
Option dialog box, while others are also accessible in the Control panel. In this exercise, you
will change some of the text frame options for a text frame on page 2.

Adjusting text inset

Inside the *Average Cell Phone Usage* text frame, the text touches the side of the text frame.
Because there is a border on the frame, this looks unappealing, and you will adjust the position
of the text.

1   In the Pages panel, double-click the page 2 icon to center the page on the workspace.

2   Using the Type tool (T), click inside the *Average Cell Phone Usage* text frame on page 2.

3   Choose Object > Text Frame Options to access the Text Frame Options dialog box.

The keyboard shortcut to open the Text Frame Options dialog box is Ctrl+B (Windows) or Command+B (Mac OS).

4 When the Text Frame Options dialog box appears, make sure the Make all settings the same button (⊗) in the Inset Spacing section is selected.

5 In the Top text field, highlight the current value, then type **.125**. Press the Tab key, and the cursor moves to the next text field. Click to select the Preview check box, and the text is inset by .125 inches.

6 Press OK. The text has moved and is no longer touching the sides of the frame. Keep the cursor in the same location for the next part of this lesson.

Setting a text inset.

Vertically aligning text

You can align text inside a frame both horizontally and vertically. With vertical alignment, you determine whether text aligns with the top, bottom, or center of a frame. You can also justify the type so that multiple lines of type are evenly distributed between the top and bottom of a text frame.

1 Choose Object > Text Frame Options.

2 In the Vertical Justification section, choose Justify from the Align drop-down menu.

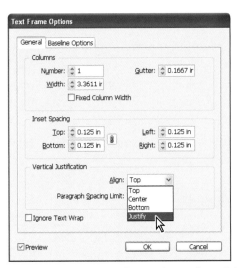

Using text frame options to set the text to be vertically justified.

3 Press OK. Notice that the text now snaps to the top and bottom of the frame. Leading is changed, but the text inset is still retained.

4 Choose File > Save to save your work.

Importing text

There are three ways to flow text into an InDesign document: You can flow text manually, and link the text boxes yourself. You can also flow text semi-automatically, which re-loads your cursor with text. And you can flow text into a document that automatically makes new frames and pages for you.

Flowing text manually

In this first exercise, you will manually flow text and practice threading text between frames.

1 In the Pages panel, locate page 3 and double-click the page 3 icon to navigate to the page, then choose Edit > Deselect all to make certain nothing is selected.

2 Choose File > Place. In the Place dialog box, navigate to the id03lessons folder, select the id0301.doc file, make sure *Show Import Options* is checked, and press Open. The Microsoft Word Import Options dialog box appears.

3 In the Microsoft Word Import Options dialog box, confirm that the *Remove Styles and Formatting from Text and Tables* option is selected, and directly under this option, that Preserve Local Overrides is not checked. Click OK to close the dialog box.

These steps make sure that none of the styles used in the Microsoft Word document accidentally find their way into your document.

If you accidentally flow text into your previously selected frame, choose Edit > Undo.

4 InDesign CS4 displays a preview of the file you are importing. The preview is located inside the loaded cursor. With the cursor loaded with text, you can preview the first few sentences of the text frame being imported. Click just below the headline text frame. Text fills the column.

Flowing text into a column.

You have successfully placed a story in the first column, but there is more type than fits into this frame. You can tell this because of the red plus sign that appears in the bottom-right corner of the text frame. This indicates that there is overset text. In the next exercise, you will thread the text from this frame to another.

Threading text between frames

As you discovered in InDesign Lesson 1, text frames contain two small boxes that let you link text between frames, allowing stories to flow between columns or between pages. At the top-left corner of a text frame is the In Port, and at the bottom-right corner of the text frame is the Out Port. You will be using the Out Port of this text frame to thread it to another frame.

Anatomy of a Text Frame

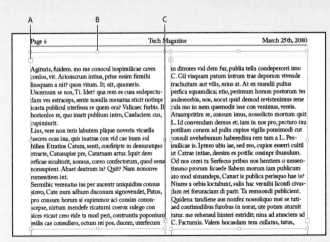

*A. In Port. **B.** Handles for resizing frame. **C.** Out Port.*

The arrow within the In Port or Out Port indicates that text flows from another frame. Choose View > Show Text Threads to display links connected to the selected frame. The arrow shows that text continues in another frame. The Out Port may also display a red plus sign (+), indicating that there is overset text that does not fit in the frame, or it may be empty, indicating that all text fits within this frame.

1. Choose the Selection tool (k) from the Tools panel.

2. Click the red plus sign in the bottom-right corner of the text frame. This is the Out Port, and the red plus sign indicates that there is overset text that does not fit in this frame. After clicking the Out Port, the cursor is ready to link to another text frame so that the story can continue.

The Out Port showing overset text.

3. Move the cursor to the second column, positioning the cursor under the headline. Starting in the top-left side of the column on the right side of the page, click and drag to the bottom-right side of the column. The two text frames are now linked.

4   Choose View > Show Text Threads. InDesign displays the link between the two frames. Choose View > Hide Text Threads to stop displaying the linked frames. Linked frames are visible only when one of the frames in the link is selected.

5   Choose File > Save to save your work.

Using semi-autoflow to link several text frames

Clicking the Out Port to link every text frame is not efficient with longer documents. You can hold down the Alt (Windows) or Option (Mac OS) key when linking or importing text so that you can place text into one frame, then move to the next frame to continue linking. This allows you to link multiple text frames without needing to click the Out Port of each frame.

1   In the Pages panel, double-click the page 4 icon to center the page in the workspace.

2   Choose the Selection tool (▸) from the Tools panel and click anywhere in the pasteboard to make sure that there is nothing selected, or choose Edit > Deselect All.

3   Choose File > Place. In the Place dialog box, navigate to the id03lessons folder and select the id0302.doc file. Deselect the Show Import Options check box, then press Open.

4   With the loaded cursor, press and hold down Alt (Windows) or Option (Mac OS), then click in the first column, just below the headline. Release the Alt or Option key.

    The text flows into the first column and the cursor is automatically loaded, so that you can link this column to another frame without needing to click the Out Port.

5   In the second column, click and drag to draw a new frame below the image of the Data Center Server. The text flows into the new frame.

Linking to an existing text frame

If you have an existing frame that you want to link text into, first click the Out Port in the frame containing the overset text. Then move the cursor over the existing text frame and click anywhere within the frame. This is common if you are linking to frames created on master pages.

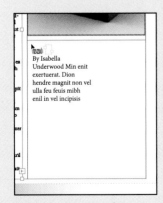

Linking the text to a new frame.

Changing the number of columns in a text frame

You can change the size and shape of a text frame at any time. You will start by making a new text frame, then you will resize it.

1 Choose the Selection tool (⬥). Click to select the column you created in the previous exercise, on the right side of the page below the image. Press the Delete key. The first column displays the symbol for overset text.

2 Continuing to use the Selection tool, click to select the text frame in the first column. Move the cursor to the center handle along the right side of the first column. Click and drag to the right, expanding the size of the column so that it overlaps the picture and extends into the right side of the page.

The text now spans the entire width of the page. You will divide this single text frame into two columns.

3 Choose the Type tool (T) from the Tools panel, then in the Paragraph Formatting Options section of the Control panel, type **2** for the number of columns (▥), then press Enter or Return.

4 Choose Object > Text Frame Options. In the Text Frame Options dialog box, type **.167 in** for the gutter, which sets the distance between the columns. Press OK.

Setting the number of columns and gutter distance.

5 The text does not flow over the image because the image has text wrap applied to it, causing the text to flow around the image. See InDesign Lesson 5, "Working with Graphics," for more on text wrap.

6 Choose File > Save to save your work.

When you automatically flow text, InDesign creates new frames based on where you click inside the margin guides. To flow text automatically, press and hold the Shift key as you place or flow text. InDesign automatically generates enough frames to flow all the text.

Baseline grid

The baseline grid allows you to align text in a layout so that text in various columns has a consistent position on the page. You will view the baseline grid, change the grid settings, and align the text to the baseline grid.

Viewing and changing the baseline grid

1 To view the baseline grid, choose View > Grids & Guides > Show Baseline Grid.

The baseline grid guides may not be visible when viewing the document below 100%.

Viewing the baseline grid.

It is a good idea to create the baseline grid with an increment or line using the same space as the leading of your body copy. You will now change the increment for the baseline grid.

2 Select the Type tool (T) from the Tools panel and click in the body text in either of the columns on page 4.

3 In the Control panel, press the Character Formatting Controls button; notice that the Leading (⟨A⟩) is set to 14.4 pt. You will enter this value inside the Baseline Grid Preferences.

4 Choose Edit > Preferences > Grids (Windows), or InDesign > Preferences > Grids (Mac OS). In the Grids Preferences dialog box, type **14.4 pt** in the Increment Every text field. Press OK to close the Preferences dialog box.

The grid now increments at the same interval as the leading. You will now align the text to the baseline grid.

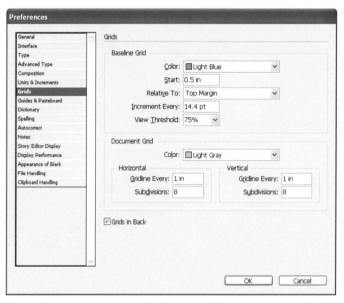

Changing the Increment Every value defines the spacing for the baseline grid.

5 Choose Edit > Select All, then press the Paragraph Formatting Controls button (¶) in the Control panel.

6 In the Control panel, press the Align to Baseline Grid button (≡≡). The selected text in both columns aligns to the baseline grid.

7 Choose View > Grids & Guides > Hide Baseline Grid, then choose File > Save to save your work.

Adding story jumps

If stories continue from one page to another within a document, you will want to direct the reader to the appropriate page where the story continues. If you type in **Please see page**, and then manually enter a page number, there is room for error, especially if the page changes.

You will use a page marker on page 2 showing that the story continues on page 5. There are text frames prepared for you to enter the marker. These frames with the Previous and Next page markers need to touch the linked text frames, and they have already been created for you. You will enter in the marker and see how InDesign displays the linked page information.

1   In the Pages panel, navigate to page 2 by double-clicking the page 2 icon.

2   At the bottom-right corner of the text frame is a small frame containing the text *Please see page*. Select the Type tool (T) from the Tools panel and place the cursor directly after the word *page* in this text frame.

3   Press the spacebar once to put a space between the word *page* and the marker you will insert.

4   Choose Type > Insert Special Character > Markers > Next Page Number. This marker displays the number 5 because the larger text frame it is touching links to page 5. Now you will add the Previous page number to advise the readers where the story originates.

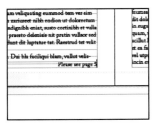

The text frame with the Next Page marker.

5   In the lower-left corner of the workspace, click the page drop-down menu to navigate to page 5. You can use this method or the Pages panel to easily move between pages.

6   Using the Type tool, place the cursor after the word *page* in the *From page* text frame.

7   Press the space bar to put a space between the words and the marker.

8   Choose Type > Insert Special Character > Markers > Previous Page Number. The number 2 appears because the text in the adjacent frame is linked from page 2.

9   Choose File > Save to save your work.

Using styles to format text

Styles save time when you're working with text that shares the same look and feel across a document. If you decide that your body text should be a different size or font, styles let you make the change in one location, avoiding the need to make changes on every page. Additionally, styles make it easy to keep a consistent design, as you can use styles to apply multiple text attributes in a single click.

Creating a headline and applying a style

In this exercise, you will create a style and apply it to a headline.

1   In the Pages panel, double-click the page 2 icon.

2   Select the Type tool (T) from the Tools panel.

3   Highlight the headline *What is the next innovation in cell phones.*

4   Choose Type > Paragraph Styles or click the Paragraph Styles button in the panel docking area. The Paragraph Styles panel opens.

5   Press the panel menu button (·≡) in the upper corner of the Paragraph Styles panel and choose New Paragraph Style. In the Style Name text field, type **Headline**, then press OK.

The new style contains the text attributes from where the cursor was located when you created the new style, including font, style, color, and spacing.

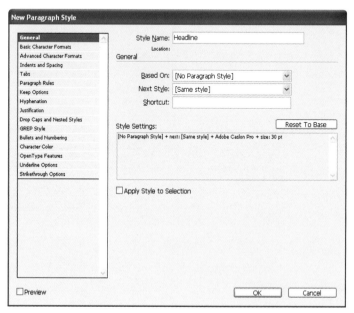

Creating a new paragraph style.

6   Select the Headline style in the Paragraph Styles panel to apply the style to the text. The appearance of the text does not change, but the text is now attached to the style. If the style is updated, the appearance of this headline will also update.

When you create a new style, you can also have InDesign apply it to the current selection. In the General section of the New Paragraph Style dialog box, select the Apply Style to Selection check box.

7   Click to place the cursor in the headline *When is the best time to update equipment?* located on page 3. In the Paragraph Styles panel, select the Headline style to apply it. The headline is formatted with the paragraph style you created.

Importing styles from other documents

You can import styles from one InDesign document to another, making it possible to share formatting across various documents, and keeping your brand identity and style consistent across multiple types of documents. In this exercise, you will import a Drop Cap style from another document and use the style in this document.

1   In the Paragraph Styles panel, press the panel menu button (-≡) and choose Load Paragraph Styles. You will locate a file from which to import a style.

2   In the Open a File dialog box, navigate to the id03lessons folder and select the id0301_done.indd file. Press Open. The Load Styles dialog box appears.

3   In the Load Styles dialog box, press the Uncheck All button to deselect all the styles, because you will only import one specific style. Select the Drop Cap check box to select only this one style.

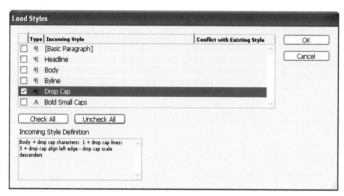

Loading the Paragraph style Drop Cap.

4   Press OK. Drop Cap is now added to the styles in the Paragraph Styles panel in your document. In the next exercise, you will update an existing style, then apply the Drop Cap style.

Redefining styles

You will now update the Body paragraph style to contain a new attribute, which will align the text to the baseline grid.

1   If necessary, navigate or scroll to view page 2.

2   Choose the Type tool (T) and click in the text frame containing the story on page 2; then choose Edit > Select All.

3   Select the Body style in the Paragraph Styles panel to apply this style to all the selected paragraphs.

4 If a plus sign appears next to the style name, press and hold the Alt (Windows) or Option (Mac OS) key and select the style name again. This removes any formatting changes that have been made since the style was applied.

Changes made to text after a style has been applied are known as overrides. If you edit a style attribute outside the Paragraph Styles panel, the style is manually overridden, and a plus sign displays in the related styles panel. If you place your cursor over the style in the Paragraph Styles panel without clicking, and pause, a tooltip appears. The tooltip identifies which attribute is causing the override.

Applying the Body style.

5 In the Paragraph Formatting Controls section of the Control panel, press the Align to Baseline Grid button (≣).

6 A plus sign next to the style name in the Paragraph Styles panel is displayed. This plus sign indicates that the style was changed since it had been applied. You will make this change a part of the style definition, and so all text using this style will include this modification to the style.

7 In the Paragraph Styles panel, click the panel menu and choose Redefine Style. All the text styled with the Body style now aligns to the baseline grid.

Redefining the Body style.

8 Click anywhere in the first paragraph of the story. In the Paragraph Styles panel, click to select the Drop Cap style. The first paragraph is now formatted with the Drop Cap style, and the rest of the story is formatted using the Body style.

9 Choose File > Save to save your work.

Type on a path

Some text can be placed outside of a text frame, and on a path. Text placed on a path can follow a line or shape, such as the outline of a circle.

1 In the Pages panel, double-click page 4 and navigate to the logo at the top of the page. If necessary, increase the magnification to zoom-in on the logo using the Zoom tool ( ).

2 Notice that there is an oval surrounding the word *Tech* in this logo. The logo should read *High Tech Corner*. You will place the word *High* on the oval.

3 Click and hold the Type tool (T) in the Tools panel until the hidden tools are revealed, then choose the Type on a Path tool ( ).

4 Move your cursor over the top center of the oval until you see a plus sign appear next to the cursor, then click once.

The cursor changes to indicate that you are able to place text on the path.

5 Type **HIGH**, then highlight the text using the Type on a Path tool by clicking and dragging or double-clicking to select the word.

6 In the Paragraph Formatting Controls section of the Control panel, press the Align Center button ( ). You will adjust the exact position of the text in the next steps, as the text is likely upside-down along the bottom of the circle.

7 Choose the Selection tool ( ) from the Tools panel. Notice that there are two vertical handles that appear directly to the left of where you clicked on the path. These handles mark the starting and ending points for the text on the path.

8 Select the left-most line and drag it clockwise, stopping when the line is vertically centered along the right half of the oval. If the text moves inside the oval, choose Edit > Undo and repeat the process, carefully following the oval as you drag counterclockwise. Be careful to not click the boxes when you move the handles, as these boxes are the In and Out Ports, which are used for flowing text, as you learned earlier in this lesson.

9   Take the top line that marks where the text starts, and drag it counter-clockwise, positioning it so it is vertically centered along the left half of the oval.

Because you had already centered the text, aligning the start and end points of the text to the opposite sides of the circle lets you know that the text is centered correctly.

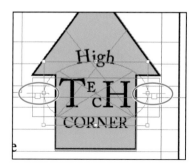

The new start and end points of the text.

10   Choose File > Save to save your work.

Importing text from Microsoft Word

When flowing a Microsoft Word document into InDesign, the default setting, Remove all Styles and Formatting from Text and Tables, automatically eliminates all the styles applied to the file in Word. The text comes into your document using the style set in the Paragraph Styles panel.

1   Navigate to page 6 in the document.

2   Choose File > Place. In the Place dialog box, navigate to the id03lessons folder and select the id0302.doc file. Select the Show Import Options check box, which is located toward the bottom of the Place dialog box, then press Open. The Microsoft Word Import Options dialog box opens.

The Show Import Options and Replace Selected Item check box.

 To open the Import Options dialog box automatically when opening a file, hold down the Shift key while you press Open.

3   In the Microsoft Word Import Options dialog box, select the Preserve Styles and Formatting from Text and Tables radio button. This maintains styles and other text formatting in the imported file. Also select the Customize Style Import radio button.

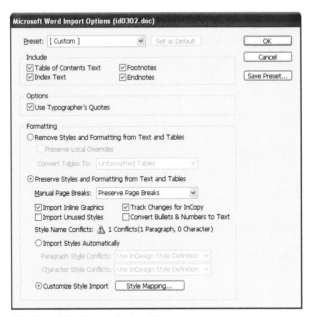

The Microsoft Word Import Options dialog box.

About Microsoft Word import options

Any Table of Contents text, index text, footnotes, and endnotes can be brought from Microsoft Word into InDesign. By default, the Use Typographer's Quotes option is checked, which changes all quotes to typographer's (curly) quotes. This means that every inch and foot mark quote will be converted as well.

If the Remove Styles and Formatting from Text and Tables radio button is selected, all text will be imported and formatted using the Basic Paragraph style for that document. If you want to keep all the character attributes that were applied in Word, select the Preserve Local Overrides check box.

If you select the Preserve Styles and Formatting from Text and Tables radio button, the styles created in Word are imported into your document, and the text adopts the imported styles, trying to mimic the styles from Word. However, if you create a template in Word that contains styles named the same as the styles in your InDesign document, there will be paragraph style conflicts upon importing, and the imported text uses InDesign's style definition by default. This means that, regardless of how text looked in Word, once imported into InDesign, the text is formatted with InDesign's styles if the Word document and the InDesign document have styles with the same names.

4 Press the Style Mapping button at the bottom of the dialog box, next to the Customize Style Import radio button. The Style Mapping dialog box appears.

Microsoft Word Import Options should show that the Body and Byline styles from the Word document have mapped to the InDesign styles with the same names. Identically named styles are automatically mapped when using the Style Mapping option.

5 The dialog box shows that the Microsoft Word style *Normal* is mapped to a style in this InDesign document. Next to Normal, select the New Paragraph Style and choose Basic Paragraph style from the drop-down menu. This causes the text in the Word document that uses the style Normal to be formatted using the Basic Paragraph style once it is imported into InDesign.

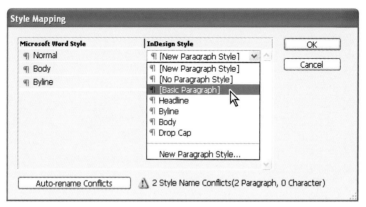

Mapping styles.

6 Press OK to close the Style Mapping dialog box. Press OK again to accept the Microsoft Word Import Options. The cursor is loaded with text that is ready to be placed with already applied paragraph styles.

7 Click in the left column on page 6 to place the text.

Missing fonts

Fonts, like graphics, are not embedded within an InDesign document. If you receive an InDesign document from a colleague, you need the same fonts that they used when creating the document. In this exercise, you will import text from a Microsoft Word document that uses a font that you probably do not have on your computer, and you will fix the font errors that occur as a result of the font not being available.

By default, InDesign highlights missing fonts in pink to alert you to the fact that the font being displayed is not the same as what was used when the text was originally formatted.

Finding and fixing missing fonts

1 In the Pages panel, double-click the page 5 icon to navigate to it.

2 Select the Type tool (T) in the Tools panel.

3 Click inside the empty text frame at the top of page 5.

4 Choose File > Place. In the Place dialog box, navigate to the id03lessons folder and select the id0303.doc file. Select the Show Import Options check box if it is not selected, then press Open.

5 Confirm the Preserve Styles and Formatting from Text and Tables radio button is selected. Press OK.

The Missing Font dialog box appears because you do not have the font Futura Bold installed on your computer.

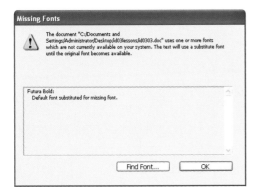

The Missing Font dialog box.

6 Press the Find Font button. The Find Font dialog box opens. Highlight the font Futura Bold by clicking on it in the Fonts in Document section. Notice the warning icon (⚠) next to the font name. This indicates that the font is missing.

7 In the Replace with section at the bottom of the dialog box, highlight the text in the Font Family text field and type **Adobe Caslon Pro**. You are going to replace Futura Bold with Adobe Caslon Pro Regular. If you do not have Adobe Caslon Pro Regular, you may use another font that is available on your computer.

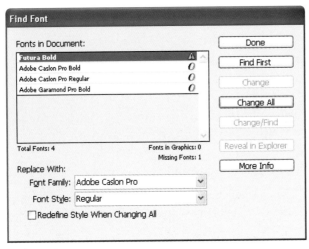

Replacing a font.

8 Press Change All. To see the missing font replaced, press Done.

9 Choose File > Save to save your work, then choose File > Close.

Congratulations! You have completed the lesson.

Self study

1 Starting on page 1, navigate though the document and apply styles to all text, including body, byline, drop cap, and headline.

2 Change the color of the body text and redefine the style.

3 Use the Selection tool (⬉) to select the story jump, the jump frame, and the frame in which it's located. Create a new page at the end of the document and drag the frames to the new page. Return to page 2 and see if the story jump automatically updates.

4 Make a new headline box on page 7 and type in a fictitious headline. Format the headline using the headline style as a starting point. You may need to adjust the size depending on how many words you enter.

Review

Questions

1   If you have a font that doesn't have the style of italic, can you make it italic?

2   Can you flow text into an existing frame?

3   Can you divide one text frame into multiple columns?

4   How can you add Previous and Next Page Markers?

5   Should you ignore missing font warnings?

Answers

1   No, you cannot create a false italic using InDesign. You need the actual font with the italic style to make this change, which is also true for other styles, including bold or outline.

2   Yes, you can flow text into existing frames, including frames that already contain text.

3   Yes, you can have many columns in a single frame. Make column adjustments in the Control panel or by choosing Object > Text Frame Options.

4   Choose Type > Insert Special Characters > Markers or use the context menus when entering the text.

5   No, you should always address warnings relating to missing fonts. Either locate and install the font onto your computer, or reassign the missing font to a similar font that is available using your computer.

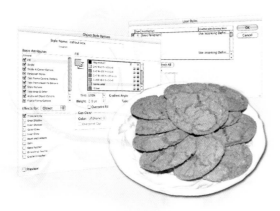

What you'll learn in this lesson:

- Defining and applying paragraph, character, and object styles

- Using nested styles

- Globally updating styles

- Loading styles from another document

- Using Quick Apply

- Organizing styles into groups

Working with Styles

Styles streamline the formatting of text and objects, making it easier to create a consistent design across text and objects. Styles also help simplify adjustments, as you can change a style and update all items that use the style.

Starting up

Before starting, make sure that your tools and panels are consistent by resetting your preferences. See "Resetting the InDesign workspace and preferences" on page XXVII.

You will work with several files from the id04lessons folder in this lesson. Make sure that you have copied the id04lessons folder onto your hard drive from the Digital Classroom DVD. See "Loading lesson files" on page XXIX. This lesson may be easier to follow if the id04lessons folder is on your desktop.

See Lesson 4 in action!

Use the accompanying video to gain a better understanding of how to use some of the features shown in this lesson. The video tutorial for this lesson can be found on the included DVD.

The project

You will discover how styles simplify the design process by using them to enhance the look of a two-page recipe layout. You will work with paragraph, character, and object styles.

Creating styles adds a bit of work at the start of a project, but the planning saves an enormous amount of time and effort as you design and format your document. If you need to make changes, styles make it a quick and easy process.

You will also discover how to import styles from other documents, allowing you to re-use design work done in other documents, or keep a consistent identity across multiple files. You will also learn how to organize your styles using style sets, along with techniques for quickly applying styles.

Style types

There are several types of styles you can use when designing and formatting your documents: these include paragraph, character, and object, as well as table and cell styles. Each type of style applies to a different page element. All these style types speed up the process of formatting and changing the appearance of text and page elements, especially when creating larger documents.

- **Paragraph styles** define text attributes that affect an entire paragraph of text, including line spacing (leading), indents, and alignment. They may also include character attributes, and apply to an entire paragraph. These styles are used for things like headlines or body copy.

- **Character styles** contain only character formatting attributes, such as typeface, size, and color. These attributes apply only to selected text. These styles are used for things such as proper names that are formatted uniquely, or technical terms that might have a different style to call attention to them within a document.

- **Object styles** apply to page elements such as boxes and lines in a layout. Sidebars or picture frames can use object styles to make them consistent.

- **Table and Cell styles** apply to various portions of a table. This lesson is focused primarily on using paragraph, character, and object styles.

InDesign includes only one style for each style type, so you will create customized style definitions for your documents. Once you create styles, you can import them into other documents, allowing you to define the formatting one time and re-use it across multiple files. You can even define the styles to be available for all future documents you create.

Paragraph styles

Paragraph styles generally include both character and paragraph attributes. When you apply a paragraph style to text, all text within a paragraph is formatted. With one click you can use a paragraph style to specify the font, size, alignment, spacing, and other attributes used in the paragraph. In this lesson, you'll start by defining the style, and then you'll apply it to text.

Defining a paragraph style

When building styles, it is useful to see what the style will look like when it is applied. You can format a paragraph, and then use the formatting as the foundation for an InDesign paragraph style. You'll start by building a paragraph style for the body text used in a cookie recipe.

1 Choose File > Open. In the Open dialog box, navigate to the id04lessons folder and select the id0401.indd file. Press Open. A two-page spread from a cookbook opens, displaying pages 72 and 73 as noted in the pages panel and in the bottom left corner of the workspace.

2 Choose Advanced from the workspace drop-down menu, or choose Window > Workspace > Advanced, to display the panels and menu options used in this lesson.

3 Choose File > Save As. In the Save As dialog box, navigate to the id04lessons folder and type **id0401_work.indd** in the Name text field. Press Save.

4 Press the Paragraph Styles button in the dock on the right side of the workspace to open the Paragraph Styles panel. The styles used in this document are listed. This document contains four styles: basic paragraph and callout large, along with two recipe-specific styles, rec_steps and rec_yield.

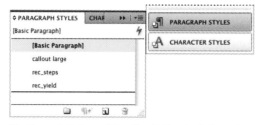

The Paragraph Styles panel lists all available styles for formatting paragraphs.

5 Select the Type tool (T) from the Tools panel. Position the cursor over the first paragraph of text located in the middle column on the left-hand page. The paragraph starts with the text, *The smell of fresh baked cookies...* Click four times to select the entire paragraph.

6   Press the Character Format Controls button (**A**) in the top left corner of the Control panel, located at the top of the workspace to display the character options. Choose Minion Pro from the Font drop-down menu, and, if necessary, choose Regular from the Font Style drop-down menu. Set the size to 10 points from the Font Size drop-down menu.

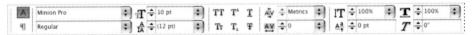

Setting the character formatting options in the Control panel.

7   Press the Paragraph Formatting Controls button (¶) in the Control panel to display the paragraph formatting options, and type **0.2** in the First Line Left Indent (⁺≣) field. Press Enter (Windows) or Return (Mac OS) to indent the paragraph by 0.2 inches.

*In the paragraph formatting options section, type **0.2** in the First Line Left Indent text field.*

8   With the paragraph still selected, press the panel menu button (•≡) in the upper-right corner of the Paragraph Styles panel and choose New Paragraph Style.

Use the Paragraph Styles panel menu to create a new style.

9   The New Paragraph Style dialog box appears. In the New Paragraph Style dialog box, type **body** in the Style Name text field, click to select the Apply Style to Selection check box, and then press OK to establish the name of the new style. The body style is added to the list of styles in the Paragraph Styles panel.

     Choosing the *Apply Style to Selection* option also links the selected text to the new style. If the style is updated, the original text will reflect any formatting changes.

10 Save the file by choosing File > Save.

Applying a paragraph style

You will now apply this new paragraph style to text in the document. To format a single paragraph, use the Type tool to place the cursor within the paragraph, then choose the paragraph style from the Paragraph Styles panel. To format multiple paragraphs, select them and then select the style you want to apply.

1   With the cursor still within the recipe, choose Edit > Select All, or use the keyboard shortcut Ctrl+A (Windows) or Command+A (Mac OS), to select all the text in the frame.

2   In the Paragraph Styles panel, select the body style to apply the style to all selected text. The entire recipe now uses the same character and paragraph formatting as the initial paragraph you formatted.

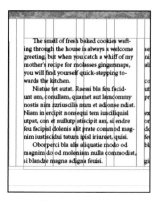

Format all the text within the text frame with the body style.

Character styles

Building character styles is similar to creating paragraph styles. You'll start by formatting text, then you'll define the character style based upon the attributes of the text you have formatted. Character styles affect only character attributes, such as font and point size. Character styles are typically used for words that need special treatment, such as bold, italics, or a unique font, and only apply to selected text.

Defining a character style

On the right page of the document (page 73), you will make the text bold at the start of each step. You'll format the first two steps, and then define a style to apply to the others.

1   Using the Type tool (T), highlight the word *Create* under the Yield section on page 73 of the recipe layout.

2   Press the Character Format Controls button (**A**) in Control panel, then choose Bold from the Font Style drop-down menu. Keep the text selected.

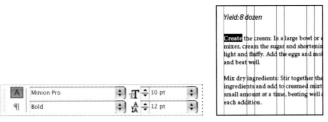

Use the character portion of the Control panel to set the type style.

3   Press the Character Styles button (A) in the dock on the right side of the workspace to open the Character Styles panel.

4   With the bold text still highlighted on the page, press the panel menu button (·≡) in the upper-right corner of the Character Styles panel, and choose New Character Style.

5   In the New Character Style dialog box, type **rec_steps_bold** in the Style name field. Press OK to create a new style. The new style name appears in the Character Styles panel.

6   Choose File > Save to save your work.

Applying a character style

Applying character styles is similar to applying paragraph styles. Highlight the text you want to format, then click the style name to apply the style.

1   On page 73 of the layout, highlight *Create the cream:*.

2   In the Character Styles panel, select the style rec_steps_bold to apply the new style to the selected text.

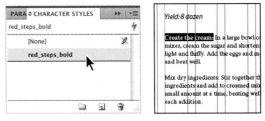

Apply the character style.

3   Highlight the phrase *Mix dry ingredients:* and apply the rec_steps_bold style by selecting it in the Character Styles panel.

Using nested styles

Nested styles combine character styles with paragraph styles, allowing you to apply both character and paragraph styles in a single step. For example, you can use a nested style to make the first word of an introductory paragraph bold and blue, while the rest of the paragraph is regular and black.

You will modify one of the paragraph styles so it also includes a character style for the initial portion of the paragraph, creating a nested style.

1 With the Type tool (T), click in the bottom paragraph on the right page, which starts with the text *Bake in oven*. If the Paragraph Styles panel is closed, click the Paragraph Styles button to open it, or choose Type > Paragraph Styles.

2 In the Paragraph Styles panel, double-click on the rec_steps style to open the Paragraph Style Options dialog box.

3 Select the *Drop Caps and Nested Styles* option along the left side of the Paragraph Style Options dialog box, then press the New Nested Style button.

4 In the Nested Styles section's drop-down menu, choose rec_steps_bold.

5 Click to select *Words* next to *Through 1*, located to the right of the rec_steps_bold style you added in the Nested Styles section of the dialog box. In the text field that appears, change *Words* to **:** by pressing the Colon key.

The rec_steps_bold style will apply to all text up to, and including, the colon (:). You can define where nested styles stop, or you can string together multiple nested styles so that different list entries can be formatted automatically.

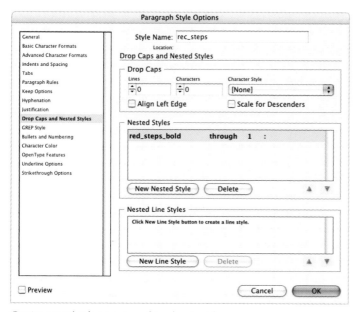

Creating a nested style automates applying character styles.

If you do not replace Words with a colon, only the first word of the recipe step will be bold.

6 Click the *Preview* check box in the lower-left corner of the dialog box to view the changes in your document. If necessary, reposition the dialog box to view your page.

7 Press OK to close the dialog box, then choose File > Save to save your work. Keep the file open for the next part of the lesson.

Globally updating styles

As you have seen, styles make it easier to apply consistent formatting to your text. You have seen how to apply multiple attributes to text in a single click. Styles also save time when you need to change or update formatting. You can modify a style definition and automatically update all text that is associated with a style. You will change the size of the recipe steps. By making a single update, all text using the rec_steps style will be updated. While you are working with two pages, the same time-saving technique works just as easily on documents with hundreds of pages.

1 Make certain the cursor is still in the bottom paragraph on the right page, which starts with the text *Bake in oven.*

2 In the Paragraph Styles panel, the rec_steps paragraph style should be highlighted, indicating that the style is applied to the paragraph where the cursor is positioned. Double-click the style to open the Paragraph Style Options dialog box.

3 Click to select Basic Character Formats on the left side of the Paragraph Style Options dialog box.

4 Choose 11 points from the Size drop-down menu, and then choose Auto from the Leading drop-down menu to change the vertical line spacing.

5 Select the *Character Color* option along the left side of the dialog box, and then choose *cookie color* from the list of available colors.

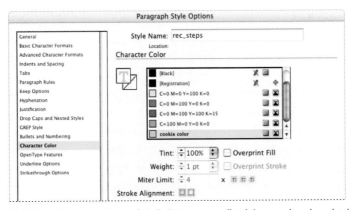

Updating attributes in the Paragraph Style Options causes all styled paragraphs to be updated.

6 If necessary, click the *Preview* check box in the lower-left corner to see the changes in the document as you make them.

7 Press OK to commit the changes and close the dialog box. All text formatted with the rec_steps style has been changed.

The updated text after the paragraph style is changed.

Loading styles from another document

After you create a style, you can use it in other InDesign documents. This lets you reuse your work in other files, keeping their appearance consistent, or simply saving time. The Paragraph Styles and Character Styles panel menus both include an option to load text styles from other documents. Here you will import previously created styles used in another recipe.

In this exercise, you'll import some new styles into the gingersnaps recipe as practice.

1 With the document open, choose Load All Text Styles from the Paragraph Styles panel menu (-≡). The Open a File dialog box appears.

In cases when you only want to use paragraph or character styles, you can choose to load only these styles by selecting either Load Paragraph Styles or Load Character Styles from the respective panel menus. For this example, you will continue to load all styles.

2 In the Open a File dialog box, choose the file id0402.indd from the id04lessons folder. This is the document from which you'll import the styles. Press Open, and the Load Styles dialog box appears.

To see the entire contents of the Load Styles dialog box, you may need to click and drag the lower-right corner until all the options are visible.

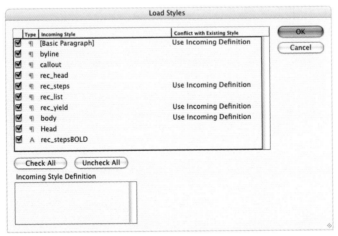

The Load Styles dialog box appears after selecting a document from which you want to import styles.

 If you want to import styles that use the same name as existing styles in your document, the Load Styles dialog box lets you choose how to handle the conflicting names. The Use Incoming Definition causes the imported style definition to be used. The Auto-Rename causes the imported style to be renamed, allowing you to use both the existing and imported styles. Click the words Use Incoming Definition to see the drop-down list you can change it to the Auto-Rename option. The Incoming Style Definition box below each style's name displays the highlighted style's definition for easy comparison.

3 Press the Uncheck All button, as this deselects all the styles in the Load Styles dialog box. Select the rec_head, rec_list, and Head styles by clicking the check box next to each respective style.

You can import all the styles in a document or only a few. By deselecting certain styles, you prevent them from being imported into your document.

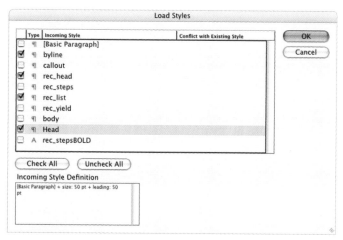

Check the styles you want to import into your document.

4 Press OK to close the Load Styles dialog box. The Paragraph Styles panel now includes the imported styles rec_head, rec_list, and Head, which can be used in this document.

5 Choose File > Save to save your work.

Quick Apply

As your list of styles grows, navigating to find a specific style can be time-consuming. If you perform editing work, you'll appreciate the ability to efficiently apply styles using Quick Apply. Using a special key command, you'll type the first few letters of a style's name and be able to quickly apply the style.

1 Using the Type tool (T), click in the *Molasses Won't Slow Eating These Gingersnaps* text box at the top of the left page.

2 Press Ctrl+Enter (Windows) or Command+Return (Mac OS) to open the Quick Apply window.

You can also use the Quick Apply button (⚡) located in the upper-right corner of the Paragraph Styles, Character Styles, or Control panels.

3 Type **hea** in the window's search field. The Head style appears at the top of the list. Press the Enter (Windows) or Return (Mac OS) key on your keyboard to apply the style to the text. The Quick Apply window closes.

Because paragraph styles format an entire paragraph, you don't have to highlight the text. Simply click in the paragraph, then apply the paragraph style.

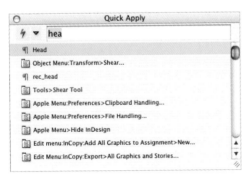

The Quick Apply window makes applying styles faster and easier.

4 Click in the box at the top of the right page, placing the cursor within the phrase *Cookie Color*.

5 Press the Quick Apply button in the Control panel and type rec in the text field. Three styles starting with rec appear in the list. If necessary, use the arrow keys on your keyboard to highlight the rec_head style if it isn't already highlighted, then press Enter (Windows) or Return (Mac OS) to apply the style.

You can use Quick Apply to apply styles and to access many commands. Use Quick Apply to access commands even if you have forgotten the menu or panel where the command is located— you need to know only the name of the command you want to access.

6 Click in the paragraph below *Cookie Color*. Press the Quick Apply button or use the keyboard command, Ctrl+Enter (Windows) or Command+Return (Mac OS), and type the letter **c** in the text field. Select the callout large style, then press Enter (Windows) or Return (Mac OS) to apply the callout large style to the text.

Applying the callout large style to the text.

7 Choose File > Save to save your work.

Organizing styles into groups

Another way to work more efficiently with a large number of styles is to organize them into groups. You can show or hide the contents of style groups, making it easier to locate the styles you need. Here you will organize the recipe's rec styles into a group.

1 Choose Edit > Deselect All to make sure nothing in the document is selected.

If the Deselect option is disabled, you have nothing selected and can proceed to the next step.

2 In the Paragraph Styles panel, click the rec_steps style to select it. Press and hold the Ctrl (Windows) or Command (Mac OS) key and select the remainder of the rec paragraph styles.

You may need to expand the panel to see all the styles. You can expand the panel by clicking and dragging the lower-right corner of the panel.

3 Press the Paragraph Styles panel menu button (‑≣). Choose New Group From Styles to create a new group from the selected styles. The New Style Group dialog box appears.

4   In the New Style Group dialog box, type **recipe** in the Name text field, then press OK. The group folder now appears open in the Paragraph Styles panel.

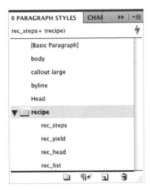

All recipe styles are now grouped within the recipe folder.

You can also manually drag styles into a group, and you can create subgroups, which are groups within groups.

5   Click the arrow next to the recipe style group to hide the styles in the group, then click it again to display the styles.

6   Choose File > Save to save your work.

Object styles

You'll now look at the overall layout of the document and work with object styles. Object styles apply to frames, lines, and other graphic elements. Object styles can include paragraph styles, but they apply to an entire frame, not just text, and can apply background color, borders, and effects such as drop shadows.

Defining an object style

In this exercise, you'll format the frame surrounding the Cookie Color text on the right side of the layout, then use this formatting as the foundation for an object style.

1   Choose the Selection tool (⬉) from the Tools panel, then click to select the Cookie Color frame on the right side of the layout.

2   Choose Object > Text Frame Options. In the Text Frame Options dialog box, type **0.125 in.** for the Top Inset Spacing and press the tab key on your keyboard. Make sure the Make all settings the same button (⬤) to the right of the Top and Bottom text fields is selected, automatically applying the same value to the Bottom, Left, and Right fields. Keep the dialog box open for the next step in this exercise.

3 In the Vertical Justification section of the Text Frame Options dialog box, choose Center from the Align drop-down menu to center the text vertically within the frame. Press OK to apply the formatting.

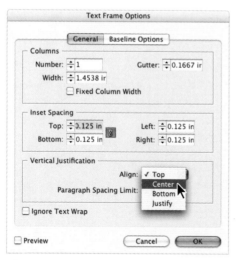

The Text Frame Options dialog box lets you format your objects.

4 Press the Object Styles button in the dock on the right side of the workspace or choose Window > Object Styles to open the Object Styles panel.

You can click and drag the bottom-right corner of the Object Styles panel to display more of the available styles.

5 With the Cookie Color frame still selected, press the Object Styles panel menu button (-≡) and choose New Object Style. The New Object Style dialog box opens.

6   In the New Object Style dialog box, type **callout box** in the Style Name text field and click the *Apply Style to Selection* check box.

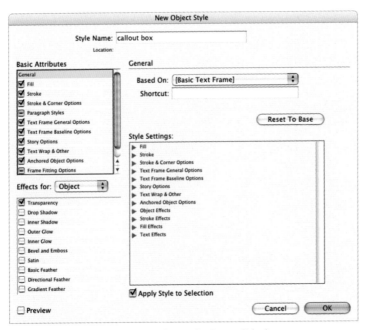

Name your new object style in the New Object Styles Options dialog box.

7   Press OK to create the new object style, then choose File > Save to save your work. Keep the file open.

Applying an object style

Applying an object style is similar to applying text styles. You start by selecting the object to be formatted, then choose the style to apply to the object. You will apply the callout box style to another frame in the layout.

1   Using the Selection tool (k), select the frames containing the headline and byline on the left page of the layout.

2   Apply the callout box style to the frame by clicking the style in the Object Styles panel.

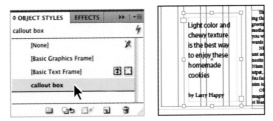

Applying the object style to the text frame containing the headline and byline.

3   Choose File > Save, or press Ctrl+S (Windows) or Command+S (Mac OS), to save
    your work.

Changing an object style

As with text styles, when you change an object style's definition, you update all elements to
which the style is applied. You will update the object style by changing the background color of
the frames.

1   With the headline and byline frames still selected, double-click the callout box style
    name in the Object Styles panel to open the Object Styles Options dialog box.

2   In the Basic Attributes section, select the Fill option. The available color swatches for this
    document appear in the Fill section.

3   Choose the swatch named cookie color to add it to the callout box object style. You may
    need to scroll through the swatches list to see this color.

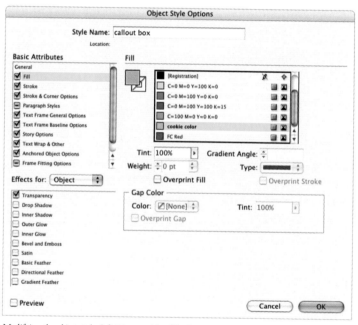

Modifying the object style definition to add a fill color.

4   Press OK. Both frames now reflect the changes to the background color.

Finishing up

As a review, you'll import some more styles and review the process of applying them to your document.

1 With the id0401_work.indd document open, choose Load All Text Styles from the Paragraph Styles panel menu. The Open a File dialog box appears.

2 In the Open a File dialog box, choose the file id0402.indd from the id04lessons folder. Press Open, and the Load Styles dialog box appears.

3 In the Load Styles dialog box, select only the styles named callout and byline to import these into your document. Press OK to close the dialog box and import the styles.

4 Choose the Type tool (T) from the Tools panel, then click and drag to select the ingredients on the right side of the document, selecting from sugar through cinnamon. In the Paragraph Styles panel, click to apply the paragraph style rec_list to the ingredients.

5 Click to place the cursor within the words *Molasses Gingersnaps* located above the ingredients; then click the rec_head style in the Paragraph Styles panel to apply the style to this text.

6 Click and place the cursor within the words by Larry Happy, then click the byline style to apply it to this text.

7 Choose File > Save to save your work, then choose File > Close.

Congratulations, you have finished this lesson.

Self study

To practice creating styles, create your own layout using your favorite family recipes. Import the styles from this lesson and apply them to the text and frames in your own recipes. Import the object styles as well.

Review

Questions

1 What is the difference between character and paragraph styles?

2 What is a nested style and why is it used?

3 What is the keyboard shortcut to access the *Quick Apply* option?

4 If there are multiple styles in a document and scrolling becomes tedious, how can you organize the styles?

Answers

1 Paragraph styles apply to all text between paragraph returns, while character styles apply only to selected text. Character styles do not include paragraph attributes such as indenting or line spacing.

2 A nested style is a paragraph style that also includes one or more character styles that format the initial portion of a paragraph style. Nested styles allow you to combine multiple formatting steps into a single click.

3 Ctrl+Enter (Windows) or Command+Return (Mac OS).

4 Style groups allow you to group together styles and determine which styles are displayed or hidden.

What you'll learn in this lesson:

- Adding graphics to your layout

- Managing links to imported files

- Updating changed graphics

- Using graphics with clipping paths and alpha channels

Working with Graphics

Graphics add depth and style to your documents. Use InDesign's powerful controls to place and enhance graphics using most common file formats, including the ability to integrate images from Adobe Illustrator and Photoshop.

Starting up

Before starting, make sure that your tools and panels are consistent by resetting your preferences. See "Resetting the InDesign workspace and preferences" on page XXVII.

You will work with several files from the id05lessons folder in this lesson. Make sure that you have copied the id05lessons folder onto your hard drive from the Digital Classroom DVD. See "Loading lesson files" on page XXIX. This lesson may be easier to follow if the id05lessons folder is on your desktop.

See Lesson 5 in action!

Use the accompanying video to gain a better understanding of how to use some of the features shown in this lesson. The video tutorial for this lesson can be found on the included DVD.

The project

In this lesson, you will work with graphics for a fictional travel magazine called *SoJournal*, adding graphics to the layout using different techniques. You will learn how to resize graphics, precisely change positioning, display quality, and wrap text around graphics. You will also learn how to manage graphics that have been updated, replaced, or are missing.

Understanding how InDesign handles graphics

When you place graphics into an InDesign layout, the graphic file remains a separate file. The imported images or illustrations are not embedded into the InDesign document, so both the separate graphic files and the InDesign document are necessary for printing, archiving, or sharing your document with collaborators who might need to otherwise manipulate the original file. InDesign keeps track of graphic files used in your InDesign documents using the Links panel, as image files are considered to be linked. This is different from text files that are imported from programs like Microsoft Word or Excel. Text files are placed into the InDesign layout, and the original file is no longer needed to manipulate the text. For every rule there are exceptions, and graphic files can be embedded within an InDesign layout—although this is generally not advisable because it increases the size of the InDesign document and limits the ability to share a graphic for use in other media, such as on the Web or as part of an interactive campaign.

You'll start this lesson by opening a document with images that have been imported, but InDesign can no longer locate the files. You will help InDesign locate the missing image files.

Locating missing images

If an image is renamed or moved from its original location after you import it into an InDesign file, InDesign loses the link to the image. Likewise, if you copy an InDesign document to a different computer, and don't take the images, InDesign will alert you that linked files are missing.

You'll use the Links panel to reconnect the InDesign layout with a missing image. In the Links panel, missing links display a red warning icon (●) next to their names, and links that have been updated or edited since they were originally placed in the layout display a yellow warning icon (△), indicating the original image has been modified. In this exercise, you will fix a link that was broken because the associated files were moved, and also fix a link to a graphic in the layout that was modified.

1   Choose File > Open. In the Open dialog box, navigate to the id05lessons folder and select id0501.indd. Press Open. As the file opens, InDesign displays a message informing you that the document contains links to missing or modified files.

2   Press the Update Links button to update the one modified link.

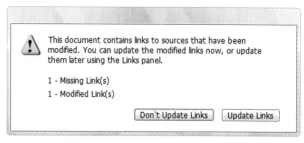

This document contains links to sources that have been modified. You can update the modified links now, or update them later using the Links panel.

1 - Missing Link(s)
1 - Modified Link(s)

[Don't Update Links]   [Update Links]

When opening a file with missing or modified links, you can choose Update Links to help reconnect the linked image files with the InDesign layout.

On the right side of the workspace, the Links panel appears. Notice the citytravel.psd file displays a red warning icon—indicating that the link is missing—while the id0507.psd file displays no icons. If you had not updated the links, it would display a yellow warning icon—indicating that the link has been changed since it was placed into the layout. In the next part of the lesson you will work with the Links panel to discover how to update image files that are missing.

When using the Update Links option any other broken links located in the folder are also updated when you update the first linked item. For example, if an entire folder containing images is relocated, you can update the link to the first missing item using the Update Links option, eliminating the need to update multiple broken links individually. You can also use the Relink to folder command from the Links panel menu.

3   Choose File > Save As. In the Save As dialog box, navigate to the id05lessons folder and type **id0501_work.indd** in the File name text field. Press Save and keep the file open.

Working with the Links panel

When you import an image into your layout, InDesign doesn't copy the complete image into your document file. Instead, it saves a reference, or a link, to the location of the original graphic file so it can access the image when necessary. This process lets you import many files into your layout without significantly increasing the file size of the document. For example, you can create a catalog with hundreds of images, but the InDesign document remains a small file with many linked images.

Because graphic files are generally linked, and not embedded within the InDesign file, you need to know how to manage linked graphic files. The Links panel lets you manage these links, find files in the document, find missing files, and update graphics in the document when changes are made to the image file. In this exercise, you will fix a link to a previously imported image that has been moved and is missing.

1   If the Links panel isn't open, press the Links button (⚭) in the panel docking area on the right side of the workspace.

2   Click once on citytravel.psd, then press the Go To Link button (⇱) at the bottom of the Links panel.

InDesign navigates to the selected image which accompanies the *City Travel* article.

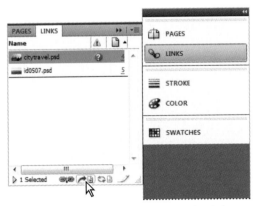

The Go To Link button displays a selected link within the layout.

3   With the citytravel.psd option still selected in the Links panel, press the Relink button (⚬) at the bottom of the Links panel. In the locate dialog box that appears, navigate to the links folder in the id05lessons folder and select the citytravel.psd. Press Open.

The Links panel now displays the list of links without any warning icons. You've updated both a missing link and a modified link.

4   Choose File > Save, or press Ctrl+S (Windows) or Command+S (Mac OS), to save your work. Keep the file open for the next part of the lesson.

When you press the Relink button (⚬) in the Links panel, the Relink All Instances checkbox appears at the bottom of the Links dialog box. Click this and all instances of the image throughout the document are relinked.

Understanding the Links Panel

The links panel displays all imported objects, the color space they use, and where they are used within the file.

A. *Show/Hide Link Information.* B. *Number of Links Selected.*
C. *Relink.* D. *Go to Link.* E. *Update Link.* F. *Edit Original.*

Customizing the Links panel

You can choose to have the Links panel display additional information regarding the Links used in your layout.

1 From the Links panel menu (-≡), choose Panel Options.

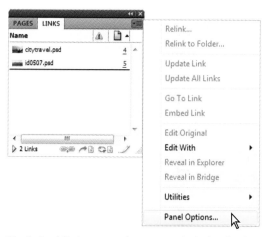

Use the Panel Options command to customize the display of Links panel.

2 In the Panel Options dialog box, click to select the Size and Color Space options in the Show Column located in the center of the dialog box. These determine which information is displayed in a column within the Links panel.

3 Press OK to close the Panel Options window. The additional information is now displayed within the Links panel.

4 To view the additional information, click the tab at the top of the Links panel, and drag it away from the panel docking area. Click in the lower right corner of the Links panel and then drag to the right, expanding the width of the panel.

5 Click the heading of each of the items displayed in the Links panel, including Name, Page, Size, and Color Space. As you click each item, the Links sort by the selected criteria.

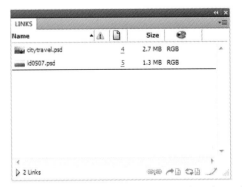

You can customize the information displayed in the Links panel and sort the display by clicking the column titles.

6 Click the Links panel tab and drag the panel over the Pages panel in the dock. When a blue border appears around the edge of the Pages panel, release the mouse to dock the Links panel with the Pages panel.

Adding graphics to your layout

You can add graphics that are created using a number of different programs or use a variety of graphic file types, such as JPEG, EPS, .PSD, TIFF, and many others. InDesign lets you import native Photoshop, PDF, and Illustrator files into your layouts. You can also import other InDesign documents (.indd format) into your layouts. In all, InDesign supports more than a dozen graphic file formats.

The most common way to add graphics to your InDesign layouts is to use the Place command, located under the File menu. In this exercise, you'll use the Place command to add an image to the front page of your travel magazine.

You can also import movies and audio in QuickTime, .avi, .wav, and .aif formats, as well as .au sound clips, into InDesign. These can be exported to the PDF file format. Oddly, multimedia files do not export to the Flash (.swf) file format from InDesign, and must be added separately to Flash files using the Flash authoring software.

1   If necessary, use the pages drop-down menu in the lower left corner of the page to navigate to page 1 of the file id0501_work.indd, then choose View > Fit Page in Window. This page displays the magazine title *SoJournal* at the top of the page.

Use the page drop-down menu to navigate to page 1.

2   To make certain that nothing is selected choose Edit > Deselect All. If the Deselect All option is unavailable, nothing is currently selected, proceed to the next step.

3   Choose File > Place and navigate to the id05lessons folder. Select the id0501.psd file to import this image. In the Place dialog box, make sure the Show Import Options checkbox is unchecked, then press Open to import the image.

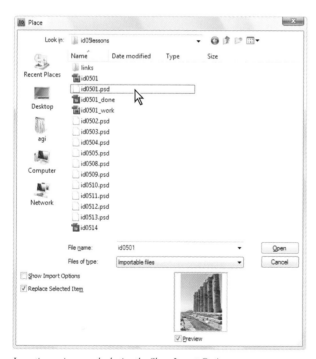

Importing an image and selecting the Show Import Options.

4   The cursor displays a thumbnail of the image you are importing. Position the thumbnail image in the upper-left corner of the red bleed guides, positioned outside the edge of the page, then click to place the image. InDesign imports the image, the SoJournal masthead, at its original size.

If you accidentally clicked in a different spot on the page and need to reposition the image, use the Selection tool (⬉) to drag the image until it snaps to the upper-left corner of the red bleed guides.

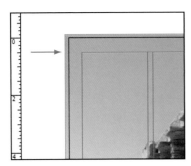

*Place the image in the upper left corner of page 1 so it
extends above and to the left of the edge of the page.*

5   Scroll down to the bottom of page 1. Notice that the image frame extends beyond the edge of the bleed guides. You will resize the image frame to fit within these guides.

6   Position the Selection tool over the lower-right corner of the image frame. When the pointer becomes a diagonal arrow (⬂), click and drag the corner of the frame to reduce the size of the frame. Stop when it snaps to the lower-right corner of the bleed. The arrowheads turn white when they are positioned over the corner of the bleed guides.

Using the Selection tool to resize the image.

7   With the cover image still selected choose Object > Arrange > Send Backward. The cover image moves behind the magazine title.

8   Choose File > Save to save your work. Keep the file open for the next part of the lesson.

Fitting options

You can use several options to get images to fit correctly to the frames on your page, including:

Object > Fitting > Fit Content Proportionally resizes the image to fit inside the frame, maintaining the original image proportions. If the proportions of the box do not match the proportions of the image, extra space will display around one or more of the frame edges.

Object > Fitting > Fill Frame Proportionally causes the smallest size to become larger or smaller to fit within the frame, eliminating any additional space around the edge of the frame.

Object > Fitting > Fit Frame to Content causes the frame to snap to the edges of the image. The frame either reduces or enlarges to fit the exact size of the image.

Be careful when using **Object > Fitting > Fit Content to Frame**, because it distorts the image to fit the frame. The proportional options are generally a better choice for most images.

These options are also available from the context menu, either by right-clicking (Windows) or Ctrl+Clicking (Mac OS) with the mouse.

Fitting an image within an existing frame

You will now explore options for controlling where graphics are placed within your layouts.

1   Navigate to page 2 using the page drop-down menu in the lower-left corner of the document window.

    Page 2 includes four image frames for pictures to accompany the paragraphs about Athens, Austin, Chicago, and Honolulu.

2   If necessary, choose the Selection tool (⬑) from the Tools panel and click the empty picture frame accompanying the Athens story at the top of the page. Handles appear around the edge of the frame, indicating the frame is selected.

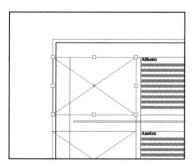

Select the empty frame to make it active.

3   Choose File > Place to import an image into the selected frame. In the Place dialog box, confirm Replace Selected Item is selected. Navigate to the id05lessons folder, select the id0502.psd image and press Open. The image appears in the selected frame, but only a part of the image is visible. You will reposition the graphic within the frame in the next part of this exercise.

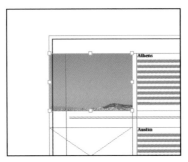

Importing an image into the selected frame.

4   Choose the Direct Selection tool (⬚) from the Tools panel and position the cursor over the image. The cursor changes to a hand icon. Click and hold the image, pause for three seconds, then drag the image inside the frame until the image is relatively centered in the frame.

While dragging the image, a light brown bounding box appears around the edge of the image that is outside the cropping area, and InDesign also displays any part of the image that is cropped by the frame. These are displayed because you clicked and held the image before dragging, known as patient user mode.

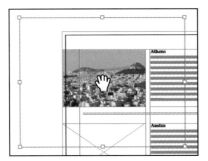

By pausing after clicking an image, InDesign displays the complete size, even any part outside of the frame.

5   Right-click (Windows) or Ctrl+click (Mac OS) the graphic and choose Fitting > Center Content. The image is centered within the frame.

6   Using the Selection tool, right-click (Windows) or Ctrl+click (Mac OS) the graphic, and choose Fitting > Fill Frame Proportionally.
These fitting options provide different ways to reposition the image. After using the Fill Frame Proportionally option, you may wish to manually refine the image position using the Direct Selection tool ( ).

Auto Fitting

Use the Frame Fitting Options to choose settings and create default options for every time graphics are placed inside existing frames. In this part of the exercise, you will create default fitting options for frames.

1   Choose Edit > Deselect All, or press Shift+Ctrl+A (Windows) or Shift+Command+A (Mac OS), to make sure nothing in your document is selected.

2   Using the Selection tool ( ), Shift+click the three remaining empty frames on page 2 of the layout.

3   Choose Object > Fitting > Frame Fitting Options.

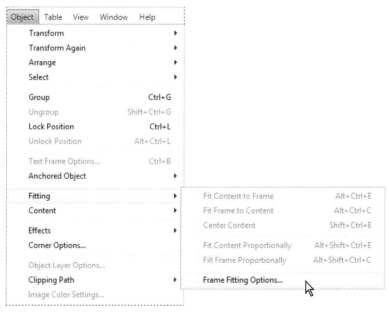

Choose Frame Fitting Options to set the defaults for placing graphics in frames.

4   Choose Fill Frame Proportionally from the Fitting drop-down menu toward the bottom
    of the dialog box, then press OK. Graphics placed into these frames will fill each frame
    proportionally.

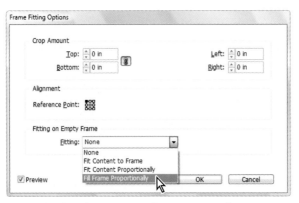

Set the default frame fitting option to Fill Frame Proportionally.

5   Choose File > Save.

Using Adobe Bridge to import graphics

Adobe Bridge is a separate application that ships with InDesign. It provides a way to manage
and view your digital assets, including images and InDesign documents. You can use Bridge to
get previews of your documents, and view information about files before you even open them.
Bridge works like a specialized version of your operating system for managing and arranging
the files you import into an InDesign layout, and files you have created using InDesign.

In this section, you will import an image into the document by dragging it from the Bridge
window directly into the InDesign document.

1   With id0501.indd still open, choose File > Browse in Bridge, or press the Go to Bridge
    button (Br) in the Control panel to launch Adobe Bridge.

2   When Adobe Bridge opens, click the Favorites tab in the upper-left corner to bring it
    forward, then click once on the Desktop listing, or click the location where you placed
    the files for this lesson.

3   In the Content tab at the center of the Bridge window, locate the id05lessons folder and double-click to open the folder.

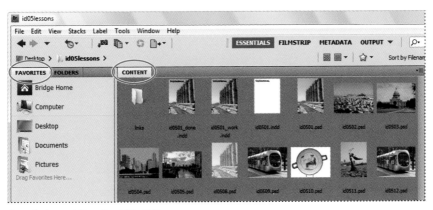

Open the lessons folder using Adobe Bridge.

4   In the upper-right corner of the Bridge window press the Switch to Compact Mode button (▤). This results in a smaller version of Bridge that allows you to work simultaneously with Bridge and your InDesign document.

5   Position the compact Bridge window so you can see the empty frame next to the second city description, Austin, located on page 2 of the InDesign document.

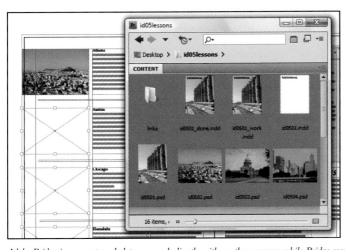

Adobe Bridge in compact mode lets you work directly with another program while Bridge remains visible.

6   Using the Bridge window locate the Photoshop image id0503.psd, an image of the Austin Capitol building. Click and hold, then drag the image into the empty Austin frame on page 2 of the InDesign document. When your cursor is positioned inside the frame, release the mouse. The photo is placed into the frame.

7   Close the Bridge window, and click anywhere within the InDesign document window to make it active, then choose File > Save.

Placing multiple graphics

You can place multiple graphics into your InDesign layouts in a single step. In this section, you will place two graphics in the remaining frames on page 2 of the layout.

1   If necessary, choose Edit > Deselect All so that nothing is selected, then choose File > Place.

2   In the Place dialog box, Ctrl+click (Windows) or Command+click (Mac OS) to select both the id0504.psd and id0505.psd images, then press Open. The cursor changes to a paintbrush icon (🖌) and displays the number 2 in parentheses, along with a thumbnail of the first image.

3   Click inside the empty frame to the left of the Chicago entry to place the first graphic. The paintbrush's number disappears, and a thumbnail of the Honolulu image appears.

4   Position your cursor over the remaining empty frame and click to place id0505.psd in the frame.

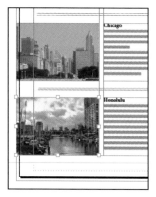

You can place multiple graphics in multiple frames using Place.

When you have selected multiple images, you can use the arrow keys on the keyboard to cycle through the various images. As you press the arrow keys, the preview of the image to be placed changes, letting you choose which image will be placed. Press the Esc key to remove an image from the list of images that is being placed.

Contact Sheet place

You can have InDesign create multiple frames and place images into a grid, known as a contact sheet. After choosing multiple images to place, press and hold Ctrl+Shift (Windows) or Command+Shift (MacOS) then click and drag to create the grid. Multiple frames will be displayed as you drag. Release the Ctrl/Command+Shift keys and then use the arrow keys to add or reduce the number of frames in the grid

5 Choose File > Save to save your work. Keep the file open for the next part of the lesson.

Adjusting the display quality of images

InDesign typically provides a low resolution preview of placed graphics. The higher resolution information is not displayed, as the high quality information is often unnecessary for layout, and displaying many high quality images can slow the performance of InDesign.

You may need to view the high quality images, and you can choose to display high quality image data for specific images, or for all images.

To change the display quality of an individual image, select the image with the Selection tool, then choose Object > Display Performance. Choose Fast Display to display a gray box instead of the image preview. Choose High Quality display to show the high resolution image information—the same data you would see in programs like Photoshop or Illustrator.

To change the display performance for all images in a document, choose View > Display Performance and select the desired quality level to use for the document.

Using object styles for images

In InDesign Lesson 4, "Working with Styles," you applied object styles to frames. You can also apply object styles to frames that contain images, quickly giving them a consistent, finished appearance. In this exercise, you'll create and apply an object style that adds a black stroke to all the frames on page 2.

1 Use the Selection tool (◂) to select the first image, the picture of Athens, on page 2 of the layout.

2 With the cursor positioned over the image, right-click (Windows) or Ctrl+click (MacOS) and choose Stroke Weight > 1 pt from the contextual menu.

3 In the dock on the right side of the workspace, press the Stroke button (≣). In the Stroke panel, press the Align Stroke to Inside button (⊠) to set the stroke to align to the inside of the frame.

Set the stroke weight to 1 pt. and align the stroke to the inside of the frame.

4 Click on the tab of the Stroke panel to collapse it back into a button. You will now use the formatting of this initial frame to create an object style, and then apply it to the other frames.

5 In the dock, press the Object Styles button (⌑). If the button is not visible, choose Window > Object Styles to open the Object Styles panel.

If the Object Styles command is not displayed in the Window menu, you may need to first choose Window > Show All Menu Items.

6 With the Athens image on page 2 still selected, Alt+click (Windows) or Option+click (Mac OS) on the Create new style button (⊒) at the bottom of the Object Styles panel to create a new object style.

Pressing the Alt/Option key when creating a new style causes the New Style dialog box to open, making it easy to confirm the settings and name the style. If you do not press the key, the new style is created and given a generic name.

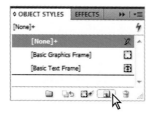

Alt/Option+click the Create new style button.

7 In the New Object Style dialog box, click the Apply Style to Selection checkbox to link the new style to the selected object.

8 Make sure the checkbox for Frame Fitting Options is selected, located along the left side of the dialog box. Next, click the words Frame Fitting Options to highlight it and display its options.

9   From the Fitting drop-down menu, choose Fill Frame Proportionally.

10 In the Style Name text field, enter the name **Image Frame** to name the style, then press OK. InDesign saves the attributes of the selected object as a new style and applies them to the selected frame.

11 Shift+click to select the remaining three images on page 2 that have not yet been formatted.

12 In the Object Styles panel, click the Image Frame style, applying it to all four images simultaneously.

To better view the one-point strokes on the four image frames, you may need to press Ctrl+(plus sign) (Windows) or Command+(plus sign) (Mac OS) to zoom in. This shortcut brings you progressively closer to the page. After you view the final result, choose View > Fit Page in Window to bring you back to a broad view of your file.

13 Choose Edit > Deselect All to deselect the images, then choose File > Save. Keep the document open.

Wrapping text around images

To force text away from graphics you can use text wrap to determine how far text should be pushed away from an object.

Wrapping text around the bounding box

When you place a graphic on a page, you might want the text to wrap around the frame that contains the graphic.

1   With the Selection tool (☜), select the image of Athens on page 2. Click, hold, and drag it to the right so the upper-left corner of the image fits into the corner where the top and left margins intersect. Part of the image overlaps the text because the image frame is positioned above the text frame at the half-inch mark.

Move the image to the intersection of the top and left margins.

2   Choose Window > Text Wrap. The Text Wrap panel opens.

3 Press the Wrap around bounding box button (▣), which causes the text to wrap around the edge of the frame.

Wrapping text around the image frame.

4 In the middle of the panel are the offset values, which determine how closely the text wraps around the image. Confirm the Make all settings the same button (⧈) in the middle of the offset values is selected. Click the up arrow, next to any one of the offset options, twice to set the offset to 0.125 inches. The text is positioned at least .125 inches away from the image frame.

5 Select the remaining three images by pressing the Shift key and clicking to select each of them. Repeat steps 2-4 for the remaining three images on the page.

Instead of selecting multiple images and repeating the process of applying the text wrap, you can instead take advantage of the object style you created in the previous exercise. Immediately after applying the text wrap to the first frame, choose the Redefine Style command from the Object Style panel, and the object style updates and the new text wrap is applied to all the image frames to which it has been applied.

6 Choose File > Save to save your work. Keep the file open for the next exercise.

Using graphics with clipping paths and alpha channels

Some images contain clipping paths or alpha channels. Clipping paths and alpha channels can be used to hide information in an image, typically the background, enabling users to wrap text around part of the image. Clipping paths are stored in the Paths panel in Photoshop, and alpha channels are saved selections stored in the Channels panel in Photoshop.

The formats that utilize paths and channels include .psd, .eps and .tif. These formats can hide parts of the image that are outside the path or channel when they are used in an InDesign layout. You will add a graphic to your layout that has a prebuilt clipping path from Photoshop, and then use the text wrap option to wrap text around the object's shape. You will place the next image in the Transportation article on page 3 of the InDesign document.

1   Press the Pages button in the dock to open the Pages panel. Double-click on the page 3 icon and page 3 centers in the workspace.

2   Choose Edit > Deselect to make sure nothing is selected then, choose File > Place, and navigate to the id05lessons folder. Click once to select the image id0509.psd, click to select the Show Import Options checkbox at the bottom of the Place dialog box. Press Open. The Image Import Options dialog box appears.

3   In the Image Import Options dialog box, click the Image tab. If necessary, click the Apply Photoshop Clipping Path checkbox so that it is checked, and confirm that Alpha Channel is set to None. Press OK to import the image.

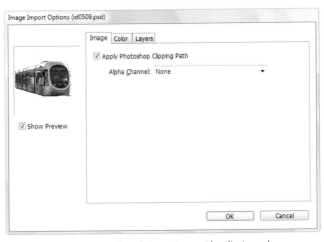

Choosing the import options when placing an image with a clipping path.

4   Position the paintbrush-and-thumbnail cursor (🖌) at the top of the left column in the Transportation article, then click to place the graphic. The train image, without a background, appears over the text. By selecting the Apply Photoshop Clipping Path option, you set the image to appear without its background.

When placing the image, be certain the cursor does not display the paintbrush inside parenthesis as this indicates the image will be placed into an existing frame on the page. If you unintentionally place the image into a frame choose Edit > Undo and repeat the process.

When Apply Photoshop Clipping Path is enabled images display only the information inside a clipping path that was created in Photoshop.

5   With the image still selected, click the lower-left reference point locator (⊞) in the Control panel.

Set the train image's lower-left corner as the reference point.

6   In the Control panel, make sure that the Constrain proportions for scaling button (🔗) is selected. This constrains the proportions to keep them equal when the image is scaled.

7   Choose 50% from the Scale X percentage drop-down menu (🔽). The resulting image is a smaller train positioned in the lower-left corner of the Transportation article.

8   Choose Window > Text Wrap to open the Text Wrap panel, if it is not already open. Press the Wrap around object shape button (⬓) to wrap the text around the shape of the image, then change the offset amount to 0.1875 inches.

The text now wraps around the clipping path that was created using Photoshop.

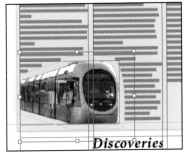

Wrap text around the object shape.

9   Choose File > Save to save your work. Keep the file open for the next part of the lesson.

Removing an image background using InDesign

You don't have to use Photoshop to remove the background from an image. You can use InDesign to create and apply a clipping path to an image. Clipping paths added to images using InDesign impact only the image in the InDesign document, and are not saved back into the original image file.

1   Choose Edit > Deselect All, to make sure nothing is selected. This keeps you from accidentally editing items in your layout. You will place a new image in the *Discoveries* article on page 3.

2   Choose File > Place. In the Place dialog box, navigate to the id05lessons folder. Select the id0510.psd image. At the bottom of the dialog box, make sure the Show Import Options checkbox is selected, then choose Open.

3   In the resulting Image Import Options dialog box, choose the Image tab. Notice that the Clipping Path options are not available. This is because no clipping path exists for this image. You will use InDesign to remove the background from the image. Press OK to place the image into your layout.

4 Position the paintbrush-and-thumbnail cursor (🖌) anywhere in the *Discoveries* article on page 3 and then click to place the image. Using the Selection tool (▶), position the image in the center of the text. Keep the image selected for the next step in the exercise.

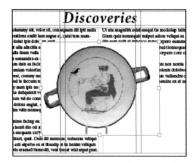

Place the id0510.psd image in the middle of the Discoveries *article.*

5 Choose Object > Clipping Path > Options. Select Detect Edges from the Type drop-down menu, leave the other settings at their defaults, and then press OK. You have removed the background using the Detect Edges option to create a clipping path.

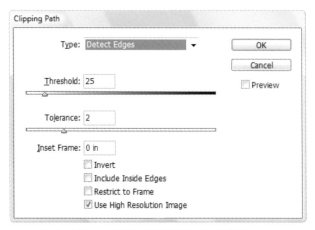

Remove the image background using Object > Clipping Path > Options.

6   If the Text Wrap panel is not visible, choose Window > Text Wrap. In the Text Wrap panel, click the Wrap around object shape button (⬛) to wrap the text around the image. You can enter a higher value to push the text away from the object shape, or set it at a lower value causing the text to follow the contour of the object more closely.

Wrap text around the object's shape.

7   Choose File > Save to save your work.

Using anchored objects

Anchored objects, sometimes called inline objects, allow a graphic to follow text that relates to the image. For example, if you are creating a dictionary and have an image associated with an entry, you want the image to move with the definition. If the text moves, the image should move with the text.

Anchoring an object attaches it to the associated text. When the text moves, the object moves with the text. In this exercise, you will explore how to create anchored objects using the skills you have already learned regarding placing images and text.

1   Use the page drop-down menu in the lower left corner of the document window to navigate to page 4.

2   Using the Selection tool (⬉), click to select the City Art frame on page 4. Press Ctrl+(plus sign) (Windows) or Command+(plus sign) (Mac OS) twice to zoom in on the selected frame.

3   Select the Type tool (T) from the Tools panel, and click to the left of the word *CHICAGO* on the fifth line. By inserting the cursor in a specific location before placing an image, you instruct InDesign to place the graphic into this location within the text, rather than into a frame that is independent of the text.

4   Choose File > Place. At the bottom of the Place dialog box, click to uncheck the Show Import Options checkbox. Navigate to the id05lessons folder, select id0513.psd, make sure the Replace Selected Item check box is selected, then press Open. InDesign imports the image to the location where the cursor was inserted.

Import the image next to the word CHICAGO, *creating an anchored object.*

5   Continuing to use the Type tool, click to position the text cursor at the end of the paragraph, immediately above the image you imported in the previous step, and then press Enter (Windows) or Return (Mac OS) one time. The text moves down, and the graphic moves with the text.

The anchored image moves with its text.

6   Press Ctrl+Z (Windows) or Command+Z (Mac OS) to undo the paragraph return, bringing the image back to its original position.

You repositioned the text to understand how the image is attached to the text, but you will want it back in its original position for the remainder of this exercise.

7   To manually control the positioning of the anchored image, switch to the Selection tool and then click once on the anchored image to select it. Choose Object > Anchored Object > Options. The Anchored Object Options dialog box appears.

8   In the Anchored Object Options dialog box, click to select the Preview checkbox in the lower-left corner. Choose Custom from the Position drop-down menu, and click the Relative to Spine checkbox. This causes the image position to remain consistent to the spine of the document if pages are added or deleted and the page on which it is placed reflows.

Although the image is now positioned outside the text frame, it remains linked to the text. If the text position changes, the image will continue to flow with the text. Leave all the other settings to their defaults, and then press OK to close the dialog box.

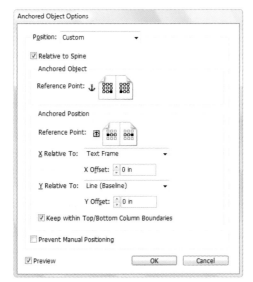 

Set the anchored image to Custom and Relative to Spine to place the image outside the text frame.

9   With the Selection tool, click and drag the graphic into the upper-right corner of the City Art box.

Reposition the anchored image manually using the Selection tool.

10 To test the spine-sensitive options, choose View > Fit Spread In Window. Use the Selection tool to select the City Art frame. Drag the frame to the empty column on the right side of the City Music box on page 5. Notice how the graphic automatically adjusts its position within the City Art box relative to the spread's spine. Likewise, if the text flowed from a left page to a right page, the anchored object would reposition itself automatically.

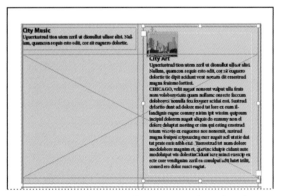

When you reposition the City Art frame to page 5, the graphic adjusts its position relative to the spine.

11 Press Ctrl+Z (Windows) or Command+Z (Mac OS) to undo the repositioning of the text frame, or simply drag the City Art frame back to its original position.

12 Save the file by choosing File > Save. Keep the file open for the next part of the lesson.

Applying a text wrap to anchored graphics is the same as applying a text wrap to any object. Click the anchored graphic with the Selection tool, choose the desired option from the Text Wrap panel, and set your offset value accordingly.

Advanced importing

You can import more advanced graphics into your layouts, including Photoshop files that use layers, and InDesign documents, without converting them to any other file type. Even if you don't work extensively with Photoshop, you can still follow along with the following steps.

Importing layered Photoshop files

In this exercise, you'll work with an imported Photoshop file that uses a group of layers that have been organized using a layer comp. Layer comps are a snapshot of the current state of the Photoshop Layers palette. Within Photoshop, you can change the visibility, position, and appearance of the layers to create different versions of a file. When you create a layer comp, it saves these settings by remembering the state of each layer at the time the layer comp was saved. You can use layer comps to create multiple compositions from a single Photoshop file.

When you import a .psd document into InDesign and use the Show Import Options checkbox, you can choose which layer comp to use from the Photoshop file within the InDesign document.

When you use layered Photoshop files in your InDesign layouts, you can change the visibility of the layers directly within InDesign. You do not need to go back to Photoshop to create different versions of an image, or save different versions of images. You can control the visibility of Photoshop layers directly within InDesign. In this exercise, you will display different versions of an image by changing the visibility of the Photoshop layers and layer comps.

1   With the Zoom tool (🔍), click and drag to draw a box around the empty frame under the Sculpture article on page 4 of the InDesign document. This increases the magnification of the page, making the frame more clearly visible.

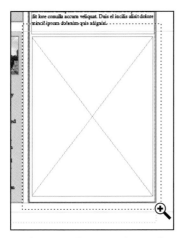

Use the Zoom tool to increase the magnification of the empty frame.

2   With the Selection tool (▸), click to select the empty frame under the Sculpture article. Choose File > Place, and at the bottom of the Place dialog box, click to select both the Replace Selected Item checkbox and also the Show Import Options checkbox so that both options are enabled. Navigate to the id05lessons folder, select id0511.psd, then press Open. The Image Import Options dialog box opens.

3   In the resulting Image Import Options dialog box, click the Layers tab to bring the layers options forward. Notice that several layers are listed in the Show Layers section. Make sure the Show Preview checkbox is selected, and then click the box next to the hsbGray layer to display that layer's option. The appearance of the image changes when you display the hsbGray layer.

4   Choose 3w/hsbGray from the Layer Comp drop-down menu to display a number of layer visibility changes which have been defined by this layer comp when the image was edited in Photoshop.

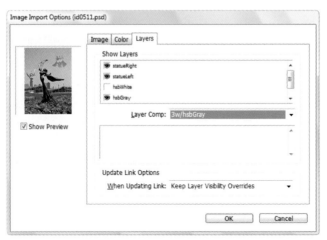

Use the layer comp visibility options to change the visibility of layers in placed Photoshop files.

5   Press OK. The image imports into the InDesign layout and displays the layers from the Photoshop image that you selected in the Image Import Options dialog box.

Now you'll explore how to change layer visibility of images after they've been placed in a layout.

6   If necessary, click the image with the Selection tool. With the image selected, choose Object > Object Layer Options. Choose Last Document State from the Layer Comp drop-down menu to return the image to its original settings, and then press OK.

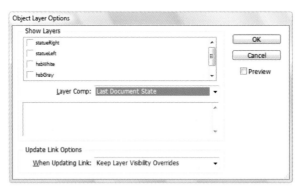

Return the image to its original state using Object Layer Options.

7   Continuing to use the Selection tool, right-click (Windows) or Ctrl+click (Mac OS) the image and from the contextual menu choose Fitting > Fill Frame Proportionally so the image fits nicely inside the frame.

8   Choose File > Save to save your work.

Importing InDesign layouts as graphics

Along with traditional image formats, you can also import other InDesign layouts into your document, placing them as graphics. You may have an ad or a flyer that was created in InDesign that you want to use in another InDesign layout. By importing an InDesign file as a graphic, you can make changes to the imported file and the modifications are automatically updated in your layout. In this exercise, you will import a CD booklet design created using InDesign into the layout.

1   Open the Pages panel from the dock on the right side of the workspace and, in the panel, double-click on page 5 to navigate to this page, then choose View > Fit Page in Window. Use the Selection tool (▸) to select the frame beneath the City Music headline.

2   Choose File > Place or press the keyboard shortcut, Ctrl+D (Windows) or Command+D (Mac OS). At the bottom of the Place dialog box, make sure that both the Replace Selected Item and also the Show Import Options checkboxes are checked, navigate to the id05lessons folder, and select the id0514.indd file. Press Open. The Place InDesign Document dialog box appears.

3   In the Place InDesign Document dialog box, click the General tab to bring it forward, and make sure the Crop to drop-down menu is set to Page bounding box, this determines how much of the page is displayed. The other two crop options for bleed and slug would be used if you wanted those additional layout options to be visible. Leave the Layers tab options unchanged, then press OK.

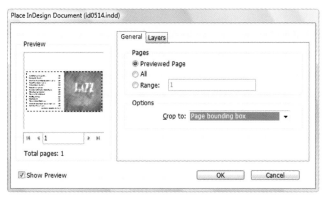

Set the Crop options to Page bounding box when importing the InDesign document into your layout.

4 After InDesign completes the import process, the program displays a warning that the file contains missing or modified links. When you import InDesign files that have links, you need to have those links available for the new layout as well. This is intentional to help you understand the import process. Press OK to import the file.

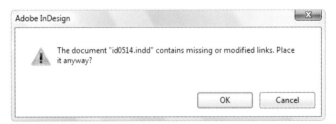

If an imported InDesign file has missing or modified links, a warning message appears.

5 The CD booklet design fills the frame. Since it doesn't fit entirely in the frame, right-click (Windows) or Ctrl+click (Mac OS), and from the contextual menu, choose Fitting > Fit Content Proportionally.

6 Choose File > Save.

At the very bottom of the Tools panel, click and hold the Normal button (⬛) to reveal more viewing options. Choose Preview, and then scroll through your completed layout. When you're finished, choose File > Close to close the document.

Congratulations! You've finished InDesign Lesson 5, "Working with Graphics."

Self study

For a different text wrap option, try placing id0509.psd in a block of text and using the Text Wrap panel, select the Wrap around Object Shape button and choose Alpha Channel from the Contour Options drop-down menu. Make sure to go to the Object menu and choose Clipping Path > Options. Change the Type field to Alpha Channel, and set Alpha to trainOpenWindow.

Use Adobe Bridge to add more images to your document. Once you get used to this workflow, you will find that it can speed up the design process.

Create additional anchored images in the text frames of your document. Explore the offset options to change the positioning of anchored objects.

Customize the display of the Links panel, and change the sorting order of the links. Then use the Links panel to collect the links used in the document by using the Utilities > Copy Links To option in the Links panel menu.

Review

Questions

1 How can you have InDesign automatically fit images to frames or frames to images?

2 To flow text around the shape of a clipping path, which panel can you use?

3 Which tool do you use to reposition a graphic inside its frame?

4 Which graphic format supports the visibility of layer comps?

5 Once a layered graphic is placed in an InDesign document, how do you change the layer visibility?

Answers

1 Object > Fitting.

2 The Text Wrap panel.

3 The Direct Selection tool.

4 The Photoshop .psd file format.

5 With the graphic selected, choose Object > Object Layer Options, or right-click (Windows) or Ctrl+click (Mac OS), and choose Object Layer Options from the contextual menu.

What you'll learn in this lesson:

- Preflighting your document
- Collecting for distribution
- Creating and customizing a PDF file
- Exporting an XHTML file
- Printing a proof

Document Delivery: Printing, PDFs, and XHTML

Designing your document is only half the job. You still need to deliver it, whether to a commercial printer, the web, or just your coworkers for review. To help you, InDesign offers multiple methods for proofing and packaging your files, as well as flexible export controls for a variety of formats, including PDF and HTML.

Starting up

Before starting, make sure that your tools and panels are consistent by resetting your preferences. See "Resetting the InDesign workspace and preferences" on page XXVII.

You will work with several files from the id06lessons folder in this lesson. Make sure that you have copied the CS4lessons folder onto your hard drive from the Digital Classroom DVD. See "Loading lesson files" on page XXIX. This lesson may be easier to follow if the id06lessons folder is on your desktop.

For this lesson, you need either Adobe Acrobat or Adobe Reader to view the PDF files you will create. If necessary, you can download the free Adobe Reader at *Adobe.com*.

The project

To sample InDesign's PDF, XHTML, and print-related controls, you will prepare a car ad for delivery to multiple customers. You'll package it using InDesign's Preflight and Package feature, match it to a printer's specifications, and convert it to XHTML for posting to a web site using the new Export for Dreamweaver feature.

Package inventory

Before you send your files to a printer or other service provider, in order to print your job professionally, it's important that you check the file for common errors that can occur during the design phase of your project. If your files aren't prepared to the required specifications, your job could be delayed or, even worse, reproduced incorrectly. InDesign CS4's Preflight feature enables you to check all the mechanics of your file to ensure that everything is in working order. You can now even define your own Preflight profiles in CS4.

For example, you're planning to submit an ad for the new IDCS3 sports car to a newspaper. In this exercise, you'll use Package to see the Package Inventory of the file, and then you'll define a Preflight setting to see how well your ad complies with the newspaper's specifications.

1   Choose File > Open, navigate to the id06lessons folder, and select CarAd.indd. Press Open.

2   Choose File > Package. InDesign analyzes the document, and displays a summary of its findings in the Package Inventory dialog box. For more information on a specific category, click its name in the list on the left side of the dialog box.

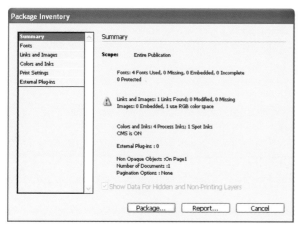

The Package Inventory dialog box displays detailed information about your file, and flags potential errors that could cause problems.

3   From the list on the left side of the dialog box, choose Fonts. The right side of the dialog box now lists all the fonts used in your document as well as their format and status. If the status is OK, the font is loaded onto your system and recognized by InDesign. A status of *Missing* indicates that the font cannot be found. Because this lesson file was created using fonts that load with InDesign, all your fonts should say *OK*.

4   Choose Links and Images from the list on the left side of the dialog box. This section displays information about the images that are used within your document. At the top of this dialog box is a caution icon (⚠), indicating that InDesign found a potential problem, specifically that one of the images uses the RGB color space. Most printing companies require images to be submitted in the CMYK color space; ask your printer for its specifications prior to sending your files.

Because you won't be printing this, you don't need to worry about this message. If you were working on a piece for printing, however, and this warning appeared, you may prefer to open the RGB file in Adobe Photoshop and convert it to CMYK or carefully check the color conversion options set within InDesign.

The Links and Images section also indicates the state of your images, linked or unlinked, as well as the actual versus effective resolutions of your images.

Actual versus effective resolution

The resolution of an image is indicated by the number of pixels per inch (ppi) that make up the image—a seemingly simple concept that can be a bit complicated. As a general rule, the higher its resolution, the higher the quality of an image. Most images that you see when browsing the Internet are 72 ppi or 96 ppi, which is the standard screen resolution of most monitors. For high-quality printing, however, image resolution should generally be around 300 ppi.

To further complicate things, the Preflight window's Links and Images section lists two different numbers at the bottom: actual ppi and effective ppi. Actual ppi is the actual resolution of the file that you are placing into InDesign. The effective ppi is the resolution of the image after it has been scaled in InDesign. For example, if you place a 300-ppi image in your document and then scale it 200 percent, the effective resolution becomes 150 ppi. As you increase the size of images in InDesign, the effective resolution decreases. The effective resolution is the number that you should pay most careful attention to, as it determines the quality at which the image is output.

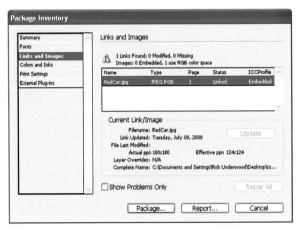

The Links and Images section of the Package Inventory dialog box.

5   Select Colors and Inks in the Preflight list to see which ink colors the document uses. This file uses a color called Pantone 187 C. Any color besides cyan, magenta, yellow, or black is considered a spot color or plate. You'll learn more about these later in the "Separation Preview" section. Press the Cancel button to close the Preflight dialog box.

Keep the file open, as you'll need it for the next part of the lesson. Now you're ready to package it to send to the newspaper running the ad.

6   Choose File > Save As. Navigate to the id06lessons folder and type **CarAd_work.indd** in the Name text field. Press Save.

Preflight checks

Like a pilot checking over his plane prior to takeoff, Preflight assesses your document, then reports potential problems—missing fonts, missing images, RGB (Red, Green, Blue) images, and more—that could prevent a printer from outputting your job properly, or hinder a customer's ability to view your file accurately. You can set up different profiles for all the different destinations you may need to make InDesign documents for. For example, you could define a Preflight profile for all the documents you create that will end up as just PDFs on the web, which are not made to print. You could define the profile to look for images that are over 100 dpi. Whenever a photo was placed that had a higher resolution than 100 dpi, an error would appear in the Preflight panel. You can also see the Preflight status in the bottom-left area of your document window. In this exercise, you will define a new profile in InDesign CS4's new Preflight panel, then check your document against the profile.

1   Choose Window > Output > Preflight. The new Preflight panel opens. Right now, the Preflight profile is set to Basic, which looks only for broken links to images, missing fonts in the document, or overset text. You will now define a new profile that will look for RGB images in the document.

The new Preflight panel in InDesign CS4.

2   From the Preflight panel menu (-≡), choose Define Profiles.

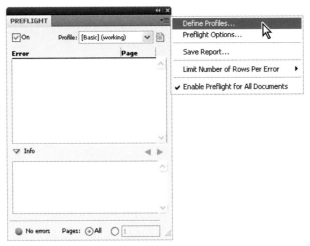

Define Profiles is located in the Panel menu on the Preflight panel.

3   The Preflight Profiles dialog box opens. You cannot change the default Basic profile, so you will define a new one that looks for RGB color in your document. In the Profiles section on the left, click on the plus sign (⊕) at the bottom to create a new profile.

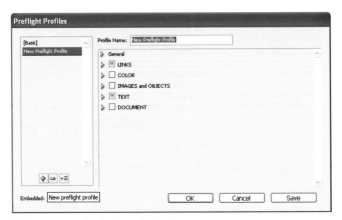

Make a new profile by clicking on the plus sign.

4   In the Profile Name text field at the top, select the text *New Preflight Profile*, then type **CMYK**.

5   In the Profile definition area, open the triangle next to Color by clicking on it. Now open the triangle next to Color Spaces and Modes Not Allowed. Check the box next to Color Spaces and Modes Not Allowed. Now check RGB.

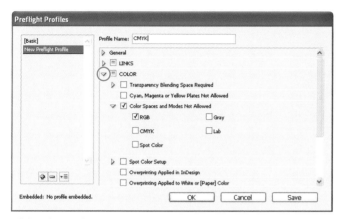

Click on the triangle next to Color Spaces and Modes Not Allowed, then choose RGB.

6   Press Save, then press OK. You have now defined a new color profile.

7   Change the profile in the Preflight panel from Basic to the new CMYK profile you have just made. Notice that the bottom-left area of your document now states that there is one error.

8   Expand the triangles to see the error it has found from within the Preflight Error window. Click on the triangle next to Color, then click on the triangle next to Color space not allowed. The Prefight profile you have just built will now give you an error message for any RGB color that might find its way into your document. To fix this issue, you would need to open the problem image in Photoshop and change the color space to CMYK. But that is only if you are sending a Package to a printer. Certain PDF settings would automatically change the color space of the RGB images to CMYK.

The Preflight panel showing you that the red car has a color that is not allowed in this document.

9   Switch the profile back to Basic and close the Preflight window.

10   Choose File > Save.

Packaging your document

When you need to send your InDesign document out for review, alterations, or printing, you must be sure you're sending all the necessary pieces. Without the font and image files used by the document, your coworkers or service provider can't accurately see and reproduce the file as you intended. To avoid this frustrating scenario, turn to InDesign's Package feature. Package gathers all the document elements the recipient needs into one folder and even enables you to include an instruction file. In this exercise, you will use Package to collect the car ad's fonts and graphics.

1   Choose File > Package. InDesign automatically runs Package Inventory and displays a warning if it finds problems. Press Package because the Package Inventory dialog box would display the same information you reviewed in the previous exercise.

2   For this exercise, press Continue when the Printing Instructions dialog box opens. For a real project, you would enter your contact information as well as any detailed instructions that the printer might need to output your file properly.

3   The Package Publication (Windows) or Create Package Folder (Mac OS) dialog box opens next; here you choose what to include in the file Package, what to call it, and where to save it. Make sure the first three options are checked: *Copy Fonts*, *Copy Linked Graphics*, and *Update Graphic Links in Package*. All others should be unchecked. Type **CarAd Folder** in the Folder Name (Windows) or Save As (Mac OS) text field, choose Desktop from the Save in (Windows) or Where (Mac OS) drop-down menu, and press Package (Windows) or Save (Mac OS).

Use the Package Publication Folder dialog box to tell InDesign which files to gather and where to save them.

4   In response to the Font Alert dialog box that details the legalities of giving your fonts to a printer or service provider, press OK to begin packaging the files. (If you don't want to see this alert in the future, click the *Don't show again* check box before you press OK.)

5   When the dialog box closes, a small progress window appears, displaying the status of the packaging process. Once it has finished, close your CarAd_work.indd file.

6   Choose File > Open, navigate to the desktop, and double-click the CarAd folder. Inside, you'll find a copy of the document file, an instructions file, a Fonts folder with all the fonts used in the job, and a Links folder that contains all the graphics—all in one easy-to-send Package. Press Cancel to close the dialog box.

When the Package process is complete, all the project's elements are grouped together in the CarAd folder.

Now that all the files required to reproduce your job have been copied to the location you specified and are contained within their own folder, you can send this folder to another person to review, or to your printer or service provider to output your job. To ensure the integrity of the files and speed the transfer, compress the packaged folder before sending the files through e-mail or uploading them to an FTP server.

Creating an Adobe PDF

The Package feature collects all your data files, but the recipients still must have InDesign to read the document. What if they don't?

The answer is to send a PDF file. PDF (Portable Document Format) is a common format that can be viewed and printed from any computer platform—Mac, Windows, Linux, and others—that has the free Adobe Reader program installed. A PDF file is an excellent way to make your project available for a wide range of users, and InDesign CS4 makes the process of creating a PDF file of your project very easy. In the following steps, you will create a PDF file of your CarAd_work.indd file so that other people can see your progress and provide feedback on changes that might need to be made before this project is sent to a printer for production.

PDFs can also be used for presentation purposes. PDFs generated in InDesign can contain sound, movies, and hyperlinks. To find out more about this, please see Chapter 12, "Creating Interactive Documents."

1   Choose File > Open Recent > CarAd_work.indd to open your work file.

2   Choose File > Export. In the resulting Export dialog box, name the file CarAd.pdf, choose Desktop from the Save in (Windows) or Where (Mac OS) drop-down menu, and select Adobe PDF from the Save as type (Windows) or Format (Mac OS) drop-down menu. Press Save.

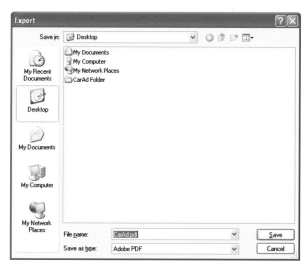

Choose the destination for your PDF file in the Export dialog box.

3   The Export Adobe PDF dialog box appears. From the Adobe PDF Preset drop-down menu at the top of the dialog box, you can choose settings that control the PDF file's size and quality, among other options. Because you will send the car ad to several people for general review, choose the *[Smallest File Size]* option from the Adobe PDF Preset drop-down menu.

PDF presets are a way of saving favorite settings for the final generated PDF file. If you own Adobe Acrobat 7.0 or a more recent version, InDesign CS4 shares these settings with Acrobat Distiller, which is included with Acrobat. Likewise, if you create a custom setting within Distiller, you'll see those settings in the Adobe PDF Preset drop-down menu when you export a PDF file from within InDesign CS4.

The Export Adobe PDF dialog box allows you to customize the PDF file you create from your InDesign file.

4 Click the Hyperlinks check box, near the bottom of the Export Adobe PDF dialog box. Activating the Hyperlinks option makes any hyperlinks created in the InDesign document clickable hyperlinks in the resulting PDF document.

5 Press the Export button. InDesign displays a warning that your document's transparency blend space doesn't match the destination color space. Because your PDF file is for viewing purposes only, this is not a concern. Press OK to begin generating the PDF file.

6 When the PDF export is finished, double-click the CarAd.pdf file on your desktop to open it. Hover your cursor over the www.idcs3.com link, and the cursor changes to a hand. Click on the link to go to the web site specified in the ad. If you receive a message warning you that the document is trying to connect to a web site, choose Allow.

The exported PDF file can contain interactive elements that are included in your InDesign file.

7 Choose File > Close to close the PDF file.

Generating XHTML

That takes care of the print and general viewing aspects of the ad campaign, but what about the web? Your client wants all the used cars listed in the ad to be published on the company web site. Although InDesign is a page-layout program, it can help you generate XHTML files from your document. XHTML is a markup language used for formatting pages on the web. In this exercise, you'll use InDesign's Export for Dreamweaver controls to publish your content in XHTML format. Greatly improved from previous versions of InDesign, InDesign CS4's Export for Dreamweaver function allows you to repurpose the content of your document to an XHTML file that is easily opened in an XHTML editor such as Adobe Dreamweaver. In several of Adobe's Creative Suite packages, Dreamweaver is included, making it easier to move content from print to the web.

HTML versus XHTML

HTML (HyperText Markup Language) has been the standard markup language on the web since the inception of the World Wide Web as you know it today. HTML allows you to describe how a page is formatted and displayed in a web browser. XHTML (Extensible HyperText Markup Language) expands on traditional HTML by separating the presentation of a page from its structure, allowing you to describe the content of a page in addition to its formatting. XHTML incorporates the power of XML in HTML, so basically an XHTML document is both a hypertext document and an XML document, making pages easier to maintain and more flexible at the same time. Some very powerful tools developed for use with XML can now also be utilized on an XHTML document. For more on XML, see Chapter 11, "Using XML with InDesign."

1 With the CarAd_work.indd file open, choose File > Export for Dreamweaver.

2 In the Save As dialog box, name the file CarAd.html, choose the desktop for its location, and press Save.

When using the Export for Dreamweaver feature, make sure that you don't have any objects or text selected in your document. If an element is selected, InDesign exports only that text or object.

3 In the XHTML Export Options dialog box that opens, leave the General settings at their defaults, as there aren't any bulleted or numbered lists in the ad.

4 Select Images in the list on the left side of the dialog box. In the image-related settings that appear to the right, choose Optimized from the Copy Images drop-down menu. For Image Conversion, choose JPEG, and for Image Quality, choose High. This generates a separate folder called CarAdFormat-web-images containing all the images formatted for the web.

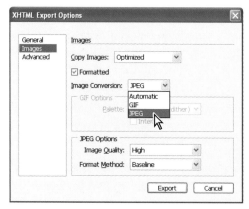

Control the quality of the images exported from your InDesign layout.

5   Select Advanced in the list on the left side of the dialog box. In the Advanced setting on the right side, click the *Empty CSS Declarations* radio button. This option inserts cascading style sheet (CSS) tags in the resulting XHTML file so that you can later add CSS definitions to format the copy. (See the next section for more on CSS.) Make sure that all other options are unselected, then press Export to save the XHTML file.

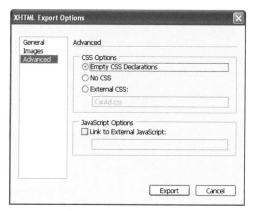

Customize the formatting of the exported XHTML file to change the appearance of the resulting file.

6   On the desktop, double-click on the CarAd.html file to view it in your default web browser. Or if your browser is already open, choose File > Open in the browser to view the file.

Adding CSS formatting

The web page you exported has fairly rudimentary formatting, because formatting in XHTML isn't nearly as flexible as in a page-layout application such as InDesign CS4. You can, however, improve the formatting of your web page by using cascading style sheets (CSS). Just as styles control element formatting in InDesign, cascading style sheets specify which elements of an XHTML file should be formatted in which way. By linking your exported XHTML file to an external CSS file, you can mimic the formatting of your InDesign styles with cascading style sheets. For your text to be properly identified in the resulting XHTML file, however, you must use InDesign's Character and Paragraph Styles to format the text and code (or have someone else code) a separate CSS file. If you format your copy manually (without styles), the CSS file cannot interpret what needs to be formatted. Try exporting the car ad again, this time linking it to a ready-made CSS file.

1   Close the CarAd.html file and return to InDesign. Choose File > Export for Dreamweaver and name the file CarAdFormat.html. Save it to your desktop.

2   In the XHTML Export Options dialog box, leave the General settings at their defaults.

3   Click Images in the list to the left, and choose Optimized for Copy Images, JPEG for Image Conversion, and High for Image Quality.

4 Select Advanced, then click the External CSS radio button and type **CarAd.css** in the text field if it's not already entered. This is the CSS file that contains the document's formatting instructions. Now you need to reorganize a few files so that the XHTML file can find the CSS file.

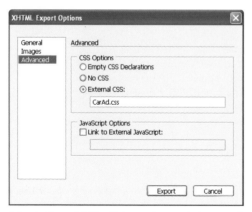

Select the External CSS radio button, then type in the name of the CSS file in the text field.

5 Press Export. Once the process is completed, navigate to the desktop. On the desktop, create a folder called XHTML. Move the CarAdFormat.html file and CarAdFormat-web-images folder from your desktop into the XHTML folder. Copy the CarAd.css file from your id06lessons folder to the XHTML folder.

6 Open the XHTML folder and double-click the CarAdFormat.html file. You should see that the text for the used cars is now formatted similarly to the text in the print ad design. Close the file when you are done reviewing it.

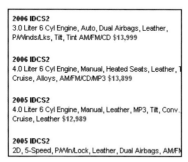

This is what the generated HTML looks like.

CSS and XHTML

Traditionally, formatting in HTML was limited to a predefined list of tags that changed the appearance of text and objects on a web page. These tags provided general formatting and were often inconsistent because different browsers' preference settings made it difficult for a designer to ensure the accurate appearance of a web page. CSS (Cascading Style Sheets), as the name implies, are similar to Styles in Adobe InDesign CS4. This feature allows you to be more specific when formatting text, images, and layout in an XHTML file and streamlines the process of applying formatting to a page. CSS can be used to apply consistent formatting to a number of pages because multiple pages can be linked to a single CSS file. This also makes formatting adjustments quick and easy, because modifications to a CSS file are automatically translated to all pages that are linked to that CSS file.

Separation preview

Designed primarily to produce print layouts, InDesign supports both traditional methods of printing color: the CMYK model and spot colors. In the four-color process model, cyan, magenta, yellow, and black inks (C, M, and Y, with black as the K) combine in various values to reproduce numerous colors. A printing press uses a separate plate for each of these four colors, laying the ink down on the substrate in separate layers. Spot colors are pre-mixed inks that match standard color values. To ensure the green in your company's logo matches across all your print jobs, for example, you could choose a specific green spot color to use consistently.

Probably the most widely used spot color system is the Pantone Matching System, which is also called PMS, or simply Pantone colors. As a companion to the system it developed, Pantone Inc. also offers a swatch book so you can see how the colors reproduce on paper. All the Creative Suite applications have the Pantone library built in, so you can add spot colors to your document easily. Spot colors each require their own plates as well.

All Pantone colors have CMYK equivalents that enable you to reproduce the color using the standard process colors, as well, should you need to conform to CMYK-only printing requirements, or reduce the number of plates.

 Keep in mind, however, that printing a Pantone color as a CMYK color may cause it to look drastically different from the spot version of that Pantone color. This is because of the limited gamut, or color range, that process colors are able to reproduce. Pantone offers a Process Color Simulator guide that compares the printed spot color against the printed process color and is indispensable when you reproduce spot colors as four-color process.

In the printing industry, printers charge customers for each plate that has to be produced for the printing job. You want to be sure that unnecessary colors aren't mistakenly sent to the printer, as extra colors increase your cost and can cause confusion. To prevent this added expense and frustration, InDesign's Separations Preview panel lets you view the separate plates, or separations, as the printer would see them before you send your file. Take a tour of the panel as you check the car ad's separations.

1   Choose Window > Output > Separations Preview, or press Shift+F6, to open the Separations Preview panel.

2   Click on the Separations Preview panel menu button (⋅≡) and choose *Show Single Plates in Black* to turn off that option and see each plate in its actual color.

3   Choose Separations from the View drop-down menu in the Separations Preview panel.

4   Click the visibility icon (👁) to the left of the CMYK entry to turn off the visibility of the Cyan, Magenta, Yellow, and Black plates in your document. InDesign now displays only the elements in Pantone 187 C.

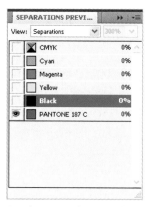

See where certain colors are used in your document.

You can tell that Pantone 187 C is a spot color because it is still visible after all the other separations have been hidden. Another way to identify a spot color in your document is to look at your Swatches panel. If any color has this icon (◉) to the right of the color name, it indicates that the color is a spot color and outputs on its own plate. Because the newspaper's specifications forbid spot colors, you must replace them in the car ad.

5   Click on the panel menu button in your Separations Preview panel, and choose Ink Manager from the list. The Ink Manager lists all the plates or inks that are currently in your document.

6   In the Ink Manager, click the spot icon to the left of the Pantone 187 C plate to change it from a spot color to a process color. You now see a process color icon (✖) to the left of the Pantone 187 C plate, indicating that the color will output as process instead of spot. Click OK. Because you mapped the Pantone 187 C plate to process and you turned off display of your process colors in step 4, no colors are currently visible.

7   Click on the visibility icon to the left of CMYK to see all the colors in your document
again. The red color that was Pantone 187 C is now a red made of the four process
colors. If you hover your cursor over different areas of your document, the Separations
Preview panel shows you the ink percentages to the right of each color in the
Separations Preview panel.

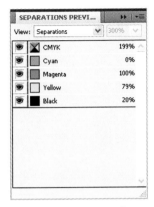

Hover your cursor over areas of your
document to see the ink percentages.

8   Toggle the visibility of various separations in your Separations Preview panel to see how
the colors in your document are combined to achieve other colors, called *builds*.

9   Choose Off from the View drop-down menu in the Separations Preview panel to get
back to your normal viewing mode, and close the Separations Preview panel. Now your
ad is properly prepared for printing in the newspaper.

Printing a proof

The best way to avoid surprises at press time is to print a proof of your document on your
desktop printer. Seeing your project on paper sometimes reveals design flaws or mistakes you
missed when viewing your document on screen. Printing out a version of your document on
a printer is referred to as printing a proof. The term *proof* is used to describe any type of output
that is generated prior to making plates for a printing press. In this exercise, you'll use InDesign
to print a proof to your desktop printer.

1   With CarAd_work.indd open, choose File > Print to open the Print dialog box.

2   From the Printer drop-down menu at the top of the Print dialog box, choose a printer
that is available to your computer.

3   Because there is only one page in your CarAd_work.indd file, leave Pages set to *All*. For
multi-page documents, however, you could specify a limited range of pages to print.

4 Click Setup in the list on the left. On the right side, choose Letter [8.5 x 11] from the Paper Size drop-down menu and click on the Landscape Orientation icon (▣) to print your document in landscape orientation on standard letter-sized paper. The preview in the lower-left corner shows your page orientation and selected printer.

5 Your ad is larger than the letter-sized paper you specified in step 4, so click on the *Scale to Fit* radio button to scale your document to fit the available space. This automatically centers your document on the printed page. (If you have a large format printer, of course, you can adjust the paper size as needed and print at full scale.)

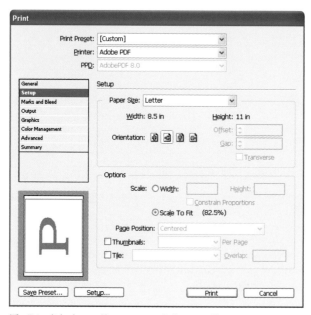

The Print dialog box enables you to control all aspects of how your page is oriented to the paper and printer.

6 In the list at left, click Marks and Bleed. Click the *All Printer's Marks* check box to tell InDesign to add the appropriate trim, bleed, and color marks to your page as you would see on a printer's proof. Leave the other settings at their defaults.

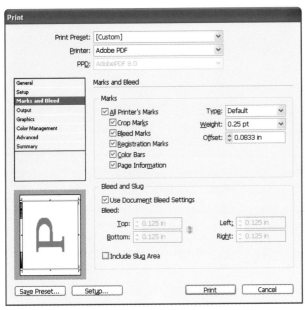

The Marks and Bleed section allows you to control the marks that are placed on your page when it is printed.

7 Click Output in the list on the left. If you are printing to a color printer that prints CMYK colors, choose Composite CMYK (or Composite RGB, if your printer doesn't print CMYK colors) from the Color drop-down menu on the right. If you are printing to a black-and-white printer, choose Composite Gray instead.

8 Click Graphics in the list on the left. In the Send Data drop-down menu of the Images section, choose the output quality of the graphics. Choose *All* for the best quality possible; choose *Optimized Subsampling* to let InDesign reduce the quality of your images slightly so the document prints faster. The higher the quality of the graphics, the more data InDesign needs to send to the printer and the longer it takes.

9 Press Print.

10 Choose File > Save to save your file, then File > Close to close it.

If you use the same set of print settings frequently, click the Save Preset button in the Print dialog box to save a preset of the current settings. The next time you need them, choose the preset from the dialog box's Print Preset drop-down menu. This streamlines the process of printing, especially when you are printing to the same printer with the same settings on a frequent basis.

Self study

Try the Find Font feature by choosing Type > Find Font to replace the fonts that Preflight or Package identifies as missing, with fonts you have loaded on your computer. Likewise, use the Links panel by choosing Window > Links to fix images that are missing or modified in your document. To find out more about how missing fonts happen, go to the Help file.

Investigate InDesign CS4's numerous tools that enable you to add interactivity to a PDF document when it is exported. For example, you can use the Button tool to add navigation to your exported PDF document, or you can add hyperlinks that are clickable links in the final PDF file.

Using the Separation Preview panel's Ink Manager, you can create an Ink Alias that maps one spot color to another. For instance, if you have two spot plates, you can map one ink to output on the same plate as the other ink. This feature is great when you realize at the last minute that you have too many spot colors in your document and need to minimize them. Practice this by creating a new document and adding at least two spot colors to your document.

Review

Questions

1 What command groups the active document and all the fonts and graphics used in the document into a single folder on your computer?

2 When creating a PDF file from InDesign, what's the easiest way to make sure that the settings for the PDF file are consistent every time?

3 What web technology is used to automatically format text in an XHTML file exported from InDesign?

4 InDesign's Preflight dialog box tells you that there is a spot color used in your document. What's the easiest way to see where that spot color is used?

Answers

1 Package.

2 Save the settings as a PDF Preset.

3 CSS (Cascading Style Sheets).

4 Use the Separations Preview panel to view only the spot color plate.

Index

Numerics

3D tools, Photoshop, 40–41

A

absolute hyperlinks, 250–252
accessibility, web design, 322
Acrobat Distiller (Adobe), 756
Actions panel, Photoshop, 55
ActionScript, Flash Lite, 461
activating layers, Fireworks, 483
Actual Pixel, 165
Add a Pixel Mask button, 26
Add Anchor Point tool, Flash, 378–379
Adjustment Brush, 170
adjustment layer, 30–32
Adjustments panel, 31
Adobe Acrobat Distiller, 756
Adobe AIR, 186–187
Adobe Bridge
    Adobe Bridge Home, 20
    automation tools, 13–18
    Filter panel, 13
    folders, 4–7
    importing graphics in inDesign, 724–726
    metadata, 7–10
    navigating through, 2–3
    opening documents in, 38–39, 61
    opening files from, 11
    overview, 1
    searching for files, 11–12
    views, changing, 18–19
Adobe Device Central
    Dreamweaver CS3, 297
    Flash, using in, 459–461
Adobe Dreamweaver CS4. *See also* cascading style sheets; web sites
    Check In/Check Out feature, 305–307
    creating documents, 203
    Design Notes feature, 308–310
    help resources, 325–328
    HTML, 191–201
    images, 257–264
    launching sites, 323–325
    new features, 182–187
    opening documents, 204
    optimizing pages, 317–323
    overview, 179–182, 187–189, 239–240, 299–300
    previewing pages in browser, 247–248
    remote connections, 300–305
    reports, 314–317
    testing site integrity, 310–312
    text, 240–255
    web sites, 189–191, 207–236
    Welcome Screen, 202
Adobe Fireworks CS4
    Auto Shapes, 477–478
    bitmaps, 464–465, 470–474
    color, 480–481
    creating documents, 466–467
    layer objects, 483–486
    layers, 482–483, 485, 487
    optimization and export process, 464, 493–500, 502–504
    overview, 463–464
    slices, 464, 487–492
    Start page, 466
    text, 478–480
    vector objects, 464–465, 474–476
    workspace, 467–470

Adobe Flash CS4. *See also* animation, Flash; drawing tools, Flash
    documents, 336–340
    file formats, 335
    help resources, 361–362
    overview, 331–334
    publishing movies, 447–461
    tools, 354–361
    workspace, 341–353
Adobe Flash Lite, 459
Adobe Flash Player 10, 334
Adobe Illustrator CS4
    color, 537–557
    cutting and pasting objects, 529–533
    drawing tools, 559–589
    layers, 527–528, 535
    overview, 507–508
    repeating resize transforms, 533–535
    selecting artwork, 516–520
    shape tools, 508–511
    shapes, 511–527
Adobe InDesign CS4
    applying using Find/Change, 607–609
    baseline grid, 679–681
    character attributes, 649–653
    character styles, 607, 697–700
    document delivery, 746–765
    globally updating, 700–701
    glyphs, 670–672
    graphics, 610–619, 713–742
    headlines, 681–682
    help resources, 619
    importing, 683
    loading from other documents, 701–703
    master pages, 621–636
    missing fonts, 688–690
    navigating, 598–601
    object styles, 609–610, 706–709
    organizing, 705–706
    overview, 591, 647–648, 693–694
    panels, 595–597
    paragraph attributes, 653–660
    paragraph styles, 606, 695–697
    paths, placing type on, 685–688
    Quick Apply, 703–705
    redefining, 683–685
    special characters, 670–672
    spelling, 660–669
    text, 648–649, 674–679
    text frames, 672–674
    tools, 592
    type, 601–605
    types of, 694
    workspace, 593–595, 598
Adobe PDF files, 754–757
Adobe Photoshop CS4 . *See also* selections, Photoshop
    3D postcard project, 22
    adjustment layers, adding, 30–32
    backgrounds, removing, 68–71
    Camera Raw plug-in, 168–174
    Clone tool, adding graphic images with, 28–30
    color, 114–122, 148–149
    combining images, 63–65
    composition, 23–25
    Curves Adjustments panel, 152–154
    fold lines, repairing, 135–145
    highlight, defining, 154–158
    histograms, 150–151
    image area, navigating, 42–51
    image size and resolution, viewing, 61–62
    images, changing size of placed, 66–68
    Mask panel, 25–27

styling, 287–289
Hypertext Markup Language (HTML)
case sensitivity, 198–200
code, 181
colors in, 197–198
data set feature, 185
document structure, 194
Dreamweaver, 190
overview, 191
placing images in, 195–197
tags, 192–194, 200–201
whitespace, 198–200
versus XHTML, 758
XHTML 1.0 Transitional standard, 201

I

Ignore White checkbox, Illustrator, 585
Illustrator CS4 (Adobe)
color, 537–557
cutting and pasting objects, 529–533
drawing tools, 559–589
layers, 527–528, 535
overview, 507–508
repeating resize transforms, 533–535
selecting artwork, 516–520
shape tools, 508–511
shapes, 511–527
image (<*img*>) tag, 197, 200, 258
image placeholders, 260–261
Image Preview feature, Fireworks, 495–499
Image Size dialog box, Photoshop, 62
Image Tag Accessibility Attributes dialog box, Dreamweaver, 196, 257
<*img*> (image) tag, 197, 200, 258
importing
bitmaps, 471
graphics in inDesign, 724–726, 738–742
In Port, InDesign, 604
Include hidden layers checkbox, Flash, 450
Incoming Style Definition box, InDesign, 702
InDesign CS4 (Adobe)
applying using Find/Change, 607–609
baseline grid, 679–681
character attributes, 649–653
character styles, 607, 697–700
document delivery, 746–765
globally updating, 700–701
glyphs, 670–672
graphics, 610–619, 713–742
headlines, 681–682
help resources, 619
importing, 683
loading from other documents, 701–703
master pages, 621–636
missing fonts, 688–690
navigating, 598–601
object styles, 609–610, 706–709
organizing, 705–706
overview, 591, 647–648, 693–694
panels, 595–597
paragraph attributes, 653–660
paragraph styles, 606, 695–697
paths, placing type on, 685–688
Quick Apply, 703–705
redefining, 683–685
special characters, 670–672
spelling, 660–669
text, 648–649, 674–679
text frames, 672–674
tools, 592
type, 601–605
types of, 694
workspace, 593–595, 598

Info icon, Camera Raw plug-in, 171
inheritance, 296
Ink Bottle tool, Flash, 343
inline style sheets, 275–276
Inner Radius slider, Property Inspector, 383
Insert panel, Dreamweaver, 180, 188
interactivity. *See* slices
internal style sheets, 276–278, 291–293
Internet Service Provider (ISP), 190
Intersect command, Combine Objects menu, 382
IP addresses, 190
IPTC Core, 8
Isolation mode, Illustrator, 520
ISP (Internet Service Provider), 190
Italic button, Property Inspector, 255

J

joining paths, 579–580
Joint Photographic Experts Group (JPEG)
Camera Raw plug-in, 168
defined, 73
Fireworks, 471
overview, 256, 501
saving files as, 74

K

kerning, 652
keyboard shortcuts, Photoshop, 127
keyframes, Flash
automatic, 416–419
F6 shortcut key, 415
Timeline, 412–415
tween span, 418
keywords
locating metadata using, 9–10
meta, 320–321
searching for files using Adobe Bridge, 12

L

Lasso tool
Flash, 343
Photoshop, 25, 39, 92–93
layer objects
deleting, 486
hiding, 485
merging, 485–486
moving, 484
naming, 483
protecting, 484–485
showing, 485
layers, Fireworks
activating, 483
hiding, 485
Layers panel, 482
organizing, 483
showing, 485
Web layer, 487
layers, Flash, 412
arranging, 401–402
folders for, 402–403
hiding, 401–402
locking, 401–402
using, 399–401
layers, Illustrator
moving objects between, 535
overview, 527–528
layers, InDesign, 615–617
layers, Photoshop
changing selections into, 88–89
stacking order, 69

Wiley Publishing, Inc.
End–User License Agreement

READ THIS. You should carefully read these terms and conditions before opening the software packet(s) included with this book "Book". This is a license agreement "Agreement" between you and Wiley Publishing, Inc. "WPI". By opening the accompanying software packet(s), you acknowledge that you have read and accept the following terms and conditions. If you do not agree and do not want to be bound by such terms and conditions, promptly return the Book and the unopened software packet(s) to the place you obtained them for a full refund.

1. **License Grant.** WPI grants to you (either an individual or entity) a nonexclusive license to use one copy of the enclosed software program(s) (collectively, the "Software") solely for your own personal or business purposes on a single computer (whether a standard computer or a workstation component of a multi-user network). The Software is in use on a computer when it is loaded into temporary memory (RAM) or installed into permanent memory (hard disk, CD-ROM, or other storage device). WPI reserves all rights not expressly granted herein.

2. **Ownership.** WPI is the owner of all right, title, and interest, including copyright, in and to the compilation of the Software recorded on the physical packet included with this Book "Software Media". Copyright to the individual programs recorded on the Software Media is owned by the author or other authorized copyright owner of each program. Ownership of the Software and all proprietary rights relating thereto remain with WPI and its licensers.

3. **Restrictions on Use and Transfer.**

   (a) You may only (i) make one copy of the Software for backup or archival purposes, or (ii) transfer the Software to a single hard disk, provided that you keep the original for backup or archival purposes. You may not (i) rent or lease the Software, (ii) copy or reproduce the Software through a LAN or other network system or through any computer subscriber system or bulletin-board system, or (iii) modify, adapt, or create derivative works based on the Software.

   (b) You may not reverse engineer, decompile, or disassemble the Software. You may transfer the Software and user documentation on a permanent basis, provided that the transferee agrees to accept the terms and conditions of this Agreement and you retain no copies. If the Software is an update or has been updated, any transfer must include the most recent update and all prior versions.

4. **Restrictions on Use of Individual Programs.** You must follow the individual requirements and restrictions detailed for each individual program in the "About the CD" appendix of this Book or on the Software Media. These limitations are also contained in the individual license agreements recorded on the Software Media. These limitations may include a requirement that after using the program for a specified period of time, the user must pay a registration fee or discontinue use. By opening the Software packet(s), you agree to abide by the licenses and restrictions for these individual programs that are detailed in the "About the CD" appendix and/or on the Software Media. None of the material on this Software Media or listed in this Book may ever be redistributed, in original or modified form, for commercial purposes.

5. **Limited Warranty.**

   (a) WPI warrants that the Software and Software Media are free from defects in materials and workmanship under normal use for a period of sixty (60) days from the date of purchase of this Book. If WPI receives notification within the warranty period of defects in materials or workmanship, WPI will replace the defective Software Media.

(b) WPI AND THE AUTHOR(S) OF THE BOOK DISCLAIM ALL OTHER WARRANTIES, EXPRESS OR IMPLIED, INCLUDING WITHOUT LIMITATION IMPLIED WARRANTIES OF MERCHANTABILITY AND FITNESS FOR A PARTICULAR PURPOSE, WITH RESPECT TO THE SOFTWARE, THE PROGRAMS, THE SOURCE CODE CONTAINED THEREIN, AND/OR THE TECHNIQUES DESCRIBED IN THIS BOOK. WPI DOES NOT WARRANT THAT THE FUNCTIONS CONTAINED IN THE SOFTWARE WILL MEET YOUR REQUIREMENTS OR THAT THE OPERATION OF THE SOFTWARE WILL BE ERROR FREE.

(c) This limited warranty gives you specific legal rights, and you may have other rights that vary from jurisdiction to jurisdiction.

6. Remedies.

(a) WPI's entire liability and your exclusive remedy for defects in materials and workmanship shall be limited to replacement of the Software Media, which may be returned to WPI with a copy of your receipt at the following address: Software Media Fulfillment Department, Attn.: *Adobe Creative Suite 4 Design Premium Digital Classroom*, Wiley Publishing, Inc., 10475 Crosspoint Blvd., Indianapolis, IN 46256, or call 1-800-762-2974. Please allow four to six weeks for delivery. This Limited Warranty is void if failure of the Software Media has resulted from accident, abuse, or misapplication. Any replacement Software Media will be warranted for the remainder of the original warranty period or thirty (30) days, whichever is longer.

(b) In no event shall WPI or the author be liable for any damages whatsoever (including without limitation damages for loss of business profits, business interruption, loss of business information, or any other pecuniary loss) arising from the use of or inability to use the Book or the Software, even if WPI has been advised of the possibility of such damages.

(c) Because some jurisdictions do not allow the exclusion or limitation of liability for consequential or incidental damages, the above limitation or exclusion may not apply to you.

7. U.S. Government Restricted Rights. Use, duplication, or disclosure of the Software for or on behalf of the United States of America, its agencies and/or instrumentalities "U.S. Government" is subject to restrictions as stated in paragraph (c)(1)(ii) of the Rights in Technical Data and Computer Software clause of DFARS 252.227-7013, or subparagraphs (c) (1) and (2) of the Commercial Computer Software - Restricted Rights clause at FAR 52.227-19, and in similar clauses in the NASA FAR supplement, as applicable.

8. General. This Agreement constitutes the entire understanding of the parties and revokes and supersedes all prior agreements, oral or written, between them and may not be modified or amended except in a writing signed by both parties hereto that specifically refers to this Agreement. This Agreement shall take precedence over any other documents that may be in conflict herewith. If any one or more provisions contained in this Agreement are held by any court or tribunal to be invalid, illegal, or otherwise unenforceable, each and every other provision shall remain in full force and effect.